THE LITERARY GUIDE
TO THE BIBLE

THE
LITERARY GUIDE
— TO THE —
BIBLE

Edited by
ROBERT ALTER
and
FRANK KERMODE

THE BELKNAP PRESS OF
HARVARD UNIVERSITY PRESS
CAMBRIDGE, MASSACHUSETTS

Copyright © 1987 by Robert Alter and Frank Kermode
All rights reserved
Printed in the United States of America
SEVENTH PRINTING, 1994

First Harvard University Press paperback edition, 1990

Set in Linotron Bembo and designed by Marianne Perlak

Library of Congress Cataloging-in-Publication Data

The literary guide to the Bible.

Bibliography: p.
Includes index.
I. Bible—Criticism, interpretation, etc. I. Alter,
Robert. II. Kermode, Frank, 1919–
BS511.2. L58   1987   809'.93522   86–32172
ISBN 0–674–87530–3 (cloth)
ISBN 0–674–87531–1 (paper)

Acknowledgments

A book of this sort is never completed without generous help from people whose names would not appear in it unless acknowledged here. At various stages of the work, and in many different ways, we have had indispensable support from Patricia Williams, the European editor of Harvard University Press, and from Maud Wilcox, editor-in-chief of the Press. Ann Hawthorne, our manuscript editor, contended patiently and skillfully with a range of problems far beyond those of an ordinary book. Dorothy Franklin in Cambridge, England, and Janet Livingstone in Berkeley, California, assisted us in correspondence and in the preparation of typescripts. Some of the secretarial costs for the project were covered by funds made available by the chancellor of the University of California at Berkeley. The hospitality of the Provost of King's College, Cambridge, and of Mrs. Williams enabled us to work together at a critical moment; and the generosity of Mishkenot Sha'ananim, Jerusalem, gave us the chance to consult directly with our contributors in Israel. And finally, we are experienced enough in work of this kind to be conscious of our good fortune in having contributors notable for their enthusiasm, good humor, and punctuality.

Contents

The New Testament

General Essays

THE LITERARY GUIDE
TO THE BIBLE

General Introduction

Robert Alter and Frank Kermode

TO most educated modern readers the Bible probably seems both familiar and strange, like the features of an ancestor. They will know, if only in a general way, of its central importance in the history of the culture they have inherited; but they will also be aware that in its modern forms that culture has denied the Bible the kinds of importance it had in the past. They will very likely see modern fundamentalism as dangerous and atavistic; yet to repudiate the biblical inheritance altogether must strike them as barbarous. Here is a miscellany of documents containing ancient stories, poems, laws, prophecies, which most of us cannot even read in the original languages, and which we probably know best, if we are English speakers, in an English that was already archaic when the King James (or "Authorized") Version was published in 1611, and may now often seem distant and exotic: "that old tongue," as Edmund Wilson once vividly expressed it, "with its clang and its flavor." Yet, as Wilson went on to say, "we have been living with it all our lives." In short, the language as well as the messages it conveys symbolizes for us that past, strange and yet familiar, which we feel we somehow must understand if we are to understand ourselves.

It might of course be argued that the centrality of the Bible in the formation of our culture is the result of historical accident. That is a view to which two centuries of modern biblical scholarship have, willingly or not, given much support. The motives of the scholars, Christians, Jews, and secularists alike, were understandable: a small body of writings, first in Hebrew, then in Greek, produced in a narrow strip of the eastern Mediterranean littoral during a period of roughly a dozen centuries, continued to have the most far-reaching consequences because these writings were accepted as revealed truth; and in the interest of *historical* truth it became a duty to try to understand the processes by which this literature emerged from its original historical situation. Broadly speaking, literary criticism was of small importance in this undertaking, which treated the biblical texts as relics, probably distorted in transmission, of a past one needed to recover as exactly as possible.

Over the past couple of decades, however, there has been a revival of interest in the literary qualities of these texts, in the virtues by which

1

they continue to live as something other than archaeology. The power of the Genesis narratives or of the story of David, the complexities and refinements of the Passion narratives, could be studied by methods developed in the criticism of secular literature. The effectiveness of this new approach—or approaches, for the work has proceeded along many different paths—has now been amply demonstrated. Professional biblical criticism has been profoundly affected by it; but, even more important, the general reader can now be offered a new view of the Bible as a work of great literary force and authority, a work of which it is entirely credible that it should have shaped the minds and lives of intelligent men and women for two millennia and more. It is this view of the Bible that the present volume seeks to promote.

It will be clear, therefore, that we do not seek to duplicate the work of traditional historical scholarship—to consider the origins of a text or to ask what may be inferred from it concerning the life and institutions of ancient Israel or early Christianity; though our contributors certainly do not neglect such considerations when they are relevant to their more literary purposes. It would be absurd to lay down the law about what is and is not relevant to these purposes, or to prohibit the use of insights deriving from comparative religion, anthropology, philology, and so forth. Nor should it be supposed that we are careless of the religious character of the material under discussion simply because our aims are not theological and not in the ordinary sense related to spiritual edification. Indeed we believe that readers who regard the Bible primarily in the light of religious faith may find instruction here along with those who wish to understand its place in a secularized culture.

If we were asked to state more positively why we have approached the subject as we have done, we should reply as follows. First of all, the Bible, considered as a book, achieves its effects by means no different from those generally employed by written language. This is true whatever our reasons for attributing value to it—as the report of God's action in history, as the founding text of a religion or religions, as a guide to ethics, as evidence about people and societies in the remote past, and so on. Indeed literary analysis must come first, for unless we have a sound understanding of what the text is doing and saying, it will not be of much value in other respects. It has been said that the best reason for the serious study of the Bible—for learning how to read it well—is written across the history of Western culture: see what happens when people misread it, read it badly, or read it on false assumptions.

The desire to read it well has broad cultural justifications which remain quite apart from religious considerations. By this we do not mean merely that the Bible is probably the most important single source of all our literature. That is certainly the case, and an increasing neglect of the Bible in our secularized times has opened a gulf between it and our general literature, a gap of ignorance which must in some measure falsify the latter. Very few of us have the unconscious assurance of an educated Victorian reading Milton; Matthew Arnold, for example, would have received as he read biblical allusions we have to look up, as well as the silent counterpoint of Greek and Latin syntax. Milton is especially biblical, but the point applies in varying measure to almost all the major writers in English. The revived interest of secular writers in the Bible does stem in part from a sense that secular literature is in some degree impoverished by this lack. But there is a more striking development: the Bible, once thought of as a source of secular literature yet somehow apart from it, now bids fair to become part of the literary canon. The coming together of religious and secular criticism has taught practitioners of the former that their studies may be greatly enhanced by attention to secular methods; the latter have benefited by discovering that the Bible, to which few of the most influential critics had of late paid much attention, is simply of such quality that they have neglected it to their immense cost.

Indeed, it seems we have reached a turning point in the history of criticism, for the Bible, under a new aspect, has reoccupied the literary culture. How have we reached this point? If we look back to the Enlightenment we notice that men of the caliber of Lessing and Herder did not suppose that they must specialize in secular or in religious literature. We remember Lessing as a dramatist, an influential critic and theorist of drama, an aesthetician; but we remember him also as a daring biblical critic. Herder's influence on the development of German literature is enormous, but his biblical studies are hardly less important. Yet it was in the time of these extraordinary intellects, and partly in consequence of their achievements, that the historical-critical method characteristic of specialized modern biblical scholarship was developed. This "scientific" criticism was of great cultural and doctrinal importance; but, as we have said, it diverted attention from biblical narrative, poetry, and prophecy as *literature*, treating them instead as more or less distorted historical records. The characteristic move was to infer the existence of some book that preceded the one we have—the lost documents that were combined to make Genesis as it has come down to us, the lost Aramaic Gospel, the lost "sayings-source" used by Matthew and Luke, and so on. The effect of this practice was curious: one spoke of the existing books primarily as evidence of what must once have been available in an original closer to what actually happened. That was their real value—as substitutes for what had unfortunately been lost.

The analytic work that goes by the name of the Higher Criticism, as well as the minute textual labors of nineteenth-century scholars, occupied minds of high ingenuity and great intellectual force. It was something new (though the methods employed owed much to classical scholarship), and it dealt in the truth, which is why it fascinated George Eliot and Matthew Arnold and others who felt that the recovery of true religious feeling required an immense detour through modern scholarship, and the establishment of forms of belief thus "demythologized." The strength of the movement seemed virtually irresistible, and the new interpretation of the Bible became for many a scientific discovery that had to be reconciled with whatever religious or quasi-religious opinions one happened to hold. Yet the fact remained that the biblical texts were valued less for what they actually were than for what they told us about other putative texts or events to which there was no direct access.

What has happened now is that the interpretation of the texts as they actually exist has been revalidated. This development has not been simple or single, and it has not been merely a reaction against the modern tradition of professional biblical scholarship. It comes of a need, felt by clerical and secular students alike, to achieve a new accommodation with the Bible as it is, which is to say, as literature of high importance and power.

A landmark in this process was the publication of Erich Auerbach's *Mimesis* (1946, English translation 1953), an extraordinary, polymathic study of European traditions of realism. It was, one might say, a providential work. Auerbach, a savant of the old European school, wrote the book in Turkey during the Second World War, with no good library except the one in his head, while just out of range European civilization was trying to destroy itself. As time goes by there are increasing reservations about much in *Mimesis*, but it was nevertheless crucial in showing the way toward a reunion of the secular with the religious critical tradition. The first chapters, comparing Old Testament narrative with Homeric narrative and meditating on the unique relation of ordinary-language realism to high "figural" meanings in the Gospels, not only offered new perspectives on the Bible itself but also suggested new connections between the achievements of the biblical writers and the entire tradition of Western literature. Auerbach showed that the old simple contrasts between Hebraism and Hellenism were misleading, that the realisms invented by the writers of the Bible were at least as important to the European future as was the literature of ancient Greece. It was no longer a matter of equating conduct with Hebraism and culture with Hellenism; and when the Bible could be seen as a source of aesthetic value, vast new questions opened, not only about revising the relations of Greek and Hebraic, but also about the exploration of texts that paradoxically had been neglected even as they were venerated and studied. And in due time scholars attended to such matters as the intellectual habits of first-century readers, while critics looked at the Bible with the eyes of the twentieth-century reader; and the two might come together to demonstrate all manner of new possibilities, a revision of past readings, a modern Bible.

Since the time of Auerbach there have been great changes in the style and method of literary criticism. Among them are the many varieties of Formalism, Structuralism, and their descendants. It is unnecessary to specify these methods here; what they have in common are a skeptical attitude to the referential qualities of texts and an intense concern for their internal relationships. Contributors to the present volume are aware of these developments, and they give a high degree of attention to the texts (studied, of course, in the original languages). "Narratology" is a word so new that it escaped inclusion in the *OED Supplement* of 1976, but the poetics of narrative is a subject at least as old as Aristotle, and poetics is the right description for what happens in this volume; indeed our contributors might, if they wished it, call themselves "poeticians," a word that postdates the *OED Supplement* of 1982. Modern criticism is a fine breeding ground of neologisms; we avoid them for the most part, and are content to call our contributors critics. We are writing to serve the interests of the educated general reader rather than those of some critical party.

We have not imposed uniformity of method on our contributors, but all involved in this project share a broad consensus of purpose as literary critics. We assume that literature is a complex language, not necessarily unique, not without significant overlaps with other kinds of language, but distinctive nevertheless, and that the constructive critic will in one way or another direct otherwise wandering attention to the operations of this language. Its syntax, grammar, and vocabulary involve a highly heterogeneous concord of codes, devices, and linguistic properties. These include genre, convention, technique, contexts of allusion, style, structure, thematic organization, point of view for the narratives, voice for the poetry, imagery and diction for both, and much else. The complexity of this interplay of elements certainly calls for expert literary appraisal and also guarantees that there will be no unanimity of approach or of interpretative conclusions. No critic, then, is an unquestionably dependable guide, but many can be helpful in different ways in showing us how to parse the language of literature. In the case of the Bible, guidance is especially necessary because so much time has intervened since this particular literary language was a living vernacular, and because so many other kinds of discourse have been superimposed on it by the subsequent tradition of interpretation.

This sketch of the operation of criticism covers much but by no means all of the ground now claimed by the various schools of contemporary criticism. It stresses the role of the critic as someone who helps make possible fuller readings of the text, with a particular emphasis on the complex integration of diverse means of communication encountered in most works of literature. An orientation of this sort seemed to us particularly appropriate for our volume because at this moment in cultural history there is an urgent need to try to learn how to read the Bible again. Certain varieties of contemporary criticism are not represented here because we think they are not really concerned with reading in the sense we have proposed. For example, critical approaches mainly interested in the origins of a text in ideology or social structure are not represented here; nor is Marxist criticism (which in any case has been applied to the Bible solely on historical issues) or psychoanalytic criticism. Given our aim to provide illumination, we have not included critics who use the text as a springboard for cultural or metaphysical ruminations, nor those like the Deconstructionists and some feminist critics who seek to demonstrate that the text is necessarily divided against itself. The general validity of such approaches is not at issue here, only their inapplicability to our project as we have defined it.

Our own notion of criticism is pluralist, and the label that best fits most of our contributors is eclectic. There are no doctrinaire proponents of a particular critical school among them. Our chief concern was to choose the contributors who would be likely to write the best essay on the subject, not what critical approach would be used. We turned with equal readiness, though with no intention of striking a numerical balance, to literary critics interested in the Bible and competent to discuss it, and to biblical scholars interested in literary criticism. The result, we should like to think, is a happy union of the two disciplines that has instructive things to say both to students of literature and to students of the Bible.

Literary criticism, long thought to be peripheral or even irrelevant to biblical studies, has emerged since the mid-1970s as a new major focus of academic biblical scholarship in North America, England, and Israel, and it has also shown a few notable signs of life on the Continent. It was natural, then, that ours should be an international undertaking. Our contributors were drawn from seats of learning (in all but two instances, secular universities) in the United States, Canada, England, Israel, Italy, and the Netherlands. They variously derive from Protestant, Catholic, and Jewish traditions. Some are committed by faith to the texts they study, and others would regard themselves as essentially secular critics. But they speak a common critical language, the differences among them stemming far more from individual sensibility and intellectual preference than from religious background. In many instances, we sought to recruit writers who had already made some notable contribution to this field of inquiry, but we did not hesitate to turn as well to several younger scholars whose initial work seemed to us to offer great promise. The volume, then, is a meeting-ground not only of nationalities and faiths but also of scholarly generations. The resulting variety of perspectives, joined with a unity of general purpose, provides a lively overview of the more than thousand years of diverse literary activity represented in the Bible.

The purpose of this book will now, we hope, be clear. We no longer live in the age when literate persons had a daily intimacy with the Bible on the basis of shared belief; individuals must now attune themselves to the book, which is today rarely assimilated in early youth. To help them do so is our main object.

In trying to accomplish it we have made certain assumptions. What we are here calling "the Bible" is really only one of several Bibles, and to some it may appear that our choice has theological implications, though the grounds of our choice are entirely literary. (The variations in biblical canons are touched on in the essay "The Canon," below.) We need say no more about the kind of scholarship that regards the biblical canons as more of a nuisance than anything else and prefers to think of the Bible as a collection of independent books more or less fortuitously assembled. There remains the difficulty that the Catholic Bible is not identical with the Protestant, nor the Bible of Greek Judaism with the Hebrew Bible. Moreover, it is obvious that Jews will not attach much religious significance to the New Testament, though as a matter of critical fact the relations between the two Testaments, so potent and interesting in the first centuries of the era, are profoundly interesting now, if not for quite the same reasons. But we have chosen what is virtually the Protestant Bible for literary reasons only; it is, more than the others, the Bible of the central anglophone tradition, the single book that most easily comes to mind when we speak of the Bible. We can claim that it includes all the books recognized by modern Jews as constituting their Bible, and all the books that Christians agree upon as parts of theirs.

THE BOOKS of the Old Testament are not treated in this volume in exactly the order familiar from the King James and subsequent Protestant versions. We have instead followed the order of the Hebrew Bible, except that for reasons of genre Ecclesiastes is joined in a single essay with Proverbs. It is for similar generic reasons that we have departed from the more familiar King James order. Whereas Ruth appears in that order after Judges, we have preferred not to interrupt the course of the so-called Deuteronomic History, which here runs from Deuteronomy to 2 Kings, as it does in the Hebrew Bible. The essays on the prophets are not interrupted by Lamentations, regarded in the traditional versions as an appendix to Jeremiah. Daniel, the last written work of the Hebrew canon, is not here treated as belonging with the classical prophets. The Hebrew Bible groups its books in this sequence: Pentateuch, Former Prophets, Latter Prophets, miscellaneous Writings; and it suited our purposes to adopt this order. The essays on the New Testament follow the conventional sequence of books, with considerations of the Pauline Epistles gathered into one general article, and the Catholic Epistles treated in the essay on Hebrews.

We have as a rule used the King James Version in translations, and our reasons for doing so must be obvious: it is the version most English readers associate with the literary qualities of the Bible, and it is still arguably the version that best preserves the literary effects of the original languages. But it has serious philological deficiencies, and its archaism may at times be misleading; accordingly, our contributors have sometimes felt obliged to revise it—indicating their changes by [AR] (author's revision)—or to provide their own translations—marked by [AT] (author's translation) or accompanied by an endnote indicating that all the translations are the author's. A few contributors have referred to the New English Bible (NEB), the Revised Standard Version (RSV), or the New Jewish Publication Society Bible (NJPS) instead of the King James Version (KJV, AV). There are two typographic departures from the King James Version. Italics are not used for words merely implied in the original, because this convention is more confusing than helpful to modern readers. When poetry is quoted, the text has been set as lines of verse. In some instances the responsibility for decisions about line breaks rests with the editor of the Old Testament section.

TRANSLITERATIONS from the Hebrew and Greek are simplified and do not correspond to scholarly convention. Diacritical marks have been limited to *ḥ* for Hebrew ḥet (roughly corresponding to the light, aspirated fricative *j* of New World Spanish) and *ō* and *ē* for Greek omega and eta to distinguish them from *o*, omicron, and *e*, epsilon. *Kh* in transliterations of the Hebrew indicates a fricative something like *ch* in the Scottish *loch*. No attempt is made in the transliterations to indicate features of the original that are primarily grammatical and the notation of which would not convey useful phonetic information to the reader. In a few instances, consistency has been set aside in the interests of what needed to be shown, as when, for example, a contributor wanted to indicate through transliteration that consonants are shared by two different forms of a word, something evident to the eye scanning the Hebrew page, though the actual pronunciation of a particular consonant may change slightly as a word is conjugated or declined (like the shift from *b* to *v* in the Hebrew bet). Transliteration between languages with partly incompatible phonetic systems is always a difficult business; what is offered here is no more than an approximation, intended to serve as an adjunct to the purposes of literary criticism.

Older scholarly convention spells out the Tetragrammaton or ineffable Hebrew name of God as Yahweh. Here we adopt a more recent convention of indicating the consonants only: YHWH. The vowels of this name are in any case somewhat conjectural, and transliterating just the consonants also accords with traditional Hebrew practice.

THE
OLD TESTAMENT

Introduction to the
Old Testament

Robert Alter

THE difficulty of getting a bearing on the Old Testament as a collection of literary works is reflected in the fact that we have no comfortable term with which to designate these books. Common usage in Western culture, following Christian tradition, calls them the Old Testament, a name originating in the assumption that the Old requires completion in the New or is actually superseded by the New. (The term itself, more properly rendered "new covenant," derives from the reading given in Hebrews 8:6–13 of a prophecy in Jeremiah 31:31, where the phrase first occurs. In Jeremiah it actually signals a grand renewal of Israelite national existence under God, but Hebrews takes it to mean the replacement of an "aging" covenant about to expire by a new one.) That is in fact how major writers from Augustine to Dante to Donne to Eliot have conceived Hebrew Scripture and absorbed it into their own work, and this conception is persistent enough to have figured centrally as recently as 1982 in a book by one of our most important critics, Northrop Frye's *The Great Code: The Bible and Literature*. The Jews collectively have rejected the term for all that it implies, and as a matter of literary history there is surely no warrant to imagine that the ancient Hebrew writers composed their stories and poems and laws and genealogical lists with the idea that they were providing a prelude to another set of texts, to be written in another language centuries later. Harold Bloom, a critic who has tirelessly studied the ways in which later writers appropriate the achievements of their predecessors for their own purposes, makes this point with witty incisiveness when he speaks of "the Christian triumph over the Hebrew Bible, a triumph which produced that captive work, the Old Testament."[1]

It is nevertheless a question what to call these books and how to think of them outside a state of captivity. The very term *Bible* (from the Greek *ta biblia*, "the books") is more a vague classification than a title. *Jewish Bible* refers to the choice and order of the texts made by rabbinic Judaism for its canon, and so in its own way it also represents an appropriation of ancient writings by latecomers, though not so egregious a one as the Christian. *Hebrew Bible*, the term which Bloom prefers and which I shall use in what follows, comes closer to the originating literary facts, though it is not strictly accurate, for three post-Exilic books, Ezra, Nehemiah, and Daniel, are partly composed in Aramaic, a Semitic tongue merely cognate with Hebrew. Postbiblical Hebrew tradition itself has never enshrined a single title but instead has wavered among several that in different ways suggest the elusive heterogeneity of the corpus. Rabbinic literature refers to the Writings and to the Twenty-four Books. Most commonly, the Hebrew Bible has been designated by Jews as *Tanakh*, an acronym for *Torah* (Pentateuch), *Neviim* (Former and Latter Prophets), and *Ketuvim* (miscellaneous Writings, or Everything Else), which is no more than a crude generic division of the books in their traditional order according to the Jewish canon. Finally, these books are often called *Miqra'*, especially in modern secular contexts, and that term simply indicates "that which is read," more or less in the sense of "the Text," and so will scarcely serve as a defining title.

Any literary account of the Hebrew Bible must recognize just this quality of extreme heterogeneity, a condition which the essays in this volume will vividly confirm. From one point of view, it is not even a unified collection but rather a loose anthology that reflects as much as nine centuries of Hebrew literary activity, from the Song of Deborah and other, briefer archaic poems embedded in the prose narratives to the Book of Daniel (second century B.C.E.). The generic variety of this anthology is altogether remarkable, encompassing as it does historiography, fictional narratives, and much that is a mixture of the two, lists of laws, prophecy in both poetry and prose, aphoristic and reflective works, cultic and devotional poems, laments and victory hymns, love poems, genealogical tables, etiological tales, and much more.

One might imagine that religious ideology would provide the principle of selection for the anthology. In some minimal sense, that must be true. There are, for example, no truly syncretistic or pagan texts included, though it is perfectly plausible that there might have been ancient Hebrew compositions written in such a spirit. The Hebrew Bible itself occasionally refers to annalistic or possibly mythological works such as the Book of the Battles of YHWH and the Book of Yashar, which have not survived. (The oldest extant scrolls, it should be noted, are those that were found in the caves at Qumran, going back to the first century B.C.E.; as far as we know, whatever else was written in the ancient period in Hebrew on parchment or papyrus has long since turned to dust, so we can only guess at the full scope of this literature.) But even within the limits of monotheistic ideology, there is a great deal of diversity in regard to political attitudes; conceptions of history, ethics, psychology, causation; views of the roles of law and cult, of priesthood and laity, Israel and the nations, even of God. Indeed, when one contemplates the radical challenge in Job not only to the doctrine of retribution but to the very notion of a man-centered creation, or Ecclesiastes' insistence on cycles of futility in place of the linear, progressive time familiar from Genesis, or the exuberant eroticism of the Song of Songs, one begins to suspect that the selection was at least sometimes impelled by a desire to preserve the best of ancient Hebrew literature rather than to gather the consistent normative statements of a monotheistic party line. In fact, the texts that have been passed down to us exhibit not only extraordinary diversity but also a substantial amount of debate with one another.

But the idea of the Hebrew Bible as a sprawling, unruly anthology is no more than a partial truth, for the retrospective act of canonization has created a unity among the disparate texts that we as later readers can scarcely ignore; and this unity in turn reflects, though with a pronounced element of exaggeration, an intrinsic feature of the original texts—their powerfully allusive character. All literature, to be sure, is necessarily allusive: as a writer, you are compelled in one way or another to make your text out of antecedent texts (oral or written) because it would not occur to you in the first place to do anything so unnatural as to compose a hymn or a love-poem or a story unless you had some model to emulate. In the Hebrew Bible, however, what is repeatedly evident is the abundance of authoritative national traditions, fixed in particular verbal formulations, to which later writers respond through incorporation, elaboration, debate, or parody. Perhaps, as a good many scholars have conjectured, these formulations first circulated in oral tradition in the early, premonarchical phase of Israelite history. In any event, literacy is very old in the ancient Near East and there is no preliterate stage of full-fledged Israelite national existence; so there is no reason to assume that the activity of putting things down on a scroll (*sefer*; see, for example, Exod. 17:14) was not part of the formative experience of ancient Israel. The internally allusive character of the Hebrew texts—not to speak of allusions in them to non-Hebrew ancient Near Eastern texts—is more like the pervasive allusiveness of Eliot's *The Waste Land* or Joyce's *Ulysses* than, say, the occasional allusiveness of Wordsworth's *The Prelude*. In this central regard, the Hebrew Bible, because it so frequently articulates its meanings by recasting texts within its own corpus, is already moving toward being an integrated work, for all its anthological diversity.

Let me offer one relatively simple example. When Boaz first meets Ruth in the field, after she prostrates herself before him in response to his offer of hospitality and protection, he praises her in the following words: "It hath been fully told [AR] me, all that thou hast done unto thy mother in law since the death of thy husband; and how thou hast left thy father and thy mother, and the land of thy birthplace [AR], and art come unto a people which thou knewest not heretofore" (Ruth 2:11). There is a strong echo here, as surely anyone in the ancient audience would have recognized, of God's first imperative words to Abraham that inaugurate the patriarchal tales: "Get thee out of thy country, and from thy birthplace [AR], and from thy father's house, unto a land that I will shew thee" (Gen. 12:1). The identical verbal-thematic cluster, land-birthplace-father, stands out in both texts, though the author of Ruth adds "mother" to the configuration, understandably enough because his protagonist is a woman and because she takes Naomi, her mother-in-law, as a kind of adoptive mother when she abandons her homeland of Moab.

What is the point of the allusion? It sets Ruth up as a founding mother, in symmetrical correspondence to Abraham the founding father. She, too, comes from a foreign country to the east to settle in the Promised Land. God's next words to Abraham—"And I will make of thee a great nation, and I will bless thee, and make thy name great" (Gen. 12:2)—will also apply directly to her as the woman from whom David will be descended. Progenitrix as Abraham is progenitor, she too will have to overcome a palpable threat to the continuation of the family line for the fulfillment of the promise. The very encounter here of a future bride and groom in a pastoral setting involving the drawing of water (Ruth 2:9) recalls a series of similar patriarchal tales. And perhaps most pointedly in regard to the complex themes of the Book of Ruth, God's very first word to Abraham, *lekh*, "get thee" (root *halak*), or simply "go," is made a chief thematic key word strategically reiterated in her story: again and again, we are reminded that her "going" from Moab is, paradoxically, a "returning" to a land she has never before seen, a return because it is now by choice her land. Thus, taking up the destiny of the covenanted people, for Ruth as for Abraham, means putting behind one the filiations of geography and biology, replacing the old natural bonds with new contractual ones, as Abraham does with God, having left his father's house, and as Ruth does with the clan of Elimelech and the land of Judea. The patriarchal text, trumpeting the departure from father and birthplace, announces a new relation to God and history; the text in Ruth, with a less theological and ultimately more political frame of reference, adopts the language of the earlier writer to define its own allied but somewhat different meanings: the tale of the foreign woman who becomes staunchest of kin through her acts of love and loyalty. Such intertextual play occurs repeatedly in the Hebrew Bible, drawing its disparate elements into a certain mobile, unpredictable unity.

My very invocation of the technique of allusion, some may object, presupposes what is most in need of demonstration—that the primary element that pulls the disparate texts together is literary. According to one common line of thought, the Hebrew Bible exhibits certain literary embellishments and literary interludes, but those who would present "the Bible as literature" must turn it around to an odd angle from its own original emphases, which are theological, legislative, historiographic, and moral. This opposition between literature and the really serious things collapses the moment we realize that it is the exception in any culture for literary invention to be a purely aesthetic activity. Writers put together words in a certain pleasing order partly because the order pleases but also, very often, because the order helps them refine meanings, make meanings more memorable, more satisfyingly complex, so that what is well wrought in language can more powerfully engage the world of events, values, human and divine ends. One hardly wants to deny the overriding spiritual earnestness of the ancient Hebrew writers; certainly what has survived of their work in the canon offers no more than occasional fleeting glimpses of the kind of playfulness often detectable in ancient Greek and Latin literature. And yet, a close study of these writings in the original discovers again and again, on every level from word choice and sentence structure to the deployment of large units of composition, a delight in the manifold exercise of literary craftsmanship. It goes without saying that these writers are intent on telling us about the origins of the world, the history of Israel, God's ethical requirements of mankind, the cultic stip-ulations of the new monotheistic faith, the future vistas of disaster and redemption. But the telling has a shapeliness whose subtleties we are only beginning to understand, and it was undertaken by writers with the most brilliant gifts for intimating character, defining scenes, fashioning dia-logue, elaborating motifs, balancing near and distant episodes, just as the God-intoxicated poems of the psalmists and prophets evince a dazzling virtuosity in their arabesques of soundplay and syntax, wordplay and image. It is probably more than a coincidence that the very pinnacle of ancient Hebrew poetry was reached in Job, the biblical text that is most daring and innovative in its imagination of God, man, and creation; for here as elsewhere in the Hebrew Bible the literary medium is not merely a means of "conveying" doctrinal positions but an adventurous occasion for deepening doctrine through the play of literary resources, or perhaps even, at least here, for leaping beyond doctrine.

The facts of the matter, however, are rather more untidy than I have indicated so far. It is our own predisposition to parcel out prose writing into fiction and nonfiction, as is done in our libraries and our lists of best-sellers; and, despite the occasional occurrence of a prose-poem, we also tend to think of prose and poetry as distinct, even opposed, categories. For the ancient Hebrews, these were not strict oppositions, and sometimes they could be intertwined in baffling ways. Fiction and nonfiction, because they seem to involve a substantive issue of the truth value of a text, pose a thorny question to which we shall have to return, but from where we stand we probably have no way of recovering what might have figured as a fact in the ancient Hebrew mind, whether the narrative data of centuries-old oral traditions were assumed to be facts, or to what extent the writers consciously exercised a license of invention. The interplay of poetry and prose is more definable because it is a formal issue, verse being scannable, even the "free rhythms" of biblical parallelistic verse. Some texts, like Psalms, Proverbs, Song of Songs, and all but the frame-story of Job, are unambiguously assemblages of poems, but there are also many mixed instances. Biblical prophecy is composed predominantly in formal verse, but there are also substantial portions of prose prophecy and passages of rhythmic prose that sometimes almost scan. The overwhelming bulk of the narrative books, in contrast to the practice of other ancient literatures, is written in prose; but the texture of the prose is studded with verse insets, most often a memorable small set piece just one or two lines long at some particularly significant or ceremonial juncture in the narrative; occasionally, a full-scale poem of fifty or more lines.

This by no means exhausts the formal untidiness of the texts with which we have to deal. For the Hebrew Bible quite frequently incorporates as integral elements of its literary structures kinds of writing that, according to most modern preconceptions, have nothing to do with "literature." I am thinking in particular of genealogies, etiological tales, laws (including the most technical cultic regulations), lists of tribal borders, detailed historical itineraries. Those who view the Bible as literature in conventional terms have quietly ignored these materials as unfortunate encumbrances, while most modern historical scholarship has seen in them either an inscrutable ancient impulse to cherish traditions for their own sake or an effort to provide quasi-documentary authentication for political realities of the later biblical period. As a result, the sundry lists have been chiefly analyzed by scholars for whatever hints of long-lost history they might preserve in fossilized form or for whatever oblique reflections they might offer of the situation of the writers and redactors. One need not reject such considerations to note, as several recent literary students of these texts have persuasively argued, that the lists are very effectively employed to amplify the themes and to effect a complementary imaginative realization, in another genre, of the purposes of the narratives in which they are embedded. Thus J. P. Fokkelman proposes that the abundant genealogies in Genesis are enactments of the theme of propagation and survival so central to that book; David Damrosch invites us to see the laws of the cult in Leviticus as a symbolic realization of an order of wholeness contrasted to the pattern of human failure reiterated in the surrounding narrative; David Gunn suggests that the lists of tribal borders in Joshua are a way of imaginatively mapping out and making real the as yet unconquered Land.[2] In any case, the Hebrew Bible, though it includes some of the most extraordinary narratives and poems in the Western literary tradition, reminds us that literature is not entirely limited to story and poem, that the coldest catalogue and the driest etiology may be an effective subsidiary instrument of literary expression.

The evidence of the texts suggests that the literary impulse in ancient

Israel was quite as powerful as the religious impulse, or, to put it more accurately, that the two were inextricable, so that in order to understand the latter, you have to take full account of the former. In all biblical narrative and in a good deal of biblical poetry as well, the domain in which literary invention and religious imagination are joined is history, for all these narratives, with the exception of Job and possibly Jonah, purport to be true accounts of things that have occurred in historical time. Let us consider one extended example of a text in which historical experience is recast, perhaps even reinvented, in a highly wrought literary art that embodies a religious perspective and that also encompasses elements which later conventions would set beyond the pale of literature.

Chapter 11 of Judges recounts the disturbing story of Jephthah's daughter. Jephthah, before going into battle against the Ammonites, makes the imprudent vow that if he returns victorious he will offer to the Lord whoever (or whatever) first comes out from the doors of his house to greet him. In the event, it is his only daughter who comes out, and Jephthah, persuaded that the vow is irrevocable, sacrifices her, first granting her request of a stay of two months during which she and her maiden friends can "bewail her virginity" (11:38). Now, the historical scholars, with some plausibility, view the whole story of the vow and the sacrifice as an etiological tale devised to explain the curious annual custom, mentioned at the end of the chapter, of the daughters of Israel going up into the mountains to lament for four days. We are scarcely in a position to decide on the historical facts of the matter. Perhaps there was a Jephthah who actually sacrificed his daughter (in contravention, of course, of the strictest biblical prohibition), and then a local cult sprang up around the death of the young woman. It may be more likely that in the region of Gilead there was a pagan cult—for the sake of the argument, let us say, of a Persephone-like goddess—which was adopted by the Israelite women; when the origins of these rites had been forgotten, the story was invented to explain them. We often think of such etiological tales as belonging to the realm of early folk traditions rather than to literature proper, being a "primitive" attempt to explain puzzling realities narratively; and such condescension has frequently been reflected in scholarly treatment of the Bible. But etiological tales are in fact essential elements of many artfully complex and symbolically resonant stories in the Hebrew Bible. The Deluge story culminates in, but can hardly be reduced to, an answer to the etiological question: how did the rainbow get in the sky? The haunting tale of Jacob and the angel (Gen. 32:24–32) is in some way generated by yet transcends the question: why do Israelites refrain from eating the sinew of the animal's thigh? And in Jephthah's story, whatever explanation is provided through the tale for the origins of an obscure practice is subsumed under the more complex literary enterprise of interrelating character, motive, event, historical pattern, political institution, and religious perspective. That art of interrelation is the hallmark of the great chain of narratives that runs from Joshua to 2 Kings.

Let us now look at just the first large segment of the Jephthah story. For reasons that will soon be apparent, the story actually begins with the last two verses of chapter 10, before the figure of Jephthah is introduced at the beginning of chapter 11.

> Then the children of Ammon were gathered together, and encamped in Gilead. And the children of Israel assembled themselves together, and encamped in Mizpeh. And the people and princes of Gilead said one to another, whosoever is the man [AR] that will begin to fight against the children of Ammon, he shall be head over all the inhabitants of Gilead.
>
> Now Jephthah the Gileadite was a mighty man of valor, and he was the son of a harlot: and Gilead begat Jephthah. And Gilead's wife bare him sons; and his wife's sons grew up, and they thrust out Jephthah, and said unto him, Thou shalt not inherit in our father's house; for thou art the son of another [AR] woman. Then Jephthah fled from his brethren, and dwelt in the land of Tob: and there were gathered worthless fellows [AR] to Jephthah, and went out with him.
>
> And it came to pass in process of time, that the children of Ammon made war against Israel. And it was so, that when the children of Ammon made war against Israel, the elders of Gilead went to fetch Jephthah out of the land of Tob: And they said unto Jephthah, Come, and be our captain, that we may fight with the children of Ammon. And Jephthah said unto the elders of Gilead, Did not ye hate me, and thrust me out [AR] of my father's house? and why are ye come unto me now when ye are in distress? And the elders of Gilead said unto Jephthah, Therefore we turn again to thee now, that thou mayest go with us, and fight against the children of Ammon, and be our head over all the inhabitants of Gilead. And Jephthah said unto the elders of Gilead, If ye bring me home again to fight against the children of Ammon, and the Lord deliver them before me, then shall I be your head [AR]. And the elders of Gilead said unto Jephthah, The Lord be witness between us, if we do not so according to thy words. Then Jephthah went with the elders of Gilead, and the people made him head and captain over them: and Jephthah uttered all his words before the Lord in Mizpeh.   (Judges 10:17–11:11)

Whether or not things happened precisely as reported here, and whether or not the ancient audience conceived this as a literally accurate account of historical events (both questions are unanswerable), it is clear from the way the text is organized that the writer has exercised considerable freedom in shaping his materials to exert subtle interpretive pressure on the figures and events. In such writing, it is increasingly difficult to distinguish sharply between history and fiction, whatever the historical intentions of the writers. Admittedly, even modern "scientific" historiography has certain rhetorical features, but biblical narrative stands at the far end of the same spectrum, the language of narration and dialogue never being a transparent vehicle to convey the events but constantly in the foreground, always intended to be *perceived* as a constitutive element of the events.[3] The very names and geographic indications in the story, whether they were happily found by the writer in his historical material or contrived for thematic purposes, form part of the pattern of meaning. Jephthah's name means "he will open," a cognate of the verb *patsah* that he uses when he says in anguish to his daughter: "I have opened my mouth unto the Lord" (11:35). The eponymous Gilead begets him, almost as though the clan itself begat him, and thus a simple genealogical datum is immediately ironized, for he is expelled by Gilead as a collective entity, then courted by its elders for reasons of frightened self-interest. He gathers around him a band of desperadoes in the land of Tob, which, however real a geographic designation, also means "good" and thus participates in another turn of irony, the land of good being the badlands from which the banished man longs to return to a home.

Jephthah's is a tale of calamitous vow-taking, and this initial section constantly plays with vows and pledges and the verbal terms they involve. At their encampment in Mizpeh the Gileadites take a vow that whoever succeeds in leading them against the Ammonites "shall be head over all the inhabitants of Gilead." When Jephthah's half brothers decide to drive him out—apparently with the threat of force, for in the next verse we learn that he has to flee—they address him with what amounts to a legal declaration: "Thou shalt not inherit in our father's house, for thou art the son of another woman." It would have been easy enough for the author to report this as interior monologue (as elsewhere in the Bible, "They said in their hearts") or as private speech among the brothers. Instead, his choice of direct discourse addressed to Jephthah (in which the narrator's plain term "harlot" is euphemistically veiled by the brothers as "another woman") sharpens the element of confrontation so important in the story and suggests that this is a binding pronouncement of disinheritance meant to be heard by witnesses. The latter suspicion may be confirmed by Jephthah's accusation of the elders, making them accomplices in his banishment ("Did not ye hate me and thrust me out . . . ?"). When the elders come to Jephthah, speaking to him quite brusquely (biblical Hebrew is rich in polite forms of address, which they pointedly avoid in their opening words), they renege on the original terms of the collective vow and offer him, instead of chieftainship over all the inhabitants of Gilead, a mere military command, not "head" but "captain."[4] As in virtually all one-sided dialogues in the Hebrew Bible, we are invited to wonder about the feelings and motives of the party who remains silent. Jephthah says nothing to his brothers, only flees; but years later, when he receives the rudely pragmatic invitation of the elders, his pent-up resentment emerges: "Did not ye hate me . . . and why are ye come unto me now when ye are in distress?" The biblical writers repeatedly use dialogue not merely to define political positions with stylized clarity, as Thucydides does, but also to delineate unfolding relations, nuances of character and attitude. The elders' brusque words trigger Jephthah's outburst. Then, caught out and trying to backpedal rhetorically, they become more voluble and more polite, introducing their remarks with a causal indication, "Therefore," that doesn't really refer to anything but vaguely seeks to give him the impression that all along they have been seeking to make amends. Their speech also underlines the thematic key words of "going" and "returning" or "bringing back" (the latter two reflect the same root in the Hebrew), which focus the story of banishment from the house and the flawed attempt of return to the house. This use of what Buber and Rosenzweig first designated as *Leitwort* (on the model of *Leitmotiv*), pervasive in biblical narrative, is still another instance of the flaunted prominence of the verbal medium. At the tragic climax of the story, when Jephthah confesses his vow to his daughter, he says, pathetically, "I cannot go back" (11:35).

But the poised choreography of words, in which formulations are pointedly reiterated and internally shifted as they are repeated, is most centrally evident in the changing language of the vow. The elders, having been exposed by Gilead, now revert to the original terms of the vow taken at Mizpeh: "thou mayest go with us, and fight against the children of Ammon, and be our head over all the inhabitants of Gilead." Jephthah accepts these terms, omitting the comprehensive flourish of "all the inhabitants of Gilead" and stipulating that he will assume the leadership only if the Lord grants him victory. Interestingly, it is Jephthah, the banished bastard and guerrilla chieftain, and not the representatives of the Gileadite establishment, who first invokes the Lord. His problem is not one of being a weak monotheist but of conceiving his religious obligations in pagan terms, not finally understanding what the Lord God requireth of him. The elders respond to Jephthah's stipulation by making still another vow ("the lord be witness between us . . ."). When Jephthah reaches the Gileadite encampment—evidently, the one referred to at the beginning of our text, the whole first section of chapter 11 being a flashback—he is, from what one can make out, spontaneously acclaimed leader by the people, despite his condition to the elders that this should occur only after the victory. They make him "head and captain over them," both president and commander-in-chief, thus carrying out equally the terms of the initial vow and those of the elders' first offer to Jephthah. The entire section of exposition then closes with still another speech-act that is continuous with the string of vows: Jephthah speaks words before the Lord, perhaps not yet the words that will bring disaster on his daughter and himself, but at least an ominous foreshadowing of them.

These interconnecting details of the text at hand then link up with a larger pattern of political themes in Judges and a still larger thematic pattern variously manifested in other narrative books of the Bible. What is above all at issue in Judges is the question of right rule and fitting rulers, the sequence of judges devolving by stages toward the state of general anarchy and civil war represented in the five closing chapters. Unlike Samson, the subject of the next major story in the line, Jephthah has a certain poise and command as a leader: he shows himself, perhaps surprisingly, an able diplomat in his negotiations with the enemy intended to avert war; he is obviously a tough and effective military leader; his exchange with the elders also indicates a quality of shrewdness. But the vow, together with his inflexible adherence to carrying it out, is a fatal flaw, and it is not surprising that after his personal catastrophe he should preside as leader over a bloody civil war (chap. 12) in which tens of thousands of fellow Israelites perish at the hands of his army. The banishment at the beginning, at the head of a band of desperadoes, looks forward to the David story, but it is the sort of similarity that invites us to contemplate an essential difference: Jephthah is a disastrously more imperfect David who exhibits some of David's gifts but will found no dynasty, build no "house," leave no lasting institutions for national unity behind him.

What can be inferred from all this about the workings of the literary impulse in the Hebrew Bible? Perhaps the most essential point is that literary art is neither intermittent in its exercise nor merely ancillary to the writer's purposes—in this central regard, our passage from the beginning of the Jephthah story is thoroughly characteristic of the whole corpus. To be sure, the writer here is deeply concerned with questions of political leadership, community and individual, the binding nature of vows and pledges, the relationship of father and daughter, man's real and imagined obligations before God; but as a shaper of narrative he engages these complex issues by making constant artful determinations, whether consciously or intuitively, about such matters as the disposition of character, the deployment of dialogue, the attribution or withholding of motives, the use of motifs and thematic key words, the subtle modification of near-verbatim repetition of phrases. For a reader to attend to these elements of literary art is not merely an exercise in "appreciation" but a discipline of understanding: the literary vehicle is so much the necessary medium through which the Hebrew writers realized their meanings that we will grasp the meanings at best imperfectly if we ignore their fine articulations as literature. This general principle applies as much to biblical poetry as to prose. A line of Hebrew verse, whether it occurs in a grim denunciation in the Prophets, in an anguished questioning of divine justice in Job, or in the exultation of a psalm of praise, is likely to evince a certain characteristic structure dictated by the formal system of biblical poetry, of which the poets, whatever their spiritual aims, were exquisitely aware. The predominant patterns within the line are in turn associated with a number of characteristic movements for developing the poem as a whole; and some poetic compositions exhibit truly intricate structural features, involving refrainlike devices, strophic divisions, rondo movements, concentric designs, and much else. This is hardly surprising to find in any poetic corpus, but these are not qualities that our usual preconceptions of Scripture have encouraged us to look for in biblical poetry; and, as with the prose, an inattention to the literary medium runs the danger of becoming an inattention to the close weave of meanings.

Let us return briefly to what can be inferred from our illustrative passage specifically about narrative, which remains the dominant genre of the Hebrew Bible. These stories, we generally assume, are part of a religious literature, but that is true only in the rather special sense that virtually every other realm of experience is implicated in the religious perspective. Hence the pungent worldliness of the Hebrew Bible. If what is ultimately at stake in Judges is the possible historical meaning of the ideal of God's kingship over Israel, what we see in the foreground here, as throughout the Hebrew narratives, are issues like the strife between brothers, the struggle over a patrimony, the opposition between legitimate wife and illegitimate mate, the bitterness of personal exile, the lines of political tension in the triangle of individual, community leaders, and populace. The narrator's extreme reticence in telling us what we should think about all these conflicts and questions is extraordinary, and, more than any other single feature, it may explain the greatness of these narratives. Is Jephthah a hero or a villain, a tragic figure or an impetuously self-destructive fool? There are bound to be disagreements among readers, but the writer draws us into a process of intricate, tentative judgment by forcing us to negotiate on our own among such terms, making whatever use we can of the narrative data he has provided. There are, of course, explicit judgments made on particular characters and acts from time to time in biblical narrative: and so-and-so did evil in the eyes of the Lord. But these are no more than exceptions that prove the rule, most frequently occurring in connection with cultic transgressions, as in Kings, with its constant concern about the exclusive claims of the Temple cult in Jerusalem. The general rule that embraces the more characteristic refusal of explicit judgment is the famous laconic quality of biblical narrative. There is never leisurely description for its own sake; scene setting is accomplished with the barest economy of means; characters are sped over a span of years with a simple summary notation until we reach a portentous conjunction rendered in dialogue; and, in keeping with all this, analysis and assessment of character are very rare, and then very brief. We have no idea what Jephthah looks like, what he is wearing, whether he is taller or shorter than his brothers, where they are standing when they pronounce banishment on him; and his feelings about being thrust out can be inferred only from his subsequent words to the elders.

Many of these habits of reticence may be plausibly attributed to an underlying aesthetic predisposition. The masters of ancient Hebrew narrative were clearly writers who delighted in an art of indirection, in the possibilities of intimating depths through the mere hint of a surface feature, or through a few words of dialogue fraught with implication. Their attraction to narrative minimalism was reinforced by their sense that stories should be told in a way that would move efficiently to the heart of the matter, never pausing to elaborate mimetic effects for their own sake. In Homer we are given, for example, a feast of feasts, these daily rituals of hospitality and degustation having an intrinsic allure for the poet and his audience. In the Hebrew Bible, we learn precious little about anyone's menu, and then it usually proves to be for a thematic point. Exceptionally, we are offered some details of the repast Abraham orders for the angels (Gen. 18) because his pastoral hospitality (as against Lot's urban hospitality at the beginning of the next chapter) needs to be underlined. We are told specifically that Jacob is cooking lentil pottage (Gen. 26) when his famished brother comes in from the hunt, so that an emphatic pun can be made on the "red red stuff" of the pottage and Esau's name Edom, the Red. David's daughter Tamar prepares a delicacy called *levivot* (the identifying recipe has not survived) for her supposedly sick half brother Amnon (2 Sam. 13:8) in order that another, more ironic pun can be introduced: he is in love, or in lust, with her, is in fact about to rape her, and she offers him a kind of food whose name points to the word *lev,* "heart." (For a verb that puns on *lev* in a related way, see Song of Songs 4:9.)

It is the often drastic reticence of the Hebrew writers that led Erich Auerbach, in a famous essay that could be taken as the point of departure for the modern literary understanding of the Bible, to speak of Hebrew narrative as a text "fraught with background."[5] Auerbach, analyzing the somber and troubling story of the Binding of Isaac, was thinking chiefly of the way that the stark surface details bring us to ponder unexpressed psychological depths and theological heights; but in more typical biblical tales, where the perspective is not the vertiginous vertical one between man and God but a broader horizontal overview on the familial, social, erotic, and political interactions among human figures, the crucial consequence of reticence is the repeated avoidance of explicit judgment of the characters. There is, in the view of the Hebrew writers, something elusive, unpredictable, unresolvable about human nature. Man, made in God's image, shares a measure of God's transcendence of categories, images, defining labels. The recourse to implicit judgment opens up vistas of ambiguity—sometimes in matters of nuance, sometimes in essential regards—in our perception of the characters.

Who, for example, is Esau? The midrash, seeing him typologically as the iniquitous Edom-Rome, proposed a black-and-white answer, but the text itself withholds such easy resolution. At first Esau figures as an impetuous hairy oaf, strong man with a bow but ruled by the growling of his own stomach; then as a rather pathetic overgrown child weeping to his father over the purloined blessing. But when, with the returning Jacob, we meet Esau again after twenty years, he seems full of princely generosity toward his brother; and though prenatal oracle, sold birthright, and stolen blessing have all confirmed Jacob's preeminence, in their final scene together (Gen. 33) it is Jacob who repeatedly prostrates himself and calls himself "servant" and Esau "master." Does all this somehow cast a retrospective light of ironic qualification on Jacob's promised destiny? Does it suggest that we have at least partly misperceived Esau, or rather that he has grown morally during all those years during which Jacob labored and struggled with Laban in Mesopotamia? As elsewhere, we are left wondering about alternatives, feeling that no clear-cut judgment is possible, because the narrator keeps his lips sealed. Meir Sternberg, who has devoted the most elaborate analysis to biblical procedures for opening up gaps and fostering ambiguities in the stories, makes the apt distinction that ancient Hebrew narrative is ideological but not didactic.[6] The story of Jacob and Esau is an especially instructive case in point. The eponymous second name attached to each of the twins, Israel and Edom respectively, sets the two up in what one might expect would be a heavily tilted political opposition: the covenanted people over against one of its notorious historical adversaries. But the story itself points toward a rather complicated balance of moral claims in the rivalry, perhaps because the writer, in fleshing out the individual characters, began to pull them free from the frame of reference of political allegory, and perhaps also because this is a kind of ideological literature that incorporates a reflex of ideological auto-critique.

What I have said so far may seem to sidestep a fundamental methodological question that has preoccupied biblical studies for a century and a half: the frequent unreliability of the received text and its accretive evolution through several eras of Israelite history. It is all very well, many biblical critics would still argue, to speak of unities and internal echoes and purposeful ambiguities in a short story by Faulkner or a poem by Wallace Stevens, because one writer was responsible for the text from beginning to end, down to the very proofreading and to any revisions in later editions. But how can we address the patchwork of the biblical text in the same fashion? By what warrant, for example, could I speak of poised ambiguities in the story of Jacob and Esau when scholarship long ago concluded that the tale is a stitching together of three separate "documents" conventionally designated E, J, and P? According to a periodically challenged consensus, the first two of these would have originated in the first two centuries of the Davidic monarchy, probably drawing on still earlier folk traditions, and all three were then cut and pasted to form a single text by anonymous Priestly redactors sometime after the destruction of the First Commonwealth, probably in the sixth or fifth century B.C.E.

I have no quarrel with the courage of conjecture of those engaged in what Sir Edmund Leach has shrewdly called "unscrambling the omelette,"[7] but the essential point for the validity of the literary perspective is that we have in the Bible, with far fewer exceptions than the historical critics would allow, a very well-made omelette indeed. Modern biblical scholarship is a product of the post-Gutenberg era, which may be one reason why it is predisposed to conceive authorship in rather narrow and exclusive terms. Collective works of art are not unknown phenomena, as we should be reminded by the medieval cathedrals growing through generations under the hands of successive waves of artisans, or cinema, where the first-stage work of director, cameraman, and actors achieves its final form in the selection, splicing, and reordering that goes on in the editing room. If in general the literary imagination exhibits what Coleridge called an "esemplastic" power, a faculty for molding disparate elements into an expressively unified whole not achieved outside of art, this power is abundantly evident in the work of the so-called redactors, so that often the dividing line between redactor and author is hard to draw, or if it is drawn, does not necessarily demarcate an essential difference. One important matter which remains undecidable is whether the redactors exercised any freedom in reworking inherited texts, or whether they felt restricted merely to selecting and combining what had been passed on to them. If the latter is true, as many scholars have tended to assume, we must conclude at the very least that the redactors exhibited a genius in creating brilliant collages out of traditional materials, though my own suspicion is that they did not hesitate to change a word, a phrase, perhaps even a whole speech or narrator's report, in order to create precisely the kind of interconnections of structure, theme, and motif to which I have been referring. If literary analysis, with the exception of one recent sectarian manifestation that radically disavows all unities,[8] is in one way or another a response to the esemplastic activity of the literary imagination, it will not be surprising that the new literary criticism of the Bible has tended to uncover unities where previous biblical scholars, following the hidden imperative "the more atomistic, the more scientific," found discontinuities, contradictions, duplications, fissures. The new literary perspective, let me stress, does not come to restore the seamless unitary character of the biblical text cherished by pious tradition, but it does argue in a variety of ways that scholarship, from so much overfocused concentration on the seams, has drawn attention away from the design of the whole. Thus, readers of this volume will find that some contributors simply set aside any consideration of hypotheses about the composite origins of the text because they find other issues more productive to discuss; other contributors explicitly use scholarly opinion about disparate elements in the text in order to see how once independent units are given new meanings, and contribute to the formation of larger patterns of meaning, by having been placed where they are in the final text continuum. In either case, the goal is to lead us toward what the biblical authors and author-redactors surely aimed for—a continuous *reading* of the text instead of a nervous hovering over its various small components.

Another difficulty, however, remains: quite frequently in the Hebrew Bible we may not have a dependable text to read. The oldest texts of single biblical books or parts of books are, as I noted earlier, preserved in the sectarian Dead Sea Scrolls, several centuries after the original composition. The oldest integral manuscript of the Hebrew Bible is a whole millennium later. Ancient witnesses beginning with the Septuagint sometimes provide help in difficult places, but their variants of the Masoretic text often reflect glosses, misunderstandings, or dubious textual traditions. There are certainly no grounds for confidence that the Bible we have is exactly the one produced by the original writers, though the degree of textual difficulties varies sharply. For long stretches of Genesis, Exodus, and other narrative books, the text seems relatively clean, with only an occasional local problem; in Job and in some of the poetic sections of the prophets, there are lines and occasionally even passages that are only barely intelligible. Most of these difficulties appear to be textual, though some are merely philological, for poetry—and in the Bible, Job above all—mines lexical resources not used elsewhere, involving terms whose meaning is uncertain. Comparative Semitic philology has made impressive progress in recovering many of these lost meanings and, in the case of more common words and idioms, in giving us a more precise sense of denotations and connotations. Since literary analysis needs at some level to respond to the nuances of words, the advances in biblical philology over the past several decades have been a necessary precondition for the development of the new literary criticism of the Bible that began to emerge in the 1970s. There are words and phrases and verses that will remain dark spots on the map, whether for philological or textual reasons, but by and large the Hebrew text now is more accessible to understanding than it has been for the past two thousand years.

Let me propose that, conversely, the application of properly literary analysis to the Bible is a necessary precondition to a sounder textual scholarship. At the beginning of his narratological study of Deuteronomy, Robert Polzin argues for "an operational priority to literary analysis at the preliminary stages of research."[9] If I may unpack that somewhat forbidding social-scientific formulation, the basic methodological issue is this: before you can decide whether a text is defective, composite, or redundant, you have to determine to the best of your ability the formal principles on which the text is organized. These are by no means the same for all times and places, as the nineteenth-century German founders of modern biblical scholarship often imagined. One has only to scan the history of a recent literary genre, the novel, to see how rapidly formal conventions shift, and to realize that elements like disjunction, interpolation, repetition, contrastive styles, which in biblical scholarship were long deemed sure signs of a defective text, may be perfectly deliberate components of the literary artwork, and recognized as such by the audience for which it is intended. There is a distinctive poetics informing both biblical narrative and biblical poetry, and an understanding of it will help us in many instances to make plain sense of a puzzling text instead of exercising that loose and derivative mode of literary invention that goes under the scholarly name of emendation.

A couple of examples should clarify the methodological point. In Proverbs 7:9, in the introductory movement of the vivid narrative poem about the gullible young man and the dangerous seductress, we are told that he goes out into the streets, where she is waiting to meet him, "At twilight, as evening falls, / in pitch-black night and darkness" [AT]. This line of verse has troubled some textual scholars because it seems a violation of logic. If it is twilight, how can it be pitch-black night? When one adds that the Hebrew word *'ishon* that I have rendered as "pitch-black" usually means the dark, or apple, of the eye and occurs in verse 2 ("let my teaching be like the apple of your eye" [AT]), we have both crux and solution. The ancient scribe, nodding, inadvertently repeated in verse 9 the word *'ishon,* which belonged only in verse 2. Then someone added "in darkness" as a gloss. What must be done to "restore" the text is to erase the whole second verset of this line and attach the first verset to the next line.

But if one considers precisely how lines of biblical poetry are generally constructed, the purported crux dissolves and the whole procedure of emendation becomes gratuitous. For it can readily be shown that in many hundreds of lines in the biblical corpus, the relation between the first verset and the second is *narrative*: under the umbrella of parallelism or overlapping meaning that covers the two halves of the line, the second action or image follows in time after the first. (For some examples, see the essay "The Characteristics of Ancient Hebrew Poetry" in this volume.) Our line from Proverbs, then, is not a break with logic but a particularly striking instance of a general principle of poetic logic observable in biblical verse: in one instant, we see the young man setting out into the streets at twilight; in the next instant, it is already totally dark, a suitable cover for the seductress as she marks her sexual target. This little temporal jump between versets may even be grounded in a mimesis of nature, for sunsets in the eastern Mediterranean seem to happen very quickly; and we should also note that the seductress's reference later, in verse 20, to a full moon evidently a couple of weeks off indicates that the action of the poem takes place at the dark of the moon. As for the occurrence of *'ishon* in verse 9, this makes perfect sense in terms of another principle of biblical poetics—the practice of tying together distinct segments of the poem (here, the framing introductory lines and then the narrative body of the poem) through the repetition of some prominent word, whether in the identical sense or in a play on two different senses. Again, this is a formal organizing principle that can be demonstrated analytically in scores of examples. Thus, in reading the poem more fully through an awareness of its poetics, we also come to see why it is absurd to rewrite the text in order to make it conform to a logic alien to it.

Let us consider one example of a supposedly defective narrative text, the first three verses of 2 Samuel 5, which report David's confirmation as king over all the tribes of Israel after the conclusion of the civil war with the tribes supporting the house of Saul. I will quote the passage in my own rather literal translation because the King James Version at this point makes some misleading choices and also takes a couple of liberties with the Hebrew parataxis.

> All the tribes of Israel came to David at Hebron and said, "Here, we are your bone and flesh. Long ago, when Saul was king over us, you were Israel's leader in battle. And the Lord said to you:
>
>> You shall shepherd my people
>>> and you shall be ruler over Israel."
>
> All the elders of Israel came to the king at Hebron, and King David made a covenant with them in Hebron before the Lord, and they anointed David king over Israel.   [AT]

The apparent difficulty here is that the last sentence is a repetition of the first. The atomistic solution of some textual scholars runs along the following lines: two traditions, using similar formulations, have been rather clumsily spliced together by the editor; in the first tradition, it was the tribes of Israel who came to Hebron, in the second tradition, the elders; the editorial compulsion to incorporate both traditions introduced both a redundancy and a contradiction in the text. This is another instance in which inattention to the organizing literary principles of the text leads to faulty scholarship. The Hebrew writers frequently use a framing technique that in fact biblical scholars have identified and designated *resumptive repetition*: if the progress of a narrative line is interrupted by some digression or specification, the writer marks the return to the point where the main line was left by repeating the statement made just before the interruption. Our passage proves to be a rather subtle adaptation of this general technique. In the first instance, a popular movement acclaiming David worthy of kingship is recorded. "All the tribes of Israel" come to him, and their support is represented by quotation of their speech, in which is embedded a quotation on their part of divine speech—appropriately, it has the solemnity of a line of formal verse—that is an explicit promise to

David of the role of leader. After these two pieces of direct discourse, the resumptive repetition takes us back to the initial narrative statement before the dialogue and continues with a summary of the political act that was consummated at Hebron. This time, however, the elders rather than the tribes are singled out as agents because, although it may be the prerogative of the populace to acclaim, it is the prerogative of the elders formally to confirm David's kingship in the ceremony of anointment. We should also note that in the initial report the tribes come to "David" and in the concluding report the elders come to "the king," who is then immediately referred to as "King David," both terms being proleptic of the end of the sentence, in this way underscoring the binding force of the anointment. The actual term *king* appears in the quoted discourse of the tribes only in retrospective reference to Saul, but God's words promising that David will be "ruler [*nagid*] over Israel" are picked up by the narrator at the end and given an unambiguous political definition when David is anointed "king [*melekh*] over Israel." Thus the technique of resumptive repetition has been joined with a still more common technique of biblical prose, minute focusing through small variations in near-verbatim repetition.[10] The supposedly composite and redundant text turns out to be a tightly woven unit in which repetition is used to frame the central dialogue and sharpen the political theme.

If the arguments I have been laying out suggest why a literary approach to the Hebrew Bible is fully warranted and in certain ways required by the nature of the material, they omit still another complicating consideration—the diachronic dimension of this literary corpus. Here, again, there is a difference between the Hebrew Bible and the New Testament that is both quantitative and qualitative. The New Testament, reflecting a particular portentous moment in history, is the work of a few generations; the Hebrew Bible spans nearly a millennium of literary activity. How much did Hebrew literature change over this period, which covers about as much time as elapsed in French literature from the *Song of Roland* to the novels of Alain Robbe-Grillet? In poetry, the changes are surprisingly minor, having more to do with certain features of grammatical forms and diction than with any underlying shift in notions of poetic style and structure. It is true that the earliest poetic texts, such as the Song of Deborah, exhibit a fondness for incantatory movements and incremental repetition that are not often found in later poems, but the formal system of versification and basic conceptions about the poetic medium do not change substantively over this whole long period. Job, the supreme poetic achievement of the era after the destruction of the First Commonwealth, probably reflects its historical moment in the abundant borrowing from Aramaic in its vocabulary, but poetically it is perfectly continuous with the poetic creations of the First Commonwealth; any formal differences are attributable to the individual genius of the poet or to the generic aims

of the genre of radical Wisdom literature for which he made his verse a
vehicle. A very late book, Ecclesiastes (fourth or third century B.C.E.)
does move toward a new horizon of literary form, but, instructively, it
does so by abandoning the system of parallelistic verse for a kind of
cadenced prose that incorporates small pieces of verse, a good many of
them wry parodies of Proverbs.

In narrative, on the other hand, though there are some strong elements of continuity, new styles and new notions of narrative art emerge
in the post-Exilic period. The golden age of Hebrew narrative was the
First Commonwealth era, when the great sequence of works from Genesis
to Kings was given its initial formulation. The brilliantly laconic style,
with its uncanny ability to intimate psychological and thematic complexities (one has only to think of the story of Joseph and his brothers, or the
David story), came to full flowering during this period. Certain features
of this classic narrative art, like the use of thematic key words and refrainlike repetitions, are still observable in a late tale like Jonah, and if the Book
of Ruth, whose dating is still disputed, is in fact late, then it represents
an extraordinary archaizing redeployment of the earlier conventions. But
from the perspective of literary history, most of the new Hebrew narratives created after 586 B.C.E. are distinctly the products of a postclassical
age. Instead of one dominant form, as in the earlier period, there is a
proliferation of forms, perhaps a kind of experimentation with different
forms by different writers over nearly four centuries of the post-Exilic
period. Ezra–Nehemiah and Chronicles represent new strategies for the
narrative engagement of history through autobiographical writing, annalistic recapitulation, the buttressing of the report of history through personal observation or, alternatively, through the citation of sources. Jonah,
Esther, and Daniel, in quite different ways, depart from the general norm
of historical and psychological realism that, despite the occasional intervention of divine agency or miraculous event, governs classical Hebrew
narrative. Jonah has variously been described as a parable, a Menippean
satire, a sailor's yarn, and it is clear that the writer has stretched the
contours of reality with a zestful overtness to suit his ends, not only in
the famous instance of Jonah's descent into the belly of the big fish but
also in such details as the dimensions of Nineveh (at three days' walk, it
would be much bigger than Los Angeles) and the animals that are made
to fast and don sackcloth. Daniel, in its insistent theme of piety (the classic
Hebrew narratives are religious but never quite pious in this way), its
intimations of an apocalypse, and some of its formal structures, is closely
akin to certain texts of the Apocrypha, and very much a work of the
Hellenistic period. (On connections with the Apocrypha, see the essay on
Daniel in this volume.) Esther, though it purportedly represents events in
the Persian imperial court in Susa, takes place in a fairy-tale never-never
land where, for example, a parade of all the fairest maidens of the kingdom

is brought to the royal bed night after night, each beauty having been exquisitely prepared for the king's delectation by being soaked six months in oil of myrrh and another six in assorted perfumes. There is broad comedy here of a sort absent from the earlier narratives, and also a rather simple didacticism one does not find in First Commonwealth writing. The stringent narrative economy of the classical literature has been replaced by a reveling in the sumptuousness of details of milieu, often cast in the form of descriptive catalogues: "Where were white, green, and blue hangings, fastened with cords of fine linen and purple to silver rings and pillars of marble: the beds were of gold and silver, upon a pavement of red, and blue, and white, and black, marble" (Esther 1:6). We need not invoke a direct influence from the Greek sphere to detect here the beginnings of a Hebrew literature that is heading toward Hellenistic horizons.

We have seen, then, that there is striking variety in the body of ancient Hebrew literature preserved in the Bible, a variety that stems from the long centuries through which it evolved, the different genres it represents, the divergent aims and viewpoints of its authors. All that notwithstanding, this is a corpus that bears within it the seeds of its own canonicity. Earlier, we noted the strong elements of internal allusion in Hebrew Scripture that at many points make it a set of texts in restless dialogue with one another. In the end, this is something that goes beyond what is ordinarily thought of in strictly literary terms as intertextuality. Although I think it is inaccurate to speak, as some have done, of a "system" of symbols in the Hebrew Bible, it is clear that the various texts exploit certain recurrent symbols which, however dictated by the topography, geography, history, and climate of ancient Israel, become a unifying way of conceiving the world, of referring the discrete data of historical and individual experience to large interpretive patterns. (This degree of symbolic cohesiveness among the Hebrew texts in turn helped make them assimilable into the new symbolic framework of the New Testament.) Thus, the act of dividing between heaven and earth, water and dry land, which is the initial definition of God's cosmogonic power, proliferates into a whole spectrum of antithetical oppositions: garden or oasis and wasteland, later recurring as Promised Land and Wilderness, or, in another variant, homeland ("the Lord's inheritance") and exile, in either case often with a necessary rite of passage through water to get from one to the other; Israel and the nations; and even calendrically, the sabbath and the six days of labor. Or, in a pattern less grounded in nature or history than in a concept, the stark initiating act of creation through divine speech from formlessness, chaos, nothingness (*tohu-bohu*) lingers in the Hebrew imagination as a measure of the absoluteness of God's power and also as a looming perspective on the contingency of all human existence and the frailty of all human exercises of knowledge and power. Although, as we have observed, there is ideological debate among the Hebrew writers, this fundamental perception is shared by all (only Ecclesiastes gives it a negative twist), and it is a central instance in which a persistent set of images also is a persistent vision of reality. A particularly memorable example is the poem about God as transcendent weigher of all creation, composed by the anonymous prophet of the Babylonian Exile referred to by scholars as Deutero-Isaiah (Isaiah 40:12–26). It would be a great poem even in isolation, but its actual richness has much to do with its ramified connections with the larger context of the Hebrew Bible. I will offer my own translation because the King James Version here abounds in errors and does very little to suggest the poetic compactness of the original. Verses 19 and 20, which depict the foolish activity of artisans making idols, are omitted because they involve several textual difficulties and in any case are not essential to the general point I want to illustrate.

> Who with his hand's hollow measured the waters,
>   the heavens who gauged with a span,
> and meted earth's dust with a measure,
>   weighed with a scale the mountains,
>   the hills with a balance?
> Who has plumbed the spirit of the Lord,
>   what man has told him his plan?
> With whom did he counsel, who taught him,
>   who led him in the path of right and told him wisdom's way?
> Why, the nations are a drop from the bucket,
>   like the balance's dust they're accounted,
>   why, the coastlands he plucks up like motes.
> Lebanon is not fuel enough,
>   its beasts not enough for the offering.
> All nations are as naught before him,
>   he accounts them as empty and nothing.
> And to whom would you liken God,
>   what likeness for him propose?
> . . . . .
> Do you not know,
>   have you not heard?
> Was it not told you from the first,
>   have you not understood the foundations of earth?
> He's enthroned on the rim of the earth,
>   and its dwellers are like grasshoppers.
> He spread the heavens like gauze,
>   stretched them like a tent to dwell in.
> He turns princes into nothing,
>   the rulers of earth he makes naught.
> Hardly planted, hardly sown,
>   hardly their stem rooted in earth—
> when he blows on them and they wither,
>   the storm bears them off like straw.

"And to whom will you liken me that I be equal?"
    says the Holy One.
Lift up your eyes on high,
    and see, who created these?
He who musters their host by number,
    each one he calls by name.
Through great strength and mighty power
    no one lacks in the ranks.

The poem not only involves the general idea of God as powerful creator but also alludes to a series of key terms from the first account of creation in Genesis. The sequence water-heaven-earth in the three initial versets recalls the three cosmic spheres with which God works on the first three days of the Creation. The reiterated assertion that there is no likeness (*demut*) that man can possibly find for God is, of course, a sound argument against idolatry, something that explicitly concerns the prophet; but the term also echoes, by way of ironic inversion, the first creation of human-kind: "Let us make man in our image, after our likeness [*demuteinu*]" (Gen. 1:26). That is to say, God is perfectly free to fashion a human creature in his own likeness, but it is utterly beyond the creature's capacity to fashion a likeness for his creator. In a related way, the background of cosmogony is present in the poet's assertion that nations and rulers are as naught, or nothing, before God, since one of the repeated pair of terms in these two sets of lines is *tohu,* the very void out of which the world was first called into being. Still another ironic crossover between human and divine is effected through an allusion to a different text. To God who is enthroned (or simply "seated") on the rim of the earth, all its inhabitants (the same word in the Hebrew as "he who sits" at the beginning of the line) seem like grasshoppers. This simile links up with the fearful report of the majority of the spies sent by Moses to investigate the land (*'erets,* the same term that here means "earth"). They were dismayed by the enormous size of "its inhabitants" (the same word as in the line we are considering), calling them "people of vast proportions," or, more literally, "people of measure" (*midot,* the same root that is reflected in the verb which begins our poem), "and we were in our own sight as grasshoppers, and so we were in their sight" (Num. 13:33). In short, the grotesque, and inaccurate, simile used by the spies in a reflex of fear here becomes an accurate gauge of the disproportion between creator and creatures, or, indeed, a kind of cosmic understatement.

The essential point, however, is not the prophet's clever use of allu-sion but the deep affinity of perception with his predecessors that his use of allusion reflects. Despite the network of reminiscences of Genesis (to which the mention of the host of the heavens at the end should be added), the dominant imagery of the poem is actually technological, in part as a rejoinder to the paltry technology of idol-making which the poet denounces. God weighs, measures, gauges, plumbs, but these activities cannot operate in the opposite direction: no man can plumb the unfathomable spirit of the Lord. To set this for a moment in relation to the poet's craft, the person who shaped these lines had a sense of familiarity with the concrete activities of quotidian reality, surveying and architecture and the weighing of merchandise, the cultivation of young plants, and the pitching of tents. The literature of ancient Israel, even in sublime moments like this one, scarcely ever loses this feeling of rootedness in the concrete realities of the here and now. At the same time, the loftiness of perspective of the poem by Deutero-Isaiah is breathtaking: "He's enthroned on the rim of the earth, / and its dwellers are like grasshoppers." The Hebrew writers in both poetry and prose were deeply engaged by the fate of nations, the destinies of individuals, and the elaborate grid of political institutions and material instrumentalities in which both were enmeshed. The contrast of perspectives that is the explicit subject of our poem is in the narratives often only implicit; but however closely the human scene is followed, there is always a potential sense, perhaps even hinted at in the challenging terseness of the narrative mode of presentation, that merely human aspirations shrink to nothing under the vast overarching aspect of eternity. One measure of the centrality of this vision to the Hebrew imagination is that the imagery and theme of our poem by Deutero-Isaiah, especially in the opening five lines, are strikingly similar to the language of the Voice from the Whirlwind, though in other respects Job (who was perhaps even a near-contemporary) reflects a much more unconsoling view of God and man, at the other end of the spectrum of Israelite thought.

Sometime in the latter part of the second millennium B.C.E., the spiritual avant-garde of the Hebrew people began to imagine creation and creator, history and humankind, in a radically new way. This radicalism of vision, though it would never produce anything like unanimity, generated certain underlying patterns of literary expression in the centuries that followed. In poetry, these were realized technically through a heightening and refinement of formal conventions largely inherited from an antecedent Syro-Palestinian tradition of verse. In the prose narratives, one may infer that these patterns became the very matrix of an extraordinary new kind of representation of action, character, speech, and motive. In both cases, the imaginative recurrence, for all the diversity, to the bedrock assumptions of biblical monotheism about the nature of reality weaves tensile bonds among the disparate texts. This endlessly fascinating anthology of ancient Hebrew literature was also, against all plausible acceptations of the word, on its way to becoming a book.

NOTES

1. Harold Bloom, "'Before Moses Was, I Am'; The Original and the Belated Testaments," in *Notebooks in Cultural Analysis,* I (Durham, N.C., 1984), 3.

2. For all three, see the essays on the respective biblical books in this volume.

3. On the perceptibility of the verbal medium as one way of distinguishing literary from historical narratives, see T. G. Rosenmeyer, "History or Poetry? The Example of Herodotus," *Clio,* 11 (1982), 239–259.

4. I was first alerted to the shrewd play between "head" and "captain" in the story by an astute paper presented by Nahum Sarna at the Institute for Advanced Studies in Jerusalem in 1983.

5. Erich Auerbach, *Mimesis: The Representation of Reality in Western Literature,* trans. Willard Trask (Princeton, 1953), chap. 1.

6. Meir Sternberg, *The Poetics of Biblical Narrative: Ideological Literature and the Drama of Reading* (Bloomington and Indianapolis, 1985), pp. 36–38.

7. Edmund Leach and D. Alan Aycock, *Structuralist Interpretations of Biblical Myth* (Cambridge, 1983), p. 3.

8. The notion that every text is divided against itself is a fundamental dogma of the critical school known as Deconstruction, which began in Paris in the late 1960s and became fashionable in America and England a decade later.

9. Robert Polzin, *Moses and the Deuteronomist. A Literary Study of the Deuteronomic History, Part One: Deuteronomy, Joshua, Judges* (New York, 1980), p. 2.

10. For a general exposition of this technique, see Robert Alter, *The Art of Biblical Narrative* (New York, 1981), pp. 97–113. Many examples are also analyzed by Sternberg, *The Poetics of Biblical Narrative.*

Genesis

J. P. Fokkelman

GENESIS is the first of the thirty-six books of the Old Testament, and much in it is used as a basis for or creatively incorporated into numerous passages further on in the Bible.[1] Genesis is the beginning of the Torah, traditionally known as the Five Books of Moses, or the Pentateuch. In the standard edition, the Hebrew text comprises well over fifteen hundred "verses," which in the Middle Ages were divided, not always happily, into fifty chapters.[2] For at least two reasons Genesis, like other narrative books of the Bible, can be hard to understand. It is very complex, and it exhibits a baffling multiformity. The difficulties have not been diminished by two centuries of the so-called Higher Criticism, a historical-critical approach[3]—an "excavative scholarship," as it has been called[4]—that subjects the text to serious reduction. Philologists and historians are apt to regard the text as a source for something beyond itself because their proper interest or attention is directed to contextual realities. And theologians tend to read the text as message, and to that end separate form from content without realizing that in doing so they violate the literary integrity of the text.

Multiformity and Discord

As readers of Genesis, we must fully respect and explore the large variety in shape and structure, tone and length, which the literary units display. This disconcerting combination of highly heterogeneous elements, which often test our tolerance, prevails in books such as Exodus, Numbers, Judges, Samuel, and Kings. The main aspects of this multiformity are as follows.

The narrator (or the creative writer responsible for the final version of the text) may, at any moment, switch from the narrative flow to a more elevated style, that is, to the compactness of formal verse. Thus a polarity arises between prose and poetry, and the body of prose functions as a setting in which, repeatedly, the gem of a poem sparkles. Sometimes the poetry consists of no more than one verse, as in the triadic line at 1:27:

> So God created man in his own image,
> in the image of God created he him;
> male and female created he them.

More often it is a two-line strophe, as in 2:23:

> This is now bone of my bones
> and flesh of my flesh:
> she shall be called Woman
> because she was taken out of Man;

or 8:22:

> While the earth remaineth,
> seedtime and harvest, and cold and heat,
> and summer and winter, and day and night
> shall not cease;

or 14:19–20a:

> Blessed be Abram of the most high God,
> possessor of heaven and earth:
> And blessed be the most high God,
> which hath delivered thine enemies into thy hand;

and compare 25:23. There are also three-line poems, such as 4:6–7:

> Why art thou wroth?
> and why is thy countenance fallen?
> If thou doest well, shalt thou not be accepted?
> and if thou doest not well, sin lieth at the door.
> And unto thee shall be his desire,
> and thou shalt rule over him;

or Lamech's song, 4:23–24:

> Adah and Zillah, hear my voice;
> ye wives of Lamech, hearken unto my speech:
> for I have slain a man to my wounding,
> and a young man to my hurt.
> If Cain shall be avenged sevenfold,
> truly Lamech seventy and sevenfold;

and compare 27:39b–40. The blessing in which God promises the patriarchs land and offspring (12:1–3) is somewhat longer still, three triadic lines, whereas subsequent passages such as 22:16–18 and 28:13 are midway between prose and poetry—the boundaries are often not very clear. Old Isaac's blessing in 27:27–29 is a double strophe (3 + 3 dyadic lines). Later the poetry recedes until chapter 49, near the end of the book, where we encounter a large composition of well over eighty versets or half-lines. In the enumerative or serial design there, Jacob concisely characterizes each of his sons (and the tribe of which he is the eponymous forefather) with a thumbnail portrait. He accords five of them only one line each; dedicates a three-line strophe to Reuben, Issachar, and Dan and a double strophe (3 + 2 versets) to Simeon and Levi together; and devotes a full stanza of eight and nine verses of praise to Judah (8–12) and Joseph (22–26) respectively.

Occasionally the switch from prose to poetry is explicitly marked. In the case of Lamech's song of revenge and Jacob's blessings, the transition is achieved by a formal beginning, an adjuration to be attentive (4:23a and 49:1b). Sometimes the discourse glides unobtrusively from prose into poetry. We suddenly realize with a little shock that the words are symmetrically aligned and that the language has become more intense; next we notice the text's poetical form; and finally we perceive that the personage who is blessed or cursed in the story has anticipated our shock of recognition in feeling the force of the poem. In the story of the Fall, Genesis 2–3, it is the figures of "man and his wife" and the serpent who through the poetry of 3:14–15, 16, and 17b–19 sense that they themselves have become the victims of God's curse.

An even greater source of heterogeneity in the composition is the use of different genres. We meet with a colorful variety of action-directed narratives in the strictest sense, genealogical registers, catalogues, blessings and curses, protocols for the conclusion of covenants, doxological and mythological texts, etiological tales, legal directives. This odd diversity is complicated still further by a third and a fourth factor of multiformity: size, that is, the difference between short and long units; and the polarity between narrator's text and character's text, that is, between report and speech. Genesis does not fundamentally differ in this regard from other narrative books of the Bible. The narrator may create a harmonious balance or variation between report and speech, as in chapters 24, 27, and 38, stories that are directly accessible and attractive to Western taste. Here report and speech together carry the plot. These instances of balance form the middle of a scale one extreme of which is represented by units consisting mostly or entirely of narrator's text (and thus lacking the charm and vivacity conferred by dialogue), and the other extreme of sections consisting entirely of character's text or dialogue. On the one hand, Abraham's outspoken haggling with God over the dwindling remnant of integrity which he hopes may still exist in Sodom and Gomorrah (18:23–33) is a textual unit that consists entirely of dialogue. Similarly, in the bargaining scene in chapter 23 the spoken word carries the plot entirely, the narrator being content with a marginal role. The body of the text consists of three rounds of dialogue, marked by bows by Abraham. It concerns increasingly concrete negotiations between him and the Hittites of Hebron which result in a purchase (vv. 3–6, 8–11, 13–15). The narrator confines himself to reporting the occasion of Sarah's death (vv. 1–2) and playing a participatory role in verses 17–20. There he speaks as the notary who is responsible for the contract of sale, for the exact description of the extent and cost of the purchased ground, and for the contractors and witnesses. In that way the narrator's text frames the dialogue.

On the other hand, the genealogical registers of chapter 5 (with the exception of 29b, Lamech's naming-speech at the birth of Noah), 11:10–26, and chapter 36 consist entirely of narrator's text. The impression of discord is especially strong where a long report stands in sharp contrast with a long speech. A similarly abrupt transition from report to speech occurs in the episode of Jacob's flock-breeding (30:37–43), followed by his flight from Laban (31:1–21). The contrast between these two units warrants a more detailed analysis. The perspective of the narrator first reveals little more than the temporal aspect of Jacob's ingenious animal-breeding, through which he is able to become wealthy. Then the perspective of the character, Jacob himself, reveals that he has in fact been victimized by his uncle Laban and providentially protected by God.

Differences in length are also a source of strong contrasts. Some of the profoundest and most exciting stories are remarkably short but are found close to a long text which moves at a very relaxed pace. Consider chapters 22 and 24. In the Binding of Isaac, Abraham is cruelly ordered by God to sacrifice his son, the bearer of the promise, whose coming he has awaited a lifetime. The immense anxieties and incalculable implications of this situation are succinctly evoked in approximately 70 lines.[5] Then, after the brief intervening episode of the purchase of the gravesite, we are pleasantly entertained by the calm flow, the epic breadth, and the poised harmony of characters, report, and speech in chapter 24, in which Abraham's servant seeks a bride for Isaac in Mesopotamia. By Hebrew standards, a great amount of space is devoted to ensuring that everything falls into its proper place—approximately 230 lines, at least four times the number found in the average story. In the last lines (v. 67), which link with chapter 23, Rebekah as a matter of course takes up Sarah's position, and we understand that a new cycle has begun. The charged story of the tower of Babel (11:1–9), hermetically composed in a symmetrical thirteen-part concentric design representing measure-for-measure justice, the mirroring of human hubris in divine nemesis, requires only 121 words and approximately 25 lines. The sinister nocturnal story of Jacob's fight and rebirth in 32:22–32 (to which we shall return later) needs only 143 words in 34 cola to develop a formidable intensity.

Another form of discord appears at the level of composition, where the narrative cycles of Jacob and Joseph constitute the second half of the book. The history of the eponymous forefather of the people of Israel extends from 25:19 to the end of chapter 35 but seems on two occasions to be drastically interrupted. During the exposition (chaps. 25–28, Jacob's youth in Canaan), an excursus in chapter 26 allows the intermediary patriarch Isaac only a few paragraphs, and in the conclusion (chaps. 32–

35, Jacob back in Canaan) chapter 34 intervenes, a brutal story about two sons of Jacob who take revenge when their sister Dinah is raped by the prince of the old and respectable city Shechem. In addition, the history of Joseph (chaps. 37–50) is interrupted in its initial phase by another harsh story, also involving sexual behavior, in which the double standard of Joseph's brother Judah is painfully exposed as he is challenged by his brave daughter-in-law Tamar. These three texts seem to be intrusions only as long as we ignore the fact that they are all separated from the boundary of their cycle by the space of one story. Thus they form hooks to the adjoining cycles. If we notice this and allow ourselves to be instructed by the key words, we can integrate these passages thematically with their context despite their superficially digressive character.[6]

Finally, in several cases discord arises through the content. For example, chapter 1, which is less a story than a solemn enumeration of the majestic deeds of creation (in a formal design of two times three days which mirrors the duality heaven/earth), presents man as created in God's image. The reader, seeing this representation of man as the crown of creation (cf. Ps. 8), may feel a certain elation. What immediately follows is the shock of the second creation story (chaps. 2–3), which portrays man as a morally shaky being who eagerly sloughs off responsibility and whose aspirations to becoming God's equal in knowledge of right and wrong are realized at the price of his own fall. Moreover, the creator is called simply "God" in chapter 1, but "YHWH God" (KJV: "Lord God") in chapters 2–3. And there seems to be a contradiction between 1:27 and 2:18–23 on the origin of nature and the relation between man and woman. Another example is 27:46–28:5: does it belong organically to the story of the deceit of the blind Isaac? The diachronic approach calls its status into question.

How are we to reconcile all these seeming contradictions, and on the basis of what criteria? Are we to declare Genesis a badly sewn patchwork? Surely such a judgment cannot be justified, certainly not on the basis of Western and modern concepts of what is whole or beautiful. Instead we must handle these contrasts supplely enough to rediscover by stages what the Hebrew standards of literary organization were and how they are embodied in the texts.

Concord or Unity

In Genesis, powerful means of integration are used at the levels of genre, theme, plot, content, and key words.

Genesis is part of a grand design which unites the books of the Torah with Joshua, Judges, Samuel, and Kings in one configuration: from the creation of the world through the choosing of the people of Israel and their settlement in Canaan up to the Babylonian Captivity. Genesis contributes two building blocks to this overarching plot: the Primeval History

(1–11) and the protohistory of the people of Israel, namely the period of the eponymous forefathers (in three cycles: 12–25, 25–35, and 37–50). These two stages prepare for the history of God's covenant with what the Hebrew Bible regularly calls "his heritage" Israel (see, for example, Deut. 4:20–21 and Ps. 28:9) in Egypt and at the foot of Mount Sinai—a history that begins in Exodus.

The characteristic contribution of Genesis to the Torah and to subsequent books is indicated by its own key word *toledot*, literally, "begettings," from the root *yld*, which is used for mothers (*yaldah*, "she gave birth"), fathers (*holid*, "he begot"), and children (*nolad*, "he was born"). The begettings provide a solid framework that supports and meticulously articulates the various sections of Genesis. The distribution of this key word is of great structural importance. Five times it occurs at the beginning of a genealogical register or enumeration, in the significant positions 5:1, 10:1, 11:10, 25:12, and 36:1. The units introduced in this manner (three chapters, two paragraphs) reveal the *toledot* as a genre in its own right and function as a conclusion; they complete two acts (chaps. 1–4 and 6–9) and two cycles (those of Abraham and Jacob). *Toledot* is also used in another way. Again it occurs five times in a strategic position, but now as an opening (with one significant exception) in a short clause, functioning as the heading of a new narrative cycle: in 6:9 (Noah and the Deluge), 11:27 (11:27–32 being the prologue of the Abraham story), 25:19 (the beginning of the Jacob cycle), and 37:2 (the beginning of the Joseph story). Thus the lives of the protagonists Abraham, Jacob, and Joseph are presented within the framework of the begettings of their fathers (Terah, Isaac, and Jacob, respectively). This image of concatenation reveals the overriding concern of the entire book: life-survival-offspring-fertility-continuity.

The one exception is 2:4a. Through its use of the key word *toledot*, it is clear that this one line, "These are the generations of the heavens and of the earth," is part of the first creation story; by forming an envelope structure together with the heading 1:1, it rounds off Genesis 1:1–2:4a and is a conclusion in itself. This exceptional usage attracts the reader's attention. Everywhere else "the *toledot* of X" refers to human beings as fathers and as subjects of begetting, but 2:4a raises the radical question whether heaven and earth may be the objects of God's begetting. The word *toledot* is, then, a metaphor which, approaching the boundaries of the taboo in Israel's strict sexual morals, carries the oblique suggestion that the cosmos may have originated in a sexual act of God. It becomes evident how daring a game the writer is playing when we consider the world from which Israelite belief wished to dissociate itself: a world characterized by natural religion, fertility rites, cyclic thinking, and sacred prostitution; a world in which the idea of creation as the product of divine intercourse was a commonplace.

The *toledot*, then, as genre (at the structural level of greater units) and as heading (at the textural level of clauses) is not distributed at random through the narrative sections, in a superficial gesture of pure technique. Its true importance becomes clear when we view it in relation to the overriding theme of most Genesis stories. Time and again, fertility in diverse and vivid variety and survival through offspring are an urgent concern in the strictly narrative material. This concern is first signaled in the choice of the name *ḥawah*, Eve, "mother of all living" (3:20), for the first woman at the end of a story in which the freshness, innocence, and harmony of man-and-wife-together have been destroyed. It recurs in Eve's pretenses in 4:1b after bearing Cain and in the enigmatic story of the Nephilim in 6:1–4. The nakedness of the first couple in 2:25 has a sequel in 9:20–27, in which the genitals of the father become taboo for the sons. The possibilities, limits, and precarious aspects of sexuality are expressly explored in, among other texts, 12:10–20; 20; and 26:1–11; in stories in which women struggle with each other for motherhood, such as 16 and 29:31–30:24; and in 19, 34, and 38, in which characters and reader are forced or invited to decide what is or is not sexually permissible under special circumstances. Tamar, who tricks her father-in-law into lying with her, is dramatically vindicated at the end of chapter 38; and it is by no means certain that the narrator condemns the curious case of incest in chapter 19 (where Lot's daughters ply their father with drink and become pregnant by him), even if he pokes fun at the dubious origin of the neighboring tribes Moab and Ammon.

Everything converges and fits perfectly at the highest level, that of theme, expressed in the words of God concerning fertility that permeate the book. From the primeval age on, God's general commandment, "Be fruitful, and multiply, and replenish the earth" (1:28), predominates, through the paradoxical intermediary episode of the Deluge (all life is destroyed except one pair of every species, which must be expressly spared to ensure continuity) to the repetition of the commandment to be fruitful in 8:17 and 9:1–3. The scores of names in the *toledot* of chapters 10 and 11 imply realization of the commandment; the scattering of humanity in 11:9 is both punishment and command.

Especially noteworthy is God's twofold blessing or promise to the patriarchs, which recurs regularly in the protohistory with the concentrated power of formal verse: 12:1–3 (the programmatic placing at the beginning of the Abraham cycle); 13:14–17; 15:18–21; 17 passim; 22:16–18; 26:3–5; 28:13–14; 35:11–12; and 46:3–4. God promises the patriarchs numerous offspring and the land of Canaan as a permanent home. Clearly, offspring are not safe without a fixed habitat, and promises of land are useless if there is no procreation. The two parts of the promise/blessing therefore presuppose each other and are intertwined. But their principal importance in terms of narrative organization is that they thematize and explicate space and time, the fundamental coordinates of life and narrative, at the highest level of meaning. Space in Genesis is divided, ordered, and sanctified by the divine promise and is also promoted to the status of a theme: the origin, wanderings, and sojourns of the forefathers. Time, too, is ordered and, because of the promise, stands under a sign of expectation and fulfillment. In its manifestation of continuity in the genealogies, time is most relevant in the Abraham cycle, where it promotes suspense. This cycle is spanned by an immense tensile arch: will Abraham get the promised son, and will he keep him? When the story begins in chapter 12, Abraham is seventy-five years old and childless. Another twenty-five years elapse before Isaac is born, and immediately afterward God seems to want to take his son away from him, directly counter to his promise. Thus continuity is also threatened with destruction, and time itself with deprivation of purpose.

The meaning of space and time in the Torah as a whole is already determined in Genesis by God himself. Their thematic importance is felt throughout the Torah (and in the subsequent narrative books, then again in the Prophets, Psalms, and Wisdom literature). And because the promises are still unfulfilled by the end of Deuteronomy, when Moses dies, the Torah points beyond itself to the sequel, longing as it were for the fulfillment which begins with the march into the Promised Land.[7] Thus Genesis, in its thematic centering of time and space, constitutes the immovable foundation of the Torah and of the entire Hebrew Bible.

When we transpose plot as planning principle from the level of the basic literary unit, the individual story, to the level of the composition of the book, it is the promises of God that carry forward the life cycles. But at this level too the writers introduce a dramatic complication. All three matriarchs, Sarah, Rebekah, and Rachel, are barren—an insurmountable obstacle to continuity. Thus a supraplot arises through and transcends the three cycles. In chapters 5, 10, and 11 the very monotony of the genealogical enumeration suggests that begetting children is a matter of course (and the hyperbolic ages of people who reached eight hundred or nine hundred years indicate that life is long). Accompanying this is a secondary theme, that of the supreme importance of the firstborn son from generation to generation, so that only his name is worth mentioning. From 11:30 on, both certainties are radically undermined. In the stories themselves, the births of Isaac, Jacob, Esau, Joseph, and Benjamin are never described in terms of a begetting (*holid*) by the father; only afterward is such paternity indicated in the concluding *toledot* lists. The conception is always represented by God's opening the womb of the barren woman, after which she can give birth (*yaldah*). Thus the birth achieves the status of a miracle, foreseen and effected by God alone. Only he can enable and guarantee continuity. In addition, the importance of primogeniture is three times subverted or handled ironically: Ishmael is older than Isaac and also carrier of the promise; Jacob outrivals Esau but pays a high price, for his maturation is marred and impeded by deceit; and at the end old Jacob's blessing of Joseph's sons, Ephraim and Manasse, deliberately reverses younger and elder. Attentive readers will compare these passages carefully and enjoy participating in the dialectic of correspondence and difference among them. Echoes of the competition between older and younger child are also present on the margin of the story, through Jacob's wives: Laban exchanges Leah and Rachel behind the bridal veil at Jacob's marriage (29:16–30—the deceiver deceived), and there is a sequel to this episode in the relation between the women, in the agreement they make to trade mandrakes for conjugal rights (30:14–24).

Whichever aspect we consider in the literary text—theme, the coordination of time and space, plot at the levels of story, cycle, or book— the means that create concord[8] are so powerful that they override the aspects of discord.[9] The differences and shifts in language and in types of text which we noted at the outset and which seemed so disturbing now fade, or rather, converge in a plane of a concord sustained from many sides. We are now in a position to reevaluate them as dynamic contrasts. The better we realize that time and space, theme and plot merge to create a synthesis of the heterogeneous, the easier it becomes to enjoy the intended play of differences and oppositions. The more we know our reading to be based on centripetal forces, the easier it is to surrender to the centrifugal movements and explore them as a system of counterpoise.

From the Whole to the Parts: A Structural Approach

A competent reader is constantly mindful of the hermeneutical principle that the whole is more than the sum of its parts, and brings this insight to bear. Just as the meaning of a word is determined not by a dictionary definition but by its context, no single element in the Hebrew narrative art can be isolated and described atomistically. Thus we should first investigate the kind of interaction between prose and poetry and the effect produced by the intersection of the two genres. Then we should examine the effect of differing lengths of episode and how the points of view of narrator and characters imitate, undermine, or enrich one another.

The short poems in Genesis have a special function in the narrative flow. By serving as crystallization points, they create moments of reflection. In a powerful and compact formula they summarize what is relevant; they condense the chief idea and lift it above the incidental. It is no coincidence that the first lines of poetry in the Bible occur at 1:27 and 2:23. Together they show that man's essence is defined by two dialogical dimensions, his relation to his partner and his relation to God. The parallelism of 1:27 ("So God created man in his own image, / in the image of God created he him, / male and female created he them") suggests that humankind is only in its twofoldness the image of God, which in its turn incorporates the fundamental equality of man and woman. The balance is represented in the concentric symmetry of 2:23b, the pattern *abcxc'b'a'*: "this (being) shall be called *'isha,* because from the *'ish* was taken this (being)" [AT]. The sin of man in chapter 3 evokes the fearful question, "Will the image of God be preserved in us?" It receives a positive answer through the thread of poetry in 5:1–2 (in 5:3 man, now called Adam, transmits the image of God to his offspring) and in 9:6.

The fascinating juxtaposition accomplished in 9:6 shows us how poetry in yet another manner distills the essential from the episodic. Verse 6a is a legal directive which prescribes an accurate balance between capital crime and punishment; 6b contains its sacral motivation (and verse 7 connects it with the theme of fertility):

> *shofekh dam ha'adam / ba'adam damo yishafekh*   (6a)
> for in the image of God / made he man.   (6b)

The first line is usually wrongly translated "Who sheds the blood of a human being, by a human being his blood shall be shed." The structure of the first line in Hebrew, however, reveals a symmetry, the concentric pattern *abcc'b'a'*. The purpose of this arrangement is of course to show that the "human being" in the first half-verse is the same person as the "human being" (that is, the victim) in the other. The correct rendering offers a precise image of balanced legal retribution: "Who sheds the blood of a human being, his blood shall (as compensation) for that human being be shed" [AT].[10] This passage is particularly instructive as the first instance of the literary, sometimes even poetic, shaping of many legal enactments and religious rules in the Torah. And this phenomenon in turn opens perspectives for the literary study of the interaction between the narrative and the legislative sections in the Torah.

The poem at 12:1–3 is a blessing from God with which Abraham is sent into the wide world, and it forms the first pillar of the tensile arch which spans the cycle 12–25. Just as programmatic, but in an entirely different manner, is the oracle-poem at 25:23. The sting lies in the tail, "and the elder shall serve the younger." God foments rebellion against the natural order. The strophe is an oracle to Rebekah, who is pregnant with twins. It is not only the center of power of the overture of the Jacob cycle (25:19–26) but also the foundation of the entire section 25–35, persisting as the matrix of Jacob's energetic aspiration for power and precedence. Jacob struggles (even during his birth, 25:22a, 26a), intrigues, and deceives in order to oust Esau from the position of firstborn. The moment the reversal becomes irrevocable, again there is poetry: in 27:27–28 two strophes evoke the blessing of God and the cosmos, and their ending (v. 29) makes a point of the polarity rule/serve. Thus the blessing of the deceived Isaac confirms the prenatal oracle. In 27:39b–40 we find the antipode, again in poetry. The "blessing" left for Esau is almost a curse and also revolves on the axis of ruling/serving.

The location of these two poems within the framework of the entire story provides structural proof that the disputed passage 27:46–28:5 forms an organic part of the whole. Note the alternation of the twins and the parents in the following six scenes.

A Isaac and the son of the *berakhah/bekhorah* (blessing/birthright), Esau (27:1–5).

B Rebekah sends Jacob onstage (27:6–17).

C Jacob appears before Isaac, receives blessing (27:18–29).

C' Esau appears before Isaac, receives anti-blessing (27:30–40).

B' Rebekah sends Jacob from the stage (27:41–45).

A' Isaac and the son of the *berakhah/bekhorah* (now, Jacob) (27:46–28:5).

The family is split into two camps in such a way that the presence of parent and child in each camp excludes the presence of the other parent and the other child. The reversal in the positions of Esau and Jacob is illustrated by the sound play *bekhorah* (= primogeniture) versus *berakhah* (= blessing). Sound play and reversal come together and become cogent in a chiasm forged by the duped Esau when he ascribes to the name "Jacob" the meaning "deceiver," in 27:36a, which can be scanned as a two-line strophe:

> Isn't he called *ya'qob*?
>   He has deceived [*ya'qebeni*] me twice:
> my *bekhorah* he took away
>   and now he takes away my *berakhah*! [AT]

But an even more powerful structural instrument than poetry, and indeed the most powerful in biblical prose, is repetition. Repetition is used at practically every level of the hierarchy which the text constitutes, from sounds, words, and clauses to stories and groups of stories. It is rarely applied mechanically or inartistically, and usually it features ingenious variations. Thus a dialectic game of identity and difference is created which challenges us to compare parallelisms at various levels and to ask questions such as: What has remained unchanged, and why? What differences occur and what do they mean? Through the instrument of repetition, Genesis is also replete with parallelisms at various levels. Indeed, it is a classic illustration of Roman Jakobson's thesis that parallelism is the main characteristic of the literary use of language. Let us consider a few examples.

When Jacob must flee Canaan and the deadly revenge of his brother, as night falls he halts at the place that will be called Bethel (28:10–22). When the narrator then states that the sun sets, we gather that this may be symbolic in this phase of Jacob's life. And yet the full function of the sunset can be appreciated only much later, when the narrator mentions the sun again (32:31). The sun rises at the bank of the Jabbok at the very moment when the hero, maimed by a night's battle and reborn as "Israel," joins his people, finally prepared to smooth matters out with Esau. This detail is part of a larger whole. The two fearful nights at Bethel and Penuel with their numinous encounter (dream and struggle) mark the voyage from Canaan to Haran and back and are counterparts in the larger design of the following cycle:

A   Jacob grows up in Canaan, displaces Esau
    birth, oracle (25:19–26)
    lentil soup/*bekhorah* (25:27–34)
    berakhah/*bekhorah* (27:1–28:5)
    Jacob in Bethel, dream (28:10–22)

X   Jacob in the service of Laban, in Haran: six units, pattern
    ABABAB (29–31)[11]

A' Jacob back in Canaan, toward Esau
    preparations (32:1–21)
    Jacob in Penuel, fight, rebirth (32:22–32)
    face to face with Esau (33)
    back in Bethel (35:1–15)
    end: birth and death (35:16–28)

The element of space, in the form of Jacob's long journey to the east and back, structures the cycle as a central panel with two flanks. The hero himself marks the end of each of the three sections with his characteristic activity of erecting a pillar of stones for a monument.

Another characteristic repetition strengthens the balance between "God's House" (Bethel) and "God's Face" (Peniel or Penuel). Immediately before and after the period in Haran, and nowhere else in the text, a large host of angels appears on Jacob's horizon. In the dream in chapter 28, angels ascend and descend the stairs connecting heaven and earth; this spectacular vision forms the prelude to a revelation from God to the fugitive. The host of angels which Jacob meets in Mahanaim (32:1–2) has at first an ambiguous influence on him, for on his way to Esau he is terrified by fantasies of catastrophe and a bad conscience. It emerges, however, that the meaning of the angels is positive and virtually the same as in chapter 28. The one group *is* the other, an escort on behalf of the God of Abraham for the new bearer of the blessing, on the verge of the Promised Land.

The element that determines the segmentation of the Abraham cycle is the narrated time; not surprisingly, for the life of this patriarch is devoted to waiting patiently for the fulfillment of the promise of God, and hence to faith and obedience. Chapters 12–21 carefully distribute a sequence of lines indicating age, mostly Abraham's.[12] These verses form a pattern by which this cycle, too, is divided into three sections. When the story begins, Abraham is seventy-five; when it ends with his death, he is one hundred and seventy-five. The text, then, covers exactly a century. The central panel, however, chapters 17–21, covers the hundredth year of his life, precisely the period in which God makes the concrete and definite announcement of the arrival of Isaac to Abraham and Sarah, and in which the ninety-year-old woman conceives, and the miraculous birth of the son takes place. At the same time, and also in the central panel, the subplot around cousin Lot is completed. The reception of guests at the beginning of 18 is parallel to that at the beginning of 19, and the annunciation of the inferno which God will draw down upon Sodom and Gomorrah stands in polar contrast to the annunciation of the birth. The aspects of sexuality at the beginning and end of 19 (Lot is prepared to cast his daughters to the sharks all around, in contrast to the daughters who get offspring from their father) are closely related to the issue of fertility, which in chapter 20 generates the following comparison of polarities: Sarah/Gerar's wives = one/all = pregnant/sterile. This reversal of the norm (normal procreation in Gerar versus previous sterility in Sarah) is placed between the annunciation and birth of Isaac. But that period partly overlaps with the one in which Sarah is brought into the harem of the Philistine king! This timing leads us to raise the impertinent question, *Is* she already pregnant when she arrives there? Surely she has not been made pregnant by . . . , has she? Not so, of course. Abimelech has not touched her (20:4a), and God himself recognizes the king's innocence in 20:6. But the point is that the coordinates of time and space create an eerie context for Sarah's sensitive condition, her only pregnancy. And the narrator keeps the time scheme obscure by revealing nowhere in chapter 20 in which weeks of the hundredth year of Abraham's life this episode occurs!

I now propose a new integration of chapter 17 into the larger structure of the cycle. Because 18 and 19 constitute antithetical parallels on essential points and, with the fulfillment in 21, frame the ambiguous chapter 20, the principal aspects of the preparation for the birth of Isaac on Abraham's side and of his annunciation have been isolated from the narrative flow of 18–21 and are provided earlier, in chapter 17. In this case, the one type of text complements the other. Chapter 17 consists almost entirely of speech: the clauses and blessings of the covenant that God confirms with Abraham and formulates, stipulating circumcision as incumbent upon the faithful. The preceding analysis of the underlying scheme of narrated time indicates that this covenant text, with its idiosyncratic use of language, forms a part of the revelation with which God turns to Abraham in 18.

A similar kind of doubling back of narration is apparent in chapter

15. If we read the chapter as an ordinary sequence, problems arise such as the following: is verse 12, after the night supposed by verse 5, to indicate the beginning of a new night, so that verses 13–21 are later revelations? Such difficulties disappear when we regard the two sections of this text, verses 1–6 and verses 7–21, as different versions of the same nocturnal vision. Then 15:1–5 is the prologue, the short, summary version (with offspring as its subject), and 15:7–21 is the main body of the unit, the elaborate, emphatic version (with its subjects the Promised Land, the future, the Covenant).[13]

When Isaac has finally been born and Abraham thinks that the terrible strain is now over, God strikes with a horrible, inconceivable demand: sacrifice your son! At the last moment, this drastic turn of the story yields a paroxysm of fearful tension. The dynamics of life and death present in 18–21 in the form of birth and holocaust, but proceeding on two different tracks (Abraham versus Sodom), are brought together to a painful focus in 22.[14] This chapter constitutes a refined fabric of binary and ternary lines. The basic pattern (the warp) is binary and is controlled by the plot, whose most fearful moment occurs at 10b, when the knife of the father hovers above Isaac's throat. Thus the chapter is divided into halves, verses 1–10 and 11–19, problem and solution, or command and execution. The opposition between the uncertainty and tension before the reversal and the relief afterward is also hidden in the following chiasm:

Abraham . . . went unto the place of which God had told him. (v. 3)	Abraham lifted up his eyes, and looked, and behold behind him a ram caught . . . (v. 13)
On the third day Abraham lifted up his eyes, and saw the place afar off. (v. 4)	Abraham called the name of that place "YHWH provides." (v. 14 [AR])

The warp of the dual composition is complicated and enriched by the weft of a triple distribution of narrative data. Three times (vv. 1b, 7a, 11) there is a short dialogue in which Abraham is hailed and promptly answers "yes?" (hineni; KJV: "here am I"). Three times there are important utterances from God: the command to sacrifice (v. 2), the prohibition against the sacrifice (v. 12), and the definite confirmation of the blessing (vv. 16–18) with which the theme of the cycle is complete. Also ternary is the key phrase "God will provide": dark and ambiguous in the mouth of the father to his son in verse 8, relieved in 14a, a proverb which perpetuates the incident in 14b. Until that moment also the variation of report and speech is ternary:

speeches: command from God (vv. 1–2)
action: preparation, material, journey + refrain line (vv. 3–6)

speeches: conversation between father and son + refrain line (vv. 7–8)
action: arrival, altar built, sacrifice prepared (vv. 9–10)
speeches: command from God not to sacrifice (vv. 11–12)
action: Abraham's substitution and slaughter of the sacrificial animal
  (v. 13)

The double naming in verse 14 underlines and concludes this sequence.
The refrain line at the end of verses 6 and 8 and in the middle of 19, "and
they went both of them together," signals a nexus in the binary-ternary
fabric. By means of this wordplay the narrator explores the possibilities
of the root *yḥd*, "one." He uses *two* derivatives from this root, *yaḥid*,
"only one," and *yaḥdaw*, "together," and places them both in *three* lines
that occupy key positions, in order to set us thinking of the *unity* of father
and son, now being threatened:

Speech	*Report*
Take now thy son, thine only one (v. 2 [AR])	and they went both of them together (v. 6)
thou hast not withheld thy son, thine only son from me (v. 12)	so they went both of them together (v. 8)
thou . . . hast not withheld thy son, thine only son [from me] (v. 16)	they went (back) together (v. 19)

This ingenious wordplay creates a paradox at the heart of the message:
by showing his willingness to give up his only son, Abraham gets him
back, and a much deepened togetherness begins, both between father and
son and between the Lord and his obedient follower.

The hardest hour for Jacob occurs during a frightful night by the
brook Jabbok (32:22–32). Here, too, the issue involves life or death, this
time in terms of displacement and definite psychic hardening versus inner
renewal. Jacob returns to his native country and must now face what he
has been able to evade for twenty years: his past as a fraud, his bad
conscience toward his brother. The imminent confrontation with Esau
puts him in a moral pressure cooker and forces him to pass through a
process of maturation at an accelerated rate. Tricks to placate or evade
Esau (32:4–5, 7–8, 14–20) no longer help; fear of death and feelings of
guilt get a firm hold of Jacob. For the first time we hear him praying to
God. Stripped of all ornament (vv. 9–10 and 12), his prayer becomes a
simple cry for help, "Deliver me" (the center, v. 11a). The reconciliation
that Jacob now attempts is still impure, for it remains in fact an effort to
bribe Esau with gifts. Jacob has still to recognize that his stand on the
back line (which is a refusal to take responsibility, 32:18, 20) must be
replaced by a position up front (acknowledgment of guilt and a plea for
forgiveness, 33:3, 10–11). But that does not happen until chapter 33. First

the impasse and self-confrontation must be complete, and Jacob's ego must undergo a horrible death (32:22–32). To demonstrate the structure of this literary unit I shall transcribe it in its entirety. The capital letters represent the five major links of the whole, which shows a design *ABXB'A'*; in the central dialogue, another concentric pattern and our chief consideration, the lowercase letters mark the subdivision. M and J stand for "man" and Jacob; the verse numbers and their subdivisions are given at the right.

A   And he rose up that night   22a
    and took his two wives, and his two womenservants, and
    his eleven sons,   22b
    and passed over the ford Jabbok.   22c
    And he took them, and sent them over the brook,   23a
    and sent over that he had.   23b
    And Jacob was left alone;   24a

B   and there wrestled a man with him until the breaking of the
    day.   24b
    And when he saw that he prevailed not against him,   25a
    he touched the hollow of his thigh;   25b
    and the hollow of Jacob's thigh was out of joint, as he wres-
    tled with him.   25c

X   *a*   M. "Let me go, for the day breaketh."   26ab
         J. "I will not let thee go, except thou bless me."   26cd
    x   M. "What is thy name?"   27ab
         J. "Jacob [Fraud]."   27cd
         M. "Thy name shall be called no more Jacob, but Israel: 28ab
         for as a prince hast thou power with God and with men,
         and hast prevailed."   28c
    a' J. "Tell me, I pray thee, thy name."   29ab
         M. "Wherefore is it that thou dost ask after my name?"   29cd
         And he blessed him there.   29e

B' And Jacob called the name of the place Peniel: 30a
    "for I have seen God face to face,   30b
    and my life is preserved."   30c

A' And as he passed over Penuel the sun rose upon him,   31a
    and he halted upon his thigh.   31b

The combination *AA'* both separates Jacob from and joins him with his family. It is marked by the key word "passed," which is also prominent in the context; compare 32:16 and 21a (Jacob hiding himself behind, v. 20) with 33:3 (Jacob finally daring to appear). With its opposition night/sunrise the pair *AA'* frames this unique night. The elements *BB'* present the action proper, a long and frightening struggle in the dark, plus the profound interpretation of the event, given by the hero himself. They embody an opposition of report and speech, concealing and revealing respectively the identity of Jacob's redoubtable opponent. The pairs *AB* and *B′A′* frame *X* as the heart, and *X* indeed has its own nature. It is a sustained dialogue showing a perfect circularity. The axis on which the circular scheme *ABXB′A′* revolves is to be found precisely in the middle of the middle, where the old Adam is defined, and Jacob's black past is for the last time summarized in the name with the association "deceiver." Then he receives the accolade from his mysterious opponent: henceforth, your name will be Israel. The act of separation (a disjunction) in *A* ensures that Jacob is left completely on his own (that is, must stand up for himself, take responsibility). The night functions not only as a cover for the opponent but also as a symbol for Jacob's dark side, with which the hero must come to terms. Repeating the key word "passed" and reuniting Jacob with his family, verse 31 represents a conjunction. This element, *A′*, deliberately and symbolically places the sun at the beginning of the main clause. The action of *B* is clarified in *B′*. Unlike Hosea 12:5, the narrator purposely does not reveal who the man of the night is, but modestly makes room for the protagonist himself, who in verse 30 draws his own far-reaching conclusions and then spells them out for us. With his announcement of his deliverance in verse 30c comes the proper fulfillment of his cry for help in 11a.

Even under the enormous stress of this *rite de passage*, Jacob remains himself in that his obsessive desire to be blessed still asserts itself. Afterward he realizes that he can symbolically surrender the blessing he has stolen from Esau. The tying off of the network of occurrences of the root *brk* ("to bless") comes in 33:10–11, when Jacob begs his brother to accept the gift, which is a *berakhah*. After one line from Esau (*A*), Jacob replies at length:

A	"I have enough, my brother; keep that thou hast unto thyself."	9
B	"If now I have found grace in thy sight,	10
C	then receive my *present* at my hand,	
D	for truly I see thy face	
X	as I have seen the face of God [AR],	
D′	and thou wast pleased with me.	
C′	Take, I pray thee, my *blessing* that is brought to thee;	11
B′	because God hath dealt graciously with me,	
A′	and because I have enough."	

Beside the Jabbok, the mirror Jacob had to look into was called "God"; this time it is called "Esau." The key-word style and concentric structure in both passages ensure that the vision of God and the actual sight of the exemplary fellow human being (the brother) flow into each other as halves of a metonymy.

Jacob had expected murder from Esau but received a long and ardent embrace. As a consequence of his doing no more than staying put and enduring the impasse, the future is open. How differently did matters end in chapter 4, where the relation of "a man toward his brother" (the Hebrew expression for human mutuality) was first explored. The result, fratricide, makes chapter 4 a kind of duplicate of the fall in 3. In chapters 32–33 it now appears that there are more constructive possibilities for solving a broken fraternal relationship. Finally, in the last cycle of the book, the psychology of crime, guilt, remorse, and compunction among brothers is worked out much more thoroughly, under the direction of the master manipulator Joseph. He puts his brothers, who once threw him into the pit, through a protracted ordeal (chaps. 42–44). Only when they have fully sympathized with the pain of young Benjamin and their old, fragile father and have broken down under the weight of their own bad conscience does he reveal himself to them as their brother who was predestined by God to ensure their survival—now in two senses, from famine and from crime. The brothers are then reconciled (chap. 45). Thus the theme of brotherhood, a metonymy for the bond that links humanity, is handled with growing complexity from the beginning of Genesis to the end.

NOTES

1. Just a few examples: the connection between Ps. 8, 104, 148 and Gen. 1; the garden as central metaphor of the Song of Songs against the background of the story of the Fall (the tangent points are systematically and fascinatingly discussed in Francis Landy's *Paradoxes of Paradise: Identity and Difference in the Song of Songs*, Sheffield, 1983, chap. 4); Jacob the deceiver and his struggle beside the Jabbok (Gen. 32) in Jer. 9:1–8 and Hosea 12.

2. The standard edition is the *Biblia Hebraica Stuttgartensia* (1967–77). In that edition the Torah occupies 353 of the 1,574 pages of the Hebrew basic text.

3. Northrop Frye pointed out in his *Anatomy of Criticism* (Princeton, 1957) that "higher" criticism actually is a kind of lower criticism and indicated what genuine literary criticism should do with the Bible. Frye has continued this line of thought in *The Great Code* (London, 1982).

4. Robert Alter, *The Art of Biblical Narrative* (New York, 1981), p. 13. Also see his humorous p. 48.

5. When I speak of lines, I suppose a so-called colometric arrangement of the prose, in roughly the same way that Buber and Rosenzweig did in their Bible translation (the so-called *Verdeutschung*, Cologne, 1954–62). An account of colometric arranging can be found in my *Narrative Art and Poetry in the Books of Samuel*,

vol. I: *King David* (Assen, 1981), pp. 462–466, and vol. II: *The Crossing Fates* (Assen, 1986), pp. 742–744. Erich Auerbach's inspiring analysis of Gen. 22 in *Mimesis: The Representation of Reality in Western Literature,* trans. Willard Trask (Princeton, 1953), is classic.

6. For Gen. 26 see my excursus in *Narrative Art in Genesis* (Assen and Amsterdam, 1975), pp. 113–115 (this book analyzes 11:1–9 and the entire cycle of Jacob). For Gen. 34 see Meir Sternberg, *The Poetics of Biblical Narrative: Ideological Literature and the Drama of Reading* (Bloomington, Ind., 1985), chap. 12; for Gen. 38 see Alter, *The Art of Biblical Narrative,* chap. 1.

7. See D. J. A. Clines, *The Theme of the Pentateuch* (Sheffield, 1978).

8. I cannot discuss here all the smaller forms which contribute to unity; one must suffice. The dream or nocturnal vision is in all three cycles a vehicle of revelation with far-reaching consequences: with Abraham (chap. 15), with Jacob (marked by the famous stairs to heaven, chap. 28), and with Joseph (who in 37 has prophetic dreams which speak for themselves and which he uses to dazzle his brothers' eyes; he is the only one who is able to interpret the prophetic dreams of Pharaoh in 41).

9. The terms *concord* and *discord* are derived from Paul Ricoeur's three-volume masterwork, *Temps et récit* (Paris, 1983–85) (an English translation by Kathleen McLaughlin and David Pellauer, *Time and Narrative,* is in progress, Chicago, 1984–). In volume I he uses these terms to define plot after providing a revealing philosophical close reading of Aristotle's *Poetics,* in particular of the notions *mimesis praxeos* and *mythos.* Ricoeur calls plot a "synthesis of the heterogeneous."

10. Note the error "by man" in the usual translations. The correct translation had already been suggested by J. Pedersen, *Israel, Its Life and Culture,* I/II (Copenhagen, 1926), 397; he recognized the so-called *bet pretii.*

11. In *A* Jacob expands: wives, children, richness; in *B* bitter conflicts take place. Under *A* I include 29:1–14, 29:31–30:24, and 31:1–21; under *B,* 29:15–30, 30:25–43, and 31:22–54. For an account of the entire construction see Fokkelman, *Narrative Art in Genesis.*

12. The places are 11:32, 12:4, 16:3, 16:16, 17:1, 17:17, 17:24, 17:25, 21:5, 23:1, and 25:7. The speech at 17:17 is the core of the sequence, an eleven-part pattern *aa'bcdxd'c'c''b'a''.*

13. Translate *wayomer* in verse 7 as a flashback: God had spoken to Abraham, etc.

14. Two memorable instances from the literature on Gen. 22: Auerbach's analysis of this story as a tale "fraught with background," in *Mimesis,* chap. 1; and, in *Fear and Trembling,* Kierkegaard's brilliantly varied, fourfold account of the trial and his elaboration on the idea that ethical and religious existence are entities and levels of completely different ranks.

SUGGESTED FURTHER READINGS

Robert Alter, *The Art of Biblical Narrative* (New York, 1981).

D. J. A. Clines, *The Theme of the Pentateuch* (Sheffield, 1978).

J. P. Fokkelman, *Narrative Art in Genesis* (Assen and Amsterdam, 1975).

Benno Jacob, *The First Book of the Bible: Genesis,* abr., ed., and trans. Ernest I. Jacob and Walter Jacob (New York, 1974).

D. Patte, ed., "Structural Readings of Genesis 2–3," *Semeia,* 18 (1980).

University of Leiden

Exodus

J. P. Fokkelman

THE second book of the Pentateuch, like the first, provides a foundation for the whole Bible. The themes and most important events of Exodus recur with regularity in later books. Exodus consists of two main sections, chapters 1–15 and 16–40, a compositional scheme that embraces the physical and spiritual birth of the people of Israel. These two stages might be called Liberation and Covenant. After a concise sketch of the book's composition, I shall examine both the extent to which Exodus represents a continuation of Genesis and the new themes and specific features that make the second book a distinctive literary text in its own right.

The caesura marking the end of the first section of Exodus is signaled by dense and powerful poetic language. Chapter 15 is a hymn to the incomparability of YHWH, who has manifested himself as supreme over Israel and Egypt. This song of Moses beside the Reed Sea celebrates the definitive liberation of Israel from slavery in Egypt, and this disjunction of two nations obsessed by each other is the issue of the whole section 1–15. The great confrontation between the leaders of Israel, Moses and Aaron (both from the priestly tribe Levi), and Pharaoh, the king of Egypt, takes place in the series of stories dealing with the Ten Plagues (chaps. 7–14). This sequence mounts to a double climax. The narrator gives much more space to the exceptional tenth plague, the destruction of the firstborn of Egypt (chaps. 11–13), than to the others and emphasizes its unique nature by interweaving two types of text. Narrative and legislative language alternate and interpenetrate as follows: 11 is narrative (annunciation), 12:1–28 gives the laws for Passover, 12:29–42 is narrative (the catastrophe itself), and 12:43–51 + 13:1–16 gives laws for Passover and the firstborn. Verses 11:10b, 12:28, 12:40–42, and 12:50–51 (and, somewhat later, 13:18b–19) mark the conclusion of each section and could easily be read as a distinct sequence of short reports, each one of which carries the line of development forward. After this, Pharaoh relapses yet again into stubbornness, which yields the decisive climax: the passage of Israel through the Reed Sea while the waters close over the pursuing Egyptian army.

The liberation is preceded by a long, also climactic preparation in three phases. After a prologue (1:6–22), which sets the tone of oppression, chapter 2 presents phase 1, Moses' education, in three short stories: birth (vv. 1–10), attempts at intervention (11–15a), and activity in Midian and marriage (15b–22). Chapters 3–4, phase 2, tell of God's revelation to Moses and his commission to demand that Pharaoh allow Israel to depart from Egypt unhindered. Phase 3 consists of Pharaoh's increased oppression as a result of Moses' and Aaron's plea (chap. 5) and God's reiteration of his command to Moses (6:2–13). The exposition concludes with the genealogy of the Levites (6:14–27), crowned with the origins and role of Moses and Aaron. By its position, this list marks the narrative change from preparation to confrontation.

The preamble to the second section relates five stories about the crises that befall Israel on the march, involving water (15:22–27), food (chap. 16), water (17:1–7), war with Amalek (17:8–16), and Jethro's advice to Moses on the delegation of power (chap. 18). These events also constitute the itinerary of the people to the most holy mountain, Sinai. Beginning in chapter 19, this summit will predominate for a very long time in the narrated world of the Torah, and Israel will remain encamped for almost fourteen months at its foot. Not until Numbers 10:11 does Israel break camp, continuing on its way toward the Promised Land, with other crises ahead. The story of the theophany (chap. 19) and the account of the conclusion of the Covenant (chap. 24) embrace a normative (legislative) section which contains the Ten Commandments (20:1–17) and the so-called Book of the Covenant (20:22–23:19), an old text containing legal rules for the rural Israel from before the time of the monarchy. A second normative section comprises chapters 25–31, in which God gives Moses instructions for making the sanctuary (the tabernacle of the congregation) and its cultic objects, as well as rules about garments and ordination of the priests. This long text in direct discourse is carefully mirrored in the narrator's text, chapters 35–39, which describes how Moses and his craftsmen follow the instructions. But there unexpectedly intervenes an immense crisis which yields another three chapters of narrative: the worship of the golden calf, Moses' mediation with the wrathful deity, renewed revelation and covenant. Finally, chapter 40 concisely recapitulates the cultic instructions and provides a follow-up: in verses 1–15 God gives instructions about the placement of the tent and of the objects within it, in 16–33 Moses obeys, and verses 34–38 imposingly conclude the book by describing how God dwells with Israel in his glory. The overall structure may be summarized as follows.

Exposition
frame	1:1–6
Israel enters slavery, Moses' youth	1:7–2:22
frame	2:23–25
YHWH reveals himself, Moses' call	3–4
oppression, command, genealogy	5:1–6:27

Confrontation
  prologue   6:28–7:13
  nine plagues   7:14–10:29
  tenth plague, Passover, Exodus   11:1–13:16
  passage of the Reed sea, Egypt destroyed   13:17–14:31
  conclusion: hymn   15:1–18

Introduction: making for Sinai
  crises in Israel over food, war, governance   15:22–18:27

Revelation on Sinai and Covenant I
  narrative text   19:1–25
  normative text, Decalogue   20:1–17
  narrative text   20:18–21
  normative text, Book of the Covenant   20:22–23:19
  narrative text   24:1–18
  instructions from God on sanctuary and worship   25–31

Revelation on Sinai and Covenant II
  crisis around idolatrous people, Moses mediates   32
  revelation and covenant   33–34
  Moses and artisans follow *instructions*   35–39
  conclusion (speech/report): sanctuary in use   40

In most prose books of the Old Testament, the story is used as a basic literary unit. But the stories combine in groups (which can be called acts); these groups often constitute a section or cycle, and the sections form a book. The arrangement of Exodus proposed here is probably not perfect, but it demonstrates the principal importance of determining a plausible arrangement through thorough analysis. An adequate schema helps us to assign accurate meanings to the literary units on the various compositional levels. Thus it is necessary first to evaluate the literary data on the higher levels (from stories to book), then to integrate them on the next-higher level, which is ruled by other networks of meaning and other rules of play. In this way we can work through the hierarchical structure of the text step by step, continuously alternating between analysis and integration.

In this process, the device of repetition is a powerful aid, as two examples from Exodus show. The deaths of Joseph and of a later Pharaoh connect 1:6 and 2:23, and this knowledge helps us realize that the short paragraphs 1:1–6 and 2:23–25 are not independent stories but bridges. Their primary function is articulative: they frame the four short stories of Exodus 1–2 and thus mark phase 1 of the exposition—a function whose importance exceeds the size and lexical meanings of these stories. Another connection with strong articulative power is formed by the substance of 2:23–25 and 4:31 versus 6:9 and 12 and 14:30–31. When we read these verses as a series, we see how the end of the three phases of the exposition and the end of the confrontation are attuned to each other and thereby provide a double theme: God's concern with Israel versus the belief or unbelief of the people. We can then reread Exodus 1–14 as a continual obstacle race for God, who wants to free his people.

Various powerful literary resources ensure that Exodus shows *a solid continuity with its predecessor Genesis*. Genesis is emphatically and clearly rounded off with the death and burial of Jacob, who as the eponymous "Israel" is *the* patriarch. Exodus links up with its predecessor in a very simple way: the opening section (1:1–5) recapitulates the names of Jacob's sons and counts the number of souls of their families, and thereby takes up the thread where it was dropped.

Two other aspects of continuity are also apparent in the prologue (1:7–22). The Egyptian kings who enslave and exploit generations of Israelites are formally grouped in an emblematic title, "Pharaoh." He makes serious attempts on the survival of Israel, first with the command that newborn males be killed, then with the command that they be thrown into the Nile. This very first story artfully extends the key notion *toledot* ("generations") from Genesis and introduces two named midwives (*meyalledot*; we can hear the rhyme) as heroines. Their courageous action turns the prologue into an arena in which immense forces of oppression and revolt clash. The midwives' refusal to execute the Egyptian orders because they "feared God" is the high point of the story. In the meantime we have recognized the theme of birth and survival: the choice of words in 1:7— "And the children of Israel were fruitful, and increased abundantly, and multiplied, and waxed exceeding mighty; and the land was filled with them"—is inspired by the Creation story (see Gen. 1:28) and is also reminiscent of God's promise of numerous offspring and his blessing of the patriarchs. Moreover, the sequel forms an iterative line containing a paradox which refers to God's support against Egyptian terror: "But the more they afflicted them, the more they multiplied and grew" (1:12a, with an echo in 1:20b). The beginning of Exodus, then, transforms the theme of the genealogical line and raises it to the level of an entire nation. The midwives and the blessing of children in chapter 1 are also emblematic, because from 12:40–41 we learn that the people's slavery has lasted four centuries. That period and its tensions are concentrated in chapters 1 and 5.

The second story describes another paradox of growth during oppression: Moses is raised by an Egyptian princess despite Pharaoh's command. Her compassion crosses the boundary dividing flock-tending Semite from Egyptian *Herrenvolk*. The issue of 2:1–10 is indicated by the key words "to bear" and "child" (both from the root *yld*). The Hebrew child, fished out of the Nile, matures quickly (the narrator virtually skips Moses' youth, 2:11–15) and finds a wife in Midian after fleeing Egypt; and the short text 2:16–22 ends with a new birth, in yet another allusion to the theme of genealogical continuation. And chapter 6 presents the genealogy of Moses, a typical successor of the registers in Genesis. The name of his son Gershom contains a pun which anticipates Israel's departure from Egypt: Pharaoh "shall surely thrust you out hence altogether [*garesh yegaresh*]" (11:1). An antithesis to this expulsion is announced later, in 34:24a: "For I will cast out the nations before thee, and enlarge thy borders." (Also see 6:1, 12:39, 23:28–31, and 33:2.)

The conclusion of Genesis and the first section of Exodus explore the question of whether the combination Israel-Egypt is a conjunction or a disjunction. At first the two nations seem to get along well. Joseph's visionary powers help Egypt through years of famine, and Pharaoh welcomes Joseph's entire family. But this conjunction quickly ends. The four-century-long oppression introduces the spectacular disjunction of the Exodus. The information from 12:40–41 on the narrated time—practically the only indication of its kind in the first section, for the narrator is not concerned with regular historiography or the individual feats of Pharaoh—supplies still another connection with Genesis. The long slavery entails the fulfillment of Abraham's haunting prophetic vision in Genesis 15. The beginning of Exodus directly signifies the ultimate disjunction between Israel and Egypt, as the water of the Nile, which to the Egyptian is in all aspects the water of life, is chosen as the site and means of death for the Israelite male babies. Thus Egypt through the agency of the Nile brings about a separation between life for Egyptians and death for Israelites, a division which should be the prerogative of the deity alone. Eventually this high-handedness leads God to intervene—the only one who has actual power over the polarities of existence. The Creator, whose first deeds consisted in establishing a division between elementary entities such as light and darkness, earth and sea, announces to Pharaoh through the mouth of Moses: "I will put a division between my people and thy people: tomorrow shall this sign be" (8:23). The words are reminiscent of the cosmogonic dividing in Genesis 1. Thus it is not surprising that Egypt's fountain of life, the Nile, in the very first of the ten plagues turns into a stream of blood—an unmistakable hint from God to Egypt that death will strike in many forms.

The first division in Genesis 1 was that between light and darkness. This polarity continues powerfully throughout Exodus and beyond. On its journey through the desert, Israel is protected and led by a column of smoke or a cloud during the day and a column of fire at night, as signs of God's presence. These are the virtuoso effects of the master of polarities, who has thus created a chiasm: light in darkness, darkness in light. These polarities occur at strategic points in the composition: in chapter 14, where the division between Israel and Egypt becomes definite, around and in the Reed Sea (13:21–22 and 14:19–20), and also in 10:23, 19:18, and 20:18, where smoke and fire dramatize the theophany on the holy mountain; in 33:9–11a, in front of the tabernacle of the congregation, where the cloud appears only in order to screen from the people Moses' contact with God; and preeminently in the climactic moment at the conclusion of the book (40:34–38), where the full polarity, day/night = fire/cloud, appears and marks how "the glory of YHWH filled the tabernacle" (v. 35b). On the one hand, this impressive moment of revelation is prepared for in the beginning of chapter 3, when Moses sees a burning bramble which is not consumed by the fire (a striking spectacle which, together with 3:4–6, introduces the long dialogue between God and Moses that begins in 3:7). On the other hand, the column of fire/smoke signals the main issue of the book: the question of whether man can behold God or not. Yes, say two passages unambiguously: 24:9–11, upon the conclusion of the first covenant, and 33:11, "And YHWH spake unto Moses face to face, as a man speaketh unto his friend." No, thinks Moses in 3:6 (although it is not at all certain whether the narrator would agree with him). No, say 19:12 and 21 and, more ambiguously, 20:19; and God himself says no in 33:20–23. The intimacy of the encounter in 33:11 harks back to Jacob's insight, beside the Jabbok, into his own truthfulness in relation to God's blessing (Gen. 32:31), and perhaps also to his nightlong struggle relieved by the break of day. Egypt is now left behind in darkness. The ninth plague *is* impenetrable darkness; the eradication of the tenth plague takes place in a horrible night; and the dawn of 14:24, which illumines the safe departure of Israel, does not extend to the Egyptian army, which is engulfed by the darknesses of deluge and death.

The moment God reveals himself to Moses in Exodus 3:6, he does so in terms from Genesis: "I am the God of thy father, the God of Abraham, the God of Isaac, and the God of Jacob." In 3:15 he even reveals his proper name, the tetragrammaton YHWH, commanding Moses: "Thus shalt thou say unto the children of Israel, YHWH God of your fathers, the God of Abraham, the God of Isaac, and the God of Jacob, hath sent me unto you: this is my name forever, and this is my memorial unto all generations" (see also 3:16, 4:5). The emphatic series in 2:23–25 characterizes the Lord unambiguously as the God who wants to keep his covenant with the patriarchs.

On the subject of primogeniture, the rights and position of the first-born, Exodus also links up with Genesis. At the same time it elevates this issue—just as with the theme of birth—to the level of peoples. This transformation occurs powerfully as early as 4:22–23, in the framework of Moses' call, when God tells him of the plagues he has in store for Pharaoh:

> Thus saith the Lord,
> > Israel is my son, even my firstborn:
> And I say unto thee,
> > Let my son go, that he may serve me:
> > and if thou refuse to let him go, behold,
> > I will slay thy son, even thy firstborn.

Here the question of primogeniture expands into the historical theme that is central to Exodus and to the whole Bible, the choosing of the people of Israel. The description of the tenth plague (11:1–13:16) contains a special section (13:1–16) on the law of the firstborn. Thus the normative is anchored in the narrative (the report of the slaughter among Egypt's firstborn). The consecration of the firstborn and the feast of unleavened bread (Passover), both manifestations of the idea of an entirely new beginning, are founded in the historical event which initiates the history of God and his people.

Within the normative context of Passover and the Passover meal, the ritual of the circumcision also reappears (12:43–48), instituted in Genesis 17 as an indispensable condition for the keeping of the Covenant. Earlier, in 4:24–26, another circumcision occurs at a frightening, almost magic moment of transition, after Moses' call but before his return to the people. Only quick and resolute interference by his wife saves Moses for Israel and the future. She turns the literal circumcision of her son into the symbolic one of Moses, who is thus saved from a demoniac attack. The attack comes from God himself, who in chapters 3–4 is apparently exasperated by the objections and hesitations of his servant. The entire incident as *rite de passage* is again reminiscent of Jacob's night beside the Jabbok.

Another religious institution, that of the Sabbath, also receives special attention in Exodus, at the prominent junctures 20:8–11 (part of the Decalogue) and 31:12–17 and 35:1–3 (the end and beginning, respectively, of blocks 25–31 and 35–39). The holiness of the seventh day was instituted in Genesis 1 after the Creation, when God turned his day of rest into one of celebration.

What is new and specific in this book? Exodus richly portrays the constitution of Israel, both physically and historically in the first section, and, in the second section, as a spiritual entity. Beginning with chapter 16 Israel enters the circle of light of the revelation and receives its spiritual statute from God. Two manifestations of this new portentous status are the conclusion of the Covenant and the two stone tablets containing the Ten Commandments. These considerations of content increase our awareness of the intimate connection between narrative and normative sections. The latter are direct discourse by God as he instructs Moses to instruct the people. Thus the legal text, in its function as spoken word, is embedded in the narrative. As elsewhere in the Bible, what we need to do here is to examine the relation of speech, using the tools of current textual and narrative theory, and not to detach embedded speech from its textural setting, even if it comes from the character God. In 12:1–12, 43–52, 13:1–16, and chapters 20–23 the enactments of God are purposefully embedded; they stand in fruitful interaction with the narrative mass around it and share their themes with it.

As a text that articulates a large spiritual vision, Exodus is defined by the three climaxes of revelation on the mountain of God, in 3:1 called Horeb, in 19–24 and 33–34 Sinai. The divine revelation in Exodus concerns God himself, both his name and his nature. Exodus 3:15, quoted above, contains the first mention of the tetragrammaton, the proper name YHWH, and makes it the focus of our attention. This mysterious and holy name is authoritatively discussed in two ways in the literary unit on the call of Moses (chap. 3). The word *yhwh*, clearly from the root *hwh* = *hyh*, "to be, become," and, like many other proper names in the Bible, an imperfect form of the verb, is uttered and explained by the bearer himself, and Exodus as a whole offers a valuable, contextual explanation for the name. God answers Moses' question about his identity in two ways in 3:14: "I AM THAT I AM" (*'ehyeh 'asher 'ehyeh*) and "Thus shalt thou say unto the children of Israel, *'ehyeh* hath sent me unto you" [AR]. Only afterward, in verse 15, does God utter his name YHWH for the first time. The entire creation has originated from God's being, which wants to stand-in-relation-to, and now God further develops this desire by designating a specific partner, the chosen people. God is the only one who can entirely develop the fullness of his being. But he cannot be happy if his creation and his creatures (among whom is the attentive listener to the story) do not get the chance to do so as well, within their appointed limits. Therefore, his freedom is also his self-chosen confinement. The Name signifies a paradox of absolute being and involvement. The "I am" poses a spiritual question to every reader taking his own growth seriously, pondering whether he can fully accept what is within and around him.

In the context of Exodus, "I am" is applied in a practical sense, in that Egypt must free Israel so that it can be/become itself, and the text plays with two sides of the key word "serving." Israel asks whether it may leave "to serve the God of the Hebrews" (key words recurring in 7:16; 9:1, 13; and 10:3), and this service is incompatible with service (slavery, the same word in Hebrew) under earthly powers because it entails actual spiritual freedom. In 3:14–15 the three *'ehyeh*-lines surrounding the revelation of the name touch on the theme of liberation. In 3:12 God says: "Certainly, I will be with thee," and in 4:12, 15 he tells Moses: "I will be with thy mouth." Together, these lines reveal the aspect of involvement and covenant in God's being, which is also implied in the probably correct translation of the name *yahweh*, "he lets be" (which includes "he creates"). Later, God as speaker uses the same construction as "I am who I am" in 33:18–19, an enheartening section on God's involvement at a moment when Moses again presses a question: "And he [Moses] said, I beseech thee, shew me thy glory. And he said, I will make all my goodness pass before thee, and I will proclaim the name of the Lord before thee; and will be gracious to whom I will be gracious, and will shew mercy on whom I will shew mercy." Similarly, in the compact poetry and archaic power of 34:6–7, after the annunciation of 33:19, the God of Israel performs a self-revelation which can serve believers as a credo:

The Lord passed before him and proclaimed:
"The Lord! The Lord! A God compassionate and gracious,
slow to anger, abounding in kindness and faithfulness,
extending kindness to the thousandth generation,
forgiving iniquity, transgression, and sin;
yet He does not remit all punishment,
but visits the iniquity of fathers upon children and
children's children, upon the third and fourth generation."[1]

The dialogic being of God, already evident in the creation of man in his own image and reflected in the man-wife dialogue, culminates in Exodus when God assigns exceptional status to his covenanted people: "And ye shall be unto me a kingdom of priests, and an holy nation" (19:6a). The blessings of the patriarchs that are so characteristic of Genesis are crowned in Exodus with the so-called covenant formula, two clauses of characteristic reciprocity: "And I will take you to me for a people, and I will be to you a God" (6:7a). This passage and the self-revelation reported in Exodus recur regularly throughout the Old Testament, and that is a proof of their major importance in ancient Israel.[2]

The full proper name of God incorporates a title: YHWH Sabaoth, which is to say, "YHWH (God) of hosts." The epithet, which usually refers to the heavenly host around God's throne, acquires another dialogic significance in Exodus within the context of covenant. God himself names Israel "mine armies" in 7:4, and the narrator uses similar words to denote the Exodus in 12:41: "all the hosts of the Lord went out from the land of Egypt." Without the hosts of the chosen people, God can no longer be complete, says the book of liberation and revelation.

God wishes to be known as much by Egypt as by Israel. For this reason, in the first section of the book the elementary and powerful line "I am YHWH" is proclaimed five times to Egypt (7:5, 17; 8:22; 14:4, 18) and five times to Israel (6:2, 6, 7, 8, 29). In the second section it recurs in strategic places, not only in 15:26 and 16:12 but also as title to the Decalogue itself. This seminal pronouncement is found further on in the Bible as well. It occurs, for example, as a key statement in Ezekiel (6:7, 10, 14, and passim), for there too God wishes to make himself known through his involvement in history.

Thus the Book of Names—as Exodus is called in Jewish tradition because of its opening words—is in effect the book of the Name. Henceforth God's care envelops the chosen people. The covenant between them has its classic formulation in Exodus; later formulations, as in Joshua 24, are only variants of this. The Covenant at Sinai remains the matrix for Israel's relationship with God. But Exodus points, beyond itself, even more clearly to the future insofar as the stories of the Exodus and the program which God lays down in his speeches to Moses anticipate the entry into the Holy Land. The blessing of the forefathers will not be fulfilled until the people take possession of the land of Canaan, and the following three books of the Torah lead us only to the threshold of that era. For all the richness of its complex formal dynamics and for all its spiritual depth, Exodus is only a part of a greater literary-spiritual conception.

NOTES

1. I quote here from the 1962 translation of the Torah by the Jewish Publication Society of America (Philadelphia).

2. The covenant formula is found, among other places, in Lev. 26:12; Deut. 26:17–18; 2 Sam. 7:24; Ezek. 11:20, 14:11, 37:23, 27; Jer. 7:23, 11:4 and 31:1, 33; Zech. 8:8. The "credo" recurs in Num. 14:18, Ps. 86:15, Joel 2:13, Jonah 4:2 (and further compare Deut. 5:9–10 and Jer. 32:18).

SUGGESTED FURTHER READINGS

Umberto Cassuto, *A Commentary on the Book of Exodus* (Jerusalem, 1967).
Brevard S. Childs, *Exodus: a Commentary* (London, 1982).
Nahum Sarna, *Exploring Exodus* (New York, 1986).

University of Leiden

Leviticus

David Damrosch

PERHAPS the greatest problem facing students of the Bible as literature is the fact that so much of the Bible is not literature at all. Amid the many and manifest glories of biblical historical narrative, prophecy, and lyric, we must also acknowledge frequent eruptions of intractably nonliterary, even antiliterary, material. In the Pentateuch, the long compilations of laws which persistently interrupt the narrative in Exodus through Deuteronomy pose the greatest such stumbling block in the reader's path. In all the Pentateuch, this problem is most clearly seen in Leviticus, composed largely of ritual ordinances which have warmed the hearts of few, if any, literary readers in any period.

Faced with such an unappetizing vein of gristle in the midst of the Pentateuch, the natural reaction of most readers is simply to push it quietly off the plate. Thus Gerhard von Rad, in a summary of the narrative contents of the Pentateuch, neglects to mention Leviticus altogether,[1] and literary studies of the book are virtually nonexistent. More polemically, Harold Bloom dismisses the Priestly regulations in Leviticus and elsewhere as pitifully belated attempts at domesticating the numinous and uncanny (in short, truly poetic) essence of the Pentateuch, the early Yahwistic source.[2]

Such neglect, whether benign or hostile, misses the central literary concern of the Priestly writers who shaped the final form of the Pentateuch, which was precisely the interweaving of law and history. Far from interrupting the narrative, the laws complete it, and the story exists for the sake of the laws which it frames. Leviticus is consequently important for the understanding of the overall role of law in the Bible. For in Leviticus the law is represented in its ideal, fully functioning form, the best model against which to assess the complicated uses and misuses of law by a Saul or a Solomon in the historical texts.

Equally, Leviticus is of great literary interest in itself, as the fullest expression of the pentateuchal effort not simply to set the law within a narrative context, but actually to subsume narrative within a larger symbolic order. An attentive look at the laws shows how it was possible for the Priestly writers to intersperse law and story so readily: in their hands, law itself takes on narrative qualities. Rather than a sterile opposition between law and narrative, the text shows a complex but harmonious interplay between two *forms* of narrative. Law and history meet on a common ground composed of ritual, symbolic, and prophetic elements. In achieving this union, Leviticus typifies a central movement in much of the Bible: the use of profoundly literary techniques for ultimately nonliterary ends.

The Ritual Order

The opening chapters of Leviticus provide one of the clearest illustrations of the narrative quality of law throughout the Pentateuch. In the earlier stages of the Priestly composition, before the Torah was divided into separate books, the material of Leviticus 1–7 was not included. The great account of the construction of the tabernacle, which now closes Exodus, would have been directly followed by the anointing of the tabernacle and the investiture of Aaron and his sons, the material which now constitutes chapters 8–10. A decisive literary decision was taken, then, to open the new book not with a direct continuation of the story from Exodus, but with seven chapters' worth of ritual prescriptions concerning sacrifices. Why was this done?

Historical criticism variously accounts for this material as an instruction manual for priests at Jerusalem or, more politically, as the result of priestly disputes at the time of the text's reformulation. On this reading, the priests from Jerusalem inserted this material in order to establish Sinaitic authority for their particular ritual practices, as against other ritual forms practiced at Shiloh or elsewhere in the country. The writing down of these laws may well have had some such impetus, but the choice to insert them here, at the start of the book, serves a literary purpose as well. Indeed, the theological meaning of the insertion is most clearly understood through the passage's narrative function.

The whole section has been constructed with considerable care. Thus, the first three chapters show a consistent triadic form. Three kinds of sacrifice are described (burnt offerings, cereal offerings, and peace offerings). Each of these offerings is in turn divided into three variants, which describe different offerings that can be made to fulfill each type of sacrifice. This tripled threefold structure gives these chapters a certain lyrical aspect. Each subsection, a few verses in length, functions stanzaically, even ending with a refrain, some variation on the formulaic phrase "it is an offering made by fire, of a sweet savour unto the Lord."

The first chapter is the most consistent, giving its refrain identically each time, and furthermore giving the refrain a three-part form of its own: "it is a burnt sacrifice, an offering made by fire, of a sweet savour unto the Lord" (vv. 9, 13, 17). The repetition of "burnt sacrifice" and "offering made by fire" is instructive. The first term is the technical term for this particular sacrifice, 'olah, whereas the second is the generic term for offerings involving fire, 'isheh. Clearly there is no real need to repeat both terms, as the first presupposes the second, but the phrasing strongly suggests the parallelism characteristic of Hebrew poetry. (In chapters 2 and 3, where the cereal offering and peace offering are also burnt, but where the poetic potential of two parallel terms for burning is lacking, the text simply uses the term 'isheh.)

Although the structure is lyric, the presentation is dramatic. Rather than simply prescribing the necessary details, the text stages the event, presenting a little ritual drama of interaction between the person offering the sacrifice, the priest, and God:

> And if his offering be of the flocks, namely, of the sheep, or of the goats, for a burnt sacrifice; he shall bring it a male without blemish. And he shall kill it on the side of the altar northward before the Lord: and the priests, Aaron's sons, shall sprinkle his blood round about upon the altar. And he shall cut it into his pieces, with his head and his fat: and the priest shall lay them in order on the wood that is on the fire which is upon the altar: But he shall wash the inwards and the legs with water: and the priest shall bring it all, and burn it upon the altar: it is a burnt sacrifice, an offering made by fire, of a sweet savour unto the Lord.   (1:10–13)

The identity of the priest(s) has been specified as "the sons of Aaron" in order to emphasize the narrative setting at Sinai, although occasional lapses into the singular indicate the use of the generalizing designation "the priest" before these rules were put into their present context. The style, though simple, is unhurried, with occasional flourishes such as "on the wood that is on the fire which is upon the altar" which emphasize the sense of ritual order and fill out the scene of ritual drama.

The presentation of the variants in each form of sacrifice reflects great skill. The burnt offering, for example, may consist of three types of animal: a bull, a lamb or goat, or a dove or pigeon. Lambs and goats are sacrificed in essentially the same way as bulls; birds require somewhat different treatment. The text could simply have mentioned the lambs and goats briefly as an alternative to bulls, but it gives them as much space as the birds, allotting to each variant a full scenic description, as in the example quoted above. These latter descriptions are slightly abbreviated from the first version, to avoid wearisome repetition, but they are full enough to impart an overall sense not so much of three choices as of a series of three sacrifices. Thus the text dramatizes the sense of orderly sequence at the heart of ritual. The singularity of the giving of the Law at Sinai is extended, through the rituals inaugurated at Sinai itself, to a narrative order of varied repetition.

The emphasis on the different forms of sacrifice allows for narrative variety within the ritual order. The rites reflect different points in the ritual year, and different problems which require the several different types of sacrifice. Equally important, the variant forms allow for differences in the circumstances of the people making the offerings. Lambs and goats are permitted for people who cannot afford a bull; birds are specified for people too poor to offer a lamb or a goat (as is explicitly stated later, in 12:8 and 14:21). The ritual order is not a millenarian order which would gloss over details of wealth and poverty; it remains linked to individual circumstance as well as to the cyclical order of the ritual calendar and the structural order of different kinds of sin.

At the same time, individual circumstance is delimited and ordered, in the implicit division of society into only three economic groups (wealthy, average, and poor). This is not an individualized narrative, or even an image of extended contingency with a multiplicity of categories (envisioning, for example, other groups of people so poor that even a bird is unaffordable, or so rich that even a bull would be too trivial a sacrifice). It remains a ritual order, but one which gives a definite place both to circumstantial variations and to narrative progression.

History

Having established this ordered ritual narrative, however, the text immediately calls it into question, in the story of the investiture of Aaron and his sons (chaps. 8–10). This is the only extended passage of full-fledged narrative in the book. In it, Moses follows the instructions given him in Exodus 29 for the anointing of the tabernacle and the consecration of Aaron and his four sons as the chief priests. The initial preparation alone takes a full week and is intricate and difficult, even dangerous, given the immense divine power with which they are dealing. Aaron and his sons perform everything flawlessly, as we are told at the end of this phase:

> And Moses said unto Aaron and to his sons . . . Therefore shall ye abide at the door of the tabernacle of the congregation day and night seven days, and keep the charge of the Lord, that ye die not: for so I am commanded. So Aaron and his sons did all things which the Lord commanded by the hand of Moses. (8:31, 35–36)

So far so good, and on the eighth day Aaron offers the final series of sacrifices (chap. 9), which culminate in a direct response from God: "And there came a fire out from before the Lord, and consumed upon the altar the burnt offering and the fat: which when all the people saw, they shouted, and fell on their faces" (v. 24).

No sooner is the ritual complete, though, than disaster strikes, for Aaron's eldest sons make the mistake of improvising an offering of their own, not specifically requested by God:

> And Nadab and Abihu, the sons of Aaron, took either of them his censer,
> and put fire therein, and put incense thereon, and offered strange fire before
> the Lord, which he commanded them not. And there went out fire from the
> Lord, and devoured them, and they died before the Lord. Then Moses said
> unto Aaron, This is it that the Lord spake, saying, I will be sanctified in
> them that come nigh me, and before all the people I will be glorified. And
> Aaron held his peace. (10:1–3)

A strange inauguration of the ritual order! Here the officiants themselves
go the way of the burnt offering just made by their father. Clearly the
episode serves, in part, a monitory purpose, warning against the invention
of new practices or the importation of practices external to the cultic
order. ("Strange fire," *'esh zarah*, can also be translated "foreign fire" and
suggests something either lying outside the prescribed order or literally
coming from another people.) The purely ritual message here stresses the
danger inherent in God's power. Like the fire, which concretely expresses
God's action in the scene, God's power is the basis of civilized life if
handled properly, but a raging, destructive force if misused. The passage
draws this ritual moral through its description of the strange fire not
actually as something forbidden but simply as something that God had
not asked for. This is also the perspective of chapter 16, when the deaths
are described as the result of Nadab and Abihu's having come too close
to God: "they drew near to the Lord and perished" (16:1 [AT]; the King
James Version and some modern translations obscure this point by assimilating this passage to the earlier one, but the Hebrew simply uses the
verb *qarav*, whose normal sense is "to approach"). Here the narrative
details drop out as unimportant to the purely ritual message, which refers
to the inherent structure of divine–human relations rather than to anything
specific to the historical incident.

Yet the shocking quality of the event, both in its timing and in the
stature of its victims, has a broadly disturbing effect. Indeed, within the
text itself, the disaster shakes Aaron's own faith in his ability to carry on
with the ritual order. The chapter ends with Moses' discovery that Aaron's
surviving sons have failed to eat the goat of the sin offering, as they were
supposed to do. He angrily reproaches them, but Aaron replies:

> Behold, this day have they offered their sin offering and their burnt offering
> before the Lord; and such things have befallen me: and if I had eaten the sin
> offering to day, should it have been accepted in the sight of the Lord? And
> when Moses heard that, he was content. (10:19–20)

A clue to the wider meaning of the episode lies in the sudden shift from
Aaron's sons to Aaron himself, and specifically in Aaron's sense that the
death of his sons is something that has befallen *him*, a sign that he himself
is not entirely worthy in God's sight. In fact Aaron is the focus of this

enigmatic episode, whose ramifications present a classic case of the biblical confrontation of the present in the form of the past.

Nadab and Abihu have no existence apart from Aaron; this is their one action in the Pentateuch, apart from accompanying Aaron on Sinai in Exodus 32. Their names, however, have a more extended referential life. In 1 Kings we read of a pair of brothers, Nadab and Abijah, the sons of King Jeroboam I. These brothers die young, both because of their own misdeeds and because of their father's sins, which have determined God to destroy his lineage (1 Kings 14–15). Now Jeroboam's signal sin is his establishment of a cult of a golden calf, at Bethel and at Dan (1 Kings 13); at Bethel he personally offers incense at the altar—just the sort of offering which brings about the death of Nadab and Abihu in Leviticus.[3]

The echo of Aaron's great moral lapse, his forging of the Golden Calf at Sinai, is clear, and the story of Jeroboam has served as a model for the reworking of Exodus 32 into its present form. Indeed, the one alteration in the names of the brothers only serves to point to Aaron as the real focus of the Leviticus story. "Nadab" is retained unchanged, but "Abijah," which means "God is my father," is altered to the more general "Abihu," "He is my father." In the present context, the father is certainly Aaron, who here receives his punishment for the forging of the Golden Calf.

It is this punishment which gives a literal point to the initial cleansing of the people at the end of the Golden Calf incident. Moses calls together all the Levites, who disperse among the people and slay the three thousand ringleaders among the other clans. Since all the Levites have rallied around Moses, they are not slaying their own clansmen, but Moses describes their feat in a striking metaphor: "And Moses said, Today you have ordained yourselves to the Lord's service, everyone at the cost of his son or of his brother, so that God may bless you this day" (Exod. 32:29 [AT]). Leviticus 8–10 presents the literal ordination, and the literal death of sons and brothers.

Four distinct layers of history are folded into the ritual order by this episode. First, the complexity of the historical moment at Sinai is encapsulated as Nadab and Abihu in effect recapitulate the Golden Calf episode and their father is brought to face the consequence of his sin. Aaron's making of the Golden Calf stemmed from the people's demand to have a tangible divinity, since Moses was remaining out of sight up on Sinai; the calf was an expression of the people's spiritual weakness.

The proleptic reference to the history of Jeroboam brings the action forward into the time of the monarchy, strengthening the association between priest and king already implicit in the regal paraphernalia given to Aaron as high priest (Exodus 28). In contrast to the weakness behind Aaron's misdeed, Jeroboam's making of the calves is an act of cynical power politics: king of the newly separate Northern Kingdom, he makes the calves in order to keep his people from returning to the shrine in Jerusalem, where he fears they will renew their allegiance to the Davidic dynasty, now represented by King Rehoboam of Judah. The episode is typical of the history of the monarchical period, with politics as the central testing ground of moral issues, whereas the premonarchical period represented by the time of the Exodus stages moral issues more directly in terms of divine leadership and ethical demands.

In addition to these specific historical references, the fact that it is Aaron's eldest sons who fail in their duty ties the scene into the family politics of the patriarchal period, when in case after case the younger brother takes the lead after the elder one is shown to lack moral strength. On the death of Nadab and Abihu, the younger brothers Eleazar and Ithamar for the first time begin to play an active role and become the forefathers of the divisions of Levites later organized by David. In its reference to Aaron, the episode of Nadab and Abihu also completes the theme of the logic of Moses' own predominance over *his* elder brother. On a deep symbolic level, this theme of the necessary triumph of the younger over the older represents, as has long been noted, one aspect of Israel's self-awareness as the people chosen by God in preference to the older and more powerful cultures around them.

These three historical levels, patriarchal, Sinaitic, and monarchical, provide resonance for the fourth, that of contemporary history. Leviticus reached its full form during or soon after the period of the Babylonian Exile. Both the fickleness of the people and the misuse of royal and priestly power under the monarchy were seen as responsible for the downfall of the nation. Nadab and Abihu serve as a warning of the importance of just leadership by the priestly class (in the absence of any formal government during the Exile) and, more generally, are an image of the justified destruction already visited on a large part of the population and a threat of even further woe to the remnant if the survivors fail to reform. In this aspect, the plaintive cry of Aaron concerning the sin offering acknowledges the shock of the Exile even while the story asserts the need to pick up the pieces and carry on.

The Symbolic Order

The fivefold interweaving of narrative orders (ritual, patriarchal, Sinaitic, monarchical, and contemporary) in chapter 10 forms a fitting conclusion to the first third of the book. Taken overall, chapters 1–10 serve as a narrative introduction to the symbolic order of cultic regulations which make up the second two-thirds of the book: the laws of purity and atonement in chapters 11–16 and the group of ordinances known as the

Holiness Code (chaps. 17–26, with an appendix in chap. 27). After long neglect, these latter sections have begun to receive attention on several fronts.[4] As the structural anthropologist Mary Douglas has observed, "rituals of purity and impurity create unity in experience. So far from being aberrations from the central project of religion, they are positive contributions to atonement. By their means, symbolic patterns are worked out and publicly displayed."[5]

A symbolic structure can be deduced, although it is not explicit in the text; but do the assorted ordinances in these chapters have any connection with what has gone before? Readers who have come to appreciate the literary value of the previous chapters are likely to view the laws of Leviticus 11–25 with dismay, for the regulations and ethical statements given here largely lack the narrative form of the earlier chapters. In fact this section presents not a nonnarrative but an *anti*narrative, whose purpose is to complete the transformation of history inaugurated in chapters 1–7.

In the context of the Primeval History as portrayed in the Pentateuch, we can say in rhetorical terms that the Eden story describes a scene of metaphorically based union with God, in whose image and likeness man is created, whereas the fall away from God and into history takes the form of a series of metonymic displacements illustrated in the major stages of prehistory (Eden, Cain and Abel, the Flood, and the Tower of Babel). This world of metonymies, of cause-and-effect relations, parts standing in for inaccessible wholeness, is the world of most biblical prose writing. By contrast, Leviticus seeks to undo the metonymic cause-and-effect relations of narrative; it struggles to recreate a metaphoric union with God in very different terms. Traditional narrative strategies are not so much abandoned as transformed, which is why Leviticus can be described as a book which uses literary methods for nonliterary ends. The narrative patterns examined above are still here—regulations are often described scenically, for example—but most of them are fractured and recombined in strange ways. The narrative order is subordinated to a conceptual order, and the surviving fragments no longer show a progressive narrative development. Instead, there are disconcerting moments such as the description in 16:3–4:

> Thus shall Aaron come into the holy place: with a young bullock for a sin offering and a ram for a burnt offering. He shall put on the holy linen coat, and he shall have the linen breeches upon his flesh, and shall be girded with a linen girdle, and with the linen mitre shall he be attired: these are holy garments; therefore shall he wash his flesh in water, and so put them on.

The narrative goes backward here, describing first the entry into the inner part of the Temple, then how Aaron is to have dressed, and finally his bath before he dresses. In an extended series of variations on this rhetorical movement, the sacrificial order creates a series of disjunctions and displacements, by which the Holiness Code seeks to reconstruct a metaphoric wholeness from the pieces of the narrative metonymies it has taken apart.

In much of the Hebrew Bible, the rhetoric of displacement is presented through the theme of exile.[6] Leviticus is no exception, and exile can fairly be said to be the very basis for the construction of the antinarrative ritual order. To be holy, *qadosh*, is to be set apart; the root means "separation, withdrawal, dedication." If a metaphoric union with God is no longer possible in a fallen world, the Law can on the other hand create a life built around a principle of separation which will serve as a metaphor for the transcendental otherness of God. God himself repeatedly makes the point that the people's separateness is to mirror his own: "Ye shall be holy: for I the Lord your God am holy" (19:2).

The separation from what is not holy paradoxically creates a close spiritual connection not only between God and man but also between man and the material world. The purity laws concerning physical disfigurements apply not only to the people but also to their clothes and even their houses, which are subject to the same purity regulations, with mildew and mold analogized to leprosy (chaps. 13–14). The people are to be separated not only from their neighbors but even, in a sense, from themselves: "Thus shall ye separate the children of Israel from their uncleanness; that they die not in their uncleanness, when they [would] defile my tabernacle that is among them" (15:31).

The text quite directly makes the connection between holiness and exile as it goes about creating a metaphoric wholeness of God, people, and land through the mechanisms of purity and avoidance. Thus the people's ritual link to the land of Israel expresses not a sense of possession but a permanence of exile. The land itself must keep the Sabbath and cannot be sold in perpetuity, for it belongs not to the people but to God: "The land shall not be sold for ever: for the land is mine; for ye are strangers and sojourners with me" (25:23). The term *ger*, "stranger," might best be translated into modern English as "resident alien" and is the term used for the Israelites during their stay in Egypt. In taking up the term, the text transforms the lament of Moses, who named his eldest son in response to a life of exile: "he called his name Gershom: for he said, I have been a stranger [*ger*] in a strange land" (Exod. 2:22). Leviticus expresses a desire for something closer than possession, a fellowship of exile, shared among the people, their servants, their cattle, their goods, and the land itself.

The transformation of exile makes alienation the basis for a renewed ethical closeness to one's neighbors and even to strangers: "thou shalt love thy neighbour as thyself: I am the Lord . . . the stranger that dwelleth with you shall be unto you as one born among you, and thou shalt love him as thyself; for ye were strangers in the land of Egypt: I am the Lord your God" (19:18, 34).[7]

Prophecy

The purpose of the Sinaitic setting for the symbolic order is ultimately not historical but prophetic. Composed after Israel's subjugation to Babylon, Leviticus presents a body of ritual which had never been fully observed and whose physical and spiritual focus, the Temple, had now been razed to the ground. Looking toward the future, the book concludes with prophecy. Chapter 26, originally the conclusion to the Holiness Code, now serves as the conclusion to the book as a whole, apart from the appendix of miscellaneous material in chapter 27. In describing the good that will follow from keeping the Law and the evils that will result from failure to keep it, the chapter looks to the contemporary history of the Babylonian Exile:

> And I will bring the land into desolation: and your enemies which dwell therein shall be astonished at it. And I will scatter you among the heathen, and will draw out a sword after you: and your land shall be desolate, and your cities waste. Then shall the land enjoy her sabbaths . . . As long as it lieth desolate it shall rest; because it did not rest in your sabbaths, when ye dwelt upon it. (26:32–35)

The devastation of the land of Israel is seen, with rich prophetic irony, as the earth's long-delayed chance to observe the fallow periods demanded by the Law but hitherto neglected by the greedy tillers of the land.

The chapter is laden with imagery of journeying, and it promises that if the people walk in the Law, God will walk with them (as he had walked with Adam in the Garden): "If ye walk in my statutes, and keep [literally, 'hear'] my commandments . . . I will walk among you, and will be your God, and ye shall be my people" (26:3, 12). In contrast to this orderly walking and hearing will be the disordered flight and aural perception of the sinful in their new exile:

> And upon them that are left alive of you I will send a faintness into their hearts in the lands of their enemies; and the sound of a shaken leaf shall chase them; and they shall flee, as fleeing from a sword; and they shall fall when none pursueth. (v. 36)

Even in the new exile, though, God will be prepared to remember his Covenant if the people repent, as the conclusion of the chapter stresses (vv. 40–45). With faith and active repentance, the people can find a new Sinai even in Babylon.

Wilderness and Promised Land merge in Leviticus. The laws are inserted into the story of Sinai not only to give them authority but still more because the Wilderness exemplifies the fullest potential of a life of exile: that the place where everything has been lost can prove to be the place where everything is gained. The stark landscape of the Wilderness seems to the people to lack any source of hope, we might say any narrative possibility, to be a dead end: "and they said to Moses, Was it because Egypt lacked graves that you have brought us out to die in the wilderness?" (Exod. 14:11 [AT]). Leviticus sees the Wilderness as the necessary lacuna, between cultures and between past and future history, in which the people can receive the redemptive symbolic order of the Law:

> And the Lord spake unto Moses, saying, Speak unto the children of Israel, and say unto them, I am the Lord your God. After the doings of the land of Egypt, wherein ye dwelt, shall ye not do: and after the doings of the land of Canaan, whither I bring you, shall ye not do: neither shall ye walk in their ordinances. Ye shall do my judgments, and keep mine ordinances, to walk therein: I am the Lord your God.   (18:1–4)

In its presentation of the Law within this vision of the redemptive potential of exile, Leviticus is the very heart of pentateuchal narrative.

NOTES

1. Gerhard von Rad, "The Form-Critical Problem of the Hexateuch," in *The Problem of the Hexateuch and Other Essays*, trans. E. Dicken (New York, 1966), pp. 1–78.

2. Harold Bloom, "'Before Moses Was, I Am': The Original and the Belated Testaments," in *Notebooks in Cultural Analysis*, I (Durham, N.C., 1984), 3–14.

3. See Roland Gradwohl, "Das 'fremde Feuer' von Nadab und Abihu," *Zeitschrift für die alttestamentliche Wissenschaft*, 75 (1963), 288–296.

4. See the pioneering studies by Paul Ricoeur, *The Symbolism of Evil*, trans. Emerson Buchanan (Boston, 1969); Mary Douglas, *Purity and Danger* (London, 1969); and Julia Kristeva, *Powers of Horror*, trans. Leon Roudiez (New York, 1982). René Girard explores the literary/social function of the sacrificial system in *Violence and the Sacred*, trans. Patrick Gregory (Baltimore, 1977), with later amplifications in *Des choses cachées depuis la fondation du monde* (Paris, 1978) and *The Scapegoat* (Baltimore, 1986). Historians of religion and biblical scholars are also showing renewed interest; see, for example, Jacob Neusner, *The Idea of Purity in Ancient Judaism* (Leiden, 1973).

5. Douglas, *Purity and Danger*, pp. 2–3.

6. See Peter Ackroyd, *Exile and Restoration: A Study of Hebrew Thought of the Sixth Century B.C.* (Philadelphia, 1968).

7. See Herbert N. Schneidau, *Sacred Discontent: The Bible and Western Tradition* (Baton Rouge, 1976), especially chap. 1, "In Praise of Alienation."

SUGGESTED FURTHER READINGS

Peter Ackroyd, *Exile and Restoration: A Study of Hebrew Thought of the Sixth Century B.C.* (Philadelphia, 1968).

Mary Douglas, *Purity and Danger* (London, 1969).

René Girard, *Violence and the Sacred*, trans. Patrick Gregory (Baltimore, 1977).

Julia Kristeva, *Powers of Horror*, trans. Leon Roudiez (New York, 1982).

Jacob Neusner, *The Idea of Purity in Ancient Judaism* (Leiden, 1973).

Paul Ricoeur, *The Symbolism of Evil*, trans. Emerson Buchanan (Boston, 1969).

Herbert N. Schneidau, *Sacred Discontent: The Bible and Western Tradition* (Baton Rouge, 1976).

Columbia University

Numbers

James S. Ackerman

THE Book of Numbers narrates Israel's departure from Mount Sinai and its journey in the Wilderness for an entire generation until reaching the border of the Promised Land. Composed of sources with exceedingly long and complex histories of development, it was probably put in its present form some time in the sixth or fifth century B.C.E., during or after the Babylonian Exile. The editors clearly assumed that life in the Diaspora had its ancient analogue in the Wilderness era. They have reinterpreted old traditions of Israel's Wilderness wandering by arranging a sophisticated collage of diverse materials into a new literary context. Much of the material is Priestly, and we can assume that Priestly circles were responsible for the final version of the book.

Although there are three major sections (10:11–25:18, containing diverse material, is framed by Priestly traditions), certain thematic concerns give literary unity to the work. The Wilderness period is depicted as an ordeal in which the Exodus generation was found wanting. What voices prolonged our sojourn in the Wilderness, pushing us back toward Egyptian bondage? How did divine guidance manifest itself, and to what extent do we still have access to it? What role does Moses play in expressing the divine will, since he too failed the test? Given our impurity, how could the Holy One be in our midst without destroying us? And how can we come near the divine presence without profaning God? These questions were of more than antiquarian interest to the religious leaders struggling to come to terms with the new realities of life in the lands of the Diaspora.

The first section (1:1–10:10) describes elaborate journey preparations that anticipate important themes of the story. Chapters 1–4 begin with a census in which nothing is left to chance. YHWH exercises tight control over the whole operation, specifying the tribal representatives who are to accompany Moses and Aaron as they make their rounds; and the narrator gives precise figures for each tribe. Every male aged twenty and above is reckoned to the military, and the numbers are overwhelming. As God lays out the order in which the tribes are to march and to encamp, we wonder who could possibly withstand such an overwhelming assault.

A second theme in these early chapters is the establishment of spatial structures and hierarchies of personnel that will permit certain groups to approach God's presence while safeguarding the rest of the people from God's holiness. After the Golden Calf incident, YHWH had decided not to accompany the people to the Promised Land. It would be impossible to dwell in Israel's midst, says YHWH, "lest I consume thee in the way" (Exod. 33:3). But Moses proves just as wily (and more successful) in negotiating with YHWH as he had been with Pharaoh: "My presence shall go with thee, and I will give thee rest" (Exod. 33:14).

There is a new tension, however, between God and people. YHWH will dwell in Israel's midst; but how can this holiness be contained, so that the people may be led and nurtured without being consumed? A carefully structured system is developed that marks clear boundaries between people and Presence. Although the tabernacle will be located in the midst of the camp, it will be surrounded at all times by a group no longer reckoned among the tribes—"that there be no wrath upon the congregation of the children of Israel" (1:53). The Levites are to be given over to the service of the tabernacle—offered to YHWH in lieu of all Israel's firstborn sons. There are further gradations among the Levitical families. Moses and Aaron and his sons encamp east of the tabernacle, and only they have direct access to the most holy objects within. Thus there are concentric circles of holiness in the camp—priest, Levite, Israelite—each protecting the outer circles from divine wrath. And this structure serves more than a prophylactic function, for from the center Aaron and his sons pronounce YHWH's blessing on all Israel: "they shall put my name upon the children of Israel; and I will bless them" (6:27).

The final major theme of the introductory section is that of divine guidance and protection, embodied in the movable cloud that veils and reveals YHWH's glory. Israel had first encountered the pillar of cloud/fire during the escape from Egypt. This pillar had protected the people from the pursuing Egyptians and guided them through the Wilderness to Mount Sinai. It reappears in conjunction with, and as a climax to, the completion of the tabernacle, as YHWH's means of fulfilling the promise to accompany Israel into the Promised Land (Exod. 40:34-38). Numbers 9:15-23 refers to that moment of YHWH's glory entering the completed tabernacle, and both sections seem to summarize the entire passage from Mount Sinai to Canaan ("throughout their journeys"). The cloud moves in mysterious ways, sometimes tarrying, at other times moving on immediately; and Israel faithfully follows the divine guidance, as relayed by YHWH through Moses.

The Numbers story has progressed calmly and smoothly to this point. The second section begins with the cloud of divine glory being "taken up from off the tabernacle" in 10:11. When Israel leaves the holy mountain and reenters the Wilderness as a covenanted people, conflict will ensue. Verse 29 introduces a new literary source, most likely preserving ancient traditions of Israel's Wilderness wandering. Read separately, this material

can be interpreted positively. But the present redaction juxtaposes disparate sources that produce a strange dissonance in their new literary setting.
For example, Moses' invitation to Hobab to accompany Israel to Canaan
and partake of the divinely promised blessings sounds like wise policy
when 10:29–32 is read out of context. Just as Moses had used the helpful
advice of his in-laws in structuring a judicial system (Exod. 18), he asks
these nomadic peoples to guide Israel through a wilderness with which
they would be quite familiar. The context here stresses absolute divine
control and guidance, however, and forces us to see Moses' request as a
breach of faith rather than as an act of prudence. Who needs Hobab when
Israel can follow the pillar of cloud? How does YHWH react? Interpreters
have long been puzzled by the twofold reference to "three days' journey"
in 10:33, and some have assumed that the second occurrence results from
dittography. But if we read 10:33–34 literally, the two symbols of divine
presence—the ark and the cloud—have split apart, so that YHWH is no
longer totally tabernacled in the midst of the camp. Has YHWH broken
away because of Moses' breach of faith?

The first three verses of chapter 11 seem to confirm our interpretation
of 10:29–36, that YHWH is at least partially separated from Israel's midst.
When the people complain, YHWH's fire devours the outer edges of the
camp. It is noteworthy that this first post-Sinai eruption of divine wrath
is not given much narrative justification. Furthermore, YHWH is located
outside the camp in the following stories. Is God still nursing grudges
because of the Golden Calf, or is this outburst partially related to Moses'
request that Hobab serve as Israel's eyes?

Chapters 1–10 have established a priestly hierarchy among the people
as to how close various groups may come to the divine presence. In 11:4–
12:16 the same theme develops in terms of prophecy, and the essential
point is this: at the absolute center of all the concentric circles stands
Moses—the unique means of revealing the divine will. Chapter 11 gives
us variations of earlier stories—the quails/manna of Exodus 16, and the
sharing of Moses' leadership burden of Exodus 18. The stories, however,
are not verbatim repetitions of the earlier ones; and we will note how the
similarities and differences contribute to the dynamics of narrative development.[1] Chapter 11 also combines into one story traditions that were
originally unrelated to one another. Such a "clumsy" integration seems
crude to Western readers, because the redactor has made little effort to
cover his tracks. We may wonder what quails have to do with the bestowal
of divine spirit on the seventy elders. In fact the redactor has created a
new context in which the stories comment on one another and thus
provide the key for their interpretation.[2]

The people long for meat as they remember their diverse, moist, and
gratis foods in Egypt. In their eyes the manna, which they must seek out,
gather, grind, beat, and boil in order to make cakes, parallels the dryness

of their existence. But from the narrator's authoritative viewpoint, the manna is anything but dry: it came as bread rained from heaven, tasting like "wafers made with honey" (Exod. 16:4, 31). Falling with the dew, it tasted like cakes made with oil. The narrative has set up a meat/manna opposition—one given by Egypt, the other by God. In Exodus 16 YHWH had brought the quails with the manna to satisfy the people's hunger. In this version a new divine strategy is introduced: God will comply with rebellious requests to such an extreme that blessing becomes judgment. The request for meat climaxes with YHWH's *ruah* ("wind") bringing quails from the sea, which the people "gather" and pile up "round about" the camp (vv. 31–32). At the point of fulfillment, however, before they have swallowed their first bite of the meat, a plague breaks out. After all, they have hankered for a taste of Egypt.

The motif of bearing the burden relates the quail and spirit-bestowal episodes to each other (11:13–17). In Exodus 18 Moses' judicial burden had been resolved by Jethro's suggestion; in this case YHWH intervenes directly. Moses is commanded to "gather" seventy elders and place them "round about" the tabernacle. As a result of Moses' request for diversity of leadership, YHWH's *ruah* ("spirit") moves out from Moses to engulf the seventy. The immediate result is ecstatic prophecy; and the consonantal text concludes enigmatically *wl' ysfw*. Depending on how we vocalize these consonants, we can read "they did not cease" or "they did not continue."[3]

Meat and manna have been set in opposition; what is the relationship between meat and spirit? Just as the people have wrongly requested a diverse diet, Moses has wrongly requested to diversify the responsibility of leadership (as with Hobab in 10:29–32 and with Eldad and Medad in 11:26–30).[4] Just as YHWH has plagued the people with quails through the *ruah*, so also the *ruah* brings the incapacitating plague of ecstatic prophecy. In the ambiguous *wl' ysfw*, both meanings apply: the elders prophesy unceasingly, but they do not speak a genuine word of prophecy.

If spirit is placed with meat/flesh at the negative pole in these juxtaposed stories, what is the second positive motif to be correlated with manna? One thematic key word in this story is *dbr*, the Hebrew root translated as "word" or "to speak." Just as the manna comes down and nurtures, YHWH comes down and *speaks* to Moses (11:17, 25). Despite Moses' doubts, YHWH says, "Thou shalt see now whether *my word* shall come to pass unto thee or not" (11:23). Deuteronomy further develops the association between manna and word: in 32:2 Moses' teaching distills like the dew; and in 8:3 God "fed thee with manna . . . that he might make thee know that man doth not live by bread only, but by every word that proceedeth out of the mouth of the Lord."

The intertwined traditions in chapter 11 correlate the people's yearning for meat with Moses' desire to broaden his lonely burden of leadership.

One move cloaks the wished-for return to the Egyptian way of life; the other, the abrogation of the concentric circles of holiness that have vested highest authority and responsibility with an inner group: "would God that all YHWH's people were prophets" (v. 29). Chapter 12 further develops the theme of authoritative leadership, when Miriam and Aaron—prophetess and priest—question Moses' unique position in mediating the divine will. Now the conflict rages in the innermost circle of holiness—the Aaronic priests—and it results in the establishment of a further inner circle: Moses alone speaks with God mouth to mouth. The pretext for the challenge is that Moses has gone outside the camp—beyond the bounds of the holy—to marry a Cushite, presumably a black-skinned woman. Again YHWH's response has an ironic yet meaningful twist: Miriam is turned white (with leprosy) and is placed outside the camp; and as long as she is separated from her people, Israel cannot proceed toward the Promised Land. Thus the text suggests that challenging Moses' unique authority, even his own desire to lighten his burden by broadening that authority, prevents progress toward Canaan and masks a yearning for Egypt.

Chapters 16–17 further develop the challenge to Moses' leadership—the situation now exacerbated by the divine judgment that the people must about-face into the Wilderness until the Exodus generation has died out. As in chapter 11, these chapters combine diverse material containing two separate themes: the priestly challenge from Korah against the unique role of Moses and Aaron, since all YHWH's people are holy; and the popular challenge from Dathan and Abiram that Moses has engineered the Exodus from Egypt as a means of grasping personal power.[5]

The redactor has again associated the longing for Egypt—Dathan and Abiram shockingly call it a "land that floweth with milk and honey" (16:14)—with the desire to cut through the hierarchical orders. The rebels claim to speak in the name of total service to YHWH—for all God's people are holy—but theirs is a false service, somehow akin to serving Pharaoh. YHWH must dwell in Israel's midst as leader and protector if the people are to enter Canaan. But such nearness to the deity will be fatal for Israel without the clearly marked gradations of holiness. In 17:12 the people express their concern that all must perish because of their fearful proximity. The text's answer, however, is the reconfirmation of Aaron and a purged Levitical order. Aaron's sweet-smelling censer stays the plague; Aaron/Levi's staff sprouts blossoms and bears fruit inside the tent of meeting.

Chapters 13–14 describe a climactic turning point in the Wilderness wandering: because of their lack of faith the entire generation that had escaped from Egypt (except Joshua and Caleb) must die before Israel can enter the Promised Land. Moses' statement here to the twelve spies should be measured both against Joshua's orders regarding the spying out of

Jericho in Joshua 2:1 and against God's commandment to Moses in this passage. Whereas Joshua's order is brief and to the point and God's command emphasizes that the land to be spied out is the long-awaited Promised Land, Moses' instructions to the spies go far beyond mediating the divine word (13:17–20). The spies are to note whether the land is good or evil, whether the people are weak or strong, and whether or not the cities are fortified. Do not these terms invite us to look askance at Moses' lack of faith? YHWH has told Moses to send spies into the land *for himself* ("send for yourself," v. 2 [AT]), and verses 17–20 reveal that Moses still doubts the goodness of the land and YHWH's ability to deliver it into Israel's hands. When the spies return, the single cluster of grapes borne on a pole by two men answers the question regarding the land's goodness; but it also colors the people's response to the spies' report about the strength and size of the land's inhabitants. The narrator terms the spies' final words (13:32–33) an "evil report" and emphasizes its fearful perspective: the land eats its inhabitants, and we are like grasshoppers before them. It was, however, the agenda of questions set by Moses and not by YHWH that prompted the spies to seek out *whether* rather than *how* the land could best be conquered. Against the majority's "a land that eateth up the inhabitants thereof" (13:32), only Caleb and Joshua maintain that the people of the land "are bread for us" (14:9).

With the command *lekh lekha*, "go thou," God had sent Abram from Mesopotamia toward the Promised Land, as well as to Mount Moriah to offer up his son (Gen. 12:1, 22:2). *Shelaḥ lekha* ("send for yourself") seems to echo that primal command. Just as God had commanded Abram to go to a land that his descendants would inherit and then commanded him to sacrifice the next generation, are not Moses and Israel facing, and failing, the same ordeal? The Exodus generation must die out because, unlike Abraham, they fear for their children's future. This younger generation will indeed suffer for the sins of the fathers by wandering for forty years; but, like Isaac's, their future is secured: they will enter the Land.

The opening chapters of Numbers have strongly emphasized divine guidance as God dwelt in Israel's midst. The census of six hundred thousand fighting men has also indicated a continuation of God's promises to make Israel a great nation. How could such a multitude feel as small as grasshoppers? Even apart from divine guidance, they could have moved into the Land like locusts. But when the Exodus generation repents and makes the abortive attempt at conquest without the presence of Moses and the ark, the people are routed: mere numbers do not suffice. The narrative makes clear that the key to conquest is faith in, and the reality of, the divine presence.

Chapter 20, which returns us to the waters of Meribah (cf. Exod. 17:1–7), explains why Moses must join the generation condemned to die in the Wilderness. In Exodus the setting was Horeb/Sinai: in response to the people's murmuring against Moses, YHWH had commanded him to strike the rock at Horeb with his staff so that the people's thirst could be quenched. In the second Meribah story Moses is again to take his staff, but this time he is to bring forth the water through the power of speech. Is this not the test: does Moses sufficiently believe in YHWH's word (see 11:23), and does he believe that his words approximate the power of that word? Ironically, the sole mediator of YHWH's word does not fully trust the word he embodies (see 27:14). He reverts to his wonder-working staff-striking form, as he had done before the divine words were spoken at Sinai. Part of Moses' "sin," therefore, is a failure to believe fully in God's power to deliver on promises—a failure we have seen developing since 10:29, when he first turns to Hobab to lead Israel through the Wilderness.

The other element of Moses' sin is his desire not to be the sole articulator of YHWH's word; but that is his destiny. He has not been self-assertive; rather he has wished to share the burden of authority. That is, he is "meek" (12:3); and in his case, this is no virtue. When Moses would just as soon abdicate, YHWH must continually insist on Moses' unique role as divine-human mediator. Finally Moses does become assertive: "must *we* fetch you water out of this rock?" (20:10). YHWH had told Moses and Aaron: "speak ye unto the rock . . . and thou shalt bring forth to them water" (20:8). Is not this a further test: will Moses attribute to himself results clearly derived from divine power?[6] He has never done this in the past (see Exod. 14:13–18). Moses finally sheds his meekness and belatedly asserts himself, but YHWH interprets the action as failure to credit the results to divine rather than to human power.

When Moses strikes the rock, "many waters" (20:11 [AT])—a term almost invariably having cosmic associations[7]—come forth to quench Israel's thirst. The Psalms often depict these waters as hostile to YHWH, typifying a chaotic world that threatens to engulf the worshiper. Yet as in other ancient Near Eastern cultures, God's victorious cosmogonic struggle had established the divine dwelling place over the many waters, transforming them into fructifying agents.[8] Paradoxically, the act that prevents Moses from entering Canaan results in divinely bestowed nourishment—"many waters"—for Israel. Chapter 20 is the culmination of a series of passages in which Moses provides Israel with water, both as test and as nourishment. In Exodus 15:22–27 Israel had come upon water that the people could not drink because of its bitterness. In response YHWH had "shewed" (the Hebrew root for "Torah") Moses a tree that sweetened the water and as a test had given them law that, if adhered to, would save Israel from the sicknesses of Egypt. This symbolism of deliverance through covenant law had been reinforced when Moses struck the rock for water at Horeb/Sinai (Exod. 17:1–7). But after the Covenant had been sealed, Israel could be held accountable for its ways: Moses had pulverized the Golden Calf, mixed it in water, and tested the people by forcing them to drink (Exod. 32:20). In Numbers 5:11–31 there is an unusually detailed description of the ritual for adjudicating a suspected adulteress. As a test of guilt or innocence, she must drink a potion of "bitter water" made up of dust from the sanctuary and ink from a scroll on which curses have been written. In chapter 20 Moses is tested: in the pre-Sinai Wilderness he had brought water from the rock with his staff. Has he grown sufficiently to believe that the words he speaks through YHWH's command have more power than the staff? Can he bear the burden of authority over Israel without claiming equal partnership with God? Psalms 106:32–33 gives the following interpretation:

> They [Israel] angered him [YHWH] at the waters of strife [= Meribah],
>> so that it went ill with Moses for their sakes;
> Because they made his spirit bitter,[9]
>> so that he spake unadvisedly with his lips. [AR]

Referring to the murmurers as "rebels" in Numbers 20:10 (a wordplay on "bitter"), Moses suffers as a result of YHWH's wrath against Israel. Because of his embittered spirit he is unable to consume the bitter waters; he is tested and found wanting (27:14).

Chapter 19, the law of the red heifer, is one of the most puzzling, anomalous, and often discussed passages in Numbers. The animal is burned in its entirety—dung, flesh, blood, and so forth—and its ashes are put outside the camp. Yet strangely, when stirred into water, these ashes constitute the "water of separation" that purifies those who are unclean. Joseph Blau comments on the rabbinic fascination with the paradox of ashes that defile making something clean.[10] There may be a thematic relationship between this Priestly legislation and the fate of Moses and Aaron at the Meribah waters. Moses' flawed humanity, hinted at in earlier episodes, comes to the surface. As a result the brothers cannot enter Canaan; but through Moses' failure Israel receives "many waters."

After YHWH's judgment that Moses and Aaron must die in the Wilderness, we might expect an eloquent speech of entreaty from Israel's great mediator. Instead, Moses proceeds with the business of bringing his people to the land his feet will not touch. Even though his negotiations with the Edomites are unsuccessful, there is a new calm, stable character in the relationship among the people, their leaders, and their God. Aaron is summoned to ascend the mountain of Hur to die, and his priestly office is given to Eleazar—foreshadowing the death of the condemned generation and the transfer of leadership to the new generation that will conquer the land. Emblematic of this is chapter 21. Verses 1–3 describe another Hormah battle against the king of Arad (cf. 14:39–45). Whereas the first engagement had been abortive, initiating Israel's return to the Wilderness for a generation, YHWH now heeds Israel's petition, giving the enemy totally into its hands. Chapter 21, in fact, foreshadows Israel's conquest of Canaan. The people receive the Transjordan following the death and burial of Aaron, as they will conquer Canaan after Moses' death. In this new context the chieftains of Israel are led by YHWH to strike for water with their staffs, apart from Moses' intervention. The judgments on Aaron and Moses seem to bring new hope for the future and new stability to relationships, though the Wilderness generation has still not been completely purged.

When the Israelites had celebrated their escape from Egypt at the Sea of Reeds, they had anticipated the trembling of those peoples who would be their neighbors in the Promised Land (Exod. 15:14–16). Now that the people are encamped at the Jordan, ready to begin the assault, the Balak-Balaam story in chapters 22–24 introduces us to a trembling Moabite king who appears as Pharaoh *redivivus*. Like Pharaoh and the Egyptians, Balak and the Moabites dread Israel as numerically superior (cf. Exod. 1:8–12, Num. 22:3–5). Balak decides to invoke powerful curses on this new enemy. Perceiving Balaam as a professional diviner whose curse can be bought if the price is right, Balak says: "for I wot that he whom thou blessest is blessed, and he whom thou cursest is cursed" (22:6). This oracle runs counter to God's promise to Abram in Genesis 12:3; and because the words used by Balak (and Pharaoh) to describe Israel's large numbers are the words of divine blessing spoken to Israel's ancestors in Genesis, we can expect a confrontation between God and this would-be curser. But much to our surprise, Balaam does not at first emerge as an adversary to God; though a Gentile, he is a seer capable of receiving divine communication from YHWH, Israel's God. And claiming that YHWH is also his God, Balaam carefully obeys every divine command and transmits every divine word that he receives.

In 22:21–35 the redactor has included the folktale of Balaam's talking ass. This story does not seem well integrated into the larger narrative, because God is suddenly angry at Balaam for complying with the divine command to accompany Balak's emissaries. However, it plays an important role in introducing Balaam's oracles.[11] Just as the she-ass three times sees what the "seer" cannot perceive—YHWH's angel standing before him with drawn sword—Balaam will three times be given a divine oracle that Balak will not accept. In response to Balak's frustration, Balaam reiterates that he can speak only the word that YHWH gives him. And the not-so-subtle comparison between the renowned seer and his more perceptive she-ass makes it clear that Balaam can see only what God reveals. Only at the third encounter between prophet and angel does YHWH finally "open" Balaam's eyes. And not until his third atttempt at revelation does Balaam introduce himself as one whose eyes have been opened (24:4). A similar pattern obtains within the oracles themselves:

A. At points far-reaching and profound, 23:7–10 shows only partial vision. Although the seer has not been taken to a point where he could see all Israel, his allusion to the "dust of Jacob" recalls the divine blessing in Genesis 13:16 and 28:14 regarding the seed of Abram and Jacob. Balaam's vision of Israel dwelling alone, not regarding itself among the nations, also recalls the earlier motif of Israel as a holy nation, set apart from other peoples. Yet he is far off the mark when he attempts to envision his own future (31:8).

B. Also equivocal is 23:18–24. The divine will to bless is inalterable by human manipulation. God has spoken—promises of blessing to the patriarchs, words of Torah mediated through Moses—and the sovereign purpose is moving toward fulfillment. Israel has been brought out of Egypt, and because of God's presence it is moving toward violent conquest. Yet we pause quizzically at 23:21: "He [God] hath not beheld iniquity in Jacob, neither hath he seen perverseness in Israel." Is God's vision focused on past, present, or future? Given what has already transpired and what will soon occur, in what sense can this oracle be true? Just as Balaam has not properly envisioned his own end, perhaps his view of Israel's future is also problematic.

C. Balaam's eyes are not "opened" until he sets his face toward the Wilderness; and 24:3–9 is an unambiguous blessing. The Exodus allusion is repeated, and the wild animal crushing the prey is now unequivocally Israel. In Balaam's vision, Israel's Wilderness encampment is transformed into a lush paradise. The dry dust of Jacob becomes his seed in "many waters"—an indication of the coming proliferation of the nation, sustained by YHWH's mastery over the waters of chaos. The result will be a king more exalted than Agag—the leader of Israel's prototypical enemies, the Amalekites (see 1 Sam. 15). And at its conclusion Balaam's oracle aligns itself with God's primal promise to Abram: "Blessed is he that blesseth thee, and cursed is he that curseth thee" (24:9; cf. Gen. 12:3).

In 24:10–14 the triadic literary pattern is broken, precipitating the final oracle. When Balak withholds payment because Balaam has not done the job, the seer—without seeking a divine word—responds by giving the Moabite king a dreadful glimpse into his own nation's future.

An extraordinary twist in the plot assigns the most far-reaching and positive visions of Israel's future found in the entire Pentateuch to a Near Eastern diviner rather than to Moses. It was Moses, after all, who had seen God at Mount Sinai and had spoken with God face to face. It was Moses who had brought forth the "many waters" at Meribah that Balaam prophesies will sustain Israel. Ironically, it is Balaam who, by precipitating the tragedy at Baal Peor, will turn out to be the cunning subverter of Israel's relationship with God. Why does the narrative give pride of place to this passive vehicle of revelation who then attempts to undermine the blessing he has spoken? Is it to demonstrate that not even a Balaam, let alone a rebellious Israel, can defeat God's sovereign purposes?

In Exodus the direct vision of God during the covenant ceremony was followed by the sin with the Golden Calf, and Numbers 25 describes a similar dramatic reversal: from the visions of Balaam, to worshiping the Baal of Peor. As in the Balaam story (22:4, 7), Moabites and Midianites are linked; and the narrative connects cohabitation with foreign women to worshiping foreign gods. The text withholds all mention of Balaam's role in precipitating the falling away at Baal Peor—probably to stress Israel's responsibility for what happened. In his oracles, however, Balaam has seen the relationship between Israel's blessing and its status as a people dwelling alone, not reckoned among the nations (23:9). And further, he has learned that divination is ineffective against God's people (23:23). Undermine Israel's separation from the nations, as at Baal Peor, and it can indeed be cursed.

Whereas the Golden Calf had been intended to honor YHWH, no such pretense is maintained with the Baal of Peor. The hint of sexual license in Exodus 32 is full-blown in Numbers 25: "the people began to commit whoredom with the daughters of Moab" (v. 1). Whereas the Levites had been the vehicle of divine judgment for Aaron's sin in making the Golden Calf, here it is a grandson of Aaron who turns back the divine wrath and saves Israel. We have already learned that only the offspring of Aaron may approach the innermost part of the sanctuary. After an Israelite takes a Moabite woman into his tent, Phinehas demonstrates his worthiness to inherit the priestly office when, in a gross parody of that office, he enters "the inner chamber" [AT] and pierces the couple with a spear— right through "her inner chamber" [AT]. With this act he makes atonement for Israel, staying the plague that has killed twenty-four thousand Israelites.

The last section of Numbers, like the first, begins with a tribal census. Chapter 26 specifies that a census took place "after the plague": and in verses 64–65 we learn that, although the figures are roughly the same, the two numberings represent two entirely separate groups of people—the old and new generations.[12] Through the first incident in the Wilderness (Exod. 15:22–27) YHWH had warned the people that adherence to divine law would spare them the sicknesses of Egypt. But with the Golden Calf and Baal Peor stories as frames, plagues had been a common experience for the first generation. A major theme within the frame is the yearning for the comforts of the Egyptian past rather than risking the dangers inherent in the promised future. The Baal Peor incident dramatizes a readiness to become like the nations and to serve their gods; but this catastrophe also becomes the divine means of hastening the purge of the older generation so that a new age can begin.

There are no plagues in the final section. Although Moses is told that he will soon die and is allowed to commission Joshua as his successor, he remains center-stage to make sure the new generation does not repeat the sins of the past. Because of the Midianite involvement in the Baal Peor sin, in chapter 31 YHWH commands Moses to engage in holy war against the Midianite people (cf. 25:17–18). Every Midianite male is slain; not one Israelite is lost. Yet Moses is angry that the women and children have been spared, fearing that Baal Peor will break out again. All the sexually mature women must also be slain (31:15–18). In the next chapter the tribes of Reuben and Gad ask to possess the already conquered Transjordan, because it is especially suitable for their cattle. Even though it is not part of the Promised Land that Israel has been commanded to possess, they say: "bring us not over Jordan" (32:5). Moses likewise turns on them for discouraging the people and threatening its fragile unity, likening their request to the spies' dismaying report at Kadesh-barnea (32:8–15). Thus for the new generation the past Wilderness experiences become paradigms for resolving new issues that arise: Israel must stay separate from the surrounding nations, and it must press on as one people toward the goal of possessing the Land.[13]

The other major theme of the final section of Numbers is an anticipation of life in the Promised Land. The stages of wandering through the Wilderness, which had seemed so random and meandering as described in Exodus and Numbers, are laid out in chapter 33 as though each place had been part of the divine plan from the beginning. The new generation is now to move in, apportioning the Land by lot among the tribes, being careful to drive out all its inhabitants. If any remain, YHWH implies, Baal Peor will repeat itself, and Israel will in turn be driven out. Chapter 34 traces the borders of the Promised Land—much larger than the land actually settled by the tribes and roughly approximating the extent of Israel's kingdom under David and Solomon. And chapters 28–29 specify the nature and amount of offerings for Israel's cultic life in Canaan. Chapter 35 describes a particular feature of Israelite law—the Levitical cities scattered throughout the tribes, with six of these cities designated to give sanctuary to any who might kill a human unintentionally.

The story of Zelophehad's five daughters (chaps. 27 and 36), which frames the final section, further develops the theme of inheriting the land. In the absence of male offspring, the daughters are to inherit; but the land inherited may not be transferred to another tribe. The introductory section of Numbers has devoted much space to the hierarchy of priest, Levite, and Israelite. But within the Israelite category, it has also given considerable attention to the unique place of each tribe in the national scheme—through the census, the orderings for march and encampment, and the dedication offerings. The final word of the book is therefore about tribal integrity. In his first two oracles Balaam has seen Israel in part and has been given a word from God to speak. But his eyes are not opened until the third, climactic vision. Only when he looks toward the Wilderness and sees Israel encamped in the prescribed tribal ordering (24:2) does he see the Israel of the future. Though dwelling in the dry Wilderness, its tent clusters conjure up the image of gardens by a river; and from those waters its kingdom will be nourished.

It cannot be definitively proved that the final formulation of the Book of Numbers took place during the sixth and fifth centuries B.C.E., and my reading does not depend on that hypothesis. Nevertheless, the work does provide at least one set of answers to the questions faced by the Jewish community in exile at that time. Through the post-Exilic Temple cult in Jerusalem, God's presence was still graciously available to the people. But a hierarchical priestly order was necessary to protect the people from divine holiness, as well as to protect that holiness from profanation. The need to enter the Promised Land had the same desperate urgency. The temptation to "return to Egypt" (settle in the lands of the Diaspora) was strong, as was the threat of assimilation by foreigners and their gods. Many will succumb to that temptation and turn aside; but this is a test, a purging. The way back to Egypt leads to sure destruction. The only hope is to press on to Canaan; and although the giants controlling the land make the goal seem impossible, divine guidance is available to the faithful. How do we learn the divine will? Prophets may arise claiming charismatic authority; but as our ancestors were nurtured by the bread from heaven and given God's instruction through Moses, we still have that word. Through that word we are nurtured and led. If we adhere to it, we will survive the ordeal: the bitter waters of divine testing will become the "many waters flowing from our buckets" (see 24:7).

NOTES

1. See especially Meir Sternberg, *The Poetics of Biblical Narrative: Ideological Literature and the Drama of Reading* (Bloomington and Indianapolis, 1985), chap. 11.

2. See Edward L. Greenstein, "The Torah as She Is Read," *Response*, 47 (1985), 17–40.

3. *Welo' yasufu* (root *swf*), the text presupposed by Targum Jonathan and the Vulgate; or *welo' yasafu* (root *ysf*), the Masoretic text.

4. David Jobling, "A Structural Analysis of Numbers 11–12," in *The Sense of Biblical Narrative* (Sheffield, 1978), pp. 26–62, especially 34–35.

5. See Robert Alter, *The Art of Biblical Narrative* (New York, 1981), chap. 7, especially pp. 133–137.

6. Aaron has been integrated into the Meribah story in chapter 20—perhaps so that this incident can be used as the reason he also may not enter Canaan, perhaps also so that ambiguity can be added to the "we" in Moses' assertive statement about bringing forth the water.

7. Herbert G. May, "Some Cosmic Connotations of *Mayim Rabbim,* 'Many Waters,'" *Journal of Biblical Literature,* 74 (1955), 9–21.

8. For example, Ps. 93; see Othmar Keel, *The Symbolism of the Biblical World: Ancient Near Eastern Iconography and the Book of Psalms,* trans. Timothy J. Hallett (New York, 1978), pp. 47–56, 113–120, and 179–183.

9. Both the KJV's "provoked his spirit" and my more literal "made his spirit bitter" follow the Septuagint and Syriac versions, which presuppose Hebrew *hemeru* rather than the Masoretic *himru* ("defied [his spirit]"); cf. Gen. 26:35.

10. "The Red Heifer: A Biblical Purification Rite in Rabbinic Literature," *Numen,* 14 (1967), 70–78.

11. See Ira Clark, "Balaam's Ass: Suture or Structure?" in Kenneth R. R. Gros Louis and James S. Ackerman, *Literary Interpretations of Biblical Narratives,* II (Nashville, 1982), 137–144; Alter, *The Art of Biblical Narrative,* pp. 104–107.

12. Dennis T. Olson, *The Death of the Old and the Birth of the New: The Framework of the Book of Numbers and the Pentateuch* (Chico, Calif., 1985), especially pp. 83–125.

13. See David Jobling, "'The Jordan Boundary': A Reading of Numbers 32 and Joshua 22," in Paul J. Achtemeier, ed., *Society of Biblical Literature 1980 Seminar Papers* (Chico, Calif., 1980), pp. 183–207.

SUGGESTED FURTHER READINGS

Robert L. Cohn, *The Shape of Sacred Space: Four Biblical Studies* (Chico, Calif., 1981).

David Jobling, *The Sense of Biblical Narrative* (Sheffield, 1978).

Nehama Leibowitz, *Studies in Bamidbar (Numbers),* trans. A. Newman (Jerusalem, 1980).

Dennis T. Olson, *The Death of the Old and the Birth of the New: The Framework of the Book of Numbers and the Pentateuch* (Chico, Calif., 1985).

Indiana University

Deuteronomy

Robert Polzin

DEUTERONOMY offers a bird's-eye view of the entire history of Israel, shortly to be recounted in detail in Joshua through 2 Kings. It is that history's opening frame and panoramic synthesis. The spatial perspectives of Moses' audience and of the narrator's implied audience are similar: Moses and his audience are in Moab, that is, outside the Promised Land, hoping to possess it with the help of God's power and mercy; the narrator and *his* audience are apparently in exile, that is, also outside the Land, hoping to get in once more through God's mercy and power. The one audience is told under what conditions they will *retain* the Land; the other audience, under what conditions they will *regain* it. The temporal perspectives of both audiences merge in the book through the phrases "that day" and "this day." Moses' "that (future) day" becomes "this (present) day" of the narrator. The separate voices of Moses and the narrator gradually fuse as the book progresses toward its conclusion.

Moses and the Deuteronomist

Deuteronomy may be described as a story told by an anonymous narrator who directly quotes only two persons, for the most part Moses, and occasionally God. When Moses is quoted, he speaks alone, except in 27:1–8 and 27:9–10, where his voice is joined with those of the elders of Israel and the Levitical priests, respectively. Only about fifty-six verses of the book represent direct utterances of the Deuteronomic narrator. Finally, since both Moses and the narrator many times quote God and others, the book is a complex arrangement of quotations within quotations.[1]

Temporally, Moses' first address (1:6–4:40) looks mostly to past events and statements, his second (5:1b–28:68) to the future; and in the rest of the book that future, both immediate and distant, is his main concern. Thus, for example, in his third address (29:2–31:6), whenever Moses quotes others directly, it is their *future* utterances he reports, coinciding with the almost complete orientation of this address toward the distant future. An even more important temporal aspect of the book's composition is Moses' and the narrator's practice of shuttling back and forth between "that day" of the speaker's past and "this day" of his here-and-now. Just as the narrator can alternate, for example, between that day in Moab when Moses set forth the law (1:3) and this day of narration (2:22, 3:14), so too Moses, the human "hero" of the book, moves back and forth in his speeches between *that day* when "thou stoodest before the Lord thy God in Horeb" (4:10) and *this day* in Moab when "I set before you [all this law]" (4:8). Both Moses and the narrator use "that day" to help them put into context this day's recitation of the law.

Psychologically, none of the words of God which Moses quotes, except the Decalogue (5:6–21), is described as also having been heard by the people. In fact in chapter 5 Moses makes the point that only when God spoke the Decalogue was he heard by the people; all the other words of God were deliberately avoided by the people as directly heard words. Rather, they were to be transmitted to the Israelites indirectly, through Moses. The only other voice in the book which quotes God directly is the narrator's: five times toward the end of the book (31:14b, 16b–21, 23b; 32:49–52; and 34:4b). That is, the narrator is a privileged observer and reporter of God's words, just as he describes Moses describing himself to be in chapter 5.

These temporal and psychological details are sometimes complicated by a more complex layering of quotations within quotations. In 2:4–7 and 32:26, 40–42, for example, the narrator quotes Moses quoting YHWH quoting himself; thus there is an utterance within an utterance within an utterance within an utterance, all in direct discourse. In fact the book deliberately presents a vast number of intersecting statements, sometimes in agreement and sometimes in conflict with one another. The result is a plurality of viewpoints, all working together to achieve a truly multi-dimensional effect. We are dealing with an unusually sophisticated and artfully constructed work of the first millennium B.C.E. Within its pages there exists habitual infiltration of the narrator's speech within Moses' speech, and vice versa, at many levels of the composition. Such artful contaminations are the basis for the deep-seated, as well as superficial, "double-voiced" nature of Deuteronomy.

The reader's first impression is that the book's superficial distinction of voices serves an underlying ideological unity, that of an overt mono-logue in which the narrator clearly states, "As far as our basic stance is concerned, Moses and I are one." However, there are clear indications that this apparent unity in duplicity is indeed only skin-deep, and that the book as a whole consists of an extended dialogue on a number of key ideological issues.

The sparse utterances of the narrator exert a powerful pull in opposite directions. On the one hand, the narrator situates the words of Moses in time and space and defines Moses' preeminent position as leader and legislator of his people (for example, 1:1–5, 34:10–12). This perspective provides an unostentatious frame that rarely distracts us from the powerful words of the book's hero. On the other hand, the narrator's infrequent words occasionally serve to "break frame,"[2] either by diverting us from Moses' main message through the insertion of a number of apparently pedantic explanatory remarks (as at 2:10–12, 20–23 and 3:9, 11, 13b–14), or by simply interrupting Moses' words without apparent reason (31:1). Moses shifts back and forth between that day at Horeb and this day in Moab; so too the Deuteronomist, by breaking frame throughout the book, subtly—almost subliminally—forces us to shuttle back and forth between the narrated past and the narrator's present. Both Moses and the narrator shift temporal gears in the process of teaching.

By such frame-breaks the narrator forces his contemporary audience, intent upon Moses' discourse, occasionally to focus upon their own temporal distance from Moses' words. In combination with a number of other compositional devices (discussed later), these frame-breaks are part of a subtle but effective strategy on the part of the Deuteronomist gradually to blur or soften the unique status of Moses at the very same time that most of the retrospective elements in the book explicitly enhance it. The narrator's utterances are spoken in two ideological voices which interfere with one another: an overt, obvious voice that exalts Moses as it plays down its own role, and a still, soft voice that nevertheless succeeds in drawing attention to itself at the expense of Moses' uniqueness.

In relation to the words of Moses that form the bulk of the book, these two ideological voices broaden the dialogue to include positions on the very nature of Israel's God and on the privileged status of his people, Israel, even as they continue to be at apparent odds with one another on the question of Moses' unique status.

The Voice of Moses

The emphasis in Deuteronomy is on the legislative and judicial word of God, and the conveyers of this word are predominantly Moses and, rarely, the narrator. The manner in which Moses conveys God's word helps to illumine the complex relationships between Moses and the Deuteronomist.

Moses' first address (1:6–4:40) is an introduction to various ways in which Moses speaks for God. More than half of this address entails his reporting of what he, YHWH, or Israel had said in the past. More significantly, chapter 4 stands apart from the first three chapters not only because its references are to future rather than past events and utterances, but also because its reported speech is predominantly in indirect discourse, whereas the reported speech in chapters 1–3 is overwhelmingly in direct discourse. Thus whereas in chapters 1 and 3 we read, for example, "the Lord was angry . . . saying, Thou also shalt not go in thither" (1:37) and "the Lord said unto me, Let it suffice thee . . . for thou shalt not go over this Jordan" (3:26–27), in chapter 4 we read: "Furthermore, the Lord . . .

sware that I should not go over Jordan, and that I should not go in unto that good land, which the Lord thy God giveth thee for an inheritance" (4:21). Since analysis of words is at the heart of indirect discourse, and their exact repetition the rule for direct discourse, these passages illustrate how, in chapters 1–3, Moses mainly *reports* the past, whereas in chapter 4 he *analyzes* it in relation to the present and the future. It is because Moses is busy commenting on, and responding to, the past in chapter 4 that his third mention of God's refusal to allow him to enter the land (4:21) switches naturally, and not accidentally, to indirect discourse.

Moses' variable practice in his first address casts light on the structure of the history introduced by Deuteronomy. This address presents (1) a "factual" look at the past, expressed predominantly by reported speech in direct discourse (chaps. 1–3); and (2) an analytical, evaluative response to the past as a means of indicating its full significance for his audience's subsequent history in the Land and in eventual exile (4:1–40). This description corresponds nicely to the overt structure of the Deuteronomic History: (1) the Deuteronomist's "factual" look at the past, formed predominantly in the reported speech of Moses expressed in direct discourse (Deuteronomy); and (2) the Deuteronomist's analytical, evaluative response to that past in order to indicate its full significance for *his* audience's subsequent history in the Land and in eventual exile (Joshua–2 Kings).

Moses' second address (5:1b–28:68) involves a compositional build-up of Moses' status as a mouthpiece of God. Whereas in the first address Moses is depicted as reporting God's word by respecting the clear-cut boundaries of that speech through the predominant use of direct discourse, in the second address this mode of reporting almost completely disappears, despite the fact that the legislative word of God predominates in quantity as well as in emphasis throughout the address. God is quoted in direct discourse only nine times in twenty-four chapters (5:6–21, 28–31; 9:12, 13–14, 23; 10:1–2, 11; 17:16; and 18:17–20). The compositional importance of this difference between the first two addresses is great. Since the Deuteronomic law code, the core of the book, is phrased as a direct address of Moses to the people, it is much more difficult to determine within the code which utterances are meant to represent the very words of God, which the commenting and responding reactions of Moses, and which a combination of both. In Moses' first address it is relatively easy to distinguish between Moses' declaring of God's word and his teaching or interpretation of that word; in the law code we can no longer tell the difference. This contrast between the subordinate style of Moses' first address and the supremely authoritative promulgation of the law code in the second address is the main compositional means by which the Deuteronomist exalts Moses' teaching authority. Whereas Moses quotes the Ten Commandments of the Lord in direct discourse (5:6–21)—that is, God is allowed to speak to the Israelites directly—in the law code of chapters 12–

28 it is Moses who speaks directly to the Israelites concerning "the statutes and judgments, which ye shall observe to do in the land, which the Lord God of thy fathers giveth thee to possess it, all the days that ye live upon the earth" (12:1). The effect of the law code's composition, therefore, is to show us that the authoritative status of the Mosaic voice is *almost* indistinguishable from that of the voice of God, whatever else the narrator—or Moses, for that matter—may tell us about the fundamental distinction between the two. If the theoretical distinction between God's word and Moses' is still clearly maintained, the practical importance of this distinction, that is, our very ability to so distinguish them, is obliterated by the law code's internal composition.

If both Moses and the narrator can quote God directly; if both of them teach by using "that day" to shed light on "this day"; if the very structure of Moses' first address mirrors, in key compositional ways, that of the Deuteronomic History itself; if, in short, as Moses speaks for God, so the narrator speaks for Moses, then, with the preeminence of Moses' word established in the law code, the very authority of the narrator is more clearly defined and enhanced. What the Deuteronomist is gradually blurring, as his narrator's long report of Moses' various addresses advances, is the distinction between the teaching authority of his hero and that of his narrator. The composition of the law code is a crucial stage in the book's overall ideological plan.

It appears, therefore, that Deuteronomy, as a panoramic preview of the subsequent history, vibrates with the following hermeneutic ratio: as the word of God is to the word of Moses, so the word of Moses is to the word of his narrator. The leveling of the words of God and of Moses in the law code serves the same purpose as the other devices that overtly exalt the status of Moses: they all contribute toward a powerful legitimation of the narrator's authority in relation to Moses. As a result, when the narrator is ready to speak at length in his own voice in Joshua through 2 Kings, the distinction between his words and Moses' is practically irrelevant. The reader has been prepared for this effect by the compositional fusion of the divine-Mosaic word in the law code.

When we move from composition to content, what precisely is Moses reported as saying about his own unique role as declarer and teacher of God's word? The answer once again involves us in an unavoidable dialogue. On the one hand, what Moses says in chapter 5 about his commissioning by God is surely his most pointed reference in the book to his own unique status. Here Moses reports in direct discourse what God told him, "Go say to them, 'Get you into your tents again.' But as for thee, stand thou here by me, and I will speak unto thee all the commandments, and the statutes, and the judgments, which thou shalt teach them, that they may do them in the land which I give them to possess it" (5:30–31). The point is clear: after hearing the voice of God speak the Decalogue, the people fear that they cannot hear more and live. Moses tells them that God sees the justice of this fear and so has commanded him to teach them his further words. The law code, then, is precisely a report of Moses teaching the people, at God's command, what God has told him. And Moses, having heard God directly, does not die.

On the other hand, Moses is depicted as raising a direct challenge to his own unique status. In the midst of the law code, Moses returns to the event of his original commissioning by God, the authenticating utterance of God first mentioned in 5:28–31. However, this second recounting of the divine commissioning uses Moses' words against himself, as it were, by revealing that *another* "Moses" is part of the package. And *his* commission is also to report God's word to the people: "And the Lord said unto me . . . I will raise them up a Prophet from among their brethren, like unto thee, and will put my words in his mouth; and he shall speak unto them all that I shall command him" (18:17–18). In 5:23–31 and 18:15–19, therefore, Moses is represented as twice relating the same incident, and presumably the same utterance of God, in response to the people's request for an intermediary to convey God's word to them. That is, Moses is described as appealing to the same occasion and to the same divine utterance to authenticate both his own prophetic role and that of a "prophet like unto him."

If we ask what specific laws, commandments, and statutes Moses is empowered by the commission of 5:31 to set forth, we are led, by the clear-cut construction of the book, to answer: the laws and ordinances introduced by the words "These are the statutes and judgments" (12:1) and concluding with "This day the Lord thy God hath commanded thee to do these statutes and judgments" (26:16). When we then ask what words precisely are referred to when God says, in 18:18, "I . . . will put my words in his mouth; and he shall speak unto them all that I shall command him," these "words" are twofold: Deuteronomy on the one hand and Joshua–2 Kings on the other. Just as Moses first relates the commandments of God in direct discourse (most often in the first address, and most pointedly in the second address with the reporting of the Decalogue) and then abruptly shifts to a much more authoritative manner of reporting that tends to blur the distinction between divine and Mosaic speech, so also the prophet "like unto" Moses first relates the words of God/Moses in direct discourse (Deuteronomy) and then abruptly shifts to a much more authoritative manner of reporting, which blurs the distinction between the words of God/Moses and his own (Joshua–2 Kings).

In effect, then, the prophet "like unto" Moses is the narrator of the Deuteronomic History, or, more precisely, that authorial presence in the text which scholars have personified as "the Deuteronomist." It is he who uses Moses' direct words to explain by a hortatory law code the wide-ranging implications of the Decalogue; in a widening circle, this same "author" will soon be using his narrator's direct words to explain in an exemplary history the wide-ranging implications of that law code.

Dialogue in Deuteronomy

So far we have seen examples from Deuteronomy which reveal through composition and content a double-voiced accent in regard to Moses' preeminent place as declarer and teacher of God's word. This "dialogue"— to use Bakhtin's term for such phenomena—was found first in the narrator's own voice, which overtly promotes Moses' eminence to the highest degree, both by explicit statement and by implicit composition, yet at the same time subtly draws attention to itself through a series of pedantic and apparently haphazard frame-breaks. Second, we found that even Moses' own words draw us in two directions in regard to his self-awareness as preeminent teacher of God's word.

The dialogue, however, turns out to be much more wide-ranging than a simple and singular disagreement over Moses' place in the scheme of things. Whether we listen to Moses' abundant utterances or the narrator's parsimonious few, composition and content combine to reveal within each voice a juxtaposition of opposing viewpoints on key ideological issues such as the nature of God and the privileged role of his people Israel.

Moses' rhetorical questions in 4:7–8, 32–34 emphasize Israel's special status in God's eyes. In 7:6 Moses again stresses Israel's unique relationship: "For thou art an holy people unto the Lord thy God; the Lord thy God hath chosen thee to be a special people unto himself, above all people who are upon the face of the earth." Israel is unique among the nations precisely because of God's special treatment. But elsewhere Moses provides disquieting evidence that casts doubt on Israel's privileged status. In chapter 2, for example, he quotes God to the effect that Mount Seir, Moab, and Ammon have been providentially allotted to the sons of Esau and the sons of Lot for their inheritance.

Apparently the Lord reserves various forms of special treatment for other nations as well—and special punishment also: "As the nations which the Lord destroyeth before your face, so shall ye perish; because ye would not be obedient unto the voice of the Lord your God" (8:20). With this statement Moses introduces us to another disquieting perspective on Israel's relation to God: "Not for thy righteousness, or for the uprightness of thine heart, dost thou go to possess their land: but for the wickedness of these nations the Lord thy God doth drive them out from before thee, and that he may perform the word which the Lord sware unto thy fathers, Abraham, Isaac, and Jacob" (9:5). The special relationship between Israel and YHWH, described by Moses elsewhere, apparently exists within a larger context. God seems to have a twofold motive for giving the Promised Land to Israel: retribution, to punish for their wickedness the nations dispossessed by Israel, and gracious fulfillment of his solemn promise to the fathers.

And what happened to those nations will happen to the Israelites also, Moses warns in 8:20. It seems, after all, that Israel is little different, at least in this regard, from the other nations that in the past have enjoyed God's blessings. Israel is now benefiting from the wickedness (could it even be the disobedience?) of some of those nations, just as other nations will eventually benefit from Israel's disobedience.

The subject matter of the narrator's frame-breaks at 2:10–12, 20–23 is a good example of how composition reinforces content in promoting this ideological dialogue on Israel's status in relation to the other nations. For example, when the narrator interrupts Moses' words with his own:

> but the Lord destroyed [the giants/Zamzummim] before [the children of Ammon]; and they succeeded them, and dwelt in their stead: As he did to the children of Esau, which dwelt in Seir, when he destroyed the Horims from before them; and they succeeded them, and dwelt in their stead even unto this day;   (2:21–22)

the content of this interruption echoes that of God's words, quoted by Moses throughout chapters 2 and 3, concerning his gift of land to the sons of Esau and of Lot.

The question, then, never answered but raised several times in the book by God, Moses, and the narrator himself, is this: If all these nations inside and outside the Promised Land have been dispossessed in the past, and are now being dispossessed, through the retributive hand of God, was their land also given to them through a divine promise similar to that made to Israel's fathers?

Also unanswered is the question about the nature of the punishment meted out to the nations dispossessed by Israel: If God is just, then does not his treatment of the nations imply some sort of previous covenant with them similar to that made with Israel at Horeb, and which, like Israel, they have violated? Whereas Moses' rhetorical questions seem to imply absolute confidence in Israel's uniqueness as a special nation unto God, his words elsewhere, as in 8:20 and 9:4–5 and throughout chapters 2 and 3, cast doubt on the absoluteness of that confidence. In these hints of a living dialogue a limited, religiously based nationalism is being cautiously expanded on an international and political scale. The succeeding chapters of the Deuteronomist's history spell out the details of this political theology.

A second major ideological dialogue fills the pages of Deuteronomy, concerning the relation between God's justice and his mercy with respect to Israel. Warning statements about the retributive nature of God's acts are so widespread and seem to be so definitive in the book that an opposing view about his fundamental mercy and abiding partiality would seem to be difficult to maintain. The key vehicle in Deuteronomy for describing God's unconditional mercy is "the covenant which God swore to the fathers," and the unconditionality of this promise is often neutralized by reference to the necessary condition of obedience. Texts such as 6:3, 10–15, 23–24; 7:6–11, 12–13; 8:1, 18–19; 10:11–13, 15–17; 11:8–9, 20–23; 12:1; 13:17b–18; and 26:14–15 reveal recurrent attempts to achieve a synthesis of the covenant with the fathers and the covenant at Horeb by making the latter a precondition for the enactment of the former. Obedience thereby becomes a condition for the fulfillment of God's apparently unconditional oath to the fathers, and God thereby becomes *fundamentally* a God of justice, not of mercy, who, as Moses says, is "God of gods, and Lord of lords, a great God, a mighty, and an awesome, who is not partial and takes no bribe" (10:17 [AR]). In Deuteronomy the *telling* of God's mercy is almost always neutralized by an immediately preceding or subsequent *telling* of his terrible vengeance or of the need for obedience.

On the other hand, whatever God, Moses, and the narrator predominantly *say* in Deuteronomy, nothing is more clearly *shown* in the book than the fact that Israel, already destined for disobedience, is going to receive a land it does not deserve. God's central decision, recounted in chapters 9 and 10, to give Israel the Land despite the people's initial and immediate disobedience, is a prelude to the entire Deuteronomic History, in which Israel exists in the Land in almost unceasing disobedience to the Mosaic covenant. Through the entire period covered in Judges, and up to the end of 2 Kings, God is nothing if not partial to Israel.

What Deuteronomy shows, therefore, as a prelude to the entire Deuteronomic History, is a God continually mindful of the promise he made to the fathers—so much so that, by the end of the history, the fall of Jerusalem becomes a climax that is the story's greatest paradox: why, after all the centuries of Israel's disobedience and God's partiality, does God at last forget the promise he made to the fathers and finally do what Moses had told them he would do? A convincing account of how brilliantly the Deuteronomist works up to this climactic mystery in 2 Kings has yet to be written.[3]

NOTES

1. V. N. Voloshinov's *Marxism and the Philosophy of Language* (New York and London, 1973) is a basic introduction to "reporting and reported speech." Just as important is Mikhail Bakhtin's essay, "Discourse in the Novel," in Michael Holquist, ed., *The Dialogic Imagination: Four Essays by M. M. Bakhtin* (Austin, 1981).

2. For an excellent treatment of the function of frame-breaks in life and language, see Erving Goffman, *Frame Analysis: An Essay on the Organization of Experience* (Cambridge, Mass., 1974).

3. Nevertheless, important work providing a partial picture of this process has begun to appear. A notable example is David M. Gunn, *The Story of King David: Genre and Interpretation* (Sheffield, 1978).

SUGGESTED FURTHER READINGS

Lyle M. Eslinger, *Kingship of God in Crisis. A Close Reading of 1 Samuel 1–12* (Sheffield, 1985).

J. P. Fokkelman, *Narrative Art and Poetry in the Books of Samuel*, vol. I: *King David* (Assen, 1981).

David M. Gunn, *The Fate of King Saul: An Interpretation of a Biblical Story* (Sheffield, 1980).

Robert Polzin, *Moses and the Deuteronomist. A Literary Study of the Deuteronomic History, Part One: Deuteronomy, Joshua, Judges* (New York, 1980).

Carleton University

Joshua and Judges

David M. Gunn

Formal Connection and Plot

VIEWED simply, the Book of Joshua recounts the entry of the people of Israel into the Promised Land, Canaan, the land of the Amorites/Canaanites. It takes up the story—a story running from Genesis to 2 Kings—where Deuteronomy leaves off: the people have left Egypt, the land of bondage, crossed the Red Sea, received the law of YHWH at Sinai, journeyed in the Wilderness, taken possession of land east of the Jordan (Num. 32), and now stand ready to possess the rest of the promise. As the Book of Deuteronomy culminates in the death of Moses, so the Book of Joshua will culminate in the death of Joshua. Thus it will begin "after the death of Moses" (Joshua 1:1), just as the Book of Judges in turn will begin "after the death of Joshua" (Judges 1:1; cf. 2 Sam. 1:1).

Chapters 1–12 tell of the ensuing war in a relatively expansive style marked by descriptive detail and reported speech, though pared toward the end to some skeletal reporting speech (see 10:28–39) intimating the characteristic prose of the next section, chapters 13–22. Woven into the Jericho and Ai accounts are first the measured, ritualistic account of the crossing of the Jordan, and then the story of Achan's transgression and execution, while another story of deception, the Gibeonites' covenant, links easily with the end of the campaign ("Now the inhabitants of Gibeon heard what Joshua had done to Jericho and to Ai," 9:3 [AR]); similarly linked are the main succeeding episodes (for example, "Now it came to pass, when Adoni-zedek king of Jerusalem heard that Joshua had taken Ai . . . ," 10:1; "And it came to pass, when Jabin king of Hazor heard . . . ," 11:1. A summary listing of the kings defeated and land possessed, east and west of the Jordan, brings the constant movement of the narrative (with its reiterated verbs of passing over/on/across, going up, returning/turning back, and so on) to a pause.

Chapters 13–22 are set off formally in parentheses, as it were ("Now Joshua was old and advanced in years," 13:1 [AR], resumed at 23:1, 2), as if formally to declare a halt, a shift from the narrative of action to the rhetoric of listing and ordering. As in Numbers (or Chronicles), listing subdues narrative here, building a land and community out of names and connectives, though occasionally narrated speech and activity push through, as when Caleb (14:6–15) and the daughters of Zelophehad (17:3–6) remind Joshua of special treatment promised by Moses, or the tribe of Joseph grumbles at its lot (17:14–18), or surveyors are sent out on behalf of seven reluctant tribes (18:2–10). But we miss something of the book's special texture if we allow our taste for action or character development to deflect us from this more static, administrative, prose. For out of it arises a powerful sense of the myriad elements that constitute "the people." "Israel" takes on substance, as does the task at hand; for the challenge to Israel is to translate those lists and allotments into an actual community in actual possession of the Promised Land. The taking of Jericho and Ai and the other campaigns dramatically recounted in chapters 1–12 sweep us along in a vision of easy success. Chapters 13–21 implicitly suggest that occupation involves much more. They also establish a sense of ambivalence which will not readily be resolved. Instructions for allotting each tribe's "inheritance," issued earlier by Moses in the prescriptive, Wilderness period (Num. 34), are now scrupulously fulfilled—perhaps. Our grasp of narrative time tends to slip with this prose. Are we dealing with the ideal or the actual? And within what time frame—with reference to narrated time, the narrator's time, or the implied reader's time—might that actuality be located? Or do we slide between prescription and fulfillment?

Chapters 23–24 bring the book to a close with a report of all Israel gathering, programmatic speeches by Joshua and YHWH (related by Joshua), the people's renewed commitment to the Covenant, and Joshua's brief dismissal of the people to their inheritance, followed by his death.

Viewed simply, Judges is an account of Israel's earliest occupation of the Promised Land, in the period before the rise of the monarchy, the period which has become known from the major characters of the book as the Period of the Judges. It is formally linked with the Book of Joshua not only by that opening phrase, "after the death of Joshua," but also by its recapitulation of Joshua 24:28–31 (dismissal and death) in Judges 2:6–9 (and cf. 2:21–22 with Joshua 23), following the reiteration of still more Joshua material in Judges 1. The book finds its continuation in 1 Samuel (according to the Hebrew Bible) or Ruth and then 1 Samuel (according to the ancient Greek versions and the Christian Bible).[1]

Whereas Joshua appears to have a recognizable, if loosely constructed, plot—Israel crosses into the Land and surmounts major obstacles (in the form of fortified cities and indigenous peoples), the Land falls within its grasp and tribal territories are allotted—Judges coheres less obviously in linear or cause-and-effect terms.[2] It has often been described as a rather randomly assembled anthology of tales, at best an illustration of a cyclical pattern of sin, oppression, repentance, and salvation, expressive of an editor-compiler's rigidly determinative theology of reward and punishment. But so to describe it is to miss or misread three salient features of the book (to which we shall return later). First, a determinative pattern of response by God is neither explicit in the so-called editorial framework or formula passages (such as 2:11–19) nor inherent in the tales themselves. Second, the tales mesh through shared motifs and themes. Third, there is a discernible tendency for the models of leadership and community developed in the earlier books (Numbers–Joshua) as well as in the opening stories of Judges itself (such as Othniel and Ehud) to become increasingly blurred and distorted as the book continues. As we bear in mind that YHWH intends to test the people's allegiance by means of the impinging "nations" (chap 2), and as we recall the fierce injunctions against forsaking YHWH (cf. Joshua 23–24 and Deut. 28–29), we may begin to see that this deterioration creates a tension transcending the constituent tales and so at least a potential plot for the whole book. Will the promise of the Land be revoked and the people cast out?

Judges 1:1–3:6 introduces the whole book. It first recounts what appear to be the final stages of the taking of the Land, thereby partly recapitulating Joshua, though the focus is now upon the inhabitants of the Land who were *not* dispossessed (see 1:27–36). This focus is then developed in theological terms by an angel of YHWH, by YHWH himself, and by the narrator: Israel's coming to terms with the Canaanites has endangered its relationship with YHWH and will lead to further deterioration, spelled out in summary fashion in 2:11–19, which we may recognize (by the end of the book) as a theological abstract of the whole work.

The next section, 3:7–16:31, recounts the tales of the judges (some are called "saviors") who judge Israel or deliver the people (some do both) from oppression: Othniel (3:7–11); Ehud (3:12–30); Shamgar (3:31—hardly a tale); Deborah (and Barak) (chaps. 4–5); Gideon (chaps. 6–8) together with the "king," Abimelech (chap. 9); Tola and Jair (10:1–2, 3–5); Jephthah (10:6–12:7); Izban, Elon, and Abdon (12:8–10, 11–12, 13–15); and Samson (chaps. 13–16). Six extended accounts are interspersed with six brief notices in the pattern 1:2:3 (Shamgar:Tola and Jair:Izban, Elon, and Abdon). This pattern in the minor accounts corresponds to the noticeable lengthening of the major tales, the inverse of what we saw in Joshua. One effect, perhaps, is focal, placing the culminating story of Samson in a special relationship with the story of Jericho and drawing attention to the movement that occurs between the taking of Jericho and the taking of Samson, at the center of which lies the "completion" (in fact, noncompletion) of the taking of the Land (Judges 1) and the theological formulations of Judges 2.

Linking the major episodes is a rhetorical framework (so-called) comprising some or all of six elements (they occur within 2:11–19 and recur within the episodes starting at 3:7, 3:12, 4:1, 6:1, 10:6, and 13:1): (1) Israel does what is evil in YHWH's sight; (2) YHWH gives/sells the people into the hand of oppressors; (3) Israel cries to YHWH; (4) YHWH raises up a savior/deliverer; (5) the deliverer defeats the oppressor; (6) the Land has rest. In fact this formula is as varied as it is constant, not only because in some cases certain elements are redundant in the particular context, but also because the pattern of responses is itself by no means adhered to rigidly. Thus neither the Gideon nor the Samson story depicts the Land as regaining "rest," nor, in the Samson story, do the people any longer remember to cry to YHWH, and, furthermore, Samson himself dies in captivity to the oppressor (in contrast to element 5). This framework, therefore, establishes a norm which can then be undermined, offering us strategic interpretive clues both to the associated tales and to the work as a whole.

Another set of rhetorical connectives within the central section of Judges derives from a pervasive chronological scheme,[3] while also detectable is a certain spatial coherence. Echoing (though not precisely) the sequence in chapter 1, from south to north, Judah to Dan, are the tribal affiliations of the protagonists in chapters 3–16, from Othniel the Judahite to Samson the Danite. With Samson in chapters 13–16, however, we are not in the north, Dan's eventual location, but in the middle (west), the allotted territory; that location allows to unfold the subsequent story of Micah and the northward migration of the Danites in chapters 17–18. The disjunction here between list and tale is thematically significant, underlining the failure of Dan in the face of the inhabitants of the Land, a paradigm of Israel's failure.

Simplest among connecting devices, in classic paratactic style, are, first, the crucial variation of the introductory formula "And the people of Israel did what was evil in the sight of YHWH" (2:11 [AR]), to read "And [they] *again* did [or "they continued to do"] what was evil in the sight of YHWH" (3:12 [AR]; cf. 4:1, 10:6, 13:1); and, second, the use of the phrase "and after [him]" to introduce and integrate sequentially the "minor" judges (3:31; 10:1, 3; 12:8, 11, 13). These devices are akin to several deployed in Joshua 1–12: first, as a connector of larger episodes, the narrator uses an introductory formula such as "And it came to pass, when all the kings which were beyond the Jordan . . . heard" (Joshua 9:1; see also 10:1, 11:1); second, for the listing of brief campaign notices while retaining an action sequence, the narrator uses chain repetition such as "And from Lachish Joshua passed unto Eglon . . . and smote it . . . as he had done to Lachish. And Joshua went up from Eglon . . . unto Hebron . . . and smote it . . . as he had done to Eglon" (10:34–37 [AR]).

Associative connectors, such as motifs or wordplay, are numerous. Some of these work to associate adjacent or nearly adjacent episodes; others function over much broader extents. In the first category is Ehud's killing of an unsuspecting Eglon, with the unexpected weapon "thrust" (*taqa'*) into the king's belly (3:21), paralleling Jael's killing of an unsuspecting Sisera with the unexpected weapon (a tent peg) "thrust" (*taqa'*) into the king's temple (4:21); or the "worthless fellows" (*'anashim reqim*) who support Abimelech (9:4), paralleled by Jephthah's followers in the next story (11:3). Likewise the Nazirite vow, implicit in the angel's speech to Samson's mother (13:3–5), conjures recollection of Jephthah's fateful and fatal vow in the preceding story (11:30–31). In another case, the song (chap. 5) that crowns the prose account of Jael's exploit (chap. 4; the two are usually treated as discrete sources by biblical critics) brings the prose narrative of Sisera's death into focus by wordplay as well as by precise repetition. "He asked for water—milk she gave" (5:25 [AT]) distills the irony of the more prosaic 4:19 ("and he said to her, 'Please give me a little water to drink, for I am thirsty'; and she opened the skin of milk and gave him some to drink" [AT]). In the prose account Jael drives the tent peg into Sisera's temple (*raqah*, 4:21, 22); the song picks up the term and plays on the syllable *raq* and the sound *q*, especially through the guttural *ḥ* (hard, as in Scottish "loch"). "She crushed his head [*ro'sh*], / and shattered and struck through [*ḥalaf*; cf. *ḥalav*, "milk"] his temple [*raqah*]" (5:26 [AT]); to Sisera's mother the wise women respond reassuringly: "Are they not finding / and dividing [*ḥalaq*] the spoil? /—a womb [*raḥam*], two wombs [*raḥmatayim*], / per head [*ro'sh*], per hero; / spoil of dyed-stuff for Sisera, / spoil of dyed-stuff, shot-stuff [*riqmah*], / dyed-stuff, two pieces of shot-stuff [*riqmatayim*], / for the neck of the spoiler" (5:30 [AT]).

As with the framework passages, motif parallels serve not only a formal cohesive function but also a typical heuristic purpose, in this case inviting comparative evaluation by drawing attention to similarities and contrasts in situations and characters. Similar functions are effected by various long-range connectors, such as the seizure of the fords at the Jordan (Ehud, Gideon, Jephthah) and the associated motif of the quarrel between east Jordan and west Jordan tribes (Gideon, Jephthah). The latter motif also finds prominent expression in Joshua (chap. 22) and in turn associates with a civil war motif in Judges (involving, in addition, the Abimelech story and burgeoning into the account of the war against Benjamin and the inhabitants of Jabesh-gilead, in chaps. 20–21). At the level of scene or episode, too, we find significant connection: for example, the angel's visitation to Manoah and his wife in Judges 13 (Samson) strongly recalls the beginning of Gideon's story in chapter 6 (which in turn evokes the paradigm of Moses at the burning bush in Exod. 3:1–12).

Chapters 17–21 have often been viewed as a supplement to Judges, with only superficial connection to the main body of the book. To be sure, the chronological scheme and the framework passages cease with the story of Samson; nor is there any further mention of a judge. Yet the term *coda* might better describe this section which does have strong thematic links with the rest of the book (see the last section of this essay).

(At the formal rhetorical level the introductory formula in 17:1 perhaps links with 13:2, the outset of the Samson story.) Other repetitions bind chapters 17–21 internally. Thus the prefatory "In those days there was no king in Israel" (18:1) associates the tale of Micah and the Danites with the succeeding one of the Levite and his concubine (see 19:1) and then serves a double function: as a concluding comment enveloping the larger tale (chaps. 19–21) into which the Levite/concubine story grows and as an invitation to continue reading into the next book. Or we may observe that the young Levite of Bethlehem who journeys to the hill country of Ephraim in the one story (17:7–8) gives place in the other to the Levite sojourning in the hill country of Ephraim, who journeys to Bethlehem (19:1–3).

Thematic Connection: Joshua–Judges 3

Viewed simply, Joshua is an account of the Israelites' entry into the Promised Land, Judges an account of their initial period of occupation. As we have already seen, however, such a description allows little glimpse of what enlivens these books, little clue to their singular complexities— and it is in the complexities that we often discover thematic significance. One major source of complication is a question that begins to arise in Joshua and is focused sharply in Judges 1–2, namely, did the Israelites wholly succeed in possessing the Land?[4]

Biblical scholars have been accustomed to discern two disparate views of the occupation: whereas Joshua presents an account of a devastating and successful conquest, all but eliminating the native population, Judges reflects a more gradual process, including a crucial failure to dislodge significant Canaanite elements. Yet this is an overly neat division, for elements of a story of partial occupation appear in Joshua itself. Certainly the Joshua narrator seems to assert explicitly YHWH's total fulfillment of his promises regarding the Land. For example, "And YHWH gave to Israel all the land which he had sworn to give to their fathers, and they took possession of it and settled in it . . . Not a word was broken of every good word which YHWH had spoken to the house of Israel; all arrived" (21:43–45 [AT]) is echoed by Joshua's own words near the close of the book (23:14–15). Yet already by the end of chapter 9 we are aware that the Gibeonites remain, protected by an Israelite covenant; from 11:22 we learn that none of the Anakim were left in the land of the people of Israel—except in Gaza, Gath, and Ashdod![5] Likewise the Geshurites and Maacathites "dwelt in the midst of Israel to this day" (13:13 [AT]), as did "the Jebusites with the people of Judah at Jerusalem to this day" (15:63 [AT]), while the Canaanites of Gezer, not driven out, "dwelt in the midst of Ephraim to this day and became forced labor" (16:10 [AT]; see also 17:11–12). At this point we should recall that, according to the prescriptions for implementing the promise (such as Deut. 7:1–2, 20:16–18), possession of the Land means not only dispossession of the inhabitants but also their total removal.

"So Joshua took the whole land, according to all that the Lord [had] said to Moses," we read in 11:23. Yet in 13:1, as the book shifts into its second phase (chaps. 13–21), YHWH intimates to Joshua that "there remains a great extent of land to possess" [AT], and if we observe both the temporal ambiguities fostered by the allotment accounts and the sporadic itemizing of the *remnant* nations, we shall be the less surprised to discover by chapter 18 that seven tribes still await even the process of allotment, let alone have taken possession of their inheritance. "How long," says Joshua to the reluctant tribes, "will you make no effort to enter and take possession of the land, which YHWH, the God of your fathers, has given to you?" (18:3 [AT]).

Faced with this range of tempering voices we may find ourselves concluding that the intimations of sweeping victory are perhaps to be taken as implying strict geographic limitations ("he took all *that particular part of* the land"), are at the very least the language of hyperbole, are even, conceivably, ironic.

Once attuned to the voices of incomplete fulfillment, we are bound to review what may have earlier passed unremarked. The preservation of Rahab and her family is, of course, an infringement of the command to "devote" ("put to the ban," "utterly destroy") those given into Israel's hand (see Deut. 7:2, 20:10–18). No matter that the agreement reached by the spies seems reasonable and reciprocal; it is an illegal covenant according to the rules governing the war of occupation, the law of YHWH, the law just mediated by the voice of Moses the servant of God in Deuteronomy, the law that lies at the heart of God's (splendidly concentric) exhortation to Joshua at the beginning of his book (1:5–9) to do according to the law which Moses commanded so that he might successfully bring the people to inherit the Land.

The uncompromising execution of the Israelite Achan and his company (chap. 7) for infringing the prohibition against taking booty reinforces the point. The sparing of the Canaanite Rahab compromises the law. It is the beginning of the account of how the Canaanites remained in the Land. Likewise the sparing of the Canaanites of Gibeon becomes another episode in the story of Israel's failure wholly to possess the Land. That agreement, too, contravenes the letter of the law.

At the heart of YHWH's speech to Joshua at the opening of the book is the law. At the heart of Joshua's final speeches at the closing of the book (chaps. 23–24) is the issue that above all else links law and Land in the commandment to dispossess the inhabitants completely (23:6–8; see also 24:14–15, 19–20):

And be very strong [says Joshua] to keep and do all that is written in the book of the law of Moses . . . that you do not go amongst these nations, these remnant ones with you; and you shall not call to mind the names of their gods and you shall not swear by them and you shall not serve them and you shall not bow down to them, but rather to YHWH your God you shall cling, as you have done today. [AT]

The speech resonates with others before it, most strikingly with Deuteronomy 20:17-18:

And you shall truly devote them to destruction, the Hittites and the Amorites, the Canaanites and the Perizzites, the Hivites and the Jebusites, as YHWH your God has commanded; that they may not teach you to do according to all their abominable practices which they have done for their gods, and you sin against YHWH your God. [AT]

The issue concerns the essence of the covenant that binds YHWH and people (hence both speeches in chaps. 23-24 issue naturally in the covenant of 24:25). Will Israel forsake YHWH for other gods? The injunction against a remnant expresses a fundamental pessimism on YHWH's part: only a people living in a world sealed off from the world seems to promise much hope of an enduring loyalty; a people rubbing shoulders with other peoples with other gods will inevitably break faith. On the other hand, the covenant itself is an expression of optimism, as is the promise which gives shape to our story. Of central interest, therefore, is how this optimistic God will confront the realization of his pessimism.

In the gap between the rhetoric of fulfillment and the rhetoric of incompletion we discover a confluence of basic questions. Is the promise of the gift of land to the ancestors truly unconditional? Or does the punishment consequent upon the people's failure strictly to observe YHWH's commandments override the promise? Does success depend upon adherence to the law (cf. Joshua 1:8)? If YHWH as covenant God allows modification or compromise of the divinely ordained commandments (cf. Rahab or the Gibeonites or the conscription of remnant Canaanites), will not this latitude threaten the very relationship that the commandments are designed to preserve, namely that YHWH alone is Israel's God? If the story of Achan models the strict application of covenant justice, what prospect is there that the people, whose propensity for backsliding has been amply narrated in the preceding books, will ever enter the Land to inherit the gift, let alone remain in it? We are but a narrative stone's-throw away from the devastating curses that buttress the book of the Law (Deut. 28:15-68; cf. Joshua 23:15-16 and 24:19-20), prominent among which is the threat of forcible removal from the Land.

Yet the gift is gratuitous, the law buttressed also with blessings (Deut. 28:1-14). The task of realizing the promise is immense in human terms, as Joshua 13–21 makes eminently plain, but a matter of merely mundane proportions in divine terms. It is truly a gift, as the narrator and YHWH are at pains to point out:

> No person shall be able to stand before thee all the days of thy life: as I was with Moses, so I will be with thee: I will not fail thee, nor forsake thee.   (Joshua 1:15 [AR])

> See, I have given unto thine hand Jericho . . . and the wall of the city shall fall . . .   (6:2, 5; see also 8:1; 10:10–11; 10:29, 32)

> And all these kings and their land did Joshua take at one time, because the Lord God of Israel fought for Israel.   (10:42; see also 24:11–12)

As even Joshua gropes cautiously for the gift ("And Joshua the son of Nun sent two men secretly from Shittim as spies, saying, Go view the land, even Jericho" 2:1 [AR]—how appallingly reminiscent of that earlier, disastrous mission in Num. 13), as Israelites treat with Canaanites, as Achan seeks the security of mammon, and as seven tribes tarry at the boundaries of the Land, we are aware that the gift is still being proffered after a journey through many books filled with much reluctance and much searching for more tangible securities than the elusive presence of YHWH. In other words, a further complicating factor in that confluence of factors is YHWH's already abundantly narrated loyalty, mercy, and propensity for compassion. In the gap between fulfillment and nonfulfillment we discover also the tension between divine justice and mercy. "YHWH is slow to anger and abundant in loyalty, forgiving iniquity and transgression; but he will not hold them innocent, visiting the iniquity of fathers upon children, upon the third and upon the fourth generation" (Num. 14:18 [AT]; cf. Deut. 5:8–10). The tension in that formulation is also one of the central tensions in the books of Joshua and Judges.

The issue of fulfillment and nonfulfillment is focused sharply in Judges 1–2, where the equilibrium shifts decisively toward the latter despite the ostensible premise upon which the story continues to be built, namely that the Land has indeed been occupied, the gift now received. Located at the center of the two books, these chapters, together with Joshua 23–24, take on a somewhat programmatic quality, influencing our reading both forward and backward.

To readers expecting neat temporal progression, this prose is puzzling; and, indeed, generations of source-critics have ingeniously unscrambled it, removing hypothetical editorial accretions and quite missing any sense of the rhetoric. There is no single way to read this text, but one that helps to expose its coherence (and to account for what otherwise may appear to be some abrupt temporal shifts) takes Joshua 23 and 24 as a starting point and observes some broad measure of correspondence between those chapters and Judges 1:22–36 and 2:1–10, respectively. Within this envelope lies a roughly concentrically shaped account of Judah (and

Benjamin) campaigning. Thus the arrangement as a whole appears broadly concentric.

A   YHWH will dispossess the remaining nations; but if Israel should join with them, YHWH will leave them to be a snare leading to the destruction of Israel from off the Land (Joshua 23).

B   YHWH (via Joshua) recounts Israel's story from Abraham; Joshua presses the people to choose between God or the gods; the people choose YHWH; a covenant is sworn (24:1–27).

C   Joshua sends the people to their inheritance; he dies and is buried; summary: Israel served YHWH all the days of Joshua and all the days of the elders who outlived Joshua (24:28–31).

D   The bones of Joseph are brought up from Egypt and buried; Eleazar dies and is buried (24:32–33).

E   Judah campaigns (with Simeon) against the Canaanites: Bezek and Adoni-Bezek; Jerusalem; Hebron; Debir—Caleb's gift (Judges 1:1–8).

F   The descendants of the Kenite, Moses' father-in-law, settle with Judah in the wilderness of Judah (1:16).

E′   Judah campaigns (with Simeon) against Zephath, Gaza, etc.; Hebron is given to Caleb; Benjamin does not drive the Jebusites from Jerusalem (1:17–21).

A′   The other tribes fail to dispossess and drive out various groups of inhabitants who are listed (1:22–36).

B′   The angel of YHWH recites the story from Egypt and reproaches the people for having broken the command to make no covenant with the inhabitants; therefore, their gods will become a snare to Israel. The people weep and sacrifice to YHWH (2:1–5).

C′   (1) Joshua [had] sent the people away to take possession of their inheritance; (2) they [had] served YHWH all the days of Joshua, and all the days of the elders who outlived him; (3) and Joshua [had] died and been buried (2:6–9).

D′   "And all that generation also were gathered to their fathers: and there arose another generation after them, who did not know the Lord or the work which he had done for Israel" (2:10 [AR]; cf. "And Joseph died, and all his brothers, and all that generation . . . And there arose a new king over Egypt, who did not know Joseph"; Exod. 1:6–8 [AR]).

Among various points of exegetical potential exposed by this ordering of the text are, first, the unmistakable decline from the possibility of optimism in *A* and *B*, to the ominous foreclosing of options, whether by Israel or by YHWH, in *A'* and *B'*; and, second, the establishment of a generational scheme—2:10 parallels, again ominously, the prelude to the story of enslavement in Egypt. The scheme signals a new story within the greater story. It also has the ambiguous effect of both confirming the nonfulfillment (or partial fulfillment) thread from the Book of Joshua and elevating the Joshua generation to model status. Whatever the faults of that generation, they turn out to be relative, bearing no comparison to the sins of the new one; and this is but the beginning of a downward spiral signaled by the narrator's unhesitating claim that each successive generation "behaved worse than their fathers" (2:19 [AT]).

Reading 1:27–35 (failure to dispossess) and 2:1–10 (the angel's accusation of covenant-breaking and his announcement that the nations would become a snare) in terms of the speeches and covenant-making of Joshua 23 and 24, as the concentricity urges us to do, makes evident what is otherwise not explicit in the Judges text, namely the confidently predicted outcome of such behavior on Israel's part—that Israel will perish from off the Land (23:12–13, 15–16; 24:20). At this point the end of the greater story (in 2 Kings 25) is brought directly into focus for the narrator's contemporary audience, not because the audience necessarily knows 2 Kings 25, but because it is almost certainly in exile, driven from the Land. In the event, Israelite and Canaanite share the same fate. Neither deserves the Land. It is a gift. That is a sobering perception for the reader who would find satisfaction in a simple story of good against evil (the chosen against the rejected) or find contemporary justification for human action in the model of ruthless dispossession. It perhaps explains why this may be a story for both possessor and dispossessed.

The pattern of decline which has already been intimated as the pattern of the new generation is spelled out in 2:11–3:6. Verses 11–13 confirm the fact of apostasy, verses 14–19 tell the spiraling tale which is to be the story of the new book. Repeating verse 14 ("And the anger of the Lord was hot against Israel") at verse 20, the narrator then explains YHWH's decision to refrain from further aid to Israel in driving out the remnant nations as a decision to "test" Israel, a somewhat ambiguous notion that leaves open whether this is punishment or opportunity for a renewed relationship, or indeed both. Repeating verse 14 yet again at 3:8, the narrator draws us back once more to the beginning of the spiral and into the first of the stories in the main body of the book, the story of Othniel.

Thematic Connection: Judges 3–21

Othniel's story is nothing if not skeletal, with just a hint of flesh on the bones—some names, a lineage, a time span. The people of Israel do what is evil in the sight of YHWH, forgetting God and serving other gods;

YHWH is angry and sells them into the hand of Chushan-rishathaim (= Chushan-Double-Wickedness?), king of Mesopotamia ("Aram of the Two Rivers," that is, northern Mesopotamia/eastern Syria); the people serve that king eight years; they cry (*za'aq*, "appeal for help") to YHWH, who raises up a deliverer, Othniel; he (YHWH or Othniel—the syntax is, perhaps deliberately, ambiguous; so, too, at 2:18, though not at 2:16) delivers them—YHWH's spirit comes upon Othniel, he "judges" them (there are obvious connotations of "rule" in this use of the term) and goes out to war; YHWH gives the king into his hand so that Othniel prevails over him; whereupon the land has rest for forty years before Othniel dies (3:7–11).

As already remarked, the story buds naturally from the antecedent narrative through verses 7–8, which imitate 2:13–14 and 2:20 (Israel's evil and YHWH's anger). The characteristic language of the spiral described in chapter 2—"raise up," "judge," "deliver" (or "save")—is immediately recognizable. Othniel we have met before.

The story is a model one not only in the sense that it gives substance or particularity to the abstractions of the chapter 2 summary but also in the sense that it is an *ideal* paradigm. Othniel is Caleb's son, a lineage hard to surpass at this point in the story (cf. Num. 14:21–24, 30; Joshua 14:6–15; Judges 1:20). YHWH's spirit initiates the action, says the narrator, and it is YHWH who gives the enemy king into his hand, inviting favorable comparison with YHWH's own earlier paradigms of war against the nations in Deuteronomy and Joshua. Above all, we notice that the people, having lapsed into the service of other gods, do belatedly cry for help to YHWH, thereby signaling that they recognize the impotence of their new gods and their dependence upon the sovereign power of YHWH.

Perhaps one reason why the Othniel episode succeeds as a model is that neither Othniel nor the people are allowed any life in it. Flesh out a character or two and there is every probability of their slipping the knots of perfection, especially if their narrator-creator is partial to a story about two people, a god, and a garden. As these tales in Judges expand, so does the picture of imperfect and vulnerable humanity, the imperfections pertaining to judge as well as to people. Moreover, beyond the end of the tale and the book and the larger story of which it is a part stands its contemporary audience, most likely Judean, in Mesopotamia, and highly conscious of that vulnerability. For them the model story of Judah and its Mesopotamian oppressor must have conveyed an especially poignant irony.

A sensitivity to variations upon, and development of, the Othniel model can help us to chart our way through the contours of the book. Thus, for example, the absence of that cry for help in the chapter 2 summary becomes immediately apparent in retrospect and the discrepancy proves proleptic. Despite recurrence in the framework to four of the succeeding stories (3:15, 4:3, 6:6–7, 10:10), the cry is significantly absent before the climactic Samson story (the last of the framework stories), where the people not only fail to address their God out of oppression but are even unable to recognize the "judge" upon whom the divine spirit has fallen. The men of Judah (Othniel's tribe!) give him into the hands of the Philistine oppressors with the exasperated comment (the irony bypasses the characters and is for the reader alone to enjoy) "Knowest thou not that the Philistines are rulers over us?" (15:11).

Here we are but one remove from the men of Israel who respond to victory over the Midianites by inviting Gideon to "rule over us, not only you but your son and grandson also [that is, rule as a king]; for you have delivered us out of the hand of Midian" (8:22 [AT]). The reader knows otherwise: it is in fact YHWH who has delivered Israel, by the hand of Gideon (see 7:7, 7:9, or 7:14, where even a Midianite knows this to be so). The consequence of YHWH's precautions "lest Israel elevate themselves over me, saying 'My own hand has delivered me'" (7:2 [AT]—his motivation for reducing the numbers of Gideon's troops) has been to deflect the adulation to Gideon! And even Gideon's reply to the men, "I shall not rule over you, and my son will not rule over you; YHWH will rule over you" (8:23 [AT]), while formally insisting on the proprieties, is delightfully reticent on the subject of deliverance. (Also ambiguous, at least momentarily, is whether the reply constitutes outright refusal or conditional acceptance on Gideon's part, meaning something like "Very well, I accept, but remember that it is not I or my son but YHWH who will truly be ruler").

The narrator teases us further. Gideon's next action is to *behave* like a king ("'give me, each of you, the earrings from your spoil' . . . and the weight of the golden earrings that he demanded was seventeen hundred shekels of gold," 8:24–26 [AT]), bringing strongly to mind Moses' injunction that a king shall not "greatly amass for [AR] himself silver and gold" (Deut. 17:17). In turn we confront a potential apostate, an Aaron at Sinai making a golden calf forged from the gold earrings of his people (Exod. 32). "And Gideon made it into an ephod and put it in his city, in Ophrah [where, ironically, stands Gideon's altar built to YHWH in the opening phase of the story, 6:24]; and all Israel prostituted itself after it there, and it became a snare to Gideon and to his family" (8:27 [AT]).[6]

"My son will not rule over you," says Gideon; but the story will recount that very circumstance in the next chapter, the bloody tale of the reign of Abi-melech (= "My Father Is King"!), son of (Gideon =) Jerub-baal (= "Let Baal Contend"; see 8:33).

That it is YHWH who delivers, YHWH who rules, YHWH who is king in Israel, is no longer a datum of consequence to the people who now populate the book. "In those days there was no king in Israel," observes the narrator in the refrain that punctuates the closing tales (18:1,

19:1), thereby prolonging the irony conjured by Samson's Judean captors. A similar irony closes the book, too: "In those days there was no king in Israel: people did what was right in their own eyes" (21:25 [AR]). We recall the formula prefacing the model tale, Othniel's, as well as all subsequent tales, but palpably absent from chapters 17–21: "And the people of Israel did what was evil in YHWH's eyes" (3:7 [AT]; see also 2:11). The evaluative standard is no longer divine, but human and individual. We are a long way from the nation of YHWH that marched in procession past the Ark of the Covenant into the Promised Land. We are a long way from the decrees of YHWH that doomed Jericho and put Achan to death.

It was YHWH who sold the people into the hand (power) of the king of Mesopotamia, and YHWH who gave the king of Mesopotamia into the hand of Othniel. The issue of sovereignty is, at least in part, a question of power, and the motif of hand/power can be traced throughout the book. It forms, for example, one of the central motifs in the story of Ehud and Eglon (3:12–30), immediately following the Othniel paradigm. Ehud the Benjaminite (that is, the "son of the right hand," or "right-handed") is a "man bound, restricted as to his right hand," that is, left-handed! The people choose to send "by his hand" tribute (*minḥah*, a "present" or "gift," or indeed an "offering") to Eglon, king of Moab, whom they have been serving for eighteen years. But Ehud has a short sword secretly strapped under his clothes to his right thigh; reaching for it with his left hand—and so unsuspected of foul play—he thrusts it into Eglon's belly. Unknowingly the people have sent Eglon, by Ehud's hand, a "gift" indeed (perhaps a pun is intended—the *minḥah*, "tribute," may point toward *menuḥah*, "rest" or "resting-place"). Escaping, Ehud summons the people of Israel to follow him, "for YHWH has given your enemies, Moab, into your hand" (v. 28 [AT]). This way of expressing what has transpired invites a telling comparison with that later exchange between Gideon and the men of Israel in 8:22–23. Ehud the deliverer moves our focus (and that of the people of Israel) away from himself to YHWH the deliverer and to the people, who are the true beneficiaries of YHWH's gift of power.

At the heart of Ehud's deliverance lies the power of words—the narrator's to shape our perceptions, Ehud's to ensnare the fat calf (Eglon connotes *'egel*, "calf"). The rare word *bari'* (v. 17), meaning "fat," has occurred before, far back in the larger story but then memorably, six times within Genesis 41, to describe the seven fat cows and ears of corn doomed to be devoured by the seven lean ones (see also 1 Kings 4:23, Ezek. 34:3, Hab. 1:16, Zech. 11:16). Eglon and *bari'* are a pregnant combination! As for Ehud, truly YHWH's person, he turns back (*shub*, "return," "repent"!) from The Images (or Idols, *Pesilim*; KJV: "quarries") near Gilgal. "I have a secret *davar* for you, king," he says (3:19 [AT]); and Eglon, expecting perhaps an oracle (*davar*, "word") from the gods near

Gilgal, commands "Silence!" Ehud's restatement confirms expectation: "I have a divine word [devar-'elohim] for you" (v. 20 [AT]). But the reader reads differently: the "divine word" (or "word of the gods") is rather the "word of God [YHWH]," or then again, as Ehud draws his sword, it becomes a "thing" (davar) of God. Like the sword which Ehud made for himself, his words are two-edged ("and [the sword] had two mouths," v. 16 [AT]). Thus against expectation is Eglon secured by a "word" that does indeed, for him, spell silence. And so Ehud "passes beyond The Idols" (v. 26 [AT]) and YHWH delivers Israel.

The story of Deborah and Barak begins with the relapse of Israel, and their being sold by YHWH into the hand of Jabin king of Canaan. Again we are told that the people cried to YHWH for help, "for [Jabin] had nine hundred chariots of iron and had oppressed the people of Israel with violence for twenty years" (4:3 [AT]). A jaundiced reader might wonder at the length of time elapsed before the renewed interest in YHWH and also at the motivation of this sudden interest. It arises out of the oppression, it does not seem to be interest in YHWH for YHWH's own sake or in recognition of any covenant obligation on the people's part. The mention of the chariots of iron, moreover, recalls Joshua's words regarding this same valley of Jezreel: "you shall dispossess the Canaanites, even though they have chariots of iron, even though they are strong" (Joshua 17:18 [AT]). Behind Joshua's words lie YHWH's words at the very beginning of his book: "Be strong and bold; for you shall cause this people to inherit the land . . . [Take care] to do according to all the law which Moses my servant commanded you" (1:6–7 [AT]). The beginning of chapter 4 (vv. 1–3) conveys a sense of the gap between those words of Moses and these people, who, oppressed once more, cry once more to the god of their convenience. The words of YHWH, Moses, and Joshua are but dimly remembered, if at all. The covenant words of Shechem (Joshua 24) are long since broken. It will not be the people who witness against themselves as they swore then (vv. 22–23), but YHWH's prophet who will first remind them of their disobedience (Judges 6:7–10).

Among the most devastating words of the book are Jephthah's—not his bargaining with the elders to secure headship over the people of Gilead (11:5–11), nor his elaborate exercise in diplomatic rhetoric (vv. 12–27) which ends with the narrator's laconic observation that "the king of the Ammonites did not listen to Jephthah's words" (v. 28 [AT]), but the vow uttered to YHWH as he crosses over to the Ammonites, with the spirit of YHWH upon him, to sacrifice whomever or whatever comes forth from the doors of his house to meet him, if YHWH will but grant him the victory.[7]

The vow encapsulates one of the great themes of the book (and of the rest of the history), namely the tension between human craving for security and the insecurity risked by allegiance and obedience to an imageless and unfathomable divinity. The larger story holds out blueprints of security—a nation (and a system of tribal affiliation), a land, institutions of leadership (judge, king, priest, prophet, and patriarchy) or cult (ark, ephod, and temple)—only to undermine and fracture them by recounting their fragility, corruption, or irrelevance. Even the law and commandments are subject to critical review, as the forbearance and compassion of YHWH erode their claim to absoluteness. Here in the Jephthah story it is perhaps the insecurity of the rejected "son of Gilead" (see 11:1–3) that goads him to play hostage to fortune in order to secure the victory and headship over the rejecters. (And there is a certain intriguing parallel between the rejection and recall of YHWH in 10:6–16 and of Jephthah in 10:17–11:11.)

To secure the victory means to secure YHWH. But the compositional scheme exposes the superfluity of the vow by isolating it through ring composition ("he crossed over to the Ammonites," v. 29 [AT], resumed in v. 32—is there irony here, that the vow should be framed by such potential ambiguity?). The sequence of "passing/crossing on/over" verbs (*'abar*) which bypasses the vow in verse 29 is prefaced by the announcement that YHWH's spirit came upon Jephthah and concludes (v. 32) with YHWH's gift of the enemy into his hand. That is to say, the movement toward victory has already begun.

The vow, however, starts a new plot line; and, like Ehud's words, those of Jephthah turn out to be two-edged as his daughter comes out (like Miriam at the Red Sea, Exod. 15:20) to meet him—his only daughter, his only child (v. 34; cf. Isaac in Gen. 22:2, 12, 16). Having risked all for the victory, he is unwilling to risk its undoing by offending YHWH through reneging on the vow; and from Jephthah's perspective the vow-victory sequence has to be captivating. He is a prisoner of his words ("I have opened my mouth to YHWH, and I am unable to return [repent?]," v. 35 [AT]), as he is a prisoner of his understanding of the immutability of both the vow (see Num. 30:1–2) and YHWH. (Is YHWH's word, too, thus immutable?) Whereas Ehud could return (repent) from the idols with a death-dealing but liberating word, Jephthah is unable to return (repent) from the death-dealing and imprisoning word-idol of his own creation. In consequence, his daughter bears his unjust rebuke (v. 35), speaks what he needs to hear (v. 36), and, receiving no paternal dispensation (see Num. 30:3–5), pays the terrible price of his bargain (for her, no hand from heaven stays the torch)—and wrenches the emotional center of the whole story from Jephthah to herself.

Juxtaposed with the story of the excess word is the farcical account of the neglected word (12:1–6), in which the men of Ephraim rebuke Jephthah for failing to call them and threaten to burn his house over him (as within a few chapters Samson's "companions" will threaten to burn the Timnite and his daughter, 14:15; cf. 15:6), and forty-two thousand

Ephraimites die at the hand of fellow Israelites, slaughtered by a word: "Shibboleth" (12:5–6).

In the Samson story many of the book's thematic interests coalesce.[8] YHWH's sovereignty is truly unfettered here. Exposed, too, is the fragility of knowledge, so susceptible to the vagaries and prejudices of perception and the nuances of language. Manoah's nameless wife, content to recognize the presence of God's messenger and not even ask his name (13:6), knows far more (and is told far more) than her husband, whose anxious inquiry seeks to secure the future. Key speeches reflect the play and power of words, which have a way of shaping action, whether they be prescriptive words, riddling words, wheedling words, ingratiating words, or prayerful words. Conjured by the speech of the visiting angel (13:3–5; see Num. 6:1–20), the Nazirite vow permeates the narrative, and through it the author manipulates both character and reader, exposing and fracturing expectations and norms. Samson, urged on by the spirit of YHWH, battles our expectation of what it is to be dedicated to/by God. The pattern of his life is indeed separation (*nazir*, "separated," "dedicated"), but not as we might have assumed. Severed from all enduring relationships, he dies, YHWH's agent, blind and alone amidst a mocking crowd. We read that Samson "shall begin [*yahel*] to deliver Israel out of the hand of the Philistines" (13:5; the use of *yahel*, from the root *halal*, "begin," plays appropriately upon the other meaning of the root, "pollute," "profane"). We look for a "judge"—for an Othniel or Gideon waging a heroic war of independence—and find instead a singular figure destroying, as he pulls down upon the Philistines the temple of Dagon, a god and a theological convention. "Our god has given into our hand Samson our enemy" [AR], they reiterate in 16:23–24. But the reader knows (and an Exilic reader might ponder) that it is not the captors' but the captive's god who has given captivity, and that in his death the captive makes known the impotence of Dagon and the power of YHWH.

If the Israel of the story recognizes this manifestation of YHWH, we are not told so. The silence is ominous. On the contrary, the only person to call upon YHWH here—or anywhere—in the story is Samson. Absent from the exposition in 13:1 is the expected cry by the people for help; subjection, moreover, is no longer "oppression" but a *modus vivendi,* which quietly mocks Joshua's tale of the possessing of the Land. So what of the ending of the tale? Does that family burial party (16:31) look upon the temple rubble and reflect upon the author of Dagon's discomfiture? Is the institution of judgeship then a failure? Has the spiral of decline been broken only to become plummeting descent? Where in all this, for the Israel of the story, lie the beginnings of Israel's deliverance?

The coda (chaps. 17–21) is bleak. Chapters 17–18 present a parody of the self-made cult. In the Levite, the Ephraimite Micah finds security. "Now I know that the Lord will do me good, because I have a Levite as priest," he exclaims with unconscious irony (17:13 [AR]). In the hijacked porta-shrine with its built-in oracle the marauding Danites find security. And at the prospect of a vastly swelled congregation the priest is elated: "And the priest's heart felt good [AR]; and he took the ephod," the narrator adds sardonically, "and the teraphim, and the graven image [*pesel*, 'image' or 'idol,' recalling the Ehud story, 3:19, 26], and went in the midst of the people" (18:20).

The story of the Levite's concubine (chaps. 19–21) echoes that of Jephthah's daughter, for she, too, falls victim to idolatrous words.[9] An extended contest in the exercise of offering and receiving hospitality (together with prejudice against the Canaanite Jebusites) leads to the travelers' late arrival in Gibeah; in turn, the words of hospitality offered by the sojourning Ephraimite lead to the sacrifice of the concubine, when Israelite Gibeah turns out to be the new Sodom. The words and security of hospitality are absolute—if, that is, one is male. This society is already divided and one part oppressed, without a foreign oppressor and even before the concubine is abused and divided and used as the excuse for the ensuing orgy of civil war and rape. YHWH, consulted only when the vital decisions have been made, plays out with ironic detachment his role as a god of convenience. "Who shall go up first for us to fight against the Benjaminites?" ask the people. "Judah shall go up first," replies YHWH (20:18 [AT]). We have come full circle. We are back at the opening of the book (1:1–2), except that now Israel battles Israel, and, trapped like Jephthah by rash words, Israelite men seize Israelite women (chap. 21; cf. 3:6).

The framework passages cease with the opening of the Samson story (cf. 13:1). With chapters 17–21 alien oppression is gone, alien subjection is gone, even the Baals and the Ashtaroth are gone. No more does the narrator need to deploy that formula to remind us that "the people of Israel again did what was evil in the sight of YHWH." For these are but stories of Israel "enjoying" the Land, stories growing out of everyday life in the Land—a little family theft, a wandering Levite seeking somewhere to stay, a domestic quarrel, and a matter of hospitality. Here, actualized in devastating detail, is the community whose mundane actuality we glimpsed in the ordering and allotting of Joshua 13–22. The narrator's earlier refrain is now unnecessary, for these stories are the formula transformed.

NOTES

1. There are no formal rhetorical links between these books and Judges as explicit as those between Joshua and Judges, but 1 Sam. 1:1 resonates strikingly with Judges 13:2, the beginning of the story of Samson, the last narrated judge;

and what follows recounts, like Judges 13, the gift of a child to a barren woman. Likewise, the Book of Ruth, "in the days when the judges ruled" (1:1), recounts the birth of a son to the bereft Naomi (4:13–17; the irony is that she already has a daughter, "better to [her] than seven sons"; 4:15).

2. For close reading of Judges, my major debt has been to my doctoral student, Barry Webb; see his pioneering study, *The Book of the Judges: An Integrated Reading* (Sheffield, 1987). Also important has been the formalist analysis of Joshua and Judges by Robert M. Polzin, *Moses and the Deuteronomist. A Literary Study of the Deuteronomic History, Part One: Deuteronomy, Joshua, Judges* (New York, 1980). Independent of my work is a stimulating study by Lillian R. Klein, *The Triumph of Irony in the Book of Judges* (Sheffield, forthcoming). A useful general commentary on Joshua is Trent C. Butler, *Joshua*, Word Biblical Commentary, 7 (Waco, Texas, 1983).

3. Details are given of time spent under the oppressor (3:8, 3:14, 4:3, 6:1, 10:8, 13:1), length of service as judge (10:2, 3; 12:7, 9, 11, 14; 15:20; 16:31; cf. 9:22), and periods of "rest" enjoyed by the Land (for example, 3:11, 3:30, 5:31, 8:28).

4. On this question as a heuristic issue, see especially Lyle M. Eslinger, "Strategy and Conquest in the Book of Joshua," in *Perspective: From Deuteronomy to Kings* (Sheffield, forthcoming); also Robert M. Polzin, "The Book of Joshua," in *Moses and the Deuteronomist*; and cf. Terence E. Fretheim, *Deuteronomic History* (Nashville, 1983), pp. 49–68. The question also emerges from a reading of Genesis–Deuteronomy: see David J. A. Clines, *The Theme of the Pentateuch* (Sheffield, 1978).

5. The cities are part of the Promised Land according to Moses (Num. 34:1–12), within the allotment of Judah in Joshua 15:1–12, and specifically allotted in 15:45–47.

6. The allusion to Exodus extends even further. "These are your gods, Israel, who brought you up from the land of Egypt," said the people on beholding the calf (Exod. 32:4 [AT]; see also v. 8). The Gideon story opened with a visitation from a prophet proclaiming, "Thus says YHWH, the God of Israel: 'It was I who brought you up from Egypt and led you out of the land of servitude' ['*avadim*, 'bondage,' playing on a key theme, that to serve other gods is to invite servitude, as now under the Midianites]" (Judges 6:8 [AT]; see also 6:13).

7. On this story see Phyllis Trible, "The Daughter of Jephthah: An Inhuman Sacrifice," in *Texts of Terror: Literary-Feminist Readings of Biblical Narratives* (Philadelphia, 1984), pp. 93–116; also J. Cheryl Exum, "Biblical Tragedy: The Case of Jephthah," *Semeia* (forthcoming).

8. In recent years the Samson story has attracted more literary-critical attention than perhaps any other of the stories in Judges. See especially James L. Crenshaw, *Samson* (Atlanta, 1978); J. Cheryl Exum, "Aspects of Symmetry and Balance in the Samson Saga," *Journal for the Study of the Old Testament*, 19 (1981), 3–29 and 20 (1981), 90; idem, "The Theological Dimension of the Samson Saga," *Vetus Testamentum*, 33 (1983), 30–45; Edward L. Greenstein, "The Riddle of Samson," *Prooftexts*, 1 (1981), 237–260; John B. Vickery, "In Strange Ways: The Story of Samson," in Burke O. Long, ed., *Images of Man and God* (Sheffield, 1981), pp. 58–73.

9. See further Phyllis Trible, "An Unnamed Woman: The Extravagance of Violence," in *Texts of Terror,* pp. 65–91.

SUGGESTED FURTHER READINGS

Lyle M. Eslinger, *Perspective: From Deuteronomy to Kings* (Sheffield, forthcoming).

Lillian R. Klein, *The Triumph of Irony in the Book of Judges* (Sheffield, forthcoming).

Robert M. Polzin, *Moses and the Deuteronomist. A Literary Study of the Deuteronomic History, Part One: Deuteronomy, Joshua, Judges* (New York, 1980).

Phyllis Trible, *Texts of Terror: Literary-Feminist Readings of Biblical Narratives* (Philadelphia, 1984).

Barry G. Webb, *The Book of the Judges: An Integrated Reading* (Sheffield, 1987).

Columbia Theological Seminary

1 and 2 Samuel

Joel Rosenberg

THE worlds bridged by the Samuel books (which I shall call simply "Samuel" when stressing their unity) are reflected in the names they assumed in the two principal ancient versions of the biblical text. The Septuagint called the books "1 and 2 Kingdoms" (1 and 2 Kings, in turn, being known as "3 and 4 Kingdoms"), whereas the Masoretic text designated them, as do our English translations, "1 and 2 Samuel." The shift in Israel's leadership from prophet-judges of Samuel's type to kings, and especially dynastic kings, is indeed the subject of these books, and it seems no accident that the canon shaped under rabbinic aegis should, in its titling, give greater weight to the figure who embodied a decentralized, theocratic, avocational, and minimalist authority rather than to the kings, the civil rulers, who replaced him. The Samuel books might more appropriately be called "Saul" and "David," respectively, or even "1 and 2 David"; yet Samuel's direct or indirect dominance of 1 Samuel and his less obvious ideological dominance of 2 Samuel (where he is otherwise never mentioned) make the appellation "1 and 2 Samuel" not only apt but a meaningful challenge for literary interpretation. Making sense of Samuel's role in the books that bear his name will do much to define the special character of the books and their argument.

Are these, however, "books" in the same clear sense as, say, Genesis, Jonah, or Ruth? And are they two books or one? The early chapters of 1 Samuel would plausibly fit into the Book of Judges, which, in the Masoretic text, immediately precedes it (indeed, its victorious seventh chapter would have given Judges a more ebullient and celebratory ending). And critics have long held that the momentous Davidic court history of 2 Samuel ends properly at 1 Kings 2. What, then, is gained, from a literary perspective, by isolating the Samuel books as they now stand? And what role do the books thus construed play in the larger narrative corpus extending from Genesis through 2 Kings? The two most widely accepted results of source-criticism—Leonhard Rost's notion of a tenth-century B.C.E. "Succession History" (2 Sam. 11–1 Kings 2) and Martin Noth's notion of a sixth- or fifth-century "Deuteronomic History" (Deut.– 2 Kings)[1] have tended to obscure the literary character of the Samuel books by depriving them both of their autonomy as books and of the commonality of texture and perspective that unites them with most other books of the Hebrew Bible. The same careful interplay of poetic fragment, folkloric tradition, archival notation, and elaborated narrative that inform biblical literature as a whole (including, somewhat differently, the chiefly poetic books) can be found in Samuel, as can the political, cultural, and religious argument that gave rise to biblical tradition itself. Samuel stands as a single "argument," one we can variously view as prophetic, Deuteronomic, or sapiential in origin, but whose consistency transcends alleged sources and books. At the same time, the Masoretic parceling of books gives Samuel a beginning and end that most fully accord with the shape of that larger argument. The best explication of the work is not one that focuses on literary techniques as isolated phenomena, but one that follows out its line of thought and unfolding story and the gradual deployment and development of its manifold themes.

Samuel and Premonarchical Israel

Samuel most resembles Genesis in its preoccupation with founding families and in its positioning of these representative households at the fulcrum of historical change. As in Genesis, the fate of the nation is read into the mutual dealings of spouses, parents, and children, of sibling and sibling, and of householder and servant, favored and underclass. And the Samuel author, like the Genesis author, weaves from these vicissitudes a complex scheme of historical causation and divine justice. Thematic movements fall into place through a series of overlapping and interlinked codes—of household, priesthood, court, and so on—in which shifts occur nonchalantly and elliptically, as if the premises of their alternation were already clear from a long tradition. Three figures in particular form the narrative focus, and in an ascending order of elaboration: Samuel, Saul, and David. Rather than viewing the three as subjects of separate story-cycles, or even of subtly interlocked story-cycles, we should understand the work as comprising three major clashes or struggles: between Samuel and Saul, between Saul and David, and between David and the combined legacy of Samuel and Saul.[2] (David's clash with Absalom, the tragic marrow of 2 Samuel, is, institutionally speaking, an expression of this third conflict, made all the more poignant by its origin within David's own household.)

The work, however, denies the historical originality of these conflicts, for they appear saturated with the resonances of similar clashes elsewhere in the Hebrew Bible. Rivalry and differential fortunes are the currency of divine plan from Genesis onward, and the opening of 1 Samuel formulates the problem with fabular elegance. We are shown some moments in the household of Elkanah and Hannah, parents of Samuel, as the family pays a visit to the covenant shrine at Shiloh. It is an Abrahamic household— Elkanah has two wives: a barren wife who is cherished and a fertile wife who is obstreperous and haughty. Here, however, it is not the husband who stands in the forefront of the narration but the distressed barren wife (Sarah's perspective is, by contrast, quite muted in the Genesis account, while her rival, Hagar, is given two whole chapters of prominence; Hannah's rival, Peninnah, for her part, is given almost no narrative elaboration). Hannah's sorrow over her childlessness and over the taunts of her rival is oddly misunderstood by Elkanah: "Why are you sad? Aren't I more valuable to you than ten sons?" (v. 8).[3] More literally, he asks: "Why is your mood bad? Am I not more good for you . . . ?" (This is the first of numerous comparative ratios by which the characters' motivations are measured throughout the work—see 2 Sam. 1:26, 13:15–16—and the first of several motivic uses of the dyad "good/bad"; see 2 Sam. 13:22, 14:17, 17:14, 19:35.) But Hannah is not consoled; a link to the future is apparently more valuable to her than the present devotions of a spouse, and her malaise leads her beyond the human arena to the recourse of prayer—indeed, of covenant: if YHWH will grant her request for offspring, she will dedicate her child to lifelong divine service.

Hannah's prayer leads to a new misunderstanding: the shrine priest Eli mistakes her tearful murmuring as drunkenness and rebukes her. Even the professional man of God is unable to detect the channels of divine-human rapport being established. Eli quickly recants his error when Hannah explains her situation, but we are already alerted that this is a priesthood in decline—a matter made clearer by the later description of the corruption of Eli's sons (2:12–17, 22–36). Meanwhile, Elkanah and his household return home, and eventually Hannah's prayer is answered: Samuel is born, and, at his weaning, he is brought to Shiloh to serve the shrine under Eli's tutelage. Upon this joyous occasion, Hannah pours forth a song of praise—one of numerous ways in which archaic and early monarchical poetry is woven into the Samuel narratives—and this exuberant psalm expresses the historical outlook both of biblical tradition in general and of Samuel in particular: YHWH is invoked as the God of surprise, bringing down the mighty, raising up the downtrodden; impoverishing the wealthy and enriching the pauper; bereaving the fertile and making barren the fruitful—always circumventing the trappings of human vanity and the complacency of the overcontented. The many turns of personal and familial fortune in the ensuing chapters are an elaboration of the compressed strophes of Hannah's song.

Indeed, the ensuing narration makes clear that Hannah's triumph and Samuel's entry into priestly service coincide with the house of Eli's fall from divine favor. As the sins of Eli's sons are detailed and Eli's ineffectual disciplining is reported, Samuel's reputation is said to grow. An anonymous prophet warns Eli of what lies in store for his own household. The young Samuel then receives a prophetic call—a remarkable event in an era when the divine word was scarce (see 3:1). The episode is modeled on the lines of traditional accounts of prophetic call (see Exod. 3:1–4:17, Judg.

6:11–24, Isa. 6:1–13, Jer. 1:1–4, Ezek. 1:1–3:15),[4] but it is ripe with unique ironies: the boy twice thinks it is Eli calling him, and when, instructed by Eli, he responds properly to the divine summons, he must report to Eli the reiterated message of his household's impending doom—a doom that will also mark the end of the shrine at Shiloh and a disastrous setback for Israel. Eli, who is under no illusions about his sons' merits, accepts Samuel's prophecy without complaint: "It is YHWH; may he do what is just in his eyes" (3:18); but we sense in this simultaneous elevation and demotion the mercurial hand of divine providence. The rise and fall of persons and families is a microcosm of the shifting fortunes of the people at large, whose attention to probity and justice has been similarly inconstant (see Judges 2:10b–23). Thus far, however, the narrative's scope has been small. We view only the interaction of the two pivotal households, one priestly, the other laic. Samuel is the bridge between the two, although he belongs, in effect, to neither. His public style as admonisher and doomsayer—unvarying in his career even past the grave—is established from his debut. Few subtleties of character are to shade Samuel's figure. Almost nothing of his personal life is recounted. He will eventually show himself to be a thoroughly ideological presence. True to the folk etymology of his name (1:20, 2:20)—in reality an etymology of the name Saul—Samuel behaves from the start as one "sought from/lent to" YHWH.

Meanwhile the narrative turns to the situation that brings down the house of Eli and that will eventually spell the end of even Samuel's type of leadership: Israel's chronic distress at the hands of the neighboring Philistines. We are already familiar with this problem from the story of Samson (Judges 13–16), and it will persist late into the reign of David (see 2 Sam. 21:15–22, 23:8–17). Chapters 4–6 remove the focus from Samuel and interpose a tale of the captivity of the Ark of the Covenant. This interlude has numerous comic touches—an odd folkloric levity for a subject normally viewed in Israel with such sacral awe: the ark, expected to strike terror into Israel's enemies, works so well that they rally to defeat Israel; the ark itself proves to be a troublesome prey, bringing plagues upon its captors and playing numerous pranks upon the Philistine shrines; finally, the chastened enemy sends it back in a wagon with a driverless oxteam, accompanied by a curious token of Philistine appeasement (symbols of the plagues they have suffered): golden effigies of mice and hemorrhoids! The ark motif is resumed in 2 Samuel 6, when David, as a symbol of his decisive victory over the Philistines, brings the ark to Jerusalem, a city newly captured from the Jebusites, where it will remain for the next four centuries. Meanwhile, its return from Philistine captivity in Samuel's time prompts an Israelite renaissance—a purification of worship, a renewed resistance against the Philistines, an extended period of peace, and a consolidation of Samuel's leadership (1 Sam. 7). This idyllic condition is well positioned: it is a final demonstration of the harmony attainable *without* kingly institutions—a pure reflex of national morale and spiritual integrity. It is a standard against which the historical events that follow will be measured.

The Founding of the Monarchy

The next five chapters (1 Sam. 8–12) recount the origin of the monarchy. The initial premise is familiar—the people complain that Samuel is old and that, as with the house of Eli, his sons do not walk in his ways (this is the book's sole indication that Samuel has a domestic life)—but the logic is uncertain: how, indeed, will a king rise above this problem? Won't the integrity of his offspring be as much a source of concern for a king as it has been for a prophetic judge? What additional stability does kingship afford? A clue is suggested by the wording of the people's request: "Appoint over us a king to judge us *like all the other nations*" (8:5). We know, of course, that, in the light of Pentateuchal doctrine, being "like all the nations" is a path of folly (see Exod. 23:23–24; Lev. 18:1–4; Deut. 4:5–8, 18:9–14); yet with the advantage of historical hindsight the Samuel author recognized the inevitability of this turn in identity for national survival. The ambivalence of the tradition on this point is suggested by the fact that YHWH, consulted by Samuel, reluctantly concedes the people's wish, threatening no direct divine retribution but warning of the natural human consequences of their choice (8:10–18—an echo of Deut. 17:14–20, as 8:6–7 carries an echo of Gen. 21:11–12). This exchange reveals two important things: that kingship is a project of the people as a whole—whatever is reported of a sovereign in books to come is indirectly *their* story—and that Israel's bid for a king is a bid for equality in the international arena—a bid, indeed, for ordinariness. Israel's previous extraordinary status among nations, its reliance on the genius of prophetic inspiration, on the sporadic efflorescence of the might of YHWH in its midst, had, in a sense, become a tiresome burden. The vertiginous swings of divine favor celebrated in Hannah's song were now—although the tradition could not say so directly—not conducive to the stability and continuity of national life. Such an awareness could be registered only in the discourse of a nation long matured, reflecting back on a more primitive and volatile innocence. Much the same loss of innocence, epitomized by the Garden story, by Abraham's expulsion of Hagar and near-sacrifice of Isaac, by Jacob's wrestle with an angel at the river Jabbok, by Israel's sojourn in Egypt and its later folly with the Golden Calf, by the nation's imperfect conquest of Canaan and by the unexpunged presence of the Canaanite in its midst, is here expressed in the Israelite elders' plea for a king. Paradoxically, presiding over the ensuing process is the man who, alongside Moses and Joshua, most epitomizes Israel's freedom from kings.

Commentators have noted the multiplicity of sources and perspectives underlying these chapters. It has been customary to view here the interplay of pro-Saul and anti-Saul or, more generally, pro- and antimonarchical sentiments. (In fact, as we shall see, both interpretations are borne out in different ways by the story.) Recently it has been suggested that the pro and con perspectives are arranged symmetrically: (*a*) 8:1–22, a warning by Samuel against kingship; (*b*) 9:1–10:16, a largely complimentary portrait of Saul and his anointing by Samuel; (*c*) 10:17–27, a renewed warning by Samuel and a public selection of Saul, who is described pejoratively as "hiding in the baggage"; (*b'*) 11:1–15, an inspired victory by Saul over the Ammonites—again, a complimentary portrait; (*a'*) 12:1–25, a final admonition by Samuel, in classic Deuteronomic style.[5] If this schematization is correct, it is all the more noteworthy that these chapters also trace the lineaments of the common Near Eastern enthronement myth: the threat from an external enemy, the clamor of the populace for a king, the secret anointing of a princely candidate (a *nagid*), his hesitation and reassurance, his public emergence, his routing of the enemy and victorious return, and the reconfirmation of his rule.[6] This pattern, which is essentially repeated (minus the hesitation motif) in the later elevation of David, is present in purer form in the poetic tradition—especially in Psalms—but in Samuel it is sharply qualified by the narrative context, where the tradition's ambivalence about kingship is allowed free expression.

"Is Saul Also among the Prophets?"

The personality of Saul is more fully developed in the remainder of 1 Samuel, which recounts the renewed incursions of the Philistines and the gradual deterioration of Saul's mental state under external and internal pressures. Saul's condition, which bears the earmarks of both depression and paranoia, is said to stem from the "evil spirit" (16:14; cf. 18:10) sent by YHWH as a punishment for his defiance of Samuel's authority. There are two versions of Saul's offense. In 13:9–14, he erroneously offers sacrifices preparatory to battle in Samuel's absence, fearing that the people will scatter before the enemy is engaged; he thus usurps a ritual function belonging to the prophet. In 15:7–9, he captures and annihilates the Amalekite populace, as Samuel has commanded him to do, but spares Agag, their king, and the choicest of their flocks of sheep—thus violating both the prophet's injunction and the norms of holy war. Both incidents are reminiscent of the account of Aaron's negligence in the Golden Calf episode in Exodus 32, and we are probably dealing with a type-scene—a traditional storytelling formula, unfolding events in a conventionally fixed sequence. Yet, perhaps for the same reason, Samuel's denunciation of Saul seems predetermined and disproportionate, especially in the light of Saul's repentant behavior in 15:24–31. The moral offenses of kingship Samuel has warned against are nowhere in evidence at this point—only a ritual impropriety, and a breach of prophetic prerogative. Despite the levels of tyranny Saul will eventually attain—especially in his treatment of David and his slaughter of the priests of Nob—the ensuing narrative retains a certain tacit sympathy for Saul that only deepens as his plight grows more tragic. There is no biblical character quite like Saul, and, apart from David's feigned madness before Achish of Gath (21:13–15), mental illness occurs as a major motif only once more in the Hebrew Bible: in Nebuchadnezzar's temporary madness in Daniel 4.

We should, however, keep in mind that Saul's torments embody effectively the hybrid and transitional nature of his institutional role. From the start, Saul's kingship is but an extension of the idioms of judgeship—including, most notably, his behavior as a battlefield ecstatic (11:6; see also Judges 6:34, 14:19, 15:14). Although he anticipates the kingly style of David in certain important ways (in his reliance on agents and informers, in his responsibility for orchestrating the instrument of war, in his fashioning the rudiments of court and dynasty), he never fully rises above the haphazard and ad hoc conditions of charismatic leadership. Saul's desire to duplicate his earliest battlefield successes leads him to fight battles frenziedly on field after field, diluting his value as a strategist and squandering his failing energies. The obscure popular saying "Is Saul also among the prophets?" (used etiologically in 10:1–12 and 19:19–24) might be understood as a comment on the paradox of a prophet-king's inability to control the conditions of his inspiration. (It is thus also a comment on the inadequacy of Israel's reliance on charismatic leadership.) And as prophecy fails him, Saul is eventually forced into a final desperate involvement with necromancy—something his own edicts and Mosaic law proscribe—only to find the spirit of the departed Samuel informing him of his own imminent doom (28:3–25).

The Young David

Against such a background should we understand the emergence of David in 1 Samuel 16–17. The youngest of the Bethlehemite Jesse's eight sons, David, contrary to his father's intentions quickly catches the eye of Samuel, who, bypassing David's older brothers, settles on the youth as his choice for the leadership of Israel in place of Saul. Samuel's secret anointing of David (who is completely silent during this phase of the narrative) does not, for the time being, unseat Saul, and David himself is to remain impeccably respectful of Saul's legitimacy for years to come, long after Saul's death. Famed as a musician, David is even engaged as a healer of Saul for a period (16:14–23; cf. 18:10–12). But from the moment David first speaks (17:26), he seems to manifest a distinctive spark of ambition that colors his actions throughout his long rise to power. His speech on the battlefield before his brilliant confrontation of the Philistine giant Goliath reveals more than a youthful religious zeal; it is sound political doctrine, flattering the people Israel as the inspired confederate army it would like itself to be (and, until that moment, most decidedly is not):

You come against me with sword and spear and javelin, but I come against you in the name of YHWH of the [celestial] armies, God of the [terrestrial] troops of Israel, whom you have insulted. This day YHWH will deliver you into my hand, and I will strike you down and remove your head from you, and give the corpses of the camp of Philistines this very day to the birds of the sky and the beasts of the field, and all the land [or world] will know there is a God for Israel; and all this community [literally, congregation] will know that not by sword or by spear does YHWH save, for the battle is YHWH's and he has given you into our hands! (17:45–47)

Yet at no point, then or ever after in the narrative, does David manifest prophetic ecstasy (although Jewish tradition understood the Psalms of David as such; see 2 Sam. 23:2). He remains a rational and farsighted architect of kingly institutions long before his attainment of actual kingship. He manages to do this while being hunted down by Saul, who early on sees the popularly acclaimed youth as a rival for the throne— a suspicion that aggravates Saul's depression and drives him to ever more desperate actions against the fugitive.

Curiously, David's very forbearance toward Saul has an element of political calculation. On two occasions (1 Sam. 24 and 26) David chances upon an opportunity to kill Saul but refuses to stretch out his hand against "YHWH's anointed" (*meshiaḥ YHWH*). David's use of this expression (see also 2 Sam. 1:14, 16) is not as traditional as it sounds. In fact Israelite custom had never accorded the anointed or charismatic leader a permanent and unconditional sacredness of person; the charismatic state ended with the cessation of battle or the death of the leader. David's usage has more in common with Canaanite or other non-Israelite conceptions of kingship and suggests that David foresees a dynastic function of kingship that goes far beyond the minimalist conception envisaged by Samuel. David knows that if Saul can be killed by an aspiring rival, any Israelite king can. Whether or not David has designs on the throne (and it is important to remember that throughout Saul's lifetime, neither David nor the narrator says so explicitly), his refusal to harm Saul is an investment in the stability of the future regime—*any* future regime.

This conservative attitude toward the person of Saul makes David's own political aspirations clearer. To judge from the situation that first kindles David's ambitions (see 17:26—as noted, David's first words), namely, Saul's offer in marriage of his daughter Michal to the slayer of Goliath, it seems possible that David might have been most comfortable not with the role of supplanter but with that of son-in-law to the king, with perhaps a secondary role in government—possibly as aide and chief protector to Saul, or to Saul's logical heir and David's dearest friend, Jonathan. If David ever foresaw the kingship passing to himself, it would preferably have been by peaceful, orderly, and constitutional means. Otherwise, it would not be a throne worth having. Saul's jealousy and suspicion of David, David's flight into exile, the course of the Philistine wars, and the eventual disaffection of Michal all prevent this more idyllic situation from evolving, but the formative role of this fantasy on David's political imagination is fundamental to our understanding of the Samuel books. The paradox that Israel's greatest king views himself as merely a kingmaker and throne-protector is an important key to much that happens in his life history. The narrator, however, never tips the balance in favor of one or the other view of David—it is only the *reader's* hindsight (or that of one who knows the tradition) that makes David an aspirant to the throne. David's *reported* behavior serves a very different self-image, even long after he attains the throne. (His apparent initial bid for kingship outside of Judah in 2 Sam. 2:4–7 seems curiously truncated and elliptical.) Moreover, even were we to assume that the premonarchic David saw himself as king, it is still fair to say that he viewed the kingly office from outside it. It is that curiously transcendent conception of royalty, as we shall see, that eventually wreaks so much harm on David's personal and domestic life.

David as Domestic Being

How, then, do we evaluate what the text says of David as domestic being—as son and brother, as spouse and father? The text's genius for informing by omission—a quality not unique in biblical literature—is particularly telling on this matter, at least at first, and there is much that is congenial to the Freud-instructed sensibilities of the modern reader. Of David's childhood environment we know little—but enough. His father views the lad either indifferently or overprotectively: David is presented to Samuel only as an afterthought. David's older brother Eliab later belittles David's efforts to get close to the action at the center of the battlefield, when Goliath issues his challenge to Israel (see 17:28). David's reply is uncharacteristically defensive and childlike: "What have I done now? Isn't it just talk?" (17:29). David's chances for a meaningful life under the roof of his father's home seem dim, and, like many a younger son in biblical history, he quickly learns that adoptive relations—of the battlefield, of the political arena, of the bed—can be the most formative and significant shapers of identity. "He turned away from [Eliab] toward someone else" (17:30) is thus a fundamental gesture in David's personal history—a departure from his father's house in all but a geographic sense. In this light we may understand the genuine affection he feels toward Saul and Jonathan (long after running afoul of Saul, David addresses him as "my father," 24:11). The homage David pays the house of Saul, almost to the end of his own rule, an homage that, from our perspective, bears much of the aura of medieval chivalric romance, seems wholly sincere, and seems, even when it is refused, to provide him with something of the security, structure, and self-affirmation unavailable to him in his own father's house. Whereas Saul seems torn by the angry departure of his patron Samuel (manifested quite palpably in the garment-tearing scene of 1 Sam. 15:27–29), David, in a less debilitated way, always carries with him the loss of his patrons Saul and Jonathan—a sense of loss that rises to a crescendo in David's great poetic elegy at the beginning of 2 Samuel:

> O, hills of Gilboa, on you let fall no dew,
> nor rain, O fields of plenty,
> for there lies loosed the shield of heroes,
> the shield of Saul without its coat of oil,
> the bow of Jonathan that shied not from the blood of its prey,
> from the fat flesh of the mighty,
> the sword of Saul that ne'er returned unused.
>
> Saul and Jonathan, beloved, sweetly remembered,
> never parted, in their lives and in their deaths, swifter than eagles,
> mightier than lions.
> O, daughters of Israel, weep for Saul,
> who clothed you in crimson and finery,
> who decked your clothes with ornaments of gold . . .   (1:21–24)

We know from 1 Samuel 14 and 31 that Saul and Jonathan were indeed parted in life and in death, but this grandiloquent blurring of reality befits the self-conscious, one could say Canaanitish, archaism that remains part of David's public style. We sense, as well, a certain incongruity between the lavishness of David's praise for his would-be adoptive family and the strange silence in the text about his relation to his own father's house. David, to be sure, retains ties with the latter (see 1 Sam. 20:6), and when he is forced into exile by the wrath of Saul he brings his parents with him and sends them into the protective custody of the king of Moab (22:6)—an ironic reversal of the dependent relation of David to Jesse conspicuously outlined in chapter 16. Beyond these scant details, nothing more is said of David's parents in Samuel, except the mention of Jesse as a patronymic. The father who nearly succeeded in keeping his son shrouded in historical obscurity is rewarded with an obscurity of his own, and we cannot escape the feeling that a certain coldness or emotional remoteness governs David's relations with his parents from the earliest days of his public career, or that an even more embarrassing situation governs the traditionary silence on the matter. Indeed, the next time we encounter the king of Moab, in 2 Samuel 8:2, he is David's captive, and the victim of an inexplicably harsh vengeance. Rabbinic and medieval Jewish commentary blame this king (who remains curiously anonymous) for the (unmentioned) death of David's parents,[7] but the text accomplishes more by omitting the exact circumstances from the narrative—as if anonymity and textual lacuna were, at these points, animate powers of their own. Were the commentators correct (and their rather fanciful suspicions are, after all, based entirely on the textual silence), then David would be indirectly responsible for the deaths of his own parents—but the text stops short of confirming this matter. In any case, the contrast between David's traditionally well-attested fervor for the house of Saul and his thoroughly unattested attitude toward his own parents' household is quite curious and adds an important dimension to our understanding.

David as Political Being

The history of David's rise and reign is political and historical as well as personal or domestic. What is interesting is the way in which David's personal life is brought into the larger context, as well as the changes in the *ratio* of personal to political history. Well into 2 Samuel, David, though he exerts a fascination and is central to the action, remains relatively undeveloped as a character—at least in relation to the development he is yet to undergo from 2 Samuel 11 onward. That development, however, must be understood on both the personal and political planes; to view either at the expense of the other is to misunderstand the work's unique perspective. Some of our misconceptions have stemmed from the tendency of otherwise responsible historians to see the story (and, in particular, the "Succession History," begun in 2 Sam. 11) as straightforward reportage of historical events by an eyewitness.[8] This view has fortunately been corrected by more recent literary study, which has shown that eyewitness reportage and narrative realism are not identical.[9] But the literary interpreters, for their part, tend to overlook the degree to which an incisive political and historical judgment—one requiring considerable historical hindsight—is part of the *literary* delight the story fosters.[10] The stories of Israel's and David's maturation are essentially the same story. This fact, more than any other, attests the literary unity of Samuel, however diverse its raw materials. The author/editor presents an almost unfathomably complex political history through a relatively limited repertoire of traditions and themes—and, in the process, renders that history clear and comprehensible.

David's political dimension should be understood on two textual planes: the report of his political actions, and the account of the deep structural changes in Israelite society that his career embodies. What source critics call "The History of David's Rise"—1 Samuel 16–2 Samuel 10—provides generous coverage at both levels, but it is only when David begins to recede to a defensive and relatively passive position as political actor, in 2 Samuel 11 onward, that the latter realm can be fully understood. Curiously, it is only here that David's domestic life comes into full view. (To call this a separately composed, eyewitness "Succession History" misses the meaning of Samuel, but it does correctly suggest that the chief issue of these chapters is the succession to David—whose entire statecraft is founded on the principle of succession.)

How, then, are we to understand the politics of the premonarchical and early monarchical David? In the political actions themselves, the dramatic interest is concentrated on David's genius under adversity. After his exile from Saul's court in 1 Samuel 21, David's political situation is desperate, and we experience a certain inevitable thrill in witnessing the consummate self-confidence with which David engineers his own survival. The great paradox of this phase of the story is that David manages to throw in his lot with Israel's enemies, the Philistines, while retaining the affection of the Israelite populace (Judean and northern alike). His sojourn among the Philistines turns out to have one important benefit: it removes David from intra-Israelite politics while the reign of Saul deteriorates, thus preserving for David a neutrality toward intra-Israelite affairs that will later work in his favor. Meanwhile he must avoid fighting alongside the Philistines against his own people, while still retaining his credibility with the Philistine leaders whom he serves as a vassal. Chapters 27–30 detail David's brilliant maneuvers to accomplish these impossibly contradictory goals.

Not until the death of Saul, at the end of 1 Samuel, and the sudden reversal of David's political fortunes does "Davidic policy" as such—the deeper structure of David's politics—come into fuller view. We have a preliminary glimpse of this dimension in the epithet "YHWH's anointed," applied by David to Saul in 1 Samuel 24 and 26. In 2 Samuel 1–10 we get a more expanded view of the monarchical revolution David has set in motion. Three episodes in particular convey with great selectivity and condensation the nature of the society now at hand. (1) In chapter 3 David rebukes his chief aide, Joab, for a blood-feud slaying of Abner (Joab's counterpart in the court of Saul's survivor Ishbosheth), a slaying that forestalls the merger of the Judean and northern Israelite monarchy and brings political embarrassment to David. David's censure of Joab establishes the role of the monarch as one who will stand above and restrain the volatile and chaotic motions of tribal conflict. (2) In chapter 6, after David's decisive defeat of the Philistines, he brings the ark to rest permanently in his newly created capital, Jerusalem (only recently a Jebusite city), amid great pomp and celebration—an echo, as noted, of the earlier return of the ark from Philistine captivity in 1 Samuel 6. David's action here is the cause of a quarrel between himself and Saul's daughter Michal, whose initial devotion to David (see 1 Sam. 19:11–17, where she helps him escape from her father) has turned to anger. Michal's forced remarriage to David (2 Sam. 3:13–16) can be seen as part of a complex scheme of political marriage, a kind of genealogical gerrymandering by which David consolidates his influence over the leading families of the realm.

The breach between David and Michal and their consequent failure to produce offspring (6:23) prevent a union of the houses of David and Saul that might have guaranteed the stability of the realm and of the dynastic succession.[11] Even David's acts of largesse toward Michal's family (chap. 9) cannot heal the rift that has developed. (3) Chapter 7, the culmination of the idyllic phase of David's career (as 1 Sam. 7 has been for Samuel's, and 1 Sam. 11–12 for Saul's), shows David to be the ideological architect of the Temple that his son Solomon will build. Divine permission for early enactment of the measure is denied, but the court prophet Nathan legitimates the notion of a permanent dwelling for the ark, as well as the principle of a Davidic dynasty. The old confederate religion is to be supplanted by the civil religion of a territorial state (one here recalls the slogan "like all the nations"), for consummate command of the idioms of civil religion is by now a chief component of David's political power.

The Political within the Domestic

Thus far the stage is set for a test of David's political ideals—and of Israel's project of postconfederate nationhood. The story now proceeds to that test, but at this point two complementary potentialities, moral and political, manifest themselves in the narrative. David's establishment of a permanent dynasty is overshadowed by the moral offense he commits with the eventual dynastic mother Bathsheba, who initially is the wife of another man, Uriah the Hittite. This immorality—and the various ensuing immoralities among David's children—can, in turn, be shown to be uniquely rooted in the political conditions David has created. Thus, although Nathan's rebuke of David at the beginning of 2 Samuel 12 establishes the narrative to come as a kind of morality fable (David, in an unguarded moment, cries that the offender in Nathan's parable should repay his transgression "fourfold"—and so it comes to pass),[12] the account of political factors in chapters 11–19 is precise and intricate.

For example, it is only David's new role as noncombatant strategist of affairs of state in chapter 11 that permits his encounter and dalliance with Bathsheba. His manner of inquiring after her identity and sending "agents" to fetch her shows that he is now at the center of a vast network of anonymous gossipers, informers, and emissaries that assist him in love and war alike. This new court society, however, renders David all the more vulnerable to public scandal, and thus necessitates the complicated and still more damaging strategy of coverup that results in the death not only of Bathsheba's husband Uriah but also of many soldiers with no connection to the scandal. In the first stage of this coverup, when David summons Uriah home from the battlefield and tries to induce him to go home to his wife (and thus, David hopes, to resume sexual relations with

Bathsheba, who is then early in her pregnancy with David's child), he extends furlough from battle duties, as one assuming an essentially secular use of the instrument of war. He is thus caught by surprise when Uriah *the Hittite* responds as one bound by the ancient confederate Israelite institution of holy war (cf. 1 Sam. 21:2–6):

> Uriah said to David: "The ark and Israel and Judah are dwelling in makeshift dwellings [*or* in Succoth], and my master Joab and the servants of milord are camping on the face of the field—and I should go to my house to eat and drink, and lie with my wife?! On your life, as your soul lives, I shall not do this thing!" (11:11)

We have no sharper expression of the clash of cultural codes. Later, when David sends Uriah back with a sealed letter instructing Joab to place Uriah in the thick of battle and to withdraw protection from him, and Joab, after carrying out the instructions, sends a courier to report the death of Uriah and other Israelites, the exchange of messages in effect displays the social structure of the nation that participates in the crime. The sedentary monarchy that the people have created (against which Samuel has warned) is the breeding ground for such outrages.

Similarly, when the events leading to Absalom's rebellion and David's second exile are set in motion (also part of the punishment foretold by Nathan), political factors supply the context. David's strategically motivated marriages have resulted in numerous offspring, initially symbols of his power, who become a gravely destabilizing force once they attain sexual maturity. Absalom's public career begins with an act of vengeance against his half brother Amnon for the latter's rape of Absalom's full sister Tamar (chap. 13)—an ironic comment on David's earlier effort to rise above the politics of blood feud. David now finds that he has created a squabbling tribal motley within his own household. The murder of Amnon politicizes Absalom in a manner that makes his eventual rebellion against his father almost inevitable. His appropriation of his father's concubines in 16:21–23 is not only a typological echo of a primordial immorality, recalling Reuben's dalliance with Jacob's concubine (Gen. 35:22), but also a calculated political act counseled by his aide Achitophel and designed to demonstrate publicly his assumption of control over Jerusalem and the kingdom.

These political considerations, however, are deepened in significance by the gradual reawakening of David's emotional life, which seems curiously suppressed in the chapters preceding the rebellion. David's capacity for a deeply expressive emotionality seems adequate to all areas of his existence but one: his interaction with his own household. Toward Saul and Jonathan, for example, toward the Judean landowner Nabal (1 Sam. 25), and toward Joab (who, however, is a kinsman, probably a nephew; see 2 Sam. 17:25 and 1 Chron. 2:2–17), David shows himself capable of a rich range of feeling which, for the most part, does not compromise the proportion and restraint in his political behavior. Toward his parents, however, we have already noted the text's silence on David's feelings, and much the same narrative inhibition governs David's relations with spouses in general, and with his children in 2 Samuel 13–14—leaving us with a sense of David's coldness or inaccessibility to those closest to him.

Some of this reserve may stem from the trauma of loss David has already experienced in the death of his first child by Bathsheba, recounted in chapter 12. Once David is informed of this loss, he breaks the fast he has been observing during the infant's illness. When his puzzled servants ask him why he now eats, David's answer is quite revealing: "While the child yet lived, I fasted and wept, for I thought: who knows? maybe YHWH will be kind to me, and the child will live. Now that he is dead, why should I fast? Can I bring him back to life? I go to him; he doesn't come to me" (vv. 22–23). These numb and dispirited words are our first indication that David's energies as parent and ruler are beginning to flag and that he has a newly tangible sense of his own mortality. This awareness, however, has perhaps begun at the end of chapter 11, where David's self-anesthetizing over the death of Uriah signals the extent to which the kingly office has truncated his humanity; significantly, there eating is also a motif: "Let not the matter be evil in your sight, for the sword eats this way and that. Strengthen your battle!" (v. 25).

Chapters 13 and 14 thus show David as newly passive—manipulated by his children and servants, remote from public events, ineffectual in his disciplining of both Amnon and Absalom, and conspicuously dry-eyed and reserved in his temporary reconciliation with the latter (14:33). It is thus a highly weighted moment when David, driven from Jerusalem by Absalom, ascends the Mount of Olives, barefoot and with his head covered, and, together with his exiled entourage, weeps resoundingly, his lost humanity restored. Only at that point is his ruptured communication with YHWH likewise restored, and David utters the prayer that will become his salvation: "Please, YHWH, frustrate the counsel of Achitophel!" (15:31; the prayer is answered in 17:1–14). Later, when Absalom's rebellion is suppressed, and Absalom, contrary to David's instructions, is slain by Joab, David receives the news of his son's death with an explosion of feeling he has never shown to the live Absalom, and here he manifests none of the measured eloquence he has shown for the slain Saul and Jonathan—only the wild, distraught grief of a bereaved parent: "My son, Absalom! O my son Absalom! If only I had died instead of you. O Absalom, my son, my son!" (18:33).

The Function of Symmetries

I have already noted that a symmetrical arrangement, common to much biblical literature, characterizes 1 Samuel 8–12. In fact, Samuel as a whole can be shown to comprise roughly a chain of several internally symmet-rical cycles.[13] Although we cannot undertake an exhaustive analysis of this pattern here, two conspicuous symmetries in particular should be noted, because they reveal, among other things, something important about David's relation to divine causality.

The first symmetry is 1 Samuel 13–31. Chapters 13–15, which cover the period of Saul's active kingship under Samuel's patronage, have their parallel in chapters 28–31, which relate Samuel's final denunciation of Saul (from the grave) and Saul's military defeat and death. In the portion of 1 Samuel where David is present as a character, chapter 11 onward, Samuel enters the story only three times: as the anointer of David (chap. 16), as having died and been buried (25:1), and as being conjured up by the witch of Endor to address the desperate and doomed Saul (28:3–19)—thus, near the beginning, middle, and end of the cycle, respectively.

Chapter 25, the midpoint in the cycle, is framed by the traditionary doublets of chapters 24 and 26, both of which illustrate David's refusal to kill Saul when he has the chance. Chapter 25, by contrast, shows David manifesting a rare lack of restraint toward the hostile Judean land-owner Nabal. He is rescued from the consequences of his precipitate near-vengeance by the intervention of Nabal's astute wife, Abigail, who con-vinces David to abandon an action that might lead to a Judean civil war. Such a war David was not then equipped to win and might have jeopar-dized the political foothold he eventually acquires in his tribal homeland of Judah. As things turn out, Nabal soon dies, and David marries Abigail, thus gaining his foothold in Judah by peaceful rather than bellicose means. David, in his remarks to Abigail in 25:32–34, recognizes the providential hand that has brought her to his rescue. In whatever other ways David is vulnerable during this phase of his history, he is most vulnerable to the consequences of his otherwise uncharacteristic display of wrath toward Nabal. That he is rescued by a woman has interesting reverberations for his later involvement with Bathsheba, when a fateful encounter with a woman has less benign consequences.

The second symmetry, in 2 Samuel 15–20, covers Absalom's revolt and, in its aftermath, the less costly revolt of Sheba ben Bichri. The two rebellions stand in parallel, as do 16:1–13 and 19:16–30, where David is confronted by several persons associated with the house of Saul: Ziba, servant of Saul's grandson Mephibosheth, Mephibosheth himself (only in the second episode), and the Benjaminite Shimei ben Gera, who initially directs curses and insults at David (only to retract them humbly after David's victory in the war). David's interaction with the house of Saul at both the beginning and end of the civil war symbolizes, to some extent, his relation to the northern tribes as a whole, whose king Saul had been, and who have been seduced by Absalom into the rebellion against David (Absalom "stole the hearts of Israel," 15:6).

The midpoint of this cycle would most likely be the moment, in

17:14, when the rebellion begins to turn in David's favor. This is one of only two points in the story (see 11:27b) where YHWH's intentions toward David are indicated by the narrator rather than by dialogue or ellipsis: "YHWH determined that Achitophel's good advice might be nullified, so that YHWH might bring evil upon Absalom" (a recurrence of the important motif of "good/evil"). Here, as in 1 Samuel 25, David's fate is conspicuously beyond his control; it is divine intervention (through human agents) that saves him. However astutely David has handled his two exiles, the two critical turning points are not his doing but YHWH's. The placement of these two moments of abject vulnerability before YHWH as the centerpiece of their respective narrative cycles preserves for us the prophetic (that is, Samuelite) perspective on kingly power.

The Closing Chapters of 2 Samuel

The so-called Succession History achieves completion outside the borders of the Samuel books, in the first two chapters of 1 Kings. There we read of the death of the aged, infirm King David and the final tense events leading to the succession of Solomon—who appears as a functioning character for the first time in the court history. Still, it is perhaps appropriate to view those events, as the Masoretic editors did, as part of the story of Solomon, and so to see the end of 2 Samuel as a well-rounded conclusion to the career of David and to the subjects of the Samuel books. Scholars have generally viewed 2 Samuel 21–24 as a late addition, with no integral role in the form and message of the book. Such a view misreads Samuel. The change from elaborated narrative to folkloric, archival, and poetic fragment accords with shifts in discourse common to most biblical literature, and here it ties together the themes of the Samuel books in a particularly effective way. Far from being late additions, they may be the archaic traditionary remnants from which the narrative was spun in the first place.

Once again, the arrangement is symmetrical. Chapters 21 and 24 record natural disasters during the reign of David that are tied to YHWH's displeasure. The causes of this displeasure are somewhat obscure, for they bear no direct relation to the preceding narratives; the connection of Saul's "bloodguilt" in 21:1 with 1 Samuel 22:6–23 is disputed, and David's apparently sinful census in chapter 24 was actually instigated by YHWH, in anger at the Land. But the measures of expiation in each case bear significant consequences for the history previously narrated. In chapter 21 David has seven descendants of Saul publicly impaled, in atonement for Saul's crimes, and later gives them a proper burial, as well as exhuming the bones of Saul and Jonathan in Jabesh-Gilead and returning them to their tribal homeland (21:10–14; cf. 2 Sam. 2:4–7). This strange mixture of barbarity and respect toward the house of Saul stands as a final reminder of David's compromised position in relation to his predecessor—for all his efforts at propriety, he is hounded, far into his own reign, by the legacy of Saul. In chapter 24 David's expiation anticipates events in the reign to follow: David purchases a threshing floor from Araunah the Jebusite (Araunah's name is, according to some commentators, actually Hittite, and the form of the scene recalls Abraham's purchase of the Cave of Machpelah in Hebron from its Hittite owners, in Gen. 23). On this site he builds an altar, whose sacrifices stay the plague. Postbiblical tradition associates the site with the eventual Temple Mount, but the presence, in any case, of an altar is sufficient to establish the typological connection. The Ark of the Covenant is not mentioned, but the name Araunah echoes the word *'aron* ("ark"), and 2 Samuel thus ends where 1 Samuel began: with a stable and functioning shrine, albeit a troubled and haunted one.

Both 21:15–22 and 23:8–39 recount the exploits of David's elite warriors and allude to Philistine battles apparently late in David's reign. The first unit records an interesting detail: David's rescue by Joab's brother Abishai causes David's men to demand that David "not go forth with us to battle any longer; you must never extinguish the lamp of Israel!" (21:17b). In addition to reinforcing the impression of a weary and aging king (see v. 15), the episode provides the etiological underpinning of the entire transition to sedentary and dynastic monarchy begun in 2 Samuel 11. The second unit presents similar quick sketches of the elite guard but culminates in a full list of the "thirty" who stood behind the chief commanders. The text is uncertain, and there may be a discrepancy between the number of names and the alleged total (23:39), counting the top men, of thirty-seven. Joab, notably, though peripherally mentioned (vv. 18 and 37), is absent from the list. (This omission is an appropriate emblem of David's long and troubled association with Joab, who eventually dies by David's deathbed command given in 1 Kings 2:5–6 and carried out in 2 Kings 2:28–34.) But the final name on the list (the thirty-first of the "thirty") is unexpected: Uriah the Hittite. The mention confirms what has previously been only implicit in the designation "Hittite": that Uriah is not an ordinary conscript but a member of the partly foreign professional military raised by and for the king. Uriah's behavior as a devout Israelite, in the manner of a simple footsoldier, is again highlighted by this incongruity and becomes all the more moving in retrospect.

The central components, chapters 22 and 23, are two songs by David. These songs stand in meaningful contrast both to each other and to the other members of the traditionary sestet. Whereas the "warrior" units show David protected by a phalanx of professional guards, the songs show him acting alone in the shelter of YHWH. Whereas the "punishment/expiation" units show a guilty monarch atoning to an angry YHWH for the sins of his predecessor or his people, the songs show the blameless protégé of YHWH and hail the deity as unstintingly gracious and benevolent. There the similarity between the songs ends. The first song, essentially a duplicate of Psalm 18, appears under the headnote "David sang this song when YHWH saved him from the hand of all his enemies and from the hand of Saul" (23:1). It is a typical "distress" psalm, common to the Near Eastern mythology of kingship, and is itself symmetrical: (*a*) recounting the singer's trials of flight, exile, and persecution, (*b*) describing the emergence of the avenging deity amid clouds, thunder, and lightning, (*c*) affirming the fugitive's innocence, purity, and steadfastness to YHWH's ways, (*b'*) reasserting the protective actions of the patron deity, and (*a'*) recounting the newly protected fugitive's nimble and mighty defeat of his enemies. Taken as a whole, the song epitomizes the first martial phase of David's career: his early period of Philistine wars and his flight from Saul. (The song's culmination in a rout of David's enemies adds a dimension withheld from the story: that David's battle with Saul was direct; cf., however, 2 Sam. 3:1.) Yet it is shadowed by the final martial phase of David's career: his flight from Absalom, the civil war, and the latter-day Philistine wars. The second song, on the other hand, appearing under the headnote "These are the last words of David, / the utterance of David the son of Jesse, / the utterance of the man who was elevated on high, / anointed of the God of Jacob, / favorite [*or* psalmist] of the songs of Israel" (23:1), shows David as the completed and sedentary monarch, serenely administering justice to the realm:

> It is he who governs righteously,
>   it is he who governs in the fear of God,
> and is like the morning of a shining sun,
>   a cloudless morning, a grassy land flourishing
>   from sunshine and from rain.   (23:3b–4)

The language of this song is exceptionally difficult, but if, as a recent translation suggests, verse 5 should be taken as a rhetorical question ("Is not my house established before God? . . . Will he not cause all my success and [my] every desire to blossom?" [NJPS]), the idyllic harmony projected by royalist doctrine remains consistent throughout. We thus have, in chapters 22 and 23, visions of the premonarchical and monarchical David, respectively—a shorthand for the more complex narrative movements we have witnessed from 1 Samuel 16 onward.

In sum, the closing chapters of 2 Samuel are an artistically wrought coda to the Samuel books as a whole, comprising most of the major themes and movements of the narrative corpus and, by ellipsis and innuendo, delicately alluding to the contradictions in the king's person and in the nation's kingly office.

The Argument of Samuel

The survey above shows that the Samuel books recount the origin of the monarchy in Israel, and that the ancient Israelite tradition perceived kingship and territorial sovereignty with great ambivalence. This ambivalence grew, in part, from the situation that surrounded the evolution and collection of biblical literature. A Jerusalemite and Judean intelligentsia, closely tied to the Davidic ruling house, preserved the traditions of Israel for posterity. These sages were the narrow bottleneck through which the Hebrew Bible's pre-Exilic tradition passed into Judaism (that is, Judahism) and the cultural traditions of the West. Yet it was the northern tribes (by then long disappeared) who made up the original "Israel." When that Israel was destroyed and absorbed by Assyria in the late eighth century B.C.E., its legacy haunted the Judean kingdom to the south, and an effort was made, during Judah's own remaining century or so of sovereignty (before it, too, was exiled to Babylonia), to affirm the cultural unity of the two kingdoms. Yet any such affirmation, if it was to be honest and mature, had to register the inner contradictions of that unity. The court circles of David's dynastic descendants were periodically influenced by an ethical prophetic movement (encompassing, but not limited to, the Deuteronomists) that called the king, priesthood, and people to task for injustice in the Land, and the prophetic standards of national integrity—essentially the standards of Samuel—left a permanent stamp on the character of biblical literature.

Samuel is thus a work of national self-criticism. It recognizes that Israel would not have survived, either politically or culturally, without the steadying presence of a dynastic royal house. But it makes both that house and its subjects answerable to firm standards of prophetic justice—not those of cult prophets or professional ecstatics, but of morally upright prophetic leaders in the tradition of Moses, Joshua, Deborah, Gideon, and Samuel. Kingship is shown as a project of the people and their tribal elders—one that represented a partial ceding of their autonomy, and so, in a sense, a loss of innocence, a fateful juncture in their history that could be represented only in the lineaments of high tragedy. (YHWH's unspecified anger toward the Land in 2 Sam. 24 becomes clearer in this light, as does the census motif there, which is arguably a mark of Israel's progress toward an organized and bureaucratized polity.) And although Saul and David are allowed to assume the forefront of the narration, the original collective protagonist is never forgotten. At the same time, the complicated interaction of Israel's first two kings, at first recounted alternately from both points of view, is allowed to stand for the troubled bond between the ancient tribal order of the north and its maverick brethren of Judah; or, on another level, between the Northern and Southern Kingdoms that emerged after Solomon's death. (In this sense, 1 Sam.'s alternation between Saul and David anticipates the parallel history of north and south in 1 Kings 12–2 Kings 25.) Once the story becomes focused on King David, still more dimensions of the history open up. The finely realistic portrait of David's household strife shows both the moral consequences of David's sin with Bathsheba and the political consequences of David's too-rapid establishment of a royal court. All these events, in turn, set the stage for the succession by Bathsheba's second-born, Solomon, in 1 Kings 1–2.

The two prophecies delivered to David by his court prophet Nathan reflect some of the ideological ambivalence in Israelite tradition over kingship and centralization of power in David's and Solomon's time. (They also recall the slogan of Sheba ben Bichri's abortive rebellion, which resurfaces when the kingdom divides once and for all: "We have no portion in David, / no share in the son of Jesse! / Everyone to his tent, O Israel!" [2 Sam. 20:1, to which 1 Kings 12:16 adds: 'Now look to your own house, David!'].) In 2 Samuel 7, David proposes to build a permanent home for the ark, a "house of cedar" to replace the archaic tabernacle tent that has served since Moses' day. YHWH, Nathan reports, registers astonishment that Israel's wandering sanctuary should come to rest in this way. Nevertheless, YHWH promises David an everlasting dynasty, and a son after him (not here identified by name) who will "build a house for my name." The Davidic scion will be a "son" to YHWH: "When he does wrong, I will punish him with the rod of men and with human afflictions. But I will never remove my favor from him as I removed it from Saul" (7:14–15). The language of the chapter is conspicuously Deuteronomic, and the prophecy suggests the conflicting trends that shaped this movement so influential to the collecting of pre-Exilic Israelite tradition. Nathan seems simultaneously to say yes and no to David's proposal. He thus encapsulates the many vicissitudes of Judean history from David's time to the Exile: Israel's tabernacle will become Judah's Temple; the Temple will be built, but by a successor to David, not by David; the dynastic successors of David will have everlasting rule (the house indeed survived in exile and passed from there into Jewish messianism) but will also suffer punishments for their moral failings; the throne will be secure, but it will also be vulnerable; it will survive the onslaughts of others, but it will not be protected from itself. The entire passage plays richly on the various senses of "house": physical shelter, temple, court, dynasty. When Nathan later (12:1–12) delivers to David a new prophecy, a stinging rebuke of David's treachery to Uriah the Hittite, we encounter the first tangible demonstration that the kingly house will be both punished and preserved: David's child by Bathsheba will die (as indeed happens later in the chapter); but when David consoles Bathsheba over this death they make love and she conceives again. "She bore a son and called him Solomon. YHWH favored him and sent a message by the prophet Nathan; and he was named Jedidiah ['beloved of YHWH,' a name cognate to 'David'] at YHWH's bidding" (vv. 24–25). Nathan's activism on behalf of Solomon/Jedidiah persists to the final hours of the succession story (1 Kings 1:11–14), where he persuades Bathsheba to intercede with the dying King David to block the accession of Solomon's half brother Adonijah.

These elaborate turns of destiny accomplish the extraordinary feat of embodying both the political complexity of the Davidic succession and the ideological ambivalence of the later tradition. Perhaps the messiness of history required that the retelling encompass so many paradoxes. But it is to the credit of the Samuel author that the story could unfold Israel's transitions on so many planes at once, through the skillful interweaving of complementary codes: theological, characterological, geographic, sacerdotal, demographic, familial. Many thematic lines thus converge: the ark, the priesthood, the prophetic movements, the Philistine wars, the rivalries of Israel and Judah and of Saul and David, the establishment of Jerusalem as a capital, the chronic presence of blood feud, the role of kingly office, the service of the king's officers and aides, the play of sexual intrigue, the ways of household strife, the conflict of sibling with sibling, the conflict of parent with child. In no other biblical books have these planes of narrative been orchestrated and sustained quite so satisfyingly and so consequentially. Both structurally and artistically, Samuel is the centerpiece of the Hebrew Bible's continuous historical account.

NOTES

1. Leonhard Rost, *Die Überlieferung von der Thronnachfolge Davids,* Beiträge zur Wissenschaft vom Alten und Neuen Testament, 3:6 (Stuttgart, 1926); translated by Michael D. Rutter and David M. Gunn as *The Succession to the Throne of David* (Sheffield, 1982); Martin Noth, *Überlieferungsgeschichtliche Studien I,* 2nd ed. (Tübingen, 1957), 1–110; translated by Jane Doull and revised by John Barton, Michael D. Rutter, D. R. Ap-Thomas, and David J. A. Clines as *The Deuteronomistic History* (Sheffield, 1981). I designate the beginning of the "Succession History" as 2 Sam. 11. Rost and later investigators have generally included one or more earlier chapters, a matter on which there is no consensus.

2. Limitations of space prevent discussion of the important theme of the destiny of Eli and his descendants. On this subject see P. Kyle McCarter, *I Samuel: A New Translation with Introduction and Commentary,* Anchor Bible, VIII (Garden City, N.Y., 1980), 91–93, 349 n. 2, 365–367; Frank Moore Cross, Jr., *Canaanite Myth and Hebrew Epic* (Cambridge, Mass., 1975), pp. 195–215.

3. Because the KJV often distorts the Hebrew, unless otherwise indicated all biblical translations in this essay are my own [AT].

4. See Uriel Simon, "Samuel's Call to Prophecy: Form Criticism with Close Reading," *Prooftexts,* 1 (May 1981), 119–132.

5. See Brevard S. Childs, *Introduction to the Old Testament as Scripture* (London and Philadelphia, 1979), pp. 277–278.

6. Among more recent discussions of kingship mythology, see Baruch Halpern, *The Constitution of the Monarchy in Ancient Israel* (Chico, Calif., 1981), pp. 1–109; Tomoo Ishida, *Royal Dynasties in Ancient Israel* (Berlin and New York, 1977); A. R. Johnson, *Sacral Kingship in Ancient Israel,* 2nd ed. (Cardiff, 1967).

7. Rashi, Radaq to 2 Sam. 8:2, based on Num. Rabbah 14:1.

8. Julius Wellhausen, *Prolegomena to the History of [Ancient] Israel* (1878; reprint, Gloucester, Mass., 1973), p. 262, speaks of events "faithfully reported"; John Bright, *A History of Israel* (Philadelphia, 1946), p. 163, of "a document with an eyewitness flavor"; Ernst Sellin and George Fohrer, *Introduction to the Old Testament,* trans. David Green (Nashville, 1968), p. 163, of an author who was "undoubtedly an eyewitness to the event and a member of the royal court."

9. See especially the admirable study by David M. Gunn, *The Story of King David: Genre and Interpretation* (Sheffield, 1978).

10. I discuss this matter at some length in *King and Kin: Political Allegory in the Hebrew Bible* (Bloomington and Indianapolis, 1986), pp. 100–112.

11. Rost, *Die Überlieferung,* thus found in this episode the etiological underpinning of the "Succession History." See, among others, P. Kyle McCarter, *II Samuel: A New Translation with Introduction and Commentary,* Anchor Bible, IX (Garden City, N.Y., 1984), 187–189.

12. J. P. Fokkelman, *Narrative Art and Poetry in the Books of Samuel,* vol. I: *King David* (Assen, 1981), pp. 411–417, shows the events of 2 Sam. 13–1 Kings 2 to be rooted in 2 Sam. 12:5–6, a connection already acknowledged in medieval Jewish commentary; see Rashi to 2 Sam. 12:6, Radaq on 12:1.

13. Fokkelman, *Narrative Art and Poetry,* provides observations on symmetrical patterns from 2 Sam. 9 on; see especially pp. 311–314, 338–341.

SUGGESTED FURTHER READINGS

Adele Berlin, *Poetics and Interpretation of Biblical Narrative* (Sheffield, 1983), pp. 23–82.

Walter Brueggemann, *David's Truth in Israel's Imagination and Memory* (Philadelphia, 1985).

J. P. Fokkelman, *Narrative Art and Poetry in the Books of Samuel,* vol. I: *King David* (Assen, 1981).

R. P. Gordon, *1 & 2 Samuel* (Sheffield, 1984).

David M. Gunn, *The Fate of King Saul: An Interpretation of a Biblical Story* (Sheffield, 1980).

———, *The Story of King David: Genre and Interpretation* (Sheffield, 1978).

W. L. Humphreys, "The Tragedy of King Saul: A Study of the Structure of 1 Samuel 9–31," *Journal for the Study of the Old Testament,* 6 (1978), 18–27.

Peter D. Miscall, "I Samuel 16–22," in D. J. McCarthy, ed., *The Workings of Old Testament Narrative* (Philadelphia and Chico, Calif., 1983), pp. 47–138.

Joel Rosenberg, "David without Diagrams: Beyond Structure in the Davidic History," in *King and Kin: Political Allegory in the Hebrew Bible* (Bloomington and Indianapolis, 1986), pp. 99–199.

John van Seters, "Problems in the Literary Analysis of the Court History of David," *Journal for the Study of the Old Testament,* 1 (1976), 22–29.

Meir Sternberg, "Gaps, Ambiguity, and the Reading Process," in *The Poetics of Biblical Narrative: Ideological Literature and the Drama of Reading* (Bloomington and Indianapolis, 1985), pp. 186–229.

R. N. Whybray, *The Succession Narrative: A Study of II Sam. 9–20 and I Kings 1 and 2* (London, 1968).

Tufts University

1 and 2 Kings

George Savran

THE writing of history, by its very nature, requires a selection of details, the imposition of a pattern of organization, and the expression of the historian's point of view. For readers who wish to uncover "what really happened," such elements of deliberate organization are a barrier to be penetrated and discarded, for they only obscure whatever historical reality can be recovered. But for those of us who feel that the truth of the text lies in the telling, the analysis of the historiographer's narrative strategies is a matter of primary importance.

The signs of a highly biased rendering of the history of Israel's monarchy are visible to even the casual reader. Unlike the practice in other biblical books, the narrator makes constant reference to other works which complement his narrative, in order to make clear that he has chosen to tell only a part of the events of a given reign. For further details about Solomon we are referred to "the book of the acts of Solomon" (1 Kings 11:41), and for the affairs of state of subsequent rulers to "the book of the chronicles of the kings of Judah" (1 Kings 14:29) or to a similar work about the kings of Israel (1 Kings 14:19). Each king is judged either good or bad in black-and-white terms, according to whether or not he "did right" or "did evil" in the sight of the Lord. This evaluation is not reflective of the well-being of the nation, of the king's success or failure in war, or of the moral climate of the times, but rather of the state of cultic worship during his reign. Those kings who shun idolatry and enact religious reforms are singled out for praise; those who encourage pagan practices are denounced. So important is this criterion that even a positive evaluation may be qualified by the king's failure to do away with worship at shrines outside Jerusalem. Thus Joash of Judah "did that which was right in the sight of the Lord" but is censured by the narrator because "the high places were not taken away" (2 Kings 12:2–3). Hezekiah, on the other hand, is singled out for praise because of the program of cultic reorganization which he sponsored (2 Kings 18:1–6).

A further indication of the narrator's bias is the categorical disapprobation of every ruler of the Northern Kingdom, regardless of his achievements. The first king of the North, Jeroboam, breaks with the political and religious authority of Jerusalem and establishes alternative shrines in the old cult centers of Dan and Bethel (1 Kings 12:25–33). He is censured severely for having had the audacity to reject the primacy of the Temple in Jerusalem and, worse, for having installed a golden calf as a cultic object in each place. The narrator is largely unconcerned with the political and social motivations of Jeroboam's revolt; he and all his successors are depicted as unrepentant idolators of the worst kind, who lead the entire nation into sin and, ultimately, into destruction and captivity.

It is possible to understand the peculiar slant of Kings toward the events it relates by seeing it in the context of the canonical books which precede it, as the final chapter of an overarching work which has been dubbed the Deuteronomic History. This collection, consisting of Joshua, Judges, Samuel, and Kings, betrays the influence of a school of thought which embraced the central tenet of Deuteronomy: Israel's presence in the land derives from its covenantal relationship with God, the breaching of which will result in the people's destruction and exile (see Deut. 28). Other themes which reflect a strong Deuteronomic influence include the ideal of the centralization of cultic worship in Jerusalem and an intensive polemic, couched in a distinctive rhetoric, against idolatry.[1] These concerns stand behind the criticism of the many kings who allow worship to continue in the "high places" and underlie the condemnation of all Northern kings as well.

Yet despite its ideological affinities with the rest of the Former Prophets, Kings is fundamentally different in style. There is no single figure, like Joshua, whose life serves as the organizing principle for the book. Nor can we isolate a few major protagonists whose interaction, like that of Saul and David in 1 Samuel, creates a dramatic framework. The overriding unity of Kings derives both from its presentation of a continuous history of Israel's monarchy from Solomon to Zedekiah and from the formulaic language with which the reign of each king is outlined and evaluated by the narrator. But at the same time there are unexpected changes in the type of material presented, with sudden shifts from dry, annalistic writing concerned with genealogy and chronology to sophisticated stories with elaborate plot and character development. Judges bears some resemblance to Kings, with its cyclical pattern of oppression and salvation spanning two hundred years. But whereas Judges spins out of control toward the end, the collapse of its literary structure mirroring the breakdown of authority in society, Kings marches steadily toward the terrible fate of the Northern Kingdom, then of the kingdom of Judah. This is a work which emphasizes the inexorability of that fate by its use of repetitive, stereotypical language and by a continuous demonstration of the reliability of prophecy.

Structure

In 1 and 2 Kings the history of the monarchy is organized into three sections. Chapters 1–11 of 1 Kings describe the United Monarchy, primarily during the reign of Solomon; 1 Kings 12–2 Kings 17 relates the synchronistic history of the divided kingdoms of Judah and Israel down to the destruction of the latter in 722 B.C.E.; and 2 Kings 18–25 recounts the subsequent fortunes of Judah through the fall of Jerusalem in 586 B.C.E. But the thematic emphases of the book suggest an additional, chiastic structure:

A	Solomon/United Monarchy	1 Kings 1:1–11:25
B	Jeroboam/Rehoboam; division of kingdom	1 Kings 11:26–14:31
C	kings of Judah/Israel	1 Kings 15:1–16:22
D	Omride dynasty; rise and fall of Baal cult in Israel and Judah	1 Kings 16:23–2 Kings 12
C'	kings of Judah/Israel	2 Kings 13–16
B'	fall of Northern Kingdom	2 Kings 17
A'	kingdom of Judah	2 Kings 18–25

The outer perimeters of the chiasm, A and A', correspond on the broadest thematic level. The beginning of the work concentrates on the founder of the Davidic dynasty, and its final chapter describes the demise of its last official king (Zedekiah) and the pardoning of his predecessor (Jehoiachin) in Babylon. As the central theme of the Solomon narrative is the building and dedication of the Temple, so the focus of the account of the kingdom of Judah is the ultimate fate of that Temple: desecration by Manasseh (2 Kings 21), renovation by Josiah (chaps. 22–23), and destruction by the Babylonians (chap. 25). The description of the despoliation of the Temple vessels in 2 Kings 25:13–17 corresponds to the order of their manufacture in 1 Kings 7.

Sections B and B' form an internal parallel to this pattern of rise and fall. The Northern Kingdom is established by Jeroboam, who is first acclaimed as a divinely chosen alternative to Solomon's son (1 Kings 11:35) but who becomes the very model of the apostate king. At the center of B is the account of his building the infamous golden calves, which are strongly condemned by narrator and prophet alike (12:25–33). In the corresponding section, B', Israel's ultimate fate mirrors that of Judah; it is destroyed by a foreign power from the east, and its people are exiled to Assyria. The link between B and B' is made explicit by the explanation of Israel's destruction as the result of the idolatry begun by Jeroboam (2 Kings 17:16–18).

Sections *C* and *C'* alternate between the reigns of Northern and Southern kings and separate the creation and destruction of the Northern Kingdom from the long narrative of *D*. This central section details the rise and fall of the Baal cult in Israel together with its royal patrons, the family of Omri, Ahab, and Jezebel; it concludes with a short coda on the demise of Baal in Judah as well (2 Kings 11–12). The exceptional length of *D* is out of proportion to the period of narrated time—eighteen chapters for about forty years. The historical importance of the Omride dynasty notwithstanding, the central position of *D* within Kings is a function of the section's presentation of a model for the victory of prophetic over monarchic forces. Much of its narrative celebrates the Northern prophets—Elijah, Elisha, and others—in their successful fight against the idolatry sponsored by the crown. In a manner parallel to the history of idolatry in *B* and *B'*, the early stories of *D* depict the establishment of Baal worship in the Northern Kingdom (1 Kings 16:31–32, 18:4), and the closing chapters describe its violent eradication in Israel (2 Kings 9–10) and subsequent reforms in Judah (chaps. 11–12). Closer to the center of *D* are Elijah's commission to anoint the leaders who will assist in this removal (1 Kings 19:15–18) and Elisha's execution of this task (2 Kings 8:7–15, 9:1–3). The midpoint of *D* is 2 Kings 2, which tells of Elijah's ascent to heaven and his succession by Elisha. Although royal succession is frequently described in Kings, this is the only account of the transfer of the mantle of prophecy in the entire Bible.[2] By placing the idea of prophetic continuity at the very center of his work, the narrator emphasizes that as long as dynastic kingship continues, there will be a corresponding prophetic response.

Characterization and Moral Judgment

While the narrator's bias is apparent in his frequent use of the refrain "and X did evil in the sight of the Lord," more detailed analysis reveals subtler techniques which provide insight into the particular narrative art of Kings. The following examples of characterization describe the interplay between such explicitly judgmental commentary and more artful techniques employed in the narrative itself.

The rending of Solomon's kingdom into the independent monarchies of Judah and Israel is explained in 1 Kings 11 as divine retribution for the king's sins. But the account of the rebellion (1 Kings 12:1–19) is told from the perspective of the people's dissatisfaction with his son Rehoboam:

> Thy father made our yoke grievous: now therefore make thou the grievous service of thy father, and his heavy yoke which he put upon us, lighter, and we will serve thee.

Their request is stated in full in 12:4 and is referred to repeatedly by Rehoboam and his advisers. The first group of counselors, the elders, receive the narrator's blessing for their affiliation with the successful Solomon, having "stood before Solomon his father, while he yet lived" (v. 6), and for their awareness of the immediate need for "good words" (v. 7) to defuse a dangerous situation. Their attention to the final words of the people's request—"If thou wilt be a *servant* unto this people this day, and wilt *serve* them . . . then they will be thy *servants* for ever" (12:7)—conveys an impression of seasoned advisers who understand the importance of exchanging temporary concessions for long-term stability.

But association and repetition can be worked both ways; the younger advisers are derogatorily called *yeladim,* "children," or perhaps "young upstarts," and are identified by age and by temperament with the new king. In 12:9–10 the king and the *yeladim* also refer to the people's words, quoting their petition in direct speech, but they cite only their call for concessions and ignore the promise of loyalty which has formed the basis for the elders' advice. Their inappropriate counsel justifies the designation "children" and suggests Rehoboam's anxiety about being able to live up to the model of his father: "My little finger shall be thicker than my father's loins" (12:10). The narrator closes the episode by highlighting the popular response to Rehoboam's inept statesmanship in word—"What portion have we in David?"—and in deed—"and all Israel stoned him with stones" (12:16–18).

The second evaluation of Rehoboam (14:21–24) is more explicitly judgmental: the narrator denounces him in the stereotypical language of Kings as an idolator, in a manner which requires no further comment. This condemnation is followed by a report of the invasion of Judah by Shishak of Egypt (14:25–28), a report which in itself is wholly neutral toward Rehoboam. The two sections are juxtaposed simply by asyndetic parataxis (the King James Version's "and" at the beginning of 14:25 is misleading), nor does there appear to be any substantive connection between them. However, the absence of any other explanation for the attack, combined with the prejudicial effect of the narrator's condemnation, creates the impression that Rehoboam's defeat is the inevitable result of his idolatrous behavior. Even the innocuous reference to the replacement of Solomon's gold shields with bronze ones takes on a negative coloration when read as part of the larger context: Rehoboam's use of an inferior metal recalls and reinforces the unfavorable comparison between father and son in chapter 12. The resulting critical portrait of the king is enriched by multiple perspectives: the people's perception of the king as insensitive to their demands, divine disapproval in 14:21–24, and the narrator's implicit linkage of sin with historical misfortune.

In the preceding example, all three perspectives reinforce one another to present a consistently critical picture of the king. The depiction of Ahab is more complex, for although the narrator's explicit judgment is highly critical, more positive aspects of the king are brought out in other sections. In the introduction to Ahab's reign the narrator, going beyond his usual condemnation of Israelite kings, denounces Ahab and his father Omri as more wicked "than all that were before them" (1 Kings 16:25, 30). Worse, Ahab surpasses even Jeroboam in displeasing God: "as if it had been a light thing for him to walk in the sins of Jeroboam son of Nebat, that he took to wife Jezebel the daughter of Ethbaal king of the Zidonians, and went and served Baal, and worshipped him" (16:31).

But in the narrative itself, the king's interaction with Elijah and other prophets seems to belie this unfavorable verdict. Ahab may have hostile words for Elijah, but he is ever obedient to the prophet's commands, gathering together the people (18:19), eating and drinking (18:41), and preparing his chariot (18:44). In 1 Kings 20 he complies with the oracles of an unnamed prophet (vv. 13, 28) and is rewarded with successive victories over his Aramean enemies. But the most surprising moment of obedience follows Elijah's vitriolic denunciation of the king in the next chapter (21:20–26), where Ahab rends his clothing and fasts in a profound display of repentance. The narrator underscores the sincerity of the king's behavior by citing God's approval in direct speech to Elijah, which includes a stay of execution till the next generation (vv. 28–29). What is the role of such servility and contrition in the portrayal of this wickedest of wicked kings?

The counterpoint to Ahab's submissiveness to God and prophet is to be found in the king's willing capitulation to *whoever* confronts him, regardless of politics or moral standards. The first hint of this occurs in 1 Kings 18:4; the persecution of the prophets of the Lord may be attributed to Jezebel, but we hear nothing of Ahab's reactions. Further, Ahab's failure to reply to his wife's threat to execute Elijah in 19:2 detracts from the sincerity of his support for the prophet in the previous chapter. The pattern continues in chapter 20, where Ahab accedes to his enemy's appeal for mercy and incurs the wrath of the anonymous prophet in verses 35–43.

The most devastating criticism of Ahab occurs in the tale of Naboth's vineyard in 1 Kings 21. Naboth rejects the king's offer of purchase because the property is *naḥalat 'avotai*, "the inheritance of my fathers," whose sale outside the family is expressly forbidden (Lev. 25:23; Num. 27:1–11, 36:7). Ahab is characteristically submissive, but the use of the words *sar weza-'ef*, "heavy and displeased" (21:4), to express his dissatisfaction recalls the king's identical reaction to prophetic criticism in 20:43. As the first signals a departure from his unqualified obedience to prophetic authority, the second indicates his impatience with the traditional religious values of his community. In recounting the conversation to Jezebel, he misrepresents Naboth's unwillingness to sell as a personal rejection. In 21:6 Ahab misquotes Naboth's refusal by substituting "vineyard"—mere property—for the all-important reference to patrimony. He also replaces Naboth's oath, "The Lord forbid it me" (21:3), with a flat personal refusal: "I will not give thee my vineyard." The placement of the indirect object immediately after the verb further indicates Ahab's sense of having been insulted, as if Naboth had said: "Perhaps I would sell to someone else, but not to *you*."[3]

From this point on, the case against Ahab is built upon his silent acquiescence in Jezebel's promise: "I will give thee the vineyard of Naboth" (21:7). He does not ask how she intends to succeed where he has failed, nor does he take any interest in the legal proceedings against Naboth. The pattern of repetition in verses 15 and 16 indicts both the murderess and her silent partner:

> And it came to pass, when Jezebel heard that Naboth was stoned, and was dead . . .

> And it came to pass, when Ahab heard that Naboth was dead . . .

Ahab's indifference to how or why Naboth has died (note the absence of the detail "stoned" in Jezebel's report) and his complete submission to the authority of Jezebel are further elements in the narrator's criticism of the king. Ahab's show of repentance in 21:27 does not rehabilitate him in the eyes of the reader but simply deepens the impression of his inconstancy. The narrative strategy has been to undercut the redeeming quality of Ahab's obedience by exposing it as weakness of character. The king is revealed to be an opportunist who will follow whoever leads him, whether for good or for bad, and he is not pushed to the wall until 1 Kings 22. The placement of this narrative at the conclusion of his portrait is crucial, for Ahab must finally choose between two mutually exclusive claims to the truth. That he chooses badly, and dies for it, is the final element in the narrator's argument.

Whereas the narrator's explicit judgments of Rehoboam and Ahab are completely negative, his evaluation of Jehu ben Nimshi (2 Kings 10:29–36) is more equivocal. Because Jehu has brought down Ahab's line and routed out the worship of Baal, he is praised by God for having done "that which is right in mine eyes" (v. 30) and is promised a continuation of his dynasty for four generations. But the narrator is a more severe critic than the deity, for whatever Jehu's accomplishments, the narrator condemns him for being guilty of the same apostasy as Jeroboam. Further, by closing with the comment "In those days the Lord began to cut Israel short" (v. 32), he implies that God not only has qualified his earlier approval of Jehu but also has passed sentence upon the entire kingdom of Israel because of his deeds. How is this ambiguous verdict reflected in the narrative account of Jehu's achievements?

In a connected series of vignettes in 2 Kings 9–10, Jehu is proclaimed king by his fellow army officers and proceeds to assassinate King Joram of Israel, the queen mother Jezebel, and their ally King Ahaziah of Judah. Continuing in an ever-widening circle of carnage which claims numerous kinsmen and supporters of the house of Ahab, the destruction culminates in a scene reminiscent of Odysseus' vengeance upon his wife's suitors, in which all adherents of Baal are trapped within their temple and mercilessly slaughtered. The intensity with which Jehu acts is reflected in his constant movement throughout the narrative in 9:14–37 (the verb *rakab*, "to ride," recurs ten times in this section). In 9:20 Joram's lookout sees Jehu "driving . . . furiously," refusing to rest until his enemies are destroyed. The repeated use of the greeting *hashalom*, "Is it peace?" by Joram and his messengers (9:17, 19, 22) serves as a foil for Jehu's repudiation of their overtures: "What hast thou to do with peace?" (9:19). The only *shalom* which is of concern to Jehu is the avenging of Naboth's death—"I will requite [*shilamti*] thee" (9:26)—in accordance with Elijah's oracle.

Jehu's victory over the house of Ahab and his elimination of Baal worship seem to make an overwhelming case for regarding him in a positive light as a divinely appointed avenging angel. But there is something suspicious in the way Jehu conveniently has a divine oracle ready to defend his every action, as he does in 9:26, 9:36, and 10:10. Oracles are nearly always spoken by a prophet or by the narrator himself, but Jehu dares to assume the authority reserved for the prophetic voice in quoting and interpreting the words of Elijah. When we realize that all those connected with the house of Ahab are the essential political targets of his coup d'état—including Joram's Judean ally, Ahaziah—the extent of divine support for Jehu's bloodbath is thrown into question. And as it becomes clear that Jehu is not a prophet, the difference between him and Elijah is brought into focus: in 1 Kings 18, Elijah the prophet is concerned with repentance; he seeks to turn the hearts of Israel back to God and executes only the prophets of Baal. Jehu the king, on the other hand, is motivated by political considerations; in 2 Kings 10 he destroys *all* those who worship Baal, for they are potential enemies of the new regime.

The narrator's strategy, then, is to speak approvingly of the destruction of Ahab and Baal but to cast doubts upon Jehu's motives as well as his methods. In order to maintain this ambivalent attitude toward the king, Jehu is censured through a variety of indirect means. The sequencing of the episodes creates the impression of a man whose enthusiasm for killing increases with every life he takes, as the tabulation of victims changes from specific "body counts" (seventy sons of Ahab, forty-two kinsmen of Ahaziah) to an inestimable number in the temple of Baal. There are constant references to the totality of the slaughter: "he left him none remaining" (10:11); "neither left he any of them" (10:14); "Go in, and slay them; let none come forth" (10:25). All this bloodshed seems to stimulate Jehu's appetite in a literal way as well. The unusually graphic description of Jezebel's death—"So they threw her down, and some of her blood was sprinkled on the wall, and on the horses, and they trampled her" (9:33 [AR])—is followed immediately by: "Then he went inside, and he ate and drank" (9:34 [AT]).

Other facets of Jehu's character are revealed by the presentation of uncomplimentary contrasts between the new king and his victims. Despite the narrator's overall disapproval of Joram, he portrays him as a wounded war hero—"Joram and all Israel had been protecting Ramoth-gilead against Hazael, king of Aram" (9:14 [AT])—whereas Jehu takes advantage of Joram's infirmity and brazenly shoots him dead with no warning. In 10:1–11 he dupes the guardians of Ahab's children into killing their wards in the vain hope of saving their own necks. Jehu's mistreatment of the remains of the victims violates the biblical ethic of proper treatment of the dead (Deut. 21:22–23, 2 Sam. 21:10–14).[4] His self-righteous condemnation of the elders for a crime which he himself has forced them to commit appears as a weak attempt to justify his own behavior: "O, you righteous people! True, I conspired against my own master and killed him, but who has slain all these?" (10:9 [AT]). In the brief account of Jehu's attack on the kinsmen of Ahaziah of Judah (10:12–14), the victims' own words emphasize their peaceful intentions: "We are going to pay our respects [*shalom*] to the king and to the children of the queen" (v. 13 [AT]). But as with Joram and Jezebel, the mention of *shalom* is the kiss of death. The lack of congruence between Jehu's words and his actions leads us to sympathize with the victims, at the expense of the "hero." His command "Take them alive" (v. 14) at first appears to respect the claims of the Judeans and to signal an end to the violence. But the immediate mention of their slaughter frustrates our expectations and makes these deaths seem all the more cruel and sadistic, as if the capture were simply for the pleasure of killing.

Even though all criticism of Jehu originates with the narrator, he sometimes camouflages its source by placing such commentary in the mouths of the characters. Thus, when Joram's watchman describes Jehu as "driving madly" (*beshiga'on*, 9:20 [AR]), he uses the same pejorative with which Jehu's fellow officers describe the "mad" prophetic disciple (*hameshuga'*) in 9:11. This technique can be effective even when the speaker is portrayed as a hostile figure. In 9:23 Joram warns of *mirmah*, "treachery," on Jehu's part; here the sudden shift to the victim's perspective garners sympathy for Joram as the object of unfair advantage. Even Jezebel is employed by the narrator to criticize Jehu. Her provocative challenge to Jehu in 9:31, *hashalom zimri horeg 'adonaw*, can be translated "Is all well, you Zimri, murderer of his master?" [AT], equating Jehu with the officer who assassinated King Elah of Israel some forty years earlier, at the encouragement of a prophet named, ironically, Jehu ben Hanani (1 Kings

16:8–12). Her words can also be rendered "Had Zimri peace, who slew his master?" as in the King James Version, making reference to the fact that Zimri ruled for only seven days before he himself was reviled by the people and committed suicide (1 Kings 16:15–18). Despite Jezebel's obvious prejudice, there is enough truth in her words to identify Jehu with the kings who commit murder to usurp the throne of Israel.

Solomon

The account of Solomon's life is far lengthier than that of any other king, at least in part because of the historical importance of his activities. But the Solomon narrative is also central to the thematic development of Kings, giving expression to key motifs which run throughout the book. Solomon serves as a prototypical figure in both a positive and a negative sense. As the ideal king, he is the legitimate heir to David's kingdom and to his covenant with God, the very model of material and political success, and the builder of the Temple. But he also exemplifies the good king whose heart is turned to idolatry, whose ultimate fate shows that the divine promise is not unconditional and can be revoked, as happens subsequently to Jeroboam, and to Baasha after him.

The first two chapters of Kings mark both a beginning and an ending; as a continuation of the account of David in Samuel, they recount the twilight years of David's reign. They focus upon his impotence in old age, his manipulation by those around him, and the last-minute recovery so characteristic of him. But as the opening chapters of the work whose topic is the period subsequent to that monarchy, 1 Kings: 1–2 should be seen as the introduction to the story of Solomon. In the first chapter he is the passive recipient of the throne, but in the second he actively demonstrates his ability to carry out his father's orders, as well as his own sense of self-preservation in finishing off his rival, Adonijah. Like his father, Solomon promotes his own chief of staff (Benaiah) and installs his own priestly family (Zadok). With the military and the cult under his control, Solomon has buttressed his position and come into his own as a ruler.

After an introduction emphasizing the determination, if not ruthlessness, with which he consolidates his authority, the Solomon who appears in the next eight chapters seems like a different person. No violence or intrigue of any sort clouds the image of the wise and successful king whose main concerns are the extent of his mercantile domain and his ambitious building projects, including the construction of a fitting temple for his God. Throughout this section there is little narrative drama. The tale of the two prostitutes in 3:16–28 is the only episode with some degree of tension, and the only text in which Solomon interacts directly with the people. Otherwise he is the recipient of praise and honor from both God and man, and the controlling force behind a wealthy empire which knows no threats to its prosperity. In chapters 3 and 4 the emphasis is on Solomon's wisdom; in a vision at Gibeon, God promises him the knowledge necessary to judge the people, to "discern between good and bad" (3:9). The story of the prostitutes demonstrates this wisdom in action; not only is the king capable of uncovering the truth, but the justice he declares is life-sustaining—"Give her the living child, and in no way slay it" (3:27). In contrast to David's reign, the kingdom is at peace, with "every man under his vine and under his fig tree" (4:25), Solomon receiving both physical tribute and considerable fame from his neighbors roundabout.

All this wealth and respite from war are now exploited for the greatest of the king's endeavors, the building of the Temple in Jerusalem. Fully half of the material on Solomon (5:1–9:9) is devoted to this project. The narrative moves slowly and with great attention to detail, giving a sense of grandeur and completeness. Unlike the text describing the building of the tabernacle in Exodus 25–40, Solomon is not instructed in the design of this sanctuary; we are spared a tedious account of the process of construction. The architectonics of the Temple is presented not as the embodiment of a heavenly blueprint but as a practical demonstration of Solomon's much-lauded wisdom. It is Solomon who claims to have built this "house" in 8:13, and the narrator attributes to him a great deal more of the credit than Moses receives for the tabernacle. The building process moves from without to within, beginning with the hewing and dressing of the great stones for the foundations, to the erection of the outer frame, the decoration of the inner walls, and the fashioning of the tools and utensils essential to the Temple service.

The majestic culmination of the whole process occurs in chapter 8, where the ark is brought inside the Temple with great ceremony before all the people, and sacrifices of unprecedented proportions are offered to consecrate the sanctuary. At the center of the account stands Solomon's long prayer, in which he gives expression to the basic theological contradiction inherent in the very construction of the Temple. "But will God indeed dwell on the earth?" The answer is both yes and no: "behold, the heaven and heaven of heavens cannot contain thee; how much less this house that I have builded?" (v. 27). Solomon continues, quoting God's own authorization, explaining God's indwelling as a state of constant attentiveness: "That thine eyes may be open toward this house night and day, even toward the place of which thou hast said, My name shall be there" (v. 29). This interpretation of God's presence is essential to Solomon's definition of the Temple as the focal point of all prayer. Even when the suppliant is physically dislocated from the site, his prayer is deemed most effective when directed toward the earthly locus of worship.

What is most unusual about Solomon's prayer is that it is not a petitionary response to a problem, an expression of thanksgiving, or praise for some moment of deliverance. It is, rather, a prayer *about* prayer. To be sure, Solomon begins by asking God to continue to fulfill his promise to David, but the greatest part of his prayer is about future petitions to be made in response to both natural and historical crises: famine, pestilence, disease, and defeat in war. God is implored to listen and respond in the future; the refrain "then hear thou in heaven" recurs seven times. There is here a mixture of optimism and fear, an intimation that God will be attentive to future prayers, as well as a sense of foreboding about future disasters. Most distressing is the final plea in 8:46–53, where captivity is mentioned, but not the return to the land, despite the reference to the Exodus in the very last verse. In light of Israel's fate at the end of Kings, the passage has a near-prophetic quality.

From this point on, the narrator's treatment of Solomon begins to change. In Solomon's second vision at Gibeon (1 Kings 9) God accepts his prayer and again affirms his dynastic promise. But in contrast to chapter 3, the threat of destruction of Solomon's line and of the Temple itself emphasizes the conditional nature of the covenant and makes that final section of his dedicatory prayer seem all the more ominous. The Temple no longer stands at the center of Solomon's world, and the projects described are undertaken for the king's own glory. Verse 26 begins a long catalogue of Solomon's wealth: his fleet of ships, shields and bucklers of gold, an elaborate ivory throne of unprecedented proportions, chariots and horses, not to mention the vast quantities of gold, precious gems, and spices received in tribute. Despite the praise of Solomon by the Queen of Sheba, this whole section is cast in a negative light by the ominous warning in 9:6–9 and by the narrator's overtly critical attitude in chapter 11. We cannot escape the impression that Solomon's marriages to "foreign women" are tied to the far-flung trading ventures which have brought him his wealth, and that the narrator's condemnation of the former implies a criticism of the latter. Solomon's straying may have been simply a policy of accommodation for his wives rather than reflecting an intrinsic belief in other gods. But in the eyes of the narrator, the size of the harem and the corresponding number of temples leave no doubt about the extent of his idolatry.

The remainder of the Solomon narrative alternates between oracles promising the rending of the kingdom and descriptions of rebellions against Solomon's authority by internal and external enemies. These first mentions of challenges to the king's authority effect a sharp change from the calm optimism that has previously characterized the narrative, reinforcing the narrator's claim that these are punishments for Solomon's idolatry. For the first time since chapter 2, Solomon has a rival to contend with, in the person of Jeroboam, and he again seeks to use violent means to deal with him. Of greater portent is Solomon's unprecedented lack of success, which presages the rebellion to come.

Three Themes

The Covenant with David

Solomon represents the actualization of God's covenant with David as it is formulated in 2 Samuel 7:11b–12:

> Also the Lord telleth thee that he will make thee an house. And when thy days be fulfilled, and thou shalt sleep with thy fathers, I will set up thy seed after thee, which shall proceed out of thy bowels, and I will establish his kingdom.

Inasmuch as the "house" referred to here means dynastic succession, Solomon's ascent to the throne is the beginning of the fulfillment of that promise. Thus everything which Solomon undertakes, from building projects to foreign trade, is seen as a concrete manifestation of the trustworthiness of that covenant with David.

The promise continues to be of central importance for subsequent generations. On a national level, the covenant guarantees the continued survival of Judah. The narrator repeatedly justifies Judah's resilience to dangers from without and within—Jeroboam's rebellion (1 Kings 11:12–13), God's anger over the sins of Abijam and Jehoram (1 Kings 15:4–5, 2 Kings 8:19), the near-fatal attack of Sennacherib (2 Kings 19:34, 20:6) —in terms of God's commitment to his dynastic promise to David.[5]

But this promise, whose unconditional and eternal quality had been stressed in the original vision in Samuel, is reinterpreted as dependent upon the behavior of the king:

> *If* thou wilt walk before me, as David thy father walked . . . *Then* I will establish the throne of thy kingdom upon Israel for ever . . . But *if* ye shall at all turn from following me . . . *Then* I will cut off Israel out of the land which I have given them . . . (1 Kings 9:4–7)

This rereading is crucial to Kings, for it indicates that what had been seen as a source of hope and reassurance to Israel serves also to foreshadow its destruction.

Although all kings are judged in terms of the good or evil they do "in the sight of the Lord," more than a third of the kings of Judah are also held up to the mirror of David's exemplary behavior. Thus Asa of Judah is praised for having pleased the Lord "as did David his father" (1 Kings 15:11), whereas his father Abijam is excoriated because "his heart was not perfect with the Lord his God, as the heart of David his father" (15:3). Solomon himself is first praised, then criticized according to this criterion (1 Kings 3:3, 11:4–6). Even Jeroboam of Israel is promised great things if he will follow in David's path, and is subsequently condemned for his failure to do so (1 Kings 11:38, 14:8). Perhaps the most striking illustration is found in the comment on Amaziah of Judah, who "did that which was right in the sight of the Lord, yet not like David his father" (2 Kings 14:3). One could please God yet still fail to measure up to the Davidic prototype.

The Temple

The central event of Solomon's rule, the building of the Temple in Jerusalem, is intimately bound up with the dynastic promise to David: "He shall build an house for my name, and I will establish the throne of his kingdom for ever" (2 Sam. 7:13). The account of the building process begins with the acquisition of materials from Hiram of Tyre, who "was ever a lover of David," that is, a treaty partner (1 Kings 5:1). Solomon's dedicatory prayer begins, appropriately, with a threefold reference to the covenant with David (8:24–26). The entire building narrative is ringed by two revelations to Solomon at Gibeon, emphasizing both his adherence to the Davidic model of obedience and God's intention to fulfill his promise to David (3:6, 9:4–5).

The presence of the Ark of the Covenant within the Temple is an essential part of the building's sanctity. The ark contains the stone tablets which are the physical representation of the covenantal relationship between God and Israel, while externally it serves as a pedestal for the deity. The relocation of the ark makes the Temple the guardian of that covenant, as well as the new resting place of God; immediately after it is brought in, the presence of the Lord fills its precincts (8:10). The Temple is a sacred center, a point of contact between man and God, whose power flows over into Jerusalem, if not into the entire nation.

The narrator's concerns with the physical well-being of the Temple and with proper worship there reflect his conviction that these matters profoundly affect the fate of the kingdom. Thus, despite all Solomon's great deeds, the idolatry of which he is accused in 1 Kings 11:1–13 is presented as the cause of the irreparable schism between North and South. The fact that his son Rehoboam permits popular worship of the fertility cult, the narrator intimates, leads to the looting of the Temple treasury by the Pharaoh Shishak (1 Kings 14:22–26). The narrator also expresses his displeasure with Ahaz of Judah by suggesting that the foreign altar which the king places in the Temple reflects both political and religious subservience to the Assyrians (2 Kings 16:10–18). But the most extensive description of contamination of Temple rites is reserved for Manasseh. He installs altars for the worship of a variety of deities within the Temple and encourages witchcraft, conjuring, and a whole range of objectionable practices. The end result of Manasseh's behavior, we are told, will be the complete destruction of Judah (2 Kings 21:13). Whatever the historical value of these judgments, in the eyes of the narrator the two greatest disasters in the life of Judah are the direct consequence of violations of the sanctity of the Temple and temple worship.

In contradistinction, Josiah is presented as the embodiment of the ideal of the good king precisely because of his cultic reforms. He orders extensive repairs on the Temple structure, removes and destroys the idolatrous cult objects associated with Manasseh, and centralizes worship in Jerusalem by outlawing other shrines (2 Kings 22–23). So great is the narrator's concern with the exclusive authority of the Temple that all the other "good" kings of Judah, who are described in general terms as having pleased God, are criticized for allowing cultic worship to continue outside Jerusalem: "But the high places were not taken away: the people still sacrificed and burnt incense in the high places."[6] Such a statement seriously undercuts whatever praise may have preceded it and heightens the achievements of the kings who did enforce changes.

The editorial judgments against Israel reflect similar concerns. In a global sense, the entire enterprise of the Northern Kingdom is considered corrupt because of its fundamental opposition to the religious authority of Jerusalem and because of the institutionalized idolatry of the golden calves. Accusations of Baal worship are particularly prominent in the stories of Elijah (1 Kings 18–19, 21; 2 Kings 1). As in the South, the kings singled out for praise are those who initiate purges of whatever idolatrous practices their predecessors have engaged in, such as Jehu's liquidation of all those associated with the Baal cult in 2 Kings 9–10. Yet, like all other Northern kings, Jehu has broken faith in the most basic way simply by following the example of Jeroboam and is forced to share the blame for the final destruction of Israel. In reflecting upon the causes of its fall, the narrator begins by outlining the full gamut of idolatrous behavior: the fertility cult, setting up "images and groves," human sacrifice, divination, and so forth (2 Kings 17:7–17). He closes, however, with harsh condemnation of Jeroboam as the one who "drave Israel from following the Lord, and made them sin a great sin" (17:21). Israel has been exiled for rejecting the two tenets which the narrator holds sacred: proper worship of the Lord (that is, without idols such as the golden calves) in the only place where God has said: "My name shall be there" (1 Kings 8:29).

Oracle and Fulfillment

One of the great tensions in nearly every biblical book is that between human initiative and divine control. Although every misfortune which befalls Judah or Israel is accomplished by a human enemy, these disasters are interpreted retrospectively by the narrator of Kings as agents of the divine. Thus the rebellions by Edom and Damascus during Solomon's reign are "stirred up" by God (1 Kings 11:14–23), and the Assyrians and Babylonians perform their destructions at the behest of God. But the narrator's primary means for expressing his understanding of the process of history is the mechanism of oracle and fulfillment. In contrast to the prophetic books, where the results of oracular prediction are generally not mentioned, the fulfillment of nearly every prophetic oracle in Kings is narrated in explicit detail. These events may take place within a short time, such as Ahijah's prediction of the breakup of the monarchy and its actualization in the subsequent chapter (1 Kings 11:31–39, 12:15). Or the time of fulfillment may span centuries, as with the prediction about the ultimate fate of the altar at Bethel during Jeroboam's time (1 Kings 13:1–10) and its realization during the reforms of Josiah (2 Kings 23:15–16).

The repeated use of this framework gives expression to the concept of God's control of history with a specificity not found in other books. All significant events, and many lesser ones, are demonstrated to be the result of divine intentions. The most important of these are:

1. Solomon's accession to the throne and the building of the Temple, which are seen as fulfillment of the promise to David delivered by the prophet Nathan in 2 Samuel 7:11–13.

2. The division of the United Monarchy as a punishment for Solomon's sins, as predicted by the prophet Ahijah in 1 Kings 11:29–39.

3. The destruction of the Northern Kingdom and the exile of her people as punishment for the sins of Jeroboam, as foretold by Ahijah in 1 Kings 14:15–16.

4. The destruction of Judah and the deportation of her people to Babylon. As this is the climactic event of the book, it merits prediction by more than one prophet. Isaiah mentions it to Hezekiah in 2 Kings 20:17–18 with reference to the king's offspring. Anonymous prophets in 21:13–14 extend the threat to the entire community, comparing its fate to that of Northern Israel. The prophetess Huldah reiterates this verdict to Josiah in 22:16–17, as does the narrator in 23:26–27. The statement of the fulfillment of the prophecy appears finally in 24:2–4. Although such "predictability" minimizes the level of suspense in the story, it serves the narrator's theological purpose admirably. The exile is not a capricious rejection by God, but a deliberate response to Israel's sins that was foretold time and again.

Another major effect of this technique is the enhancement of the role of the prophet. There is no prophetic figure in Kings (except those who are intentionally proved false) whose words do not come to pass, either as predicted or with some degree of reinterpretation.[7] The ideal of prophecy invoked here is that of Deuteronomy 18:22: true prophecy is that which actually comes about, but "if the thing follow not, nor come to pass, that is the thing which the Lord hath not spoken." The classic power struggle in Kings is that between prophet and king, and the former is always shown to be the person of greater authority, even though political and military might resides with the monarch. The triumph of prophetic over royal authority is illustrated by Nathan's role in the very first chapter of Kings. Although no oracles are involved, it is the prophet who coerces David into honoring an oath (which he may or may not have sworn) promising the throne to Solomon. Despite the imbalance of power, the prophet is usually impervious to the threats of the king, as Elijah proves victorious over Ahab and over his son Ahaziah. But the example of Micaiah ben Imlah in 1 Kings 22 presents a more ironic vision. Enraged at the prophet's prediction of his impending death in battle, Ahab orders him jailed "until I come in peace" (v. 27). Ahab does not return, nor do we hear anything further of Micaiah; the accuracy of his prophecy has sealed his own fate as well as that of the king.

Most of the prophetic figures in Kings exist primarily for the oracles they deliver, but Elijah and Elisha stand out as more complex characters whose careers extend beyond their political involvements. Both are strongly associated with the common people, and many of the tales about them have a legendary or folktale quality.[8] In a book which is almost entirely about the ruling classes, these stories restore a sense of everyday reality and suggest something of the popular support for the prophet's authority. The styles of the two figures are very different. Elijah is aloof, if not mysterious, in his comings and goings, constantly at odds with the crown, even forced to flee for his life in 1 Kings 19. He has a flair for the dramatic, best illustrated by the contest with the Baal prophets in 1 Kings 18. By contrast, Elisha is involved in the daily affairs of the prophetic guild of which he is the leader. He is rarely hostile to royal authority, even serving as an adviser to the king in 2 Kings 3 and 6.

Although the narrative style of prophecy and fulfillment heightens the importance of the Mosaic prophet, Elijah carries this idea further. Not only is he like Moses in his prophetic role as messenger to the people, but he is portrayed as a Moses *redivivus*. Elijah experiences a divine revelation at Mount Sinai (Horeb) after a journey of forty days in the desert (1 Kings 19). Like Moses, he is fed in the wilderness by God (1 Kings 17:4, 19:5–7) and provides food for others as well (17:14–16). The slaughter of the priests of Baal as a response to idolatry in 1 Kings 18 is reminiscent of the aftermath of the Golden Calf incident in Exodus 32:26–29. Most striking, however, is the series of events surrounding the prophet's death in 2 Kings 2. Accompanied by Elisha, he crosses the Jordan to die on the other side. Unlike any other prophet but Moses, his death is mysterious, and his place of burial is unknown (Deut. 34:6). In an unprecedented move, he appoints his own successor in the person of Elisha, whose similarity to Joshua in this story is unmistakable: he splits the waters of the Jordan in order to cross into the land and then assumes command of his "people," the band of prophets who were formerly loyal to Elijah. That his first stop along the way is Jericho helps to round out the analogy.

The purpose of this extended parallel is primarily theological. By invoking the figure of Moses, the narrator also recalls the Covenant at Sinai as the point at which all Israel bound itself to God in response to a fiery revelation. At that same moment, the people empowered Moses to act as the mediator of that covenant (Exod. 20:18–21, Deut. 5:24–29). In 1 Kings 18 the people return to their covenant with the God of Israel and favor Elijah over the political authority of the king. But this new revelation is also intended as a repudiation of the god Baal, who, as a storm god, was perceived as showing himself in thunder and lightning, in a manner too close to the traditional image of the Sinaitic revelation. The crucial redefinition of the manifestation of Israel's God appears in 1 Kings 19, where he is explicitly located beyond the strong wind, above the earthquake and the fire, in the "still small voice" (v. 12). "The *qol Baal*, the thunderous voice of Baal, has become the *qol demama daqqa*, the imperceptible whisper."[9]

NOTES

1. See Moshe Weinfeld, *Deuteronomy and the Deuteronomic School* (Oxford, 1972), pp. 320–324.

2. Although Joshua is sanctified as Moses' replacement (Num. 27:18, Deut. 34:9), he himself is not a prophet.

3. Meir Sternberg, *The Poetics of Biblical Narrative: Ideological Literature and the Drama of Reading* (Bloomington and Indianapolis, 1985), p. 431.

4. Benjamin Uffenheimer, *Hanevu'ah Haqedumah Beyisrael* [Ancient prophecy in Israel] (Jerusalem, 1973), pp. 260–262.

5. Gerhard von Rad interprets this continued appeal to the Davidic covenant, as well as the release of King Jehoiachin from prison at the very end of Kings, as an optimistic counterpoint to the theme of inevitable destruction; "The Deuteronomic Theology of History in I and II Kings," in *The Problem of the Hexateuch and Other Essays*, trans. E. Dicken (New York, 1966), pp. 219–221.

6. This statement is made of Joash (2 Kings 12:3) and, with variations, of Asa, Jehoshaphat, Amaziah, Azariah, and Jotham (1 Kings 15:14, 22:43; 2 Kings 14:4, 15:4, and 15:35, respectively).

7. One such example of reinterpretation is found in 1 Kings 21:27–29.

8. Alexander Rofé finds a variety of different genres in these tales; "The Classification of the Prophetical Stories," *Journal of Biblical Literature*, 89 (1970), 427–444.

9. Frank M. Cross, "Yahweh and Baal," in *Canaanite Myth and Hebrew Epic* (Cambridge, Mass., 1973), p. 194.

SUGGESTED FURTHER READINGS

Robert L. Cohn, "Form and Perspective in 2 Kings 5," *Vetus Testamentum*, 33 (1983), 171–184.

Robert L. Cohn, "Literary Technique in the Jeroboam Narrative," *Zeitschrift für die alttestamentliche Wissenschaft*, 97 (1985), 23–35.

David Jobling, "Ahab's Quest for Rain: Text and Context in 1 Kings 17–18," in *The Sense of Biblical Narrative* (Sheffield, 1978), pp. 63–88.

Yair Zakovitch, "The Tale of Naboth's Vineyard: 1 Kings 21," in Meir Weiss, ed., *The Bible from Within* (Jerusalem, 1984), pp. 379–405.

Jerusalem

Isaiah

Luis Alonso Schökel

THE Book of Isaiah is a collection of collections, like a lake into which the waters of various rivers and tributaries flow. It is customary to divide it into three parts: Isaiah, chapters 1–39; Deutero-Isaiah, chapters 40–55; and Trito-Isaiah, chapters 56–66. The first part may be subdivided into six units: chapters 1–12, a series of oracles, largely by Isaiah; 13–23, oracles against pagans, many of which were composed later; 24–27, eschatology, added very late as a conclusion to the series of oracles against the pagans; 28–33, a new series of prophecies by Isaiah with several late insertions; 34–35, a diptych, eschatological in character, linked to chapter 13 and to the style of Deutero-Isaiah; and 36–39, a narrative section, with poems inset.

The second part (chaps. 40–55) is the most compact and homogeneous and responds to the historical situation of the Exile, anticipating the return to Zion. The third part (chaps. 56–66) continues some themes of the second, following its style while introducing oracles whose subject is judgment. It closes with a new eschatology, chapters 65–66, repeating almost fifty words from chapter 1 and thus enclosing the entire book in a gigantic envelope structure.

Isaiah, one of the richest and most important books of the Old Testament, brings into focus centuries of historical experience and poetic concerns. The events covered by Isaiah himself unfold between about 767 and 698 B.C.E., as is indicated in the list of kings' reigns in the superscription. The prophetic calling, according to 6:1, occurred in 740 B.C.E. Deutero-Isaiah is situated about 553–539 B.C.E. Trito-Isaiah appears to be post-Exilic.

Isaiah

Today few scholars regard Isaiah as the work of a single poet. Even a substantial part of chapters 1–39 has been attributed to other authors, and, of the remaining oracles, numerous verses may be considered as layers of later sedimentation. No one today attributes to Isaiah chapters 24–27, most of 13–14, a good part of 31–33, or the second half of 11. From chapter 10 we must exclude at least verses 10–12. But if we also eliminate the doubtful or disputed verses, such as 2:2–5 and 11:1–9, where shall we encounter sufficiently important poems? A compromise solution consists in moving through the book, stopping to take note of the most important poems, regardless of authorship. Our concern is the book rather than its author, though we do not wish to overlook him entirely. In the following paragraphs I shall concentrate on the stylistic elements commonly employed in chapters 1–39 and on the poetic world of chapters 40–66.

Although in the prophetic collections we cannot speak about personal styles because the tradition tends to concentrate on common themes and forms, some special traits permit us to consider Isaiah as a classical writer: classical because of the distance he places between experience and the poem. That is, rather than allowing the experience, however traumatic, to break out spontaneously like a scream, he transforms it consciously into poetry. Similarly, Isaiah does not insert himself into the poem in order to express his own reactions; he is much more objective than subjective. He does not use the "lyric irruption" so characteristic of Jeremiah. Add to this a formal perfection and a particularity of style, achieved by numerous resources which he handles masterfully. The poetic distance and concern with form tell us that we are very far from ecstatic, half-conscious, spontaneous outbursts. The prophetic "oracles" may be brief, but they are considerably more than loose oracular phrases.

Although the poetry of Isaiah is objective, in that it does not seek to express personal emotions, it is an intensely rhetorical poetry. The prophet wants his words to create a particular reaction in his listeners: he wants to affect them, shake them, motivate them by confronting them with transcendental issues. From the first, he implores, "Hear, O heavens, and give ear, O earth: for the Lord hath spoken" (1:2), instead of "Hear, O Israel," as if the people of Israel were not listening and the speaker had to implore nature to be the witness of God. Note the emphatic, initial alliteration, *shim'u shamayim*. In the second oracle (1:10–20) he confronts the "rulers of Sodom, the people of Gomorrah"—no *captatio benevolentiae*, no currying the goodwill of the audience, but—a violent shaking, uniting the people with their vicious overlords. The third oracle (1:21–26) begins with a lyric complaint that is in reality a denunciation seeking a change of heart, if not the prognostication of an inevitable punishment.

A noteworthy example of the movement from the lyrical to the rhetorical within a single poem is 5:1–7. The lyric tone is announced in the title, "A Song of My Beloved," and in the modulations of the first person, singing the trials of love's labors lost. A song of love is disguised as a worksong. Suddenly, in the third verse, shifting toward the audience, the poem appeals to the jury in a legal dispute on love: look at all he has done for her and yet she refuses to reciprocate. The rhetorical artifice creates an ironic twist: the listeners become the judges of their own conduct (like David listening to Nathan's parable, 2 Sam. 12).

Another rhetorical device consists in evoking the response of the listeners in order to turn it back against them, creating a boomerang effect. In 28:9–13 the listeners mock the prophet, reducing his oracles to the level of a grade-school lesson in the ABCs. Isaiah picks up the joke, transforms it into the unintelligible language of an implacable enemy, and hurls it back at the speakers.

Between the lyrical and the rhetorical is mockery—the taunting description, the satire—seen, for example, in the vignette describing in detail the coquettish walk and wanton glances of the women of Zion (3:16), listing their physical adornments and personal belongings (3:19–23). A related satiric scene, the representation of the drunken magistrates (28:7–8), is frankly brutal.

In accord with the rhetoric and the culture of the epoch, the prophet composes poetry destined for oral recitation, perhaps as a ballad or song (see Ezek. 33:37). The oral character of the poetry—the auditory effects and the great importance given to the sonorous quality of the words—affects the composition. Modern scholars should try to listen to it. Repetitions or similar sounds link words and parallel phrases which then unite or contrast with one another. A dominant sound or a play on words may become serious and even tragic; paronomasia draws out of a name an entire destiny. The sound delights, surprises, emphasizes, and aids the memory. Here are a few examples from the first chapters:

1:4 *hoy goy* ("ah, nation"): the noun rhymes with the interjection, as if it were the echo of a shout.

1:10 *'am 'amora* ("people of Gomorrah"): "people" appears almost as if it were a part of "Gomorrah."

1:18 *kashanim . . . kasheleg* ("like scarlet . . . like snow"): the sounds are linked here in order to contrast the opposed meanings.

1:19–20 *to' khelu . . . te' uklu* ("shall eat . . . shall be eaten" [AR]): a play of antonyms.

2:12 *heharim haramim* ("high mountains"): an effect something like "*mountains eminent*" in English.

3:6 *simlah lekha . . . hamakhshelah* ("you have a mantle . . . heap of ruins" [AT]).

The Hebrew phrase, because of the simplicity of syntactical articulation and the scarcity of adjectives and adverbs, is customarily short. Only a few oratorical texts resort to an elaborate phrasing, with subordinate clauses (a good example is Deut. 8:7–18). Likewise, the best Hebrew narration advances in a succession of brief phrases. This syntactic simplicity can present a challenge for the poet who has to shape, concentrate, oppose, surprise, or provoke his audience. He may select a phrase suggesting a solemn beginning, a polished closing statement, or a phrase which halts and wounds the listener in its cleverness, its emotional charge, or its enigmatic reference.

The third oracle (1:21–26) begins with a complaint of five words rhymed in *ah*: *'eikhah haytah lezonah qiryah ne' manah*, "How is the faithful city become a harlot," and concludes: "You shall be called Faithful-City, Justice-ville" [AT].

Here are a few more instances of compact phrases that have an arresting or epigrammatic force.

> If you don't believe, you won't survive.   (7:9 [AT])
>
> I will trust and not fear.   (12:2 [AT])
>
> For the cry is gone round about the borders of Moab.   (15:8)
>
> Let us eat and drink; for to morrow we shall die.   (22:13)
>
> We have made lies our refuge and in falsehood we have taken shelter. (28:15 [RSV])

Many of these phrases are paralleled by others and reveal their force in context. Logically, they impose a slow, emphatic delivery. On the other hand, there are verses that occur more than once, so that they begin to etch themselves into one's memory. Perhaps there may even have been music that accentuated the impact of such phrases. This style of composition is conceived for oral recitation but it is not improvised. It reveals a conscious and controlled craft that makes enormous formal demands on the poet.

The short Hebrew phrase lends itself to *parallelism* in poetry. Parallelism is, above all, a formal resource for the articulation of discourse, and in its most basic form is dyadic, though three- and four-part divisions are not uncommon. Beyond four begins a series. Parallelism consists in the formal correspondence of two consecutive brief utterances. The degree of correspondence may vary, and should, to avoid monotony. By means of parallelism the poet is able to analyze one situation in two ways; he can dwell upon and show first one side and then the reverse of the same reality. In the corresponding half he may introduce an alternate rhythm. Because parallelism is found so frequently in all genres of Hebrew poetry, it is best to focus on those examples composed with a particular end in mind. Isaiah is a master in the original use of this method.

Verse 1:4 presents, after an interjection which governs everything that follows, four nouns each with its adjective. They proceed in an order of increasing proximity to God. The final adjective rings with the most force: "Ah, sinful nation, people laden with iniquity, offspring of wicked men, sons degenerate" [AT]. In verse 7 we hear the articulation of parallelism of the $a + a' + b$ type, containing rhymes which do not respond to the formal division. There are four possessive "your"s and three nouns, "country," "cities," "land." By departing from the rigorous form, the fragment "in your presence" adds a tragic element. Listen to the effect:

> Your country is desolate, your cities burned out,
> your land, in your presence, aliens devour. [AT]

The oracle 1:2–10 ends with a parallelism whose extreme incisiveness, reinforcing rhyme, and evocation of the wicked cities cause listeners to shudder: "we should have been like Sodom, become like Gomorrah" [AT], *kisdom hayinu la'amorah daminu* (1:9).

There is nothing more conventional than the opposition of good and bad which Isaiah takes advantage of in 1:16–17 in order to join density with urgency. Two alliterative verbs and two nouns say it all: *limdu heytev dirshu misphat*, "cease to do evil, learn to do good."

In one line (29:1) the poet concentrates the swift advance of time and its inexorable repetition: "Add year to year, / let the feasts run their round" [AT]. An imperative and jussive, the duplication of "year," the feasts converted into an autonomous subject of the annual cycle—one could hardly pack more material into six words.

More complex is 29:15, which contains secondary bifurcation in the third line and crossed correspondences or chiastic elements: counsel/deeds, deep/hide/darkness; these are words of challenge, and YHWH stands alone. The translation gives some idea of the original asymmetry:

> Woe to those who hide deep from the Lord their counsel,
> whose deeds are in the dark,
> and who say: Who sees us? Who knows us? [AT]

Compare this calculated asymmetry with the regularity found in 30:1: "who carry out a plan, but not mine; / and who make a league, but not of my spirit" [AT].

The regularity of parallelism achieves a special effect in a kind of military advance. After an introductory line, the rhythmic march files by rapidly, like its theme, indefatigable and precise (5:26b–29):

> and lo, swiftly, speedily it comes!
> None is weary, none stumbles,
> none slumbers, none sleeps;
> not a waistcloth is loose,
> not a sandal thong is broken;
> their arrows are sharp, their bows bent,
> their horses' hoofs seem like flint,
> their wheels like the whirlwind:
> Their roaring is like a lion,
> they roar like young lions:
> they growl and seize their prey,
> they carry it off, and none can rescue. [RSV]

Enumerative series in poetry are a potential weakness because of their tendency to become reduced to simple catalogues. The poet has to control the art of selection and combination. He must be vigilant to insure against monotony that will destroy the efficacy of the verse. An excellent example is found in the enumeration of the lofty objects doomed for destruction in 2:12–19. It is as if the poet had erected two rows of imposing, even towering, objects and, stirring against them a fierce wind, had brought them down effortlessly. In the end, only God towers. An anaphoric repetition evokes the assault in ten cadences: tall objects in general, cedars and oaks, mountains and hills (nature), towers and walls (the civilized world), ships and boats (the commercial world). Rhymes and alliterations gather, level out and smooth over the series of obstacles. The final contrast is man brought low and the Lord exalted. Compare with this the simple enumeration in 3:2a. In an oracle against Egypt the poet recounts the misfortunes that will afflict the land and the various professions (19:5–10): sea, rivers, canals, streams; reeds, rushes, herbs, sown grasses; hook and net fishermen, wool workers and weavers, masters and day laborers. The series gives the impression of unity, without particular distinction in detail, except the sole, effective annotation: "its canals will become foul" (19:6 [AT]).

Many poetic descriptions bring together a series of features which stylize and recreate the image of an object or action. The description may contain only a single pair of salient features capable of representing or evoking the whole. An example is the characterization of the adversary in 9:5 as "all boots trampling with thump, / all garments rolled in blood" [AT]. An auditory account and a visual evocation conjure up the war in the reader's fantasy. A siege is concentrated in two details: "I will besiege you with towers, / and I will raise siegeworks against you" (29:3 [AT]). A whole action is described in two rapid strokes: "He will cast to the earth with the hand, / with the feet he will trample the proud crown of the drunkards of Ephraim" (28:3 [AT]). We find both the tranquil description, executed stroke by stroke, and the kind of compressed description we call characterization. Isaiah is a master of the second type, as two verses in chapter 5 show:

> Shame on you! you who rise early in the morning
>   to go in pursuit of liquor
> and draw out the evening inflamed with wine.   (v. 11 [NEB])

> Shame on you! you mighty topers,
>   valiant mixers of drink.   (v. 22 [NEB])

Onomatopoeia, a form of description in which the arrangement of phonemes in a given language imitates in sound the meaning of words, naturally is difficult to translate. The Revised Standard Version translates 5:24 as "the tongue of fire devours the stubble," missing the sound of the

crackling and the hissing in the original Hebrew: *ke'khol qash leshon 'esh*.
The deep roar of the sea sounds in the King James Version's 5:30, "They
shall roar against them on that day like the roaring of the sea," though it
is very far from the original, with its repetitions of *h* and *m* and its sonorous
ending: *weyinhom 'alaw bayom hahu kenahamat yam*. A famous instance of
onomatopoeia is the chirping of nestlings in 10:14: *potseh peh umetsaptsep*;
and, likewise, the very obvious comparison of 17:12: "Ah, the thunder of
many peoples, they thunder like the thundering of the sea!/ah, the roar
of nations, they roar like the roaring of mighty waters" [RSV]. The sound
of the original makes this evocation of roaring waves quite awesome: *hoy
hamon 'amim rabim kahmot yamim yehmayun ushe'on le'umim kishe'on mayim
kabirim yisha'un*.

An even more subtle form of reinforcement of meaning by sound is
the sonorous metaphor which suggests movement or action by a phonetic
assimilation of clustered words. Verse 18:2 describes the rapid movement
of the messengers, with perhaps sounds similar to *galgal*, "wheel": *lekhu
melakhim qalim 'el goy*, "Go, ye swift messengers, to a nation."

The shaping of an imaginative world is strongly felt in the poetry of
Isaiah, as in almost all the biblical prophets. He creates from nature,
domestic or city life, observed in significant moments. The imaginative
elements pass into the poem with relative objectivity, except when the
poem turns to the fantastic with theophanies of mythical origin. Metaphor
is rare; simile is frequent.

Isaiah usually develops comparisons with sobriety. "As when a hun-
gry man dreams he is eating and awakes, the stomach empty; or when a
thirsty man dreams he is drinking and awakes, the throat dry" (29:8 [AT]).
A vision not understood is like a closed book that neither the illiterate nor
the educated can read (29:11). The sudden catastrophe, though expected,
is compared to a wall that collapses; the poet describes it with precision:
"like a break in a high wall, bulging out and about to collapse, whose
crash comes suddenly, in an instant" (30:13 [AT]); to this he adds another
comparison from daily life, the breaking of pottery (30:14). The routing
of a squadron is announced with a hyperbolic comparison: "till ye be left
as a beacon upon the top of a mountain/ and as an ensign on a hill" (30:17).
This may be contrasted with a fantastic vision of the theophany: the
elemental fire raging torrentially and unceasingly (30:27–28, 33):

> Behold, the name of the Lord comes from far,
>   burning in anger, in dense rising smoke [AR]:
> his lips are full of indignation,
>   and his tongue as a devouring fire:
> And his breath, as an overflowing stream,
>   shall reach up to the neck . . . [AR]
> a burning place . . . is made ready [RSV],
>   he hath made it deep and large:

> the pile thereof is fire and much wood;
> the breath of the Lord,
> like a stream of brimstone, doth kindle it.

The line omitted from verse 28 above contains qualifiers of unusual forcefulness and originality. Two fascinating images say that the Lord is going to sift out and then bridle the nations; that is, to separate them in order to break, to bridle their fury. Isaiah adds to these two surprising modifiers: "the sieve of destruction and the bridle of misguidance" (30:28).

A curious and surprising technique for comparison bases itself on the following development. Normally an equation is formed by a subordinate clause, A, and then the principal clause, B. At times clause B is amplified or clarified. But Isaiah occasionally abandons B and amplifies A in a way that illumines the latter obliquely. The normal form of what amounts to a biblical cliché would run like this: Wickedness is like a devouring fire which destroys the evildoer. Isaiah turns from the evildoer to the fire (9:18):

> For wickedness burneth as the fire:
> it shall devour the briers and thorns,
> and shall kindle in the thickets of the forest,
> and they shall mount up like the lifting up of smoke.

(For a more concentrated example of this technique, see Sirach 9:10 and Ps. 127:4–5).

The most interesting literary aspect of Isaiah, as with many other biblical poets, is the transformation of an experienced reality into a new, coherent, poetic universe. Although we do not have the facts to reconstruct the genesis of particular poems because the prophet did not leave us the requisite information, the evidence of the text allows us the following heuristic maneuver. The poet contemplates an actual pilgrimage of the tribes to a liturgical festival at the central sanctuary of Zion (Passover, Pentecost). A variety of tribes, perhaps with an array of different accents and garments, converge or assemble, ascending the mountain in response to the allure of the sanctuary where the Torah is read and the word of God proclaimed; peace and harmony mingle within diversity. This view transforms itself into a vision: the hill recedes into the temporal distance of the future, then grows and stands out in a landscape of mountains; nations and peoples converge, flowing together like rivers, the children of the house of Jacob (fraternal tribes born of the same father) ascend; peace reigns, not imposed by arms but by sheer force of attraction to the Law and to the Word. Such is the vision brought together in 2:2–5 (with a variant in Micah 4:1–4), the famous evocation of a future when the peoples will "go up to the mountain of the Lord" and learn how "nation shall not lift up sword against nation, neither shall they learn war any more."

A different example of this visionary faculty is in 8:7–8, where the invading enemy army is transformed into a rising, relentless flood:

> The Lord bringeth up upon them
> > the waters of the river, strong and many . . .
> and he shall come up over all his channels,
> > and go over all his banks;
> And he shall pass through Judah;
> > he shall overflow and go over,
> > > he shall reach even to the neck;
> and the stretching out of his wings shall fill
> > the breadth of thy land, O Immanuel.

In another passage (7:18–19), invading troops give way to swarms of horseflies and bumblebees that "shall come, and shall rest all of them in the desolate valleys, / and in the holes of the rocks, / and upon all thorns, and upon all bushes." Jerusalem is a bride (a symbol taken from Hosea): at first she is loyal, later an adulteress, and, later yet, purified and loyal once more (1:21–26). The examples here are coherent images with no propensity toward intellectual allegory.

In 11:1–9, the celebrated vision of the ideal king who will spring from the stem of Jesse, the author creates a wide and harmonious universe through the pronounced use of more regular parallelisms. The elements all come into play: the four winds (KJV: "spirits"; 11:2) alight upon the budding sprout; the sea is sheer plenitude; the plant world is a cut stump that resprouts; the animal world is peaceful; wild beasts and domestic animals mingle together in one dwelling watched over by a small child; even the old enemy serpent is soothed by the child. In the midst of all this, the heir of David governs justly.

There is a magnificent satire (14:4–21) in the form of an elegy to an anonymous king which, because of its very anonymity, addresses itself to many. The powerful aggressor has died and celebration fills the land: there are shouts of jubilation; cypresses and cedars rejoice: "no hewer comes against us" [AT]. Likewise, in the habitation of the dead, the news is received with a chorus of mocking salutations, proclaiming the fall of one who aspired to scale heaven's ladder but instead descended to the uttermost reaches of the abyss.

On the other hand, the proclamation of 30:18–26 (probably not the work of Isaiah) does not achieve a successful imaginative coherence, and thus illustrates by way of contrast how effective are the more characteristic creations of a coherent poetic world. Here, the people undergo trials as a chastisement for their evildoings, but, it is said, if they cast off their idols and convert, God will change their fortune. Oppressors will die; their towers—symbols of power—will be destroyed. The fields will blossom. Rivers and streams will furrow through dry mountains. Abruptly, the poet jumps from the domestic world to wondrous eschatological images: "the light of the moon shall be as the light of the sun, / and the light of the sun shall be sevenfold, as the light of seven days" (v. 26). The image in itself may be striking, but the poem as a whole does not cohere.

The narrative section, chapters 36–39, includes several poems. The most interesting are the satires of the prophet against the haughty and arrogant king of Assyria, and the supplication of Hezekiah in his affliction. The final lines of the satire reduce the emperor to the status of an animal (37:29):

> therefore will I put my hook in thy nose,
>   and my bit [AR] in thy lips,
> and I will turn thee back on [AR] the way
>   by which thou camest.

Hezekiah's oration after recovering from his near-fatal illness describes the brevity of his unfortunate life and demonstrates the intertwining of eloquent, reflective poetry with the narrative strands of the book (38:12):

> My dwelling is plucked up and removed from me
>   like a shepherd's tent;
> like a weaver I have rolled up my life;
>   he cuts me off from the loom. [RSV]

Deutero-Isaiah

The anonymous prophet known as Second Isaiah (Deutero-Isaiah), because his work is incorporated in the Book of Isaiah, ranks among the great religious poets. He is the poet of the return, the poet of hope. At first reading, we are struck by the rhetorical flow of the words: the broad, four-part parallelisms with a corresponding richness of vocabulary. It is a rhetoric directed to and against the audience, based on an enthusiastic and contagious lyricism. For the attentive ear, there is an exquisite sonorous quality which at moments reaches true virtuosity. Beyond this, there is a richness of imagery and a greatness of vision—greatness, not grandiosity. The poetry exhibits a freedom and joy sufficient to close distances, boldness that reaches to the sky. All of this is joined by a passion that touches the heart and succeeds.

The beginning (40:1–11) is like a brief overture in which the major themes, tonality, and poetic procedures are announced. The double imperative of the opening verse repeats like a musical motif. It woos or "talks to the heart," with a penetrating gentleness rather than with aggressiveness. Immediately, the theme of return enters in the prodigious transformation of the desert highway on which the "Glory of the Lord" will appear (the glory that Ezekiel saw departing Jerusalem and vowed would return). Then the wind or breath (*ruah*) of God is mentioned: it is a powerful wind, capable of withering all vegetation and all human production hostile to his project. The word of God follows which "is always fulfilled" (v. 8). Glory, spirit, word. There is fear neither of obstacles on the road nor of the opposition of men: "All flesh is grass" (v. 6). The prophet is a herald approaching Jerusalem to announce the great news from his mountain pulpit: "Here is your God" (v. 9 [AT]). He comes as a pastor, guiding his people, guarding especially the multitude of the weak and the lame. The scene is limited on the one side by a Jerusalem (a personification of the people) that suffers in exile, and on the other side by a Jerusalem that awaits in the homeland. Crossing the huge and marvelous scene, anonymous voices interweave with one another. This is, preeminently, the poetry of hope.

The two following examples display both a sonorous quality and strong correspondences. In 40:4, *wehaya he'aqob lemishor weharekhasim lebiq'ah*, "the tortuous will be straight, the rugged will be plain [AT]," a chiasm of sound, *'qb-bq'h/mshr-rks*, reveals the radical reversal prophesied.

'al har gaboah 'ali lakh	*mebaseret tsiyon*
harimi bakoah qolekh	*mebaseret yerushalem*
harimi 'al tira'	
Climb up to a mountaintop,	you who bring Zion good news
lift up your voice aloud	you who bring Jerusalem good news
lift up, fear not. (40:9 [AT])	

This prophet readily clambers up a mountain, eager to sing forth and proclaim. His message has a dramatic quality that defies all manner of resistance: idols, empires, nature, the weakness of the exiled, the distrust and dispiritedness of those to be liberated. Each of these obstacles will be discussed in turn.

Were we to judge from the historical evidence at the time, we might have supposed that the Babylonian gods had overpowered the God of Israel. Perhaps they were "rival gods"—in violation of the First Commandment. The poet approaches this theme on two levels: the first is ironic, picturesque, and superficial, the other radical and profound. To identify idolatry with the adoration bestowed on a manufactured work of rock or wood is a superficial vision which may answer to an unreflective form of popular religion, but it provides the poet ample opportunity for satiric development. In 44:12–20 we read a prose version with considerable descriptive flair: the realism of the scene underscores the nature of mere manufacture and justifies the poet's withering view of idolatry. Such a presentation of the problem must have made an impression on some of the listeners. More convincing, however, is the other poetic recourse: the depiction of a lawsuit or challenge by God to the other gods. The poet grants these gods a fictitious reality for the sake of creating a public contest. He does this to show their ontological nullity—their total incapacity to foretell or to bring events to pass. These gods, "the rivals of God" (Exod. 20:3), who exist by means of poetic concession, are not just less than the God of Israel; simply, they do not exist. Their feigned existence and works are unmasked and annulled. This analysis goes to the theological root of the issue. The literary device of a lawsuit is ingenious. Who would not be interested in a dispute, a challenge, a tournament? It is a guaranteed crowd-pleaser. Suggested by the basic concept of rival gods, it may recall the historical contest at Carmel between Elijah and the prophets of Baal (1 Kings 18).

Babylonia is the conquering and dominating empire. What power can a handful of exiles wield against her? "Shall the prey be taken from the mighty?" (49:24). Yet Babylonia is defenseless before God and before his historical ambassador, Cyrus (41:1–5, 43:14, 45:1–6, 48:12–15). "Who are you that you fear a mortal, / a man who is like the grass?" (51:12). It is as if a man had no right to fear another human, when he has God on his side. To fear under such circumstances is an offense to the Protector:

> And forgettest the Lord thy Maker,
>   that hath stretched forth the heavens and laid the
>   foundations of the earth;
> and hast feared continually every day
>   because of the fury of the oppressor,
> as if he were ready to destroy? (51:13)

Just as Jerusalem is the focus and personification of the whole Judean community, so the Babylonian capital represents the entire enemy nation. In the vein of the classical oracles against empires and pagan rulers, the poet composes a satire against Babel (chap. 47). Babel was a rich, powerful mistress, tender and delicate, sure of herself: "you felt secure in your wickedness," "you reigned securely"; she considered herself superior to everyone and unique: "I shall be mistress forever . . . I am, and there is no one besides me" (vv. 7, 10 [AT]). Such claims are virtually a pretense to deification against the background of the author's own language. Among her counselors, she consults magic, sorcerers, and the bureaucratic predictions of astrologers. Later, the mistress is sentenced to public shame and isolation:

> Take the millstones, and grind meal:
>   put off thy veil, strip off thy robe [AR],
>   uncover the thigh, pass over the rivers.
> Thy nakedness shall be uncovered,
>   yea, thy shame shall be seen. (47:2–3)

The oracle is dedicated to what was then the capital of the world, the superpower of its time. The satire is meant to be read as a complete contrast to the loving messages directed to the mistress, Jerusalem, the disloyal wife, once rejected but now forgiven and reconciled. This is a poet who revels in powerful contrasts.

The way back from Babylonia to Jerusalem is neither easy nor comfortable for a displaced community. But the poet is not interested in describing the trek realistically. Quite to the contrary, in order to engage the imagination of his countrymen, he conjures up a miraculous journey, a transfigured peregrination, a new Exodus. From the old Exodus—which paradoxically he invites the people to forget (43:18)—he takes numerous motifs in order to transform them. Above all, the leaving:

> Go ye forth of Babylon, flee ye from the Chaldeans. (48:20)

> He who is bowed down shall speedily be released. (51:14 [RSV])

> Depart ye, depart ye, go ye out from thence,
>   touch no unclean thing;
>   go ye out of the midst of her;
>   be ye clean, that bear the vessels of the Lord.
> For ye shall not go out with haste,
>   nor go by flight:
> for the Lord will go before you;
>   and the God of Israel will be your reward. (52:11–12)

> For ye shall go out with joy,
>   and be led forth with peace. (55:12)

What in reality will be an exhausting march is converted into a joyous procession, with water abounding in the wilderness. What was miraculous in the hands of Moses is no more than ordinary this time:

> I will open rivers in high places,
>   and fountains in the midst of the valleys;
> I will make the wilderness a pool of water,
>   and the dry land springs of water. (41:18)

(Note the quadruple synonymy, as if these were four rivers in a recreated paradise.) The desert is transformed into a vast park of copious wood and shade, with seven species of trees—a new paradise: cedar, acacia, myrtle, olive, cypress, plane, pine (41:19). The obstacles on the road are paved over, like the path of a sacred procession: "and a highway shall be there, / and it shall be called The Sacred Way" (35:8 [AT]). Even more, nature, in an act of ecological solidarity, pays homage to the caravan of repatriates: "break forth into singing, O mountains: / for the Lord hath comforted his people" (49:13); "the mountains and the hills shall break forth before you into singing, / and all the trees of the field shall clap their hands" (55:12). The entire chapter 35 synthesizes the transformation as seen in themes and styles characteristic of Deutero-Isaiah (being, it would seem, a poem by the prophet of Exile that somehow was slipped into the first forty chapters). It could be titled a "Hymn of Joy." Four-part synonyms measure the movement of the procession through the wilderness. The transformation revives barren nature, restores mutilated bodies, and revitalizes the broken spirit. In the poet's hyperbolic language, the cripple does not walk, but leaps; the mute does not speak, but sings. A singular current of joy cuts across, irrigates, and gives life to everything. Lions, jackals, all ferocious beasts will disappear. There is no room for sadness in this caravan; at the vanguard, a personified Happiness leads, while Joy brings up the rear.

In Deutero-Isaiah the fatalistically resigned and obstinately dispirited people become imbued with hope. Believing that God had wearied of them, they had nothing to hope for. Swiftly and concisely, the poet reverses the argument, rallying the people while explaining the flight: it is not God, the imaginative and all-powerful, who wearies, but the people, even the strongest and most agile among them. God gives strength to the weak:

> they that wait upon the Lord shall renew their strength;
>   they shall mount up with wings as eagles,
> they shall run, and not be weary;
>   and they shall walk, and not faint.   (40:31)

A great enemy of hope is nostalgia: the dream of a golden past, never to return. Devoting excessive time to the past, the people neither see the present nor plan for the future. The prophet denounces this paralyzing nostalgia, and against the traditional teaching about memory (Ps. 78:5–7), he boldly instructs them, "remember ye not the former things" (43:18), so that they may comprehend the approach of a new future. At this point, the poet introduces one of his central symbols of fecundity: the future emerges as a seed shooting forth and opens for itself a way upward. It is, at the same time, a touching reality and a promising one. We observe thoughtfully and with emotion this sprout, this sign of hope. In another passage (42:14) the symbol of fecundity is more forthright: the poet presents God as a pregnant woman who "will gasp and pant" [AT] as she gives birth. God, pregnant with the future, is going to bring forth a new time, in a new creation.

Deutero-Isaiah sees the future as a new creation because, in effect, the future does not yet exist. A free and glorious future seems impossible. For God, however, nothing is impossible. The creator of the universe will transform nature, renew her and recreate her. The God of history will create a new era in historical time. This God, creator of the world, and of a people, is the ultimate guarantee of hope. This is the meaning of the hymnlike fragments scattered and seemingly floating through this great and torrential poem. Singing praises is both the foundation and the actualization of hope.

But the people resist in another way. "I already knew it," says one man without illusions. "Nothing is new; everything repeats itself; I no longer spin out illusions in order not to have to suffer further disillusionment." The prophet interrupts:

> I have shewed thee new things from this time,
>   even hidden things, and thou didst not know them.

> They are created now, and not from the beginning;
> > even before the day when thou heardest them not;
> > > lest thou shouldest say, Behold, I knew them. (48:6–7)

In effect, the lack of hope is like a blindness that prevents seeing and discovering deeply:

> Hear, ye deaf;
> > and look, ye blind, that ye may see . . .
> Seeing many things, but thou observest not;
> > opening the ears, but he heareth not. (42:18, 20)

The people must set forth and change inwardly so as to become witnesses of God: "Bring forth the blind people that have eyes,/and the deaf that have ears . . . Ye are my witnesses" (43:8, 10).

Related to the symbol of fecundity is the conjugal relationship, which occupies a prominent position in this body of prophecy. In Deutero-Isaiah's vision, God is the husband and Jerusalem the wife. The symbolic union is translated into sublime poetry. In the first instance, 49:14–26, the wife complains that the husband has forgotten her. God, indignant, responds, adding maternal love to marital love: a mother cannot help loving her child. (By coupling the two images, the poet intensifies and relativizes both.) As a mother she cannot object to this argument which the poet uses to intensify the symbol. She is surprised to see her children surrounding her, and God tells her that he has enabled them to return honorably. She objects, saying that the children were taken away as legitimate spoils of war. God, in turn, appeals to his lordship over history. In this exchange, the intimate matrimonial symbol expands to a social and historical horizon. By poetic association, society and history become imbued with an amorous passion in their personal relationship with God—something that the symbol alone is able to capture and bring forth from the ineffable sphere where divinity, humanity, and history are joined.

In 51:9–52:6 a bold and affectionate dialogue unfolds. Jerusalem, the humiliated wife, shouts to her husband, "Awake, awake!" reminding God of his former prowess (vv. 9–10). "Awake, awake, stand up!" he answers, signaling the end of her humiliation (vv. 17–23). It is she who must awaken, rise up, and dress herself for celebration, fully aware "that I am he that doth speak: behold, it is I" (52:6).

In 54:1–10 the husband once again addresses his wife. Jerusalem is pictured as a woman in whom all possible feminine disgraces are concentrated: she is unmarried, forsaken, barren, repudiated. But all this is no more than a fit of anger now ended. "For a small moment have I forsaken thee;/but with great mercies will I gather thee" (54:7).

Whether attributable to the same author or to a faithful imitator, the material after chapter 55 contains beautiful embellishments of the same theme. In chapter 60 we find the great poem of light: the day which begins and never ends, rich with exquisite moments; the dawn over the city shining from above, against a panorama of darkness; the ships flying "as the doves to their windows" (v. 8).

In 61:10–62:9 the king (sun) returns victorious. His dawn has illuminated the city crowned with battlements. He has married her, giving her his name, and in a poignant phrase, confesses: "as the bridegroom rejoiceth over the bride, / so shall thy God rejoice over thee" (62:5). As the book closes, one charming domestic image reemerges (66:7–14). The mother has brought forth a people painlessly. While her friends gather to feast her, the husband surrounds her with comforts. The children are "dandled upon her knees" (v. 12) and begin to grow strong.

Without discussing here the historical identification of what the exegetes call the Servant of the Lord, we must give some attention to the remarkable poem in chapters 52:13–53:12. Its contents are pathetic and its expression restrained. After a solemn introduction, in which God announces "something inexplicable and most strange" (52:15 [AT]), an anonymous chorus sings and evokes the biography of an anonymous person. (A prologue and epilogue set the piece apart.) This antihero of whom they sing lacks a graceful appearance and good health. He is cut off from society, with neither the strength nor the will to carry out his duties. A failure in life and condemned to death, he is finally buried among evildoers. What more is there to say? The person described remains silent throughout the poem, up to the point where the silence becomes painful, even intolerable. At the end (53:9) the anonymous chorus offers a belated tribute: "he had done no violence, / neither was any deceit in his mouth." What, then, becomes of the theory of retribution in the poem? First, the anonymous chorus has taken pity on the person, crying out when he is silent. It has understood his plight, and as a result its members have undergone an inner change. If the Servant has accomplished this, he cannot have been a failure in life. Moreover, God himself, after the man's death, will restore him to life and honor: he will see the light and be reinstated. God will give him men as a reward, making him the instrument of salvation.

The poet has completely avoided identifying his antihero turned hero. He has wanted neither to smooth over nor to mitigate this tragic, enigmatic, and intense vision. There could be no better poetic expression of triumph through failure, glory through humiliation. There could be no better rescue from the anguish of exile than demonstrating the fecundity of suffering accepted without violence. The poet could not bequeath to posterity a meditation more profound or paradoxical. In order to understand it and accept it, it is necessary to cast one's lot with the anonymous chorus of spectators and participate with them.

Such is the richness of the word of God that the anonymous poet of the Exile, the singer of hope, proclaims. In his conception, a word is as fertile and prolific as the rain or the snow (55:10). The poet is conscious of his transcendental mission, to which service he has put his consummate literary talent.

CHAPTERS 24–27 form a special, late block that some call apocalyptic but is more appropriately called eschatological. The apocalypse, as we know it through the Book of Daniel, proposes a periodization of history—corresponding to the four metals of one statue, or four beasts—which issues into the one impending, decisive moment, giving way to a new definitive stage. Periodization is lacking in Isaiah 24–27. Its material is so heterogeneous that some scholars regard it as merely an anthology of autonomous pieces drawn from diverse epochs. Other examples of this genre, however, indicate that these materials may belong to a single, reasoned, unitary vision.

God is the king and judge who decides the destiny of his people and of his enemies. One group from among his people will save themselves by trial and purification in the midst of a catastrophe. A remaining group is similar to the olives clinging to an already harvested tree, grapes left on the gleaned vine, or an ear of grain still in the field after the harvest (24:13, 27:12). The others will be saved on the land (24:13), first dispersed, then summoned and reunited (27:13), including the dead, "thy dead" who will return to life (26:19).

The enemy is presented in diverse forms—kings on earth and stars in the sky (deified rebels?); there are evildoers and killers (24:21, 26:10, 26:21). The enemy is also the primordial and mythical serpent (27:1). And it is, like a leitmotiv, a hostile city, a "lofty city," a fortress (26:5, 27:10–11); and at one point, emblematically, it is called Moab (25:10).

Opposite this city rises the city into which "the just people" enter (26:1–2 [AT]). From his mountain the Lord reigns; on it he receives the homage of his worshipers (25:6, 27:13). Because God is the protagonist, his enemies are brought down; the hostile city is razed and the serpent is slain (26:5–6, 27:1). He judges the world and protects his people. He invites all peoples to a marvelous banquet. All this develops into a cosmic scene: the earth and its inhabitants, city and country (represented by wine), the floodgates of heaven.

Stylistically, the composition of these chapters is confusing, with repetitions and twists and violent juxtapositions. Only the first part makes things easier for us. There is a universal catastrophe in the midst of which one group is saved (24:1–6, 7–12, 13–16a, 16b–18a, 18b–20); there are images of imprisonment and judgment, reigned over by God, then a hymn of acclamation, and the banquet of the king (24:21–23, 25:1–5, 25:6–8). In the last part of this section the Lord's great sword and trumpet usher us in to witness the purification and renovation of the people (the vineyard) and the destruction of the enemy (27:1–13).

The actual poem includes relatively weak fragments (like 26:1–13) alongside effective passages. An instance of the latter is the comparison in 25:10–11:

> Moab shall be trodden down under him,
>> even as straw is trodden down for the dunghill.
> And he shall spread forth his hands in the midst of them,
>> as he that swimmeth spreadeth forth his hands to swim.

Frequently the poet strains for an effect, especially with an accumulation of sonorous qualities. The implacable and successive elimination of the inhabitants is described with the alliteration of *pahad, pahat, pah* (something like "scare, snare, snag" in English). The earthquake is an onomatopoeic parade that must be heard in Hebrew:

> *boqeq . . . bolqah . . . hiboq tiboq ha'arets*
>> *hiboz tiboz . . .*
> *'abela nabela ha'arets*
>> *'umlalah nabelah tebel.* (24:1–4)
>
> *ro'ah hitro'e'ah ha'arets*
>> *por hitporerah 'arets*
> *mot hitmotetah 'arets*
>> *no'a tanu'a 'arets.* (24:19–20)

A rough English equivalent to all this might sound something like "the earth shivers and staggers, stumbles and tumbles, quivers and quavers and quakes, jars and jerks and jolts." Similar clusterings of onomatopoeic effects are rare in classical Hebrew texts, so it is difficult to say if this is a successful model.

Similarly straining for effect is the appropriation of three adjectives to describe the executing sword: "hard and great and strong," which rhyme in the Hebrew. The descriptions move away from realism through accumulation of details and intensification; they are patently hyperbolic. Isolated realistic strains mix with fantastic visions difficult to understand: the dungeon for kings and stars, the blush of the Burning (sun) and White (moon), the hand of God supported on a mountain, the seafaring dragon, and more of the same.

Two fragments illustrate the impressive strength of this unknown poet of last things. Here is the poet's evocation of the eschatological banquet (25:6–8):

> And on [AR] this mountain shall the Lord of hosts
>> make unto all people
> a feast of fat things,
>> a feast of wines on the lees,
> of fat things full of marrow,
>> of wine on the lees well refined.
> And he will destroy in this mountain

the face of the covering cast over all people,
    the veil that is spread over all nations.
He will annihilate [AR] death for ever.
    and the Lord God will wipe away tears from off all faces;
and the ignominy [AR] of his people shall he take away
    from off all the earth:
        for the Lord hath spoken it.

It is the definitive victory of the God of life over the supreme enemy. If he kills the murderers (26:21), he destroys with them future deaths. What will become of those already dead, locked lifeless in the earth? In a splendid image of mythic ascendance, the sovereign power of God is affirmed supreme above the spoils of Death: mother earth, fertilized by a luminous celestial dew, feels herself pregnant; sitting up, she brings forth the dead, alive:

Live, indeed, shall your dead,
    their bodies shall rise;
the dwellers of the dust shall awake
    and sing for joy.
For your dew is a dew of light,
    and the Land of Shadows shall give birth. (26:19 [AT])

NOTE

This essay was translated from the Spanish by Jacqueline Mintz.

SUGGESTED FURTHER READINGS

Joseph Blenkinsopp, *A History of Prophecy in Israel* (Philadelphia, 1983).
F. J. Delitzsch, *Biblical Commentary on the Prophesies of Isaiah* (Grand Rapids, 1980).
W. L. Holladay, *Isaiah, Scroll of Prophetic Heritage* (Grand Rapids, 1978).
Otto Kaiser, *Isaiah 1–12: A Commentary* (Philadelphia, 1983).
———, *Isaiah 13–39: A Commentary* (London, 1974).
Claus Westermann, *Isaiah 40–66* (London, 1969).

Pontifical Biblical Institute

Jeremiah and Ezekiel

Joel Rosenberg

THE books of Jeremiah and Ezekiel—representing the two prophets who most epitomized Israel's transition to exile—pose literary problems different from those of more purely narrative biblical books. A literary reading must try to make sense of how the books have chosen to unfold the words of their alleged authors, for it is fair to say that Jeremiah and Ezekiel are less the authors of their books than personages or voices within a text. Despite the common ancient practice of attributing authorship of a work to one or another chief figure within it (a practice that critical scholarship sometimes perpetuates), it is likely that ancient readers were at least subliminally aware of another presence—anonymous, narrative, and traditionary in character—by whose intelligence the prophet's words acquired additional shape, coherence, and historical resonance for a later community. This interplay of prophecy and traditionary memory is our key to the literary dimensions of Jeremiah and Ezekiel, and accordingly we must beware of overvaluing any one part at the expense of the whole. Once we understand the carefully modulated montage of utterance and narrative in the two works, we will be better able to see the complementary relation of the two prophets and to comprehend the role they played in the formation of biblical tradition as a whole.

Jeremiah

A chief paradox of the Book of Jeremiah is a kind of reciprocal ambiguity between the earlier and later chapters: the closer we are to the prophet's indisputedly original words, largely identified with the poetic material, the farther we are from biographical specifics; and, conversely, the more deeply immersed we become in the details of Jeremiah's life, the more likely we are to encounter either prose synopses of the prophet's utterances or stereotyped recapitulations, which are no less integral to the total composition. The poetic material in Jeremiah is most concentrated at the beginning (chaps. 1–25), middle (chaps. 30–31), and end (chaps. 46–51), and this fact supplies our initial clues to the structure and meaning of the book.

Before we examine that structure, however, we should try to apprehend the separate styles and apparent sources as they present themselves and to gain a better sense of their uniqueness and internal progressions, so that later we can appreciate the distinctive way in which they are combined. We may here dispense with the chronological categories proposed by scholarship[1] and instead view the alleged sources as voices within the work, of which there are essentially three types: poetic oracles, prose sermons, and biographical prose.

Poetic Oracles

Although meter and parallelism are no longer criteria as certain as they once seemed for identifying biblical poetry, it is still possible to assert that a distinctly poetic style predominates in Jeremiah 1–25, 30–31, and 46–51:[2] staccato exclamations, rapid changes of scene and vantage point, frequent shifts of voice and discourse, use of invocation, plural command, and rhetorical question, a propensity for assonance and wordplay, a rich array of metaphors and similes from the natural landscape and from human crafts and trades, and precision of metonymy and synecdoche. Here we come closest to the mind of the prophet, and it is clear that the book has been constructed to allow the voice of Jeremiah to dominate the beginning, end, and core of the text.

The opening chapters convey a sense of the prophet's panoramic purview and his brilliant reversals of mood and tone. The book begins with a starkly simple commissioning scene (a bold contrast to Moses' commissioning in Exodus 3 and to those of Isaiah 6 and Ezekiel 1–3), in which YHWH drafts the reluctant prophet ("Before I formed thee in the belly I knew thee . . . and I ordained thee a prophet unto the nations," 1:5), who is initially shown two symbolic visions: the almond branch (*shaqed*), a symbol of the watchful (*shoqed*) deity (1:11); and the molten caldron pouring destruction from the north (1:13), symbol of the imminent terror from northern peoples who will descend upon the hapless nation—an image that will dominate the whole book. The prophet now turns to plead with his audience, personifying a God who remembers the former love of his favored people (2:1–3—the influence of Hosea is especially marked here) and reciting the milestones of its early history. Intermittently he flares up in wrath over the defilement of the Land, the faithlessness, superstition, and folly of the people, the futile alliances of their leaders. The nation is personified as a wanton woman, lustful in her passion (2:23–24), contriving schemes to grasp her lover (2:33), lying with paramours on roads and hilltops (3:23). Momentarily, the prophet imagines a scene of reconciliation, first calling to the people to turn back (3:2) and articulating their hypothetical heartfelt confession (3:22–25), then again in the voice of YHWH promising forgiveness and future blessing (4:1–2). Visions of doom resurge in 4:3–9, and the wrathful deity is now sketched as the awesome divine warrior of Near Eastern myth (4:11–13). In a characteristic etiological flourish, the prophet pauses to pronounce the causal nexus between human misdeed and bitter punishment: "Your ways and your doings have brought this upon you" (4:18 [AT]). Then, suddenly, we are plunged into the moaning despair of one who must witness such devastation:

> My anguish, my anguish!
> I writhe in pain!
> Oh, the walls of my heart!   (4:19 [RSV])

Is it the prophet who speaks here, or is it YHWH speaking figuratively of himself? No connectors enable us to know for sure. This mingling of divine and prophetic persona (punctuated only occasionally by first-person markers such as "and the Lord said to me") is frequent in Jeremiah and illustrates the extent to which God's sorrow and the prophet's suffering are seen as two sides of the same coin. As the prophet surveys the devastation of the Land as if it were already an accomplished fact (4:25–31), first and third person mingle with fluid ease; then, just as easily, the prophet turns again to the populace ("And when thou art spoiled, what will thou do? Though thou clothest thyself with crimson, though thou deckest thee with ornaments of gold . . ."; 4:30), and, shifting voice once more, depicts Daughter Zion's cry of despair: "Woe is me now! for my soul is wearied because of murderers" (4:31).

The chief themes of the early chapters, despite much geographic specificity, are unique to no particular moment of the prophet's mission and, indeed, display much the same feel for the typical and typologically recurrent that characterizes Hebrew prophecy as a whole. Jeremiah appears to have learned from his predecessors—from Amos and Micah the preoccupation with social injustice and the indifference to cultic propriety; from Hosea the feminine personification of Israel and the nostalgia for the days of the Exodus and the Wilderness wandering; from Isaiah the panoramic vision, the sharpness of satire, and the gift of paronomasia and linguistic musicality. The prophet moves around the Land with the certainty of a stage director, calling forth the sights, sounds, and exclamations of his tortured era, posing legalities and claims, mocking the self-exculpations and self-pity of the populace, and expressing anguish and despair over their devastation and its aftermath, only to call the enemy down upon them anew, as new offenses of the people come to mind. We notice a certain hardening of the prophet's position, as he moves from the hope of repentance to a sense of the inevitability of retribution. As this happens, we find increasing expression of prophetic and divine pathos—at first without distinction between the celestial and earthly perception; then, as the prophet's social encounters increase, with a growing sense of the prophet's isolation from God and man alike.

The lamentation passages in 11:18–20 and later are perhaps the most distinctive feature of the book, from which alone we would be entitled to view Jeremiah as our most self-revealed prophet. Much akin to Job's outcries, Jeremiah's tortured confessions alternate between plea, accusation, and anticipation, now begging for divine vindication in the face of his mockers and enemies, then, at a particularly raw moment of desperation (20:7–10), complaining of deception by the deity and of the cruel absence of respite or relief. After a brief glimmer of renewed trust (20:11–13), the prophet curses the day he was born, implicitly repudiating the mantle of prophecy that was laid upon him in the womb (1:5). Gradually we come to see the enormous toll and burden on one who was once granted the freest mandate and the most dextrous hand:

> to root out, and to pull down,
>   and to destroy, and to throw down,
>   to build, and to plant.   (1:10)

Many have noted the symbolic, exemplary nature of Jeremiah's sufferings—"a speaker of parables and himself a parable."[3] This impression is strengthened by the numerous ways in which Jeremiah is called upon to act out mimetically some aspect of the nation's fate: standing at the Temple gate (7:2), wearing and destroying a loincloth (13:1–7), refraining from marriage (16:1–4), witnessing a potter at his wheel (18:1–4), smashing a potter's jug (19:1–12), holding forth a winecup of wrath (25:15–17), attaching a yoke to his neck with thongs (27:1–4), and so on. But there is no need to view the prophet's anguish as purely teleological and didactic, or as a kind of shamanistic dramatization of the torment of an era. The lavishness of prophetic pathos flows more from the breakdown of missionary purpose than from an enactment of it. Even YHWH must confront this unforeseen faltering of his plan. Had Jeremiah remained but a mannequin of heavenly design, a disembodied oracular voice, we would not have sensed as fully the desperation and extremity of the time and place in which he moved. His sharp departure from prophetic tradition and custom in setting forth his complaint so elaborately is wholly his own innovation, and there is nothing else quite like it in biblical prophetic literature.

Prose Sermons

Extensive prose of a sermonic nature invades the Book of Jeremiah as early as chapters 3, 7, and 11, and it punctuates the oracles in briefer ways in the form of eschatological pronouncements ("In that day, there will be . . .") and etiological justifications ("for the people of Judah have done what displeases me"). Scholars have long noted the diction and cadences of the Deuteronomists in these prose segments—"Hearken to his voice," "to do right in the eyes of the Lord," "the stranger, the fatherless, and the widow," "provoke me to anger," and many related turns of speech.[4] The prophet could be revealing his own familiarity with the so-called Ur-Deuteronomy; or he could be using phrases that were later imitated by the Deuteronomists; or the affinity could rest in commonality of language, era, and heritage; or there could have been interpolations by a Deuteronomistic hand in order to claim Jeremiah for the movement. Though the precise textual relation between the Book of Jeremiah and Deuteronomy may elude us, there is a certain convergence of interest between Jeremiah and the Deuteronomist. Both simultaneously affirm and deny the uniqueness of Israel among the nations; both call the people to strict accountability for their wrongdoings; and both reflect a similar sense of historical and divine causality. That the nation's fate was to become a proverb and a byword in the discourse of later generations, as Deuteronomy and the Deuteronomistic portions of Jeremiah would have it, accorded well with the idiom of this most emblematic of prophets—indeed, he, too, was a symbol of ridicule: "I have become a constant laughingstock—everyone jeers at me" (20:7 [AT]).

On the other hand, investigators seeking to challenge or downplay the influence of Deuteronomistic ideology in the prose sermons have suggested a useful model for recovering from them the authentic voice of the prophet. They have spoken of a remembered gist and of "demetrified" copies of the prophet's original utterances.[5] If we shift our interest here from source-criticism to literary interpretation, we find an excellent model for understanding the voice of the prose sermons—for it is not the first-hand voice of the prophet but a voice filtered through memory and tradition, and thus a sign of the baroquely tortuous chronological sense that informs the book as a whole. The prophet speaks and is remembered speaking. As Jeremiah looks forward to the era of the survivors, eyes and ears from that era harken back to him. The mutuality of prediction and fulfillment is repeatedly affirmed. The wider arc of divine purpose is repeatedly made explicit.

Biographical Prose

The history of Jeremiah's life and times, like the Deuteronomic voice, builds gradually in the Book of Jeremiah. Indeed, anticipations of the biographic voice begin within the Deuteronomic material itself, in chapters 7 and 11. There we find reference to Jeremiah's famous Temple sermon in the fourth year of Jehoiakim; to the prophet's clashes with the Jerusalem leadership during their apparent efforts to reverse the reforms of Josiah; and, most significantly, to Jeremiah's estrangement from his own village of Anathoth as a plot against his life arises there. The poetic oracles that accompany and follow this material underscore this biographical interest by presenting the prophet's laments over his many enemies and ridiculers. The narratives that accompany these laments represent the first of the various symbolic actions commanded of Jeremiah (discussed above), and so bring into focus the specific public confrontations that will later be given historical concreteness. Only from chapter 20 onward do references appear to specific names of officials and dates, and to controversies of late pre-Exilic Jerusalem. Up to that point, we experience the issues only typologically—in the homiletic rhythms of preachment and the compressed synecdoche of oracle. After that time, the history of Jeremiah's life gradually comes into full view, and the prophet is finally revealed as an engaged historical actor, uncompromising but relentlessly committed to persuasion and debate, mingling with the highest ruling circles, able to mobilize allies among them, and, most important, exercising, despite his vulnerability to persecution, considerable public influence, enough to have made himself a threat to the national leaders.

The biographical prose should be understood as stemming from two fundamentally different documentative processes—one arising as an amplification of sermonic situations, and the other as part of a more purely historiographic or biographical project. There seems to have been an evolution from the one to the other, and that history of discourse on Jeremiah is preserved in the layout of the book as a whole, where we find a progression from oracle to sermon, from sermon to sermonic setting, and from sermonic setting to personal and court history.

Why was it important to include the historical material on Jeremiah? He is, after all, the most fully documented literary prophet in the Hebrew Bible, even without chapters 37–44. But the latter amplify the sparsely reported events of 2 Kings 24–25 in an exceptionally illuminating way. It is a stirring account, detailing Jeremiah's troubles during Jerusalem's final days, with fascinating glimpses of the uncompromising prophet and the tragically vacillating King Zedekiah. Here, we learn of the rescue of Jeremiah from starvation in a mud pit by an Ethiopian slave named Ebed-Melech, of the capture of the city and the humiliation and exile of Zedekiah, of the defeat of the conspiracy and the stormy aftermath in Judah and Egypt. It is not a "passion" narrative, as some have maintained. If anything, it portrays the prophet's vindication and rescue; and the final setbacks he experiences, in his failure to convince the surviving Judean leaders to abandon their conspiratorial course against Babylon, serve only to accentuate the folly and perverseness of the very persons he is trying to rescue. Our clue to the function and significance of the history in the Book of Jeremiah can be found in the return of the Deuteronomic style in the later chapters, especially in 44. There an elaborate, almost ceremonial dialogue occurs between Jeremiah and the Judean exiles in Egypt, in which the prophet affirms that he has been sent as the last in a line of prophets mandated to warn the people "to turn from their wickedness, to burn no incense to other gods" (44:5). We see that a biography of Jeremiah—or, more accurately, a detailed report of his repeated rejection by court and community alike—underscores the Deuteronomic theme of an embattled prophetic tradition and sets the destruction of Jerusalem and Judah firmly into the framework of reciprocal justice that shaped the Deuteronomistic history as a whole (Deuteronomy–2 Kings) and, indeed, the entire narrative history from Genesis through 2 Kings.

Structure

The structure of Jeremiah, and especially of its apparently chaotic chronology, has proved elusive to critical investigators, many of whom have declared the text to be in disarray and have attempted a reconstruction of an "original."[6] The great divergence between the Masoretic and Septuagint versions of Jeremiah has intensified this perplexity, for the Greek translation places the oracles against the nations (46–51) after chapter 25 (which seems to introduce the international theme). But by relying on the distinction among poetic oracles, prose sermon, and prose history, we can make a very plausible case for adhering to the Masoretic arrangement. That arrangement not only has a symmetrical pattern quite common in biblical literature but also helps us to make sense of a number of odd details that might otherwise seem obscure. Allowing for some crossover or interfixing common to biblical redaction, we thus find a poetic central segment, bracketed by two long, chiefly prose segments; these, in turn, are bracketed by two more bodies of chiefly poetic oracle. The whole is then placed into a redactional framework introducing and concluding the prophet's mission. Parallel segments match up thematically as well as, for the most part, formally, although considerable overlap of elements occurs in the actual sequence of texts. The theoretical pattern is summarized as follows:

a Historical headnote (1:1–3).

b Commission (1:4).

c "Prophet to the nations" theme introduced (1:5–10).

d Doom for Israel; poetic oracles predominate (chaps. 1–10).

e Prophet cut off from Anathoth; focus on prophet's trials and conflicts; prose predominates (11:1–28:17).

f Optimistic prophecies; renewal of Israel; prose brackets poetic center (chaps. 29–31).

e' Prophet returns to Anathoth; focus on prophet's trials and conflicts; prose predominates (32:1–45:5).

d' Doom for the nations; poetic oracles predominate (chaps. 46–51).

c' "Prophet to the nations" theme culminates (chaps. 50–51).

b' Prophet's concluding message (51:59–64).

a' Historical appendix (chap. 52).

The outermost parallel is fairly self-evident: both sections are concerned with setting the book in the context of the Deuteronomic History and more or less presuppose the reader's acquaintance with that history, specifically with its last four chapters (2 Kings 21–25) or their substance.

The second parallel is more problematic—first, because *b'* does not seem to end the whole book but only the Babylonian oracles that immediately precede it in chapters 50–51; second, because its purported date (see 51:59) is the fourth year of Zedekiah's reign, not the end of Jeremiah's career. Thus, his last *mentioned* prophecy is not his last *delivered*. Yet there are good reasons for ending Jeremiah's prophecies to the nations with the Babylonian oracles: Babylonia is presented as Israel's nemesis throughout the book, and she is now the most powerful of nations and the symbol of political might as such. One other episode in the book is dated to the fourth year of Zedekiah's reign, namely Jeremiah's confrontation with the court prophet Hananiah. Curiously, Hananiah's theme is the fall of Babylon, and Jeremiah expresses reserve on the truth of this oracle, stating that it can be verified only if and when it comes true (27:7–8), and later (27:15) he criticizes Hananiah for having provided false assurances to court and kingdom. Assuming that both chapter 28 and 59:59–64 have a basis in fact, we learn something quite intriguing about Jeremiah: that at the same time that he was telling his own people not to expect the immediate fall of Babylon, he was telling the Babylonians (at least symbolically—no recipient is designated) that their kingdom would indeed fall.

The fall of Babylon, then, if authentically Jeremiah's prediction, seems to have been a secret prophecy, not intended for the prophet's contemporaries back home in Judah, and possibly not even for the Babylonians of his era, since Jeremiah (51:59) gives Seraiah ben Neriah the scroll of his Babylon prophecies without designating any recipient (though it is to be read aloud). This is quite odd, and Jeremiah's further instructions to Seraiah suggest that the delivery is to be a purely magical act, not intended to persuade any crowd or official—only to notify "Babylon" as a whole. Recipients are not to be ruled out, but their locale and identity are unimportant. With the delivery of this message, Jeremiah's ministry is logically complete, even though he has some eight more years of documented preaching.

These considerations enable us to understand the significance of *c* and *c'*, which focus on Jeremiah's mission "to the nations." Much debate has arisen as to whether this means "to" or "concerning," but we need only assume that his mission embraces *all* nations, though it is also quite likely that most of his internationally oriented oracles were intended chiefly for recipients beyond his own era, Judean or otherwise. The mission is not to be understood as a serious program to preach to foreigners, in the manner of, say, Paul in the New Testament epistles. It is sound Deuteronomic doctrine and also authentically Jeremianic. It affirms the central tenet of Jeremiah's whole prophetic mission: that the God of Israel and Judah controls the destinies of all peoples with thorough impartiality and vigorous justice. In chapters 50–51 the full design of Jeremiah's mission "to the nations" becomes clear for the first time: even the great devourer will be devoured; even the great nemesis, which throughout the book has been seen as the spearhead of "the enemy from the north," has its *own* enemy from the north (50:41–43).

The relation of the three bodies of poetic oracle (*d*, *f*, *d'*) can now be seen more clearly. These are the three classic components of most prophetic books of the Hebrew canon: prophecies of doom for Israel; prophecies of doom for the surrounding nations; prophecies of restoration for Israel. Unlike, say, Isaiah or Ezekiel, where these three orders of prophecy are put into a relatively simple sequential relation, in Jeremiah they are placed in a polar and symmetrical opposition: *d* is opposed to *d'* and both are contrasted with *f*. The symmetry all the better underscores that we are not dealing with simple historical prediction, but with a dialectical system in which changes in one area—most specifically, Judah/Israel's repentance—can set off a chain of consequences in the others. All is contingent on human behavior, all is subject to the same impartial standard, and all is reversible in the fullness of time. Between (and partly overlapping) these three elements are two long sections dealing with the life of the prophet, each introduced by an episode illustrating some aspect of his relation to his home village, Anathoth. As chapter 32 makes clear, the prophet's relation to Anathoth is a touchstone of larger events coming to pass—his return is a minuscule and possibly uncompleted token of Israel's eventual return from exile—and thus shows us in an oblique and quiet way that two major progressions in the nation's history are being comprehended: from prosperity to ruin, and from ruin to (still distant) prosperity.

One further and striking symmetry in Jeremiah 20–40 sheds light on the otherwise quite confusing chronology of the book.

a	Jeremiah's first imprisonment is recounted (20:1–18)	no date given, but probably in reign of Jehoiakim
b	An official of Zedekiah asks Jeremiah to pray to YHWH; broad survey of Jeremiah's dealings with various kings (21–24)	reign of Zedekiah

c	Jeremiah summarizes orally 23 years of preaching (25:1–14)	fourth year of Jehoiakim's reign
d	Cup of wine (gloss: "of wrath") is forced on neighboring nations (25:15–38); Jeremiah's troubles with official circles are recounted (26:1–24)	fourth year of Jehoiakim's reign beginning of Jehoiakim's reign
e	Jeremiah predicts that nations will be enslaved to Babylonia (chap. 27)	beginning of Jehoiakim's reign, but real referent is Zedekiah's anti-Babylonian conspiracy
f	Jeremiah's rival Hananiah predicts short-term vindication of the nation (chap. 28)	fourth year (or "beginning") of Zedekiah's reign
g	Jeremiah tells exiles to settle permanently in Babylonia (chap. 29)	shortly after exile of Jehoiachin (Jeconiah); thus, beginning of Zedekiah's reign
h	"Book of Consolation" addressed to Northern Israel (chaps. 30–31)	
g'	YHWH tells Jeremiah to settle permanently in Anathoth (chap. 32)	tenth year of Zedekiah's reign, during siege of Jerusalem
f'	Jeremiah predicts long-term vindication of the nation (chap. 33)	tenth year of Zedekiah's reign, slightly later than g'
e'	Judean slaveowners renege on releasing slaves, and Jeremiah predicts death for them (chap. 34)	during siege of Jerusalem, but possibly earlier than g'
d'	Cup of wine is refused by Rechabites; authentic (but nonofficial) servants of YHWH are praised; the nation's disobedience is denounced (chap. 35)	"in the days of King Jehoiakim"
c'	Jeremiah summarizes in writing 23 years of preaching (chap. 36)	fourth year of Jehoiakim's reign
b'	An official of Zedekiah asks Jeremiah to pray to YHWH; Jeremiah's dealings with Zedekiah's court are set forth in detail (37:1–39:18)	early in Zedekiah's reign
a'	Jeremiah's final release from prison is recounted (40:1–5)	after the Babylonian capture of Jerusalem

It can be seen that the reigns of Jehoiakim and Zedekiah are interspersed in something of a checkerboard pattern, and that, starting with *b/b'* inward, parallel pairs fall within the same reign (the apparent exception, *e/e'*, at least yields *messages* applicable to the same reign). Just as the overall layout of oracles stresses that prophetic prediction is not a matter of sequential chronology but rather of dialectical interdependence, this deployment of episodes suggests that the prophetic vocation is not a matter of steady augmentation of the prophet's doctrine or of increasing acceptance by his public, but rather one of continual reversal, deadlock, setback, and resurgence. The restlessness and apparent aimlessness of the prophet's career is thus captured in a unique and profound way. Patterns emerge in his ministry which are hard to see in the short run (for the reader as much as for the prophet or his contemporaries), but which, over the long run, show simultaneously a deep consistency of vision and an immense versatility of expression. The relativity of the historical hour, the alteration of preachment to context and circumstance, are stressed as the prophet is shown churning about in relentless movement—adapting, clashing, revising, retrenching, threatening, pleading, promising. Yet one thread of argument runs through this Heraclitean swirl of change. The only human power that transcends all circumstances, all nations and alliances, all empires and kings, is the power of repentance. It is this power alone that grants insight into history, for it is here shown as the force that shapes history. And behind all motions and changes is the voice of Jeremiah, whose book characteristically leaves us in the dark about where he spent his final days—a not untypical ending for prophetic cycles (consider Moses' unknown gravesite, Elijah's exit in a chariot of fire, Jonah's silent perplexity before a divine question). In Jeremiah's case the omission creates a sense of the prophet's freewheeling ubiquity "to root out, and to pull down, / and to destroy, and to throw down, / to build, and to plant" (1:10), which can now be seen as an emblem for the double opposition, between national and international calamity and between calamity and restoration, that informs the design of the book as a whole, and which defines the parameters of historical understanding within the Hebrew Bible at large.

Ezekiel

Ezekiel is simultaneously more homogeneous a composition than Jeremiah and more opaque about the origins of its components. As is the case with practically every other biblical book, there is widespread disagreement on Ezekiel's unity, authorship, and historicity.[7] Nevertheless, a significant number of modern interpreters recognize throughout the distinctive stamp of an individual mind.[8] The pervasive dominance of the "I" voice, the persistence of precise dates and of an almost purely sequential chronology, and the private, literate, and bookish manner of the language and idioms give the text much of the quality of a journal, with all the disjunction and heteroglossia that characterize journals. Otherwise we have few clues concerning the flesh-and-blood Ezekiel, though perhaps even fewer grounds for distrusting the book's own testimony.

Whether or not Ezekiel lived when and where he says,[9] he was an astute observer of political events, possessing an extensive knowledge of geography, human commerce, priestly lore, and foreign literature and mythology. He was a philosopher of history of the first magnitude. Whatever its historical authenticity and claims to prophecy, the book is a remarkable fiction, most of all in its own purported context, anticipating in imaginative power and in boldness of allegorical vision the major works of Dante, Milton, and Blake, to cite three on whom Ezekiel's influence seems considerable.

It may be best to begin where Ezekiel himself begins, on 31 July, 593 B.C.E., along the banks of the Babylonian Chebar canal. There, according to the prophet's testimony, "the heavens were opened, and I saw visions of God." The verses that follow (1:2–3) give the book's sole narrative reference to Ezekiel in the third person (24:14 occurs within quoted speech),[10] and we may, with a wide consensus of premodern and modern commentators, choose to regard it as a gloss: "In the fifth day of the month, which was the fifth year of King Jehoiachin's captivity, The word of the Lord came expressly unto Ezekiel the priest, the son of Buzi, in the land of the Chaldeans by the river Chebar; and the hand of the Lord was there upon him." But to call it a gloss misses the point of its presence: that someone in the book's internal tradition knew that the prophet's enigmatic formulation in 1:1—"in the thirtieth year"—meant the fifth year of the Captivity, that is, 593 B.C.E. Curiously, the dating system followed throughout the book—by Ezekiel himself, presumably—is that of 1:2–3, not of 1:1. The opening verse's "in the thirtieth year," if it is not a scribal error, is there for a reason. What, then, is meant by "the thirtieth year"? Of what? Why are obliqueness and ellipsis called for here? Why start with a different calendrical system and then withdraw it?

We may leave this question unanswered until the full trajectory of the book justifies the answer. We may also allow the text's details of the prophet's vision to speak for themselves, for the text addresses itself amply and uninhibitedly to the lineaments of the divine chariot-throne and its angelic bearers. Let us confine ourselves to two matters comprehended by the account: that the apparition occurs outside the land of Israel (while, despite the reference to exile, the nation's sovereignty is intact and the Temple still stands), and that the word used for the divine presence is *Kavod* ("Glory"), the priestly term for a manifestation of the deity during the ongoing sacerdotal operations of the cult (see Lev. 9:6, 23). The vision is here not, as is sometimes assumed, a proclamation or assurance that YHWH can manifest himself outside the land of Israel, for that possibility was taken for granted in ancient Israelite belief. Nor does it seem to announce a transplanting of the cult to foreign soil, since at the time of the vision the Jerusalem cult in fact still stood and would never, in the belief system of the priestly prophet, operate anywhere but Jerusalem (see chap. 6). No, this quasi-cultic manifestation can be seen only as an extraordinary occurrence, one not welcomed by the prophet, and which we could call a state of emergency. Not until chapters 8–11 does it become fully clear that a presence of the *Kavod* in Babylon foretokens its removal from Jerusalem, and nowhere in chapters 1–7 does the prophet say—dare to say—that the punishment of Israel will entail the end of its chief site of worship. People might suffer, surely—about this Ezekiel is unhesitatingly precise: "parents shall eat their children, and children shall eat their parents" (5:10 [AT]). But his delicacy and restraint regarding the effects on the divine Glory itself are all the more striking, and they flow from the deepest and most sensitive taboo in the priestly tradition: the inviolability of the sacred site par excellence, the Holy of Holies in the Jerusalem sanctuary. Only a shocking and unprecedented change in Israel's historical situation could bring the unthinkable into the open, and when the prophet comes to describe the Glory's awesome departure, in 10:18–22 and 11:22–23, there is a mood of almost hypnotic calm in his words, as if the grounds for this event were by now self-evident. No wail of mourning, no heightened expression whatever, accompanies the report. It is the book's first firmly unequivocal declaration that the national sovereignty has come to an end.

Much has been speculated on the prophet's psyche and personality, but, restricting ourselves to the plane of literary expression, we need note only that the book, at certain crucial junctures, stops distinctly short of revealing the prophet's feelings, despite its lush generosity in rendering divine pathos, and even despite its willingness otherwise to render the prophet's astonishment and dismay over things coming to pass. This radical subordination of the prophet's human feelings to divine intention is already implicit in the mode of address that prevails in divine speech throughout the book: *ben-'adam* ("human being," literally, "son of Adam"), a term hierarchic in force, and one that accentuates the prophet's mortal, earthbound, and subservient status. It is implicit as well in the first symbolic act commanded of the prophet: his eating of a scroll (or book) containing "lamentations, and mourning, and woe" (2:10; see 2:8–3:3), whose ingestion yields a taste "as sweet as honey." There is much that we could say about the semiotic subtleties inherent in this merger of the prophet with his message (or, given the contents of the scroll, with Jeremiah's), but let us focus on the paradoxical skewing of the affective domain described here: that a scroll of woe tastes sweet (3:3), and that the prophet is instructed (2:8) not to disobey or balk at what is offered. It helps to explain why Ezekiel, unlike Jeremiah, is so inseparable from the unfolding of his book, and yet simultaneously why he is so self-effacingly circumspect about his own feelings. He is not, as such, required to *suppress* his feelings, only to make their expression coextensive with what is written—to maintain a silence that is analogous to the silence of a text. The taste of honey thus signifies not a sensation of the prophet's tastebuds, still less his reaction to the inscribed woes—only a typically emblematic and allegorical affirmation of the objective "sweetness" of that most precious commodity, obedience to divine imperative. This terrifying reign of objectivity in Israel's darkest hour sets the tone for the entire book, transcending all alleged sources and genres. As we shall see, the prophet's personal life is not irrelevant to the book's argument, but it gains its relevance and poignancy only as a sign within the argument—"for I have set thee for a sign unto the house of Israel" (12:6).

Our sense of paradox is compounded in chapter 3, where the prophet receives two diametrically opposed commands. He is first told that, as a watchman over Israel, he is personally responsible for the fate of his charges should he fail to warn one who is capable of repentance (3:17–21). He is then told (3:22–27) that he is to keep silent and remain within his house: "I will make thy tongue cleave to the roof of thy mouth, that thou shalt be dumb." Several times further in the book (see 24:27, 29:21, 33:22), the prophet's dumbness is alluded to, and we must appreciate the puzzle in the fact that though prophetic messages flow aplenty through the prophet during his entire alleged period of silence, and even though we know that in fact the prophet does make public declarations during that time (indeed, is *commanded* to—see, for example, 14:6 and 20:3), some aspect of that ministry is held unrealized, is judged or ordained to be a type of muteness. Are we to assume that Ezekiel is incurring the penalty of a negligent watchman, or that YHWH is contriving to punish the very man he commands? Or is this perhaps a way of saying that repentance is no longer possible—or, more pertinently, that the time ripest for repentance, the time when the watchman's call can be heard, has not yet arrived? Before the watchman can be heard, the heart must first be broken; the seal of sovereignty must be ripped away.

Understanding the book in this manner helps make clear much that is otherwise peculiar about its contents or design. It explains, for example, the overwhelmingly legal orientation of the book's doom oracles in a work otherwise so preoccupied with repentance, mercy, and restoration. Unlike Jeremiah's, Ezekiel's discourses commence not with pleas for turning, but with pronouncements of punishment that may, somewhere far down the line, elicit a retrospective repentance. Virtually all of the discourses, however elaborate and however varied in theme, unfold in the same basic rhetorical pattern, constructed out of the words *ya'an* ("because") and *lakhen* ("therefore").[11] Expansions of this elegant structure are afforded by the many phrases that underscore the causal nexus thereby proclaimed between action and consequence: "and when they ask you why . . . you shall say . . . ," "for thus says the Lord God" "and now behold, I shall . . . ," and, above all, the most ubiquitous of the book's motivically repeated phrases, "and they [or you] shall know that I am the Lord." Only completion of the trajectory of promise and fulfillment can truly convince those capable of being saved where their true interests lie, and who YHWH is. Ezekiel is perhaps unique and unprecedented in its preoccupation with the *conditions* of repentance. No prophetic book has formulated the problem in such a nuanced manner. So many of Ezekiel's discourses in the first half of the book—before the destruction of Jerusalem—are retrospective visions: Israel's whole pre-Exilic history is repeatedly reviewed, as if in a kind of premature postmortem. The house of Israel is given a hindsighted depiction of its life in the Land, which will make full sense only once the dire predictions come to pass and the people—their remnant—are sufficiently motivated to reflect backward and understand. This expository strategy helps explain why a number of the deity's anticipations of repentance among the populace are envisaged only after the punishment has run its course—and thus why the prophet's mouth is not yet fully opened:

> Yet will I leave a remnant, that ye may have some that shall escape the sword among the nations, when ye shall be scattered through the countries. And they that escape of you shall remember me among the nations . . . and they shall lothe themselves for the evils which they have committed in all their abominations. And they shall know that I am the Lord, and that I have not said in vain that I would do this evil unto them. (6:8–10)

But did Ezekiel *preach* this, and if so, where?

There is some suggestion that Ezekiel was in regular contact with the elders among his own Exilic community in Babylon, and on numerous occasions was compelled to preach to them or to their constituents things they might not have liked to hear about the fate of their homeland (see 14:1–11 and 20:1–44). Any preaching "for Israel," that is, for the Land and its inhabitants, was just as relevant to the ears of his colleagues and compatriots in Babylon. This double applicability flows from the unique situation of the exiles of 598 B.C.E. Those deported with King Jehoiachin were not in exile in the fuller sense of the term that prevailed after 587, but were a kind of hostage community of leading citizens, who were apparently valued enough by at least some of the population who remained that their detention could be used to enforce the submission of the home populace to Nebuchadnezzar's political sway (see 2 Kings 24:10–17). In such a setting, eyes and ears among the exiles were, at least from 598 to 587, trained on the land of Israel and its fate, and all preaching to them was, literally or figuratively, a preaching to the land and to Jerusalem.

And for the time being (given what we know of Jeremiah's experience), the detainees alone, among the nation as a whole, could be in a position to hear or appreciate the prophet's message. Only they had the foretaste of exile; only they knew firsthand the might (or even, given their relatively lenient treatment, the "sweetness") of the Babylonian yoke. Given this anomalous audience, Ezekiel, unlike Amos, Isaiah, or the poetic Jeremiah, rarely surveys his contemporary Judean society with the detailed eye of the social commentator or of the anguished deity, for the historical setting in which such a survey would have force and cogency has passed away. It is not the trial but the moment of sentencing that most animates the prophet, and the post-sentencing search for perspective and insight over what has been lost. Curiously, Ezekiel's most expansive poetry, verses in the grand manner of his great predecessors, occurs not in the Israelite phase of his mission, but in his diatribe on foreign nations (which we must assume to have been spoken to his own countrymen), where he could be more uninhibited (though still retrospective) in his invective, and more certain of enlisting the agreement of his listeners.

This last matter brings us one step closer to understanding both the structure of the book and the special character of Ezekiel's symbolic discourses in the book's first half, especially the parables of Israelite history. Both phenomena flow from the unique conditions of the first Exilic community, as we have seen. This group was torn by great dissension. The exiles had no way of knowing what would come about for themselves, or how history would turn. A bad but eloquent prophet might easily be preferred to a good but blunt one. A priestly prophet was by heritage and training a conciliator, a consoler, a sealer of consensus. It was at times necessary for a blunt prophet, one with an adamantine brow such as Ezekiel's (see 2:9), to moderate or disguise his message for the ears of his less reflective constituents by fashioning a discourse difficult to pin down, addressed past the emotional multitudes to those who shared his concerns. Whence the riddle (ḥidah), the proverb (mashal), and the dirge (qinah), all of which are oblique discourses. This is not to say that Ezekiel was comfortable with the role of esoterist; indeed, he chafed under criticism by his contemporaries of his abstractness and indirection: "Ah, Lord God, they are saying of me, 'Is he not [just] another maker of allegories?" (20:49). (Allegory, parable, and proverb are the same word in Hebrew, mashal). We may see more than dismay at persecution shaping this discouragement: the prophet is straining at the bit. For all their analogical brilliance, the parabolic addresses in chapters 13–24 seem crabbed and claustrophobic. Ezekiel is prevented from exercising his most cherished priestly mission, one for which his birth and schooling have most conditioned him to serve, as dispenser of absolution and consolation. For this his mouth is closed, his hands are tied. It is significant that just before his

complaint about the ridicule of his allegories we encounter Ezekiel's masterful effort (in chap. 20) at abandoning the *mashal* mode and expounding
the *nimshal*, the thing analogized.

Such, at any rate, is what emerges from the scant biographical hints
throughout the book's first half (chaps. 1–24). The book's structure requires this interpretation, for the beginning and end of his so-called silence
are very clearly marked: in 3:24–27 he is told to keep silent until God is
ready; in 24:25–27, at the close of his prophecies on Israel and just before
his prophecies on the surrounding nations, he is told that when news
comes of the city's fall, his mouth will be opened and he will no longer
be dumb; in 33:21–22, at the close of his prophecies on the nations and
the beginning of his prophecies of Israel's restoration, he records that "in
the twelfth year of our captivity" (586 B.C.E.) a survivor of the debacle
came to announce that the city has fallen, and we are told that the prophet's
mouth was hereby opened. It is not the quantity of biographical material
that is significant, but its placement. Still, the progression would amount
to but a dry formalism were it not for one further biographical detail
placed just before the second of the three announcements noted above:

> Also the word of the Lord came unto me, saying, Son of man, behold, I
> take away from thee the desire of thine eyes with a stroke: yet neither shalt
> thou mourn nor weep, neither shall thy tears run down. Sigh, but not aloud
> [RSV]; make no mourning for the dead, bind the tire of thine head upon thee,
> and put on thy shoes upon thy feet, and cover not thy lips, and eat not the
> bread of men. So I spake unto the people in the morning: and at even my
> wife died; and I did in the morning as I was commanded.
>
> And the people said unto me, Wilt thou not tell us what these things are
> to us, that thou doest so? Then I answered them, The word of the Lord
> came unto me, saying, Speak to the house of Israel. Thus saith the Lord
> God; Behold, I will profane my sanctuary, the excellence of your strength,
> the desire of your eyes, and that which your soul pitieth; and your sons and
> your daughters whom ye have left shall fall by the sword. (24:15–21; see
> 24:22–27)

The stoic silence and lucidity of Ezekiel the man are here most astonishing—as is the grotesqueness of his didactic exchange with the people.
(It is difficult here to imagine how this scene would have played with
flesh-and-blood actors.) This is the only place in the book where the
prophet's domestic life is brought into view, and it rounds out our vision
of the man in an unexpected way. Ezekiel is not, as his visions might lead
us to expect, a shamanistic recluse, but rather a devoted family man. He
is a full sharer in the sufferings allotted to his people. The death of his
eye's delight, or desire, is now the text, an object lesson, as the adultery
of a similarly precious companion had been for Hosea, and it must here
serve as a sign of the precious city and Temple that will now fall. "Sigh,
but not aloud" could be the watchword of the prophet's entire career, and

no phrase better captures the raging torrent of emotions that must, as when Abraham had told Isaac, "God will provide himself a lamb, my son" (Gen. 22:8 [AR]), remain unspoken. Paradoxically, Ezekiel's enforced muteness concerning his personal loss coincides thematically with the opening of his mouth concerning the nation's loss. The entire first half of the book is now revealed as the prehistory of a wider and more significant mission, to be unfolded in chapters 25–48, where we have the feeling that Ezekiel, whatever problems of expression might arise, is more in his element.

As noted earlier, the "nations" oracles are among Ezekiel's richest poetry, in a narrower sense of that term. Translators are accustomed to render most of Ezekiel in prose rather than in strophic format, but it is clear that much of what they have deemed prose is capable of being cast as verse. Yet even by the conventional reckoning, chapters 25–32 abound in verse, and here we find Ezekiel's masterful command of geography, commerce, and mythology. He pictures Tyre as a huge ship with Lebanon's cedars and Bashan's oaks for its planks and oars; the men of Zidon and Arvad at the helm and among the rowers; those of Persia, Lud, and Phut, and Arvad manning troops and towers; Javan, Tubal, and Meshech trading bronze for merchandise (27:5–13). "The heart of the seas" teems with mariners, pilots, caulkers, and merchantmen, while the king, having enclosed himself "in Eden the garden of God" (28:13), and encrusted with an abundance of gemstones as the symbols of his royal status, believes himself as wise as a god. Pharaoh, for his part, is seen as a dragon of the Nile whom God will hook by the jaw, and as a verdant world-tree, rooted in the waters of the deep, shelter of birds and nations, whom the hand of foreigners will now fell. The section moves logically, surveying the neighboring countries from the more provincial and proximate—Ammon, Edom, and Philistia (chap. 25)—to the more maritime and cosmopolitan: Tyre (26:1–28:23) and Egypt (29:1–32:32). We must here recall the oracle in which God has promised Ezekiel that from Jerusalem will go forth a fire that will consume in a progressively widening arc (3:4).

That the bulk of invective is reserved for Egypt and its maritime arm Tyre is no surprise, for Ezekiel, like Jeremiah, sees Egypt's duplicitous leading role in the abortive western cabal against Babylonia as the linchpin of Israel's troubles. This perspective helps account for Ezekiel's sense of Egypt as a place of depravity and vicious corruption. Unlike Jeremiah, Ezekiel spares Babylon from censure, a measure of his different vantage point, and, unlike in Jeremiah, the censure of nations occupies a midpoint rather than the finale of the book. At least one of the oracles (29:17–21) is dated *after* the book's final oracles—indeed, is the latest of the book's dates, 571 B.C.E.—and it is doubly interesting for being the book's sole indicator that Ezekiel's prophecies on Tyre and Egypt were left unfulfilled. Whether this frankness emanated from Ezekiel or an editor is unclear (it is a decidedly Ezekielian touch), but it has the effect of making 29:17–21 the centerpiece of the foreign oracles, and indeed of the entire book. Curiously, this lone contradictory oracle strengthens rather than weakens the force of what surrounds it, for we are thus notified that Ezekiel has left the realm of his normally astute political and historical wisdom and entered, true to his preferred mission, into the riskier realm of utopian fantasy, magic, and myth—though myth here is a vehicle of satire and belittling, not yet the more earnest paradisiacal consciousness that will dominate chapters 40–48. We have here (especially at 28:12–19) what seems an older, more mythological prototype of the Garden story, not yet pressed into the cadences of homily and fable, but unequivocal in its rejection of false paradises. The motifs of cosmic centers that are prominent in these chapters throw into relief one glaring omission: the panorama embraces the two maritime powers flanking Israel but omits Israel, the geographic center. This omission sets the stage for the final use of cosmic-center imagery in chapter 47, where from the Temple threshold flows a river eastward to the Dead Sea, fostering teeming new life in its hitherto uninhabitable waters. But in this last image there is an instructive difference, which we should now consider in the context of Ezekiel's restorative visions as a whole.

It has been customary to view chapters 33–48 as the third and final movement of the book, comprising in its broadest sense a body of redemptive prophecies for Israel of an unprecedentedly radical, supernaturalist cast. This interpretation needs some qualification. First, a good deal of textual space is still allotted to prophecies of woe or admonition. If a redemption is coming to birth, its birth pangs are still considerable, even before Gog's appearance in chapter 38. Second, two contradictory attitudes toward the redemption seem to occur side by side: on the one hand, divine judgment of righteous and unrighteous in Israel and a general mood of conditional divine blessing continue even as the people's fortunes are restored (so, for example, 35:17–22 and 43:11); on the other hand, the people's perennial unrighteousness is no longer a stumbling block to their redemption—it is not for their sake that the God of Israel acts, but for his holy name (32:22–32; cf. 37:23). Indeed, just as disaster was once necessary to create the conditions for repentance and soul-searching, now unmerited redemption is expected to do the same. We have, in a sense, been cut loose not only from our moorings in political facts and historical likelihoods, but from logic itself. We find the God of Israel sanctifying himself before a world audience in a setting that no longer bears the familiar earmarks of a world. From here on the representational powers of language, even allegorical language, break down. Myth, which came alive so palpably in the foreign oracles, is no longer serviceable, and what replaces it, whatever its origins and its outlandish lineaments, is not mythic—a type of gnosis, to be sure, but one mobilizing contradictory potentials in the prophet's imagination: a severe and solemn precision, on the one hand, as in the measuring out, down to the cubit and the hand-breadth, of the dimensions of the restored Temple (40:5–44:3); and at the same time an airy insubstantiality about the whole, a kind of abstractness, going all the way back to chapter 33, that somehow seems related to the odd fact that Jerusalem's fall per se is unrepresented—it is signified only by an announcement from without (33:21–22). In this Exilic perspective, we are far from the ambience of Lamentations and the poetic Jeremiah. We find instead a baroquely artificial diction, a frenzy of labeling and cataloguing—a celebration, almost, of the naked functionality of language, somewhat analogous to our modern architectural style, rooted in Vladimir Tatlin, that allows pipes, tanks, and service scaffolds to play a role in a building's artistic form.

Yet there is no faltering here in the expository structure of the book. This dramatic shift in the role of language, while anticipated as far back as the opening chapters, is comprehensible solely in the light of the limitations imposed on the prophet in 24:15–17. Just as the city's cries cannot be heard, the prophet remains ever apart from his newfound freedom of pronouncement. We have, in the fullest sense, a "sigh, but not aloud."

For this reason, even the momentous miracles of chapters 37–39 have a kind of geometric starkness and paradoxicality, which are further sustained in chapters 40–48. Though the bones of Israel are clothed with flesh and animated by the spirit, they remain nameless, faceless soldiers in the army of YHWH. Gog and his infamous hordes are slain in a mysterious conflagration that leaves the Land strewn with the invaders' corpses but also leaves the inhabitants strangely unscathed. The Land is purified, but only by suffering the grossest of defilements. The invaders are buried, but they are also carrion for birds and beasts. The Temple sanctuary is readied for the return of the Glory, but only after the deity himself, glutting the maw of chaos, offers "sacrifice" of flesh and drunkenness of blood to the scavenging animals (39:17–20). Later, the Land is allotted to the renewed tribes, but according to no known geographic or historical imperatives. Clearly, the world has been turned upside down; no familiar norms of mimetic representation or prophetic tradition now prevail, and the mythic language of chapters 28 and 31 now appears as the crudest kind of literalism, the language of the historically ephemeral. With his array of charts and blueprints, the prophet moves into uncharted domains for biblical tradition—the audacious textuality of a broadly architectonic allegory. It remains tantalizingly uncertain whether it is the national or the personal loss that most guides him. Looked at one way, the book of Ezekiel is a silent tribute to his deceased wife; viewed in another way, it is an object lesson in which the prophet's personal tragedy is but a sign of larger events.

One further key to the meaning of the book's final chapters (40–48) is found, naturally enough, in the section's headnote: the date "in the twenty-fifth year of our exile," namely in 573 B.C.E. Here, we may take a simple but important suggestion from medieval Jewish exegesis. As Rashi notes on 1:1, the mysterious "thirtieth year" is that of Israel's final Jubilee cycle—one begun but not ended in the Land. Thirty years before the inaugural vision in 593 was 623—the eve of Josiah's reform. Twenty-five years after that, in 598, King Jehoiachin was exiled. Twenty-five years after that was Ezekiel's Temple vision. Ezekiel's affinities with the Code of Holiness are well known, and in that document (quite coincidentally, in Lev. 25) the laws of Sabbatical and Jubilee are set forth. There (25:9), the Jubilee is designated to begin on the Day of Atonement, that is, on the tenth day of the seventh (or New Year) month. The vision in Ezekiel 40–48 is likewise dated "in the twenty-fifth year of our exile, at the beginning [sic] of the year, on the tenth day of the month." (The number 25 likewise appears motivically throughout the Temple vision.) In the Jubilee year, all land and property must revert to their original owners. Likewise, in the vision, the Land will return to Israel and to the protective aegis of Israel's God. It matters not whether the Jubilee reckoning (or even the Exilic reckoning in the headnote dates) was authentically Ezekiel's— it is part of the book's internal tradition, and it adds an extraordinary coherence to the reported events, setting Ezekiel's era in a vaster frame-work of history and metahistory. The Jubilee reckoning must remain unexplicit because, in the ritual-legal code of the priest, it is an ambiguous category: a fifty-year sacred cycle that was uncompleted in the Land, begun but not ended by the Israelite inhabitants, transferred from the custody of priestly law to the redemptive designs of the self-sanctifying deity. If the more familiar contours of biblical (essentially, Deuteronomic) justice, of the human-centered cycles of reward and punishment, have fallen by the wayside and been replaced by a more apocalyptic causality, it is the extreme desperation of the era that has made it so. If Ezekiel, consummate journeyer of the spirit, has left behind the flesh-and-blood environment of Land and people, he may be forgiven by force of events that have left him triply bereaved. We may think of his book as a form of farewell to the household, priestly calling, and land he has known and loved. It is a form of silent sigh, and it had the benefit, perhaps unforeseen by Ezekiel, of nurturing within his fellow Israelites a concretely restorative hope.

NOTES

1. For classic source analysis of Jeremiah, see especially Sigmund Mowinckel, *Zur Composition des Buches Jeremiah* (Kristiana [= Oslo], 1914) and *Prophecy and Tradition* (Oslo, 1946). On more recent trends, see T. R. Hobbes, "Some Remarks on the Composition and Structure of Jeremiah," *Catholic Bible Quarterly*, 34 (1972), 257–275, reprinted in Leo G. Perdue and Brian W. Kovacs, eds., *A Prophet to the*

Nations: Essays in Jeremiah Studies (Winona Lake, 1984; henceforth cited as "Perdue and Kovacs"), pp. 175–191.

2. On the problem of poetry and prose in Jeremiah, see, in general, W. McKane, "Relations between Poetry and Prose in Jeremiah, with Special Reference to Jeremiah iii 6–11 and xii 14–17," *Vetus Testamentum*, supp. 32 (1981), 220–237 (reprinted in Perdue and Kovacs, pp. 269–284), and note 4, below. On the Jeremianic authenticity of chapters 30–31, see John Bright, *Jeremiah: A New Translation with Introduction and Commentary*, Anchor Bible, XXI (Garden City, N.Y., 1965), 284–287. On the authenticity of chapters 46–51, see Umberto Cassuto, "The Prophecies of Jeremiah Concerning the Gentiles" [1917], in *Biblical and Oriental Studies*, vol. I: *Bible*, trans. Israel Abrahams (Jerusalem, 1973), pp. 178–226.

3. James Muilenburg, "Jeremiah the Prophet," in *The Interpreter's Dictionary of the Bible*, II (New York and Nashville, 1962), 824, col. 1.

4. See J. Philip Hyatt, "Jeremiah and Deuteronomy," *Journal of Near Eastern Studies*, 1 (1942), 156–173 (reprinted in Perdue and Kovacs, pp. 113–127); idem, "The Deuteronomic Edition of Jeremiah," in R. C. Beatty, J. P. Hyatt, and M. K. Spears, eds., *Vanderbilt Studies in the Humanities* (Nashville, 1951), pp. 71–95 (reprinted in Perdue and Kovacs, pp. 247–267). Cf. John Bright, "The Date of the Prose Sermons of Jeremiah," *Journal of Biblical Literature*, 70 (1951), 15–35 (reprinted in Perdue and Kovacs, pp. 193–212), especially Appendix A.

5. See, for example, William L. Holladay, "A Fresh Look at 'Source B' and 'Source C' in Jeremiah," *Vetus Testamentum*, 25 (1975), 394–412 (reprinted in Perdue and Kovacs, pp. 213–228), and sources reviewed there.

6. See, for example, Bright, *Jeremiah*, pp. lv–lxxxv, especially lvi–lxiii; idem, "The Date of the Prose Sermons," in Perdue and Kovacs, pp. 198–199.

7. For a summary of critical opinion on the book's composition, see Walther Zimmerli, *Ezekiel 1: A Commentary on the Book of the Prophet Ezekiel, Chapters i–xxiv* (Philadelphia, 1979), pp. 3–8; Brevard S. Childs, *Introduction to the Old Testament as Scripture* (London and Philadelphia, 1979), pp. 357–360.

8. See, for example, Walther Eichrodt, *Ezekiel: A Commentary*, trans. Cosslett Quin (Philadelphia, 1970), pp. 11–22; and compare the "holistic" approach of Moshe Greenberg, *Ezekiel 1–20: A New Translation with Introduction and Commentary*, Anchor Bible, XXII (Garden City, N.Y., 1983), especially pp. 18–27.

9. More extreme views of the book's date include C. C. Torrey, *Pseudo-Ezekiel and the Original Prophecy* (1930; reprint, New York, 1970) (the Hellenistic period), and James Smith, *The Book of the Prophet Ezekiel: A New Interpretation* (London, 1931) (northern Israel, eighth century B.C.E.).

10. See Zimmerli, *Ezekiel 1*, p. 24.

11. On the "proof-saying," see ibid., p. 38 and n. 195.

SUGGESTED FURTHER READINGS

Peter R. Ackroyd, *Exile and Restoration* (Philadelphia, 1968).

Joseph Blenkinsopp, *A History of Prophecy in Israel* (Philadelphia, 1983).

Umberto Cassuto, "The Arrangement of the Book of Ezekiel," in *Biblical and Oriental Studies*, vol. I: *Bible*, trans. Israel Abrahams (Jerusalem, 1973), pp. 227–240.

Michael Fishbane, "'A Wretched Thing of Shame, a Mere Belly': An Interpretation of Jeremiah 20:7-12," in Robert M. Polzin and Eugene Rothman, eds., *The Biblical Mosaic: Changing Perspectives* (Philadelphia, 1982), pp. 169–183.

Moshe Greenberg, "On Ezekiel's Dumbness," *Journal of Biblical Literature*, 77 (1958), 101–105.

Geoffrey Hartman, "Jeremiah 20:7-12: A Literary Response," in Robert M. Polzin and Eugene Rothman, eds., *The Biblical Mosaic: Changing Perspectives* (Philadelphia, 1982), pp. 184–195.

Abraham J. Heschel, *The Prophets* (Philadelphia, 1962).

H. van Dyke Parunak, "The Literary Architecture of Ezekiel's Mar'ot Elohim," *Journal of Biblical Literature*, 99 (1980), 61–74.

Timothy Polk, *The Prophetic Persona: Jeremiah and the Language of the Self, Journal for the Study of the Old Testament*, Supplement 32 (Sheffield, 1984).

Shemaryahu Talmon and Michael Fishbane, "The Structuring of Biblical Books: Studies in the Book of Ezekiel," *Annual of the Swedish Theological Institute*, 10 (1976), 129–153.

Tufts University

The Twelve Prophets

Herbert Marks

THE Book of the Twelve Prophets, the most heterogeneous of the twenty-four that make up the traditional Hebrew canon, is a prophetic anthology, containing writings composed over a period of almost five hundred years. As such, it presents problems and opportunities for reading similar in many ways to those posed by the Bible as a whole. Not only the individual books, but informal sections within the same book, adjacent verses, and even words within a single verse are the work of various hands, reflecting different historical contexts, different rhetorical conventions, different or flatly incompatible ideological perspectives. Such a text challenges our common habit of construing meaning with reference to the intentions of an imagined author.

Interpreters generally resort to one of several fictions to replace this missing figure of the author, including the supreme fiction of a divine intentionality or spirit, embracing incompatibles and transmuting the accidents of juxtaposition into a unique plenum. Weaker alternatives include the attempt to focus on a particular stage of the text's history: perhaps to isolate an "original" core in each book going back to the prophet himself; or, since this involves the loss of much material, to posit instead a final editor of great perceptiveness and subtlety, responsible for the extant form of the text, whose vagaries may thus be recovered as meaningful. Perhaps the fullest reading is the one that alternates between these latter extremes, compassing the contraries of voice and text—though recognizing at the same time that there are more than two stages, the "final" one no less elusive than its predecessors.

The earliest mention of "the twelve prophets" occurs in the deuterocanonical Wisdom of Jesus ben Sirach, written early in the second century B.C.E. (The common designation "minor prophets," referring to the relative brevity of the individual books, not to their importance, probably derives from Augustine, *City of God* 18.29.) The collection is thought to have assumed its unitary form sometime in the century before. The compilers of the Hebrew text apparently aimed for a chronological arrangement. The first six—Hosea, Joel, Amos, Jonah, Obadiah, and Micah—belong, or were thought to belong, to the eighth century, a period which saw a resurgence of Assyrian power and the fall of the Northern Kingdom.

The critically dubious placement of Obadiah and Joel, which lack historical superscriptions, may be based on verbal association (Hosea 14:1 followed by Joel 2:12, Joel 3:16 by Amos 1:2, Amos 9:12 by Obad. 19). In the case of Jonah, the most anomalous member of the collection, the placement accords with the chronological setting of 2 Kings 14:25, the verse that gave the book its protagonist. (In the Septuagint, the order within the chronological division is by length: Hosea to Obadiah, with Jonah last, where it stands as a sort of commentary on the entire collection.)

The next three books—Nahum, Habakkuk, and Zephaniah—belong to the years of Assyrian decline at the end of the seventh century B.C.E. Again, verbal association probably affected the order within the chronological division (Hab. 2:20 and Zeph. 1:7, with Nahum placed first because of the subtler connection of 1:2–3 with the final verses of Micah). The last three books—Haggai, Zechariah, and Malachi—all belong to the beginning of the Persian period (late sixth and early fifth centuries), which saw the rebuilding of the Temple and the consolidation of Israel's cultic and legal traditions under the control of the priesthood. Because the biblical writings at the time of their final compilation were already approaching the status of Scripture, the two distinct principles of literary organization—representation or mimetic verisimilitude in the effort to recreate a historical schema, and formalization in the reliance on verbal ties—did not appear incompatible. Both the text and its ostensible subject matter were God's *davar*, his "work" or "word."

It is a striking fact that, with the exception of the pseudonymous Jonah, none of the Twelve is mentioned anywhere in the Book of Kings, which covers the same period as the pre-Exilic prophets (although the mysterious "man of God" from Judah who prophesies against Jeroboam in 1 Kings 13 has been compared to Amos of Tekoa). This raises questions about the motives for the collection, which in other respects shows signs of Deuteronomic shaping. Perhaps the editors intended it as a supplement to the history books. Yet the final count of twelve prophets seems less a reflection of the material available than a deliberately imposed convention, designed to enforce a radical kind of closure. The book of Jonah, a didactic or satirical narrative rather than a collection of prophetic sayings, fits awkwardly with the rest of the Twelve (see the following essay by James S. Ackerman); and there is some question whether Malachi, which begins with the same distinctive phrase—"oracle of the word of YHWH"—found elsewhere only in the two anonymous collections belatedly added to the book of Zechariah (see Zech. 9:1, 12:1), was not broken off from them to make a separate unit. In the Hebrew arrangement witnessed by Sirach, the Twelve come immediately after the three "major" prophets, Isaiah, Jeremiah, and Ezekiel. The pattern of three plus twelve recalls the three patriarchs and the twelve sons of Jacob—one of the basic paradigms of Israelite historiography, repeated again among the apostles of Jesus and among the twelve "tribes" at Qumran with their council of twelve laymen and three priests. By accommodating the prophetic corpus to such a type, the editors were in effect assimilating prophecy to a canonical rule, solidly rooted in communal tradition. (A similar imposition is probably responsible for the final shape of the book of Psalms, whose five sections correspond to the "five fifths of the law," as the Pentateuch is called.) From this perspective, "The Book of the Twelve" may well be an anti-prophetic document, restricting prophecy to a limited number of sources, whose authority depends on established precedent. In a famous passage, Amos likens the call to prophesy to an irresistible and unsolicited natural force: "The lion hath roared, who will not fear?/the Lord God hath spoken, who can but prophesy?" (3:8); and in the account of the debate at Bethel with the priest Amaziah, the prophet appears as an ordinary herdsman, compelled against his will to leave his flock and declare God's judgment (7:10–17). The elaboration of a fixed canon of prophetic writings forecloses, even as it enshrines, this charismatic tradition, in which the vested authority of an Amaziah could be set at nought. Yet its internal discrepancies and the power of its discordant voices have continued to inspire successive waves of reform—political, religious, and literary.

Text and Voice

Compilation is, of course, only the final stage in the complex compositional process by which the prophetic books as we know them evolved. Amos and those who came after him are called the "writing prophets" to distinguish them from others such as Nathan and Elijah whose acts are recounted in the Deuteronomic History, but it is likely that the majority of them delivered oral speeches, which often went through several stages of transmission before being written down. Scholars sometimes postulate a series of hypothetical layers, beginning with the actual words of the prophet, for the most part short sayings or oracles prompted by a particular historical situation and addressed to a particular audience. Such sayings conform to one of a limited number of formal models, similar in many respects to literary genres, although, as with more familiar genres, the boundaries between them are by no means clear. Preserved by his followers, the words of the prophet would eventually have been combined into small collections, supplemented in a few cases by short biographical narratives, such as the account of Amos's conflict with Amaziah (Amos 7:10–17) or the third-person account of Hosea's marriage (Hosea 1). At a later stage, the collections would have been brought together into something like the current books, often with the addition of framing material, which, like the revisions and interpolations at each step in the process, reflected the new perspective of the editors.

The relevance of this general scheme varies from book to book.

Nahum, Habakkuk, Zechariah, Malachi, and Joel were probably written compositions from the outset. Even with books that did evolve in the manner just described, critical reconstruction requires a verse-by-verse analysis, often based on a circular series of inferences. Yet a few characteristic patterns are still apparent. The most obvious reflect the change in perspective that followed the collapse of the Northern and Southern Kingdoms. In the face of these catastrophes and the ensuing harshness of exile, the old prophetic burden of condemnation and warning gave way to new tasks of encouragement. Concurrently, the emphasis on specific transgressions and actual historical circumstance receded in favor of a freer orientation toward an unspecified future resonant with eschatological overtones. In the case of Amos 9:11–15, for example, we may infer that stylistically distinctive expressions of hope or comfort were simply appended to the end of an extant collection, thereby transforming the prophecies of judgment—now fulfilled—into a provisional movement in the drama of eternal deliverance. This revisionary tendency was confirmed by Jewish tradition, which, as the early reference in Sirach suggests, remembered the Twelve principally as agents of comfort:

> May the bones of the twelve prophets
>   revive from the place where they lie,
> for they comforted the people of Jacob
>   and delivered them with confident hope. (49:10)

The Book of Micah has perhaps the most extensive redactional history among the Twelve, and it will be instructive to consider both its final form and the hypothetical stages in its composition. The superscription permits us to identify Micah as a contemporary of Isaiah, likewise active in the kingdom of Judah before and after the fall of Samaria to the Assyrians in 722 B.C.E. The invectives and threats in the first three chapters are, except for minor expansions, generally accepted as "genuine" sayings of the prophet, who shows a particular sympathy for the poor of the land, referred to as "my people" (2:4, 8, 9; 3:2, 3), and a corresponding hostility to the institutions of power centralized in the capital. Corruption and injustice among the princes, landlords, priests, and guild prophets have provoked YHWH's judgment of doom against Jerusalem, which Micah here proclaims in defiance of the complacent Temple theology (3:9–12).

A similar ethical perspective seems to motivate the covenant lawsuit in 6:1–5 (cf. Hosea 4:1) and the oracles immediately following, including the repudiation of ritual sacrifice in favor of the personal virtues of justice, kindness, and "humility" (6:6–8; cf. Amos 5:21–24, Hosea 6:6). By contrast, the pseudonymous prophecies of redemption from exile, of Jerusalem's future glory and hegemony over the nations, and of a Davidic ruler who will shepherd his people "as in the days of old" (chaps. 4–5 and 7) clearly reflect a post-Exilic setting (note the explicit reference to Babylon in 4:10).

From these antithetical traditions the redactors have created three literary units, each introduced by an injunction to "hear" (1:2, 3:1, 6:1), in which oracles of judgment are followed by oracles of salvation. As in Isaiah 2–12, which shows a similar pattern, the transitions are abrupt. For example, Micah's oracle against Jerusalem, which ends by reducing the Temple mountain to a wooded height, is followed immediately by the prophecy of Zion's exaltation when the Temple mountain "shall be established in the top of the mountains . . . and people shall flow unto it" (4:1). (The same oracle of eschatological triumph appears in Isa. 2:2–4, which, alongside the many thematic and stylistic features shared by the two collections, points to a common history of redaction.) Theologically, the unmotivated reversals suggest the absolute freedom of YHWH. At the same time, they seem to reflect the psychological paradox of power in vulnerability, or of anxiety generating strength, of which the "confessions" of Jeremiah and certain psalms of lament are the most prominent Hebrew models, analogous to the infernal descents of epic and the passions of classical tragedy and the New Testament.

The confessional paradigm is most evident in chapter 7, which reproduces the disjunctive logic of the previous sections in a quasi-liturgical setting. As with so many prophetic passages, how we read the chapter depends in the first instance on where we locate the original units and thus, by inference, the marks of literary elaboration. Were verses 8–20 (or some part of them) once a separate liturgy in which sequentially responsive expressions of human trust and divine promise, of petition and praise, were arranged for choral recitation? Or were the "responses" composed, or collected and ordered, by the same anonymous hand that published them as Micah's? How are they related to the hymnal introit (1:2–4) which now opens the entire book? Can we assume the unity of even the opening lament (7:1–6), with its bitter, and perhaps incongruous, outburst of imperatives (7:5) reminiscent of Jeremiah 9:4? What, in either case, is the relation of its first-person speaker to the feminine "I" of the ensuing confession (7:8–10), whose references to sin and judgment recall the divine lawsuit that opens the larger redactional section (6:2), and whose gender (apparent in Hebrew from the feminine possessive in the quoted taunt at 7:10) suggests a collective personification (compare the personified city of 6:9)? Finally, what are the relations between both these figures and the "I" of the pivotal verse that links them—perhaps a redactional hinge, mediating the transition from judgment to salvation with a declaration of patience and faith: "But as for me, I will look unto the Lord;/I will wait for the God of my salvation:/my God will hear me" (7:7 [AR])? The text as we have it resists univocal answers; nor need we suppose that its indeterminacies were foreign to the sensibility of the redactors. At the least, the allusiveness with which "wait" (*'oḥilah*) at the midpoint of the passage gestures toward the anxious "writhing" (*ḥuli*) of the daughter of Zion (4:10), while the verb translated "I will look" (*'atsapeh*) picks up the stem elsewhere associated with the prophetic "watchman" (7:4), suggests a deliberate convergence of desperation and confidence, of individual and communal identity.

As the example of Micah illustrates, redactional "order" in the Prophets is not always perspicuous. The received texts are cluttered and chaotic, and the signs of literary shaping have studiously to be recovered from under a welter of vestiges and interpolations. Even where deliberate patterns may be confidently traced, they frequently overlie one another, like the superimposed figures of paleolithic cave art—the successive tradents, authors, and editors having valued polyphony and suggestive density more than formal decorum. The persistence of discordant features that resist assimilation may result in part from the peculiar status of the Israelite literature as evolving Scripture, a repository of collective traditions that could more safely be expanded or rearranged than canceled. But regardless of its cause, it contributes largely to the aesthetic impact of the collections, which in the self-occlusion of their rough formal structures, as in the sheer abundance of their "difficult ornaments," are the reflection or perhaps the model of Israel's image of the divine.

Although it was shaped in different circles and attained its approximate form earlier than Micah, the Book of Hosea also comprises three smaller collections, each of which tempers inexorable judgment with a final promise of forgiveness. The main collection in chapters 4–11, framed by call and messenger formulae (4:1, 11:11), is composed of short, mostly isolated oracles, which Lowth compared to "the scattered leaves of the Sibyl" (*Lectures on the Sacred Poetry of the Hebrews*, lect. 21). They seem to proceed from accusation to threat to promise, though there is also evidence of chronological grouping, and local organization is frequently determined by theme or catchword (see especially 4:4–5:7, where the various sayings all denounce religious syncretism under the figure of "whoredom"). Throughout, there is a unifying concern with fidelity (*ḥesed*) to the Covenant, equated with "knowledge of God" (4:1). Religious abuses, ranging from violation of covenant law (4:2 may represent an early form of the decalogue) to idolatry (8:5) and participation in the Canaanite fertility rites (4:13–14), have led YHWH to reject his people: they shall be "swallowed up" among the nations (8:8), "smitten" and "dried up" (9:16), their king "utterly . . . cut off" (10:15); in short, "they shall return to Egypt" (8:13; 9:3, 6).

The later sayings especially are dense with allusions to Israel's history, presented both to accuse and to remind the audience of the special legacy they are in danger of forgetting. This historical bond is the basis for the moving depiction of YHWH as a troubled father unable to forget his wayward son, which has been placed near the end of the collection, where it prepares for the final promise of restoration at 11:11:

> When Israel was a child, I loved him,
>   and out of Egypt I called my son.
> The more I called them, the further they went from me;
>   they sacrificed to the Baals and burned incense to graven images.
> Yet it was I who taught Ephraim to walk,
>   taking them up in my arms;
>   but they did not know that I cared for them.   (11:1-3 [AR])

In the lines that follow, the conjunction of judgment and promise has been enlarged by the successive arrangement of disparate oracles into a dramatization of divine pathos, in which the rhetorical turns reflect the turning against themselves of YHWH's wrath and compassion: "my heart turns against me ['alay], / my repentings are kindled together" (11:8 [AR]). Such conjunctions defy the pressure of events, enacting a deep though often inaccessible human reality, here troped as the freedom of radical otherness: "for I am God, and not man; / the Holy One in the midst of thee" (11:9).

The last three chapters repeat the general movement of the main collection, beginning with illustrations of Jacob/Israel's legendary "deceit" (11:12; see also Gen. 27:35, 29:25) and ending with a series of salvation oracles that expand on the reciprocal relationship between Israel's "return" and YHWH's "turning." Return is also the burden of the composite narrative of Hosea's marriage in chapters 1-3, which in its present form serves as an introduction and hermeneutical guide to the collected oracles. This is one of the most heavily interpreted sections of the prophetic literature, although much of the discussion has centered on moral or supposedly biographical questions: Are the women in chapters 1 and 3 the same? Are all three children in fact Hosea's? Is Gomer a common prostitute, and, if so, how could God have commanded his prophet to marry her? Concern over Hosea's moral purity is equally evident in the many allegorical interpretations, which date back to the Targums, and in the rationalizations of Origen and Maimonides, who treated the passage as a prophetic vision.

Somewhat more to our purpose are the modern debates over the relation between the biographical memoir in chapter 1 and the first-person narrative in chapter 3. The most reasonable solution—and the most exegetically productive—is to treat the two as originally independent versions of the same tradition, which the editors here arranged in narrative sequence with the addition of the adverb "again" in 3:1 ("Go again") so as to create a story of alienation and reconciliation against which Hosea's own prophecies to Israel must now be read. (In the received text this pattern is partly obscured by subsequent expansions, identifiably addressed to Judean and post-Exilic audiences and more eschatological in tone; examples include 1:7, 1:10–2:1, and 3:4–5.) The emphasis in the first chapter, taken by itself, is not really on marriage or harlotry, but on the naming of the three children, a typical form of symbolic action (see Isa. 7–8). The sequence is cumulative and leads to cancellation of the covenantal bond based on YHWH's self-revelation at Sinai: "for ye are not my people, and I will not be your God" (1:9, literally, "I am not your I am," a punning allusion to the divine name; cf. Exod. 3:14). The pairing of the two accounts, however, puts the focus on the marriage, and specifically on the wife's "whoredoms," a loose figure for Israel's infidelities, very probably based on Hosea's own trope in the main collection, which develops the sacred marriage of Canaanite ritual into a figure for religious apostasy.

Accordingly, the redeemed "adulteress" of 3:1 is identified with Gomer, but in place of the history of estrangement needed to motivate the reconciliation, the editors have inserted a collection of oracles (chap. 2) depicting Israel's religious apostasy under the erotic figure of the faithless woman. A close reading of this apparently homogeneous material reveals several traditionary strands and a good deal of editorial stitching, but the clearest break is at 2:14, where accusation and threat suddenly give way to promises of comfort:

> Therefore, behold, I will allure her,
> and bring her into the wilderness,
>   and speak comfortably unto her . . .
> and she shall sing there, as in the days of her youth.   (2:14–15)

The transition, willful despite its conjunction, simulates the unconditioned generosity of YHWH—conveyed in the surrounding narrative through the actions of his prophet—and thus dictates our reading of the marriage story as a parable of divine forgiveness. In this reciprocal glossing of symbolic action and prophetic discourse it is impossible to say which takes precedence, just as it is impossible to say whether the three-chapter unit, which could conceivably have circulated on its own, would have provided the model for the arrangement of the main collection or have been elaborated in its wake. Moreover, its double plot, for all its persuasiveness, does not annul the severity of the original traditions, still discernible beneath the redactional arrangement, but rather leaves their ultimate authority in suspense.

The powerful short Book of Nahum, which Lowth judged "without equal in boldness, ardour, and sublimity," provides a different model of the way redactional mediation can loosen a prophetic message from its original historical context. The core of the book, chapter 2, is a poetic tableau describing in vivid language the destruction of Nineveh, last capital of the Assyrian Empire. The dramatic details—chariots, torches, plunder, massed corpses—are all typical and reproduce the language of Near Eastern treaty curses. Whether the sack of the city was an accomplished fact or only actively anticipated at the time the poem was written is thus uncertain. The destruction is presented in process, a technique distorted by the King James Version, which translates the imperfect verbs as future, but appreciated by the Deuteronomic editor, who in the superscription introduces the book generically as a "vision." The description culminates in a magnificent cadence in which the repetition of "all" enforces the note of finality, and the conversion of splendor to ruin is represented not in itself, but more powerfully by its effect on those who suffer it:

> She is empty, and void, and waste [*buqah umebuqah umebulaqah*]:
>   and the heart melteth, and the knees smite together,
>   and much pain is in all loins,
>   and the faces of them all gather blackness.   (2:10)

An ironic coda (2:11–12) generalizes the action, moving from description to the emblematic association of Assyria with the lion, while the *ubi sunt* motif converts lament to taunt in accordance with a pattern characteristic of Hebrew victory odes (cf. the Song of Deborah, Judges 5:28–30).

Chapter 3, though not integral with the preceding vision of the sack, continues it, beginning with a conventional woe oracle addressed to the "bloody city" Nineveh but modulating immediately into another cinematic montage of battle scenes. The juxtaposition of moral category and visual image works like a medieval emblem, the final "heaps of corpses" standing as a translation of, and judgment on, the rapacity that here seems to be its cause, while "none end of . . . corpses" (3:3) likewise comments upon "none end of . . . store" (2:9) in the previous section. The subsequent series of variations includes an ironic recollection of mighty Thebes, destroyed fifty years earlier by Assyria with a ruthlessness now transferred back upon Nineveh.

It has been suggested that the original Nahum was a cult prophet attached to the Jerusalem Temple and that the linked poems in chapters 2 and 3 are extensions of the nationalistic genre of oracles against foreign nations. Similar material is common throughout the prophetic writings and forms a distinct section of the books of Nahum's contemporaries Jeremiah (46–51) and Zephaniah (2:4–3:8). In the latter, these oracles are the central section in a tripartite structure that moves from threats against Judah (1:2–2:3) to promises of salvation (3:9–20). The same dialectical arrangement is found in the Greek text of Jeremiah and may have helped shape the convention of the apocalyptic battle that ushers in the millennium in such late writings as Zechariah 14, Joel 3, and Revelation 20. It is a powerful schema which gives narrative organization to Israel's inherently ambivalent relation to YHWH, a God "merciful and gracious . . . and [who] will by no means clear the guilty" (Exod. 34:6–7). In psychological terms, it projects guilt and consequently the feared judgment onto the nations before introjecting the desired presence, now relieved of its threat.

We see this structure most clearly in the Book of Zephaniah, where the imminent "day of YHWH" is conceived, following Amos 5:18–20, as a "day of wrath" on which Judah will be judged and the whole earth "devoured [te'akhel] by the fire of his jealousy" (Zeph. 1:18). At the end of the central section of oracles against the nations, ending with Assyria, the same phrase recurs (3:8); but now the judgment has been displaced onto the foreign nations who are the object of the preceding oracles. The ensuing gospel of redemption then concludes with a literal image of internalization in which YHWH the "devourer" assumes a place "in the midst" of Israel (3:15, 17). This internalization is reciprocal, for YHWH promises to "gather [in]" the afflicted (3:18), a figure related to the remnant motif which runs through the book (2:3, 7, 9; 3:12) in keeping with the example of Zephaniah's Jerusalemite predecessor Isaiah. Like the recurrence of the key word "devour" ('kl), the distribution of the verb "gather" reinforces the three-part movement of the book. The Hebrew stem 'sf has two nearly antithetical senses, on the one hand "ingathering," on the other "removal" or "destruction," and the prophet's message, like the fate of Judah, is suspended between them. The promises of salvation culminate in the "ingathering" in 3:18 (a conclusion enlarged in the brief post-Exilic coda); but this is only the merciful counterpart of the threatened decreation with which the opening doom on Judah began: "I will utterly destroy ['asof 'asef] all things from the face of the earth, says the Lord. I will destroy ['asef] man and beast; I will destroy ['asef] the birds of the air" (1:2–3 [AR]). The effectiveness of the wordplay is of course just as great whether we derive the irregular forms in 1:2–3 from 'sf, "gather," or take them as homonymous forms of the stem suf, "cease." If the latter, we gain an added dimension of verbal play, in which historical and etymological alternatives are both resolved in favor of "ingathering" rather than "cessation." Between the two terms, the threatening sense is again projected onto the nations, which YHWH determines to "gather" for destruction (3:8) as part of the definitive "devouring" that terminates the book's middle movement.

The destruction of Assyria in Nahum corresponds to this second movement taken in isolation from the theological context, the condemnation and remission of Israel's sin, which gives the nation oracles their meaning in the other pre-Exilic prophets. Readers who value the austere emphasis on cultic purity and social justice in Amos, Hosea, and Micah have thus tended to depreciate a prophet who seems content to glorify vengeance. Yet it is precisely here that we must distinguish between the early strata of the book and the final setting; for in the edited collection, the reader comes to Nahum's vision of martial triumph by way of an independent hymnic composition, celebrating God's supernatural power and presenting his ultimate control of historical ends as an aspect of his primal authority over all creation:

> He rebuketh the sea, and maketh it dry,
>> and drieth up all the rivers . . .
> The mountains quake at him,
>> and the hills melt,
> and the earth is burned at his presence,
>> yea, the world, and all that dwell therein.   (1:4–5)

In this context the destruction of Nineveh is no longer an aggressive vindication of Jewish nationalism but, more generally, an illustration of God's universal government. As in Obadiah, a specific prophecy may now be read either with reference to its historical setting or within a revisionary frame that tends toward eschatology.

The hymn proper is an acrostic covering the first half of the Hebrew alphabet and ends at 1:8, but the short oracles that follow, adjoined to the hymn by the repetition of *kalah*, "utter end" (1:8, 9), and punctuated with the definitive phrase *lo 'od*, "no more" (1:12, 14, 15; see also 2:13), reinforce the eschatological orientation. The two locutions are conjoined in the final verse of chapter 1, which occupies an ambiguous position between the hymnic material and the anti-Assyrian poems which it may be read as introducing:

> Behold upon the mountains the feet of him
>> that bringeth good tidings,
>>> that publisheth peace! .
> O Judah, keep thy solemn feasts,
>> perform thy vows:
> for the wicked shall *no more* pass through thee;
>> he is *utterly cut off.*   (1:15)

The opening verset is a direct echo of Isaiah 52:7 (cf. 40:9), and thus an indication that the final form of the book (as of Micah) may have been shaped by the same late-Exilic circles responsible for the transmission of the Isaianic material. There are good grounds for supposing that these editors may have been moved by an incipient sense of a biblical canon, that they tried to free the extant traditions and writings from their historical anchors, to open them to continual reinterpretation within a dialectical context created by the aggregate of Israel's literary heritage. Here the echo both invites assimilation to the cosmic theology of Deutero-Isaiah and invokes by association the characteristic emphasis on salvation. Taken in isolation, the messenger's proclamation is related to the command in the same verse to keep the feasts. But within the larger context of the book, the tidings appear to refer to the visionary poems that follow. In this way the vindictive account of Assyria's destruction is redefined as a consequence or aspect of the promise of eschatological peace. In light of the echo, the very name of the prophet comes to recall the message of comfort—*naḥamu naḥamu 'ami,* "Comfort, comfort, my people"—with which Deutero-Isaiah begins (40:1).

Redactional use of an independent hymn is also discernible in Amos and in the final chapter of Habakkuk. In Amos, three "strophes" of what may originally have been a single composition celebrating YHWH's power over creation in implicit refutation of the claims of Canaanite deities (hence the refrain "YHWH is his name") are introduced into the collection at moments of exceptional severity, as though to solemnize the words of divine judgment (4:13, 5:8–9, 9:5–6). In Habakkuk, as in Nahum, the hymn helps to relocate the contingent or historical action at the core of the book. Against the turmoil and uncertainty of human affairs—the world of existential immediacy which is the traditional scene of prophecy—the compilers set the elemental features of the phenomenal world (light and darkness; earth, sea, and sky) in their timeless sublimity. The two orders so juxtaposed have almost nothing in common except the dominion of YHWH, personified in the hymns where the approach is descriptive, and represented in the oracular forms by the dynamic force of the word, a dramatic figure for the grammatical modes of command, dread, and desire, as for the principle of causal succession. It is for the reader to specify more precisely the relation between cosmology and history, and thereby to define the nature of their common term. But since no simple formula (inside-outside, above-below, whole-part, cause-effect) can explain the relation, one is thrown back on the human motives generally associated with the different genres, alternating between the willful impulses of desire and fear expressed in the oracles and the contemplative impulse to praise, accept, and endorse magnified in the hymn.

In Nahum this absolute order is encountered at the beginning of the book. It provides a theocentric perspective from which to interpret the historical action that follows, approaching the contingent by way of the absolute. In Habakkuk, which has a more complex structure and compositional history, the pattern is reversed. The first section (1:2–2:5) has been organized as a dialogue in which YHWH answers the prophet's complaints about the fate of the righteous. A series of woe oracles against an unnamed enemy (2:6–20) is then followed by the hymn in chapter 3. Further seams are evident in each of the three sections, and the scattered historical allusions are inconsistent, making dating extremely difficult. In its attempt to reconcile the facts of suffering and injustice with the idea of divine governance, the book reflects the tradition of Israelite Wisdom literature (cf. Ps. 73), while in overall structure it resembles certain psalms of lament, beginning with petition and ending with hymnic celebration. The parallel with Psalms 74 and 77 is particularly close, the hymnic conclusion to the latter echoing almost word for word in Habakkuk 3:10–11.

The opening dialogue is itself a liturgical form, rooted in the responsorial patterns of Temple worship—a mode which Deutero-Isaiah develops most fully. By lending a new animation to the prophetic voice, it focuses attention on the person of the prophet. In Habakkuk, however, its suggestiveness depends largely on the dramatic inconsistencies which result from the composite structure. Scholars have tried to construct a unified scenario for the section, but it is precisely the disjunctions—the fact that prophetic complaint and divine response appear to be at cross-purposes—that account for its resonance.

Habakkuk's initial complaint concerns YHWH's silence before the demise of justice:

> O Lord, how long shall I cry,
>   and thou wilt not hear?
> or cry out to thee of violence,
>   and thou wilt not save? . . .
> So the law fades,
>   and judgment slackens;
> for the wicked surround the righteous;
>   so judgment goes forth perverted.   (1:2, 4 [AR])

The violence here is evidently internal, a continuation of the abuses attacked by the classical prophets. YHWH's response, however, announces an imminent military invasion, a violence of a different order, which, although it does not dull the issue of theodicy, shifts it into the international arena: "lo, I raise up the Chaldeans, / that bitter and hasty nation" (1:6). The response is equally surprising from a formal perspective, for by generic convention the prophet's petition ought to have been followed by a divine word of comfort. Habakkuk's second complaint (1:12–2:1) renews the emphasis on social justice, but the appeal is now set within the larger context of national defeat, which the prophet first accepts as a chastisement (1:12) and then decries (vv. 15–17). The final response reconciles without resolving the disparate perspectives by reorienting the prophet toward a future event of indeterminate content which the righteous must faithfully attend:

> And the Lord answered me and said,
> Write the vision, and make it plain upon tables,
>   that he may run that readeth it.
> For the vision is yet for an appointed time,
>   but at the end it shall speak, and not lie:
> though it tarry, wait for it;
>   because it will surely come.   (2:2–3)

For all its surprising shifts and sublimations, the dialogue manages to generate a logic of its own, or to goad us into constructing one. It is a logic that in fact points toward the hymn of chapter 3—a redactional appropriation of a bolder sort—which extends and completes the responsorial pattern, but in at least two different ways. On the one hand, the description of YHWH the divine warrior driving forth from Mount Paran functions like the theophanies in the Psalms or the appeal to the splendor of creation at the conclusion of Job. It commands assent beyond the logic of theodicy by convincing us, rhapsodically rather than discursively, that the power of YHWH is incommensurate with human notions of purpose and, by extension, with human notions of justice. It thus fills the place of the withheld vision which the prophet was commanded to write (2:2–3). On the other hand, the conclusion of Habakkuk's second complaint has left us in anticipation not only of God's answer but also of the prophet's subsequent reaction:

> I will stand upon my watch,
>   and set me upon the tower,
> and will watch to see what he will say unto me,
>   and what I shall answer when I am reproved.   (2:1)

From this second perspective, the hymn expresses the personal reconciliation of the prophet. The succession of complaints has established a pattern of prophetic answering which the hymn now forgoes. Like Job's final speech, it marks Habakkuk's acceptance of the divine "reproof" and so follows movingly on the injunction to "keep silence" before YHWH enthroned in his Temple, which concludes the intervening woe oracles (2:20; cf. Zeph. 1:7).

This second function of the hymn is underlined by the expansions (3:2, 16–19) which link it to the watchtower speech (2:1) and, via the key word "hear," to the prophet's opening lament:

> O Lord, I have heard thy speech, and was afraid.   (3:2)

> When I heard, my belly trembled;
>   my lips quivered at the voice . . .
> Yet I will rejoice in the Lord,
>   I will joy in the God of my salvation.   (3:16, 18)

Together with 1:2 and 2:1, these verses constitute the autobiographical frame within which the original traditions have been assembled. The choice of such a structure suggests again that for the final editors the troubled status of prophecy itself was an urgent issue. The concern is evident already in the several sections. The command to "write the vision" (2:2) echoes the similar command in Isaiah 30:8, where the issue is precisely the indifference of the people to the prophetic word. Likewise, the parallel between "law" (torah) and "judgment" (mishpat) in the first complaint (1:4) suggests that judgment may refer as much to a languishing genre of prophetic speech as to social justice. Hence the "judgment" of the lawless Chaldeans which "goes forth from themselves" (1:7 [AT]) becomes not only a corrective but also an ironic replacement for the "judgment" that "doth never go forth" from the beleaguered prophet in Judah (1:4). The word used in that context is not "prophet" but tsadiq, "righteous one," and it is difficult to hear the famous verse at the end of the dialogue, directing the "righteous" to "live by faith" ('emunah, 2:4), without recalling those in Judah who would not "believe" (1:5, same stem), though YHWH, or his prophet, spoke the word.

The autobiographical frame dramatizes this predicament by attaching it to the personal experience of a typical figure. As the divine warrior is finally a personification of divinity, so the watchman on the tower is finally a personification of prophecy, erected more likely than not in the face of rising skepticism and disaffection with the tenets of prophetic religion. Psalm 74, which also moves from petition to celebration, fixes at its nadir on the cessation of prophecy: "there is no more any prophet:/ neither is there among us any that knoweth how long" (74:9). One might say that the Book of Habakkuk, which is structured according to a liturgical form, supports the traditional view of the prophet as messenger against such despair. It does so in part through its formal indeterminacies, which allow the concluding hymn to be read simultaneously as God's response or the prophet's. On a smaller scale, the pivotal image of Habakkuk looking forth from his watchtower to catch both YHWH's word and his own response conflates the two voices dramatized in the dialogue. The final phrase—literally, "what I shall answer concerning my reproof ['al-tokhaḥti]"—is ambiguous: does "reproof" refer to the prophet's challenge to YHWH or to YHWH's challenge to the prophet? In the context of the book as a whole, the ambiguity marks a fusion and so reaffirms the place of the prophet as the divine spokesman.

WHEN THE AGING Goethe began the *West-Oestlicher Divan*, his commemorative journey back to the sources of lyric, he envisaged a return to "the air of the patriarchs," to a primordial world in which "the word carried such weight because it was a spoken word." As we have seen, the prophetic collections are far from being the loose *diwan* form to which they are sometimes compared, yet in our preoccupation with their specifically literary features we tend to overlook the more difficult questions of representation and inflection, which in prophecy as in lyric are figurations of voice. Ezekiel consumes a written scroll as a sign of his prophetic vocation; but the pre-Exilic prophets, who to the best of our knowledge indeed delivered their sayings orally, depend for their power on fictions of presence, on effects of invocation and evocation, which strain against all forms of literary fixation.

A full description of these effects might begin with the combination of rhetorical mobility and thematic restraint: the exuberant crowding of violent and often incongruous figures, reminiscent of the boldness of popular speech, and the narrow repertoire of themes and referents (YHWH, Israel), which sustain such ceaseless variety. More subtle perhaps are the agitated shifts of grammatical markers, especially tenses and pronouns, which project the ambiguities of the divine messenger form into the domain of syntax; and the marked insistence on patterns of causal motivation, the incessant "therefore," which becomes, paradoxically, a figure for the unentailed power of YHWH (and hence of prophetic speech). Each of these effects is animated by a strong antithetical impulse, and scholars have dedicated entire monographs to its ethical corollary, the "prophetic no." The characteristic will to negation was already obvious to the disciples of Amos, who epitomized it in the argument or motto to his collected sayings—

> The Lord roars from Zion,
>   and utters his voice from Jerusalem;
> the pastures of the shepherds mourn,
>   and the top of Carmel withers   (Amos 1:2 [AR])

—where the prophet's own figure for the irrepressibility of prophetic voice (the lion's roar, 3:8) is wedded to natural figures of ruin and desolation.

Amos's voice, supreme among the Twelve, is "the voice of honest indignation," identified by Blake as the genius of prophecy, and his magnificent rhetoric is consistently, even monotonously, antithetical. The first section of the book (chaps. 1–2) shows his deployment of the well-attested prophetic genre of oracles against the nations. The standard messenger form, "thus saith the Lord," introduces the specific accusations, and these are followed in turn by an announcement of judgment. The denunciation of Israel's enemies was a standard task of official prophecy. Amos, however, turns it to his own purpose. At an earlier stage, the section probably comprised five oracles (compare the five visions in chaps. 7–9 and the five forms of self-indulgence castigated in the woe sayings of chap. 6). Damascus, Gaza, Ammon, and Moab were all long-standing enemies; but Amos goes on, extending the list to Israel itself:

> Thus saith the Lord;
> For three transgressions of Israel,
>   and for four, I will not turn away the punishment thereof;
> because they sold the righteous for silver,
>   and the poor for a pair of shoes.   (2:6)

The traditional terms by which YHWH's messenger assured his people of their God's special protection are here used to declare that no special bond exists. Israel is similar to the other objects of YHWH's wrath, only more culpable. The Wisdom formula "three transgressions and four" suggests a pattern of cumulation and surfeit in accordance with which Israel, in the larger scheme of the whole oration, is the supernumerary term. Thus the cited atrocities of the nations—including the ripping up of pregnant women by the Ammonites and the desecrations of the Moabites—are only preliminaries to the more severe transgressions against social justice perpetrated in Israel.

To group Israel with the nations is to negate the whole history of salvation and thereby to upset the foundations of communal identity. The same disavowal determines the reinterpretation of the Exodus which is placed toward the end of the book, just before the eschatological coda. That YHWH led Israel "out of the land of Egypt" is the basis of the earliest credos, providing the frame within which even the Law is promulgated (Exod. 20:2). Amos dismisses it:

> Are ye not as children of the Ethiopians unto me,
>   O children of Israel? saith the Lord.
> Have not I brought up Israel out of the land of Egypt?
>   and the Philistines from Caphtor,
>   and the Syrians from Kir? (9:7)

Amos's campaign against inequity, his zealous pursuit of social justice, thus leads to a paradoxical repudiation of the covenant relation itself, which in Israelite tradition determines the very possibility of justice.

It is difficult to comprehend this ecstatic fury of the negative. Where does the energy for the prophet's wrath come from? How and why does he persist against all odds in rejecting accommodation? To speak of the social context of prophecy, of schools or support groups, only evades the central question of a poetic power which in its hallucinatory intensity recalls the megalomania, the magic words and obsessional ideas, of the paranoiac. Like paranoid delusions, prophetic zeal may be a function of repression, or, more precisely, of the failures of repression, which allow the will to break through in disguised forms and to elaborate, in place of the forbidden world, its own structures of psychological and social affliction. The aggression at the root of all poetic enthusiasm has been recognized since Longinus, the first literary critic to mention the Bible, but it burns hottest in the prophets, who, themselves afflicted, inflict their word on everything about them. Indignation includes but is not limited to social criticism. The poetic ire of Amos extends to poetry itself, consumed with other expressions of human capability, in a universal leveling:

> I hate, I despise your feast days,
>   and I will not smell in your solemn assemblies.
> Though ye offer me burnt offerings
>   and your meat offerings, I will not accept them:
>   neither will I regard the peace offerings of your fat beasts.
> Take thou away from me the noise of thy songs;
>   for I will not hear the melody of thy viols.
> But let judgment run down as waters,
>   and righteousness as a mighty stream. (5:21–24)

Beyond the aptness of water as a figure for leveling, righteousness in Amos is catastrophic. "Judgment" (*mishpat*) is translated "justice" in all the modern versions, and the parallel references to those who convert justice and righteousness to wormwood (5:7, 6:12) seem to confirm this social emphasis. But the Hebrew sustains the fuller range of meanings preserved in the King James Version, where "judgment," like its older synonym "doom," may suggest condemnation or even calamitous visitation (see also Hosea 5:1, 11; 10:4; Isa. 4:4, 26:9). The association of justice and cataclysm, reinforced by the metaphorical depiction of Israel's fate in the rise and fall of the Nile (8:8) and by allusions to the Flood in two of the three late hymnic passages scattered through the final redaction (5:8, 9:6), resembles the antithetical treatment of the "day of YHWH" in the preceding verses. Again the word is directed with an almost vindictive ferocity against the structure of communal defense and presumption, which by Amos's time had modified the old tradition of the divine warrior into a vision of eschatological victory:

> Woe unto you that desire the day of the Lord! to what end is it for you? the day of the Lord is darkness, and not light. As if a man did flee from a lion, and a bear met him; or went into the house, and leaned his hand on the wall, and a serpent bit him. Shall not the day of the Lord be darkness, and not light? even very dark, and no brightness in it? (5:18–20)

Such reversals, which cut the prophet's polemic off from its institutional foundations, amount to an anticreation, more radical for being less systematic than the deliberate cancellation of the priestly ordering found, for example, in Jeremiah 4:23–26. Anticosmic gestures are a basic strategy of much Western literature, but the force of Amos's negations is foreign to literature, where aggression is typically converted into *contemptus mundi*, iconoclastic quest, or the rage for aesthetic order, while its object is subsumed into some ulterior reality—often a book, a similitude or "mesocosm" which preserves the world it would resolve. This sublimation is thematized in Dante's *Divine Comedy,* in Spenser's *Mutabilitie Cantos,* in Proust's *Remembrance of Things Past,* but it is implicit to one degree or another in every poetic or fictive work, beginning with the elegiac eighth book of the *Odyssey,* where we first feel the loss of the heroic present, its liminal vulnerability, by way of its immortalization in the song of the rhapsode Demodocus. In the later prophetic writings, we are given something similar. A book, or its visionary prototype, usually an apocalypse or dream text, subsumes the perceptual reality negated by the prophetic word. By contrast, the oral rhetoric of early prophecy refuses to convert its passion, whether for an artifice of eternity or for a seat in the apocalyptic theater. The negations of Amos make their own amends.

Vision and Revision

Among the techniques productive of "grandeur, magnificence and urgency," one of the most notable, according to Longinus, is *phantasia* or visualization, "the situation in which enthusiasm and emotion make the speaker see what he is saying and bring it visually before his audience" (*On the Sublime,* 15). Hosea describes God as multiplying visions when he speaks to the prophets (12:10), and word and vision are frequently grouped together in the Deuteronomic superscriptions: "the word which Amos [Isaiah, Micah, Habakkuk] saw." We have seen the use Nahum makes of *phantasia* in his vision of the destruction of Nineveh. In later Hebrew prophecy, the extended vision or apocalypse becomes a distinct literary genre with its own special conventions. The most developed instance of it among the Twelve occurs in Zechariah, often called the most obscure of the prophetic books.

From the point of view of its composition history, Zechariah is really several books, but our chief concern here is with the late sixth-century prophet represented in chapters 1–8, who, together with his contemporary Haggai, actively promoted the reconstruction of the Temple under Zerubbabel (see Ezra 5:1–2, 6:14). Support for the Temple project was by no means universal in Judah, despite the Persian policy of encouraging the restoration of local forms of worship throughout the empire. From what we can gather, control of the YHWH cult following the return from exile had come increasingly under the domination of a single class of priests who traced their authority through Zadok from Aaron. Consequently, the disfranchised, including many of the Levites and Temple prophets, opposed the Zadokite program with eschatological fervor, expressing their hostility to institutionalized religion through the antithetical and visionary rhetoric of classical prophecy (see, for example, Isa. 66:1–4).

The "night visions" of Zechariah, in their final form as an integrated sequence, are designed on the contrary to lend divine legitimation to the Temple program of the Zadokites. At least some of the eight visions must originally have served a different function. The vision of the divine horsemen (1:8–17) presumes that Jerusalem and the cities of Judah are still suffering the afflictions of the conquest. Likewise, the vision of the four horns (1:18–21) seems to be an allegorical judgment against Babylonia, and the vision of the man with the measuring line (2:1–5) a possible warning against fortifying Jerusalem for revolt. By contrast, the visions of the flying scroll (5:1–4) and of the woman in the ephah (5:5–11) appear to address conditions after the return, when reclamation of property rights and exclusion of the *gerim,* or foreign colonists, were crucial issues (see Ezra 4:1–5). The flying scroll is particularly striking: on the one hand it is a figure, derived from Ezekiel, for the word of God incarnate in the scroll of the Law; yet its vast dimensions are those of the vestibule of the Temple of Solomon (1 Kings 6:3; see also Ezek. 40:14), the implication being that the two dispensations, word and Temple, are coextensive.

In Zechariah as it now stands, these visions have all been assigned the same date: shortly after the laying of the Temple foundation in the second year of Darius (520–19), the same year in which Haggai was exhorting Zerubbabel to get on with the work of building (Zech. 1:7, Hag. 1:2–4). It seems likely that they were first arranged in a group of seven, symmetrically distributed about the central figure of the menorah, whose seven lamps, interpreted as "the eyes of the Lord, which run to and fro through the whole earth" (4:10), represent God's presence enshrined in the Temple. From this center the divine power radiates out through Jerusalem and Israel (the visions of the wall and the scroll) to the nations (the visions of the horns and the ephah) and on to the ends of the earth, patrolled by the two tetrads of horsemen in the first and last visions. The vision of the filthy garments in chapter 3, which is formally distinct and upsets the symmetry, may represent a subsequent and more directly polemical response to the accusations of the antihieratic party, here identified with Satan, who is rebuked for challenging the high priest Joshua. Several short passages, such as the word to Zerubbabel focusing on YHWH's "spirit" (4:6–10) and the eschatologically oriented prophecy of YHWH's glory "tabernacling" (*shkn*) in the midst of Zion (2:8–12; cf. Ezek. 37:27, 43:9), also seem to be expansions on the basic composition, which is traditionary rather than charismatic in emphasis.

The Book of Zechariah marks an important step toward the full-fledged apocalyptic prophecy of Daniel, Second Esdras, and the Book of Revelation. These works were the models for the view of prophecy as "visionary theater" which dominated the thinking of the Middle Ages and the Renaissance, influencing the conception of the prophetic vocation shared by Dante and Milton. There is a certain logic, even an inevitability, in the way the symbolic vision emerges as the final stage in prophecy's historical development. Given the highly imagistic texture of the pre-Exilic oracles, apocalyptic might even be considered the generic expression of a visual pressure latent already in classical prophecy, where the dominant tropes (prosopopoeia, apostrophe) work to personify the abstract and to make the absent present. Hosea, for example, represents YHWH in dizzying succession as husband, lion, healer, birdcatcher, father, leopard, she-bear, cypress, and even pus and rot; and his figurations of Israel are still more visual and prolific. Moreover, prophetic forms probably evolved in part from the practice and rhetoric of divination, including of course the interpretation of dreams, common in Israel as throughout the ancient Near East.

The affinities with divination are particularly evident in the visual puns and associative techniques deployed by Amos in one of the earliest examples of the genre subsequently developed by Zechariah. Amos's five visions compose a carefully graduated series. In the first two (7:1–3, 4–6), the prophet recognizes figures of imminent destruction (locusts and fire), which he succeeds in deflecting by a moving appeal to YHWH's mercy. In the next pair (7:7–9, 8:1–3), interrogation replaces intuitive understanding as he is forced to acknowledge the inevitability of YHWH's judgment in the appearance of the plumb line and the summer fruit. (The shrewd placement of the encounter with Amaziah between visions three and four both provides a fuller context for Amaziah's hostility and hints at Amos's ultimate vindication.) Interpretation of the fourth vision depends on a rebus, the "basket of summer fruit" (*qayits*) suggesting by paronomasia the "end" (*qets*) of Israel. A similar instance of audiovisual play occurs in Jeremiah 1:11–12, where the prophet is shown a rod of almond (*shaqed*) to signify that YHWH is watching (*shoqed*) over his word. In both examples the prophetic word must be inferred from its revelatory image, and in Amos the vision even terminates in a repudiation of speech: "corpses scattered everywhere; be silent [*has*]" (8:3 [AT]). The final vision (9:1–4), following a series of oracles which enlarge on the theme of judgment, concludes the series by showing *how* the announced end will come, beginning with the destruction of the sanctuary and extending outward. In five structurally parallel versets the prophet reproduces the fivefold pattern of the larger sequence, the formal reiteration intensifying the sense of finality. Each line depicts a different attempt at evasion. The first four (hell, heaven, mountain, and sea) are again composed into pairs, while the isolated fifth (political captivity) reconfirms the historicity of the threat, and hence the reality and immediacy of the vision.

Prophecy is thus, from the very beginning, a matter of visual no less than aural hallucination—or at least its rhetorical simulation. According to Maimonides, for whom all prophetic revelation was a form of imaginative vision akin to dreaming, the superior imagination, when not receiving and imitating things perceived by the senses, can receive and imitate the intellectually mediated "overflow" of the divine presence (*The Guide of the Perplexed*, 2.36). A modern writer might be more inclined to substitute "the unconscious" for "the divine," but the functional observation still holds. From a Freudian perspective prophecy could be described as "archaic" or "regressive"—a displacement of thought by hallucination along a metaphorical chain which begins with sensations and proceeds via mnemic images through words to verbal complexes or thought. If mnemic images are more primitive than words, we can understand the tendency of the prophets, oriented ethically as well as psychologically toward the primordial, to displace or confuse word with vision. Thus, in the first vision of Zechariah, seeing and showing are interwoven with speaking and answering in what seems, semantic flexibility notwithstanding, like a deliberate synesthesia: the "vision" being prompted by an initiatory "word of YHWH" and having at its center a dialogue and a command to "cry out" (Zech. 1:7–15).

FOR THE MOST PART, the visions in Amos depend on the prophet's direct apprehension of verbal and visual associations. In Zechariah, by contrast, we see the emergence of a new intermediary figure, the interpreter angel, influenced perhaps by the heavenly messenger that guided Ezekiel (Ezek. 8:2, 40:3). It is he who now exercises the traditional prophetic prerogatives of intercession and proclamation (Zech. 1:12, 14–15). The change signals a shift in emphasis from the direct transmission of YHWH's word to greater reliance on the revelations of the past, which, with the acceleration of scribal activity, are beginning to acquire authoritative status. Henceforth, the word of YHWH will be increasingly mediated by a textual tradition until, in the stories of Joseph and Daniel, interpretative skill is itself represented as charismatic.

Even from the beginning, however, vision and revision were inseparably fused, not only in the prophets' tendency to exploit historical ideals against contemporary norms, but also in their adaptation of specific tropes and forms. Amos refers repeatedly to his prophetic forerunners, as do Hosea, Isaiah, and Micah, who moreover echo either Amos or one another with impunity. Jeremiah, whose early sayings are strongly indebted to Hosea's, even has YHWH complain about the prophets who steal divine words "every one from his neighbour" (23:30). The revisionary impulse extended to legal and narrative traditions as well. Thus Hosea's interpretation of the Jacob saga as a parable of rebellion and reconciliation reads like an aggadic transformation of the Genesis story (or of the underlying traditions):

> The Lord hath a controversy with Judah [originally "Israel"?],
>   and will punish Jacob according to his ways . . .
> He took his brother by the heel in the womb [cf. Gen. 25:26],
>   and in his strength he strove with God [cf. Gen. 32:22–32]:
> Yea, he strove with the angel, and prevailed [cf. Gen. 32:28]:
>   he wept, and made supplication unto him . . .
> So thou, by the help of thy God, return [cf. Gen. 28:15, 21];
>   hold fast to loyalty and justice,
>   and wait on thy God continually.   (Hosea 12:2–6 [AR])

Here Hosea's concern with the possibility of forgiveness has converted the wily patriarch into a type of the wayward son of chapter 11, an example to the rebellious nation of the efficacy of reform.

A more narrowly verbal appropriation is evident in the hymnic conclusion to Micah, where the key words are all borrowed from the traditional list of divine attributes, which YHWH proclaims to Moses before his renewal of the Sinai Covenant. Since much of the final section of Micah is cast as a covenant lawsuit, the echoes are particularly appropriate:

> The Lord, the Lord, a God *compassionate* and gracious, slow to *anger,* and abundant in goodness and truth, keeping *mercy* for thousands, *pardoning iniquity* and *transgression* and *sin* . . . (Exod. 34:6–7 [AR])

> Who is a God like thee, that *pardoneth iniquity*
>   and passeth by *transgression* . . . ?

> he retaineth not his *anger* for ever,
>> because he delighteth in *mercy*.
> He will again have *compassion* upon us . . .
>> thou wilt cast all our *sins*
>> into the depths of the sea.   (Micah 7:18–19 [AR])

The same formula undergoes a somewhat more complex transformation, with the emphasis turned from forgiveness to vengeance, in the brief segment that interrupts the acrostic hymn at the very beginning of Nahum (1:2b–3a).

In late interpolations such as these, and in the writings of the post-Exilic prophets, we can see the revisionary gestures becoming more deliberate, the network of echo and allusion increasingly dense. Such persistent reference to earlier texts is an active part of the circular process of canon formation. Sources, elevated by virtue of being cited or echoed, lend back their growing authority to the writings that appear to sustain their tradition. The obsession with a textual heritage which animated the founders of Judaism and Christianity at the turn of the era thus has its origins in the later layers of the Bible itself. When Haggai (who alludes to Amos and Jeremiah as well as to the Holiness Code) is directed to "ask . . . the priests concerning the law" (2:11), the word *torah* probably signifies a mere point of "instruction," but both the juxtaposition of accepted formulas, presumed binding, in the passage that follows (2:11–14) and the style of reasoning from them to a current moral exigency anticipate the methods of rabbinic exegesis.

For Zechariah, likewise, the authority of the scriptural word outlives the cry of its occasion, as is evident from the editorial introduction, in which YHWH speaks with the voice of the Deuteronomists: "Your fathers, where are they? and the prophets, do they live for ever? But my words and my statutes, which I commanded my servants the prophets, did they not overtake your fathers . . . ?" (1:5–6 [AR]). Such long-suffering words help to generate the visions themselves; for the prophecies of the seventy years' captivity (Zech. 1:12; see Jer. 25:11, 29:10), of the avenging smith (Zech. 1:20; see Isa. 54:16), of the man with the measuring line (Zech. 2:1; see Ezek. 40:3), and of the righteous Branch (Zech. 3:8, 6:12; see Jer. 23:5, 33:15) all have their source in "the former prophets" (Zech. 1:4; 7:7, 12), revised by the deferred action of an "interpreter angel."

In contrast to Haggai and Zechariah, who combine messianic rhetoric with a dedication to the Temple cult, the author of Malachi uses intertextual echoes to sharpen his protest against current abuses. Malachi 1:6–2:9, the second and longest of the book's six disputations, is a virulent attack on the Zadokite priesthood, who in elevating themselves above the other Levites "have corrupted the covenant of Levi" (2:8). On the surface, the passage is a critique of ritual misfeasance, but its denunciations are sharpened by a pattern of ironic references to the words of the Priestly blessing

(Num. 6:23–27), whose authority, according to how one interprets the echoes, is either mocked or directed against its own custodians. The priests, solemnly bound to "put [YHWH's] name upon the children of Israel" (Num. 6:27), have come to "despise [his] name" (Mal. 1:6), and consequently their "blessings" have been "cursed" (2:2). YHWH's protection or "keeping" (Num. 6:24) has become the priests' failure to "keep" his ways (Mal. 2:9); the "shining" (from *'or*) of the divine countenance (Num. 6:25) has become their vain "kindling" (same stem) on the sacrificial altar (Mal. 1:10). Polluted offerings have so vitiated their rote appeals for "grace" (Num. 6:25, Mal. 1:9) that YHWH will no longer "lift up his countenance" upon them (Num. 6:26, Mal. 1:9); instead he will cover their "countenances" with dung (Mal. 2:3 [AT]), for they have corrupted the covenant of "peace" (Num. 6:26, Mal. 2:5) and have been partial in administering the Law (literally, "lifted their countenances against the *torah*"; Mal. 2:9).

The allusive texture is probably densest in the late Book of Joel, sometimes called the "learned prophet," who, though sedulous in his recreation of the old oral forms, must have composed his prophecies in writing toward the close of the Persian period (early fourth century B.C.E.). Like the authors of the two pseudonymous collections sometimes known as "Second Zechariah" (Zech. 9–14), Joel appeals to textual traditions in support of an eschatological vision which will supersede the theocratic reliance on ritual and law. His picture of the endtime, later adopted by the author of Acts for Peter's speech at Pentecost (Acts 2:1–21), includes a radical democratization of spiritual authority:

> And it shall come to pass afterward,
>   that I will pour out my spirit upon all flesh;
>   and your sons and your daughters shall prophesy,
>   your old men shall dream dreams,
>   your young men shall see visions.   (Joel 2:28)

Yet this very passage is itself heavily indebted to at least two literary models: Ezekiel's prediction of the outpouring of spirit upon the house of Israel (Ezek. 39:29), which also underlies the transition from the previous oracle (cf. Joel 2:27 and Ezek. 39:28), and Moses' defense of unauthorized prophecy in the Wilderness camp (Num. 11:29)—a parodoxically mediated projection of unmediated experience.

As in the Book of Obadiah, Joel's vision of the coming day of YHWH supervenes on a historical event. The disastrous plague of locusts, described in chapter 1, gives way in chapter 2 to a vision of divine hosts leaping upon the mountaintops and darkening the heavens as they gather to execute the word of judgment. Following a call to "return to YHWH with all your heart" (2:12 [AT])—based not, as for the Deuteronomists, on a devotion to *torah*, but rather on a full acceptance of the prophetic threat, such that YHWH himself will "return and repent" (2:14; cf. Amos 4:6–11; Hosea 3:5, 14:1; Mal. 3:7; Jonah 3:9–10)—the second half of the book announces a new season of plenty before depicting, in what may be a secondary expansion, the final day when YHWH will judge the nations in the valley of Jehoshaphat ("YHWH judges") and at last "utter his voice from Jerusalem" (3:16) as Amos 1:2 had promised. Every episode in this sequence is so rich in prophetic echoes that it would take an extensive commentary even to begin to unravel them. Worth noting, however, for its theoretical interest is the way Joel presents the words of an earlier prophet as divine speech (2:32b, quoting Obad. 17a), while at the same time taking liberties with established texts, as in his inversion of the beautiful oracle of peace found in Micah and Isaiah—"Beat your plowshares into swords, and your pruninghooks into spears" (Joel 3:10; see Micah 4:3, Isa. 2:4)—or of the Isaianic prophecy of a wilderness transformed into Eden (Joel 2:3; see Isa. 51:3).

The danger of such bold revisionism is the growing burden it places on those who would extend the chain of supersessions. Amos, the earliest of the writing prophets, already expressed an impatience with prophetic forms, and it was perhaps inevitable that the prophetic corpus would ultimately include, together with its diatribes against priestly abuses, the anticipation of a day in which prophecy itself would cease:

> And it shall come to pass, that when any shall yet prophesy, then his father and his mother that begat him shall say unto him, Thou shalt not live; for thou speakest lies in the name of the Lord . . . And it shall come to pass in that day, that the prophets shall be ashamed every one of his vision. (Zech. 13:3–4)

By the time this was written, the evolving canon of prophetic writings had long begun to displace direct revelation as an imaginative force within Israelite culture. The wonder is that the theocratic circles, having established the Torah as a bulwark against charismatic religion, failed to suppress the emerging collections. The antagonism is especially evident in the coda to the Pentateuch, which chooses oddly to stress the uniqueness of Moses, "whom the Lord knew face to face" (Deut. 34:10), thereby putting the revelation at Sinai and the Deuteronomic law beyond the reach of prophetic supersession.

The conclusion to the Book of the Twelve seems in many ways to be a deliberate counterpart to this passage in Deuteronomy. As such, it testifies again to the wisdom of the final compilers, who recognized that the future of the collection required not the suppression of divergent ideas but their juxtaposition under the most extreme reciprocal pressure. The new coda begins with an exhortation to preserve the authoritative body of scribal traditions: "the law of Moses my servant, which I commanded unto him in Horeb for all Israel" (Mal. 4:4). But this injunction is then balanced by a final glance toward the eschatological future, of which the prophets rather than the scribes were the appointed wards. In Malachi 3:1, YHWH has already announced the coming of a divine messenger who will purify the priesthood: "Behold, I will send my messenger [mal'akhi]"—a revisionary conflation of the Deuteronomic "prophet like [Moses]" (Deut. 18:18) with the divine messenger mentioned first in the Covenant Code (Exod. 23:20) and again in the anti-Aaronic context of the Golden Calf episode (Exod. 32:34). In the coda, this figure is identified with Elijah, the archetypal prophet, who, like Moses, heard the divine voice at Sinai (see 1 Kings 19):

> Behold, I will send you Elijah the prophet before the coming of the great and dreadful day of the Lord: And he shall turn the heart of the fathers to the children, and the heart of the children to their fathers, lest I come and smite the earth with a curse. (Mal. 4:5–6)

The late version of this passage in Sirach speaks of Elijah's coming "to turn the heart of the father to the son, / and to restore the tribes of Jacob" (48:10), and it is tempting to carry the parallel back and to see in Malachi too an allusion to the twelve tribes, of which the Twelve Prophets may have been a reflection. Of course, in the order most frequently attested, these verses conclude not only the Book of the Twelve but the prophetic corpus as a whole. From this perspective, both the prophecy of the eschatological forerunner and the closing threat take on ulterior meanings—the "curse" in particular reflecting the long succession of failures, which from the Garden of Eden through the Wilderness wanderings, and again, for the Deuteronomists, from the conquest of the Land through the defeat of Judah, had characterized sacred history.

Later generations were sensitive to the implications of such a perspective. For most English readers, the last verse of Malachi is followed directly by the "good news" of the Gospels. In its proclamation of the word made flesh, the New Testament represents the abrogation of the open-ended or endlessly self-perpetuating revisions of prophetic literature. It propounds its central presence once and for all. Likewise, Jewish Bibles regularly repeat the promise of Elijah's coming in small print following the final verse, thus ending the collection on a hopeful note and converting the anxiety of succession into a figure of eternal return or of timeless expectation. Sheltering in the comfort of these traditional responses, the solitary reader may occasionally look beyond to the prophets' more ominous alternative.

SUGGESTED FURTHER READINGS

Joseph Blenkinsopp, *A History of Prophecy in Israel* (Philadelphia, 1983).
———, *Prophecy and Canon* (Notre Dame, Ind., 1977).
Martin Buss, *The Prophetic Word of Hosea* (Berlin, 1969).

Brevard S. Childs, *Introduction to the Old Testament as Scripture* (London and Philadelphia, 1979).

Michael Fishbane, *Biblical Interpretation in Ancient Israel* (Oxford, 1985).

James Luther Mays, *Micah: A Commentary* (Philadelphia, 1976).

Robert R. Wilson, *Prophecy and Society in Ancient Israel* (Philadelphia, 1980).

Hans Walter Wolff, *Hosea: A Commentary*, trans. Gary Stansell (Philadelphia, 1974).

———, *Joel and Amos: A Commentary*, trans. Waldemar Janzen, S. Dean McBride, Jr., and Charles A. Muenchow (Philadelphia, 1977).

Indiana University

Jonah

James S. Ackerman

ALTHOUGH the Book of Jonah appears among the Minor Prophets in the biblical canon, it differs considerably from all the others as a piece of literature. Whereas the Major and Minor Prophets are essentially collections of oracles, Jonah recounts the adventures of a prophet who struggles against his divine commission. The story rather recalls the prophetic legends in 1 and 2 Kings that focus on Elijah, Elisha, and others. Scholars have struggled with the problem of genre, and there is no consensus. I prefer the general label "short story," and I will later try to point out elements in the narrative that bring it close to classical satire.

The story was probably written during the sixth or fifth century B.C.E., when Jews were struggling to adjust to and recover from the Babylonian Exile. How were they to perceive the nature of God in the light of what had happened? By what means could the community transform its institutions and traditions in order to adapt itself to the changed circumstances? Drawing on a wide range of biblical allusions, as well as on a bit of Mediterranean folklore (the fish episode), the writer scrutinized some of the answers that were evolving. In doing so, he created a literary masterpiece that has captivated its readers and stirred artistic imaginations from the Midrash to Melville—long after the particular issues faced by the post-Exilic community had been resolved.

"Jonah son of Amittai" (1:1) is surely a reference to the eighth-century Northern Kingdom prophet briefly described in 2 Kings 14:25 as a popular prophet who, in the context of the Israelite king's sin, proclaims divine mercy and support for that kingdom. The name means "Dove son of truth," and the dove has two major characteristics in the Hebrew Bible: it is easily put to flight and seeks secure refuge in the mountains (Ezek. 7:16, Ps. 55:6–8), and it moans and laments when in distress (Nahum 2:7; Isaiah 38:14, 59:11). Will these characteristics, we wonder, also apply to our hero? And what meaning will the story give to "son of truth"?

The formula in 1:1 makes it clear that Jonah is a prophet, but we are surprised and intrigued by the divine command. Prophets had pronounced judgment on enemy nations within the safe confines of Israelite territory. But commanding a prophet to enter a foreign city with a word of judgment from the Lord—given the mistreatment and misunderstanding the prophets suffered when they spoke to God's own people Israel—is, to say the least, an expansion of the prophetic vocation! Jonah is commanded to "arise . . . go . . . and cry against" (1:2); he immediately "rose up to flee" (1:3). Reluctance to serve is a conventional feature of the genre of prophetic call (cf. Jer. 1:6). But Jonah's total disobedience puzzles us, especially when we learn that his flight is "from the presence of YHWH."

Nineveh and Tarshish are geographic antipoles. Nineveh, to the east, is the later capital of Assyria, the very nation that would destroy and carry off Jonah's people—the ten tribes of the Northern Kingdom—sixty years later. The Assyrians were renowned for their power and gross cruelty, and allusions in our story recall the Flood and the judgment on Sodom and Gomorrah. Thus we know Nineveh as a city whose power is a threat to Israel's existence and whose evil is antithetical to God's will. Tarshish, on the other hand, lies somewhere in the far west and is a place where YHWH is not known (Isaiah 66:19). Jonah, a servant fleeing his master's sovereignty, also sees Tarshish as a refuge beyond YHWH's domain. Since the story depicts YHWH as the almighty creator God, it has placed Tarshish at the ends of the earth, where death and chaos begin. Strangely, Tarshish also connotes luxury, desire, delight. C. H. Gordon suggests that "whatever the original identification of Tarshish may have been, in literature and popular imagination it became a distant paradise."[1] For Jonah, therefore, Tarshish may paradoxically represent a pleasant place of security that borders on nonexistence.

Prophets were thought to be servant-messengers who attended the divine court, "standing before YHWH's presence" (as in 1 Kings 17:1), just as royal servants stood "before the presence" of their king. Jonah's flight from YHWH's presence is described as a series of descents (Hebrew *yarad*): he "went-down"—to Joppa, into the ship, and into the innermost part of the ship. He then lay down and fell into a deep sleep, the latter term again echoing the *yarad* descent pattern. This motif—extremely common in Psalms—is continued in Jonah's prayer, which describes his entering Sheol, the world of the dead (2:2–9). The narrative, therefore, seems to be depicting Jonah's flight from YHWH's presence as a descent to the underworld. Our prophet is taking a path that leads to death as he seeks to avoid the road to Nineveh.

The unusual term *yarketei hasefina* ("the innermost parts of the ship," 1:5 [AT]) seems to be a wordplay on *yarketei tsafon,* which in Psalm 48 is equated with Mount Zion (the city of our God, the final refuge for Israel against the attacking nations) and in Isaiah 14:12–19 is described as God's dwelling place in the heavens (the antipole of Sheol, the Pit, into which Lucifer has been brought down). Why is the writer asking us to think of Zion, God's dwelling place, as we read of Jonah's descent into the hold of the ship? Is the ship both a mini-Sheol and a mini-Zion, or is there an antithetical relationship? We are also given clues that this is no ordinary ship that is leaving the Joppa seaport. Jonah pays "her fare" [AT]; and when the storm hits, "the ship thought to be broken up" [AT]. Nowhere else in the Hebrew Bible are "fare" and "thought" used with inanimate objects. What kind of a maw has our hero entered in his descent from YHWH's presence?

The ship's captain and crew are depicted quite sympathetically. In contrast to our sleeping prophet, they resourcefully pull out all the stops in order to stay alive—praying to their gods, jettisoning their cargo, casting lots. They know that their fate is in the hands of higher powers whose workings they cannot fathom ("if so be that God will think upon us, that we perish not," 1:6; "for thou, O Lord, hast done as it pleased thee," 1:14). They also do everything possible to save Jonah's life. Jonah had descended, lain down, and slept. The captain tells him to "arise"; the crew tries to "return" [AT] to dry land. Describing death, Job says "so man *lieth* down, and *riseth* not: till the heavens be no more, they shall not awake, nor be raised out of their *sleep*" (14:12); "so he that *goeth down* to the grave shall come up no more. He shall *return* no more to his house" (7:9–10). Ironically, the captain's appeal to Jonah ("arise, call upon") echoes the divine command in 1:2. The captain is appealing to Jonah to "get up" and pray to his God; but by implication he is pointing the way by which Jonah can "arise" from his death descent. The crew are trying to steer the ship to shore, so that he can obey his divine commission; but by implication they are attempting to "return" him to the land of the living.

The sailors' frantic activity highlights Jonah's inactivity. Unlike Jesus (see Mark 4:35–41), his sleeping in the storm suggests paralysis rather than faith. We must assume that, in response to the captain's appeal, he continues to lie low and snore on. Taken out of context, his response in 1:9 sounds like a wonderful confession of faith. But he omits any confession of his disobedience, and his claim to fear YHWH rings hollow when contrasted with the growing piety of the sailors (see especially 1:16). We must join the crew and read the entire statement ironically: how does one escape "the God of heaven, which hath made the sea and the dry land," by embarking on the high seas? Although Jonah does not mention his flight, the sailors immediately realize what he has done.

Some interpreters see 1:12 as reflecting growth in Jonah's character. He now has more compassion for the crew, and, ready to accept God's judgment for his disobedience, he is willing to give up his life that the crew may survive. But Jonah's search for refuge from YHWH has been depicted as a descent toward death. This subconscious death wish is now reinforced by his request to be thrown into the sea. And even at the end of the story Jonah will still be claiming that death is preferable to life. Just as a lion summarily slays the disobedient prophet in 1 Kings 13, YHWH sends a great fish after Jonah; and the verb "to swallow up" never has a positive connotation in the Hebrew Bible. Korah and his followers were swallowed up by the earth/Sheol, as were Pharaoh and his chariots (Num. 16:28–34, Exod. 15:12). Thus YHWH seems to be reinforcing Jonah's descent pattern—three days and three nights being the traditional time it takes to reach the underworld.[2]

Much to our surprise, Jonah prays; and the Hebrew word denotes an appeal for help in which, if appropriate, divine forgiveness is sought. We expect the prayer to be a lament, and indeed the 3/2 stress pattern of the lament genre dominates. The tense of the opening verb is ambiguous, so we don't know at first whether to read "I cried" or "I cry." Since laments begin with an appeal for help, we assume that we are reading Jonah's cry for help. But as we read further, we discover that the prayer is a song of thanksgiving for *having been delivered* from death's domain. Scholars have made various attempts to naturalize this part of the story. The majority maintain that Jonah's prayer is a later insertion. But both in terminology (going down, calling out, steadfast love, vows and sacrifices) and in theme (casting, presence of God, idol worship, divine sovereignty) the song is closely tied to the rest of the story.

By setting us up to receive Jonah's song as a lament, the narrative forces us to question how a prophet heading toward the underworld could sing of his deliverance from Sheol. Jonah has feared drowning; he describes his sinking into the seas as a descent to the city of the dead (2:6). Why, then, does he feel so secure in the belly of the fish which he thinks is delivering him from the belly of Sheol? We know from 1:9 that Jonah is capable of making wonderful statements of faith in a context that turns every word to parody. Both the inner part of the Tarshish-bound ship and the belly of the fish give Jonah the same false, deathlike security. The prayer begins "I cried"—precisely the same action that Jonah had been commanded, by both YHWH and the captain, to carry out against Nineveh and in behalf of the ship. Having refused to cry out to save the others, he changes his tune when he himself faces the prospect of violent death. And when 2:3 continues: "for thou hadst cast me into the deep . . . I am cast out from thy presence" [AR], remember that it is Jonah who fled from the divine presence and who requested to be hurled into the sea.

Jonah regards idolaters (and there is a clever wordplay in 2:8 that associates them with the sailors of chap. 1) as deserters of *ḥesed*—a term indicating a chief characteristic of YHWH (translated as "mercy"), denoting a loving response performed within a covenant relationship. In some songs of thanksgiving, as in Jonah's, *ḥesed* can be virtually synonymous with God. But the idol-worshiping sailors have forsaken their gods and fear YHWH! It is Jonah who has forsaken his God; and, we will later discover, the main reason for his flight is God's superabundant *ḥesed* (4:2). In case we have missed this subtle contrast, the narrative permits Jonah

to conclude his prayer with a promissory note: someday he will perform
that which we know the sailors have already accomplished one thousand
leagues above (1:16).

Is it not strange that Jonah expresses his eagerness to return to the
Temple, especially when there is no mention of his repentance or willingness to go to Nineveh? Where is the fear of YHWH that he had owned
to in 1:9? Does he perceive his near-death in the waters as sufficient divine
punishment? Is he counting on divine *hesed* to overlook his disobedience
and cancel his commission? Is not the piety reflected in this song a bit too
cozy? To what extent is the story aligning the Temple with the ship's
hold and the fish's belly—as yet another deathlike shelter that he hopes
will protect him from fulfilling his divine commission?

In the Jonah story there are structural parallels between chapters 1
and 3, as well as between chapters 2 and 4. Chapter 4 also begins with a
lament appeal from Jonah, to which YHWH responds with actions and
questions. Although YHWH appoints the great fish in chapter 2, there is
no verbal response to Jonah's prayer. The divine response, though muted,
is still eloquent: YHWH commands the great fish to *vomit*; and if the
narrative had wanted to achieve any effect other than satire, there are
many other Hebrew words for "bringing forth" our hero onto dry land.
Again we are disoriented. The fish which we had thought was carrying
Jonah to his doom has indeed rescued him. Does Jonah's deliverance
confirm the viewpoint articulated in the prayer? I think not. The prayer
closes with "Salvation is of the Lord" (2:9)—a key theme of the story;
and to dramatize this very point, YHWH and the writer deliver Jonah by
a means that our imagination cannot naturalize—by simply letting the text
say that it is so. We have been subtly prepared for the just-as-miraculous
deliverance that will soon take place in Nineveh.

The second half of the story seems to return us to the beginning; but
there are some differences, and we are asked to account for them. This
time God gives the prophet a specific message, and Jonah now goes to
Nineveh. We cannot be certain that Jonah's oracle to the Ninevites is a
faithful repetition of God's words. Because the verbal repetition in 3:2–3
implies that Jonah is now complying with God's commands, and because
he will later turn on the deity for canceling the judgment he had pronounced, we can reasonably assume that "yet forty days . . ." (3:4) is
indeed the divine proclamation. Knowing that Nineveh will be "overthrown" in "forty days"—words that, along with others, recall the un-
leashing of divine judgment in the Flood and Sodom and Gomorrah
stories—Jonah may be more willing to comply.[3] From his foiled flight he
has learned that God is unrelenting in carrying out the divine will; thus
he can assume that the oracle he brings will indeed come to pass.

The response of the Ninevites is unprecedented in the prophetic
tradition: Jonah barely enters the city and speaks five Hebrew words (not

even introduced by "thus says the Lord"), and thereby instigates the most frantic reform ever heard of. In a scene that is both comic and moving (we can imagine animals and servants in sackcloth; unwatered flocks and nobility "crying mightily unto God"), the sinful city instantly and completely turns itself around. Through Jonah God "has cried unto" [AT] Nineveh; and now Nineveh "cries unto" that God. The Ninevites have "turned from" their "evil"; and now God "turns away" from the "evil" that had been planned for the city. This episode is replete with allusions to Jeremiah 36, in which the king of Judah scorns Jeremiah's warnings of impending judgment on Jerusalem. The narrative suggests a contrast between the bitter experience of the prophets in Jerusalem and the amazing success of Jonah in Nineveh. Had the writer used realistic narrative to depict Nineveh's repentance, we would have wondered whether the city's new heart could possibly be genuine and whether the remission of divine punishment was deserved. But the story's comic exaggeration permits us to accept the amazing transformation as "fact" precisely because we are asked to imagine it as a beautiful fantasy. We will soon learn that Jonah is unwilling to accept what has happened; thus the narrative has driven a wedge between reader and prophet—between the justice we had hoped would fall on the sinful city and the mercy we are made willing to imagine.

The story establishes a relationship between the great fish (in which Jonah remains three days and nights) and the great city (which requires three days to traverse). Both function as enclosures, and Jonah perceives them antithetically. The great fish is aligned with the ship's hold, Tarshish, and perhaps the Temple in Jerusalem—shelters that offer the illusion of security but in fact result in a deep sleep that brings one down to the city of Death. For Jonah the only negative enclosures are the city of Death, from which he barely escaped in the heart of the sea, and the city of Nineveh, from which he attempted to flee. As readers we begin the story by sharing Jonah's perception; but the possible Temple/fish/ship/Tarshish equation, coupled with the amazing conversion of Nineveh, prompts a realignment of these images. The narrative has consistently called Nineveh "the great city"; but in 3:3b the Hebrew reads "and Nineveh was a great city *for God*" [AT]. Jonah made the traditional equation between city of Nineveh and city of Death; but the story suggests that the opposite is potentially true. The key feature of Nineveh's reversal is its turning away from violence. The larger context, however, is the community's symbolic association with the world of the dead—through ashes, sackcloth, and fasting. Whereas Jonah's disobedience precipitated his descent to the world of the dead, Nineveh's symbolic death is part of a return from its evil way and an appeal to God that it be spared.

No prophet within the biblical tradition has ever had such success. Jonah flees his divine commission, and the entire crew ends up worshiping YHWH. He speaks five words in Nineveh, and the whole city instantly turns away from its "evil." But as God repents of the "evil" that has been planned for the city, this "evils" Jonah "a great evil" (4:1) [AT]. In the context of a petition prayer (the same word used for his activity in the belly of the fish in 2:1) we finally learn why Jonah has fled his divine commission. For the third time he proclaims a statement of faith from Israel's religious traditions (4:2; see Exod. 34:6, Joel 2:13). The first two, taken out of context, may initially be understood as positive affirmations. The narrative does not permit such a reading this time: I attempted to flee your realm because I knew that, ultimately, you are a merciful God. But why is Jonah so upset? A strong line of interpretation that goes at least as far back as the early rabbis proposes that Jonah is angry because he has been made to look foolish. When the judgment oracle does not come to pass, the prophet and his deity become the objects of taunting abuse. But we find no hint of this in the story.

It seems more likely to me that Jonah's problem is theological. Unlike Israel's ancient Near Eastern neighbors, who perceived their gods as capricious monarchs, the Exodus-Sinai experience convinced Israel that its God—the creator and redeemer God—was also a just God. Divine justice could sometimes take three or four generations to work itself out; but ultimately, Israel believed, people would receive their just deserts. And there could be no question about what Nineveh deserved. How could God possibly be swayed by one sudden change of heart, blotting out long generations of iniquity? If divine mercy can so easily cancel out divine justice, then life is arbitrary and capricious. Jonah's theological problem is the reverse of Job's. Whereas suffering causes Job to probe the caprice of divine sovereignty, the sparing of Nineveh drives Jonah to do the same. For both protagonists YHWH's rule must be expressed through a well-ordered universe. The story has satirized Jonah as a prophet whose piety is out of sync with his behavior. But Jonah, strangely, is also depicted as a man of faith driven to challenge and disobey God out of a zeal for divine integrity. Echoing the descent theme of chapters 1–2, Jonah would rather die than live in a world where a just God no longer reigns (4:3, 9).

In 4:5–11 we find that Jonah has not given up: he camps out east of the city, probably in the hope that Nineveh will falter (can a leopard change its spots?) and that divine judgment will finally fall.[4] The booth the prophet builds for himself reminds us of the shelter images that have recurred throughout the story. Israel is commanded to build and dwell in booths annually as an act of worship ("rejoicing"; see Deut. 16:13–14, Neh. 8:15–17); and the fact that Jonah also "rejoices a great rejoicing" [AT] in his booth suggests an association between shelter and worship. Psalms 31:20 uses the booth as a figure for the divine presence in which those who "fear" God are "hidden" (Hebrew *tsafan*; compare the *yarketei hasefina* in which Jonah hides); and Isaiah 4:6 envisions YHWH's covering Zion with a protective booth to "shade" it from the heat. Is Jonah's booth a dim reflection of Zion—of the Temple that had been the hoped-for destination of his song?

If Jonah has shaded himself with the booth, why does YHWH add the shade of the gourd? And how does that "deliver" (the Hebrew has a wordplay with "shade") Jonah from his "grief" (Hebrew "evil," that is, anger)? We should note that the first half of the story has concluded with a divine "preparation" that functions as a thematic resolution: Jonah had repeatedly "descended," so YHWH "prepared" a great fish "to swallow [him] up." Paradoxically, however, the fish *both* took Jonah all the way down *and* spewed him forth toward his commission. The same pattern obtains in chapter 4 if we interpret the three divine "preparations" in verses 6–8 as one interrelated sequence. Jonah has become hot-angry after YHWH had spared Nineveh; now YHWH intends to "deliver/shade" him from his anger by really heating things up.

Of the many protective shelters in the Jonah story (Tarshish, ship's hold, fish's belly, Temple, booth), three have allusive connections to Mount Zion. Ancient Near Eastern iconography is replete with figures of the tree of life that flourishes atop the divine mountain but is attacked by a serpent.[5] Is it possible that gourd and worm are caricatures of tree of life and serpent, appropriate images in a satiric story? Psalms strongly connects Mount Zion with the cosmic mountain;[6] and the Jerusalem Temple—YHWH's dwelling place on Zion—may contain symbolism associated with the Edenic tree of life.[7] Moreover, the author now introduces the form "Lord God" (4:6)—the divine name in the Eden story. Lord God, it would seem, has reestablished and then destroyed both Zion and Eden in order to "deliver" Jonah from his "evil." How is this a deliverance? The prophet who in 4:3 would rather die than live in a capricious, amoral universe now asks for death rather than live in a world without divinely provided shelter.

Chapter 4 begins with Jonah's complaint about the divine *ḥesed* (mercy). YHWH concludes the story, using the same number of words as Jonah, with a lesson on "pity" (Hebrew *ḥus,* perhaps used because of its phonetic associations with *ḥesed*). Jonah is told that his pity for the withered gourd is misdirected, as he is forced to contrast his feelings for "Nineveh, that great city," with the pity that God has shown (4:9–11). YHWH, as creator, has the prerogative of showing compassion for the world in its entirety—including creatures that don't know up from down. Jonah may still seek secure enclosures and perceive all that is outside as life-threatening. But God's world—even Nineveh—is able to repent its evil. In fact, as the fate of the exposed Nineveh suggests, it is more life-threatening to seek out a secure refuge. The gourd (like Tarshish, Eden, and perhaps Zion) has been blown away; the ship and the fish spew one forth. In a world that offers no eternally secure shelters, Jonah is urged to understand (and perhaps emulate) the divine pity.

The Judean community had a very difficult time reestablishing itself in Jerusalem after the Exile. The eschatological hopes of Isaiah 40–55 did not come to pass, even after the Temple was rebuilt (see Haggai). The resulting despair and anger are reflected in the book of Malachi, where the primary issue is divine justice: perhaps we Israelites deserved the exile in Babylonia; but how can YHWH hold back judgment on the other nations that deserve it even more? Jonah's paralysis and withdrawal also seem to result from his anger over divine injustice (see 4:2). He seeks secure shelters that inhibit his fulfilling the divine will and thus separate him from God and humanity; and yet, paradoxically, these same shelters have strong allusive associations with the divine cultic presence, in which the prophet can rejoice and feel protected from the rest of the world. Since the story's conclusion invites us to side with God over against Jonah, we can guess that one of its targets was the Zadokite priesthood—with its strong Temple Presence theology—which was rising to power soon after the return from the Exile (ca. 538–400 B.C.E.).[8]

The prayer sung in the belly of the great fish provides the key to the story's genre. What appears to be a supplication for help becomes a song of thanksgiving as it is sung by a man descending toward Sheol. When the song's piety becomes sickeningly sweet or unwittingly perceptive ("Salvation is of the Lord"), the prophet is vomited onto dry land just as he is about to hit the sea bottom. Such a scene is close to farce; since the story is also quite serious, however, I would argue that satire is a more appropriate designation of genre. There is no evidence of cultural contact between the writer and the classical satire that was probably evolving in other parts of the Mediterranean world at the time. But it does seem to give the modern reader the most useful handle on the story.[9] In satire we find incongruous, distorted events; a mixture of literary genres; an image of violence at the heart of the story; journeys as typical settings; and relatively little emphasis on plot or character development. The author of Jonah has skillfully used irony in order to distance us from the hero while also keeping the story on its narrow path between invective and farce.

NOTES

1. "Tarshish," in *The Interpreter's Dictionary of the Bible,* IV (New York and Nashville, 1962), 517–518.

2. See G. M. Landes, "The 'Three Days and Three Nights' Motif in Jonah 2:1," *Journal of Biblical Literature,* 86 (1967), 446–450.

3. Compare Jonah 1:2 with Gen. 18:20–21; Jonah 3:4 with Gen. 7:17; 19:21, 25, 29; Amos 4:11; and Jonah 3:8 with Gen. 6:11, 13.

4. The final scene makes many clear allusions to 1 Kings 19, which describes Elijah's flight from Jezebel. The prophet sits under a broom tree and asks for death. When he seeks out God's protective presence on the divine mountain, he

hears a still voice that commissions him to return and carry out YHWH's will in the arena of Near Eastern politics.

5. Othmar Keel, *The Symbolism of the Biblical World: Ancient Near Eastern Iconography and the Book of Psalms,* trans. Timothy J. Hallet (New York, 1978), pp. 51–52 (figs. 45–47).

6. Richard J. Clifford, *The Cosmic Mountain in Canaan and the Old Testament* (Cambridge, Mass., 1972), pp. 131–160. Note especially Ps. 68:15–16, 48:1–8, 2:6; and Isa. 2:2–4.

7. Keel, *Symbolism of the Biblical World,* pp. 186–190, especially 163–164. Two Temple pillars (Jachin and Boaz; see 1 Kings 7:15–22) were freestanding and must have served a symbolic rather than an architectural function. Their capitals were decorated with pomegranates—an ancient fertility symbol. These pillars have been construed as symbolizing, among other things, trees of life; mountain-pillars supporting the cosmos and, by extension, the Davidic monarchy; and the pillars of fire and cloud that led Israel through the Wilderness. Also, Ezekiel's description of the Temple of the new Jerusalem depicts cherubim guarding a palm tree as a repeated decorative motif (41:17–20) and envisions a river flowing from the temple that waters and gives life to the wasteland (47:1–12; cf. Gen. 2:10–14, Ps. 46:4, Zech. 14:8, and Rev. 22:1–2). To me this constitutes sufficient evidence that Zion and Eden—both related to the cosmic mountain in biblical texts and ancient Near Eastern parallels—were associated with each other in biblical thought.

8. See Paul D. Hanson, *The Dawn of Apocalyptic* (Philadelphia, 1975), especially pp. 1–31, 161–186, 369–401.

9. For a discussion of satire and irony, see A. Kernan, *The Cankered Muse* (New Haven, 1959), and W. C. Booth, *A Rhetoric of Irony* (Chicago, 1971).

SUGGESTED FURTHER READINGS

James S. Ackerman, "Satire and Symbolism in the Song of Jonah," in Baruch Halpern and J. D. Levenson, eds., *Traditions in Transformation: Turning Points in Biblical Faith* (Winona Lake, Ind., 1981), pp. 215–246.

Terence E. Fretheim, *The Message of Jonah* (Minneapolis, 1977).

Edwin M. Good, *Irony in the Old Testament* (Philadelphia, 1965), pp. 39–55.

André Lacocque and Pierre Emmanuel Lacocque, *The Jonah Complex* (Atlanta, 1981).

George M. Landes, "The Kerygma of the Book of Jonah," *Interpretation,* 26 (1967), 3–31.

Jonathan Magonet, *Form and Meaning: Studies in Literary Techniques in the Book of Jonah* (1976; reprint, Sheffield, 1983).

Indiana University

Psalms

Robert Alter

PSALMS, together with Proverbs and perhaps the Song of Songs, is
distinguished from all other biblical books by its manifestly anthological nature. We know little about how the anthology was made or when
most of the pieces included in it were composed. Some rather general
inferences, however, about the contexts of these poems can be drawn and
may help us get a bearing on the kind of literary activity reflected in the
collection.

The composition of psalms was common to most of the ancient Near
Eastern literatures that have come down to us. (See the essay by Jonas C.
Greenfield, "The Hebrew Bible and Canaanite Literature," in this volume.) From the Ugaritic texts that antedate the earliest biblical psalms by
at least three or four centuries, we may conclude that the Hebrew poets
did not hesitate to borrow images, phrases, or even whole sequences of
lines from the Syro-Palestinian pagan psalmodic tradition, written in a
language closely cognate to Hebrew. The borrowing occasionally may
have gone in the opposite direction as well: a recently deciphered text
from second-century B.C.E. Egypt, composed in Aramaic and written in
Egyptian demotic characters, looks as though it might be a pagan, or
rather syncretistic, adaptation of Psalm 20.

As these two widely separated instances of borrowing in different
directions may suggest, psalms were a popular poetic form in the ancient
Near East for a very long stretch of time. The biblical collection is composed of poems probably written over a period of at least five centuries.
A few late poems, such as Psalm 137 ("By the waters of Babylon . . ."),
refer explicitly to historical conditions after the destruction of the First
Temple in 586 B.C.E. Other psalms may well go back to the early generations of the Davidic dynasty, that is, the tenth and ninth centuries B.C.E.
It may not be an anachronism, moreover, for the author of the Samuel
story to put a psalm of thanksgiving (not one included in the canonical
collection) in the mouth of a pre-monarchic figure such as Hannah, Samuel's mother (1 Sam. 2), though the reference to the king in the last line
(v. 10) is obviously anachronistic. It seems plausible enough that psalms
quite similar to the ones in our collection were already in use at local
sanctuaries such as Shiloh before the cult was unified in Jerusalem; and

the recitation of the psalm by Hannah, a woman of the people who in her barrenness had improvised her own simple and touching prose prayer (1 Sam. 1), may reflect an assumption by the writer that the psalm was a profoundly popular form, a vehicle accessible to all for crying out in distress, or, as here, for expressing gratitude to God.

Precise dating of most psalms is impossible, though certain features of later biblical Hebrew can be detected in some of the poems. (Some psalms appear to allude to specific historical events, but in ways so teasingly elliptical that scholars rarely agree about what the actual events might be.) In any case, psalm composition through the whole Old Testament period is stylistically conservative; there is a sense of a densely continuous literary tradition, evolving very slowly over the centuries. In narrative, when you read a late book like Esther or Daniel, you at once know you are engaged with a different style, a different set of literary techniques and conventions, from those that inform Genesis or Samuel. On the other hand, you can read two psalms that, for all anyone can tell, may be as far apart in time as Chaucer and Wordsworth, and yet justifiably perceive them as virtual contemporaries in idiom, poetic form, and generic assumptions.

Authorship, as with all biblical books except the Prophets, is even more of an unsolvable puzzle than dating. Although the tradition embodied in 1 and 2 Samuel in fact conceives King David as both poet and warrior, scholarship long ago concluded that the superscription "a psalm of David" which heads many of the poems is the work of a later editor, as are the ascriptions of other psalms to Asaph, Ethan the Ezrahite, and so forth. Indeed, it is not at all clear that these superscriptions were intended to affirm authorship, for the Hebrew particle *le* in these formulas that is usually rendered "of" does not necessarily imply an authorial "by" and might rather indicate "in the manner of," "according to the standard of," or sometimes "for the use of."

The sociology of psalm composition also remains a matter of conjecture. It has been proposed that there was a professional guild of psalm-poets associated with the Temple cult in Jerusalem and probably recruited from Priestly or Levitical ranks. Such poets would have composed liturgical pieces for the rites in the Temple and would have also produced supplications and thanksgiving psalms for the use of—perhaps for purchase by—individual worshipers. All this is plausible but undemonstrable. In any event, the popular character of the Psalms, the fact that the psalm-poets never developed the kind of complex and innovative style found in Job or the shrewd intellectuality of the poetry of Proverbs, makes one suspect that psalm composition may not have been exclusively limited to a small professional circle in Jerusalem.

The organization of the book is the work of editors in the Second Temple period. That work was completed by the time the Septuagint translation of the Bible into Greek was prepared in the second century B.C.E., because the Septuagint has essentially the same order and chapter divisions as those that have come down to us in the Masoretic text. There is, in the various traditions of late antiquity, a little wobbling as to whether certain individual psalms are actually single poems or conflations of more than one psalm, and so the total number of pieces in the collection wanders between 147 and 150, with the normative Hebrew textual tradition finally settling for the roundness of the latter number. It is highly likely that there were originally competing anthologies of psalms which the later editors then spliced together, occasionally leaving a little duplication between different groups of poems (as in the doubling of Ps. 14 in 53). The oldest of these collections is thought to be the so-called Davidic Psalms (Ps. 3–41, with Ps. 1 and 2 serving as a preface to the whole collection), and the most recent, Psalms 107–150. Tradition divides the poems into five books, marking the end of all but the last with an editorial formula of closure that begins with "blessed" and ends with "amen." It would appear that this division into five was superimposed on what was initially an assemblage of four small collections in order to effect an alignment with the Five Books of Moses. For the ancient Hebrew literary imagination, numbers had more of a symbolic than a purely quantifying function, and this piece of editorial symbolism would have borne witness to the centrality that Psalms had come to enjoy in national consciousness by the time of the Second Temple.

Genre

Probably no single aspect of Psalms has received more scholarly attention in recent generations than the issue of genre. The pioneer studies were done early in the century by the German founder of biblical form-criticism, Hermann Gunkel.[1] He discriminated seven general categories of psalms and a variety of mixed types. As might have been expected, his successors tried to refine his divisions and variously multiplied or redivided the categories. The efforts of form-criticism have clearly enhanced our understanding of Psalms because in no other area of biblical literature is genre so pronounced, with such compelling consequences for modes of expression. There are, nevertheless, certain ways in which the form-critics misconceived the phenomenon of genre in Psalms.

Gunkel himself, being concerned with dating and development, like so many modern biblical scholars, tended to assume one could plot a curve from simple versions of a particular psalmodic genre, which must be early, to complex versions, which must be late. By this logic, of course, one could demonstrate that Imagist poetry considerably antedated *The Faerie Queene,* and Gunkel's evolutionist notions of literary history have been generally rejected by subsequent scholarship. His determination to uncover the so-called life setting for particular psalms has proved more stubbornly contagious.

Now, it is obvious enough that some of the Psalms were designed for very specific liturgical or cultic occasions. A particularly clear instance is the pilgrim songs, which appear to have been framed to be chanted by, or perhaps to, worshipers as they ascended the Temple Mount and entered the sacred precincts (Ps. 24) or as they marched around the looming ramparts of Zion (Ps. 48). But there is surely a good deal of misplaced concreteness in the energy expended by scholars to discover in psalm after psalm the libretto to some unknown cultic music-drama. The result in some instances has been to weave around these poems a kind of historical romance under the guise of scholarship, using the tenuous threads of comparative anthropology, as in the persistent conjecture that the psalms referring to God's kingship were used for an annual enthronement cere- mony in which the Lord was reinvested as king. In fact it is by no means self-evident that all the psalms were used liturgically, just as it is far from certain that they were all actually sung, though of course some obviously were, as the indications in the text of musical instruments, antiphonal responses, and the like make clear. Though some of these poems were surely "performed" in various Temple rites, we need to bear in mind that the psalmists, like other kinds of poets, often expressed a strong vision of reality through the imaginative leap of metaphor, and it is surely unwise to seek to reduce all these metaphors to literal cultic facts.

The most pervasive form-critical misconception about psalmodic genre is the notion that genre, apart from the occasional mixed type, is a fixed entity. This leaves the critic chiefly with the task of identifying formulaic sameness from one instance of the genre to the next. The evidence of literary history elsewhere and later suggests that, quite to the contrary, writers tend to be restive within the limits of genre, repeatedly find ways to juggle and transform generic conventions, formulaic or otherwise, and on occasion push genre beyond its own formal or thematic limits. We are likely to perceive the poetic richness of Psalms more finely if we realize that there is a good deal of such refashioning of genre in the collection, even when the recurrence of certain formulas tells us that a particular generic background is being invoked. I shall try to make this process clearer through illustration, but first a brief outline of the principal genres of Psalms may be helpful.

The usual Hebrew title for the collection is *Tehillim*, "Praises," a noun derived from a verb frequently used by the psalmists, *hallel*, "to praise," and familiar to Western readers in the form *hallelujah* ("praise the Lord"). Perhaps this designation was chosen because of the prominence of poems celebrating God's greatness in the Temple rites, or even because of the sequence of five hallelujah poems (Ps. 146–150) that forms a kind of coda to the collection. In fact, however, the total number of supplications—

well over a third of all the poems in the collection—is slightly larger than the number of psalms of praise. These two categories are the two principal kinds of psalms; together they make up more than two-thirds of the collection. Each may reasonably be divided into subcategories. Some supplications have an individual character (for example, entreaties to God in the throes of physical illness) and some are collective (pleas for help in time of famine, plague, siege, or exile). Psalms of praise may be general celebrations of God's majestic attributes, of his power as Creator manifested in the visible creation, or they may be thanksgiving poems, which, again, can be either individual or collective in character.

In addition to these two dominant categories, there are various lesser genres, most of which are represented by only half a dozen or so psalms: Wisdom psalms (there are actually a dozen of these, Psalms 1 and 37 being particularly clear examples, and Wisdom motifs also appear in a good many supplications); monarchic psalms (for example, Ps. 21 and 72); pilgrim songs (in addition to the two mentioned above, the most poignant is probably Ps. 84); historical psalms (essentially, catechistic recapitulations of the major way-stations of early Israelite history, such as Ps. 68 and 78). One might also argue for the profession of faith or innocence (for example, Ps. 23 and 62) as a distinct genre.

A brief consideration of the supplication will suggest the range of uses to which a single psalmodic genre may be put. The supplication is essentially a poetic cry of distress to the Lord in time of critical need. It may be short or long; it often refers to enemies, but these may be either actual military adversaries, or shadowy underhanded types somehow scheming against the speaker, or simply mean-spirited detractors who would crow in triumph were he to succumb to physical illness. Psalm 6, in which the enemies bridge the second and the third of these three types, offers a neat generic paradigm of the supplication:

> For the leader, with instrumental music on the *sheminith*,
>   a psalm of David
> Lord, chastise me not in your anger,
>   punish me not in your wrath.
> Have mercy on me, Lord, for I languish,
>   heal me, Lord, for my bones are shaken.
> My very life is sorely shaken,
>   and you, O Lord, how long?
> Return, O Lord, and rescue my life,
>   deliver me for the sake of your faithfulness.
> For there's no praise of you in death,
>   in Sheol who can acclaim you?
> I am weary from my groaning,
>   each night I drench my bed,
>   with tears I melt my couch.

> My eyes waste away with vexation,
>   are worn out from all my foes.
> Depart from me, all evildoers,
>   for the Lord hears the sound of my weeping.
> The Lord hears my supplication,
>   my prayer he will grant.
> Let all my enemies be shamed, sorely shaken,
>   let them turn back, be shamed, at once![2]

This supplication begins with a plea that God relent from his fury, making abundant use of verbal formulas that also mark many other instances of the genre: "Have mercy on me," *honeini*, a verb cognate with the noun *tehinah*, "supplication," in verse 9; "heal me"; "return, O Lord"; and that most imperative formula of the genre, often used elsewhere with repetitive insistence, "O Lord, how long?" The argument that God should save the suppliant because in the oblivion of the underworld none can praise the Lord is a conventional motif shared by dozens of supplications. Equally conventional is the concluding affirmation of the Lord's responsiveness to the suppliant's prayer and the evocation—the verbs of the last verse could be construed as either a wish or an actual prediction—of the enemies' dismay. Another, final instance of convention is the neatly antithetical closural effect in which the evildoers are "sorely shaken," just as the speaker's bones and inner being were shaken at the beginning.

Psalm 6 thus gives us a clear picture of the supplication in terms of structure, theme, and formulaic devices; and in fact a good many psalms are built on precisely this plan. But more interesting are the repeated divergences—sometimes rather surprising ones—from the paradigm. Psalm 13 begins with an anaphoric series of "how long" and conjures up a desperate image of the suppliant's imminent demise, yet it concludes on this note:

> But I trust in your faithfulness,
>   my heart exults in your deliverance.
> I sing to the Lord,
>   for he has requited me.   (vv. 5–6)

There is nothing optative or predictive about the verbs here: the deliverance is stated, in the surge of faith at the end, as an already accomplished fact. What this means is that the poem, though it is an exemplary instance of the supplication, is retrospectively transformed by the last verse into a thanksgiving psalm. The poetic process at work here is more dynamic, less mechanical, than what is implied by the usual scholarly notion of hybrids or mixed types.[3]

Often, when the types are in fact mixed, there is actually a tight interweaving of different generic strands from the beginning of the poem to the end, which produces a mutual reinforcement of different thematic emphases and expressive resources. Thus, Psalm 26 strongly qualifies as a supplication, for the speaker begins by asking God to vindicate him, invokes the malicious enemies from whom he pleads to be rescued, and concludes with a prayer that he will once more be able to walk a smooth way, praising the Lord. But the poem is also formally a profession of innocence; and in the language the speaker uses, proclaiming that he has never sat with the wicked or entered the assembly of evildoers, Wisdom motifs are prominent as well. These introduce a notion of causal logic into the supplication, for one knows from the Wisdom psalms proper (compare Ps. 1), as well as from Proverbs, that he who avoids the council of the wicked will, by virtue of the divine scheme of justice, be blessed with length of days.

The most intriguing instances of the expansion of the limits of genre in Psalms involve a displacement or reordering of the expected themes. Psalm 39 is a supplication in time of sickness, properly concluding with a plea that God hear the speaker's prayer, but the sole mention of illness does not occur till the tenth of the psalm's thirteen verses. Before that, the suppliant stresses his need to stay silent and the impossibility, in his anguish, of doing that, and from silence he moves to a meditation on the terrible transience of all human life. Instead of the formulaic imperatives "have mercy on me," "heal me," he implores God, "Let me know my end / and what is the measure of my days, / I would know how fleeting I am" (v. 4). The last note of this somber, moving poem, then, is not an image of frustrated foes but an evocation of the speaker's own imminent end, the final word in the Hebrew being "I-am-not" (*'eyneni*).

Psalm 90 pushes still further this realignment of emphases in the genre. By degrees, we learn that the poem is a collective supplication—first, from the allusions to God's wrath and then, late in the poem, through the use of the formula "return, O Lord—how long?" (v. 13). But before we become aware of the occasion for the plea, which is some unspecified affliction that has befallen the community, the psalm is manifestly one of the great biblical evocations of the ephemerality of mere human existence against the backdrop of God's eternity, and this, rather than the plea for help, seems its most urgent subject: "For a thousand years in your eyes / are like yesterday gone, / like a watch in the night" (v. 4).

One final example should suffice to illustrate the general principle that genre in Psalms is very often not a locked frame but a point of departure for poetic innovation. Psalm 85 is a collective supplication, imploring God to restore Israel to its land after the nation's defeat and exile. But, quite remarkably, it begins not with a plea but with a series of verbs in the perfect tense, confidently presenting the restoration as an accomplished fact:

You have favored, Lord, your land,
　　you have restored Jacob's condition [others: turned back
　　　the captivity of Jacob],
　　you have forgiven the iniquity of your people . . .　(vv. 2–3)

It is only in verse 4 that the poet finally uses the expected imperative "return, God of our deliverance," followed by the formulaic "will you forever be incensed against us?" But just four brief verses are devoted to such language of actual entreaty, and then, in keeping with the ringing optimism of the initial lines, the last half of the poem (vv. 7–13) is a luminous vision of national restoration, very much in accord with the messianic theme of the literary Prophets, and hardly what one would expect in a supplication:

Faithfulness and truth will meet,
　　justice and well-being kiss,
truth springs up from the earth,
　　justice looks down from heaven.　(vv. 10–11)

Style

What most characterizes the style of Psalms is its pointed and poignant traditionalism. Figurative language is abundantly used (though occasionally there are poems, such as Ps. 94, that avoid it), but there are few surprises of the sort encountered in the imagery of Job or of the Prophets. Wordplay and other virtuoso effects of invention are less prominent than in other kinds of biblical poetry, and for the most part the power of the poem does not depend on brilliant local effects but builds cumulatively through sequences of lines, or from the beginning of the poem to the end.

There are, to be sure, individual lines that are in themselves quite arresting and as such have become part of the Western treasure-house of memorable bits of poetry. But even a single instance of these will suggest the link between the force of such striking moments and the traditionalism of the poetic idiom:

As a hart yearns for channels of water,
　　so my soul yearns for you, God.
My soul thirsts for God, for the living God.
　　O when shall I come to appear before God?　(42:1–2)

In a semiarid climate where wadis turn into dry gulches in the summer and the parched, rocky landscape is enlivened by the occasional lush miracle of an oasis, it is understandable that poets should make running water a conventional figure for refreshment, restoration, life itself. Animal imagery is also common enough in Psalms, though it is more often attached to beasts of prey and used to represent situations of menacing violence (for example, in an urgent supplication, such as Ps. 22, the speaker's enemies are a pack of sharp-toothed curs). It is not so common to compare the soul or inner being (*nefesh*) to an animal, and in the first line here that simile gives the conventional image of longing for water a small but crucial shock of immediacy. The thirstiness is then spelled out in the second verse with a simple, striking metaphoric equation: the living God equals fresh water, which in fact would be called "living water" in biblical Hebrew. And since, for the Israelite imagination, the living God has chosen for himself in Zion a local habitation where one "appears before God" at the pilgrim festivals, Jerusalem itself, in the implied metaphor of the second half of the line, is conceived as a kind of oasis in the wilderness of the world, the sacred wellspring of water/life/God.

As happens at later points in literary history—there are analogues, for example, in medieval Arabic and Hebrew poetry, French neoclassical drama, English Augustan verse—this is a kind of poetry in which the strength and beauty of the individual poem are usually realized through a deft restatement or refashioning of the expected. Thus the speakers in these various poems represent the state of protection they seek from God or for which they thank him as a shield or buckler, a tower or fortress, a sheltering wing, a canopy or booth, cooling shade; the dangers that beset them are ravening beasts, serpents, arrows, burning coals, pestilence. The poets seem perfectly comfortable with this set repertoire of images, only rarely attempting to reach beyond it. Indeed, the familiarity of the metaphors and of the formulaic locutions through which they are often conveyed is precisely their chief advantage. The counters of poetic idiom have been worn to a lovely smoothness by long usage, and that is why they sit so comfortably in the hand of the poet, or—perhaps more relevantly—in the hand of the ordinary worshiper, in biblical times and ever since, for whom these poems were made. Psalm 91 is a characteristic instance of how a psalmist shapes from the elements of this traditional repertoire a poem with an individual character stamped with the eloquence of faith.

> You who dwell in the shelter of the Most High,
>   in the shadow of Shaddai abide!
> I will say of the Lord: my refuge and fortress,
>   my God in whom I trust.
> For he will save you from the fowler's snare,
>   from the blighting plague.
> With his pinion he will cover you,
>   beneath his wings you'll take refuge,
>   his faithfulness, a shield and buckler.
> You shall not fear from terror at night,
>   from the arrow that flies by day,
> From the plague that stalks in the dark,
>   from the scourge that despoils at noon.

A thousand at your side will fall,
   ten thousand at your right,
      yet you it shall not reach.
You will soon see it with your eyes,
   the requiting of the wicked you'll see.
—For you, O Lord, are my refuge!—
   The Most High you have made your abode.
No evil will befall you,
   no illness enter your tents.
For he will order his messengers
   to guard you on all your ways.
They will bear you on their palms
   lest your foot be bruised by stone.
You will tread on cub and viper,
   trample the lion and asp.
"Because he delighted in me, I shall deliver him,
   I shall safeguard him for knowing my name,
Let him but call me and I shall answer—
   I am with him in distress,
      I shall rescue him and grant him honor.
With length of days I shall sate him
   and show him my saving strength."

The poem's imagery is a kind of small thesaurus of the very stockpile of coventional figures we have just reviewed, but the effect of the whole is a strong and moving poetic statement, not a facile rehearsal of the familiar. This power may be due at least in part to the mutual reinforcement that occurs among related images. If there is a hidden nerve center in the poem, it is the verb "cover" (*yasekh*) in verse 4, a cognate of the noun *sukkah*, a thatched booth in which one takes shelter from the sun. The poem begins with "shelter" (literally, "hiding place") and "shadow," terms of protection that are immediately stepped up into "refuge" and "fortress," just as the gentle covering of "wings" in the first two versets of verse 4 becomes the weightier "shield and buckler" of the end of the line. This local move participates in a general tendency of biblical poetry toward an intensification or concretization of images and themes both within the line and in the poem as a whole. (See the essay "The Characteristics of Ancient Hebrew Poetry" in this volume.) In a similar fashion, the repeated assertion of shelter in the opening lines becomes a more sharply focused representation of the divinely favored man walking about untouched as thousands fall all around him. This is followed by the active intervention of an agency of protection, God's messengers or angels, who carry the man on their palms, allowing no sharp stone to hurt his feet—which, in a final intensifying maneuver, in fact can safely trample the most savage beasts. The psalm then ends climactically with three lines of direct discourse by God—who, in the shifting grammatical voices of the poem, was referred to only in the second and third person until this point. The divine source and guarantor, in other words, of all the remarkable safeguarding that has been imaged in the poem, now reveals himself directly, affirming his immediate involvement with the God-fearing man ("I am with him in distress") and the unswerving resolution to protect him and grant him long life.

What often accompanies this traditionalism of poetic idiom in Psalms is a bold simplicity of language. The notion of simplicity, however, must be adopted with caution because it has been used too readily to attribute to these poems a kind of sublime naïveté, to see in them a purely spontaneous outpouring of feeling. In fact many of the psalms show evidence of fairly intricate rhetorical and structural elaboration. The "simplicity" of Psalms is rather the ability of subtle poets, sure in their tradition, to call on archetypal language, to take unabashed advantage of the power of repetition, and, when the occasion seems to require it, to displace figuration by stark literal assertion. Psalm 121, a very different sort of poem about divine protection, displays just these stylistic features:

> A song of ascents
> I lift my eyes to the mountains—
>   from whence will my help come?
> My help is from the Lord,
>   maker of heaven and earth.
> He will not let your foot stumble,
>   your guardian will not slumber.
> Look, he neither sleeps nor slumbers,
>   the guardian of Israel!
> The Lord's your guardian,
>   the Lord's your shade at your right hand.
> By day the sun will not strike you,
>   nor the moon by night.
> The Lord will guard you from all evil,
>   he will guard your life.
> The Lord will guard your going and coming
>   now and forevermore.

The archetypal sweep of the poetic landscape in this brief piece is remarkable. The speaker lifts his eyes to the mountains and, in a characteristic biblical association of terms, moves from mountains to heaven and earth and their Maker. A second binary pair that harks back to Genesis 1 is quickly introduced, day/sun and night/moon. The poem is a powerful realization of the meaning of "guarding" and "guardian," the terms recurring, with anaphoric insistence, six times in eight lines. Metaphoric elaboration is not allowed to intervene in this process of realization. The only weak candidates for figures of speech in the poem are the minimal synecdoche of the slipping foot in verse 3 and the conventional "shade" for shelter in verse 5, which is immediately literalized in the next line as a protection against sunstroke and moonstroke (the latter perhaps referring to madness supposedly caused by exposure to the moon). The point of the poem is that the Lord is quite literally a guardian or watchman who never sleeps, who always has his eyes open to keep you from harm. The concluding note of benediction on "forevermore" is, it might be argued, a formulaic device for ending a psalm, but here it ties in beautifully with the beginning of the poem because an arc has been traced from the eternity behind mankind when heaven and earth were made to the eternity stretching out ahead. Altogether, the poem is a quintessential expression of the poetic beauty of Psalms in its artful use of a purposefully limited, primary language to suggest a kind of luminous immediacy in the apprehension of the world through the eyes of faith.

Structure

Elsewhere in the biblical corpus, the boundaries of poems are often ambiguous. Where the traditional chapter divisions might seem to imply a single poem in Proverbs or the Prophets or the Song of Songs, scholars have often argued for a splicing together of two or three poems or for a collage of fragments from several poems. In Psalms, on the other hand, there are very often clear markers of beginnings and endings in the formulaic devices we have already noted in connection with genre, and in almost all instances the chapter divisions dependably indicate individual poems. Since many of the psalms were, after all, fashioned for public use, it is not surprising that the psalm-poets should by and large favor symmetrical forms in which poetic statement is rounded off or tied up by an emphatic balancing of beginning and end.

The most common expression of this formal predilection is the so-called envelope structure—in fact a structure popular in many biblical genres—in which significant terms introduced at the beginning are brought back prominently at the end. The extreme version of the envelope structure would be the use of a refrain at the beginning and end of a psalm, as in Psalm 8, which opens with the declaration "Lord, our master, / how majestic is your name in all the earth," then scans creation vertically from heaven to man at the midpoint to the land and sea "beneath his feet," and concludes by repeating the opening line.

A longer and more complicated instance of envelope structure is offered by Psalm 107. This thanksgiving psalm, which reviews God's mercies in rescuing his people from the trials of exile on land and sea, begins with a formula that occurs in other poems: "Praise the Lord, for he is good, / for his faithfulness is forever." The division between the first and second movements of the poem (verse 8) is marked by a refrainlike variation on this opening line: "Let them praise the Lord for his faithfulness, / his wondrous deeds for the sons of man." These words recur verbatim as a refrain marking discrete segments of the poem in verses 15, 21, and 31. The very last verse (43) sums up the imperative to celebrate God's many bounties in the following words: "He who is wise will heed these things, / he will take note of the faithfulness of the Lord." The poet thus avoids the regularity of an explicit concluding refrain, but the key concept that began the poem, the *faithfulness* (or "loving-kindness," *ḥesed*) of the *Lord,* rings forth at the end, with the order and syntactic relation of the two component nouns changed, and "faithfulness" used in the plural (in the Hebrew), perhaps as a concluding indication of all the different mercies of the Lord that the poem has evoked.

The role of the refrain in Psalm 107 points to a more general possibility of structuration in Psalms, the subdivision of individual poems into strophes. This is an aspect of Psalms that we are just beginning to understand, but it may be that there are strophic divisions in many of the longer poems. The perception of such formal poetic structure could in some cases provide a key to otherwise elusive meanings. To cite an extreme instance, Psalm 68 has posed such problems of seeming incoherence that many scholars have embraced W. F. Albright's suggestion that it is not a poem at all but a catalogue of first lines from no longer extant psalms. J. P. Fokkelman, on the other hand, makes a plausible case for a cogent structure here in formal divisions: going from small to large, he designates them as strophes (a term he uses to designate a cluster of two or three lines), stanzas, and sections.[4] Almost all of the small units he discriminates are marked by a term for God—usually, *'Elohim*—at the beginning of the first line and at the end of the last line, and triadic lines are used to indicate the ends of many of the strophes. The three large sections Fokkelman identifies in the poem (vv. 2–11, 12–24, 25–36) are organized thematically around three different mountains, first Sinai, then Bashan, then God's new chosen abode, Zion. The atomistic habits of philological analysis have tended to divert attention from such larger principles of organization, but formal symmetries of this sort may be present in a good number of the longer psalms.

In any case, envelope structure is the one clearly discernible structural pattern that recurs with inventive variations in many different psalms. Beyond that, it is probably not very helpful to attempt a taxonomy of psalmodic structures (chiastic, antiphonal, and so forth), because the evidence of the poems suggests that for the most part structure was improvised in the poet's impulse to create an adequate form for the subject at hand in the individual poem. Envelope structure, in other words, is an explicit convention of biblical literature, a recognized way of organizing material in both poetry and prose, and it could be exploited with emphatic effect in the closed form of the psalm. Other structures, by contrast, seem to have been tailor-made for particular poems rather than applied as a convention, and so our task as readers is not to attempt to classify them but to observe their varying operations in shaping the meanings of individual psalms. Let me illustrate this point briefly.

Psalm 12 is a supplication spoken by someone beset by insidious schemers. What the suppliant stresses is the treacherous use of language by his adversaries, who seem to him in his distress to be virtually all of mankind: "Lies do they speak to each other, / smooth talk, / with a double heart do they speak" (v. 3). In the semantic parallelisms from line to line, "tongue" and "lips"—both of which mean "speech" in biblical idiom—recur, the suppliant praying that the Lord "cut off all smooth-talking lips, / every tongue speaking proudly" (v. 4), while the arrogant are imagined saying, "By our tongues we'll prevail, / with these lips of ours, who can lord over us?" (v. 5). The poem pivots neatly on verse 6, as we hear, after this characterization of the treacherous language of humankind, God speaking in direct discourse that affirms divine justice, announcing his resolution to rise up and rescue the oppressed from their persecutors. In the balanced antithetical structure of the poem, the duplicity of human speech, to which the first four verses are devoted, is set off by the redemptive emergence of God's perfect speech in the last four: "The words of the Lord are pure words, / silver purged in an earthen furnace, / refined sevenfold" (v. 7).[5] The point of the neat antithetical structure is to embody in the shape of the poem the speaker's sense that, all dismaying appearances to the contrary, there is in the very nature of things an ethical counterweight to the triumphal arrogance of the wicked.

Psalm 48, a pilgrim song, works out a tripartite poetic structure for the poet's perception of the double paradox of the particular and the universal, the historical and the eternal, focused in God's chosen city, Jerusalem. Zion, concretely imagined here as a distinctive stronghold towering on a Judean promontory, is also "the joy of all the earth" (v. 2), and the poem sweeps impressively from the particular site to a large geographic panorama, and back again to the particular site. After the introductory verses celebrating the bastions of Zion (1–3), the poem moves back in time (vv. 4–8) to the routing of a naval expedition at some unspecified point in the past, within which is recessed the memory of a more distant and archetypal past, since the report of the naval victory uses language alluding to the drowning of the Egyptians as it is described in the Song of the Sea (Exod. 15). Geographically, the poem moves not only down to the Mediterranean shore but to the known ends of the earth, for the invading fleet is said to come from Tarshish (Jonah's distant destination), in Cilicia, Spain, or who knows where to the west. The last of the poem's three segments (vv. 9–14) takes us back to Zion, "in the midst of your temple" (v. 9) and once more all around those ramparts that are testimony in stone to God's protection of his people. Moreover, the safeguarding that he provided in the event just recalled and at the time of the Exodus before it, will continue for all time: thus the pilgrims are enjoined to tell of God's power to "generations to come" (v. 13), for he who has elected this city will remain "our God forever" (v. 14).

Finally, it is well to bear in mind that the architectural metaphor of structure, with its implication of something solid and static, inevitably does a certain injustice to poetic form, which reveals itself to us progressively in time as we read from line to line. The dynamic character of structure in Psalms is particularly evident in those poems where the utterances are organized in an implicitly narrative sequence. Thus Psalm 97 is not just an acclamation of God's variously manifested majesty, as it might seem to the casual eye, but a vivid narrative enactment of his power as the world's king. As in victory poems devoted to the Lord of Battles (compare Ps. 18), God is first seen on his throne enveloped in cloud, then sending forth fire and hurling lightning bolts across the earth (vv. 2–4). The very mountains melt like wax before this onslaught of divine effulgence (v. 5), and all peoples then acclaim his greatness; every conscious creature, from idolators to divine beings, does fealty to him (vv. 6–7). Israel is now inserted in this global picture, exulting in its God who is the God of all the world, as his fiery epiphany has just demonstrated. Furthermore, a nice symmetry of envelope structure is superimposed on the entire narrative sequence. The poem begins: "The Lord reigns!/Let the earth exult,/let the many islands rejoice." To mark the transition of the second half of the poem from all the earth to Israel, the paired verbs of the beginning recur: "Zion hears and *rejoices,*/the towns of Judea *exult*" (v. 8). The final verse picks up one of these two verbs, "rejoice," which as a noun, "joy," ends the previous verse:

> Light is sown for the righteous,
>   and for the upright, joy.
> Rejoice, you righteous in the Lord,
>   and praise his holy name.   (vv. 11–12)

Thus the double structure of the poem, narrative and envelope, exemplifies the psalmodic fashioning of specific forms to match specific perceptions. We experience through the significant shape of this psalm a just order in creation, events moving in a sequence that compels appropriate response: Israel, the nations of the earth, the very angels above, are aligned in a hierarchy of correspondences that bears witness to the universal majesty of the Creator.

Themes

The Book of Psalms reflects certain distinctive and recurrent thematic concerns. These are not, as one might at first think, coextensive with psalmodic genre but, on the contrary, tend to cut across the different genres. Many of the characteristic themes share the archetypicality we observed in psalmodic imagery, and the power with which these archetypal themes are evoked may explain a good deal about why the poems have continued to move readers, both believers and nonbelievers, in cultural and historical settings far different from those in which the poems were first made. Little will be served by attempting a comprehensive catalogue of the themes of Psalms, but a few representative illustrations may suggest something of this power of timeless reference that so many of the poems possess.

One of the most common themes in the collection is death and rebirth. It is equally prominent in the supplication and in the thanksgiving psalm, a fact that makes more understandable the element of fluidity or dialectic interplay noted earlier between these two seemingly opposed genres. The prehistory of the theme might justifiably be viewed as a monotheistic—and metaphoric—reworking of a pagan mythological plot, the death and miraculous rebirth of a god (in the Mesopotamian tradition, Tammuz). Most of the poems draw on a common repertoire of images: the gates of Sheol (the underworld), the darkness of the pit populated by mere shades, or, in an alternative marine setting, as in Jonah's thanksgiving psalm, the overwhelming breakers of the sea. Illness and other kinds of dangers, perhaps even spiritual distress, are represented as a descent into the underworld from which the Lord is entreated to bring the person back or, in the thanksgiving poems, is praised for having brought him back. The effectiveness of this vestigially mythological plot is that it can speak powerfully to so many different predicaments, in the psalmist's time and ever since—for those who believe in resurrection, for those who feel the chill threat of literal extinction here and now, for those who have suffered one sort or another of inward dying. Thus in a memorable line by that most psalmodic of English poets, George Herbert, "After so many deaths I live and write," the metaphor has the virtual effect of literal fact. In much the same way, the poet of Psalm 88, as his language makes evident, has a clear sense that he is conjuring with a metaphor, and yet his tale of descent into death has the force of experiential truth:

> for my soul is sated with troubles,
>   my life's reached the brink of Sheol.
> I'm counted with those who go down to the Pit,
>   I'm like a man with no strength,
> Abandoned among the dead,
>   like bodies that lie in the grave
> whom you remember no more,
>   from your hand are cut off.
> You've thrust me into the bottommost Pit,
>   in darkness, in the depths.
> Your wrath lies hard upon me,
>   with all your breakers you afflict me. (vv. 3–8)

It goes without saying that whatever themes the various psalms treat are caught in the heavily charged field of relationship between man and God. Thus, longing, dependence, desperation, exultation become elements in a series of remarkable love poems—once more, cutting across psalmodic genre—addressed by man to God. Religious experience attains a new contemplative and emotive inwardness in these poems. The radically new monotheistic idea that God is everywhere is rendered as the most immediately apprehended existential fact:

> If I soar to heaven, you are there,
>   if I make my bed in Sheol, again you're there.
> If I take wing with the dawn,
>   dwell at the end of the West,
> there, too, your hand guides me,
>   your right hand holds me fast. (139:8–10)

The hiding of God's face or presence is one of the greatest terrors the psalm-poets can contemplate, and the cry of many a suppliant in these poems is impelled by the urgency of a desperate lover: "I stretched out my hands to you, / my soul's like thirsty earth to you" (143:6).

One of the most ubiquitous themes in the various genres of Psalms is language itself. There seems to be a development from a formal organizing device to the self-conscious investigation of a theme. That is, as befits poems which may often have been recited in a cultic setting, many of the thanksgiving psalms begin and end with the declared intention of praising, extolling, thanking God, and many of the supplications begin and end by entreating God to hear the plea, pay heed, and rescue. But the poets very often proceed from these formulas of inception and conclusion to ponder the uses and power of the medium of language they employ. The supplication often quite explicitly raises questions about the efficacy of man's speech to God, the possibility of an answering speech from God to man, the tensions between speech and silence, the different functions of language for crying out in anguish and for exploring the enduring enigmas of man's creaturely condition. (Psalm 39, which we glanced at earlier, strikingly unites all these concerns.) The thanksgiving psalm stresses speech/song as the distinctive human gift for recognizing God's greatness, a gift that God in some sense seems almost to need. Psalm 30 is an instructive case in point because it juxtaposes the two kinds of discourse, entreaty and praise, underlining both the efficacy of the former (the speaker in his former plight had "cried out" to the Lord) and the necessity of the latter. Embedded in the narrative structure of this poem are two different instances of direct discourse—what the speaker said to himself in his complacency before disaster overtook him, and a brief "text" of his actual entreaty to God in the time of his distress. The common psalmodic theme that the dead cannot praise God is given special conviction here: to be humanly alive is to celebrate God's bounties, which is what God has enabled this speaker to do by rescuing him from the underworld.

Finally, many of the psalm-poets, especially those who draw on Wisdom motifs, are acutely aware of the contradictory character of language. Psalm 12, which we touched on in considering possibilities of structure, nicely illustrates this consciousness of the double nature of speech. There is never any radical skepticism about the efficacy of language in the Bible because God, the cosmogonic language-user and the planter of the linguistic faculty in man, remains the ultimate guarantor for language. But if speech can be used to express true feelings (the supplication) and to name the truth (the thanksgiving psalm), it may also be turned into a treacherous instrument of deception. These two divergent possibilities are often expressed through two opposing clusters of images—language as a weapon, a sharp-edged arrow, or burning coals (compare Ps. 120), and language as a perfect vessel, a beautifully unalloyed substance, "refined sevenfold" (12:7).

All in all, the preoccupation with language tells us a great deal about the kind of poetry that has been brought together in the Book of Psalms. The vision of a horizon of "pure speech" suggests a confident effort to make poetry serve as adequate, authentic expression, from the lips of man to the ear of God, and hence the frequent sense of powerful directness, of unadorned feeling, in these poems. But the awareness of language as an instrument, an awareness often made explicit in the texts, reflects a craftsman's knowingness about the verbal artifices through which the poet realizes his meanings. Both these perceptions about language and poetry need to be kept in mind if we are to be able to gauge the greatness of the poems. The sundry psalms are finely wrought with the most cunning turns of poetic artifice, subtly and consciously deploying and reworking a particular set of literary conventions; and yet in their stylistic traditionalism and archetypal range they often manage to convey the persuasive illusion of a perfect simplicity beyond the calculations and contrivances of art.

NOTES

1. For a concise English summary of Gunkel's views, see Hermann Gunkel, *The Psalms: A Form-Critical Introduction,* trans. Thomas M. Horner (Philadelphia, 1967.)

2. All translations in this essay are my own [AT] because the KJV does not sufficiently represent the formal design of the poetry.

3. Jack Sasson has pointed out to me that this fluidity between genres is nicely reflected in the insertion of a thanksgiving psalm into the Book of Jonah

at a point in the story which actually calls for a supplication, when Jonah is in the belly of the fish.

4. Professor Fokkelman has been kind enough to show me an outline of an unpublished study of this psalm.

5. This antithetical structure has been aptly observed by A. L. Strauss, *Bedarkhei hasifrut* [In the ways of literature] (Jerusalem, 1970), pp. 89–94.

SUGGESTED FURTHER READINGS

Robert Alter, *The Art of Biblical Poetry* (New York, 1985), chap. 5.
Hermann Gunkel, *The Psalms: A Form-Critical Introduction,* trans. Thomas M. Horner (Philadelphia, 1967).

University of California, Berkeley

Proverbs and Ecclesiastes

James G. Williams

PROVERBS and Ecclesiastes are the two chief works of the ancient Israelite Wisdom tradition. The Book of Job is usually included among the Wisdom writings, and occasionally the Song of Songs. In addition to these works, we find Wisdom compositions among the psalms (for example, Ps. 1 and 119), as well as proverbs and folk sayings scattered throughout various books of the Old Testament. In the Apocrypha, Sirach (Ecclesiasticus) and Wisdom of Solomon are important expressions of ancient Jewish Wisdom.

Wisdom as a Way of Looking at the World

Different as these works are from one another, they all presuppose a way of looking at the world that was characteristic of ancient Israelite Wisdom literature and, to a great extent, of all ancient Near Eastern Wisdom literature. This Wisdom perspective was quite different from that of the grand narratives of the Pentateuch and the Former Prophets, which told of the beginnings of the world and of Israel, related the establishment of cultic institutions, and included many tales of founding figures, prophets, and kings. Wisdom is dedicated to articulating a sense of order. The world is viewed as an order informed by a principle of retributive justice.[1] As one turns to the world and gives to it, so one receives from it. The world is vitally retributive in the sense of the Latin *retribuare,* "to pay, grant, repay." In Proverbs this principle is stated in one line, which unfortunately reads in translation as a stuffy moralistic maxim:

> Treasures of wickedness profit nothing:
> but righteousness delivereth from death. (10:2)

The clever play on consonants does not come through in English. "Treasures of wickedness" translates a Hebrew phrase constructed of sibilants which are interrupted only by the *r* sound: *'otsrot resha'.* Wickedness is immediately contrasted with righteousness, and the contrast is strengthened with two sibilant combinations and a concluding sibilant: *utsedaqah tatsil mimawet,* "and righteousness delivereth from death." A sound-meaning relation is thus created between "treasures" and the "righteousness" that "delivereth from death."

The principle of retribution is given a more dramatic form in this proverb about overweening pride:

> Those haughty of heart are loathed by YHWH;
>> A matter sealed! They shall not be acquitted.   (16:5 [AT])

The second half of this proverb represents a future certainty through a dramatic image. "A matter sealed"—literally, "hand to hand"—is an expression evidently derived from the practice of striking hands as a sign of sealing a bargain (also 11:21; see 6:1, 11:15). What is "struck" or sealed is the guilt of those who are overbearing, which suggests a judgment scene.

Of course, the fact that the world is a marvelous order does not mean that human thoughts, schemes, and words are really under human control. From a human point of view the world is ultimately a maze:

> A man's heart deviseth his way:
>> but the Lord directeth his steps.   (16:9)

(See also 16:1, 19:21, 20:24, 21:30–31, 26:27.) But in spite of the fact that the human mind cannot finally fathom the way of the world and the way of God, the Wisdom tradition tends toward confidence in the dependability and bounty of the world.

This dependable world is revealed and sustained in the proper appreciation and use of language. It is through speaking that relationships are established and the world is opened up. This is put most vividly in Proverbs 18:21:

> Death and life are in the power of the tongue:
>> and they that love it shall eat the fruit thereof.

Language gives human beings the capacity to create ideas and symbols that constitute a human world. But this capacity is simultaneously the ability to bring about evil situations and harm others. Words can both damage and heal:

> A soft answer turneth away wrath:
>> but grievous words stir up anger.   (15:1)

In the mouth of the fool, the proverb, the chief form of wise language, is useless:

> Legs dangling from the lame
>> and a proverb in the mouth of fools.   (26:7 [AT])

The theme of language is so pervasive in the Wisdom tradition that it is central in sexual ethics, dominating the characterization of the "stranger woman," the seductress who lures the man trying to steer his way through life's hazards. It is her coaxing, flattering speech that holds the power of entrapment (2:16, 5:3, 6:24). She symbolizes the most destructive kind of folly. Her seductive, and ultimately destructive, use of language leads to utter disorder, as we see in the allegory of Dame Folly (9:13–18).

In order to be wise, to understand the principle of retributive justice and the necessity of wise utterance, one must heed the "fathers," who are first of all one's parents, and by extension all of those who have the role of elder in the present and past generations:

> My son, hear the instruction of thy father,
>   and forsake not the teaching [AR] of thy mother.   (1:8)

This traditional attitude is stated by Bildad in Job:

> For inquire, I beg you, of a former generation
>   and ponder what their fathers have searched out,
> for we are but of yesterday and do not know,
>   for our days are a shadow on the earth.   (Job 8:8–9 [AR])

Everything in traditional Wisdom, from its basic ideas to its literary forms, affirms order. What this means when the principle of retribution, the necessity of wise utterance, and the authority of the fathers are brought to bear on the individual is the imperative of discipline and self-control. Wisdom has no systematic view of the human self, but the individual is seen as a complex order held in check and guided by wisdom. The wise person will be cautious and moderate (Sirach 18:27, 30), will plan ahead and not be lazy (Prov. 10:5), and is able to take orders from a superior (Prov. 10:8). One of the most interesting indications of this emphasis on discipline and self-control is the way in which words denoting temperature become metaphors of restraint and undesirable license.

> An angry man [man of heat] stirs up strife:
>   but the patient person settles disputes.   (15:18 [AT])

> He that hath knowledge spareth his words:
>   and a man of understanding guardeth his temper
>   [is cold of spirit].   (17:27)

To summarize, Wisdom as a way of looking at the world depicts a vital order informed by retributive justice and given human expression in wise utterance. The sayings of the wise have been transmitted by the elders, who are to be held in respect, and this world-sustaining wisdom of the sages is maintained through individual and social discipline. Wisdom thus affirms a divine cosmic order and represents folly as disorder. It does not, however, impose a systematic view of order on the world and human behavior. Although human existence and the surrounding world are placed within the framework of order, individuals and situations are conceived of in their particularity and are not methodically organized into a system of abstractions.

This basic outlook, consistently espoused in the rather conservative wisdom of Proverbs and Sirach, and also incorporated in the talmudic tractate Abot, is a way of seeing the world which most of the Wisdom texts of ancient Egypt and Mesopotamia assume and advocate. But the ancient Israelite wisdom of order became inadequate for some thinkers and was transformed in their writings into a "wisdom of counterorder." This change occurred when the disorienting effects of three related conditions shook the tradition. (1) Wisdom's generalizations about typical individuals and situations seemed to be contradicted by individual experience and particular situations. (2) The tradition consequently lost its power to inform feeling and thought and exert social control. (3) The representing function of language was subverted by new questions issuing from a skeptical or paradoxical frame of mind in the late Old Testament period, from the Babylonian Exile (586 B.C.E.) into the Hellenistic period and Diaspora (from about 330 B.C.E.). This new situation is reflected in the later phase of Wisdom literature.

The Book of Job gives expression to the most radical doubt concerning the sapiential tradition in this later phase. The Job poet draws upon the principle of retribution and attendant Wisdom themes, and his work is heavily stamped with traditional Wisdom poetics. But Job's radical innovation is its challenging new view of divine justice and human suffering. In this central regard, the Job poet does not employ the literary forms of conventional Wisdom. The climax of Job is a revelation of YHWH which is presented within a narrative dialogue frame. The combination of narrative dialogue and divine speeches is characteristic of the Law and the Prophets, but not of the Wisdom literature of the ancient Near East.

Ecclesiastes, in contrast, both presupposes and attacks the conventional wisdom represented by Proverbs. Ecclesiastes' style, outlook, and conclusions on the meaning of life radically question received wisdom. Ecclesiastes sees polarities in creation but subordinates them to a skeptical questioning of what the ancient sages taught. Its litany of the "right times," for example (3:1–8)—the poetic enumeration of the right seasons to do and not to do certain things—reads as though it were straight out of the pages of the Wisdom of order. Yet the question with which the poet follows the enumeration shows that he perceives this sapiential teaching of the times as vain: "What profit has the worker in his toil?" (v. 9 [AT]). A sad irony emerges, for the obvious answer to the rhetorical question is "none," as indicated both in the following verses (3:10–15) and in what he says earlier about profit (1:3; 2:11, 13). The world is not an arena of gain; there is no retribution that is satisfying.

The literary foundation of Wisdom poetry is the proverb, which we shall consider at length in the next section. The proverbs of traditional Wisdom and ritual have a similar function, in that both represent an ideal present which recurs constantly in accordance with a specific model of the world. Myth and proverb also operate similarly, both placing their respective subjects outside of time. One concrete expression of this relationship of myth, ritual, and the kind of proverb current in a folk tradition is a tendency people have to repeat a saying in order to identify with its truth, though the truth remains something for which they need not take responsibility. The saying comes from the past and the authority of the tradition, so in repeating it one simply states "what is said." Thus, when David says to Saul outside the cave at En-gedi, "Wickedness proceedeth from the wicked" (1 Sam. 24:13), he makes a point about his own good intentions by repeating ancient wisdom. His intention is to reestablish peace and equilibrium between himself and Saul, which is one of the primary uses of the Wisdom saying. The saying quoted is also a good example of the kind of principle that shows the common basis of Wisdom and law. In this instance, a person's motives, which the community must trust in order to maintain stable social life, are to be inferred from what he actually does. Since the legal tradition has effect only from the starting point of observable behavior, it must build up elaborate mechanisms to deal with possible lack of evidence and the nature of the suspect's intentions (both handled, for example, in Exod. 22:7–13).

The part that proverbs and sayings play in righting social situations and supporting legal statutes is closely related to what has been uncovered in some modern theories of the self; these theories offer certain insights into the function of Wisdom. Henri Bergson argued in his essay *Laughter* that laughter acts primarily to correct a social situation riddled with tension. Sigmund Freud, in *Wit and Its Relation to the Unconscious,* also stressed the tension-relieving work of wit, analyzing it in terms of his theory of the unconscious and the pleasure principle. The lifting of constraints is an act of *disorder,* whether momentary or sustained. Social constraints will give license to engage in approved forms of momentary disorder, such as jokes in certain tacitly agreed-on settings. But if disorder is sustained, it must be placed within a new frame of reference, a "counterorder" that calls into question the dominant tradition. One such counterorder point of view is set forth in Ecclesiastes, which is directed against the Wisdom tradition presented in Proverbs.

Proverbs

None of the biblical writings is strictly speaking a "book" in the modern sense, which carries a connotation of final form—something the ancient works did not have until a canon or normative version was fixed by the tradition. Moreover, in the earlier period scrolls were used that had to be rolled and unrolled. Even the later codex did not have a binding to enclose its contents. The necessary fluidity of what we retroactively call a book in the Bible is especially evident in Proverbs, which, it is generally agreed, is a collection of literary proverbs and Wisdom poems.

There is a consensus on the outline of Proverbs and also on a very broad chronology. Chapters 10–22:16 and 25–29 probably come from an earlier period, before the Babylonian Exile. Chapters 22:17–24:34 may be later and are thought to be heavily dependent on an Egyptian Wisdom text, the Instruction of Amenemopet. Chapters 1–9 are later, probably post-Exilic, and form an introduction to the rest of the collection. This segment is made up of Wisdom poems of varying lengths, including narratives in which Lady Wisdom speaks (1:20–33, 8:22–31). Chapters 30–31 are a kind of appendix and may be late, like chapters 1–9. This way of outlining the contents indicates a continuous tradition reflected in the construction of a longer and longer scroll. But who composed it, and for whom?

Answering this question is difficult. When we consider a work like Abot in the Talmud we are aided by our knowledge of the rabbinic tradition. Abot was evidently intended as a compendium offering a summary of what the "fathers" (sages and rabbis) taught. It presents primarily maxims, but these maxims are obviously related to the legal cases catalogued in other tractates of the Mishnah, as well as to issues later taken up and tales in the Gemara (the extension of the Mishnah). Concerning Proverbs, however, we cannot say as much. Perhaps Proverbs was "a source book of instructional materials for the cultivation of personal morality and private wisdom."[2] It could have served as a source of *loci communes* or "commonplaces" for speakers and sages. The different collections in chapters 10–29 would have been especially appropriate for such a use.

The introduction to the entire collection (1:1) attributes the proverbs to Solomon. Chapters 10–22:16 are headed "the proverbs of Solomon," and chapters 25–29 are identified as "proverbs of Solomon, which the men of Hezekiah king of Judah copied out" (25:1). In fact, although there are few allusions in Proverbs to the national religious traditions and cultic institutions, the attribution of the entire work as well as parts of it to Solomon shows the mythic tendency of the later Wisdom tradition. The legend of Solomon as the wise ruler of Israel's golden age (1 Kings 3:16–28, 4:20–34, 10:1–29) resulted in his becoming the "patron saint," so to speak, of the Wisdom tradition in post-Exilic and Hellenistic times. His name is also associated with the Song of Songs in the Old Testament and the Book of Wisdom (or Wisdom of Solomon) in the Apocrypha. We have also the Psalms of Solomon from the same period as the Wisdom of Solomon, about the first century B.C.E. A still later work, the Odes of

Solomon, was probably written after 100 C.E. It may have been written by a Jew and revised by a Christian, though this is uncertain. In style and theme it is akin to the Gospel of John.

The mythical principle at work in bringing these texts under the aegis of Solomon is a truth cherished in every traditional society, namely that only the *archē* or beginning is valuable. In this case, Solomon's reign is viewed as the beginning and point of orientation of Israelite Wisdom. Although this mythic tendency has little to do with the specific form and content of the proverbs and collections in Proverbs, it underwrites the voice of the elders that the transmitters believed was speaking through the proverbs and allies this voice of authority, albeit tenuously, with a great figure of Israel's history.

One problem in reading the actual proverbs of the collection is that they have indeed become proverbial, especially as translated in the King James Version.

> Pride goeth before destruction,
>> and an haughty spirit before a fall.   (16:18)

> A soft answer turneth away wrath:
>> but grievous words stir up anger.   (15:1)

> Wine is a mocker, strong drink is raging:
>> and whosoever is deceived thereby is not wise.   (20:1)

These renderings in the King James Version are part of our cultural heritage and still retain their literary force. Yet even when the effect in English is pleasing, the Hebrew poetry may not be adequately conveyed. A literal rendering of Proverbs 16:18 would be something like this:

> Before breaking [is] pride
>> and before falling [is] haughtiness of mind.

What gives this proverb its punch in Hebrew is a quick juxtaposition of images, an almost stroboscopic effect. First there is a rapid flash of words: "before breaking," followed by "pride" without a verb; then a second phrase flashes: "before stumbling" (or "reeling"), followed by "haughtiness of mind" (or "spirit"). The King James Version is not bad, though it misses the total effect. But some of the modern translations merely compound the boredom readers may feel for the commonplace and their resistance to it when it is associated with the voice of authority. The New English Bible, for example, is accurate enough, but it practically turns the proverb into pale prose:

> Pride comes before disaster,
>> and arrogance before a fall.

Here all the vividness, the *picturing* power of the proverb, is lost.

It would be wide of the mark to argue that all the proverbs are literary masterpieces. But they *are* poetic compositions; that is, they are clearly intended as elevated speech which has marked features of special linguistic ordering. Some of them are artful to the point of being real literary art, so that it is possible to speak of a "poetry of Wisdom." The literary foundation of this Wisdom poetry is the binary proverb, which is composed of two members or phrases drawn together into a sort of parallelism. The various forms that are typical of Wisdom literature may be viewed as extensions and variations of this formal base. Here are two proverbs which I have translated more or less literally in order to suggest this rapid, binary, juxtapositional form:

> Despiser of his neighbor: lacking of mind
> and man of discernment: keeps still.   (11:12 [AT])

> Goer as gossip: concealer of counsel
> and faithful of spirit: concealer of speech.   (11:13 [AT])

The King James Version, in a comfortable prose amble, renders:

> He that is void of wisdom despiseth his neighbor:
> but a man of understanding holdeth his peace.

> A talebearer revealeth secrets:
> but he that is of a faithful spirit concealeth the matter.

The two proverbs just cited are instances of what biblical scholarship calls the "sentence" or "sentence proverb": an observation or assertion composed of two members or phrases that are usually in synonymous or antithetical parallelism. One scholar has recently called into question the very existence of parallelism as the basic structure of ancient Hebrew poetry;[3] and indeed, the standard definitions, which usually emphasize compositional elements of equal importance, balance, and antithesis, are doubtless inadequate. Nonetheless, parallelism is a convenient descriptive word when properly qualified, as I shall show later in this section.

Another kind of proverb is the "instruction" or "instruction proverb." It is characterized by a verb in the mode of command or prohibition, with a second member, or set of members, that gives an explanation. Here are two examples:

> Speak not in the ears of a fool:
> for he will despise the wisdom of thy words.   (23:9)

> Remove not the old landmark;
> and enter not into the fields of the fatherless:
> For their redeemer is mighty;
> he shall plead their cause with thee.   (23:10–11)

The second text is clearly an expansion of the instruction form, and it illustrates concretely how closely related the Wisdom and legal traditions were in their concern for the right ordering of human life. The first member of the proverb is a prohibition which is almost exactly the same as the one in Deuteronomy 19:14.

The literary proverbs were composed from the stuff of life, the concerns of different spheres of existence. The common ground shared by Deuteronomy 19:14 and Proverbs 23:10 illustrates this principle. Two forms that were derived from folk traditions are particularly interesting and merit mention here. One was the folk saying. In the Old Testament there are some folk sayings that are generally recognized by biblical critics (for example, Gen. 10:9; Judges 8:21; 15:16; 1 Sam. 10:11, 12; 24:13, 14; 2 Sam. 20:18; 1 Kings 20:11; Jer. 13:12, 23; 17:11; 31:29; Ezek. 18:2). They are typically very concise, use alliteration and assonance, and often employ wordplay. Like the literary short forms of Proverbs, these sayings presuppose the principle of retributive justice. These literary and conceptual features are shared with the proverbs of the Book of Proverbs, though the latter display a refined poetic development within the constraints of parallelism and the explanatory clauses of the instruction form.

It is instructive to find folk sayings in Proverbs that are expanded into binary proverbs. Here are two examples:

> When pride cometh, then cometh shame:
>   but with the lowly is wisdom. (11:2)

> In all labour there is profit:
>   but the talk of the lips tendeth to poverty. (14:23 [AR])

In the first one, the folk saying is pithy and assonant, its point reinforced by internal rhyme (ba' zadon wayavo qalon, "comes pride then comes shame"). That could be followed by any number of second phrases, but what actually follows offers a vivid poetic contrast, one far removed from the ambience of the folk saying. The contrast would be comparable to taking one of our own sayings, "Birds of a feather flock together," and adding to it "but fools fare ill with the wise." In the second member of Proverbs 11:2 the image of the "lowly" is a subtly clever contrast to "shame." The latter word in Hebrew, qalon, comes from a root meaning "light" or "worthless." The form of the proverb suggests that truly weighty people, those who have wisdom, make themselves light or apparently worthless in another sense—they humble themselves. In our second example, Proverbs 14:23, the first member has a familiar meaning, like the German Arbeit macht Freude, "Work brings joy," and similar sayings in other cultures. The second member, while not producing a highly nuanced effect, comes across with a certain vigor by the use of the contrasting "poverty" ("penury" in the King James Version). The effect is more sparkling in the Hebrew words motar/maḥsor: profit is set against lack, plus against minus, and the opening and closing consonants of the two words are the same. Perhaps "profit" and "privation" would give a better sense of the soundplay in Hebrew.

The other form derived from folk traditions that merits attention is the riddle. In the Old Testament the only full quotation of what we normally call a riddle is ascribed to Samson in Judges 14:14, but the Israelites may have understood their word *hidah* much more broadly than our ordinary usage. The Hebrew word is used in Numbers 12:8 as the contrary of YHWH's communication with Moses: "With him will I speak mouth to mouth . . . and not in dark speeches [*behidot*]." In two psalms the word is connected to the word for parable or proverb (*mashal*) (Ps. 49:4, 78:2). The introduction to Proverbs states that a wise person will learn "the words of the wise, and their dark sayings" (1:6). There is therefore no doubt that the riddle or "dark saying" was one of the literary forms associated with Wisdom, and since riddles are always popular at the folk level, their use offers another example of the relation of literary proverbs to popular culture.

To what extent are there riddles in Proverbs? Given the broad semantic range of the Hebrew term *hidah,* there are certainly many enigmas or dark sayings among the proverbs. But even with the common usage of the English term in mind, we can discern partially concealed riddles that have been adapted to the form of the binary proverb. It may have been a great challenge to take a riddle, form a riddling assertion from it for the first member of the proverb, then fashion the answer into the second member. This could take the form of an arresting metaphor in the first phrase, which is then answered with a conventional teaching in the second phrase.

> As a jewel of gold in a swine's snout,
>> so is a fair woman which is without discretion.   (11:22)

In other words, "[What is as amazing or incongruous as] a gold ring in a swine's snout?" The riddle is answered in the second line. Exactly the same in form is this proverb:

> Clouds and winds and no rain
>> is a man who boasts of a gift not given.   (25:14 [AT])

A riddle is employed within a longer poem in 6:27–28:

>> Can a man take fire in his bosom,
>>> and his clothes not be burned?
>> Can one go upon hot coals,
>>> and his feet not be burned?

These questions presuppose the riddling form, "Who is it that?" or "Who is the man?" Whatever the correct response might be to a riddle like this in the folk setting, the answer in this poem is "he that goeth in to his neighbour's wife" (6:29). As a *hidah* in the context of a short poem it is understandably more complex than the popular riddle would be. The right answer intimates that yes, in one respect the man's clothes are not burned, nor are his feet. There is no observable sign of his escapade—immediately. But he is bound to be "burned" by dishonor (6:33), one of the worst things possible in the world of traditional Wisdom. He may also have to face the wrath of the woman's husband, who burns with his own fire, the fire of jealousy (6:34)!

The dynamic elements of the literary proverb are intensification, narrativity, and metaphoric play. Intensification refers to the strengthening or sharpening of the second phrase of the binary form.[4] The second member is often not a simple parallel to the first, but augments it. The following two proverbs illustrate intensification.

> By the blessing of the upright the city is exalted:
> but by the mouth of the wicked it is overthrown. (11:11 [AR])

> The tiller of the soil has his fill of bread:
> but the pursuer of vanities has an empty head. (12:11 [AT])

The first member of Proverbs 11:11 reads initially like a vague and somewhat ambiguous generalization. Does a city grow and prosper because the upright are simply present in it (see Ezek. 14:14), or because they pronounce a blessing upon it? Even if the second meaning is intended, the thought seems rather abstract. But with the completing antithetical phrase the total image becomes concrete and vivid. It is the *mouth* of the wicked—their concrete acts of speaking—that destroys a civilized community. In 12:11, the first member has the style of a folk saying. The second member sets up a contrast with the first and so makes the binary proverb a more inclusive comment on life in the world. It does this by depicting a type of human being who is removed from everything solid and substantial. This person pursues "vanities" (in Hebrew *reqim*, "empty things") rather than working his soil; rather than being full or satisfied he is empty or lacking. The Hebrew expession, *ḥasar-lev,* literally "lacking of mind," is a way of saying "empty-headed." The extreme contrast between this pursuer of vanities and the tiller of his soil results in a revised view of the latter. Now he is not simply the model of an able farmer, but a paradigm of the prudent person.

In the binary proverbs that work by intensification there is a kind of silent adverbial emphasis implied at the beginning of each member which is more effective by not being stated. "[As is well known,] by the blessing of the upright the city is exalted/[even more so,] by the mouth of the wicked it is overthrown." One confirmation of the actuality of intensification lies with the two proverbs which utilize *af-ki,* "how much more [or less]," rather than the simple conjunction "and" (15:11, 19:10).

> Delight is not seemly for a fool:
> how much less for a slave to rule over princes. (19:10 [AR])

Narrativity is the telling of a process of acts, events, or experiences. It would obviously not be present except in very compact form in proverbs, which make up a genre lying to the contrary extreme of narrative forms. But the use of tightly controlled narrative phrases empowers many of the proverbs. Narrativity often also involves intensification, but the object is to depict an orderly process moving from one state to another along a path of consequences.[5] For a little humorous scene I would cite Proverbs 19:24:

> The sluggard hides his hand in the dish—
> he won't even lift it to his mouth!   [AT]

The two phrases here are not parallel. In fact the juxtaposition is a little surprising: we would expect the sluggard to be pictured as a glutton in the second member, or to be told that he expends no effort to work for his food. Instead, we leave him with his hand buried in the bowl. This is pointedly aborted narrativity: we would expect an action or further action, but nothing happens—an apt fate for the sluggard.

A more typical example of narrativity is a proverb which is a paradigm of the role of language in the world of Wisdom.

> Death and life are in the power of the tongue:
> and they that love it shall eat the fruit thereof.   (18:21)

In the first phrase we are given a tableau which then comes alive with movement in the second phrase. The tongue is a feminine noun in Hebrew. The expression "in the power of" is literally "in the hand of." We glimpse a picture of a woman who holds death and life in her hand. We sense a mythic allusion, and the second phrase verifies this intuition: her *'ohavim*, her friends or lovers, shall eat of the fruit she offers. We are reminded of the woman in the paradisaic garden. The fruit is taken by those who love language. The outcome of their action is ambiguous—or perhaps one should say her fruit is ambiguous. Is it good fruit, the fruit of life, or is eating language's fruit always a partaking of life and death together? Perhaps the proverb intends to say more or less what Lady Wisdom says in 8:17: "I love them that love me" (see 8:21).

If a proverb achieves its effect by means of narrativity, the key to reading it may reside in the second phrase or member, especially if the first member makes a general assertion or states a general principle. "The memory of the just is blessed" (10:7a) is a line well known to the Jewish tradition in its Hebrew form (*zekher tsadiq livrakhah*). But the narratival contrast of the second member may have been the proverb's source of appeal in the biblical period: "but the name of the wicked shall rot" (10:7b). Similarly, the explanatory clauses of two instruction proverbs (23:17–18, 24:19–20) both begin with a traditional truism about the principle of retribution, which is then filled out by a compact narration of consequences:

> For surely there is a future [AR];
> and [even more surely] thine expectation shall not be cut off.   (23:18)

> For there shall be no reward to the evil man;
> [surely] the lamp [AR] of the wicked shall be put out. (24:20)

I have added adverbial qualifiers to the second members in order to bring out the intensification that reinforces the narrative quality.

As significant as narrativity and intensification may be, metaphoric play is the most important element of Wisdom poetics, as it is of language in general. My starting point is Benjamin Hrushovski's illuminating argument that metaphor is not merely one imaging word that expresses concretely a reality absent from the text.[6] Most biblical scholars approach the role of metaphor in this limited way, finding a few images that are clearly metaphorically rich (such as "a soft tongue breaketh bone," Prov. 25:15), but missing the total metaphor in many proverbs. Consider Proverbs 14:11:

> The house of the wicked shall be overthrown:
> but the tent [AR] of the upright shall flourish.

The words "house" and "tent" are metonyms that stand for the family or clan. As discrete words they are insipid. But the two phrases as a total poetic line paint a vivid verbal picture: the house of the wicked is torn down, whereas the tent of the upright flourishes. Some contemporary commentators and translators understand "tent" as an exact poetic parallel to "house" that does not change the meaning of a permanent, solidly structured dwelling place (see, for example, the New English Bible). But the second half of the proverb offers more than a contrast of the upright person and his prosperity with the wicked and his ill fortune; it also juxtaposes a temporary shelter to a house. The upright and his family fare better in a tent than do the wicked in a house!

Metaphor is better understood as a *pattern* that functions within the interplay of *frames of reference*. Hrushovski defines a frame of reference as "any continuum of two or more referents to which parts of a text or its interpretation may relate . . . Its ontological status is immaterial; it is anything we can talk about."[7] An important aspect of Hrushovski's concept of frame of reference is indeterminacies, places in a text that are not covered by the detailed representation of language. Some of these indeterminacies become *gaps* which the reader has to fill in.[8] Sensitivity to gaps is particularly important for interpreting aphoristic language, whose very "gappiness," or dearth of connections and context, is generically inherent.

Let us consider as an illustration of metaphoric play 18:21, which we cited earlier as an expression of the importance accorded to language. The proverb begins with the grand abstractions "death and life," but the combination of the two is a way of saying "everything important and real." This pair is followed by very concrete referents from the everyday world, "in the hand of the tongue." It is strange to put this combination together in English, but "in the hand of" was probably such a basic colloquialism that the Hebrew ear would have experienced no dissonance—at least in the first half of the proverb, for through the second half the initial expression takes on new life. The word "tongue," moreover, suggests concrete acts of speaking as well as language generally. We see, then, in the first member, two frames of reference: *fr1*, the concrete world of bodily members (hand, tongue); *fr2*, the surrounding cultural world (life and death as everything important, language). The second member of the proverb offers a third frame of reference, that of the mythical world of the garden where a woman offers fruit to her lovers. The upshot is that we *reread fr2* in light of *fr3*. The tongue is no longer an organ or a dead metaphor for language, but something more and in between the two. Like a woman, it has lovers who seek its fruit; like the mythical woman in the garden, its fruit is a reality that involves human destiny.

Clearly, there is one word here that is the metaphoric key, *lashon*, "tongue," but the metaphoric reality encompasses an interplay among the frames of reference. *Fr1* suggests *fr2*, which is reread in light of *fr3*. But once we reread through the window of *fr3* we are led back to *fr1* by virtue of the "sound-meaning interactions."[9] The semantics of the text saturate the sounds of the words with certain implications, which in turn reinforce a total pattern of meaning or meaning-tone. To illustrate this it is necessary to transcribe the Hebrew words:

mawet	*weḥayim*	*beyad*	*lashon*
death	and-life	in-hand [of]	tongue

we'ohaveha	*yokhal*	*piryah*
and-her-lovers	will-eat	her-fruit

Once we notice the lovers eat fruit and the predominance of labial sounds (consonants requiring lip articulation: *m, w, b, v,* and *p*) in the two members, we are brought back to the concrete world of hand and tongue in a new way. The use of language is as immediately real, as significantly consequential, as eating and holding something in the hand. Eating suggests speaking, and vice versa, and the intimation of sexual intercourse suggests that language is not only communication but also pleasurable connection and correspondence.

We are left, to be sure, with an indeterminacy that becomes a gap for the seeker of wisdom. What is this life and death that we are ingesting as language's fruit? Knowing a proverb is not a substitute for the search. We could, of course, look to Proverbs 1–9, whose expansion of the proverb and use of narrative include the representation of Lady Wisdom's appeal to humankind. She cries out in the streets (1:20), she is the very companion of God and delights in the sons of men (8:22–31). But Lady Wisdom's is not a voice that the skeptical Ecclesiastes heard. For him the ambiguity of "death and life" was weighted in death's favor.

Ecclesiastes

Ecclesiastes is known as the "Preacher" in the English-speaking tradition, owing to the influence of the King James Version. In the Christian tradition *ekklēsiastēs* was understood as "one of the church" or "churchman" because the Greek word for church is *ekklēsia*. The Greek title, however, is a translation of the Hebrew *qohelet* (Eccles. 1:1, 12; 7:27; 12:9, 10), whose exact import eludes us. It comes from a Hebrew root meaning "to gather" or "to assemble," and it is related to the noun *qahal*, "assembly" or "congregation." Perhaps it refers to gathering people together, as a teacher would, or it may be an allusion to the function of composing words or assembling one's teachings (see Eccles. 12:9: "and [he] set in order many proverbs"). But the title is a feminine participle, a form of this root that occurs nowhere else in the Old Testament. The odd use of the feminine gender, together with the fact that the term is associated with Solomon (though without naming him; see 1:1, 12), suggests the author wanted his work to be recognized as part of Israel's Wisdom tradition but not taken literally as the wisdom of Solomon.

However we translate the word, the speaker in the book is the skeptic par excellence of the Old Testament. Since the title Ecclesiastes has become misleadingly associated with the Church and the role of the preacher, I shall refer to the voice speaking in the book by the Hebrew Qohelet. Qohelet is a kind of "preacher," but a preacher of skepticism who sets himself against the Wisdom of order.

Ecclesiastes is a collection of teachings. No analysis of its design has gained a scholarly consensus. It seems clear that development of thought does not occur after chapter 3. We must look for guiding metaphors and take note when these metaphors emerge as thematic patterns. The author's style and outlook were probably influenced to some extent by the Hellenistic culture of the third century B.C.E. He was acquainted with a notion that resembles the Greek idea of the immortality of the soul (see 3:21), and his writing may have been affected by Greek literary forms, such as *parainesis* (exhortation). But all in all, it is best to see Ecclesiastes as a work composed of ancient Hebrew literary forms, which the author employs in both conventional and unconventional ways.

For example, Qohelet often quotes proverbs:

> That which is crooked cannot be made straight:
> and that which is wanting cannot be numbered. (1:15)

> For in much wisdom is much grief:
> and he that increaseth knowledge increaseth sorrow. (1:18)

It is possible, of course, that the writer, both in these verses and elsewhere, has composed his own proverbs and presented them in a deliberately archaizing manner.

In general, the writer uses poetic parallelism, even when he is writing rhythmic prose rather than verse. A reflection-fragment such as 4:1 is actually built up out of the kind of parallelism that both adds to and intensifies what has already been stated:

> So I returned, and considered all the oppressions that are done
>   under the sun;
> And behold, the tears of the oppressed,
>   and they had no comforter:
> and on the side of their oppressors there was power,
>   but they had no comforter. [AT]

This same dynamic of incremental repetition is beautifully wrought in the introductory poem on the cosmos and human existence, 1:3–11. Consider verses 3–6:

> What profit hath a man of all his labour
>   which he taketh under the sun?
> One generation passeth away, and another generation cometh:
>   but the earth abideth forever.
> The sun also ariseth, and the sun goeth down,
>   and hasteth to his place where he arose.
> The wind goeth toward the south, and turneth about unto the north;
>   it whirleth about continually,
>   and the wind returneth again according to its circuits.

Human labor (*fr1*) is placed within the context of societal and cosmic cycles (*fr2*). The latter could be a source of comfort, for they are enduring and perpetual. But they are not comforting to Qohelet, who asks what one can gain from them. In the thematic pronouncement just before this poem he has said, "Vanity of vanities . . . vanity of vanities; all is vanity" (1:2). This point of view clarifies the second frame of reference. The Hebrew word behind "vanity" is *hevel*, which means "vapor" or "breath." "'Vapor of vapors,' says Qohelet." If everything is vapor, then the round of generations and the turnings of sun and wind and waters are but the recycling of a mist or a breath whose reality is this: it disappears. The fiction of Qohelet as "the son of David, king in Jerusalem" (1:1; see also 1:12) establishes still another frame of reference, that of the royal patron of wisdom, who informs the reader by verse 11 that there is nothing profitable to know!

This voice of the royal patron of Wisdom is obviously a fiction. It is not to be identified with the writer's own position any more than Moses in Deuteronomy is identical with the author(s) of the Torah, or Jonathan Swift with Gulliver, or Joel Chandler Harris with Uncle Remus.[10] Indeed, if we think in terms of personas or roles in the literary work, there are three in Ecclesiastes:

1. The frame-narrator who presents Qohelet (1:1). His voice slips in, perhaps inadvertently, at 7:27, and he speaks in an epilogue which serves partially to mitigate the effects of Qohelet's skepticism (12:8–14).

2. Qohelet the narrating voice who observes the world and recounts his experiences (for example, 1:3–6, 1:12, 2:1).

3. Qohelet the experiencing subject, whose experiences are narrated by the reviewing voice. The clearest example of this is 2:1–17, the experiment with three ways of life.

The appeal of this work of Wisdom is therefore not to the authority of an ancient tradition, but to the voice of individual experience. The focus on individual experience and the rhetoric of argumentation build up a massive case against the foundations of traditional Wisdom. One of the most common devices of this rhetoric is to use a proverb or a proverblike form to undercut conventional conclusions. When Qohelet the narrating voice says aphoristically,

> The thing that hath been done, it is that which shall be;
> and that which is done is that which shall be done:
> and there is no new thing under the sun.   (1:9)

he is really arguing against the thought of gain or comfort from the recurrence of all things (see 1:2–3, 11). When he reflects that living a long life is not necessarily satisfying (6:1–6), he adds:

> All the labour of man is for his mouth,
> and yet the appetite is not filled.   (6:7)

The author was probably familiar with a proverb like the one in Proverbs 16:26. But whereas there the appetite works for the laborer to motivate him, Qohelet avers that the appetite (*nefesh*, or "soul") is insatiable. Qohelet finds in human experience a craving for something more than is presently possessed, a desire for an excess, a profit. What would this profit be, and what is the lack that Qohelet cannot satisfy for himself?

A hint at the answer is given in 7:1, which is the most paradoxical use of the offsetting saying in Ecclesiastes (see also 4:5–6):

> A good name is better than precious ointment;
> and the day of death than the day of one's birth.

The first phrase reads like a traditional saying. A good name or reputation carries with it all the desirable connotations of virtue and wisdom: discipline, judicious use of language, industriousness, respect for the tradition. A name is a power in its own right that perpetuates the reality of the family. A very similar line is found in Proverbs 22:1, but in Ecclesiastes the thought has the clever simplicity of a folk saying. In Hebrew it is a chiasm:

tov	*shem*	*mi-shemen*	*tov*
good	a-name	from-oil	good

but the effect is as jarring as a Zen *koan* when it is joined to the second phrase. The day of death better than one's day of birth? Yes, that is what the persona Qohelet says. Since fortune is fickle, one cannot count on preserving a good name. And even if one is able to hold on to this precious possession, a good name amounts to vapor if the bearer of the name must face a fleeting existence that hurries toward death.

Qohelet makes no bones about his agony at the prospect of death, which means for him that there is no profit of any sort, material, intellectual, or spiritual. One passage where he says this quite clearly also illustrates another aspect of his rhetoric, one which is more straightforward than the use of proverb against proverb. Here, as frequently, he presents a conventional Wisdom idea in the form of a proverb and then contradicts it with his view of the truth of human experience that the proverb does not comprehend.

> Then I saw that wisdom excelleth folly,
> as far as light excelleth darkness.
> The wise man's eyes are in his head;
> but the fool walketh in darkness;
> and I myself perceived also that one event happeneth to them all.   (2:13–14)

Everything is in order about the wise person, who has eyes where they should be. He has the light of wisdom, which directs him. The context of the verses is the threefold experiment of the king. Pleasure and achievement have been tried and found wanting (2:1–11); and, given what we know from the still larger context (chap. 1), we suspect that wisdom will be found wanting too. This is exactly what happens when the Wisdom sayings are confronted by the "I" of the experiencer: "and I myself perceived that one event happeneth to them all." The one "event" is death. Wise person and fool both share the same fate (2:15), as do humans and beasts (3:19–21).

For the voice that speaks and relates its experiences in Ecclesiastes, existence is like vapor, insubstantial; one cannot gain anything of lasting value from it. There may be right times for everything, as Qohelet enumerates in poetic lines (3:1–8). It was certainly common wisdom that there is a proper time for everything, and the sagacious person will know how to discern it and use it (see Deut. 11:14; Jer. 5:24; Ps. 1:3, 31:15, 104:27; Prov. 15:23). But then comes the question that arrests the poetic repetition of 3:1–8: "What profit hath he that worketh in that wherein he laboureth?" (3:9). In fact, it is as though God has played a trick on humankind in making the human creature a divided being:

> [God] hath made every thing beautiful in its time; also he hath set the everlasting [ha'olam] in their heart, so that no man can find out the work that God maketh from the beginning to the end.   (3:11 [AR])

The Hebrew word I have translated as "the everlasting" should perhaps be rendered "world," as in later Hebrew and in the King James Version. It is understood as "love of the world" in a rabbinic source, the Midrash Rabbah on Ecclesiastes. The word 'olam means "world, age, distant time." In context, it signifies something basic, something at the heart of things, "what God maketh from the beginning to the end." In other words, man bears within his heart or mind the very secret of the ongoing life that surrounds him and in which he participates. (In fact some commentators render 'olam as "secret" or "hidden thing.") Yet a human being, certainly one like Qohelet, does not *feel* like a participant and lacks any satisfying control over his destiny (see 1:15, 7:13). The creature man is trapped between the secret of the divine work planted in his mind and the vaporous existence that is his lot. He cannot grasp the 'olam, even though it is within him.

In this predicament of a vaporous existence pursued without profit there is one recourse that Qohelet advocates: to enjoy the *portion* (ḥeleq) that one may find or receive. This portion is happiness or joy, the joy of the immediate experiences of eating and drinking, work, and conjugal love (2:10; 3:22; 5:17–18; 9:6, 9). This happiness should be accepted, one may rejoice in it, but it may not be kept as "profit" for the future. The sage Qohelet thus sets immediate, pleasurable experience against the order of thought and discipline transmitted in Israel's traditional Wisdom.

> Behold that which I have seen: it is good and comely for one to eat and to drink, and to enjoy the good of all his labour that he taketh under the sun all the days of his life, which God giveth him: for it is his portion.   (5:18)

In Proverbs 10–31 the tradition offers the power of language and a set of assumptions and metaphors which form the human world, providing a bridge between the self and the world. In the poems of Proverbs 1–9 Wisdom itself becomes a mediating symbol between God and the created order. For Sirach it is the priesthood, the custodians of the tradition, and Wisdom as Torah that offer direction and the good life. For the rabbinic tradition the Torah, as guarded and cherished by the covenant people, enables the Jew to find a passage to life through the chaos of evil and human divisions. For the Christian tradition it is the Christ, Jesus as the Anointed One, who opens the way from the human predicament to divine salvation. But Qohelet can articulate no way, no bridge or mediating reality from the predicament of profitless vanity to the everlasting work of God. Wisdom with a capital *W* is impossible for him. The world is simply too much to think and say (1:8). His one real affirmation—besides the counsel to be prudent, which does not involve a real yea-saying to life—is to enjoy one's portion as it may be given.

> Truly the light is sweet, and a pleasant thing
>   it is for the eyes to behold the sun:
> But if a man live many years, and rejoice in them all:
>   yet let him remember the days of darkness;
>   for they shall be many.
> All that cometh is vanity.   (11:7–8)

NOTES

1. For a fuller treatment of the world view of the ancient Jewish Wisdom tradition see James G. Williams, *Those Who Ponder Proverbs: Aphoristic Thinking and Biblical Literature* (Sheffield, 1981), chap. 1.

2. R. B. Y. Scott, *Proverbs–Ecclesiastes*, Anchor Bible, XVIII (Garden City, N.Y., 1965), 3.

3. James L. Kugel, *The Idea of Biblical Poetry: Parallelism and Its History* (New Haven, 1981), chap. 6.

4. See Robert Alter's essay "The Characteristics of Ancient Hebrew Poetry" in this volume and Kugel, *The Idea of Biblical Poetry*, chap. 1.

5. On narrativity in proverbs see Robert Alter, *The Art of Biblical Poetry* (New York, 1985), chap. 7.

6. Benjamin Hrushovski, "Poetic Metaphor and Frames of Reference," *Poetics Today*, 5 (1984), 5–43.

7. Ibid., p. 12.

8. Ibid., p. 13.

9. Ibid., p. 9.

10. These examples are used by Michael Fox in "Frame-Narrative and Composition in the Book of Qohelet," *Hebrew Union College Annual*, 48 (1977), 83–106 (see 93–96 and 104). I am also indebted to his analysis of voices or dramatis personae in Ecclesiastes, pp. 83–92 and 104–106.

SUGGESTED FURTHER READINGS

Robert Alter, *The Art of Biblical Poetry* (New York, 1985), chap. 7.

Benjamin Hrushovski, "Prosody, Hebrew," in *Encyclopedia Judaica* (New York, 1971), pp. 1200–02.

James L. Kugel, *The Idea of Biblical Poetry: Parallelism and Its History* (New Haven, 1981), chap. 1.

James G. Williams, *Those Who Ponder Proverbs: Aphoristic Thinking and Biblical Literature* (Sheffield, 1981).

Syracuse University

Job

Moshe Greenberg

THE prophet Ezekiel mentions Job alongside Noah and Daniel as a paragon of righteousness (Ezek. 14:12–20); from this we know that Job was a byword among the sixth-century B.C.E. Judahite exiles whom the prophet addressed. But from Ezekiel and from the late passing reference to Job's patience (or perseverance) in James 5:10–11 one would never guess the complexity of the character set forth in the book that bears his name. Indeed the book's representation of Job seems to some modern scholars so disharmonious as to warrant the hypothesis that two characters have been fused in it: "Job the patient," the hero of the prose frame of the book; and "Job the impatient," the central figure of the poetic dialogue. In the prose story, Job the patient withstands all the calamities inflicted on him to test the sincerity of his piety and is finally rewarded by redoubled prosperity. The moral is: piety for its own sake is true virtue and in the end is requited. It is this old story—often called a folktale—that is supposed to have been known to Ezekiel's audience. Later, the hypothesis continues, a far more profound thinker (perhaps a survivor of the Babylonian Exile and its crisis of faith) used the temporary misfortune of the hero as the setting for his poem, in which the conventional wisdom of the tale is radically challenged.

This theory is based on expectations of simplicity, consistency, and linearity that are confuted by the whole tenor of the book. Reversal and subversion prevail throughout—in sudden shifts of mood and role and in a rhetoric of sarcasm and irony. The dialogue contains much response and reaction but no predictable or consistent course of argument. When to these disconcerting features are added the exotic language (loaded with Aramaisms and Arabisms) and the uncertain state of the text in many places—from apparent corruption of words to unintelligible sequences of verses—the confidence of some critics in their ability to reconstitute the original text by rewriting and rearrangement seems exaggerated. This essay discusses the book as we have it.

The chief literary (as distinct from theological or literary-historical) problem of Job is its coherence: do the prose and the poetry or the speeches of Job and his Friends hang together? How are they related? We must gain an awareness of the complexities of interplay among the elements of the book. The truncation of the third round of speeches and the integrality to the book of Elihu's speeches have been treated by most critics as problems to be solved by a theory of textual dislocation or adulteration. I shall try to describe how these elements in their present shape work upon the reader. This is not to assert the infallibility of the text in hand, but rather to confess our inability to justify on grounds other than individual predilection the alternatives proposed to it. It also reflects a conviction that the literary complexity of the book is consistent with and appropriate to the nature of the issues with which it deals.

The background of the dialogue is established in chapters 1 and 2 in five movements. The first movement introduces the magnate Job, one of the "dwellers in the east" (1:3)[1]—that is, east of the Land of Israel—in the uncertainly located country of Uz (connected with Aram to the north in Gen. 10:23, but with Edom to the south in Lam. 4:21). He is a "blameless and upright man, one who fears God and shuns evil" (1:1). His wealth and family are described in numbers typifying abundance—seven sons and three daughters, seven thousand small cattle and three thousand camels, and so forth. The happiness of the family is epitomized in the constant round of banquets held by the children; Job's scrupulousness is shown by his sacrifices on their behalf, lest in a careless moment they "bless" (euphemism for "blaspheme") God in their hearts (1:5).

In the second movement, the action that shatters this idyll starts. "One day," at a periodic assembly of the divine court (1:6), God singles out Job for praise to the Adversary (the antecedent of the later Satan and anachronistically so called in the King James Version; in Hebrew Scriptures an angel whose task is to roam the earth and expose human wrongdoing). This commendation virtually invites the Adversary to suggest that since God has built a protective hedge around Job, his piety may not be disinterested ("for nothing," 1:9): only deprive him of his possessions and see whether he won't "bless" God to his face! God accepts the challenge and empowers the Adversary to carry out the test.

The third movement takes place "one day" as a round of the children's banquets begins and they are gathered in the house of the eldest son (1:13). A terrible chain of calamities befalls Job: one messenger after another arrives to report the destruction of every component of Job's fortune, culminating in the death of his children. Job goes into mourning, but with a blessing of God on his lips (the Adversary is thwarted, but his expectation is literally realized!). The movement concludes, "In all this Job did not sin or impute anything unsavory to God" (1:22).

The scene of the fourth movement is heaven again. "One day," at the periodic assembly of the divine court (2:1), God repeats his praise of Job to the Adversary, adding, "and he still holds on to his integrity, so you incited me to destroy him for nothing" (2:3). The Adversary proposes the ultimate test: afflict Job's own body and see whether he won't "bless"

God. God agrees, with the proviso that Job's life be preserved, and the Adversary hurries off to inflict a loathsome skin disease on Job, driving him to constant scratching with a sherd as he sits in the dust (the Greek translation reads, "on the dungheap far from the city"). His wife protests: "Do you still hold on to your integrity? 'Bless' God, and die" (2:9). Job remonstrates with her: "Should we then accept the good from God and not accept the bad?" (2:10). The question is rhetorical, but in every rhetorical question lurks the possible affirmation of what is ostensibly denied. Moreover, by bluntly calling what he has received from God "bad," Job has moved from his nonjudgmental blessing of God after the first stage of his ruin. The movement concludes with a variant of the preceding conclusion: "In all this Job did not sin with his lips." Is "with his lips" a mere equivalent of "did not impute anything unsavory to God," or did the talmudic sage correctly perceive in it a reservation: with his lips he sinned not, but in his heart he did![2] Is the impatient Job of the poem already foreshadowed in the closing stage of the narrative?

The last movement brings the three Friends of Job (also of Abrahamitic, extra-Israelite stock) into the picture. Coming from afar to comfort Job, they assume his condition—they sit on the ground with him, having torn their clothes and thrown dust on their heads. They keep him company in silence for seven days until he starts to speak.

The contrast between the simple folktale and the artful poem must not be overdrawn. In fact the artistry in the narrative is considerable. The representation of time in the first to the fourth movements progresses from duration to instant. In movement one, the regularity of happy, uneventful lives is expressed by verbs in the durational mode: "would go and would make a banquet," "would send word," "always used to do." The decision in heaven to test Job and its earthly realization in calamities (the second and third movements) occur each on separate days. Moreover, temporal disjunction is accompanied by disjunction of agent: although the Adversary is empowered to ruin Job, he is not mentioned in the subsequent story of disasters. But in the climactic fourth movement, the pace is stepped up and the events are concentrated. Events in heaven and their effect on earth occur on one and the same day; God licenses the Adversary to afflict Job's body, and the Adversary sets to work immediately and in person, as though eager to win his wager. The parallelism of the second stage of Job's trial to the first is expressed with the intensification and focusing that are characteristic of the second verset of poetic parallelism.

Dialogue and elements of poetic diction permeate the prose tale, further diminishing the contrast between the frame and the poem. Only the last movement of the story is speechless—owing to the courteous silence of the Friends. The first movement ends with Job's internal dialogue of concern lest his children blaspheme in secret. The second movement and the corresponding first half of the fourth movement consist almost entirely of dialogue between God and the Adversary, with the latter employing markedly elevated speech: parallelism ("roaming the land and walking about in it," 1:7; "the work of his hands you blessed, and his cattle abound in the land," 1:10); proverbs ("Skin for skin; all a man has he will give for his life," 2:4), emphatic repetition ("a hedge about him and about his household and about all he has," 1:10). The chain of calamities in the third movement is conveyed entirely through reports of messengers all of which exhibit the same pattern. The details of the accounts of disaster are artfully disposed: human and natural destroyers alternate, and the loss of Job's children is delayed to the end. Job's acquiescence in God's decree, with its parallelism, its compression, and its balanced lines, is poetry proper:

> Naked came I forth from the belly of my mother
> and naked shall I return thither:
> The Lord gave, and the Lord took away;
> blessed be the name of the Lord.   (1:21)

The terrestrial scene of the fourth movement is dominated by the sharp exchange between Job and his wife in which an ironic touch is visible. Job's wife unwittingly advocates the Adversary's cause to Job ("'Bless' God, and die") while expressing her exasperation with her husband in the very terms used by God to praise him ("still hold on to your integrity"). Such reuse by one character of the language of another is a constant feature of the poem; its occurrence here in the narrative is another bond between the two parts of the book.

The preliminary narrative establishes Job's virtuous character and so provides us with inside information known to heaven and Job alone. Our judgment on what Job and his Friends will say about his character must be determined by this information. We also know—what neither Job nor his Friends do—that Job's sufferings are designed to test him. These circumstances are fertile ground for irony; their impact on our reception of the arguments put forward in the poetic dialogue is an open and intriguing issue. If we now follow the debate step by step, we will get a clearer sense of the artful interplay between statements and positions, of the elements of progression in the arguments, and of the overarching ironies of the book as a whole.

AFTER BROODING over his fate for seven days, Job breaks his silence with a bitter diatribe against his life and its symbol, light (chap. 3). He wishes that the day of his birth would be reclaimed by primeval darkness and imagines the peace he would have enjoyed in Sheol had he been stillborn. Why does God give life to the wretched, whom he has "hedged about" (that is, obstructed—a reversal of the meaning of the very phrase used by the Adversary to describe Job's security)? He recollects his lifelong fear of calamity (one thinks of his anxious sacrificing on behalf of his children) which did not avail to prevent it.

This outburst takes the Friends by surprise. They had come to commiserate and encourage, not to participate in a rebellion against God's judgment. Their first spokesman, Eliphaz, opens softly (chaps. 4–5), reminding Job of his custom of cheering victims of misfortune, and gently chiding him for breaking down under his own calamities. He preaches the doctrine of distributive justice: no innocent man was ever wiped out, while the wicked reap their deserts. He reports a revelation made to him "in thought-filled visions of the night" (4:13); man is by nature too base to be innocent before God—even the angels are not trusted by him! Shortlived as he is ("cut down from morning to evening," 4:20), man cannot acquire the wisdom to comprehend his fate. Will Job seek vindication from some (other) divine being? Only fools let vexation kill them; "taking root" for a moment, they suddenly lose everything they own through their blindness to the truth that "man is to misery born as the sparks fly upward" (5:7). In Job's place, Eliphaz would turn to God, who works wonders and benefactions and who constantly reverses the fortunes of men. It is a lucky man whom God disciplines, for if the man—here Job—accepts it and repents, he has good hope of being healed and of living prosperous and happy to a ripe old age. All this has been proved by experience.

In this first exchange, each party starts from advanced positions: Job vents his death wish with untempered passion, becoming the spokesman of all the wretched of the earth. Eliphaz's carefully modulated reply sets the pattern for all subsequent speeches of the Friends: a prologue, demurring to Job, followed by a multithematic advocacy of the conventional view of God's distributive justice. Most of the themes of the Friends' argument are included in Eliphaz's speech: man's worthlessness before God; man's ephemerality and (consequent) ignorance; a call to turn to God in penitence; praise of God; the disciplinary purpose of misfortune; the happiness of the penitent; the claim to possess wisdom greater than Job's.

The rhetoric of debate pervades the speech of Eliphaz and all that follow. Themes are introduced by expressions of interrogation ("Is/Does not . . ."), demonstration ("look, behold"), exhortation ("Remember! Consider! Know!"), and exception ("but, however"). Among the rhetorical questions peppering Eliphaz's speech, one exhibits the unconscious irony typical of many in the Friends' speeches: "Call now, will anyone answer you;/to which of the divine beings will you turn?" (5:1). Eliphaz is scoffing, but in the event Job will not only call upon a heavenly witness, arbitrator and vindicator; he will ultimately be answered by the greatest and holiest of them all.

A constant difference between the general and particular observations of Job and the Friends is already evident in this first exchange. Both parties pass back and forth from the particular case of Job to the general condition of mankind. But in Job's speeches his particular misfortune governs his vision of the general; his unmerited suffering opens his eyes to the injustice rampant in society at large. In the Friends' speeches, on the other hand, the general doctrine of distributive justice governs their judgment of Job's case: he must be wicked in order to fit into their scheme of things. Job's empirically based generalities reflect reality; the Friends' perception of the particular is as fictive as the general doctrine from which it springs.

Echoes of Job's speech may be heard in that of Eliphaz. Job's "roarings" (3:24) reflect his anguish; Eliphaz speaks of the "lion's roar" (4:10). Birth and misery figure prominently in Job's speech; Eliphaz combines them in his epigrammatic "man is born to misery." Countering Job's wish for a direct passage from birth to grave, Eliphaz holds out hope of a penitent Job reaching the grave happy and in ripe old age. Such echoes and allusions pervade the dialogue, arguing against a commonly held opinion that the poem of Job consists of a series of disconnected monologues.

Job begins his reply to Eliphaz (chaps. 6–7) with a reference to ka'as, "vexation" (which Eliphaz warned kills fools, 5:2); overwhelming vexation has caused Job to speak so intemperately (6:2–3). He is the victim of God's terrors; to hold out hope to him is mockery, for his only wish is to be speedily dispatched ("crushed" he says in 6:9, using Eliphaz's language in 5:4). He is not made of stone so as to be able to tolerate his suffering any longer (6:12; in 5:17–18 Eliphaz called it God's benign discipline). He is disappointed that his Friends have deserted him. As when thirsty travelers seek out a wadi and find it has run dry in summer heat, so now when Job looks to his Friends for support they fail him. All he asks of them is to pay attention to his case, show him his fault, and stop producing vapid arguments. Job turns Eliphaz's theme of man's ephemerality to his own use: man's life is like a hireling's term of service; his only relief is night and wages. But Job's life is a hopeless agony; night brings him only the terrors of his dreams and night visions (a bitter echo of Eliphaz). Since human life is so brief, it is a wonder that God fills it with such suffering. Job parodies a verse in Psalms: "What is man, that you are mindful of him: / mortal man, that you take note of him?" (8:4; cf. 144:3: "Lord, what is man, that you should care about him, / mortal man, that you should think of him?"). This is skewed sardonically into:

> What is man, that you make much of him,
>   that you fix your attention upon him—
> inspect him every morning,
>   examine him every minute? (7:17–18)

If only the "watcher of men" would look away for a while and let Job live out his few remaining days in peace!

Establishing here the pattern for the following dialogues, Job's answer is longer than his predecessor's. He has been goaded by Eliphaz's pious generalities and oblique rebuke into itemizing his experience of God's enmity and its universal implications. In this way all the replies of the Friends arouse Job to ever-new perceptions of his condition and of the divine governance of the world.

Job's complaint scandalizes Bildad, the next interlocutor (chap. 8). "Will the Almighty pervert justice?" he asks rhetorically (v. 3), and proceeds to ascribe the death of Job's children to their sins. Thus Bildad lays bare the implications of the speeches of both his predecessors. Job ought to supplicate God contritely rather than assert a claim against him. Since we are so shortlived, it behooves us to consult the ancient sages; they teach that as it is nature's law that plants wither without water, so the course of the godless leads to perdition (the moral law). God will not repudiate the blameless or support the wicked; hence if Job repents, a joyous future, better than his past, is in store for him.

In his reply (chaps. 9–10), Job exploits the forensic metaphor in the rhetorical questions of Eliphaz and Bildad ("Can mortals be acquitted by God?" 4:17; "Will the Almighty pervert justice?" 8:3). It expresses the covenantal-legal postulate of ancient piety with its doctrine of distributive justice, shared by all the characters in the dialogue. God refuses to follow the rules, Job asserts: "Man cannot win a suit against God!" (9:2). God indeed works wonders (echoing Eliphaz)—mainly in displays of his destructive power in nature (a parody of Eliphaz's doxology). Such aggression he directs against any who seek redress from him for calamity inflicted on them undeservedly. In language suffused with legal terms, Job denounces God's disregard of his right: he terrorizes Job into confusion; even if Job could plead, his own words would be twisted against him. Contrary to Bildad's assertion, God indiscriminately destroys the innocent and the guilty, for "he wounds me much for nothing" (9:17; ironically, Job has unwittingly stumbled on the true reason for his suffering). If God would allow him, Job would demand of him a bill of indictment. He would charge him with unworthy conduct: he spurns his creature while smiling on the wicked; he searches for Job's sin, though he knows Job is not guilty. He carefully fashioned Job and sustained him through the years—only to hunt him down with a wondrous display of power (themes of Psalm 139 are sarcastically reused here).

It is now Zophar's turn (chap. 11). After denouncing Job's mockery and self-righteousness, he speaks as one privy to God's counsels: if God would answer Job, he'd show him his ignorance; the fact is that God has treated Job better than he deserves. God's purpose is unfathomable:

> higher than heaven,
>> deeper than Sheol,
> longer than the earth,
>> broader than the sea.   (vv. 8–9)

Job should pray to God and remove his iniquity; then he will enjoy the hope, the light, the peace and the sound sleep of the righteous.

Each of the three Friends having had his say, Job now delivers his longest answer yet (chaps. 12–14). Goaded by Bildad, he mockingly acknowledges their monopoly of wisdom, but claims he is no less wise. A shower of irony and sarcasm follows. Borrowing terms from Bildad's invocation of the ancient sages and Zophar's celebration of God's boundless wisdom, Job grotesquely invokes the dumb creatures of sky, sea, and earth to teach the commonplace, "With him [God] are wisdom and power; his are counsel and insight" (12:13), followed by another parodic doxology depicting divine power exercised with sheerly destructive results in the social realm. In this context the stock praise of God that he "uncovers deep things out of darkness, brings deep gloom to light" (12:22; cf. Dan. 2:22) suggests that he tears the lid off submerged forces of death and chaos, allowing them to surface and overcome order.[3] As for the Friends, they are quacksalvers, liars, obsequiously partial to God; they ascribe false principles to him and ought to be in dread of his ever subjecting them to scrutiny. Job, despite his ruined state, will stand up to God, convinced God must recognize integrity.

> Let him slay me; I have no [or in him I will] hope;
>> yet I will argue my cause before him.
> Through this I will gain victory:
>> that no godless man can come into his presence.   (13:15–16)

This burst of confidence collapses into the mournful realization of his vulnerability to God's terrors. Again he asks to be allowed to converse with God, to be informed of his sin (13:20–23; cf. 6:24, 10:2). Again he complains of God's enmity, wonders at his petty keeping of accounts and his persecution of "a driven leaf" (13:25). Again he implores God to let him live out his term of service in peace, for, unlike a tree, which after being felled can still renew itself from its roots, man once cut down sleeps eternally in Sheol.

But must containment in Sheol be final? Might it not be a temporary shelter from God's wrath? "If a man dies, can he revive?" (14:14)—hope wells up in the question, and the fantasy of reversal continues: When wrath subsides, God would call and Job would answer, God would long for his creature. But this anticipation of a doctrine whose time was not yet ripe, this flight of a mind liberated by the collapse of its concept of order, is a momentary flash. Job falls back into despondency.

When the first round of dialogue began, Job rejected life; by its conclusion, he is clinging to it and longing for renewed intimacy with God. Lamentation, anger, despair, and hope succeed each other in waves, but a clear gathering of energy is visible in his speeches. The Friends, hurt by Job's challenge to their concept of the moral order, have turned from comforters to scolds, each harsher than his predecessor. Eliphaz only implies that Job is a sinner; Bildad openly proposes that his children have died for their sins; Zophar assures Job that his suffering is less than he deserves. Yet each ends with a promise of a bright future if Job will only acknowledge his guilt and implore God's forgiveness. Though they provide no direct comfort to Job, by blackening his character they rouse him out of the torpor of despair and kindle in him the desire to assert himself.

Eliphaz opens the second round (chaps. 15–21), deploring Job's mockery of his Friends' counsel. His pernicious arguments undermine piety. Is Job Wisdom personified ("Were you born before the mountains?" at 15:7 evokes Prov. 8:25 in reference to Dame Wisdom); does *he* have a monopoly of it (cf. 12:2–3)? Job's ridicule of sapiential tradition rankles with Bildad and Zophar as well ("Why are we thought of as brutes?" 18:3; "reproof that insults me," 20:3). One would think Job had listened in on God's council when in fact it was to Eliphaz that insight into man's true condition was vouchsafed in a night vision (15:14–16 repeats with slight variation the oracle on man's baseness in Eliphaz's first speech, 4:17–21). Eliphaz proceeds to depict the life and exemplary fate of the wicked as taught by the sages. This theme, briefly touched upon previously, is elaborated at length throughout the second round of the Friends' speeches. Since they cannot persuade Job to withdraw his arraignment of God, his very perseverance in his claims appears to them to convict him of sin. Hence they endeavor, in this round, to frighten him into recanting by describing in detail the punishment of the wicked. That these descriptions, ostensibly generic, contain items identical with Job's misfortunes, is of course not accidental. The poet exhibits virtuosity in playing variations on this single theme. He has Eliphaz focus on the tormented person of the wicked man (chap. 15); here the most blatant allusions to Job's condition occur. Bildad concentrates on the destruction of his "tent" and progeny:

> Light has darkened in his tent;
>   his lamp fails him . . .
> Generations to come will be appalled at his fate [and say],
>   "These were the dwellings of the wicked;
>   here was the place of him who knew not God." (18:21)

Zophar (chap. 20) develops an alimentary figure: the ill-got gain of the wicked are sweets he tries to swallow but must vomit, or they will turn to poison in him and kill him.

Job answers the monitory descriptions of the fate of the wicked with pathetic descriptions of his misery (chap. 16). In response to Eliphaz he figures God as an enemy rushing at him like a hero, setting him up as his target—inverting Eliphaz's picture of the wicked playing the hero and running defiantly at God (15:25–26). He has been afflicted despite his innocence, and this very thought moves him to plead that the wrong done to him not be forgotten ("Earth, do not cover my blood," 16:18). In a transport of faith he avers he has a witness in heaven who will arbitrate between him and God, then descends again into despair.

Responding to Bildad's depiction of the wicked man's loss of home and kin, Job relates (chap. 19) how God has stripped him of honor; how friends, wife, and servants have abandoned him till only his flesh and bones remain attached to him. He implores the compassion of his Friends, wishes for a permanent record of his arguments, and consoles himself with the assurance that although he is forsaken in the present, his redeemer-kinsman (go'el) lives and will in the end appear to vindicate him.

In his reply to Zophar (chap. 21), concluding the second round of dialogue, Job bids his Friends be silent and listen to something truly appalling (Job spurns as specious the horror over the pretended destruction of the wicked described by Bildad, 18:20), namely the real situation of the wicked. Contrary to the Friends' doctrine, the wicked live long and prosper, surrounded by frolicking children; they die without pangs. They flaunt their indifference toward God with impunity. How often is their light extinguished (contrary to Bildad's claim)? Their children will pay for their sins?—why doesn't God pay *them* back! The Friends have reproached Job with insolence toward God: "Can God be instructed in knowledge—/he who judges from the heights?" (21:22; the verse seems to cite the Friends, but it is a pseudo-citation since in fact they never said this; in the heat of debate Job ascribes to the Friends what can at most have been implied in their speeches). Job answers: What sort of judge distributes well-being and misfortune according to no standard? The Friends have admonished: "Where is the tent in which the wicked dwelled?" (see the end of Bildad's speech, 18:21); Job retorts: every traveler (that is, worldly-wise person, not necessarily old) knows that even in death the wicked are honored.

In the second round the Friends dwelt one-sidedly on the punishment of the wicked, intending Job to see in the wicked a mirror of himself. What they succeed in doing is to move him to particularize his own suffering and—equally one-sidedly—the success of the wicked, thus at once proving he is not one of them and confirming again God's perversity. In this round, too, Job experiences sporadic moments of hopefulness and intimations of vindication. Significant of things to come in round three is the frequency (especially in Job's last speech) with which Job cites the Friends or anticipates their responses to him. In the first speech of this round he says that were he in their place he would mouth the same sort of platitudes (16:4); in his last speech he begins to show he can do it.

Eliphaz returns to the arena yet a third time (chap. 22). Is your righteousness of any interest to God? he asks Job (v. 3); the implication seems to be that Job's clamor for a hearing is arrant presumption (Eliphaz cannot know that God indeed has a stake in Job's righteousness). In fact, he continues, you are very wicked—behaving in a cruel and callous manner toward the weak and defenseless. Eliphaz has been driven to this extreme by his tenacious adherence to the doctrine of distributive justice, the threat to which may be gauged by his incredible accusation. In the sequel, Eliphaz misconstrues Job's pseudo-citation (21:22) to mean that God cannot see through the cloud-cover to judge mankind; but, he affirms, the wicked are punished. Job must return to God, give up his trust in gold (another fabricated charge), and pray to God; reformed, he will be God's favorite, capable of interceding with him on behalf of the guilty. Once again Eliphaz suggests he knows God's counsels; he cannot know that in the end his prediction will come true when Job prays to avert God's wrath from Eliphaz and his companions!

Job replies in a soliloquy (chaps. 23–24) indirectly relating to Eliphaz. He would like to find God, not in order to repent, but to argue his case before him, for he is sure he would be cleared; but he finds him nowhere. He would emerge as pure gold from a test, and God knows it, yet the deity capriciously harasses him. A list of crimes committed by the wicked now appears, intertwined with a description of the downtrodden, and ending with the cutting reproach "Yet God does not regard it unseemly!" (24:12). After describing a trio of "rebels against the light"—murderer, thief, and adulterer, who shun the light of day—the speech becomes unintelligible till its last defiant line: "Surely no one can give me the lie / or set my words at naught" (24:25).

Bildad's third speech (chap. 25) is a mere six verses, a doxology consisting chiefly of a repetition (for the second time; see 15:14–16) of Eliphaz's threadbare oracle (cf. 4:17–21). The following speech of Job contains a doxology that might well continue this one (26:5–14); indeed many critics have taken it for the misplaced end of Bildad's speech. But an alternative interpretation is commendable for its piquancy: "Bildad's speech is short and sounds like what Job says in reply precisely because Job cuts him off and finishes the speech for him."[4] Such mimicry accords with the tenor of the beginning of Job's speech, in which he derides Bildad's rhetorical impotence and suggests that even his banalities are not his own ("Whose breath issued from you?" 26:4). Job demonstrates with great flourish that he can better anything Bildad does. When the Friends are reduced to repeating one another and Job can say their pieces for them, we know that the dialogue has ended.

And indeed Zophar has nothing to say in this third round. To be sure, critics have identified his "lost speech" in the next speech of Job: 27:13 is a variant of the conclusion of Zophar's last speech (20:29)—picking up as it were where he ended—and the subsequent description of the doom of the wicked continues Zophar's specific theme of dispossession. That these two passages are connected can hardly be in doubt, but is the latter an alien intrusion into Job's speech? Its context permits another explanation.

After waiting in vain for Zophar to speak, Job (chap. 27) resumes his address (aptly not called a reply) with an oath invoking (paradoxically) "God who has deprived me of justice" (v. 2). He affirms his blamelessness against his Friends' vilification. He will hold on to this integrity (an echo of 2:3, 9) as long as he lives, for God destroys the impious who contend with him. He offers to teach his Friends "what is with God" (27:11)—perhaps a reference to wisdom (cf. "It is not with me," 28:14, and "[What do] you understand that is not with us?" 15:9), in respect of which the Friends held themselves superior to Job (15:9–10). For now, they must stop talking the nonsense that their own experience contradicts (27:12). As an example of such nonsense Job then offers what Zophar might have said had he spoken, in a second display of expert mimicry.

Still formally part of Job's speech is the sublime poem on wisdom that follows (chap. 28)—the wisdom by which the world is governed, by which the meaning of events is unlocked. Man knows how to ferret precious ores out of the earth; he conquers the most daunting natural obstacles in order to obtain treasure. But he does not have a map to the sources of wisdom. The primeval waters, Tehom and the sea, do not contain it; farsighted birds of the sky do not know its place; Death (the realm next to divinity) has heard only a rumor of it. God alone, whose control of the elements of weather exemplifies his wide-ranging power, comprehends it. For man he has appointed, as its functional equivalent, the obligation to fear God and shun evil—wherewith he adjusts himself to the divine order.

The topic of this poem and its serene resignation seem out of place at this juncture. Critics generally excise the poem from its context, though some ascribe it nonetheless to the author of the dialogue. It is a self-contained piece having only tangential connections with its environment; but these may account for its location. The mention of silver in the first line links the poem to the preceding description of the wicked man's loss of his silver (27:16–17). More substantial is the possible connection with Job's undertaking to teach his Friends "what is with the Almighty" (27:11), preparatory to which they should stop talking nonsense. If, as was suggested above, this is a reference to wisdom, which is with God alone, then the Friends' parade of assurance that they know the reason for Job's suffering is sheer presumption. As the medieval exegete Naḥmanides put it, "He instructed them to say, 'I don't know.'"[5] A closer paraphrase might be: abandon your futile doctrine; it is a reproach to you and will not gain you God's favor. This is Job's last word to his Friends.

Job's speech in chapters 27 and 28 is framed by phrases that echo his initial characterization in the prose tale. At the beginning, the expressions "I will maintain my integrity / I will hold on to my righteousness" (27:5–6) recall God's praise: "he still holds on to his integrity" (2:3). At the end, the human equivalent of wisdom is "to fear the Lord and shun evil" (28:28), the very traits of which, according to the story, Job was a paragon. Between these appears Job's arraignment of God and his friends, and the denial that wisdom is accessible to man. Taken together, these evince the sheer heroism of a naked man, forsaken by his God and his friends and bereft of a clue to understand his suffering, still maintaining faith in the value of his virtue and in the absolute duty of man to be virtuous. The universe has turned its back on him, yet Job persists in the affirmation of his own worth and the transcendent worth of unrewarded good. Perhaps this is the sense of the difficult passage in 17:8–9:

> The upright are appalled at this [Job's fate];
> The innocent man is aroused against the impious [Job's Friends];
> The righteous man holds to his way [despite it all];
> He whose hands are pure grows stronger.

If such is the gist of this complex speech, it marks a stage in Job's reconciliation with God, undercutting the climax in chapter 42. But did the ancient poet share our predilection for the single climax? He has depicted Job attaining to peaks of confidence several times, only to relapse into despondency. The same may hold true for Job's making his peace with his fate and with God.

Job's final speech, a long soliloquy (chaps. 29–31), reverts even more explicitly to his former state as "the greatest of all the dwellers in the east." He recollects pathetically his past glory, the awe in which he was held, his regal patronage of the needy and helpless (a pointed refutation of Eliphaz's gratuitous accusations); how he looked forward to living out his days in happiness, surrounded by his family and honored by society "like a king among his troop, as one who comforts mourners" (29:25). Instead he now drinks bitter drafts of insult from a rabble "whose fathers I would have disdained to put among my sheepdogs" (30:1). Once again he describes his suffering—God's cruel enmity toward him—ending his lament with a line contrasting with the conclusion of the previous picture: "My lyre is given to mourning, / my pipe to accompany weepers" (30:31).

In the last section of the soliloquy (chap. 31), Job forcefully affirms his blamelessness in a form derived from the terminal curse-sanctions of covenants. The biblical models are Leviticus 26 and Deuteronomy 28: if Israel obeys the stipulations of the Covenant, it will prosper; if not, it will suffer disaster upon disaster. Attention is directed to this traditional pattern by allusion to a "covenant" Job made with his eyes not to gaze on a maiden (31:1). In the immediate sequel he spells out the classic covenantal doctrine by which he has guided his steps: "Surely disaster is appointed for the iniquitous:/trouble for the wrongdoer" (31:3). (In the retrospective light of this conception, all of Job's speeches assume the character of a "covenant lawsuit" in reverse: man accusing God, instead of God accusing man [Israel] as in the books of the Prophets.) In the thin guise of self-curses Job recites a catalogue of his virtues—the code of a nobleman who does not allow his status to weaken his solidarity with the unfortunate. The virtues come in bundles and are interrupted by an only occasional self-curse ("If I did not practice such and such a virtue, may this or that calamity overtake me"), indicating that the pattern (in which normally the curses are prominent) is more form than substance—a vehicle serving the double purpose of marking a conclusion (the function of covenant curses) and of manifesting the unbroken spirit of Job. The latter is under-lined by Job's wish that his Litigant produce a bill of indictment: he would display it as an ornament, so sure is he that it would prove him righteous!

Having played out their parts, the Friends fell silent; now Job falls silent, and the scene assumes the form it had before the dialogue began. But there is a tension in the air: will the Litigant respond?

Resolution of the tension is delayed by the sudden appearance of a new character: angry at the Friends for their inability to answer Job otherwise than by declaring him a sinner, and at Job for justifying himself against God, brash young Elihu the Buzite takes possession of the stage (chaps. 32–37). He excuses his intervention by citing the impotence of his elders and delivers himself of three highly wrought speeches, full of obscure language and not always to the point. Though insisting he will not repeat what has been said (32:14), he does go over familiar ground; new are the grandiloquence and the occasional argument in favor of positions already taken. Thus to Job's charge that God does not answer, Elihu replies (off the point) that God speaks to man through dreams and illness designed to humble man's pride and turn him from his bad course (Eliphaz said as much in 5:17–18, but without elaborating the suffering and later confession and thanksgiving of the penitent). He counters Job's complaint of God's injustice by affirming, tautologically, that the sole ruler of the earth cannot do wrong, since it is of the essence of rulership to be just. From the transcendence of God Eliphaz had argued that man's works cannot interest him (22:2–3); Job had reasoned from the same fact of transcendence that even if he sinned, it could scarcely matter to God (7:20); Elihu advances the thought that the good and evil that men do cannot affect God, but only other men. Hence—if we understand 35:9 rightly—human misery has its cause in human evil; yet God is not indif-ferent, and in the end he punishes the guilty. Elihu's last speech opens with an interpretation of the suffering of the virtuous as disciplinary, and concludes with a rhapsodic paean to God's greatness as evidenced in the phenomena of rain, thunder, and lightning.

Elihu has indeed championed God's cause without condemning Job (except in 34:8: Job makes common cause with the wicked); his ornate eloquence has contributed color but little substance to the debate. Critics consider his speeches redundant and hence from another hand or at least outside the original plan of the book. But if repetition is an indication of unoriginality, considerable tracts of the dialogue of Job and his Friends would have to be declared secondary. The pattern of alternating dialogue is absent in Elihu's section, but it has already lapsed in the last spell of Job's oratory. Elihu's style is different from that of his predecessors, but might not that difference be intentional, to distinguish impetuous youthfulness from more deliberative age? Our author may simply have sought another character through which to display rhetorical invention. Indeed, can a better reason be given for the extension of the dialogue for three rounds than the delight of the poet in the exercise of his gift? This very motive animates the ancient Egyptian composition called "The Eloquent Peasant," whose thematic similarity to Job has been observed: a peasant who has been robbed pleads his cause before the governor; the king, who is told of the peasant's eloquence, deliberately delays judgment of the case so as to enjoy more and more of it. By this device the author gains scope for exercising his skill in playing variations on a few themes. (A modern editor's evaluation of the piece recalls evaluations of Elihu's speeches: "The peasant's speeches are, to modern taste, unduly repetitive, with high-flown language and constant harping on a few metaphors.")[6] Be that as it may, the unconventional representation of youth outdoing age bespeaks the author of the rest of the poem, whose hallmark is subversion of tradition. Elihu has marginally surpassed the Friends in affirming that God does speak to man, that not all suffering is punitive, and that contemplation of nature's elements opens the mind to God's greatness—a line of apology for God that does not entail blackening Job's character. We are on the way to God's answer from the storm.

The chief problem raised by God's answer to Job (chap. 38–41) is to relate the panorama it paints of God's amazing creativity to the issues the interlocutors have been wrestling with.

In opening his speech (chaps. 38–39), God exchanges roles with Job: till now, Job has demanded answers from God; now God sets unanswerable questions to Job about the foundations of the universe. Does Job know anything about the fashioning and operation of the cosmic elements—earth, sea, the underworld, and darkness? Has he knowledge of, can he control, the celestial phenomena of snow, hail, thunder, and lightning, or the constellations? From these spectacles of nature God turns to wilderness animals and their provisioning: the lions, who lie in ambush for their prey; the raven, whose young cry to God for food; the mountain goats, whose birth only God attends; the wild ass, who roams far from civilization; the wild ox, who mocks man's attempt to subjugate him; the silly ostrich; the war horse, with his uncanny lust for battle; the soaring falcon and eagle, who sight their prey from afar. None owe man anything; the ways of none are comprehended by him.

How different this survey of creation is from that of Genesis 1 or the hymn to nature of Psalm 104. Here man is incidental—mainly an impotent foil to God. In Genesis 1 (and its echo, Ps. 8) teleology pervades a process of creation whose goal and crown is man. All is directed to his benefit; the earth and its creatures are his to rule. In Psalm 104 nature exhibits a providential harmony of which man is an integral part. But the God of Job celebrates each act and product of his creation for itself, an independent value attesting his power and grace. Job, representing mankind, stands outside the picture, displaced from its center to a remote periphery. He who would form a proper judgment of God cannot confine himself to his relations with man, who is, after all, only one of an astonishing panoply of creatures created and sustained in ways unfathomable to the human mind.

Instead of confessing his ignorance and, by implication, his presumptuousness, in judging God, Job replies (40:3–5) that he is too insignificant to reply; that he can say no more. This response, as Saadya Gaon observed in the tenth century, is ambiguous: "When one interlocutor says to his partner, 'I can't answer you,' it may mean that he acquiesces in the other's position, equivalent to 'I can't gainsay the truth'; or it may mean he feels overborne by his partner, equivalent to 'How can I answer you when you have the upper hand?'"[7] In order to elicit an unequivocal response, God speaks again.

In language identical with that of the first speech, God declares he will put questions to Job: "Would you impugn my justice, / condemn me, that you may be right?" (40:8). Job has dwelt on the prosperity of the wicked, attributing it to divine indifference or cruelty. God invites Job to try his hand at righting wrongs, if he has the hand to do it: "Have you an arm like God's? / Can you thunder with a voice like him?" (40:9). If he can do better, God will sing his praises. Once again, Job's ignorance and impotence are invoked to disqualify him from arraigning God; only one who comprehends the vastness and complexity of God's work can pass judgment on his performance. To drive home Job's powerlessness, two monstrous animals are described that mock the Genesis notion of man's rule of terrestrial and sea creatures. Behemoth, a land animal, is briefly described: his muscles are powerful, his bones like metal bars. Leviathan, a denizen of the waters, is a living fortress, whose parts evoke shields and military formations; flames and smoke issue from him; no weapon avails against him; his tracks are supernally luminous; he lords it over the arrogant.

The effect of this parade of wonders is to excite amazement at the grandeur and exotic character of divine creativity. By disregarding man, the author rejects the anthropocentrism of all the rest of Scripture. God's governance cannot be judged by its manifestations in human society alone. Had the moral disarray evident in society been tolerated by a mere human ruler, other humans of like nature and motives would have been entitled to judge him as vicious. But no man can comprehend God, whose works defy teleological and rational categories; hence to condemn his supervision of human events because it does not conform to human conceptions of reason and justice is improper.

Man's capacity to respond with amazement to God's mysterious creativity, and to admire even those manifestations of it that are of no use or benefit to him, enables him to affirm God's work despite its deficiencies in the moral realm. Such deficiencies, like so much else in the amazing cosmos, stand outside human judgment. Chapter 28 has already anticipated the conclusion at which Job must arrive in the face of God's wonders: for mankind wisdom consists of fearing God and shunning evil; more than that he cannot know.

Job now submits unequivocally (42:2–6). He confesses his ignorance and his presumptuousness in speaking of matters beyond his knowledge. Now that he has not merely "heard of" God—that is, known of him by tradition—but also "seen" him—that is, gained direct cognition of his nature—he rejects what he formerly maintained and "is consoled for [being mere] dust and ashes" (v. 6). Lowly creature that he is, he has yet been granted understanding of the inscrutability of God; this has liberated him from the false expectations raised by the old covenant concept, so misleading to him and his interlocutors.

The Adversary has lost his wager. Throughout his trial Job has neither rejected God (he has clung to him even in despair) nor ever expressed regret for having lived righteously (cf. Ps. 73:13–14). He thus gave the lie to the Adversary's insinuation that his uprightness was contingent on reward. Yet this last word of the poet does not pull all things together. God's answer does not relate to the issues raised in the dialogue; it seeks rather to submerge them under higher considerations. Although the poet rejects the covenant relation between God and man with its sanctions of distributive justice, he offers no alternative. In effect, he puts the relation entirely on a footing of faith—in the language of the Adversary, "fearing God for nothing" (1:9).

The narrative epilogue (42:7-17) relates Job's rehabilitation. God reproaches Eliphaz, the chief and representative of the Friends, for not having spoken rightly about him as Job did. God thus seconds Job's protest in 13:7-10:

> Will you speak unjustly on God's behalf?
>> Will you speak deceitfully for him? . . .
> He will surely reprove you
>> if in your heart you are partial toward him.

God forbids a conception of himself as a moral accountant, according to which the Friends interpreted Job's suffering as punishment and Job ascribed injustice to God. Since the prayer of the injured on behalf of those who injured him is the most effective intercession (cf. Abraham's intercession for Abimelech, Gen. 20:7, 17), God orders the Friends to seek Job's intervention with him on their behalf (ironically, Eliphaz promised Job this power, 22:30). With this act of mutual reconciliation, Job is restored to his material and social position: his possessions are doubled (cf. Bildad's promise, 8:7), and he has children equal to the number of those reported dead by the messenger. Unlike 1:2, 42:13 does not state that the children "were born to him"; Naḥmanides infers from this difference that the original children were restored, having been only spirited away by the Adversary[8]—a laudably humane, if unpersuasive, piece of exegesis. The story pays unusual regard to Job's daughters, noting their incomparable beauty, their exotic names—which may be rendered "Day-bright" (so ancient tradition understood *Yemima*), "Cassia" (a perfume-herb), and "Horn of Eye-Cosmetic"—and their equalization with their brothers as heirs, an egalitarian touch worthy of our unconventional author. Job dies at a ripe old age surrounded by four generations of his family (cf. 5:26, 29:18).

Critics have deemed this conclusion, yielding as it does to the instinct of natural justice, anticlimactic and a vulgar capitulation to convention; the common reader, on the other hand, has found this righting of a terribly disturbed balance wholly appropriate. In its reversal, the conclusion is of a piece with the rest of the book, so consistently subverting expectations and traditional values. Thus the story is set in motion by the Adversary's undermining the value of covenant-keeping piety, casting doubt on its disinterestedness. This instigates the immoral exercise of dealing the deserts of the wicked to pious Job in order to try his mettle—a perverse measure that cannot be avoided if doubts about his motives are to be allayed. Job, true to his character, blesses God even in adversity; however, soon thereafter he awakens to the moral disarray in the world and comes near blasphemy by accusing God of indiscriminate cruelty. Job despairs, yet continues to look to God for vindication. The Friends came to console, but exhaust themselves in vexatious arguments with Job; seeking his repentance, they incite him to ever bolder protest. They propose to teach him traditional wisdom; he ends by teaching them the inaccessibility of true wisdom. Job calls on God to present his bill of indictment, believing and not believing he will respond, and eager to present his defense. God does actually respond, but not to Job's questions; and Job has no answer at all. God rebukes Job for presumptuousness, but he also rebukes the Friends for misrepresenting him. Finally, when Job has resigned himself to being dust and ashes in the face of the cosmic grandeur revealed to him, God reverses his misfortune and smiles on him to the end of his life.

The piquancy of these incessant turns of plot, mood, and character is heightened by the overarching ironies resulting from the union of the frame story and the dialogue. We see a handful of men striving vainly to penetrate the secret of God's providence, guessing futilely at the meaning of what they see, while we know that behind this specific case of suffering is a celestial wager. The effect of keeping the background setting and the foreground dialogue simultaneously in mind is almost vertiginous. For example, the Friends appear so far right in insisting, and Job so far wrong in denying, that God discriminates in his visitations—for a reason none can know. All are wrong in asserting that whether Job (man) sins or not is of no account to God. Job's sardonic charge that he is persecuted just because he is righteous is truer than any of the human characters can know. At the same time, the surface meaning of the dialogue is not invalidated: appearances do support Job's contention that God is indifferent to those who cling to him and smiles on the wicked; the Friends' depiction of society as a perfectly realized moral order is really nonsense. The beacon of the righteous is not hope of reward but the conviction that, for man, cosmic wisdom is summed up in the duty to fear God and shun evil, whether or not these virtues bear fruit. The misfortunes of the righteous ought not to imply a condemnation of God, in view of the grandeur and mystery of God's creative work at large.

Vacillating between the "truth" of the story and the arguments of the dialogue, the reader may be inclined to harmonize the two: the suffering of the righteous is, or may be, a test of the disinterestedness of their virtue. This of course can never be known to the sufferers or their neighbors; the case of Job is a stern warning never to infer sin from suffering (the error of the Friends), or the enmity of God toward the sufferer (the error of Job). Although such a harmonization may offer some consolation to Job-like suffering, it is not spelled out in the book. With its ironies and surprises, its claims and arguments in unresolved tension, the Book of Job remains the classic expression in world literature of the irrepressible yearning for divine order, baffled but never stifled by the disarray of reality.

The Poetry of Job

The poetry of Job is a sustained manifestation of the sublime, in the classical sense of "exhibit[ing] great objects with a magnificent display of imagery and diction" and having "that force of composition . . . which strikes and overpowers the mind, which excites the passions, and which expresses ideas at once with perspicuity and elevation."[9] It embraces an extraordinary range of objects of universal interest: emotions of serenity and terror, hope and despair; the contrasting characters of men; doubts about and affirmations of cosmic justice; the splendors and wonders of animate and inanimate nature. To be sure, these appear elsewhere in biblical literature, but only in the Book of Job are these themes expressed with such concentration, such invention and vivid imagery.

The poet makes use of the various genres of biblical lyric and sapiential poetry: the personal complaint of Psalms in Job's self-descriptions; the moral character portraits of Proverbs (the lazybones, the drunkard) in the depictions of the righteous and the wicked; the psalmic hymns in the doxologies, which in Job are sometimes straightforward and sometimes parodic. However, Job's brilliant descriptions of weather and animal phenomena and the evocation of man's exploration and exploitation of earth's resources have only rudimentary antecedents in earlier biblical poetry.

Innovative imagery pervades the book: the tree cut down that renews itself from its roots (14:7–9) as a metaphoric foil for man's irrevocable death; humanity's kinship with maggots (17:14) and jackals (30:29) as an image of alienation and isolation; the congealing of milk (10:10) as a figure for the formation of the embryo; the movement of a weaver's shuttle (7:6), of a runner in flight, or of the swooping eagle (9:25–26) as similes for the speedy passage of a lifetime; God's hostility figured as an attacking army (19:12); God's absence represented in the image of a traveler's unfound goal in every direction (23:8; a striking reversal of the expression of God's ubiquity in Ps. 139:7–10).

The diction of the poems is distinguished by lexical richness, with many unique, unusual, and "foreign" expressions, lending color to the non-Israelite setting and characters. For example, 'or, besides its normal Hebrew sense of "light," seems to bear dialectical Aramaic senses of "evening" (24:14) and "west wind" (38:24); and there are many other terms that occur only in this book. There is much expressive repetition of sound (alliteration, assonance); the explosive p sound, for instance, dominates 16:9–14, a passage in which Job pictures himself as a battered and shattered object of God's pitiless assaults. Verbal ambiguity is abundantly exploited: be'efes tiqwah in the weaving image of 7:6 can mean "without hope" or "till the thread runs out"; in 9:30–31, the opposites bor, "soap," and shaḥat, "muck," are homonyms of two synonyms meaning "pit," thus conveying the suggestion "out of one pit into another." Contrariwise, the same expression recurs in different contexts, effecting cohesion while at the same time producing variety: the pair "vision/ dream" serves as the vehicle of oracular experience (33:15), nightmares (7:14), or a figure of ephemerality (20:8); the pair "dust (dirt)/clay" expresses the qualities of insubstantiality (4:19), lifeless malleability (10:9), worthlessness (13:12), and multitude (27:16).

What quality in poetry makes it the preferred vehicle for this author's vision? Poetry was the form taken by sapiential observation and speculation throughout the ancient Near East. With its engagement of the emotions and the imagination, it was the usual mode of persuasive discourse. Through its compression, poetry allows stark, untempered expression that, while powerful in impact, awakens the kind of careful reflection that leads to the fuller apprehension of a subject. Moreover, the density of poetic language, compelling the reader to complement, to fill in gaps, fits it peculiarly for representing impassioned discourse, which by nature proceeds in associative leaps rather than by logical development. Spontaneous debate, too, is characterized by zigzag, repetitive, and spiral movement in which sequence is determined more by word and thought association than by linearity. Someone listening in to debate must supply the connections in a manner not very different from the complementing required for the comprehension of poetry. Such passionate argument is precisely reflected in the poetry of Job, as each interlocutor links theme to theme without troubling to arrange them according to logical sequentiality, and by that very liberty enriching the connotations and multiplying the facets of the argument.

The poetry of Job is continually astonishing in its power and inventiveness. Its compression allows multiple possibilities of interpretation, corresponding to the open, unresolved tensions in the author's vision of reality. It is a beautifully appropriate vehicle for a writer bent on compelling us to see things in new ways.

NOTES

1. All translations in this essay are my own [AT].

2. Rava, in Babylonian Talmud, Bava Batra 16a.

3. Based on an interpretation of 12:22 in J. Gerald Janzen, *Job* (Atlanta, 1985), pp. 104–105.

4. P. W. Skehan, "Strophic Patterns in the Book of Job," *Catholic Biblical Quarterly*, 23 (1961), 141.

5. Charles Chavel, ed., *Kitve Rabbenu Moshe ben Naḥman*, I (Jerusalem, 1964), 86 (comment to 27:14).

6. W. K. Simpson, ed., *The Literature of Ancient Egypt* (New Haven, 1972), p. 31.

7. Yosef Kafaḥ, ed., *'Iyyov 'im Targum u-Ferush Ha-gaon Rabbenu Saadya . . .* (Jerusalem, 1973), pp. 198–199.

8. Chavel, *Kitve . . . Naḥman*, I, 128.

9. Robert Lowth, *Lectures on the Sacred Poetry of the Hebrews*, trans. G. Gregory (London, 1847), p. 155.

SUGGESTED FURTHER READINGS

L. L. Besserman, *The Legend of Job in the Middle Ages* (Cambridge, 1979).

Eugene Goodheart, "Job and the Modern World," *Judaism,* 10 (1961), 21–28.

J. Gerald Janzen, *Job* (Atlanta, 1985).

Jack Kahn, *Job's Illness: Loss, Grief and Integration* (Oxford, 1975).

R. B. Sewall, *The Vision of Tragedy* (New Haven, 1956), pp. 1–24.

Meir Weiss, *The Story of Job's Beginning, Job 1–2: A Literary Analysis* (Jerusalem, 1983).

J. W. Whedbee, "The Comedy of Job," *Semeia,* 7 (1977), 1–39.

Hebrew University of Jerusalem

The Song of Songs

Francis Landy

THE discourse of love, of which the Song is a distillation, is created not only by the lovers, is not only the basis of a community predicated on love, first developing from the family, the mother–child relationship, and then the society of lovers to which the Song appeals, but also draws into its orbit things, plants, animals, geography. It can do nothing else: lovers can communicate only through the world, through metaphor. The lover explores the other person and finds in the body affirmation, response, and also solitude. Something happens that is beyond speech, and it enters language only through displacement. For this reason sexual interpretations of the Song are both fascinating and boring; they exemplify the pornographic desire to name and appropriate pleasure, to have it at imaginative command, and they miss the point. If the Song were a continuous allegory of sex, no matter how ingenious the techniques or subtle the allusions, it would be nothing more than a riddle or a tease.

The lover is a stranger who represents, in his or her heterogeneity, the world that we must make our own; the lover's body is explored, with all its multifarious possibilities of significance and action, its extremes of revulsion and attraction, its vulnerability and peril. The body is subject to death, and thus to a concern in which there is always an element of anxiety.

The lovers are two persons, with presumably their own separate biographies, but the poem is their composite speech, expressing a common personality to which they both contribute, to which each is opened up, and which is experienced in relation to the other. Further, each is, of course, an aspect of a single person, namely the poet. One of the features that gives the Song its coherence is the consistency of voice within it, shared by both lovers and engendering them.

The germinal paradox of the Song is the union of two people through love. The lovers search for each other through the world and through language that separates them and enfolds them. The body is the medium for this search and is the boundary between the world and the self. Thus the body comes to represent the self to the world, and the world to the self. It becomes the focus of metaphor, the conjunction of differentiated terms.

Metaphor links self and other, man and nature, sign and referent. Hans-Peter Müller, in a recent book on the imagery of the Song,[1] argues that metaphor, a projective identification with the world, is necessary to establish the reality of the self as an object. Thus, exploring the body is equivalent to exploring the world, a point made in verse after verse. Beyond this, the Song is concerned as much with the relationship between man and nature—his alienation from it through language and consciousness, and his participation in it—as it is with that between human beings.

The union of lovers is, then, a means for the discovery of a common identity between discrete terms; it is a metaphor for the poetic process. The subject of the poem is not just or simply human love, but also everything that enters into relation with it in the poem, the whole world as it is experienced or animated through love. The Beloved (my term for the woman in the poem) is, for example, addressed in 2:14 as a dove, whose voice communicates not only her presence but also the world it inhabits; the preceding description of the spring (2:10–13), in which the Lover (my term for the man) woos his beloved with primaveral beauty, gains much of its rhetorical power from its apparent impersonality and objectivity; it is as if the spring were wooing on his behalf. As a result the words of the poem have an element of redundancy; they are the forms adopted by a voice whose message is even simpler than their ostensible "I love you" or "You are beautiful," a voice that is a call, human and universal, announcing its own presence and desire. Many passages in the Song are likewise motivated by the need to speak for the sake of speaking. In the dialogue of 1:7–8, for example, the mellifluous exchange of cross-purposes, in which the Beloved's attempt to make a rendezvous meets with ambiguous evasion, is developed through a series of circumlocutions one of whose functions is to protract the conversation. A unit whose theme is absence keeps the lovers present to each other; between them they construct a duet. Similarly, the formal portraits that take up much of the poem have a repetitive component; they hold the image and, it is hoped, the attention of the loved one.

Analyzing the imagery of the Song is consequently both mandatory—since the poem is essentially concerned with metaphor—and only one aspect of the work of interpretation. For the Song appeals to the sensual ear as much as to the intellect; the reader may be baffled by the words and still respond to their emotional and physical connotations; in fact the difficulty reinforces this appeal to an uncritical pleasure. The poem has an enchanting quality, whatever the precise meaning of the words, that derives in part from its musical quality, its function as voice; and in part from its imaginative play with the beauty of the world, corresponding to our own reverie on the sensations with which it continually surrounds us.

The poem is, then, an abstract succession of verbal images, an order of sounds as well as sensory impressions, linked perhaps through synesthesia. Words are selected because they sound beautiful; one at least, *semadar* (KJV: "tender [of grape]," 2:15, 7:12), has survived in modern Hebrew as a girl's name, and its precise meaning is unknown. Another, *pardes*, "orchard" or "paradise" (4:13), is phonetically very similar to it; as a borrowing from Persian it is both exotic and has an astonishing subsequent career, replacing "the garden of God" or "the garden of Eden," for reasons that might not entirely preclude the aesthetic. Verbal magic, whose extreme is glossolalia, is very close to incantation and hence to the roots of the lyric;[2] euphony is achieved among differentiated sounds.

Hebrew poetry has, as far as we know, no equivalent of meter.[3] Instead, compositional skill tends to be directed toward rhetorical structure, such as parallelism, and to alliteration. Alliteration is a persistent and elaborate feature of both Hebrew verse and prose, though with different effects and frequencies. Moreover, clusters of consonants are nearly always permutated, alliterate in tandem (it is more speculative to talk about vowels, because these were first recorded only in the early Middle Ages). Thus, at a purely abstract level, patterns develop, are transposed, and are modulated as elements drop out of a cluster and are replaced by others. Consider an example generated by the word *pardes*, referred to above.

(Shelaḥayikh) pardes rimonim 'im peri megadim keparim 'im neradim nerd wekarkom qaneh weqinamon

> [Thy plants] are an orchard of pomegranates,
>> with pleasant fruits;
>>> camphire with spikenard,
>> Spikenard and saffron,
>>> calamus and cinnamon . . . (4:13–14)

The combination *prd* of *pardes* is repeated in *peri megadim* and *keparim 'im neradim*; in the last phrase, *k* is added to the cluster, and *p* drops out in *keparim 'im neradim nerd wekarkom*; the two *ks* in *karkom* are matched by two *qs* in *qaneh weqinamon* (phonetically very similar in Hebrew), which are then coupled with *n* (*qaneh weqinamon*), thereby incorporating the submotif of nasals that alternates with the *k/prd* cluster.

"Words similar in sound are drawn together in meaning"[4]—alliteration acquires a metaphoric dimension. The Cratylean concept, that a word has an intrinsic relation to the object it designates, represents a poetic ideal. A word expresses the identity of a thing not through its overt function as sign, but through paralinguistic connotations; its constitutive sounds are the elements from which the object is fashioned. A beautiful word metaphorically suggests a beautiful thing; this is a reciprocal process, since it may also acquire beauty from its associations. A beautiful language implies a beautiful world; the latter, in turn, can be properly articulated only in a beautiful language.

In the Song, alliteration connects linguistic units that are syntactically divided. For example, in the catalogue of spices, the alliteration coordinates phrases in apposition and suggests a common denominator. The *pardes* produces "pleasant fruit," specified as or alongside with "camphire and spikenard." Each contains the essence of the *pardes*, the paradise of the Song. Likewise, in the formal portraits of the lovers, the overt structure, which fragments the body into disconnected parts, overlays a hidden cohesion through wordplay. Take, for instance, the following passage:

> Thy teeth are like a flock of sheep that are even shorn,
>   which came up from the washing,
> whereof every one bear twins,
>   and none is barren among them.
>
> Thy lips are like a thread of scarlet,
>   and thy speech is comely;
> thy temples are like a piece of pomegranate
>   within thy locks.
>
> Thy neck is like the tower of David
>   builded for an armoury,
> whereon there hang a thousand bucklers,
>   all shields of mighty men.
>
> Thy two breasts
>   are like two young roes
> that are twins,
>   which feed among the lilies.   (4:2–5)

Syntactically, each sentence with its images is separate, its stillness marked by a complete absence of main verbs in the Hebrew; the only relationship between utterances is one of proximity and the progression from the face to the neck and then to the breasts. There are many alliterations: for example, the word "twinned" (KJV: "bear twins"), *mat'imot* in Hebrew, corresponds to its referent through its duplication of *m* and *t*. In the same verse, "whereof every one," *shekulam*, is almost identical to its opposite, "barren" (literally, "bereaved"), *shakulah*, the loss that does not befall them. Moreover, each verse except 4 begins or ends with a verbal echo. "Thy teeth," *shinayikh*, in verse 2 is correlated with "like a thread of *scarlet*," *shani*, in verse 3, and "Thy two [*shenei*] breasts are like two young roes" in verse 5. The sequence concludes with an intensification of the same combination: *shoshanim*, "lilies," is framed by words alliterating on *sh* and *n*.[5] The series *shinayikh*, *shani*, *shenei*, and *shoshanim* ("teeth," "scarlet," "two," and "lilies") contrasts white and red, duplicity and division. The two breasts, a pair emphasized by repetition, are like twin young roes; symmetrically, in 4:2 the teeth—a dual form in Hebrew—are like ewes that twin. In between, the thread formed by the two lips, the mouth or speech that is lovely, and the split pomegranate emphasize the possibility of fracture. Just as the passage began with a fecund flock of sheep (in Hebrew specified as "ewes"), it concludes with an image of multiplicity, the lilies scattered profusely in the field, spots of color against the terrain. The interplay of white and red evokes a powerful symbolic contrast (purity versus sexuality). The description, with its precise visual images, is a guise for a meditation on the formal relations of the body; the alliteration serves to couple opposites, such as the teeth and the lips, the two fawns and the lilies on which they feed.

The metaphors of the Song are wonderfully perplexing, sometimes surreal in their juxtaposition of extreme incongruities, their baroque development, their cultivation of disproportion. "Thy hair is as a flock of goats, that appear from Mount Gilead" (4:1); "thy nose is as the tower of Lebanon which looketh toward Damascus" (7:4); and "thine eyes like the fishpools in Heshbon, by the gate of Bath-rabbim" (7:4) are three examples among many. They have entered the repertoire of biblical absurdities. Yet they are not intrinsically funny, despite the analogy between metaphor and wit, since there is no sudden release of embarrassing truth; instead what is perceived, for example, in the formal descriptions, is an intricate series of connections between the beauty of the Lover or the Beloved and the world. The more elaborate and remote the comparison, the more universal a figure he or she will be. The breasts are likened to young roes, the Lover to a roe; the word translated in the King James Version as "roe" is in Hebrew a synonym for beauty. Likewise, there are pervasive images of intoxication: the Lover's caresses are better than wine (1:2), the Beloved regales him with her pomegranate juice (8:2), which in Hebrew probably means liquor. Thus the lovers possess and communicate all beauty and pleasure.

An image in the Song always evokes a combination of sensory qualities, which are selected according to their relevance in context, and of associations of ideas, deriving from common experience and literary tradition. Thereby it fulfills two functions—communicating the emotions of the lovers and reflecting upon their meaning and value.

From the pool of possible correlatives, often only one is selected for comparison by the text. "This thy stature is like to a palm tree" (7:7) is one example; "and the smell of thy garments is like the smell of Lebanon" (4:11) is another. At other times, even if not explicitly stated, the basis for comparison is clear—for example, the teeth are white as sheep, the redness of lips is as a scarlet thread (4:2-3). Only one property effects the metaphorical transfer. We have, then, a surplus of information that either develops or detracts from the image. For instance, the detail that the ewes twin in 4:2 adds an analogy of symmetry to that of whiteness; the specification of the scarlet as a thread might reduce the erotic appeal of the lips. Thinness, however, focuses attention on the demarcation between the lips, as the point of exploration, compounded by the succeeding "and thy speech is comely" (4:3).

Sometimes the comparison is less precise. "Thy two breasts are like two young roes" (4:5), for instance, has puzzled some critics; relevant correspondences, of color, warmth, grace, and animation, contribute to a diffuse parallel, in which no one element predominates. Other images for the breasts, "clusters of the vine" (7:8), and "towers" (8:10), conform more closely to the distinctive attributes of the body-part they represent. The former introduces an element of synesthesia, of taste and touch as well as of vision. Sometimes the scope of an image is limited to one particular aspect, as when the Beloved's stature is compared to a palm tree (7:7), generating further analogies of taste and grasp. Simile both renders the object palpable and distances it.

Sight and smell are the dominant sensations of the Song; taste is both associated with the latter and participates in the alimentary metaphorical complex, whereby the absorption of food is correlated with amorous delectation. Sight is contrasted with smell: whereas sight, involving distance, defines things in their difference, and is the most articulated and hence most conscious of senses, smell is pervasive, attached to sexuality and to extremes of intoxication. The clarity of vision that enables us to perceive things objectively is augmented by olfactory diffusion, as a means of identification. Thus the two aspects of the simile—recognition of a common property and insistence on separation—are duplicated in the interplay of the senses.

Only one metaphor actually refers to voice, that of the Beloved as dove in 2:14; significantly, that voice is reticent: "let me hear thy voice; for sweet is thy voice."

An image will acquire significance from its context, its relation to other images in the vicinity, and from our empirical knowledge. We bring to the metaphor of the vineyard notions of agriculture and social value. Thereby it joins a paradigm, in other words a class of related terms, such as those deriving from the realm of agriculture. Sequence and paradigm interact; the sequence, which represents the principle of time in the Song, the progression of its argument, is the intersection of innumerable paradigms from all parts of the poem, which represent timelessness, the poem as meaningful space. Every word brings with it the associations deriving from its previous occurrences and changes them retrospectively.

The *roe* in 4:5, for example, belongs to the paradigm of wild creatures in the Song—a class including lions, leopards, and foxes—and a further subset of gentle wild creatures, including doves. There is a relationship of opposition with the domestic ungulates of the first part of the description in 4:1–2. The image of breasts as young roes suggests an association of justified timidity; like the young roes, the breasts are delectable and the object of male pursuit. But here they are in repose between the lovers; they have found a safe haven, as if we have perceived them unawares, or fear has not yet interposed itself between men and animals.

An image stands for that which is unknown and unknowable; there is always a surplus of associations and meaningful contexts, hence a certain indeterminacy. It may, for example, draw some of its material from ancient Near Eastern art. There is a pictorial motif of fawns drinking from stylized lilies; fawns were sacred to Astarte, the goddess of love. If a word or phrase is ambiguous, both possibilities may contribute to the semantics of the poem; they may augment or counterpoint each other.

The image of the roe in 4:5 brings with it, together with its natural properties, associations drawn from the rest of the poem. Elsewhere it is an emblem for the Lover, suggesting his grace and speed. Between the lovers and the breasts he looks at there is a shared metaphor. In 2:8–9 the Lover, as roe, hastens toward his Beloved; here, in the breasts, he sees a quiescent image of himself, grazing among the lilies, as his eyes feed on the Beloved's image. We thus begin to find images that embody the personality that grows between the lovers, and hence their common human identity.

The final image of 4:5, the *lily,* with its associated flower image "the rose of Sharon" (2:1), is a figure for the Beloved in the poem. Elsewhere it is said of the Lover that "he feedeth among the lilies" (2:16, 6:3), but here it is the breasts, as "young roes," "which feed among the lilies" (4:5). In 5:13 lilies are emblematic of the Lover's lips: "his lips like lilies, dropping sweet smelling myrrh." In this way this image, too, permits the interchange of identity between the lovers.

The imagery also implies a reversal of function. Throughout the Song, sense becomes sensation. The tongue and palate are tasted, the eye is seen, and the nose is smelled in the simile "and the smell of thy nose [is] like apples" (7:8). The Lover tastes honey and milk under his Beloved's tongue (4:11); for her, "his mouth is most sweet" (literally, "his palate is sweets") (5:16); there is consequently an exchange of succulence. The eyes drink in each other; the nose breathes in the air and the fragrance of the other; the Lover is thus infused and vitalized by his Beloved's breath.

The roes are twins, like the lambs in 4:2; twins suggest a pair of sexually undifferentiated siblings. Elsewhere in the Song it is the lovers who are figuratively siblings. In 8:1 the Beloved wishes that her Lover were "as my brother, that sucked the breasts of my mother!"; in 4:8–5:1 the Lover insistently calls her "my sister, my spouse."[6] The first image, in particular, is reminiscent of the two young roes who are the breasts, a clear case of projective identification. Here there is an unrealizable conflation of the Lover, a stranger encountered in the world, with the brother, who has shared her earliest experience, her mother's love, of which the primary symbol is milk. She reenacts this first love by bringing him to her mother's house and entertaining him with her own intoxicating fluids (8:2). She adopts the roles of mother and sister but also that of child, since someone—in Hebrew it is ambiguous whether the subject is the Lover or mother—instructs her: "I would lead thee, and bring thee into my mother's house, who [thou/she] would instruct me: I would cause thee to drink of spiced wine, of the juice of my pomegranate." She acquires ancestral wisdom and in return gives of her alcoholic beverages,[7] which quench thirst and communicate ecstasy; in the Song ecstasy is ambiguously identified with true wisdom. Wine is the product of the cluster of the vine, to which her breasts are likened in 7:8; likewise she is "an orchard of pomegranates" in 4:13. What she gives, then, is herself. But the familial intimacy is possible only through make-believe; the particle "as" (*ke* in Hebrew) serves to identify fantasy and reality, a wistfulness reinforced by the initial exclamation "O that thou wert." "O that thou wert as my brother, that sucked the breasts of my mother! when I should find thee without, I would kiss thee; yea, I should not be despised" (8:1). In reality, if they did display their love openly, she would be shamed, as happens elsewhere in the Song (5:7); or if he were really a brother, the incest taboo would prevent consummation. The subversive desire, that he should be both lover and brother, can be expressed only through a fantasy of infantile regression, to a time before there were prohibitions and before society imposed secrecy on lovers.

What is unattainable in 8:1–2 is stated as fact in 4:8–5:1. The Beloved is "my sister, my spouse." One or both of these epithets must be a metaphor. The spouse who comes from far away, from Lebanon in 4:8, is identified with the sister who shared his origins; in her are invested incestuous feelings, whereby a sister is metaphorically a wife. Lebanon, the cold inhospitable region, the haunt of lions and leopards (4:8), is also the source of the streams (4:15) that water the garden of love (4:12–5:1). The Beloved is both the garden that ultimately encloses both lovers and is possessed by them (5:1), and the fountain that animates it (4:12, 15). The lovers unite—having come from afar—in the garden that identifies them as siblings as well as an exogamous couple, sheltered in its embrace and nurtured by its fruit (5:1). The garden, with its extension, its spices and fruit, represents the body of the Beloved—the woman as a source of sexual appeal; it is also differentiated from her, since she is the essence that causes it to flourish. Thus the fountain is both immanent, the very center of the garden (4:12, 15), and apart from it, rising in Lebanon (4:15). But Lebanon is also ambiguous. If Lebanon is the barren and perilous terrain from which the Beloved is summoned in 4:8 and, correspondingly, the source from which the streams flow, it is also the Beloved herself. Verse 4:11 ends "and the smell of thy garments is like the smell of Lebanon," providing a contrast between the luxuriance of its forests—proverbial for their fragrance[8]—and its desolate summits. The clothes express and conceal the woman as the forests do Lebanon.

Accordingly, Lebanon and the garden are antithetical yet interdependent poles of a movement from death (the consuming lions of 4:8) to life, from emergence from origins to submergence in re-creation. Both are associated with and differentiated from the woman. The Beloved who is a locked garden and sealed spring in 4:12 opens to admit the Lover, and finally all lovers and friends—"eat, O friends; drink, yea, drink abundantly, O lovers [KJV: beloved]" (5:1). Self-fulfillment, then, is achieved through self-surrender. The two phases are interdependent; the woman has grown, immersed in her spices, safe and still, waiting for the Lover, as for a Prince Charming, to "awaken" her—a verb applied to the north wind that first disturbs the serenity of the garden (4:16). But this interdependence is also equivalent to the metaphoric process, whereby the illusion of two separate people enclosed in their bodies is replaced by the numerous correspondences discovered between them, perceived as a congeries of loosely cohering features allied with strange landscapes. At the heart of the metaphor is the paradoxical relationship sister-spouse: the opposite with whom the Lover identifies and who is in his likeness. That which is unknown, the concealed, mysterious garden, is another aspect of himself, with which he was born. Together they unite, male and female, to form the collective human personality.

The double epithet "my sister, my spouse" frames the passage, linking the Lebanon sequence (4:8–11) to the garden sequence (4:12–5:1). It is a constant statement of paradoxical relationship which gives assurance, amid the prevailing turbulence, that the object of desire is an intimate part of ourselves. Likewise, as Hans-Peter Müller has shown, the description of the sealed garden in 4:12–15 is a still center, characterized by an almost total lack of verbs, that contrasts with the surrounding verbal energy.[9] In 4:9 the Beloved, through ravishing her lover's heart, gives him a heart, since the rare verb employed, *libavtini,* may mean both; it also echoes the word *Lebanon* (*Levanon*) in the previous verse. It is as if Lebanon is infused in his heart. In 5:1, as we have seen, possession is mutual. The exercise of power transmits power and is thus an image of the sexual relationship. What is striking here is the primacy of the woman. Her impact in 4:9 is deflected only by metonymy ("with one of thine eyes, with one chain of thy neck") and verbal artifice; in 5:1 the Lover's self-glorification is subverted by intoxication.

The mother, as we have already seen, is a prominent figure, with whom both lovers identify; the Lover, for example, compares his Beloved's uniqueness to him, among all his queens and concubines, with her mother's delight at her birth (6:9). Mother love is the archetype of love, which all subsequent loves reconstitute; the lovers reenact this primordial relationship. We have seen, for example, that in 4:5 the Lover imagines himself as an infant at the breast, and that in 8:1 the Beloved imagines him as a fellow suckling. The breasts coordinate adult erotic feelings with an infantile correlate. The Beloved brings her lover back to the intimacy of the matrix (3:4). She awakens him at the birthplace, where he first opened his eyes to the world; she imagines his mother's labor: "I awakened thee under the apple tree: there thy mother travailed with thee; there she travailed with thee that bare thee" (8:5 [AR]). But in 2:3 it is the Beloved who is under the apple tree, which is a symbol for the Lover: "I sat down under his [*or* its] shadow with great delight, and his [*or* its] fruit was sweet to my taste." The apple tree gives protection and nourishment; it shelters mother and baby, and both lovers. Love in the Song is an awakening of consciousness, but it is also a return to birth, and that is a prelude to the encounter with death that immediately follows, in 8:6.

There are no father images in the Song; its nuclear family consists of mother, brother, and sister. Only the tower of David in 4:4 and metaphors such as the apple tree indirectly allude to a male procreative force. In 1:6, where the Beloved is the victim of fraternal animosity, the brothers are called, in the Hebrew, "my mother's sons." The absence of the father makes the mother a global parental figure, combining the attributes of both sexes. But the absence of the father is also that of the authoritative patriarchal society outside the Song.

The Beloved is associated with the earth, a link reinforced by allusion. For example, "honey and milk are under thy tongue" (4:11) is almost identical with the familiar epithet of the land of Israel, the land flowing with milk and honey. In the Bible, the earth is the feminine complement of God: the two combined to form man, who articulates their relationship, for example, in sacrifice. Through the Beloved's hair may be seen Mount Gilead and flocks of goats (4:1); the pastoral landscape is no less the object of affection than the hair it supposedly illustrates. The elaborate combinations of parts of the body and geographic features, like those between the lovers' bodies, assert the indissolubility of man and the earth, man as part of nature, and his representative status. Through the lovers and the poet, all creatures find their voice and are consummated through love.

The woman as the earth is the trope that underlies the formal portrait of 7:2–5, which, with all its extravagant imagery, is in fact a single extended metaphor of the Beloved as the kingdom:

> Thy navel is like a round goblet,
>   which wanteth not liquor:
> thy belly is like an heap of wheat
>   set about with lilies.
>
> Thy two breasts are like two young roes
>   that are twins.
>
> Thy neck is as a tower of ivory;
>   thine eyes like the fishpools in Heshbon
>   by the gate of Bath-rabbim;
> thy nose is as the tower of Lebanon
>   which looketh toward Damascus.
>
> Thine head upon thee is like Carmel,
>   and the hair of thine head like purple;
>   a king is held in the tresses.   [AR]

The face evokes peripheries: Lebanon is in the north, Heshbon in the east, Carmel in the west. The landscapes complement one another: the mountain fastness matches the city on the edge of the desert and the promontory overlooking the sea. Each suggests power and prosperity in its dealings with the outside world: the tower of Lebanon watches over Damascus;[10] the "gate of the many" in Heshbon is the focus of busy traffic; the sea is dominated by the Carmel, and from it is extracted the royal purple.[11] The toponyms signify abundance: Heshbon means "computation, account," hence a fortune; Carmel is the "fruitful land"; in contrast, Lebanon is the "white one" and correspondingly impressive. At the center of the body is the belly, which is associated with harvest. All this wealth is for the sake of the king, and for the Lover who feasts his eyes; yet the king, in the climactic phrase, is overcome by weakness: in Hebrew it reads "a king is imprisoned in tresses" ("galleries," KJV, is impossible). The king is dependent upon the kingdom and is captivated by it. There is an ideal harmony of king and realm, expressed in the sacred marriage, and in the Song by the overall scheme whereby the king falls in love with a country girl; analogously, the poet/Lover who controls the object becomes absorbed by it. But the king cannot escape his role. Throughout the Song there is a tension between his humanity and his function, between his inaccessibility, behind his curtains (1:5), and his attempt to woo the Beloved. Whether the sacred marriage can work is always ambiguous.

There is also an opposition between the woman and the country; she is its equivalent, and its rival for the king's attentions. As prisoner of her hair, he is emblematic of the vulnerability of kings, and hence of the whole body politic, to sexuality, the ultimate power of women that is the object of repression.

The metaphors of the Song reinforce its unity through an intricate web of cross-references, whereby an image is coupled with another at some distance from itself. Larger units also parallel, complement, and transform each other. We have seen, for example, that 8:1–2 abbreviates but also develops 3:1–4; another variant of this group is 5:2–7. Two formal portraits of the Beloved (4:1–7, 7:1–6) bracket one of the Lover (5:10–16); two garden sequences interact and contrast with each other (4:12–5:1, 6:1–12). There is thus a certain circularity in the Song; the second half reflects the first. Beyond this, however, there is a unity of theme, a wider metaphoricity of which the underlying motif of the lovers as king and kingdom is an example. The union of lovers through metaphor, their discovery of correlates, and of themselves, in and through each other, is the poetic process. The poem is integrated as the lovers are integrated; through its work all the fragments of the world cohere, and are granted significance, in a single vision.

Yet there is also an element of disunity in the Song, in the violence with which it dismembers the body, its total disregard for logical connection, the abruptness with which it embarks upon and abandons episodes in the lives of lovers. The disunity is also that of the lovers, whose work of integration can never be completed. Constantly they assert differences and distances. One is a lily (2:2), the other an apple tree (2:3); one is a roe (2:9, 17; 8:14), the other a dove (2:14). The dove has to be cajoled from the rocks (2:14); the Beloved seeks the Lover through the streets of the city (3:2, 5:6); he waits impatiently outside her door (5:2), snatching glimpses through the lattice (2:9). Finally, he is excluded from the garden in which she is singing to her friends (8:13–14).[12] This concluding scene suggests the status of the poem; the discourse of the lovers separates them. It is a displacement of love, in which foreplay—seduction, sweet-talk— repeatedly defers fusion.

The differentiations between the lovers are also those of language, between words and letters that represent things in their multiplicity. The violence of fracture testifies to the intensity of desire to unite even the most disparate phenomena. But these remain obstinately intractable. Between the words, sounds, and episodes are silences; the poem verges always on the limits of language, which points to that which cannot be spoken. For example, in the elaborate portraits of the lovers that stretch both the poet's and the reader's imaginative capacity, the poetic energy is suddenly abandoned in inarticulate acknowledgments of beauty ("Thou art all fair, my love; there is no spot in thee" (4:7; and compare 7:6). Correspondingly, each episode moves toward a climax that cannot be fulfilled in the poem. There is a pattern of expectation and frustration, a pressure in time that cannot be exhausted. Consequently, the Song functions also as a sequence; it has a dramatic quality as the lovers alternately converge and withdraw. Each new beginning and each loose end promises and leaves a residue of unsatisfied hope, a debt owed by the narrative.

There are two structural foci in the poem, corresponding to its two coordinates, the time of reading or listening, with its gradual increase of tension, and the timelessness of its composition, the poem as tableau, which is also that of its fictional world. Each incident takes place in a temporal vacuum. There is no "story" in the Song, no truth, only a set of anecdotes, hovering between reality and dream, that exemplify the relationships of lovers.

One structural focus is the center, the midpoint between corresponding halves of the poem. Concentricity is not strict, not mechanical, but it is nevertheless pervasive. In general, large central units complement each other (for example, the two descriptions of the woman in 4:1–7 and 7:1–6, and the two episodes in the garden, 4:12–5:1 and 6:1–12), as do smaller peripheral ones. The center is the point of transition between two entirely different moments. The first is the entrance of the Lover into the garden of love which is the Beloved in 5:1; his possession and enjoyment of its fruits constitute the one act of consummation in the poem, and hence its emotional center. Round it all the other scenes are grouped. The other moment is the waking of the Beloved's heart to the Lover's knocking in 5:2, under cover of her sleep; this suppression of consciousness allows him to steal in, if only, ambiguously, in hallucination; her solitude is compounded in the ensuing scene by abandonment and humiliation. Between the two moments is a pause, a silence; therein all "friends" and "lovers" [AT] have been invited to participate in the joy of the couple. Correspondingly, the Song closes with the "companions" (in Hebrew the same word as "friends") listening to the Beloved's voice, in the gardens, which are gardens not only of love but of poetry (8:13). The Beloved's voice is of course associated with, and survives only in, the Song; the friends listening to her could then include the entire audience of the Song, all of whom participate sympathetically in the experience of the lovers.

The garden is the longest episode as well as the central image in the poem; its relation to the poem corresponds to that of the garden to the world. The fountain that waters it gives it life and is the invisible presence in all its manifestations. The other structural focus is the climax, in which the poem's narrative pressure—its work of comparison, its alternation of promise and postponement—is released. It is the assertion that love is as strong as death, that jealousy/passion is as harsh or enduring as Sheol, and that its sparks or coals are the flame of God (8:6). In this credo, the poet seems to speak in his own voice and not through the protagonists. The image of fire, an element that appears nowhere else in the Song, is contrasted with that of water. Both are fluid and verge on the transparent or invisible. The spring that is the Beloved animates all the fruits of the garden, and correspondingly the words of the poem, whose abundant metaphors are inflections of her fecund voice; the fire is fed by the lovers' desire to unite and by their ineluctable separation. The flame turns substance into energy, the visible into the invisible; therein the world, in all its multiplicity, is reabsorbed in the creative speech from which it emerged. It is a metaphor for poetry, the fusion of the phenomena of the world in the voice and vision of the poet. The lovers ignite the divine flame between them. In this way, love is as strong as death, an assertion that could be understood facilely as referring to generation, or to the transcendence of a brief moment, in which all time and all creatures participate and find their value, over transience.

As we have noted, the dominance and initiative of the Beloved are the poem's most astonishing characteristics. Metaphorically aligned with a feminine aspect of divinity, associated with the celestial bodies, the land, and fertility, the Beloved reverses the predominantly patriarchal theology of the Bible. Male political power is enthralled to her. The lovers live, however, in a patriarchal world; the Beloved suffers the humiliation that attends sexually adventurous women. She is cast out of her family (1:6), despised by shepherds (1:7),[13] beaten by watchmen (5:7). The lovers can only find or imagine an enclosure, secluded from the world: a garden, a forest bed, or the poem itself. The poem is unfailingly critical of a society that does not know the true value of love and that imposes shame on lovers. The affirmation that love is as strong as death and is not quenched by the great floods (8:7), that it alone is not transient and illusory, is followed at once by the ironic comment: "if a man would give all the substance of his house for love, he [KJV: it] would utterly be condemned." In the eyes of the world, to give one's entire fortune for love is folly; from the perspective of the Song, in which riches are ultimately worthless, it is wisdom.

Yet the poem is also ambivalent. Love is the bond of a vital society; its message is transmitted by the daughters of Jerusalem, by friends and lovers, and ultimately by ourselves as readers. Nevertheless, it also threatens social order: a king falls in love with a country girl and forsakes his kingdom. Lovers seek differentiations between each other, to preserve their separate identity. Civilization devotes itself to the cultivation of a beauty that both communicates and distances the object of desire.

The Song of Songs may be contemporaneous with Ecclesiastes;[14] to Ecclesiastes' thesis that everything is illusory the Song answers with its one possible antithesis. Like Ecclesiastes it is a work of comparison, though one that results not in confusion but in cumulative affirmation. Like Ecclesiastes, it uses the figure of Solomon as the type of the most fortunate man. More centrally, the Song is a reflection on the story of the garden of Eden, using the same images of garden and tree, substituting for the traumatic dissociation of man and animals their metaphoric integration. Through it we glimpse, belatedly, by the grace of poetry, the possibility of paradise.

NOTES

1. H.-P. Müller, *Vergleich und Metapher im Hohenlied* (Göttingen, 1984).

2. H.-P. Müller, "Die lyrische Reproduktion des Mythisches im Hohenlied," *Zeitschrift für Theologie und Kirche,* 73 (1976), 23–41.

3. This is one of the most contentious issues in modern biblical poetics. I would agree with Robert Alter, who cites Benjamin Hrushovski that it is characterized by a "semantic-syntactic-accentual rhythm"; *The Art of Biblical Poetry* (New York, 1985), p. 8. For a full history of the debate and a powerful critique of metrical theories, see James L. Kugel, *The Idea of Biblical Poetry: Parallelism and Its History* (New Haven, 1981). For a restatement of the metrical hypothesis, see W. G. E. Watson, *Classical Hebrew Poetry: A Guide to Its Techniques* (Sheffield, 1984), pp. 87–113.

4. Roman Jakobson, "Linguistics and Poetics," in *Selected Writings,* III (Mouton, 1981), 43.

5. In contrast to more recent translations, the King James Version is sensitive to the verbal play and rhythm of the Hebrew and is successful in finding

some English equivalent. For example, in 4:2–5, quoted earlier, each verse is balanced around three- or four-stress lines; alliteration is marked: "*like* a *flock*," "*sheep* that are even *shorn*," "*bear* . . . *barren*" (a play very similar to *shekulam . . . shakulah*), "a *piece* of *pomegranate*."

6. In 5:2 the term "my sister" occurs again, in conjunction with the more familiar epithet for the Beloved, "my love."

7. In Hebrew the erotic *sous-entendre* is overdetermined by a wordplay between *'ashqekha* ("I would cause thee to drink") and *'eshaqekha* ("I would kiss thee") in 8:1.

8. Cf. Hosea 14:7.

9. H.-P. Müller, "Poesie und Magie in Cant. 4:12–5:1," *Zeitschrift der deutschen morgenlandischen Gesellschaft,* supp. III/1 (1977), 157–162.

10. For Damascus as a thorn in Solomon's side see 1 Kings 11:25.

11. Purple dye was extracted from a shellfish (the murex) harvested in vast quantities in the Mediterranean.

12. Where the KJV has "Make haste" in 8:14, the Hebrew actually reads "Flee away."

13. The obscure word *'oṭeya,* which the KJV translates as "as one that turneth aside," probably means "as one veiled," possibly as a prostitute.

14. Third–fourth centuries B.C.E. The evidence is linguistic (Persian and Greek loanwords) and stylistic.

SUGGESTED FURTHER READINGS

Michael Fox, *The Song of Songs and Ancient Egyptian Love Poetry* (Madison, 1985).
Francis Landy, *Paradoxes of Paradise: Identity and Difference in the Song of Songs* (Sheffield, 1983).

University of Alberta

Ruth

Jack M. Sasson

THE literary analysis of Ruth differs significantly for those who treat it as a folktale with an earlier, oral form and for those who examine the fine elaboration of its literate narrative art, although one approach rarely excludes the other. An earlier generation of scholars, given to charting the metamorphosis of tales from single folkloric prototypes, saw Ruth as a recasting of certain incidents in the saga of the goddess Isis, as a Hebraized version of the Eleusinian mysteries, with Naomi and Ruth taking the roles of Demeter and Persephone, respectively, or as a historicized version of the epic of the Canaanite goddess Anat. All these hypotheses theorized amply about why the Hebrew story would adapt foreign myths; the general tendency was to see in Ruth an effort to create a mythological or epic backdrop for the ancestry of David.

A more recent approach has drawn on the folklorist work of the Russian formalist Vladimir Propp in order to show that Ruth follows a pattern common to folktales and as such cannot be a reliable source for information of a legal and historical nature, since folktales ordinarily eschew all such information in favor of easily accessible testimony for exemplary behavior.[1] In any event, even among the artful narratives of Scripture, Ruth stands out in the power of its concentration, in the limpidity of its vocabulary, in the versatility of its language, in the balanced proportion of its scenes, and, above all, in the vividness and integrity of its main characters.

The narrator of Ruth may well have had an orally circulating tale with which to work, but we have only his written version to inspect for signs of its original form. The fact that the tale divides naturally into four major episodes, each of which ends with summarizing and previewing lines, may suggest a technique by which to hold the attention of a listening rather than a reading audience. The plot is advanced mostly through dialogue, which accounts for fifty-five of its eighty-five verses, a technique that makes every scene intimate. This, the highest ratio of dialogue to narrative in any of the biblical books, is certainly rich in dramatic potential, and the audience is obliged to infer the story's meaning from minute clues in the words exchanged by the characters. On several occasions the language in Ruth also reflects an interaction between the storyteller and his audience. For example, the famous aside in 4:7 ("Now in Israel's past days, in order to validate any legal act")[2] gains in impact when heard in a tone that differs from that of the flanking narratives.

Ruth is replete with examples of oral wordplay and of thematic key words meant to stimulate an audience's memory. With the exception of Genesis, another book full of folktales with versions which may have circulated by word of mouth, this type of paronomasia is nowhere else as densely deployed in Hebrew narratives. On the other hand, Ruth also requires patient visual study to unlock a few examples of gematria (a cryptograph with hidden numeric values); and this condition shows that the narrator adapted whatever came to his disposal for a learned readership.

More impressive as testimony for the narrator's skill in handling his tale, however, are the various devices he uses to structure his material. Perceptive recent writings (some more convincing than others) have uncovered carefully developed and ordered series of patterns, often guided by a reliance on sets of binary oppositions: famine/plenty, escape/return, barrenness/fruitfulness, isolation/community, reward/punishment, tradition/innovation, male/female, life/death. The narrator often distributes these themes far apart and realizes the thematic opposition only after a span of time and activity. On the other hand, he achieves intensity in each of his scenes by placing in a central position the verses which provide crucial information or development.

Much of the story's charm derives from its language. Although there are a number of words and idioms unique to Ruth, none of them is obscure enough to impede the flow of the narrative. The harmonious alliteration and repetition of key words in many clauses generate a reassuring sense of patterned thematic development. The absence of martial terminology, the underplaying of theological diction, the frequency of gently couched greetings and blessings (ten times), the constant recall in the dialogue of vocabulary that accentuates noble sentiments and compassionate motives—all these have allowed Ruth to work its magic on countless generations.

Each of Ruth's four scenes, equivalent to the four chapters in our Bible, is provided with a coda meant to summarize past activities even as it prefigures future ones. The first of these contains an initial unit (1:1–6) which serves as prologue to the story, and the last has a ballast unit (4:14–17) which provides a satisfying epilogue. The last coda anticipates a future beyond the story's immediate frame and includes a genealogy (4:18–22) trimmed unmistakably to place the story's main male character, Boaz, in the favored seventh slot, thereby conveying a moral that was of particular interest to the historically minded Hebrew: common people achieve uncommon ends when they act unselfishly toward each other.

The narrator sets the scene in the prologue with remarkable economy.[3] Time is at once specific and diffuse ("When the Judges used to judge"), conveying more than the actual words imply, since during that period—as any Hebrew would know—people were constantly losing God's grace before earning it again. This initial clause wrenches Ruth from the world of folk or fairy tales (where gods and magic reside comfortably), setting it within Israel's chronicle of its troubled relationship with God. For the story's immediate purpose, however, geography acquires controlling power: the narrative is specific when it mentions Bethlehem, within Israel's orbit, and becomes diffuse when it speaks of the other world, Moab, where Judeans ought to have no business. Sandwiched between these temporal and spatial elements is an impersonal force, *ra'av*, "famine," which in Israel could only have been God's instrument for judgment and cannot, therefore, be thwarted by human acts. Moab, where the god Chemosh reigns, may not be experiencing famine when a Judean family seeks shelter there; but its fields will eventually kill a father and his sons and render their wives sterile.

At first this family is introduced anonymously: "a certain man from Judah," his wife, and his two sons trek eastward; and only when they reach Moab do they acquire personal names. Given their abandonment of God and his land, the parents' names must certainly be ironic (Elimelech, "My God Is King"; Naomi, "Winsome" or "My Lovely One"), while those of the sons could be foreboding—even sinister, given their crackly rhyme: Machlon and Chilion ("Weakening and Pining" or "Blot Out and Perish"). Symbolic names of this sort are not typical of Hebrew narrative and may once more betray an edifying purpose in Ruth.[4]

The remaining portion of introduction has four short verses that nicely emulate the relentlessness of fate. Naomi loses her husband, and, without the guidance of a father, the boys marry two Moabite women whom the narrator deceptively presents in conventional Hebrew style. Orpah is introduced first: "Nape (of the neck)," according to some who read the name prefiguratively; "Scented" or "Cloudy," according to some philologists. As is common in Hebrew narrative technique, Ruth, a major character, gets second mention. Her name, edifyingly but falsely understood to mean "Friendship," is related to a Semitic root meaning "to be soaked, irrigated," or the like. As is to be expected, the marriages have no issue, for there could be no future for the sons of Israel in Moab, and the narrator reverts to Naomi, the only Judean to survive this calamity. The gloom, inaugurated so impersonally with the word "famine," gives way to hope as Naomi hears of the restoration of God's bounties to her homeland. The language here (1:6) is rich with assonance and alliteration (*latet lahem lahem*), ending with the word for food, *lehem*, which unsubtly directs Naomi, as well as the reader, back to Beth*lehem*, "Storehouse for food." The story of Ruth really begins here. Because it is a deceptively simple tale whose themes, loyalty and love, are manifest, Ruth is accessible to all on first reading. However, its intricately worked out plot relies on an awareness of legal and social mechanisms obtaining among the Hebrews, and the best way to clarify these is simply to follow the narrative.

Her future limited by the days remaining to an old woman, her survival severely compromised by the absence of male helpers, her past totally obliterated as long as she remains in Moab, Naomi resolves to go back home. As a widow, *'almanah* (a term which in biblical Hebrew is applied only when women are bereaved of husbands, sons, *and* fathers-in-law), Naomi must depend on Ephrathites for minimal help; but she has to be in Bethlehem to receive it. She could not wish for her daughters-in-law to accompany her, for in Bethlehem each of them would be a *nokhriyah,* a "foreign woman," too distant from her own kin to receive care and sustenance. Luckily for us who cherish noble sentiments and beautiful rhetoric, Naomi cannot easily persuade them to face this reality.

She pursues on three levels her arguments against taking Moabite women back to Bethlehem. She first (1:8–9) wishes them godspeed and good remarriages—a powerful indication that levirate marriage (discussed below) is not at stake in this story. When Orpah and Ruth "break into loud weeping" and insist on accompanying her, Naomi turns mordant and self-pitying: she is too old to bear the sons who could revive their marriages; bereft though they may be, her daughters-in-law cannot match the sheer misery God has inflicted on her.

Wisely, Orpah understands the predicament and, after much weeping, goes home. That later legends made her an ancestress of Goliath shows, however, how reasonable decisions can nevertheless be remembered as betrayals. Ruth, on the other hand, "clings" (the verb *dabaq,* repeated with slightly differing meanings four times in two chapters) to Naomi, thereby holding center stage for the next three major scenes.

Ruth's supplication to accompany Naomi is not registered in poetic language; but it does reach a lyrical perfection rarely matched in other Hebrew narratives. She cannot be persuaded to desert Naomi, and will go with her anywhere; she will share her shelter, whatever its quality (so; rather than, as commonly translated, "where you lodge, I will lodge"); her fate will be with Naomi's people and with God, and she will never return home, for she expects to be buried by Naomi's grave. Ruth invokes a powerful oath, placing herself in her mother-in-law's bondage: "May the Lord strike me anytime with afflictions, if anything but death parts us" (v. 17). Because of the oath, Naomi has no choice but to accept Ruth's decision.

Bethlehem hums (the city is here personified, and the verb is onomatopoeic) at their arrival, but we cannot be sure to what effect. The inhabitants' reported speech—"Could this be Naomi?"—is brief, but it conveys bewilderment, sadness, puzzlement, excitement, shock, delight, or any combination of these and a dozen more emotions. Naomi's response, though obscure in its Hebrew construction, nevertheless shows that the bitterness she previously displayed has not faded. "Call me Mara ['Bitter One'],'' she says, and allows them no time to ask why before she delivers her second tirade against God's injustice. Bethlehem's women do not attempt to soothe her rage: when two impoverished women enter a town with no men to lead them, the tragedy of the situation needs no elaboration.

The first scene ends here. In his summary of these events, the narrator adds that "they reached Bethlehem at the beginning of the barley harvest" (v. 22) and thus assures us that famine is not a deprivation that Naomi will experience again. This notice also allows us to gauge the time spanning the remaining scenes as no more than about ninety days, when the winnowing seasons for barley and wheat come to an end.

Chapter 2 opens by introducing a rich landowner, Boaz, who is kin to Naomi's husband. His name may include "strength" (*'oz*) as part of its meaning; but it is more relevant to recall that Boaz was the name of one pillar in Solomon's temple, and hence may have had a dynastic implication. Boaz, then, is related to Elimelech and can be a potential redeemer of his deceased kinsman's land; but his kinship is not so immediate as to give him first opportunity to do so. At any rate, it is Ruth who suggests a way of linking her fate to him: "Should I go to the field and glean among the ears of grains, *in the hope of pleasing* him?" (v. 2);[5] for Ruth urgently needs to find a way to change her situation, from being a *nokhriyah* to becoming a *shifhah,* a "maidservant." Lowly as this last status may be within a clan, it nevertheless affords its holder protection from hunger and from violence.

Ruth actually wants permission to gather the grain from among the sheaves, a privilege (we learn from v. 15) reserved for members of the clan, which only a landowner can grant. Boaz notices the woman as she stands waiting for his reply. An overseer identifies Ruth and even attempts a weak jest. "Notice," he tells Boaz, "she had little time to stay at home" (v. 7). Boaz asks no questions from this unprivileged soul but readily offers advice: stay in my field, stick to my girls; even drink a little water if you care to. However, he does not respond to her original request. Ruth is not ready to give up. With a gesture of exaggerated servility—usually only kings and gods receive such prostrations—Ruth gently cloaks her expectations: "Why is it that I pleased you enough to notice me? I am but a foreigner [*nokhriyah*]" (v. 10). Boaz responds with another speech but is now more personal: you are wonderfully loyal and brave; God will surely reward you for seeking his protection.

Ruth, who has yet to receive permission, tries again, this time with more *chutzpah*: "I must have pleased you, my lord, since you have comforted me and have spoken tenderly to your maidservant [*shifhah*]. Yet I am not even considered one of your maidservants" (v. 13). Finally grasping Ruth's intent, Boaz waits until lunchtime to make up his mind. Then, in full view of his workers (an act which may well have a legal implication), he seats her among them, personally fills her bowl with grain and mash, and gives her the permission he has not granted previously. In short, Ruth has come to be a member of Boaz's clan and need no longer be a burden to her mother-in-law.

As she returns home, loaded with twenty kilograms of grain through Boaz's generosity, Naomi praises her deed and blesses Boaz, invoking a delicious pun as she lauds his goodness: "Boaz [bo'az] . . . who has not withheld ['azab] his kindness" (v. 20). When Naomi reveals that Boaz is also in a position to redeem the land left her by her husband, the stage is set for the next encounter between Ruth and Boaz, for the story of Ruth cannot end when hunger is replaced by satiety; there is yet the matter of perpetuating the memory of men who left no sons behind.

It is Naomi who provokes the next meeting. She wants Ruth to enter Boaz's home, perhaps not as a wife but certainly as a concubine. Were this to happen, the bonds of kinship that kept the two women together would surely be broken. Yet this could not be acceptable to Ruth, whose oath demanded otherwise. The rest of the story tells how Ruth resourcefully resolves her dilemma.

Harvest time has just come to an end, and owners of fields are customarily celebrating God's bounty on the threshing floor, under the warm and cloudless sky of a Judean spring. Boaz has drunk enough to feel free from daily care. Ruth, handsomely dressed and fetchingly scented, waits until midnight before approaching the sleeping Boaz. Naomi's instructions at this point are hard for us to establish: Is Ruth merely to remove the covers at his feet? Or is Naomi asking her to risk a bolder move?

Whatever the charge, we learn that Boaz momentarily panics at finding a woman so close to him, and the scene is obviously meant to be humorous. Ruth quickly opens with a twofold proposal. "I am Ruth your handmaid," she says (3:9), using the term 'amah, which ordinarily denotes a woman who can be taken by a freeman as either concubine or wife. Her next statement, "spread your robe over your handmaid," may well be teasing Boaz, who earlier praised her for seeking shelter under God's wings but who ignored her request. The statement's implication, however, could not be plainer, for it is an appeal to be brought into Boaz's immediate household (see Deut. 23:1 and Ezek. 16). When, finally, Ruth entreats Boaz to become Naomi's redeemer, his turn comes to rebuke her gently. Her last request, he tells her, is better than the preceding one, for she urged him in behalf of Naomi only *after* she had made a plea for her own future. Whatever their sequence, these two requests betray Ruth's strategy for a happy ending to all concerned: by entering the household of the man who redeems Naomi, Ruth can retain kinship to her, though in a different fashion.

Boaz assures her on all counts. She need no longer look for other men to protect her. Indeed, because of her marriage to Machlon, her reputation as an *'eshet ḥayil*—a woman married to a man of standing—is well known to the whole town. Therefore, there is nothing to prevent her from entering his household as an *'ishah*, a *primary* wife. The matter of becoming Naomi's redeemer is more complex, since another man has prior rights to redeem her land. Nevertheless, he will do all that is in his power to fulfill the obligation himself. To all this, Boaz invokes a powerful oath and asks Ruth to stay the night.

Ruth has triumphed; but she needs to persuade Naomi that Boaz will be a suitable redeemer, and it is only in the last verses of the third chapter that this occurs. Naomi herself has no cause to meet Boaz, let alone to prefer him to another redeemer. Ruth therefore uses the enormous bounties (another twenty kilograms or so of grain) that Boaz gave her at dawn to frame her last persuasive act. "He gave me six measures of barley, telling me not to return empty-handed to my mother-in-law," she reports to Naomi (v. 17). Boaz, of course, has said nothing of the sort; but what better way to sway her mother-in-law than to recall at such an auspicious moment a term (*reyqam*, "empty-handed") that Naomi used in her deepest despair ("but the Lord had brought me back *empty*," 1:21)?

For the last episode, the narrator switches from a series of intimate encounters to a crowd scene. Again, chance occurrences are made to seem natural. Just as Boaz reaches the city gate, where business transactions take place, the potential redeemer steps into the limelight. In a tale in which names enhance characters and prefigure their development, the potential redeemer is anonymous, for his future, unlike Boaz's, will ultimately be anonymous: an interesting fate for someone who will shortly fret about his estate. He is asked to purchase the land available to Naomi and thus become her redeemer. Otherwise, Boaz will do so. The man readily accepts, for Elimelech's land will become his after the death of a widow without issue. Boaz then plays his trump card.

He tells the assembly that on the very same day that the redeemer acquires Naomi's land, he, Boaz, will acquire Ruth, widow of Machlon, "*in order to perpetuate the memory of the deceased upon his estate*" (4:5). I have italicized this clause because it explains how Boaz persuades the redeemer to give up his land. Boaz uses the verb *qanah* to declare what must be done with Ruth. When the Masorites vocalized this verb centuries after the tale was written, they made it read "You must acquire," *qanita*, whereas the verb's consonants are *qnyty*, "I have acquired." For this reason, generations of readers have thought that laws regarding levirate marriages were at stake: Ruth had to marry this anonymous redeemer unless he gave up his rights to Boaz. But this could not be the case, since levirate marriages were in fact no marriages at all, and a widow who found herself in this situation automatically entered her brother-in-law's household, at least until she bore a son for her dead husband. In fact, as Boaz himself previously acknowledged (3:10), Ruth was free to select her own protector.

Before a lawfully constituted assembly, Boaz appeals to an old custom, fully and legalistically formulated in 4:10, which encouraged a man to beget a child on a widow so that "the memory of the deceased may not be obliterated from among his kinfolk." The union's first child would therefore be Machlon's, and when he grew up, the land redeemed from Naomi would revert to that child. This is why, when the redeemer hears of Boaz's resolve, he gives up his claim to redemption. In all these details, then, the nice distinctions of social and legal institutions become an integral part of the storyteller's subtle art.

The story of Ruth could end here. The narrator, however, uses a few more verses to refresh his audience's memory of past customs of validation and attestation (4:7), to record Boaz's legal declarations (4:9–10), and to savor the beautiful blessing—actually a royal blessing—with its rich promises for the couple's future (4:11–12). The coda is deftly used to tie up loose ends and to recapitulate themes. After Boaz makes Ruth his wife (*'ishah*), God allows her to conceive, but the boy that she bears is really Naomi's. Women in chorus praise God for preventing the end of Elimelech's line and thus overturning a fate that seemed so sinister in the prologue. They laud Boaz as an ideal redeemer, the child Obed as a perfect comforter and a solicitous sustainer, and Ruth as Naomi's beloved.

A curious notice follows, alerting the audience to unfoldings exceptional in Scripture: "female neighbors"—and not the parents—invent a name for Obed; Naomi adopts him and becomes his keeper. In the ancient Near East, these acts symbolize the legitimacy of royal power. It is, however, enough simply to pursue the text a few more verses (18–22) to discover that the child born to Ruth eventually fathers Jesse, who in turn fathers King David.

NOTES

1. I have explored possible avenues of interpretation when Ruth is assessed as a folktale in *Ruth: A New Translation with a Philological Commentary and a Formalist-Folklorist Interpretation* (Baltimore, 1979).

2. All translations in this essay are my own [AT] and are based on my philological analysis of Ruth in the commentary cited above.

3. The reading of Ruth offered below is defended at length in my commentary, cited above. E. F. Campbell's commentary to Ruth, Anchor Bible, VII (Garden City, N.Y., 1975), provides a different interpretation of the plot's structure. Both contain extensive bibliographies.

4. Gen. 14 is another text whose unfolding acquires fuller meaning when we recognize the symbolic character of the names mentioned in v. 2.

5. This sentence does *not* imply that Ruth is trying to trap Boaz into marriage, for at this stage her hopes are much more modest.

SUGGESTED FURTHER READINGS

Robert Alter, *The Art of Biblical Narrative* (New York, 1981), pp. 58–60.

Adele Berlin, *Poetics and Interpretation of Biblical Narrative* (Sheffield, 1983), pp. 83–110.

D. F. Rauber, "Literary Values in the Bible: The Book of Ruth," *Journal of Biblical Literature,* 89 (1970), 27–37.

University of North Carolina

Lamentations

Francis Landy

LAMENTATIONS is as historical as the Song of Songs is ahistorical; it marks, with untempered immediacy, the focal calamity of the Bible, the destruction of Jerusalem in 586 B.C.E. The lyric discharges the cumulative emotions suppressed in the narrative and anticipated or recalled in the Prophets. The alienation, temporal and social, of the Prophets suddenly becomes a collective experience. There is no more need to persuade, to find communicable symbols; the voice simply bears witness to its failure, turns over broken images and hopes. The barrenness and desolation of the poem are, then, also matters of rhetoric; the descriptive voice is direct, unenigmatic, as if the scene spoke for itself, and uses rhetorical techniques—repetition, metaphor, personification, and so forth—in the service of negation.

Laments must be as old as love poems; we find laments for the destroyed cities of Sumer, laments for the dying god Tammuz, and, in the Bible, David's laments for Saul and Jonathan and for Abner. The Prophets, especially Ezekiel, compose derisive laments for the cities whose doom they foretell. Grief tries to find expression in an order of words that will restore the dead to the human community, articulate the inexpressible, turn death into beauty.

Thus the lament closes and echoes back the narrative, as it does in Gilgamesh; it consummates the prophecy. It preserves for us the direct impact of the fall of Jerusalem. But with one reservation: there are five laments. Each has its own perspective, its own vocabulary and rhetorical technique, linked by the form (the acrostic, whereby each verse begins with its corresponding letter of the Hebrew alphabet) and by verbal and thematic correspondences. The effect is both of overwhelming plangency, finding the solace of repeated poetic expression, and of polysemy, as the inarticulate initial cry, *'eikhah*, "how," generates linguistic divergence. The discourse attempts to explain, illustrate, and thus mitigate the catastrophe, to house it in a familiar literary framework; it must also communicate its own inadequacy. Its success, in a sense, depends on its failure. This happens, for example, if a poem fades out in a whimper or an ineffectual cry for revenge, and it has to recognize the silence that exhausts it, the power of the enemy, and the necessity of starting again. But this success through the enactment of inadequacy is also reflected, as always, in the details of language.

Let us take the superb beginning: *'eikhah yashvah badad ha'ir,* "How doth the city sit solitary." *Badad,* "solitary," is ambiguous; the city may be solitary because it is unpopulated or because it is isolated among the nations; its uniqueness turns into its nemesis. This ambiguity is compounded by *rabati-'am,* "that was full of people," which could also mean "mistress of people," linking the present misery of the city to its former grandeur as *rabati bagoyim sarati bamedinot,* "mistress of the nations, princess of the provinces" (that is, countries [AR]). The populace (*'am*) could refer either to Zion's citizens or to the world, and hence to psalms such as 48, quoted in Lamentations 2:15, in which Jerusalem is called "the joy of the whole earth." But this magnitude is perilous, since the city's pretensions to grandeur and its illicit relations with the world—hence the loaded terms "mistress . . . princess"—are held responsible for its fate. Thus the culminating simile of the first line, "she has become as a widow" [AT], is also ambiguous: is she bereft of her people, of YHWH, of her lovers, or of all three? This simile complements "she has become tributary" [AT] at the end of the second line; the repeated verb "has become," together with the opening "doth sit," imposes a stillness and finality on the verse that also permeates the second: "She weepeth sore [literally, 'Weeping she weeps'] in the night, and her tears are [literally, 'tear is'] on her cheeks [literally, 'cheek']: among all her lovers she hath none to comfort her." The repetition of the verb "weep," though a Hebrew emphatic idiom, suggests reiteration, an ever-replenished plaint: it could well be a model for the book. The sorrow is silhouetted by the quiet of the night and the destroyed city. But the figure of continuity and repetition is juxtaposed with one of arrested time: "her tear is on her cheek." It is as if she will never escape this moment. This introduces a powerful motif of the first chapter, "There is none to comfort her." What, then, is the function of the poet and the poem, as an attempt at response and consolation? And further, what is the function of the archcomforter, God?

We come to the central dilemma of the book. It draws on the ready-made explanations of the calamity—Jerusalem has sinned, its prophets lied, they shed innocent blood, and so forth—without apparent question (at least until the very end, 5:20), as if a bad explanation were better than no explanation, and juxtaposes them with descriptions of misery. Parataxis works to establish not connections but dissonances. This is very clear in chapter 2, the second poem in the sequence, where God's wrath is contrasted without comment with the grief of the aged and the young girls, the incessant weeping of the poet, and the starvation of children. The same images repeat themselves at intervals, as if fixated in the memory, only to be carried ultimately to a logical inversion. The mothers eat their children, to whom they cannot give suck; the mourners, covered in ritual ash, lie dead in the dust. But this is God's work: "Thou hast slain them in the day of thine anger; thou hast killed, and not pitied" (2:21). In the first half of the chapter, which is an unremitting, frightening, yet almost objective account of God's onslaught, the focus is essentially on physical destruction and the paradox of God's violation of his own holy place; in the second half of the chapter, the catastrophe is solely and gratuitously human. Yet the sacrilege and the human suffering cannot be entirely dissociated, because the victims are God's children. The chapter begins its conclusion with a rhetorical question, "Behold, O Lord, and consider: to whom hast thou done this?" (2:20 [AR]). Among the victims are priest and prophet, killed in the sanctuary (2:20), although the prophets have ceased to receive visions (2:9) and have prophesied falsely (2:14). Thereby God has fulfilled his ancient purpose, "that he had commanded in the days of old" (2:17). Not only are the false prophets, then, agents of his will—a persistent and traumatic biblical theme (for example, in the story of Micaiah, 1 Kings 22)—but also God is being induced to recognize that despite their wrongdoing they are his servants, equated through parallelism in 2:20 to the starving and cannibalized children. But this might also be a metaphorical equivalence: like the children sucking dry breasts, the prophets receive no vision, there is no Torah (2:9), and God greedily swallows— just like the death-god Mot in Canaanite myth—his people (2:2, 5, 8).

The first part of chapter 2 is controlled by the metaphor of God as an enemy who destroys what is his. The fortresses of the daughter of Judah (v. 2) are really his fortresses (v. 5), over which she laments (v. 5). He substitutes for his *mo'ed*—meaning both "festival" and "appointed time"—the celebration of the victors in the Temple (v. 7). The shifting of terms is insistent. The enemy are summoned to this convocation by God, whose instrument they are; God, however, is only apparently an enemy— hence the simile *ka'oyev*, "*like* an enemy" (vv. 4, 5)—and will ultimately, so the poet hopes, invite them to a festival or appointed time of retribution (2:22). The compounding of illusions tactically displaces the reality of horror and the hardly concealed conceptual chasm when all the symbols of religious identity have vanished. Another example of this predicament is "The Lord hath caused the solemn feasts and sabbaths to be forgotten in Zion" (v. 6), which also uses the word *mo'ed*. But festivals and sabbaths are seasons of remembrance, points of contact between contingent time and mythic time, and hence assertions of cosmic order. In erasing this memory, God implicitly annuls the symbolic links through which we situate ourselves in the world; amnesia is a reversion to chaos.

The pitiless sequence is interrupted only twice, once by the grief of the daughter of Judah (2:5), and a second time by that of the walls of Jerusalem, in a lovely alliterating phrase *waya'avel ḥel weḥomah yaḥdaw 'umlalu,* "therefore he made the rampart and the wall to lament; they languished together" (2:8). The weeping of stones (see 2:18) appeals against God's relentlessness.

Chapter 3 attempts to escape from these quandaries through transposition to another mode. In it, the central chapter of the book, the poet grieves over his own fate, in terms very reminiscent of Jeremiah, Job, and the anonymous Psalms of Lament. The particular catastrophe, with its vivid immediacy, is replaced by a genre. The eyewitness of the first two chapters gives way to a series of stock metaphors. This may be illustrated by the initial words of the poems. *'Eikhah,* "How," the sheer response to something beyond words, is opposed in chapter 3 by *'ani,* "I," a self-definition as "the man that hath seen affliction by the rod of his wrath" (3:1), whose uniqueness is unconvincing because of its conventionality. The tradition is, however, being used as a resource and a foil. Its evocation affirms that the difference between individual and collective calamity is one of degree, not of kind, that language which was efficacious in the past may also be of service now. It is thus a search through old formulas for a context through which to comprehend this new catastrophe, a search that does not work because it never worked. It is not as if the tradition were directly criticized. The poet talks like Job one minute, and like one of Job's friends the next. He seems unaware of the contradiction—that a God who refuses to listen to prayer may be persuaded by it. But the appeal is to no avail: the end of the poem is as desperate as the beginning, with a passionate but as yet impotent cry for vindication.

The fourth chapter returns to the theme of the first two, the fall of Jerusalem, and to their initial word, *'eikhah;* it repeats much of their material. It is, however, more understated and shorter; two-line acrostic strophes replace three-line ones. It lacks the pathos of the first chapter, with its personification of weeping Jerusalem, and the dramatic sweep of the second. Instead there is a note of returning reality. The dominant figure of speech is comparison, which here operates as a powerful distancing device, in contrast to the metaphors of the first two chapters. Mothers are as cruel to their children as the proverbial ostriches; the sin of Jerusalem was worse than that of Sodom; its Nazirites were whiter than snow, are now blacker than black. These insistent comparisons set the catastrophe in a context that is partly literary, partly historical. The carelessness of ostriches (4:3) effects a spatial displacement to the wilderness, to the absurdity of nature, as in God's speech from the whirlwind in Job, and the comparison is of course unfair to the mothers of Jerusalem, and consequently a conceit. Alongside these rhetorical devices that idealize and divert is a simple account of the fall of the city. We experience the defenders waiting in vain for relief, the growing claustrophobia, the celerity of the enemy, the capture of the king. A feature of this description is emotional economy; for example, the king is depicted as "the breath of our nostrils, the anointed of the Lord" (4:20). (The image is very ancient, and has been found in the Tel-el-Amarna letters, written a thousand years earlier.) He signifies at once the vitality of the state through which his subjects live, and a divine effluence, as the one who directs his kingdom. The perception is appropriate and comprehensive; elsewhere in the book, however, it might have been greatly expanded. Finally, there is a curse against the daughter of Edom, which is reminiscent not only of Obadiah but of the imprecation against Babylon in Psalm 137. The absence of specification of the real enemy, the Babylonians, is perhaps evidence of political expedience, of a people living under occupation; at any rate, Edom, the brother-cum-enemy, is of far greater symbolic import. We see here (as in Malachi) the possible beginning of Edom's career in Hebrew literature as the archetype of Rome and all the enemies of Israel.

The final chapter is an evident coda, distinguished from the others by its brevity and its lack of a formal acrostic. It is a prayer to YHWH to remember all Israel's sufferings, which are summarized in rapid detail. The language calls to mind that of Job as well as of chapter 3, but without any of Job's subversive implications. From the appeal to the memory of God and the desolation of Zion, the poet evokes his eternity and apparent forgetfulness, concluding with a plea—despite God's continuing wrath and utter rejection—for a reversal and renewal of time, a time fraught with ambiguity from the beginning.

Lamentations is one of the most obtrusively formal books in the Bible. On each side, two chapters of twenty-two verses each surround one of sixty-six verses; each except the last is an alphabetic acrostic (the third chapter is a triple acrostic; hence its sixty-six verses). This formal arrangement is useful for the study of Hebrew metrics, since for once we know where verses begin and end. The acrostic provides a purely external structure for the poem, predictable and yet open to all the possibilities of expression and fragmentation. This assurance and freedom counteract the loss of political and religious structure described in the poem. They may be seen as an ironic wish-fulfilling gesture, an ineffectual assertion of control over language, and hence over thought, in the face of devastating reality. But this formal structure works on a deeper level. The acrostic is a sign of language—the system of signs—in which all the letters of the alphabet cooperate to generate meaning. Beyond this it is a sign of language as play, free of signification, of the multiple word games that permeate Hebrew poetry. Language is self-fulfilling, self-gratifying. We return to the theme of the first chapter: "She hath none to comfort her." Out of the dark night, in which Jerusalem's tear is on her cheek, the voice rises, turning the weeping into differentiated poems and words, human desolation into grandeur. That plangent phrase recurs through the chapter, changing context, seeking a corresponding phrase of consolation from God as well as from Zion's faithless lovers, eliciting identification and appeasement from us. So the phrase, like the poem, speaks of our solitude amid our ruins, that the destruction to which it bears witness should turn to hope.

SUGGESTED FURTHER READINGS

N. K. Gottwald, *Studies in the Book of Lamentations* (Nashville, 1954).

W. F. Lanahan, "The Speaking Voice in the Book of Lamentation," *Journal of Biblical Literature,* 93 (1974), 41–49.

Alan Mintz, *Hurban: Responses to Catastrophe in Hebrew Literature* (New York, 1984), chap. 1.

University of Alberta

Esther

Jack M. Sasson

THE Book of Esther tells Jews that their national liberation festival originates in a historical event. It explains to them why such a festival bears the non-Hebrew name Purim and instructs them how to observe it. It also seeks to imbue them with pride at the accomplishment of Jewish ancestors who lived in a strange land and faced ruthless foes.

The teller spares no effort to convince his audience of the story's historical setting: he frequently adopts the style of an archivist, giving dates for specific activities and providing genealogies for his main characters; he flaunts his (imperfect) knowledge of the Achaemenid Empire and its administration, scattering Persian words for which he gives Hebrew equivalents; he invents a few of the names he needs, imitating Persian nomenclature; he challenges readers to check his facts in the chronicles of past Persian kings—certainly an impossible assignment for the average reader.[1]

The exotic behavior of the foreigners and their court is also stressed. The storyteller makes observations on details in passing, as with the crowning of royal horses at parade time (6:8), or he builds a major subplot around them, as with the procedure for securing an audience with the Persian king (4:11). In telling how the king finds a replacement for Vashti (2:8-15), the storyteller lingers over stylized elements which are better known in the *Arabian Nights*: the need for two semesters to prepare a young woman physically for just one night with the king, and the tribulation of a king who must nightly rise to the occasion until he is released from it by the one true love.[2] This particular scene may not be the teller's most successful invention, for it is neither crude enough to arouse prurient interest nor focused sharply enough to keep us mindful of Esther's bounteous charm and appeal. It does, however, remain typical of Jewish romances of the Hellenistic period (such as Judith, Tobit, Susanna, and segments of Daniel) in exaggerating the manners and mores of others, and thus it vividly illustrates why Esther cannot be judged on its distortion of Persian practices.

The tale can be heard or read in a single session. It alternates action and description, although the two are rarely allowed to merge. The storyteller has in mind an audience who will not grow tired of repetitions, and he adopts a chatty, possibly vernacular, Hebrew. Although sometimes lackluster and often prolix, this idiom nevertheless promotes ambiguity by depending on certain verbal forms which lack temporal precision (for example, the infinitive absolute). The teller is careful to use a language with a restricted vocabulary only when narrating action. However, when lingering on descriptions of specific scenes (such as the banquets or the search for a new queen) he uses a cataloguing style, rich in a vocabulary for luxurious living, often without conjunctions. The narrator often masterfully juxtaposes simultaneous activities within the confines of a single verse. An excellent example is the brilliant contrasts afforded in 3:15: "As the couriers swiftly fanned out with the king's resolution and as the decree was proclaimed in Susa's citadel, the king and Haman settled down to drink while Susa was struck dumb."[3]

The Book of Esther has far less dialogue than other narratives in Hebrew Scripture, and the storyteller sometimes attributes statements to groups rather than to individuals (as in 3:3, 5:14). Occasionally the teller flaunts his omniscience when revelation of a character's inner thoughts is important to the plot (as at 6:6). He is not beyond expecting his audience to suspend plausibility for the sake of a brilliant ending. Thus the story requires that Haman know nothing of Esther's relationship (let alone kinship) to the Jew Mordecai. In this ignorance he may be alone: Mordecai, after all, himself paced daily in front of the harem before Esther was chosen, and afterward everyone seems to be transmitting information between the two and among the Jews of Susa (see especially 2:22). There are other ambiguities, especially in the dialogues, whose precise import cannot easily be assessed. For example, Mordecai warns Esther that although she may feel safe within the palace, the help which comes to the Jews from "another quarter" could lead to her death and to that of her "father's household" (4:14). Esther, of course, is an orphan and may well be an only child.

Except for four central figures—the king, Mordecai, Esther, and Haman—persons who are given little or no background (Vashti, Memucan, Hegai, Hatach, Zeresh, Harbona) enter the story, carry the plot forward, and leave it without unduly burdening the audience's memory. The main characters themselves are deceptively static; but the development they exhibit as they interact with each other is not expected to alter the audience's attitude toward them.

Ahasuerus is a caricature of a king who is swayed by the first advice he hears; but this trait is required by the plot: all the multiple reversals that are featured in the story could not occur easily were the king single-minded in perspective or conviction. On the contrary, the king must be totally open to suggestion. Thus, except when the intoxicated monarch brashly asks for Queen Vashti's presence at the second banquet honoring the palace personnel (1:10–11), he never acts without some expressly stated or subtly intimated advice. Indeed, the frequency with which advice is offered from all sources and to every character is such a major feature of Esther's plot structure that it has led some scholars wrongly to locate Esther's origins in Wisdom circles.

Ahasuerus is not without his droll moments, and the writer assigns him what may be the story's most comic line. When Esther denounces the man who has sold her and her people into slavery, the accused, of course, could be the king as well as Haman. Yet the events of barely a fortnight earlier are so hazy in his memory that Ahasuerus can answer: "Who is he and where is he who dares plan such a thing?"

The writer assigns Haman a rich assortment of postures befitting his evil character. He is proud of his subordination to a capricious king; yet he is so insecure that he brandishes his *vita* even before those who must know it well (5:9–12). Haman so obsessively needs to destroy Mordecai that he departs from his own plan in order to hasten the death of his archenemy. His vanity turns him into a buffoon (6:6); so does his panicked reaction to Esther's accusation (7:8). Yet Haman is not one-dimensional. During one brief moment, in fact, he even comes to realize the consequences of his own acts, and in this regard he may well deserve to be termed "antagonist." This occurs when Haman is told: "If Mordecai, before whom you have begun to fall, is of Jewish stock, you will not overcome him; you will certainly come to ruin in his presence" (6:13). Haman, however, is hardly a Persian Shylock, and his fall remains comic, never eliciting audience sympathy.

Esther enters the scene already favored by circumstances. A Jewish orphan raised by her cousin Mordecai, she is pretty and winsome; but she responds to what others expect of her. She becomes a queen because she lets others make decisions crucial to her future, and she can be browbeaten by Mordecai's threat even when assured of her husband's attachment (4:13–14). Yet, like many other women in Hebrew Scripture who come into their own after men create crises they cannot resolve themselves, Esther does rise to the occasion, and even after Mordecai has become the king's main adviser, she finds the means by which to save her people (8:1–6). That she returns to Mordecai's control after her moment of triumph tells us much about the circumscribed range of movement antiquity allowed women.

The writer's fondness for Esther is obvious at all stages of the story, and he gives her the most personal voice of any character. Esther can show anxiety about her cousin's welfare (4:4) as well as elicit pathos at the burden she carries in behalf of her people (4:16). She can be feminine and mysteriously coquettish (5:8), but she can also be ministerial (8:5, 9:13). Her most brilliant lines, however, are delivered at the second banquet, when she flatters, pleads, deplores, then turns sarcastic—the last, admittedly lost on Ahasuerus—all within two verses (7:3–4):

If you favor me, O king, and if it please you, may my own life be given me as my wish, and my people as my request; for we have been sold—I and my people—to be destroyed, massacred, and exterminated. Had we been sold just to become male and female slaves, I would have kept my silence; for about such a trifle, it is not worth troubling the king.

The teller sustains tension for two more verses, allowing Esther to deliver the coup de grace: "the man, the malevolent enemy, is this evil Haman!" (7:6).

Mordecai is played like a theme in a Sibelius symphony, with fragments of his personality occurring scattered in the early chapters; only after Haman's fall are they integrated into a full version to represent the writer's perfect image of a partisan Jew in a position of mastery: "Indeed, Mordecai the Jew ranked just below King Ahasuerus; he was highly regarded by the Jews and was very popular among his brethren, constantly seeking his people's welfare and interceding in behalf of his kindred" (10:3).

From the moment he first appears, Mordecai is a courtier, and his battles are with his colleagues at the royal court. The writer does not judge Mordecai when he brings his brethren to the brink of disaster either because of rancor (he had just saved the king and felt that he deserved better than to be forgotten) or because of insubordination and misplaced pride (it is the king, after all, who determines how to treat Haman). The storyteller is deadpan as he reports Mordecai's quick forsaking of his mourning garb when Haman calls for him with royal attire and chariot (chap. 6). Mordecai has come to represent the Jew who will not be bowed by circumstances and who will seize unforeseen opportunity. Moreover, the teller, who is certainly familiar with Israel's history, knows that under no circumstances would a descendant of Saul—in this case Mordecai (2:5)—allow a descendant of Agag—in this case Haman (3:1, 11; 9:24)— once again to escape God's will and thus avoid extirpation (see 1 Sam. 15). Mordecai himself seems aware of the momentous aspect of this confrontation when he berates Esther: "Even if you maintain silence in this situation, relief and liberation will come to the Jews from another source, while you and your family will perish. Who knows, you may well have come to the throne just for this occasion" (4:14).

The characterization of Mordecai changes radically in the other version of Esther available from antiquity: the redaction in Greek preserved in the Septuagint and containing 107 additional verses not found in the Hebrew.[4] Mordecai of the Greek version is a more detached person, more obviously aware of the cosmic struggles in which Jews are mere pawns. This version is set a full year before the Hebrew text begins its tale, and precisely ten years before Haman casts lots. Mordecai receives a dream full of enigmatic visions. He awakes and cannot resolve them but stumbles upon the plot to kill the king. He is immediately rewarded by the king, for which he earns Haman's jealousy and hatred. The Greek text intimates Haman's involvement in the plot, and his Agagite descent is made Macedonian (Greek A:1–12). Mordecai's refusal to treat Haman as the king had commanded is given a noble reason in one of the many prayers inserted in the text: "You know, Lord, that it was not because of insolence or arrogance or vanity that I . . . did not bow down before arrogant Haman . . . But I did this in order that I might not put the glory of man above the glory of God" (Greek C:5–7). When, after many self-conscious prayers (not available to the Hebrew version), Mordecai reaches the pinnacle of power, he can recall his dream and find correlations to the events of the past ten years (Greek F:1–10). The reader of the Greek version, therefore, never needs to delve into Israel's past to appreciate fully the book's many mysteries; they are all resolved for him by a didactically explicit Mordecai.

In either version, the fate which overtakes Haman is predetermined, and in the ensuing triumph of Mordecai the writer gives his audience opportunity to hope for the future of the Jews. In the Greek account, the storyteller suppresses all that is comic, delivering his grave lesson in a serious tone; and his stylistic and structural imitation of apocalyptic literature (Daniel and the many apocalypses of the Hellenistic period) serves his purpose perfectly. In the Hebrew rendering, however, the comic potential of the story is richly exploited, and laughter at human vanity, gall, and blindness becomes the vehicle by which the writer gives his tale integrity and moral vision. Were it not for its modern pejorative connotation, "travesty" (wherein serious subjects are treated lightly) would suit Esther as a literary category. Setting aside the questions of intellectual influence or contact, we can say that this is essentially the same literary mode adopted by Hellenistic romances (for example, Apuleius' *Golden Ass*), by the medieval fabliaux, and by Voltaire in his satiric *Contes philosophiques* (such as *Candide, Zadig,* and *Micromégas*). In all such stylized, farcical narratives, the laughter is broad and comes from the incongruity of situations and from the sharp reversals of fate.

In the Hebrew version of Esther, banquets are a key to the tale's structure. This version opens with two successive banquets (the second also includes Vashti's own) set in Ahasuerus' third regnal year (1:3–9), and it ends with two others, set in his twelfth year, wherein the Jews celebrate their victory over their enemies (9:17–18). These parallels bracket the tale, of course, but, more important, they complete a gradual shift of interest from generalities regarding the Persian Empire to particularities of Jewish concern. The lavish descriptions of Ahasuerus' commemorative banquets are therefore balanced by the reasoned prescriptions for festivities perpetually imposed upon the Jews by Mordecai's edict (9:20–23) and by Esther's letter (9:29).

The banquet in honor of Esther's installation as queen occurs (appropriately enough, given the formulaic importance of the number) in the king's seventh year (2:18). The king's munificence on this occasion contrasts sharply with his moody response at the end of Vashti's banquet. The primary purpose of the king's banquet, however, is to establish the time for Mordecai's thwarting of the attempted regicide (2:21–23), an act which ultimately will affect Haman's fate more than any other. It is not surprising, therefore, that the Greek version places it at the beginning of the story, thus subordinating plot to pedagogy.

Five more years will pass before Mordecai openly clashes with Haman. In this central section of his tale the teller perceptibly quickens the narrative pace. On the first month of Ahasuerus' twelfth year, Haman casts his fateful lot, determining that the year shall not end without the Jews' full destruction. The private banquet that Haman and the king enjoy at the end of their conclave (3:15) not only is set against the despair that obtains among the Jews in Susa but also contrasts sharply with Mordecai's mourning and the Jews' three-day fast at Esther's bidding (4:15–16). These events themselves are but background for the most brilliantly conceived of the tale's banquet scenes; for within a week's time, the festivities offered by Esther will bring about a complete reversal of fortunes between Mordecai and Haman.

The Hebrew version exploits a motif that was all too familiar and even realistic to audiences in antiquity: a usurper murders a king and seeks legitimacy by forcibly appropriating the reigning queen.[5] These crucial scenes (chaps. 5–8) change so rapidly and are filled with so much movement that the audience hardly realizes how carefully they are plotted. In fact, some scholars have mistakenly tried to use these chapters to prove that Esther is formed of two separate strands, one focusing on the harem intrigues involving Vashti and Esther, the other on the court struggles involving Mordecai and Haman. In order to appreciate the artistry of these scenes, we should recognize that Haman's fall requires the conjunction of *three* separate factors. By itself, Esther's accusation of personal malice might only have led the king to investigate the matter, as he did earlier in similar circumstances (2:23). The king himself might not have decided instantly to impale Haman if he had not very recently remembered Mordecai's loyalty. With Harbona's revelation, right after Haman's clumsy lurch at the queen, that Haman has prepared a (seventy-five-foot!) stake for Mordecai, the evidence for a conspiracy fully crystallizes in the king's mind. Moreover, the scene realizes its comic potential through the contrast between two separate points of view: that of the king, who grows increasingly suspicious, and that of Haman, who, even to the last, never knows why the king, let alone Esther, turns against him.

Esther's first appearance before the king and the latter's offer to place at her disposal half his kingdom (repeated almost moronically later) may well have erotic implications because of the submissive tone she adopts, for the king lapses into unseemly familiarity when he talks about "Esther" (without her title "the queen") to his aides (5:5). What this first visit does, however, is to prepare us for the king's acceptance of Esther's second banquet invitation. We cannot know how Esther's deferential remarks in extending her second invitation, this time within earshot of Haman, affect the king: do they arouse his jealousy and alert him to Haman's future behavior? In Haman's case, however, Esther's words certainly raise his self-confidence and lead him to cast prudence aside in order to seek Mordecai's immediate death. It is at this point, therefore, that the noose opens wide for Haman.

Chapter 6, which tells of the king's insomnia and Haman's misplaced advice, contains a first-rate example of rude comedy and reversal of expectation. However, it also adds a bit of information that will be crucial in the next scene. When Haman advises that he whom the king wishes to honor be dressed to look and act like royalty, he is in effect proposing treatment (we know from extant cuneiform evidence) reserved for substitute kings.

Haman returns home to receive his supporters' forecast of doom. This vignette is pivotal. The mourning with which he is clothed harks back to Mordecai's own, but the language at 6:12 (*ḥafuy ro'sh,* "crestfallen") prefigures his despair (*peney haman ḥafu,* "ashen faced") when Ahasuerus accuses him of assaulting the queen (7:8).[6] It is not surprising, therefore, that, badly shaken by the crowning of Mordecai and by his own family's evil prognoses, Haman is not able to react coolly to Esther's accusation.

Everything falls together at Esther's second soirée. She denounces Haman; the king is angered and rushes out to reflect; a terrified Haman turns to Esther for succor; the king returns to find his vizier prostrate on his wife's couch and suspects the worst. When Harbona comes in with the announcement that Haman had planned to kill the very man whom the king recently honored for loyalty, Haman's fate is sealed. As befits the crime, the punishment is severe: the king orders the execution of Haman's whole family. Any audience in antiquity would recognize the annihilation of a whole clan as standard punishment for treason. Any Jew would find in Haman's discomfiture an excellent instance of measure given for measure; if cognizant of Scripture, a Jew would moreover realize that Haman's downfall finally completes the job of destroying the Agagites that God imposed on the Benjaminite Saul. Anyone else, including all those who now read the tale purely for pleasure, will find in it unambiguously drawn characters and fully resolved situations. In Esther, unsubtle villains meet with brutal fates; proud partisans are fully vindicated; lovely heroines retain the affection of all; and stolid, dim-witted monarchs are there to be used by all.

NOTES

1. For an evaluation of the narrator's knowledge of Persia and its customs, see L. B. Patton's thorough study in his *International Critical Commentary to Esther* (New York, 1908), pp. 64–77. Such assessments are repeated in almost every major contribution on Esther, since the book is constantly—and, I might add, unnecessarily—subjected to historical analysis.

2. In 2:19 the text ought to read "when various [*shonot* rather than *shenit,* 'a second time'] young women were gathered," thus removing the likelihood of another such trial for the king. Thus 2:19–20 synchronizes with 2:12–15.

3. All translations from the Hebrew are my own [AT].

4. The Greek version is readily available in any Roman Catholic translation of Scriptures (Jerusalem Bible, Douay) or any Protestant rendering which includes the Apocrypha (New English Bible). I have relied on C. A. Moore's fine Anchor Bible commentary, *Daniel, Esther and Jeremiah: The Additions* (New York, 1977).

5. As noted above, the Greek version presumes that conspiracy is at stake and declares it to be such from the outset of the story. The Greek narrative is more obvious in this respect, and therefore less playful and interesting.

6. The Hebrew of the phrase in 7:8 is difficult.

SUGGESTED FURTHER READING

Sandra Beth Berg, *The Book of Esther,* Society for Biblical Literature Dissertation Series, 44 (Missoula, Mont., 1979).

University of North Carolina

Daniel

Shemaryahu Talmon

THE linguistic and literary diversity of Daniel reveals a composite structure. The opening and concluding parts (1:1–2:4a and 8–12), in Hebrew, frame a portion in Aramaic which is itself a composite (2:4b–6:28 and 7:1–28). A smooth transition from the opening Hebrew section to the Aramaic part is deftly achieved by the introduction in Hebrew (2:4b), of some Chaldean soothsayers who speak Aramaic: "Then spake the Chaldeans to the king in Syriack [Aramaic]." This linguistic structure resembles that of Ezra; there, too, a composite Aramaic passage (Ezra 4:7–6:18 and 7:1–26) is sandwiched between two pieces of Hebrew narrative (Ezra 1:1–4:6 and 7:27–10:44). This combination may indicate the writers' decision to use both languages spoken by Jews in the post-Exilic period.

It remains a matter of debate whether or not the entire book was originally written in one language (Aramaic or Hebrew), with parts subsequently translated into the other. Likewise it cannot be determined whether a translator into the vernacular Aramaic was addressing himself to a wider reading public or whether the translation into Hebrew was intended for a scholarly audience. In any event, the very fact that parts of the book were translated appears to indicate an increasing interest in apocalyptic speculations and literature among Jews before the turn of the era.

The first half of the book (chaps. 1–6) uses a narrative style. It is composed of a series of six court tales about Daniel and his three friends Hananiah, Mishael, and Azariah. The tales are linked by common motifs and literary imagery and by an apparent concentration on human affairs. All four men are introduced as young Judean nobles who were exiled by the Babylonian king Nebuchadnezzar when he conquered Jerusalem in the third year of the reign of Jehoiakim, king of Judah. Because of their beauty, wisdom, and righteousness (chap. 3), they are chosen to serve at Nebuchadnezzar's court. When Daniel successfully interprets the king's enigmatic dream, he is elevated to a position of exceeding prominence (2:48), and at his request his three friends are also given high offices in the imperial administration (2:49). Daniel's position is further strengthened when he interprets another dream of Nebuchadnezzar's (chap. 4). Later, in the reign of Belshazzar, he explains a cryptic inscription which appears on a wall in the palace during a banquet given by the king (chap. 5; a vivid scene described by Xenophon in his *Cyropaedia* and captured by Rembrandt in his famous "Belshazzar's Feast").

Although these tales are obviously intended to be read as historical reports, their fictitious character is revealed by several flaws in the historical references: Belshazzar, for example, was not the son of Nebuchadnezzar, as stated in 5:2, but rather of Nabonidus, the last Babylonian king. No evidence is available to support the affirmation that Jerusalem was taken by the Babylonians in the third year of Jehoiakim's reign (1:1). This datum was probably extrapolated from the report in 2 Chronicles 36:6 of the undated deportation of Jehoiakim by Nebuchadnezzar. Nor is there a historical record of a King Darius the Mede, son of Ahasuerus, mentioned in 9:1, or of a Median empire between the fall of Babylon under Nabonidus and the rise of the Persian Empire under Cyrus the Great (chaps. 6 and 9).

Quite different in style and outlook from the pseudo-historical narrative is the second part of the book (chaps. 7–12). It consists of four units of dreams and visions in which future world events are revealed to Daniel, leading up to the persecution of the Jews in the reign of Antiochus Epiphanes (second century B.C.E.) and their ultimate salvation (12:1). The first unit speaks of Daniel in the third person, whereas in the remaining three Daniel himself is the narrator. These units, too, are conjoined by recurring motifs and expressions and by their apocalyptic character. Both halves of the book contain poetic passages of varying length 4:23–26, 12:1–3 (Hebrew); 2:20–23; 4:10–12, 14–18; 6:27–28; 7:9–14; 8:23–26 (Aramaic). These common elements indicate that notwithstanding the internal linguistic, stylistic, and literary diversity, which has led some scholars to suggest that the book was written and made public in serial fashion, Daniel has conceptual unity. The writer presents a religious philosophy of history which links the past with the future—a future which is in fact the writer's own present. With trust in God, he assures us, and obedience to his commandments, the Jewish people will overcome all setbacks in the present age, as in the past, and pave the way for the ultimate triumph of God and Israel in history. Or, as Philo of Alexandria would have phrased it (*Life of Moses* 2.278), the fulfillment of promises in the past guarantees their realization in the future.

The quite different character of the two halves of Daniel seems to have caused the different positioning of the book in the Hebrew and the Greek canons. In the latter, which became the Bible of the Church, Daniel is regarded as a prophet, and his book follows that of Ezekiel, the last of the great prophets. This tradition shows in a florilegium of biblical passages from Qumran (4Q 174),[1] in New Testament texts (Matt. 24:15, Mark 13:14), and in Josephus (*The Antiquities of the Jews* 10.11–12), all of which refer to "Daniel the Prophet." This inclusion of Daniel among the prophets was suggested by the visionary character of chapters 7–10.

The Jewish Sages expressly rejected the designation of Daniel as a prophet, declaring: "they [Haggai, Zechariah, and Malachi] are prophets, while he [Daniel] is not a prophet" (Babylonian Talmud: Sanhedrin 93b–94a). Accordingly, in the Hebrew canon Daniel comes after Esther and before Ezra–Nehemiah, that is, between books which are considered historiographies. Maimonides, the most prominent Jewish authority in the Middle Ages, confirmed the correctness of this order: "the entire nation is agreed that the Book of Daniel should be placed among the Writings and not among the Prophets" (*The Guide of the Perplexed* 2.45). In this instance it was obviously the narrative character of chapters 1–6 which caused the book to be placed among the post-Exilic historiographies.

Historicity

Daniel is said to have lived through the days of the last Babylonian kings Nebuchadnezzar (chaps. 1–4) and Belshazzar (chaps. 5, 7–8), into the reigns of the Persian kings Cyrus (chap. 10) and Darius I Hystaspes (if indeed this is the ruler referred to in 11:1 as Darius the Mede; but see 9:1), that is, from about 600 to about 520 B.C.E. However, its historical inaccuracies support other indications that the book should be dated much later. The writer, who presumably lived in the second century B.C.E., wove his tales and visionary dreams around a legendary figure, in a literary fashion popular in his time. He was probably acquainted with traditions to which the prophet Ezekiel alludes, about a Daniel unequaled in wisdom (Ezek. 28:3) and righteous like Noah and Job (Ezek. 14:13–14, 19–20). These allusions are possibly the immediate cause for the placement of Daniel after Ezekiel in the Greek canon. Further, the caves of Qumran have yielded not only fragments of the biblical Book of Daniel but also a fragment of a composition entitled by its editor "Prayer of Nabonidus." The latter bears a telling resemblance to a central theme in Daniel 4 (which there, however, focuses on Nebuchadnezzar): King Nabonidus, plagued by maladies and exiled to the oasis of Taima, is exhorted by a Jewish sage to relinquish his "idols of gold, silver [bronze, iron], wood, stone, and clay" and embrace the faith in the one true God, so that he will be healed and reinstated to his royal office.[2] The biblical Daniel may also be linked with the figure Dnil/Dnel known from the Ugaritic epic *Aqht* (not later than the fourteenth century B.C.E.).

While no definite connection between the Ugaritic Dnil/Dnel and the biblical Daniel can be established, the combined evidence from the Book of Ezekiel, the "Prayer of Nabonidus," and the epic *Aqht* makes it seem likely that the author of the biblical Book of Daniel knew of traditions concerning an antediluvian "wise and just Dnil/Dnel." He shifted that figure from its original Mesopotamian or Phoenician-Canaanite setting into Palestine-Judea and made him the kingpin of his own literary creation. Such shifts in period and location are common in comparable specimens of apocryphal and pseudo-epigraphical literature, including the Book of Jubilees, in which Noah is the central dramatis persona; the Book of Enoch, ascribed to the godfearing ancient known from a tradition in Genesis 5:18; the "testaments" allegedly composed by the twelve sons of the patriarch Jacob; and the Book of Baruch, said to have been composed by the scribe of the prophet Jeremiah (Jer. 45). By a similar literary maneuver, King Solomon was made the author of the apocryphal Book of Wisdom and of a collection of "psalms," possibly in emulation of the ascription to him of Proverbs (Prov. 1:1; cf. 25:1), the Song of Songs (Song 1:1), and Ecclesiastes, said to have been written by "Koheleth the son of David, king in Jerusalem" (Eccles. 1:1). Likewise, rabbinic tradition saw King David as the author of the Book of Psalms.

It appears that in this respect as in others (discussed below), Daniel represents both the earliest and the most accomplished example of a genre which achieved wide currency in the Judeo-Christian literature of the Hellenistic-Roman (or intertestamental) period. This genre, which could be designated "inverted plagiarism," was emulated by much later writers: an author bent on attaining public acclaim of his writings would willingly suppress his own name, ascribing his creations to a worthy figure of old whose name alone would suffice to assure them of general acceptance.

Style and Imagery

The author of Daniel incorporates motifs, imagery, and phraseology from biblical, and to some degree also from nonbiblical, literature. The text is shot through with literary allusions, paraphrastic quotations, and borrowed phrases which were presumably current when the book was made public.

Daniel, especially in its Hebrew sections, contains original phraseology which demonstrates considerable stylistic innovation. Some of this novel phraseology is echoed in the writings of the Covenanters of the Judean desert, the Qumran scrolls. But the book is also replete with imagery and turns of phrase which appear to be lifted from a variety of canonical Hebrew writings, as even a small selection of examples illustrates: The expression *kalah weneheratsah,* "utter desolation" (9:27 [AT]), occurs only once elsewhere in the Hebrew Bible, in Isaiah 10:23. In Daniel 11:7, 10, and 36 we find still more expressions from Isaiah (11:1, 8:8, 10:25). Daniel 10:14 is seemingly made up of phrases taken from Genesis 49:1 and Habakkuk 2:3. The opening paragraph in 11:30 is adapted from Balaam's oracle in Numbers 24:24. "Daniel sat in the gate of the king" (2:49) echoes "Mordecai sat in the king's gate" (Esther 2:21). Daniel and his fellow ministers are appointed to ensure proper taxation, so that "the king['s treasure] should have no damage" (6:2). Likewise, the Persian officials warn the king of the exiles who have returned to Judah lest their activities "endamage the revenue of the kings" (Ezra 4:13). And Esther would acquiesce in anything but the destruction of her people, so as not to "cause damage to the king['s interest]" (Esther 7:4; compare 3:8–9).

The humanlike figure that touches Daniel's lips (10:16) is described in imagery that appears to be derived from the inauguration visions of Jeremiah (Jer. 1:9), Ezekiel (Ezek. 1, esp. v. 26), and possibly Isaiah (Isa. 6:6–7). Folklore furnishes numerous parallels for a (world-) tree which provides nourishment to all beings and shelter to beast and fowl, such as that seen by Nebuchadnezzar in his dream (4:10–14). The image also shares striking details with the portrayal of the primeval Behemoth in Job 40:15–24.

Patterns and Motifs

Daniel shares with other biblical writings a predilection for the ascending numerical pattern 3 + 1, observable in other ancient Near Eastern literatures. Whatever the roots of this pattern, it signifies a basic "complete" unit of three, topped by a fourth of special standing and importance.

The tale of Daniel and his three friends immediately brings to mind the parallel tradition concerning Job and his three Friends. In both instances, the names of all four dramatis personae are carefully recorded (Dan. 1:6; Job 2:11, 42:9). This is also the case in one strand of tradition which records David as the youngest of his father's sons, who, despite his youth, outranks his three oldest brothers: "the three eldest sons of Jesse went and followed Saul to the battle: and the names of his three sons that went to the battle were Eliab the firstborn, and next unto him Abinadab, and the third Shammah. And David was the youngest" (1 Sam. 17:13–14a). Solomon is the fourth of David's sons who were born to him in Jerusalem (2 Sam. 5:14). Solomon vies for the succession to the throne and prevails over his three older brothers, Amnon, Absalom, and Adonijah. Again, after two of the four sons of Aaron the high priest, Nadab and Abihu, are consumed by a fire from heaven (Lev. 10:1–2), and Ebiathar, a descendant of the third, Ithamar, is banished to Anatoth (1 Kings 2:26–27; cf. 1 Chron. 24:1–5), the priestly office at the Temple in Jerusalem reverts to the fourth son, Eleazar, and his descendants.

The 3 + 1 pattern also underlies the episode of Daniel's appointment by Darius as the first of "three presidents" whom the king put in charge of 120 princes who oversaw the affairs of his kingdom (6:2). We are specifically told that "Daniel was preferred above the presidents and princes, because an excellent spirit was in him; and the king thought to set him over the whole realm" (6:3). The stereotyped wording makes it seem likely that the original version of this tale spoke of 120 governors of the empire, superintended by three ministers, with Daniel controlling the entire administrative hierarchy, second only to the king himself. Understood thus, this administrative scheme would be an exact replica of the one ascribed to Nebuchadnezzar in 2:48–49: "the king made Daniel . . . ruler over the whole province of Babylon, and chief of the governors . . . of Babylon . . . and he set Shadrach, Meshach, and Abednego, over the affairs of the province of Babylon: but Daniel sat in the gate of the king" (cf. Esther 2:21).

The 3 + 1 pattern is well represented in biblical Wisdom literature. An entire series occurs in Proverbs 30:15–31. Some of the "topped triads"—"three things . . . yea, four"—derive from the animal world, exemplified by the smallest creatures (Prov. 30:24–28) or larger beasts (Prov. 30:29–31). Another proverb starts out with an enumeration of three inscrutable facts in the animal and the inanimate world, leading up to an even more unfathomable fourth phenomenon in human life: "There be three things which are too wonderful for me, yea, four which I know not: The way of an eagle in the air; the way of a serpent upon a rock, the way of a ship [better: a fish] in the midst of the ocean; and the way of a man with a maid" (Prov. 30:18–19). An additional series is set altogether in human experience. Three things are unbearable: a slave who becomes king, an evildoer who prospers, a hated wife who conceives (and therefore triumphs), but worst of all, "an handmaid that is heir to her mistress" (Prov. 30:21–23).

The same model recurs also in visionary or prophetic literature. Balaam the seer blesses the people Israel three times instead of cursing them as the Moabite king Balak had commissioned him to do (Num. 24:10), and then adds a fourth blessing which surpasses the previous ones (Num. 24:15–24). Likewise, on the journey from Pethor, Balaam's ass sees three times "the angel of the Lord standing in the way, and his sword drawn in his hand, and . . . turned aside" to avoid him (Num. 22:23–30), until the seer's eyes are opened, and the fourth time he perceives the angel who threatens his life (Num. 22:31–33).

The pattern 3 + 1 finds a most salient expression in Amos's oracles against foreign nations (Amos 1:3–2:3) and against Judah and Israel (Amos 2:4–16). The phrase "for three transgressions . . . and for four," which recurs in every instance, shows the fourth to be more damnable than the preceding ones: "Thus saith the Lord . . . I will not turn away the punishment thereof" (Amos 1:3, 6, 9, 11, 13; 2:1, 4, 6). In this as in many other instances, the quintessence of the pattern is to be sought in the "fourth" item in which the series culminates, and which is intrinsically different from the preceding unit of "three" which serves as its antithesis. Therefore, the component "three" cannot be interpreted as referring to a precise number, but rather should be viewed as a schematic literary figure. Such an understanding would remove a difficulty in the explanation of Daniel's visions of "four kingdoms" that shall arise (chap. 11; cf. 8:18–

26), likened to "four beasts" (7:1–8; cf. Prov. 30:29–30) and culminating in the fourth, the Greek Empire (8:21, 10:20, 11:2).[3] While the immediately preceding third kingdom is obviously Persia and the first is Babylon, the exact definition of the second has been subject to speculations since antiquity. But these speculations may be unnecessary. If we view these visions of Daniel as further examples of the 3 + 1 pattern, their thrust and the clue to their meaning would lie in the fourth, the Greek Empire, with the preceding unit of "three" supplying the indispensable foil required by the traditional schema.

Similarly, the puzzling mention of an otherwise undocumented Babylonian siege of Jerusalem in the third year of the reign of Jehoiakim, king of Judah, which opens the book (1:1) may reflect another literary convention. It cannot go unnoticed that the book dates two of Daniel's visions in the third regnal year of a king: one in the third year of Belshazzar (8:1) and one in the third year of Cyrus (10:1). Likewise, Ahasuerus gave his banquet, which was to become of crucial importance in Esther's life history (compare Belshazzar's feast in chap. 5 and Pharaoh's in Gen. 40:20), in the third year of his reign (Esther 1:3).[4] Although the possible exactitude of this date cannot be categorically ruled out in this or the other case, its recurrence in visions and tales in Daniel and Esther appears to reveal a predilection for this literary convention among post-Exilic writers (see further 2 Chron. 17:7).

Use of Traditions

The author of Daniel adopts and develops certain biblical traditions, moving from the genre of prophecy to that of apocalypticism. Building on Jeremiah's divinely inspired assurance that Israel would experience a restoration of its fortunes seventy years after the destruction of the Temple (Jer. 25:11, 12; 29:10; cf. Zech. 1:12, 7:5; Ezra 1:2; 2 Chron. 36:21–23), he foresees a new redemption of his people after seven times seventy years (9:2, 25–26). But his pronouncements are intentionally veiled, as if to prevent his readers from fully fathoming the apocalyptic visions. In this he appears to imitate Ezekiel's equally mystifying description of his vision of the heavenly chariot (Ezek. 1). He takes from Ezekiel 3:1–2 and Zechariah 5:1–4 the motif of a celestial scroll in which are spelled out divinatory matters that the prophet is commanded to assimilate or even to ingest, though with an interesting and significant variation. Ezekiel digests the contents of the scroll by physically eating it. To the post-Exilic prophet Zechariah, the content of the scroll he sees is explained by a heavenly interpreter (Zech. 5:1–4), probably identical with the angel who interprets for him the ensuing visions (Zech. 5:5–6:8) as in Zechariah 1–4. Daniel, too, is enlightened by a heavenly messenger: the angel Gabriel explains the meaning of what he has read in "books" of an obviously revelatory nature (chap. 9) and later interprets a vision of Daniel's (chap. 10). But revealed matters of ultimate significance must remain unintelligible to Daniel (12:8) and to other men, securely hidden away in sealed books until the appointed time of revelation (12:4, 9).

This mystification seems to indicate a theological trend, the roots of which are discernible in late biblical writings but which comes into full bloom in apocryphal, Qumran, and early rabbinic literature: the unbridgeable chasm which increasingly separates man from the divine sphere. In the biblical past, a prophet could bring God's word to man. Now, the seer requires a celestial interpreter to explain his visions to him. Mediator upon mediator intervenes between man and God. And even then the meaning of the revelation may remain hidden.

The Type-Plot of "The Successful Exile"

Scholars have accurately recognized traits in the Daniel story which it shares with other biblical tales of a destitute (fatherless) young Judean or Israelite exile who rises to an unprecedented height at a foreign court.[5] Some focal events and circumstances in the progress of Joseph in Egypt, of Esther and Mordecai, and of Nehemiah and Ezra at the Persian court are unmistakably reflected in the alleged life history of Daniel and his friends. Like Joseph, who was "stolen away out of the land of the Hebrews" (Gen. 40:15) and found favor with his master, an Egyptian official (Gen. 39:1–4), and the orphaned Esther (Esther 2:7), who gained the support of the overseer of Ahasuerus' harem (Esther 2:9), the expatriate Daniel wins the goodwill of the Babylonian courtiers charged with his education (1:3–18). Because of their good looks, intelligence (cf. Ezra 7:25), and modesty (Gen. 39:2–12; Esther 2:8–10, 15–16; Dan. 1:4; cf. Neh. 2:5–8), all three attract the attention of those in authority and ultimately of the ruler of the foreign land into which they have been abducted (Gen. 41:37–39; Esther 2:17; Dan. 1:6–7, 19–20). They soon attain the highest positions in the realm: Joseph becomes viceroy of Egypt (Gen. 41:40–44); Esther is made queen of the realm (Esther 2:17); Mordecai (Esther 2:21–23, 6:3, 10:2), Ezra (Ezra 7:6, 11–26), and Nehemiah (Neh. 1:1, 2:1–9) are given important appointments at court. Likewise, Nebuchadnezzar elevates Daniel to the rank of "ruler over the whole province of Babylon, and chief of the governors over all the wise men of Babylon" (2:48); and Belshazzar makes "a proclamation concerning him, that he should be the third ruler in the kingdom" (5:29).

The elevation to such exalted office is marked by an installation ceremony which in all three instances is described in almost identical terms: "Then commanded Belshazzar, and they clothed Daniel with scarlet, and put a chain of gold about his neck" (5:29); "Pharaoh said unto Joseph, See, I have set thee over all the land of Egypt. And Pharaoh took off his ring from his hand, and put it upon Joseph's hand, and arrayed him in vestures of fine linen, and put a gold chain about his neck; And he made him to ride in the viceroy's chariot [AR]; and they cried before him, Bow the knee" (Gen. 41:41–43). In the case of Mordecai, Ahasuerus instructs Haman to conduct the ceremony exactly as the latter has specified, erroneously assuming that he himself is to receive these honors: "For the man whom the king delighteth to honour, Let the royal apparel be brought which the king useth to wear, and the horse that the king rideth upon, and the crown royal which is set upon his head . . . Then took Haman the apparel and the horse, and arrayed Mordecai, and brought him on horseback through the street of the city, and proclaimed before him, Thus shall it be done unto the man whom the king delighteth to honour" (Esther 6:7–11; cf. Esther 8:15).

Joseph starts out as a dreamer (Gen. 37:5–11) to become a successful interpreter of dreams (Gen. 40). Thanks to this faculty he achieves highest distinction in the Egyptian kingdom (Gen. 41). Likewise, Daniel makes his way to the top in Babylon by convincingly explaining the dreams of Nebuchadnezzar (chaps. 2, 4) and the mysterious writing which appears on the wall during Belshazzar's feast (chap. 5). But in contrast to the story of Joseph, he starts out as an interpreter of dreams and only later becomes a dreamer and a visionary (chaps. 7, 8, 10–12).

Both Joseph and Daniel succeed where all Egyptian and Chaldean wise men fail (cf. Gen. 41:8 with Dan. 2:1–13; 4:1–4, 15). Similarly, in the final event, Mordecai and Esther prove to be wiser than the scheming Haman (Esther 6:13, 9:24–25).

The full integration of the foreigner in the very hub of his new milieu requires one additional adjustment: the change of his Hebrew name to an appellation which conforms with local usage. (The renaming may also be considered a status symbol, comparable to a throne name sometimes adopted by kings at the beginning of their reign.) The Judean Hadassah takes on the pagan name Esther (Esther 2:7); Pharaoh confers upon Joseph the Hebrew (Gen. 40:15) the meaningful appellation *Zaphenath-paneaḥ,* interpreted by tradition to mean "Riddle Solver" (Gen. 41:45); and a high-ranking official at Nebuchadnezzar's court renames Daniel and his friends Belteshazzar, Shadrach, Meshach, and Abed-nego (1:7).

The rise of the exile at the foreign court does not proceed altogether smoothly. The type-plot setting requires that on his way to the top, the stranger will have to overcome obstacles placed in his path by envious adversaries. Being unable to attack him openly because of his excellent reputation and good standing, his enemies conspire to bring about his fall and temporarily succeed in their aim. This turn of plot is variously manifested in the stories of Joseph, Mordecai, and Nehemiah. Like Ahasuerus (Esther 3), Nebuchadnezzar is easily persuaded by his advisers and has Daniel's three friends thrown into the blazing furnace (3:19–23). They are saved, however, by divine intervention (3:24–27), while their tormentors are consumed by the flames that leap out of the furnace (3:22).

The motif "from pit to pinnacle" is enacted once more in an episode of court intrigue against Daniel, set in the reign of King Darius the Mede (chap. 6). Unable to find any malpractice in Daniel's administration of the kingdom, his adversaries scheme to devise a charge involving his religion. Knowing that Daniel prays three times a day to his God, they induce the malleable ruler to proclaim himself the only divinity to whom the citizens of the realm may present a petition for the next thirty days. They catch Daniel making supplication to his God and report him to the king. Unable to act against his own ordinance, Darius reluctantly gives orders to have Daniel thrown into the lion's pit, comforting himself and the victim with the thought that Daniel's God will surely save him. And indeed, when the sealing stone is removed from the mouth of the pit the next morning, Daniel answers Darius' anxious call with a declaration of his loyalty to him (6:22) and emerges unscathed from the pit. Overwhelmed by the greatness of this miracle, Darius offers homage to Daniel's God and decrees that all men in his royal domain shall revere him (6:25–27). Applying retributive justice, he orders Daniel's accusers to be thrown into the lions' pit with their wives and children (cf. Esther 9:6–10, Num. 16:32). They are immediately set upon and consumed by the wild beasts (6:24).

As a symbol of mortal danger, lions play an important role in Hebrew Scriptures. Shepherds tremble before the lion's roar (for example, Isa. 31:4; Amos 3:4, 8; Zech. 11:3; Ps. 22:13; Job 4:10), which is compared to the noise made by armies on the march (Isa. 5:29–30) and to the tempest which manifests God's intervention in nature and history (for example, Jer. 25:30, Hos. 11:10, Joel 3:16, Amos 1:2, Job 37:4). Lions mete out divine punishment, ravaging transgressors and recalcitrants (1 Kings 13:24–28, 20:36; 2 Kings 17:24–26; Jer. 50:17). Only exceptional men can vanquish a lion (2 Sam. 23:20), like the divinely inspired Samson (Judges 14:5–9) and David (1 Sam. 17:34–37).

But the lions of the Daniel tradition are a different breed. They are the only specimens of their kind in biblical narrative which are turned from ferocious beasts into docile animals.[6] They recall Isaiah's visionary lion that in a future ideal age "shall eat straw like the ox" and forage together with calves, a little child leading them to the pasture (Isa. 11:6–9, 65:25). The depiction of that era of universal peace is enfolded by means of ring composition between two sections of a complementary vision of the future ruler of the appeased world, "a rod out of the stem of Jesse" (Isa. 11:1–5, 10) on the one hand, and on the other the restitution of Israel's fortunes and its victory over its historical enemies (Isa. 11:11–16).

This thematic similarity with Isaiah spells out the "message" contained in the episode of Daniel in the lion's den. At the same time, it links the narrative part of the book, which centers on the person of Daniel (chaps. 1–6), with the series of dreams and visions (chaps. 7–12) which center on world history and, in this framework, on the fate of the people of Israel and their ultimate redemption (12:1–3). It is because of this message that the two tales of Daniel's and his friends' rescue from the blazing furnace and the ferocious lions became paradigms of divine deliverance in the repertoire of Western literature and visual art inspired by the Hebrew Scriptures.

A Diaspora Novel

The Exilic setting of the type-plot and the motifs which Daniel shares with the stories of Esther, Joseph, and, to a degree, with Ezra–Nehemiah— as well as with some features of the Moses-in-Egypt tradition—have given rise to the attractive supposition that these narratives are representative examples of a distinct biblical genre—the Diaspora Novel.[7] However, despite their persuasive commonality, there are some telling differences among these narratives. The Book of Esther in particular is, in certain respects, quite unlike the other specimens of the presumed genre in that it is almost totally devoid of specifically Israelite historical reminiscences and religious-cultic traditions. Esther is the only book of the Hebrew Bible in which the name of God is not invoked even once. God is, in fact, altogether absent from the scene on which the drama is acted out by human antagonists to the best of their skill and cunning. There is no mention of prayers, which one would have expected Esther, Mordecai, and the Jews of Persia to have uttered in times of mortal distress. Such prayers were, not unexpectedly, supplied by the author of the additions to the Greek translation of the Hebrew book. Mordecai, Esther, and probably also some of their compatriots revel at the king's table, seemingly without paying attention to the dietary prescriptions which regulate the consumption of food in Jewish tradition. In view of the post-Exilic date of the book, when Israel certainly abided by a particular religious-cultic code, the silence on such matters is highly significant. It may be explained by the Wisdom coloring of the Esther tale, which accentuates the human and the general rather than the religious and the particular.[8]

The Joseph story similarly exhibits conspicuous Wisdom traits.[9] But in this instance the "Land of the Hebrews" serves throughout as a visible backdrop of scene, and the God of Israel determines the progress of events in the unfolding drama. This presence is fully explicated by Joseph when he reveals to his brothers the hidden propitious significance of their evil deed: "Now therefore be not grieved, nor angry with yourselves, that ye sold me hither: for God did send me before you to preserve life" (Gen. 45:5; see also Gen. 45:6–8; 50:19–20; 41:16, 32). The absence of any mention of the observance of food taboos or any other cultic prescriptions by Joseph or, for that matter, by Moses while at Pharaoh's court, is in keeping with the setting of these traditions in the pre-Sinai (revelation) period, that is before the issuance of the laws, beginning with Exodus 20, which pertain to these matters.

How different, predominantly from the Esther tale, is the atmosphere which prevails in the other Diaspora Novels. Ezra–Nehemiah is pervaded by an awareness of Jewish history, a wholly Jewish religious outlook, and an unrelenting endeavor to make tradition the mainstay of the reconstituted community's public and private life. The civic and cultic leaders offer prayers of confession and thanksgiving to Israel's God (Ezra 9:3–10:1; Neh. 2:4, 9:4–37). Life is regulated by the ordinances of "the Law" (for example, Ezra 10:4–44; Neh. 8:1–3, 10:1–39, 12:44–47). There is no mistaking the Jewish character of the book and of the community whose history it portrays.

The "Jewishness" of the chronicle of Daniel and his friends comes even more to the fore because of its biographical character, which makes for a more graphic presentation of the religious way of life. The divine immanence, the young men's reliance on Israel's God, and their trust in his efficacy pervade the narrative. The young men meticulously observe the food taboos, subsist—even flourish—on a diet of seeds and water, rather than partake of the king's provision of unclean meat and wine (1:5–16). Daniel prays three times a day, "his windows being open in his chamber toward Jerusalem" (6:10), and makes supplication for his people (9:3–19), like Ezra (Ezra 9:5–15) and the Levites or the entire community (Neh. 9:4–37).

The pronounced Jewish piety which permeates the Book of Daniel invites a comparison with the similarly oriented apocryphal Book of Judith, also set in the reign of Nebuchadnezzar, although there he is presented as king of Assyria, not of Babylonia (Judith 1:1). Judith, a beautiful and wealthy widow, meticulously observes all ritual rites incumbent on her. She prevails upon her compatriots not to lose faith in God, who will surely have mercy on his people. Like Daniel and his friends, Ezra and Nehemiah, and unlike Esther, Mordecai, and the Jews of Susa, Judith and her compatriots profusely offer prayers to the God of Israel. Like Esther, Judith uses her beauty and her cunning to save her people. She tricks Holofernes into believing that, spurred by a prophetic revelation, she fled from Betuliah to lead him and his army victoriously into the city of Jerusalem. But whereas Esther feasts at Ahasuerus' table, Judith refuses to partake of the Assyrians' food and drink. She brings with her her own ritually clean provisions, just as Daniel and his friends avoid defilement by eating the king's meat and drinking his wine, and subsist on "pulse and water" (1:12). Ultimately, Judith accomplishes her mission by killing the lusting Holofernes (Judith 12:16–13:8) rather than by becoming the consort of a Gentile as Esther does.

THE ABUNDANT EVIDENCE of literary and intellectual dependence on earlier biblical writings and the religious-conceptual affinity with apocryphal literature confirm the late date of Daniel, arrived at on the strength of other (for example, historical) indices. The range of quotations, allusions, and paraphrases demonstrates the writer's familiarity with the Hebrew Scriptures. Since it may be assumed that his audience was also familiar with the biblical texts, the very makeup of the book may reflect on the learning of the ancient audience, and may help explain the book's attainment of popularity.

Daniel must be classified as a fictional tale rather than as a historical narrative; but a comparison with Chronicles and Ezra–Nehemiah, which together with Daniel constitute the closing triad of the Hebrew canon, shows that it is also a distinctive variant of late biblical historiography. Whereas the Chronicler's outlook is altogether retrospective, and the compiler of Ezra–Nehemiah records contemporaneous events, the author of Daniel professes to be concerned with "prospective" history. It is presumably this visionary perspective that made the motifs, imagery, and episodes of Daniel a source of inspiration to writers and artists of much later generations. The apocalyptic, utopian—that is, nonhistorical—character of the visions facilitates their use as prototypes. By applying, in essence, the same technique so well known from the Qumran pesher writings, the ad hoc interpretation of prophetic pronouncements which the author of Daniel had himself practiced, later readers could discern their own situations prefigured in the ancient tales and visions of Daniel.

NOTES

1. J. M. Allegro, ed., *Discoveries in the Judaean Desert*, V (Oxford, 1968), 54.

2. J. T. Milik, "Prière de Nabonid et autre écrits d'un cycle de Daniel: Fragments araméens de Qumran 4," *Revue Biblique*, 63 (1956), 407–417; F. M. Cross, *The Ancient Library of Qumran and Modern Biblical Studies* (New York, 1958), pp. 123–124; B. Jongeling, C. J. Labuschagne, and A. S. van der Woude, eds., *Aramaic Texts From Qumran I* (Leiden, 1976), pp. 123–131; Geza Vermes, *The Dead Sea Scrolls: Qumran in Perspective* (London, 1982), pp. 72–74; J. A. Fitzmyer, "The Contribution of Qumran Aramaic to the Study of the New Testament," *New Testament Studies* 20 (1974), 391–394.

3. This image may also reflect an Iranian tradition of four world empires (Assyria, Media, Persia, Greece) and may be compared with the schema of four world eras represented by four metals (gold, silver, copper, iron), preserved by Herodotus (fifth century B.C.E.).

4. Medieval exegetes, followed by some modern commentators, see a reference to Belshazzar's feast in Dan. 5 in Isa. 21:5. See Rashi and Kimchi on Isa. 21:5, Rashi on Dan. 5:1, and H. L. Ginsberg, *Studies in the Book of Daniel* (New York, 1948).

5. The term *type-plot,* suggested to me by Robert Alter, designates a more comprehensive art form than the type-scene, illustrated by him in "Biblical Type Scenes and the Uses of Convention," in *The Art of Biblical Narrative* (London and New York, 1981), pp. 47–62.

6. They resemble the benevolent lion that saves the life of the fugitive slave Androcles. The story by Aulus Gellius is told by Seneca, *De beneficiis* 2.19.1, and inspired Shaw's play *Androcles and the Lion.*

7. W. L. Humphreys, "A Life Style for the Diaspora: A Study of the Tales of Esther and Daniel," *Journal of Biblical Literature,* 92 (1973), 211–233.

8. Shemaryahu Talmon, "Wisdom in the Book of Esther," *Vetus Testamentum,* 12 (1963), 419–455.

9. Gerhard von Rad, "Josephsgeschichte und ältere Chokma," *Vetus Testamentum,* supp. vol. 1 (1953), 120–127.

SUGGESTED FURTHER READINGS

E. J. Bickerman, "Daniel *or* The Fulfilled Prophecy," in *Four Strange Books of the Bible* (New York, 1967), pp. 51–138.

A. A. di Lella, Introduction to *The Book of Daniel,* Anchor Bible, XXIII (New York, 1978), 3–110.

H. Lusseau, "Daniel," in André Robert and André Feuillet, eds., *Introduction to the Old Testament,* II, translated from the second French edition (New York, 1970), pp. 164–177.

Hebrew University of Jerusalem

Ezra and Nehemiah

Shemaryahu Talmon

EZRA and Nehemiah are our main sources on the period of the return
from the Babylonian Exile, a time of transition between the First
Temple period, which came to an end in 586 B.C.E., and the emerging
Second Commonwealth.

Ezra–Nehemiah, Chronicles, Daniel, and Esther, are the latest works
in the canon of Hebrew Scriptures, and together they manifest the Hebrew
literary genius of the age. The authors of these books could draw upon a
wealth of traditions and literary techniques which had developed in the
era of the biblical monarchies and use them in trying to shape the social
and religious awareness of their contemporaries. But notwithstanding their
preoccupation with adapting exemplary tradition to the changed religious
and political circumstances, they were genuinely innovative in the spheres
of literature, religious thought, and cultic and societal organization. The
writings of this period also reveal the development of the exegetical principles of the legal (halachic) and possibly also the narrative (aggadic)
midrash which were subsequently refined by the Sages and applied to the
interpretation of Scripture. (See the essay on Chronicles in this volume.)

In early Jewish tradition Ezra and Nehemiah were considered one
work, written (together with most of Chronicles) mostly by Ezra but
completed by Nehemiah. This ascription may have resulted from the
prominence which the Jewish Sages accorded Ezra, whom they viewed as
a second Moses. Ezra and Nehemiah are counted as one work in the
traditional tally of twenty-four books that make up the Hebrew Bible, in
the Septuagint, and in the earliest roster of the books of the Old Testament, by Melitto of Sardis (second century C.E.). Origen (third century)
and Jerome (fourth century), however, refer to two separate books, named
First Ezra and Second Ezra. This division prevailed in the Vulgate, whence
it made its way into a Hebrew manuscript dated 1448 and subsequently
into most printed editions of the Bible. It may well be the original arrangement, for the Book of Ezra bears no superscription, whereas the
Book of Nehemiah is introduced by the caption "The account [AR] of
Nehemiah the son of Hachaliah" (1:1). If Ezra and Nehemiah are indeed
two separate works by different authors, we could better explain the du-

plication of certain passages such as the roster of returning exiles (Ezra 2 = Neh. 7) and the apparent dislocation of the section dealing with "the reading of the Law," a tradition clearly attributable to Ezra but contained in Nehemiah 8–9.

Another possible index of different authorship is language. Nehemiah, like Chronicles and Esther, is written entirely in Hebrew. In contrast, Ezra contains a passage in Aramaic dealing with the building of the Temple, between the account of the initial stage of the return (1:1–4:5) and the chronicle of Ezra (7:1–10:44), both written in Hebrew (with the exception of the Aramaic decree issued by Artaxerxes to Ezra, 7:12–26).

Composition

The present literary complex Ezra–Nehemiah comprises three narrative units, each focusing on a central character. The first six chapters deal with the initial stage of repatriation under the leadership of the Davidic scion Zerubbabel and the high priest Jeshua (538–515 B.C.E.). This stage ends with the inauguration of the rebuilt Temple (Ezra 6:16–18) and the celebration of the Passover festival (6:19–22). In view of its content, this section could appropriately be designated "The Book of Zerubbabel" (BZ).

The next four chapters (Ezra 7–10) pertain to Ezra the priest and scribe, who is reported to have headed the return of another contingent of Judeans in the seventh year of the reign of the Persian king Artachshast (Artaxerxes Longimanus, 458 B.C.E.). Ezra's activities in the province of Jehud (Judea) are recounted, including the expulsion of "foreign women" from the community of those who returned. The section culminates in the account of "the reading of the Law," which for reasons that cannot be ascertained was inserted as a self-contained passage in Nehemiah 8–9. Thus the "Ezra Memoirs" (EM), the Book of Ezra proper, consists of Ezra 7–10 and Nehemiah 8–9.

The third unit, the "Nehemiah Memoirs" (NM), which corresponds to Nehemiah 1–7 and 10–13, relates the history of Nehemiah son of Hachaliah. Nehemiah, we are told (2:1), came to Jerusalem in the twentieth year of the reign of Artaxerxes I (445/44 B.C.E.), having been appointed governor of the province of Jehud (5:14–19). The presentation of the march of events suggests that Nehemiah returned to Persia in 433/32 after having served as governor for twelve years. A year later he came back to Jerusalem for a second term of office (13:6). Though the duration of this second term is not known, it seems likely that the period of Nehemiah ended about 420 B.C.E.

All three constituent blocks display a similar structure and, with one exception, are composed of the same four types of subunits:

1. In Ezra only, royal documents worded in Aramaic for the use of the Persian bureaucracy (4:17–23; 6:3–5, 6–12; 7:11–26) or in Hebrew for Judeans in the Diaspora (1:1–4).

2. Letters in a common epistolary style, written in Aramaic by Persian officials to the king (Ezra 4:8–16, 5:6–17) and in Hebrew in an exchange between Nehemiah and Sanballat, the governor of Samaria (Neh. 6:2–9).

3. Diverse lists, all in Hebrew, perhaps from Temple archives or the files of the provincial governors of Jehud: inventories of Temple vessels (Ezra 1:9–11, 8:24–28); rosters of returnees (Ezra 2:2–64 = Neh. 7:7–66; Ezra 8:1–14) and of those among them who had married "foreign wives" (Ezra 10:18–44); lists of the inhabitants of the resettled cities of Judah and Benjamin (Neh. 11:25–36) and of Jerusalem (11:3–24), of the builders of the city wall (3:1–32), and of the signatories to Nehemiah's covenant (10:1–27).

4. Passages of a cultic or devotional nature, such as the account of the reading of the Law (Neh. 8), the dedication ceremony of the city walls (12:27–43), and the celebration of the Passover festival (Ezra 6:19–22a). Especially significant is Ezra's confessional prayer (9:6–15), which is a forerunner of the later Jewish *widuy,* or public confession (Ezra 10:11); Nehemiah's invocation (1:5–11; compare Dan. 9:4–19); and the Levites' recitation after the reading of the Law (Neh. 9:5–37), which resembles the genre of the "historiographical psalm," such as Psalms 78, 105, and 106.

Structural Devices

The complex composition of Ezra–Nehemiah suggests an intricate and possibly multiphase process of literary structuring. A close reading of the text reveals some of the redactional techniques used and helps us trace the contours of originally independent components.

In Nehemiah's Memoirs, for example, the end of a topical unit is recurrently marked by the *closing invocation* "Remember me/them, O my God" (13:22, 29; 5:19; 6:14), which is also used to close the book as a whole (13:31).

Throughout Ezra–Nehemiah the extent of a textual unit is sometimes delineated by a *summary notation,* which recapitulates the major issues mentioned in that unit in a catalogue of catchphrases. Like the recapitulation of themes at the end of a musical composition, it produces a sense of significant closure. In its simplest form, such a notation occurs in Nehemiah 12:26, condensing the roster of priests and Levites named in 12:10–25 (see also 12:47 in respect to 12:44–46).

A more elaborate concluding formula appears in Ezra 4:4–5a, summarizing the obstacles hindering the returnees' efforts to rebuild the Temple: "Then the people of the land weakened the hands of the people of Judah, and troubled them in the building, And hired counsellors against

them, to frustrate their purpose." The first half of the summary recalls
3:3: "and they [could only] set the altar upon its bases, for fear was upon
them because of the people[s] of the land" [AR], while "[they] hired counsellors" presumably refers to "the adversaries of Judah and Benjamin"
who originally offered to participate in the building operations but became
"adversaries" when their offer was rejected (4:1–3). The summary in Ezra
4:4–5a enables us to recognize 3:2–4:3 as a textual unit. A similar instance
of summary notation appears in Ezra 6:13–14, recalling details reported
in the Aramaic account of the building of the Temple (5:1–6:12).

Most revealing is the tersely phrased catalogue of Nehemiah's reform
measures (13:29b–31a), lodged between the closing invocations (13:29a
and 31b) at the end of the book. Here, only matters mentioned in Nehemiah 10–13 are enumerated: those who "have defiled the priesthood" are
the priests who have intermarried with the house of Sanballat the Horonite
(13:28); "the covenant of the priesthood, and of the Levites" refers to
Nehemiah's reinstitution of the payment of dues to the cultic personnel
(10:36–39, 12:44); "thus cleansed I them from all strangers" recalls his
battle against marriages with "foreign women" (10:30; cf. 13:23–27); "[I]
appointed the watches of the priests and the Levites, each in his function"
[AR] relates to the restitution of the priestly and Levitical watchers who
served their turns in the Temple (12:44b–45; cf. 13–22); and "the wood
offering, at times appointed, and . . . the firstfruits" brings to mind the
corresponding provisions made in the covenant (10:35, 36, 39). Because
it echoes only matters described in chapters 10–12 and, to a lesser extent,
in chapter 13, the summary notation in Nehemiah 13:29b–31a supports a
prevalent hypothesis that chapters 10–13 should be viewed as an entity
separate from the rest of the Nehemiah Memoirs.

Another structural device, *resumptive repetition,* marks the extent of a
self-contained unit inserted in a longer passage: the resumption of the
original narrative interrupted by the insertion is indicated by the partial
repetition of the last verse before the insertion. In Ezra 4:6–24a, for
example, the cluster of "accusations" leveled against the returnees "all the
days of Cyrus king of Persia, even until the reign of Darius king of Persia"
(4:5b) is revealed as an insertion by the repetition of the latter part of this
statement in an Aramaic variant in 4:24b: "So it [the work of the Temple]
ceased unto the second year of the reign of Darius king of Persia." Likewise
Ezra 2:70 (= Neh. 7:73)—"the priests, and the Levites, and some of the
people . . . dwelt in their cities"—marks a resumption of the narrative
broken off at 2:1b (= Neh. 7:6b)—"Now these are the children of the
province that went up out of the captivity . . . and came again unto
Jerusalem and Judah, everyone unto his city"—and indicates that the "list
of returning exiles" (Ezra 2:1–70 = Neh. 7:7–70) was originally a separate
unit, subsequently inserted into EM and NM.

Biblical Historiography

All three units of Ezra and Nehemiah are representative examples of biblical historiography, characterized by straightforward prose narration. This genre was deliberately nurtured by the Hebrew writers, who deemed it more suitable for the recording of historical events than either the epic or the annals which predominated in the surrounding cultures of the ancient Near East, especially in Mesopotamia. Epic singers are bound by formulaic language, traditional motifs and themes, poetic parallelism of members, and other fixed structural devices. The epic mode mirrors a synthetic past, shot through with myth and legend. Prose narration, on the other hand, provides a stylistic flexibility which is indispensable in relating historical fact. Biblical historiography is not altogether free from elements of historicized fiction. This tendency toward fiction may reflect the influence of ancient Near Eastern myths and epic songs, especially on early biblical literature. But such influence diminishes appreciably in the post-Exilic period. By then the epic genre was waning in the Near East, and, saturated as it had been by pagan ideals, the repatriated exiles were hardly likely to incorporate it in their cultural heritage.

Although all three units of Ezra–Nehemiah adhere to straightforward historiographical prose narration, they progress from straight historical narrative in the Book of Zerubbabel, to partly historical and partly autobiographical narrative in the Ezra Memoirs, to predominantly autobiographical narrative in the Nehemiah Memoirs.

An example of this autobiographical genre, which may be considered an innovation of the post-Exilic period, occurs in Ezra's speech of thanksgiving to God for the decree he received from Artaxerxes:

> Blessed be the Lord God of our fathers, which hath put such a thing as this in the king's heart, to beautify the house of the Lord which is in Jerusalem: And hath extended mercy unto me before the king, and his counsellers, and before all the king's mighty princes. And I was strengthened as the hand of the Lord my God was upon me, and I gathered together out of Israel chief men to go up with me.   (7:27–28)

Nehemiah exhibits this autobiographical style from the very outset:

> And it came to pass in the month Chisleu, in the twentieth year, as I was in the citadel of Shushan [AR], that Hanani, one of my brethren, came, he and certain men of Judah; and I asked them concerning the Jews, the remnants that remained there [AR] of the captivity, and concerning Jerusalem. And they said unto me, The remnant that are left of the captivity there in the province are in great affliction and reproach: the wall of Jerusalem also is broken down, and the gates thereof are burned with fire. And it came to

pass, when I heard these words, that I sat down and wept, and mourned for [AR] days, and fasted, and prayed before the God of heaven. (1:1–4)

Thereupon follows the wording of Nehemiah's supplication (1:5–11).

The historical account in Ezra–Nehemiah is distinguished throughout by stylistic features that make for vivid biblical prose narration and set it off to advantage in comparison with the listlike Mesopotamian annals. Action predominates over description: verbs often outnumber nouns, adjectives, and adverbs. The resulting dramatic effect is heightened by the close temporal and spatial limits circumscribing the scene of action. Dialogue, as a form of "verbalized action" everywhere central in biblical narrative, is skillfully employed to enliven the continuous prose tale. A good example is Nehemiah's colloquy with some groups of poor citizens who complain about the heavy payments of interest exacted for loans from their richer compatriots (5:1–5). The dialogue is arranged in two corresponding series of speeches, moving from the bitter outcries of the totally destitute to the complaints of those who are suffering economic hardship but not yet dire poverty:

Round one	Round two
	First group
"We must pledge our sons and daughters so that we can buy corn, eat, and live." (v. 2 [AT])	"Yet now our flesh is as the flesh of our brethren, our children as their children: and, lo, we bring into bondage our sons and our daughters to be slaves [AR];" (v. 5a)
	Second group
"We have mortgaged our fields, vineyards, and houses, that we might buy corn, to save us from hunger." (v. 3 [AR])	"and some of our daughters are brought into bondage already, neither is it in our power to redeem them;" (v. 5b)
	Third group
"We have borrowed money for the king's tribute . . ." (v. 4a)	"for other men have our fields [AR] and vineyards." (v. 5b)

This verbal exchange prompts Nehemiah to rebuke the oppressors and make them swear to restore to the poor their fields, vineyards, and houses: "And the people did according to this promise" (5:13).

Another example of dialogue dynamically integrated into the plot is found in Nehemiah's report on his defense measures to ensure the safety of the inhabitants of Jerusalem:

When Sanballat, Tobiah, the Arabs, the Ammonites, and the Ashdodites heard that the walls of Jerusalem were being restored and the breaches being filled up, they fumed; and all conspired to come and attack Jerusalem and cause her harm. We prayed to our God and set a watch against them day and night. The Judeans [literally, Judah] said: "The strength of the carriers is failing and there is much rubble; we cannot build the wall." Our adversaries said: "They will not know nor notice until we come into their midst and slay them and stop the work." When the Judeans who lived among them came and told us ten times that they were planning to steal up against us, I stationed my men by families, armed with their swords, their lances, and their bows, opposite the open places, behind the wall, and on the ramparts.   (Neh. 4:7–13 [AT])

Once again, the dialogue advances the development of events by dramatically defining the stances of the participants. At the same time, it serves as a bridge between two sections of narrative.

Historical Scope

In its entirety Ezra–Nehemiah is generally regarded as a narrative compilation in which diverse documents and sources are inserted at appropriate junctures. This feature explains the discontinuity in the historical account, which covers approximately one century. Some sixty years between the end of the period of Zerubbabel (Ezra 6:18 or 22) and the return of Ezra (7:1–10) remain uncharted. There are probably further breaks between Ezra 2 and 3, and within chapter 3, which make it difficult to ascertain the chronological progress of events. The problem is compounded by the lack of any date at all for some events (for example, Ezra 2:1, 68 = Neh. 7:6, 73; Ezra 3:10; 4:1, 7, 8; 9:1; Neh. 4:1, 7, 15; 9:38; 11:1; 13:1) and the provision of only a month and a day for others (for example, Ezra 3:1, 4, 6, 8; 6:19; 9:15; Neh. 9:1). In only a few instances is an event dated by reference to the regnal year of a Persian king (for example, Ezra 1:1—compare 5:13—4:6; Neh. 5:14, 13:6), occasionally with the addition of the day and the month (for example, Ezra 6:15, 7:7–9; Neh. 1:1, 2:1). This lack of exactness and the stringing together of episodes in the text sometimes create the impression that one event follows directly upon another, whereas they may in fact have been chronologically quite remote from each other.

The impression of an immediate chronological sequence is intensified by the repeated use of the common biblical expressions "Now after these things" (Ezra 7:1), "Now when these things were done" (Ezra 9:1), and "And before this" (Neh. 13:4), with which the compiler links independent episodes. These terms, however, are simply formulaic literary connecting devices, rather than indications of true historical sequence.

The compiler of Ezra–Nehemiah recorded events of which he had immediate knowledge. In this respect, the difference from the earlier biblical historical books is noteworthy. The chronological limits are clearly set out in a summary notation which concludes the account of religious and societal regulations introduced or reinstituted by the leaders of that period: "And all Israel in the days of Zerubbabel, and in the days of Nehemiah, gave the portions of the singers and the porters, every day his portion" (Neh. 12:47). This notation is significantly preceded by a comprehensive roster ranging from "the priests and the Levites that went up with Zerubbabel the son of Shealtiel and Jeshua" (12:1) to those who officiated "in the days of Nehemiah the governor, and of Ezra the priest, the scribe" (12:26). Thus, even when the writer is reporting on the earliest phase of the return from the Exile (538–515 B.C.E.) the lapse of time between the actual occurrences and the time of writing in about 400 B.C.E. is probably the shortest in biblical historiography.

The chronological proximity of historical event to historical record puts certain restraints on the literary license of the compiler of Ezra–Nehemiah. Although his religious, social, and political convictions are certainly discernible in his exposition, his account still bears the stamp of factuality. The writer's influence is less evident in the selection and the coloring of historical facts reported than in the order of their presentation.

Because the compiler's audience also had immediate knowledge of the events reported and a sense of their intrinsic meaning or else had access to the same sources of information, the distance between reader and text would necessarily have contracted; the contemporary audience could identify with or seek to enter into and be entered into by the text. In this respect Ezra–Nehemiah differs both from the older narrative sequence that runs from Genesis to Kings and from the contemporaneous Book of Chronicles, in both of which personages and events are seen from a certain distance, through the strong mediation of tradition, folklore, and literary invention.

SUGGESTED FURTHER READINGS

L. J. Liebreich, "The Impact of Nehemiah 9:3–37 on the Liturgy of the Synagogue." *Hebrew Union College Annual,* 32 (1961), 227–237.

H. Lusseau, "Esdras and Nehemias," in André Robert and André Feuillet, eds., *Introduction to the Old Testament,* II, translated from the second French edition (New York, 1970), pp. 178–190.

Shemaryahu Talmon, "Ezra and Nehemiah (Books and Men)," in *The Interpreter's Dictionary of the Bible,* supp. vol. (New York and Nashville, 1976), pp. 317–328.

H. G. M. Williamson, "The Composition of Ezra I–IV," *Journal of Theological Studies,* 34 (1983), 1–30.

———, *Ezra, Nehemiah,* Word Biblical Commentary, 16 (Waco, Texas, 1985), pp. xxi–li.

Hebrew University of Jerusalem

1 and 2 Chronicles

Shemaryahu Talmon

CHRONICLES presents a survey of biblical history from the creation of the world to the destruction of the First Temple and the conquest of the Kingdom of Judah by the Babylonians in 586 B.C.E. Thus it parallels and on the whole depends upon the more detailed account contained in the first two components of the Hebrew Bible, the Pentateuch and the Former Prophets. Like other biblical historiographies, such as Joshua, Judges, Samuel, and Kings, Chronicles is made up of originally independent narrative sections of varying length. These sections, relating events in the lives of outstanding personalities, predominantly kings, were combined to form a connected chronological sequence. Into this framework of historical prose a variety of additional elements were inserted: lists (such as 1 Chron. 12:1–40; 15:4–10, 17–24; 23:3–27:34; 2 Chron. 17:14–18; 21:2–3; 31:2–3, 11–15), short prophetic tales (such as 2 Chron. 12:5–8; 15:1–7; 16:7–9; 20:37; 21:12–15; 25:7–8, 15–16; 28:9–11), poetic pieces of a psalmodic nature (such as 1 Chron. 16:8–36, 29:10–19; 2 Chron. 14:11, 20:21), and some orations (such as 2 Chron. 13:4–12; 20:5–12, 14–17; 29:4–11; 30:6–9). These insertions are missing in the parallel account in Samuel–Kings.

Altogether, Chronicles exhibits the chronological breadth which characterizes biblical historiography and is unequaled in the literatures of the ancient Near East or, for that matter, in the early postbiblical Hebrew writings. In the cultures of ancient Mesopotamia the prevailing literary genre was the annalistic form, which covered a restricted period of time by recording historical events in the form of terse notations arranged in dockets. We may have allusions to this historiographic roster in the references to "the book of the chronicles of the kings of Media and Persia" (Esther 10:2; see also 2:23, 6:1), "the chronicles of King David" (1 Chron. 27:24), and "the book of the acts of Solomon" (1 Kings 11:41). The very comprehensiveness of the biblical historiographies invites a comparison with the great works of history known from the classical world, with which they served as prototypes for later historians.

Content

Chronicles centers on the Davidic dynasty and the religious and socio-political constitution of the kingdom of Judah. Only passing reference is made to the history of the Northern Kingdom (Ephraim-Samaria). In this presentation King David, his heir King Solomon, and Mount Zion with its Temple overshadow Moses, who, with Mount Sinai, predominates in the biblical traditions about Israel's early days. A similar shift of emphasis is observable in many psalms which extol the greatness of the Davidic house and of Jerusalem. It is possibly this similarity in outlook that prompted the Chronicler to adorn his work with pieces of cultic poetry culled from the Book of Psalms: 1 Chronicles 16:8–36 = Psalms 105:1–15 + 96:1–13a + 106:1, 47–48. It is of interest that a short quotation from Psalms 132:8–10 in 2 Chronicles 6:41–42 is not found in the parallel version of Solomon's prayer in 1 Kings 8.

The Chronicler's attitude toward the house of David is apparent when his account of Israel's history in the First Temple period deviates from the mostly parallel account in Samuel–Kings: he omits all references to David's rebellious war against Saul and to his alliance with the Philistines, whereas in Samuel both events are recounted in great detail (1 Sam. 19:18–26:25, 27:1–29:11). Similarly, there is no mention in Chronicles of David's dispute with Nabal the Carmelite or of Nabal's rather mystifying death, after which David married his widow, Abigail (1 Sam. 25:1–42). Likewise omitted is the tale of David's illicit affair with Bathsheba, the wife of Uriah the Hittite (2 Sam. 11:2–12:25), though there is brief reference to the wider context of Israel's war against the Ammonites (1 Chron. 20:1–3). In Samuel the Bathsheba episode constitutes a self-contained unit inserted into the more comprehensive battle report, as is clear from the envelope structure (2 Sam. 11:1 and 12:26–31). Therefore, the Chronicler could easily drop this piece of court intrigue without disrupting the flow of his narrative.

The entire string of stories relating to the succession is missing: the murder of David's son Amnon by Absalom (2 Sam. 13), the latter's rebellion and death (2 Sam. 15:1–18:18), the court cabal which led to the enthroning of Solomon (1 Kings 1:11–40) and to the execution of his rival Adonijah (1 Kings 2:13–25). There is no reference to David's testament to Solomon (1 Kings 2:1–9) nor to incidents which occurred early in Solomon's reign partly as a result of the implementation of that will: the execution of Joab (1 Kings 2:28–46) for his slaying of Abner ben Ner, commander of Saul's army, which David himself had been unable to avenge (2 Sam. 3:26–39); and the death of Shimei ben Gera the Benjaminite (1 Kings 2:36–46), who had sided with Absalom in his abortive rebellion against David (2 Sam. 16:6–12). Nothing is said of Solomon's taking in marriage foreign women from neighboring nations nor of the cultic high

places which he built for them. These deeds are most critically viewed in
1 Kings 3:1–2 and 11:1–10, where they are seen to have precipitated the
rebellions that marred the end of Solomon's reign and to have sparked
the internal strife that after his death led to the division of Israel into two
separate kingdoms (1 Kings 11:11–12:20).

Chronicles is not, however, simply a parallel version of Samuel–Kings
that edits out court intrigues and other material critical of the monarchs.
There are also significant additions and alterations. For example, 1 Chronicles 23–28 describes in great detail David's preparations for the building
of the Temple; in contrast, Kings credits Solomon with the entire operation (1 Kings 6:1–9:1; compare 2 Chron. 3:1–7:10), after David is prevented by divine command from carrying out his building plans (2 Sam.
7). The divine intervention is significantly muted in Chronicles (1 Chron.
29:1, 2 Chron. 2:2–6). The Chronicler also gives an account of a campaign
mounted by Pharaoh Shishak against Solomon (2 Chron. 12:9–12) which
finds no mention in Kings. Equally, Kings contains no evidence for a
cultic reform instituted by Hezekiah, which the Chronicler describes extensively (2 Chron. 29–31). The Chronicler seems to imply that he has
culled the additional information from one of the many sources to which
he refers (discussed below).

Given this pronounced orientation toward the Davidic dynasty and
the Southern Kingdom, it is not surprising that the Septuagint entitled
Chronicles *to paraleipomena tōn basileōn Iouda,* "miscellanies concerning the
kings of Judah."[1]

Historical Scope

The Chronicler records only relatively remote history. He deals with
nothing more recent than the conquest of Jerusalem by the Babylonians
in 586 B.C.E., some two centuries before his own time. The only exceptions to this retrospective framework are the collection of genealogies
relating to the post-Exilic generations and the reference to the onset of
the Persian period appended at 2 Chron. 36:22–23.

Since the Chronicler's audience was as far removed as himself from
the events he reports, he was not subject to the literary restraints imposed
by a directly involved and knowledgeable readership. He had considerable
latitude in the arrangement of events and in the adjustment of their presentation to his own historical and theological outlook. The resulting gap
between the historical facts and their presentation probably did not escape
the notice of his audience. It could well be that precisely to bridge this
gap, the Chronicler, more than any other biblical writer, profusely and
ostentatiously cites otherwise unknown works (the total runs to about
twenty), stating explicitly that they served him as source material for his

full-scale survey of the history of Judah (1 Chron. 11:1–2 Chron. 36:21). This is in marked contrast to the historiographic approach of Ezra–Nehemiah, which makes no attempt to establish the credibility of the account by referring to earlier histories only by their titles. There, by contrast, relevant sources are quoted verbatim and lists, documents, and official reports are incorporated into the narrative.

Some of the earlier Hebrew works referred to in Chronicles appear to be of a historiographic nature. They may be identical with or similar to those cited in Kings: "the book of the kings of Israel" (1 Chron. 9:1; 2 Chron. 20:34, 33:18; compare, for example, 1 Kings 14:19; 15:31; 16:14, 20, 27), "the book of the kings of Judah and Israel" (2 Chron. 16:11, 25:26, 32:32), or "the book of the kings of Israel and Judah" (2 Chron. 27:7, 35:27, 36:8). It is likely that all these titles designate the same work. Other purported source-texts are ascribed to prophetic authors: the books of "Samuel the seer" and "Gad the seer" (1 Chron. 29:29), "Nathan the prophet" (1 Chron. 29:29, 2 Chron. 9:29), "Shemaiah the prophet" and "Iddo the seer" (2 Chron. 12:15), and "Jehu the son of Hanani" (2 Chron. 20:34). There is reference to "the prophecy of Ahijah the Shilonite" (2 Chron. 9:29) and to "the vision of Isaiah the prophet, the son of Amoz" (2 Chron. 32:32), who also is reported to have written "the rest of the acts of Uzziah" (2 Chron. 26:22). These latter writings cannot be identified with the canonical Book of Isaiah. It may be assumed that all these prophetic tracts, which are sometimes mentioned side by side (as in 1 Chron. 29:29; 2 Chron. 9:29, 12:15), were parts of a comprehensive collection entitled "sayings of the seers" (2 Chron. 33:19).

Of special interest are two works which bear the heading *midrash*: "the story [*midrash*] of the prophet Iddo" (2 Chron. 13:22), whose "book" is mentioned in 2 Chron. 9:29 and 12:15, and "the *midrash* of the book of the kings" (2 Chron. 24:27). These may be alternative titles for the above-mentioned "book of Iddo the seer" and "book of the kings of Israel (and Judah)," respectively. The term *midrash*, which in later times came to refer to a specific genre of rabbinic exegetical literature, is sometimes understood in this context as mere fiction and taken to disclose the imaginary character of the Chronicler's sources and, consequently, the spuriousness of his entire work. But this type of biblical "narrative midrash" may be considered a forerunner of the rabbinic *midrash aggadah*, an authentic literary genre, just as the apparent examples of "legal midrash" in Ezra–Nehemiah may be seen to foreshadow the rabbinic *midrash halakhah*. (See the essay on Ezra and Nehemiah in this volume.)

Structure

The book is made up of two main parts—1 Chronicles 1–9 and 1 Chronicles 11:1–2 Chronicles 36:21—which are distinguished from each other by both content and genre. They are best discussed in reverse order. The second part, which concerns the history of the Davidic kingdom, parallels the historical account in 2 Samuel 1:1–2 Kings 25:17. Within this section are three large segments: the accounts of David's reign (1 Chron. 11–29), of Solomon's reign (2 Chron. 1–9), and of the reigns of the kings of Judah until the destruction of Jerusalem and the Temple (2 Chron. 10:1–36:21). There is no parallel to 2 Kings 25:18–30, which relates events after the destruction of the Temple.

This entire complex is preceded by a compilation of various genealogical lists and episodes (1 Chron. 1:1–9:44) which provide a comprehensive but condensed history of Israel from the antediluvian ancestors to the establishment of the monarchy. In its entirety this section parallels the far more detailed history contained in the Pentateuch and the Former Prophets. The genealogy begins with the forefathers of mankind and culminates in the early days of the monarchy: Samuel and his sons (6:28), Saul and his progeny (8:33–9:39), and David and his offspring (3:1–9). Occasionally, however, the records extend into Exilic and post-Exilic times (for example, 3:10–24; 5:23–26; 9:1–34 = Neh. 11). Such references prove that the final redaction occurred in the late Persian or the early Hellenistic period.

This genealogical compilation focuses on the tribes of Judah (including Simeon) and Benjamin, which together formed the nucleus of the Persian province of Jehud in the post-Exilic age. Another indication of this orientation is the inclusion of Edomite genealogical records (1:34–54; cf. Gen. 36:1–43), Edom, to all intents and purposes, having been merged with Jehud at that time.

The individual items in this section are derived in part from the Pentateuch and from Joshua and Ruth (see 1 Chron. 2:11–12 and possibly 4:22). But certain elements, such as the census lists and battle reports in 1 Chronicles 4:19–23, 38–43 and 5:1–26, are otherwise unknown. Their presence suggests that the compiler of the genealogical rosters, and indirectly the Chronicler, had access to sources of information not tapped by earlier biblical writers. Such sources, however, are not explicitly mentioned in this section, in contrast to the historical account (1 Chron. 11:1–2 Chron. 36:21), where they abound. Consisting of strings of genealogies interspersed with a few episodic tales, 1 Chronicles 1–9 portrays history as a series of static pictures, and thus lacks the dynamism in which biblical historiography generally excels and which is apparent in the rest of Chronicles and in Ezra–Nehemiah.

The two parts of Chronicles are connected by a cluster of notations and brief records concerning King Saul. These commence in 1 Chronicles 9:35–44 with a repetition of Saul's genealogy, already recorded in 8:29–40. There follows a report of Saul's last days, a slightly paraphrased version of the parallel account in 1 Samuel dealing with his defeat at the hands of the Philistines, his death and the death of his sons (1 Chron. 10:1–7), and the burial of their corpses by the men of Jabesh-Gilead (10:8–12; cf. 1 Sam. 31:8–13). A summary notation (see the Glossary and the essay on Ezra and Nehemiah) refers to the "Witch of Endor" episode (cf. 1 Sam. 28:3–25), culminating in the divine announcement of the transfer of kingship from Saul to David (1 Chron. 10:14b): "So Saul died for his transgression which he committed against the Lord, even against the word of the Lord, which he kept not, and also for asking counsel of a necromancer [AR]; And inquired not of the Lord: therefore he slew him, and turned the kingdom unto David the son of Jesse" (= 1 Sam. 28:17).

Together these notations form a transition between the genealogical records of the premonarchical era and the extensive account of the history of Judah and the Davidic dynasty. This compositional bridge demonstrates the skillful use of literary techniques and conventions to weld a variety of sources into one coherent framework and thus present "the chronicle of the whole sacred history" (as Jerome called it; see note 1).

Authorship and Date of Composition

No author or compiler is named in the book. Rabbinic tradition considers most of Chronicles, together with Ezra–Nehemiah, to have been written by Ezra and completed by Nehemiah. This attribution reflects the prominence accorded to Ezra the scribe, whom the Jewish Sages viewed as a second Moses. Many modern Old Testament scholars likewise attribute Ezra–Nehemiah and Chronicles to one author, generally to the unnamed compiler of Chronicles. However, differences in historical outlook, language, and style between Ezra–Nehemiah and Chronicles make the presumed common authorship questionable. The scholarly debate on this issue persists.

Although some scholars would date the composition of Chronicles to the Hellenistic era (300–200 B.C.E.), prevailing opinion holds that the book achieved its final form in Persian times, in the first or, at the latest, the second half of the fourth century. The Chronicler's almost exclusive interest in the history of the kingdom of Judah in the First Temple period is seen as a reflection of the actual situation of the community of repatriated exiles, which was comprised entirely of former Judeans and Benjaminites (see, for example, Ezra 1:5, 2:1, 4:1, 10:9; Neh. 4:10; 7:6; 11:4, 7, 25). These were citizens of the Persian province Jehud (Ezra 5:1, 8; 7:14, cf. Dan. 2:25, 5:13, 6:13), that is, *Jehudim* (see, for example, Neh. 1:2; 4:1; 5:1, 8, 17; 6:6; 11:3, 4, 25; 13:23; cf. Esther 2:5; 3:4, 6, 10, 13; 4:13, 16) or Aramaic *Jehudaje* (Ezra 4:12, 23; 5:1, 5; 6:7, 8, 14; cf. Dan. 3:8, 12), translated "Jews." Likewise, the Chronicler's silence regarding the history of the Northern Kingdom in the same period can be taken to indicate his opposition to the erstwhile Samarians whom the returnees encountered in the Land and refused to admit into their body politic (Ezra 4:1–3). His preoccupation with genealogies and family rosters discloses a concern to ensure that all members of the "reconstituted Israel" could prove their Israelite, or rather, Judean-Benjaminite, descent (see Ezra 2:59 = Neh. 7:61). Lineage was of special significance where cultic personnel were concerned (see Ezra 2:61–63 = Neh. 7:63–65).

Place in the Canon

In most manuscripts and printed editions of the Hebrew Bible, Chronicles closes the canon and immediately follows Ezra–Nehemiah. Chronologically, however, Ezra–Nehemiah is a sequel to Chronicles: the latter concludes by quoting the decree of Cyrus (2 Chron. 36:22–23), and Ezra opens with the same text (1:1–3a). And indeed, in some medieval manuscripts, significantly the famous tenth-century Aleppo Codex, Ezra–Nehemiah comes at the end of the canon while Chronicles is the first book in the collection of the "Writings" (Hagiographa). This same order is possibly reflected in the apocryphal Book of Ezra, which begins with an account of the reigns of the last kings of Judah (1 Esdras 1:1–55, paralleling 2 Chron. 35:1–36:21). Thereupon follows the text of Cyrus' decree and the report on the first stage of the return (1 Esdras 2:1–14), an almost word-for-word translation of chapter 1 of the canonical Book of Ezra.

It is likely that these traditions preserve the original arrangement. At some stage in transmission, Chronicles was transposed and became the last book in the Hebrew canon. Then the opening verses of Ezra were appended to it. This resumptive repetition (see the essay on Ezra and Nehemiah) served as a signpost, alerting readers to the proper chronological sequence: Chronicles, Ezra–Nehemiah. We may assume that, like the Fifth Book of Moses, which recapitulates salient parts of the Tetrateuch and therefore came to be known as "Deuteronomium" or "second law" (Hebrew, *mishneh torah*), Chronicles was considered a "Deutero-Biblia," indeed, "the chronicle of the whole sacred history." Tradition made it then the finale of the Hebrew Bible.

NOTE

1. Chronicles is called *dibre hayamim* in Hebrew, that is "events of the times" (*or* "days"), *libri paralipomenorum* in Latin. Its modern name derives from the title "Chronicon totius divinae historiae," used by Jerome in his *Prologus galeatus*.

SUGGESTED FURTHER READINGS

R. L. Braun, "Chronicles, Ezra and Nehemiah: Theology and Literary History," *Vetus Testamentum,* supp. vol. XXX (Leiden, 1979), 52–64.
J. M. Meyers, *I Chronicles,* Anchor Bible, XII (New York, 1965), xvi–lxiii.

R. H. Pfeiffer, "Chronicles, I and II," in *The Interpreter's Dictionary of the Bible,* I (New York and Nashville, 1962), 572–580.

H. Lusseau, "The Books of Paralipomenon or the Chronicles," in André Robert and André Feuillet, eds., *Introduction to the Old Testament,* II, translated from the second French edition (New York, 1970), pp. 191–206.

Hebrew University of Jerusalem

THE
NEW TESTAMENT

Introduction to the
New Testament

Frank Kermode

THE Introduction to the New Testament is recognized by biblical
scholarship as a genre in its own right; the typical and authoritative
modern Introduction of W. G. Kümmel contains a history of the genre
since the Enlightenment.[1] The purpose of such works is to give an account
of the formation of each of the constituent books and of their interrela-
tions, together with a history of their collection into a canon. The literary
criticism characteristic of the Introduction is of the kind which concerns
itself with sources, or with the prehistory of literary forms found in the
New Testament. The chronological sequence of the books is a matter of
importance; for instance, an author may treat the Pauline Epistles first
because they were the earliest to be written. The relations between the
four Gospels, and especially between Matthew, Mark, and Luke, are a
perennial concern.

Such Introductions have over the past two centuries served many
different historical and theological presuppositions, none of which is particularly germane to the present enterprise, though some of the problems
encountered by more orthodox introducers recur in our more literary
approaches, especially in relation to the Gospels.

What is a gospel? Mark announces in his opening verse that his book
is "the gospel of Jesus Christ." The Greek, *to evangelion,* means "the good
news" and was used of imperial proclamations. Before the Gospels were
written the gospel was presumably an oral proclamation of the teaching
and the resurrection of Jesus—the sense in which Paul uses the word, as
in I Corinthians 4:15 ("I have begotten you through the gospel," *dia tou
evangeliou*). But after Mark wrote his book the word acquired another
sense, for the book itself became *a* gospel. Traditionally the four canonical
examples of the genre were known as "the Gospel according to Mark,
Matthew, etc."; but by the second century the word "gospel" is found in
the plural, indicating that people were no longer thinking of the four
merely as different versions of one gospel, but as four Gospels. There
were certainly many more than four, but only four were received, and
it is from them, and not from surviving apocryphal works which bear

the name of gospels, that we derive our sense of what sort of book a gospel is.

New literary genres are continually formed from existing ones. We should have difficulty in understanding any book which bore no family resemblance to any other; we need, as it were, to take our bearings from the known, which will provide us not so much with an exact pattern as with a norm enabling us to understand both what is familiar and what is original in the new work. Many conjectures have been offered as to the antecedents of the Gospels. Some say they derive from Hellenistic forms such as the aretology, or life of a divinely endowed man, or the *bios,* about great men more generally; others propose a Jewish archetype.[2] What seems clear is that the Gospels were shaped by a need to record in writing something of the life and teaching of Jesus; existing ways of writing biography would affect the ways in which this could be done without compelling them to be in any formal sense biographies. Mixtures of narrative and lawgiving were, after all, familiar enough from the Old Testament, to which all the Gospels continually refer; much of their narrative is built upon it, as is much of their doctrine. The way they use Jewish techniques—of scriptural rewriting, of parable, and so on—might well, given the cultural dominance of Greek, be affected by Greek styles and forms, but the first readers or hearers would understand them as products of ways of writing they already knew, however ad hoc the new combinations. Their appropriateness to what in time showed itself to be a new religion, growing away from the Judaic origins, is shown by the divergence, soon to be obvious, between rabbinic and Christian uses of the Hebrew Bible.

It is of course very difficult for modern readers to imagine themselves in the position of a first-century Jew or Christian, or to understand in what sense the Christian dependence on the Hebrew Bible resembled and differed from the Jewish.[3] The resemblances include a shared belief that biblical texts contained mysteries and prophecies; there were messianic texts, and the two parties might not agree exactly what they were, but both assumed their existence. The coming of the Messiah would at last make the Torah plain; but whereas the Jews waited for that event, the Christians had already experienced it, and one purpose of their Gospels was precisely to show the Torah clearly, not through a glass darkly. There is a very great difference between the way one sees the past, its events and its promises, from a point of view close to the end of time—the point of view of first-century Christians—and the way one sees it when fulfillment is still in the future. Early Christian writing has the ends of the world upon it. Hence its emphasis on fulfillment, fullness of time; the shape of the world-plot can now be seen. The Old Testament types are crowned by their antitypes—Moses by Jesus, Melchizedek by Christ. The Law is transformed; and the New Testament contains much discussion of the differences that grew up between those who wanted it observed in its literal and those who adopted its spiritual form. Paul expresses very boldly the typological sense of the Mosaic narrative: our fathers "were all baptized unto Moses in the cloud and in the sea . . . and did all drink the same spiritual drink: for they drank of that spiritual Rock that followed them: and that Rock was Christ" (1 Cor. 10:2–4). And he contrasts the new covenant (Greek *diathēkē,* also "testament") with the old—the spirit that gives life against the letter that kills. Moses, he says, was veiled because the Israelites could not bear "the glory of his countenance," but although unconverted Jews still read "the old testament" with "the same vail untaken away," Christians know it is "done away in Christ" (2 Cor. 3:6–14). And although there is no comparably explicit announcement in the Gospels, these statements give us a sense of the manner in which the evangelists, each in his own way, approached their main source—how they read their Bible.

Matthew's Jesus preaches the Law transformed and fulfilled, though without the abatement of one jot or tittle of it. And Matthew seems to have had most authority in the early Church, supplanting Mark; and his continued primacy is witnessed by the Anglican liturgy, which nearly always chooses its lections from Matthew rather than from Mark, no doubt in part because Matthew records many more sayings (so, for that matter, does Luke).[4] Augustine notoriously described Mark as the follower and abbreviator of Matthew, and this view largely prevailed for many centuries. And here we are confronted by the "Synoptic problem": what is the relation between the first three Gospels? Which came first, and so was closer to the historical realities?

Discrepancies between the Gospels were noticed very early, but the main effort of scholars was to bring them into harmony. It was only in 1776 that J. J. Griesbach produced a synopsis of the three, setting them out in parallel columns to facilitate the study of mutual dependence and difference. Since then they have come to be known as the Synoptic Gospels. No one doubts that they are intimately related, but the exact nature of that relationship is extremely difficult to determine, and it remains a topic of subtle controversy. Very little in the way of new evidence can be expected, and there seems no end to the possible interpretations of the internal relations of the three texts. The main argument is about whether Mark or Matthew came first. Beginning in the 1830s the view gained ground that priority must be accorded to Mark, and it is probably still the majority opinion that Matthew and Luke used Mark, augmenting him from a collection of sayings (Q) and also from sources peculiar to themselves; there are many variants of this view. Recently, however, inconsistencies and improbabilities in the standard explanation have led to a revival of the old assumption that Matthew came first. Other scholars retain the Marcan priority but dispense with Q. Fortunately the purposes of the present volume do not require us to decide between competing opinions. Disagreements among the contributors declare themselves only rarely, and in unimportant ways; for example, John Drury, who writes on Luke, does not believe in Q, whereas James Robinson, writing on Acts, does; but although they are talking about the work of the same author the disagreement creates no dissonance in what they say. In the few cases in which there was an expository need to back one side or the other we have accepted the priority of Mark; that is, we assume Matthew and Luke to have been dependent upon Mark, whatever else they may have used. And we take John to have been largely independent, though he probably knew Luke.

However, our main purpose in mentioning these matters is to emphasize that they are not as important to us as they are to the writers of formal Introductions and to practitioners of traditional historical criticism. Their concern is inevitably with hypothetical forerunners, lost documents underlying the ones we possess, or perhaps with preliterary forms inherited by the evangelists and incorporated into the Gospels at a later time. Emphasis on such inheritances is less exclusive than it once was, for there has of late been much more attention to the evangelists as writers, as individuals with their own social and theological settings and interests. Here our prime interest is in what they wrote, and in the relation of what they wrote to the whole of the book in which they find themselves.

In considering these questions we have again to remind ourselves that the Bible of the New Testament writers was the Hebrew Bible (and its Greek and Aramaic translations and paraphrases). Upon this founding text was superimposed a strong oral *kerygma*, the Christian proclamation, but the Scriptures, the written foundation, were especially important to the evangelists as writers. With them they were supplementing the oral tradition (which was given precedence well into the second century); they did not suppose themselves to be writing Scripture (the author of Revelation is a late exception). Their attitude to the Bible must have been that, properly interpreted, it would confirm the oral tradition, which they knew to be true, since the Torah was also absolutely true for all time. There must accordingly be harmony between old and new. Their habit of reading would in some ways have closely resembled that of the Qumran community, which, as we know it from the Dead Sea Scrolls, interpreted Scripture as having an intimate and immediate application to its own concerns. From the Scriptures the early Christians could infer the only possible ways in which the career of Jesus could be described. The Old Testament therefore shapes the narratives of the New, which cannot be fully understood without reference to its sacred predecessor.

The modernity of the applications made by the evangelists is indicated by their probable use of the codex instead of the scroll; the codex—its leaves arranged quite like those of a modern book—was up-to-date, a businessman's aid to easy reference, whereas the biblical scroll, venerated not only for its contents but also as a physical object, had a time-defeating permanance.[5] Yet the modern record of the codex had to comply with the message of the ancient scroll.

Given these assumptions, and the certainty that the Old Testament contained meanings that time and interpretation would reveal (with the corollary that whatever time revealed must be detectable by interpretation in the Old Testament), it is not difficult to see that although the evangelists wrote under some common constraints there was plenty of scope for the exercise of personal preference and individual talent. It is particularly obvious that John has his own interests, his own manner; he is so different from the others that some have wanted to deny his book the title of a Gospel. The story of Nicodemus and the account of the raising of Lazarus, for example, are very different from anything in the Synoptics; the long discourses of John's Jesus are totally different from Matthew's Sermon on the Mount. But even the Synoptics, despite the family resemblances, have their own predilections and idiosyncrasies; one need think only of the way Matthew tones down what is in Mark fierce and abrupt, as in the account of Jesus' visit to his home town (Mark 6, Matt. 13) or the explanation of the purpose of the parables (Mark 4, Matt. 13). These may be attributed to varying theological attitudes; but they are also differences of personal style.

For example, the Synoptics all attach evident importance to the Temptation in the Wilderness (Mark 1:13, Matt. 4:1–11, Luke 4:1–13), which intervenes between the baptism of Jesus and the beginning of his ministry. It is a kind of initiation, a threshold experience; John does not have it, but his account of the first Cana miracle serves a similar end. Mark allows the Temptation only one verse (1:13), though that verse includes the information that the time in the wilderness was forty days, that Jesus was with wild beasts, and that he was tempted by Satan. Matthew leaves out the beasts but extends the narrative, specifying three temptations (to turn stones into bread, to throw himself off the pinnacle of the Temple, to receive the kingdoms of the world) and recording three refusals, all in the form of texts from Deuteronomy. Luke also recounts three temptations, spreading them over the forty days instead of having them all at the end, as Matthew does. He alters the order of the temptations, putting the challenge of the pinnacle last. And he says more than Matthew about the devil's departure from the scene: "when the devil had ended all the temptation, he departed from him until an opportune time [AR]" (4:13).

Mark is terse and mysterious; Matthew and Luke here give him narrative expansion. Matthew's version represents the testing of the second Israel in the same wilderness as the first (it *must* follow that pattern). Luke's expansion is partly a product of his more highly developed narrative sense: he places the most violent and desperate of the temptations last. He also links this episode to the larger narrative plot of the book, predicting the next, the conclusive, encounter with Satan that must follow in its due season. After his ordeal Luke's Jesus returns "in the power of the Spirit into Galilee" (4:14), ready to begin his ministry. We may note by the way that Luke's expression "all the temptation" or "every temptation" (*panta peirasmon*) had its effect outside the limits of his Gospel, for it was taken to mean that Jesus, having suffered every conceivable temptation, was a model for tempted Christians (cf. Heb. 2:18, James 1:12).

Matthew and Luke do not invariably extend Mark—indeed they often reduce him. But here is a relatively simple instance of narrative expansion. Mark's germinal episode is enlarged; Matthew has three temptations, folktale style, and Luke improves on Matthew's order, strengthens the narrative connection of the episode to the whole story, and emphasizes not only the initiatory aspect of the ordeal but also its exemplary character.

Narrative is of course not the only concern of the Gospels, but it is a very important one. It is almost impossible to imagine a gospel without narrative (we cannot really think of the so-called Gospel of Thomas, a collection of sayings and parables that turned up at Nag Hammadi in 1945–46 as a gospel, any more than Q, if it existed, was a gospel). Indeed it is impossible to imagine a totally nonnarrative Christianity or a nonnarrative Judaism or indeed a nonnarrative life. We have also seen that a first-century Christian narrative could not have been constructed independently of the Hebrew Bible. As the example above suggests, the narrative impulse took individual forms, and the evangelists enjoyed a considerable measure of compositional freedom in the invention and disposition of narrative elements. One more instance of variation between the Synoptics will emphasize this point.

The story of the demoniac of Gerasa is common to Mark, Matthew, and Luke (Mark 5:1–20, Matt. 8:28–34, Luke 8:26–39). Mark tells it immediately before the anecdote of the raising up of Jairus' daughter and the interpolated narrative about the cure of the woman with an issue of blood (5:21–43). Just as the story of the woman is inserted between the beginning and the end of the story of the girl, the story of the demoniac is placed between that double episode and another, the stilling of the storm (4:35–41); so it is the middle member of the triad of tales about the divine power over nature and death. Mark often uses this device of intercalation—it is probably the most conspicuous structural principle in his Gospel.[6] By saving the little girl from death and returning the diseased woman to adult normality, the supernatural orders the natural in human life, as it orders the rest of creation when the storm is stilled. In between, the madman is saved from spiritual disorder, demoniac possession. The demoniac's narrative is elaborate. The demons recognize Jesus as the Son of God (they, and they alone, always do in Mark). They give the man enormous strength; nothing can bind him, he roams among the tombs, crying out and bruising himself with stones. When the demons are expelled he is no longer savage and naked but civil and clothed. The Gerasenes, alarmed by this display of power, urge Jesus to leave their district.

The story affords several parallels with that of the woman with an issue of blood. A divine power proceeds out of Jesus to cure the woman, a demoniac power leaves the stricken man; he is restored to normality after suffering a diseased excess of male violence, she from a disorder related to female sexuality. The girl also provides an antithesis to the demoniac. She is the daughter of a ruler of the synagogue, whereas the madman is a Gentile; and they inhabit opposite sides of the lake, which the Gerasene is not permitted to cross. All these parallelisms and intercalations are characteristic of Mark, and to work them out he needs space. Matthew, with his different aims, seems to have been uneasy about Mark's telling of the demoniac's story. He has two demoniacs, and they are described as merely "fierce"—there is no detail of chains and self-bruising. He omits Mark's memorable line, "My name is Legion, for we are many." Matthew does not say the Gerasene townsfolk came out to see the cured demoniac; and his demoniac does not ask to be allowed to accompany Jesus. It seems that Matthew at this point is not interested in vivid narrative. It is as if he is content to record this piece of tradition and pass on. So, too, with the raising of Jairus' daughter (Mark 5:38–43, Matt. 9:23–26, Luke 8:51–56). Mark, with a storyteller's desire for verisimilitude, gives us the Aramaic command, *talitha cumi*; but Matthew omits it. Luke follows Mark rather more closely, but even he cannot accept the bold saying "My name is Legion, for we are many"; he substitutes "for many devils were entered into him." Like Matthew, Luke omits the detail that the woman with the hemorrhage had spent all her money on physicians; but some ancient authority, seeking harmony between the accounts, put it in, which is why the King James Version still makes Luke (traditionally known as "the physician") include a detail that only Mark did not think too trivial to mention.

What this demonstrates is that Matthew and Luke were aware of (perhaps disapproved of) some of the peculiarities of Mark's narrative style and found them unsuited to their different literary purposes. Possibly Matthew was looking for economies in narrative to allow himself more space for sayings. In any case he seems to have felt free to make what changes he pleased, and perhaps put in two demoniacs to balance the pair of blind men (9:27–31), as Michael Goulder has proposed.[7] To each his own manner.

Mark represents the point at which the oral tradition was first challenged by the written; and it has been persuasively argued that the conditions of oral and script transmission differ so greatly that Mark's Gospel institutes a critical change in the early history of Christian teaching and narrative.[8] Nevertheless it retains some of the style and the vivacity of oral story. Oral tradition is essential to all accounts of the life of Jesus; but each unit of the tradition may be differently valued and given a different setting in the whole. John, for example, whatever his access to the preliterary tradition, is more selective than the Synoptics, and more artificial, if that word can still be used in a eulogistic sense. As one sees from the story of Nicodemus, he likes to give a structural value to what might be simply a disconnected episode. The raising of Lazarus is quite unlike the raising of the daughter of Jairus, since it has an important function in the plot of the Gospel as a whole. The manner in which they assemble the pre-Passion material is a good indication of the differences among the four writers.

The remainder of the story—the Passion narrative—rests much more heavily on scriptural references. It has been calculated that the last five chapters of Mark contain 57 quotations from, and 160 allusions to, the Old Testament, not to mention 60 places where there is influence from the Old Testament.[9] We must suppose then that the preliterary versions of the Passion narrative had their origins in written Scripture, even if they reached script via oral recitation. How much credit for the composition of the first written Passion narrative should go to Mark cannot be determined; some think a separate account of the Passion existed beforehand. The broad outlines of the four accounts are very similar, but there are important variations; and this is what one would expect, for the writers who exercised such freedom in the handling of the pre-Passion material would assume certain liberties in the narrative interpretation of the Old Testament testimonies, liberties for which there were precedents in the Jewish narrative tradition. What is remarkable is that the vivid realism of the stories is not affected by their dependence upon another book, namely the Hebrew Bible. The writers practiced what is sometimes called "protomidrash." Midrash updated the old stories, adjusted them to the need of the moment; properly speaking it was practiced only later, but the habit of mind that produced midrash certainly existed earlier. A simple instance of the practice is the story of the birth of Jesus, differently told by Matthew and Luke. Here they had to work without guidance from Mark, who starts the whole story at what was for him its beginning, namely the baptism. So Matthew and Luke each constructed his own quite distinct version of the circumstances surrounding the birth of the divine child, drawing freely on Old Testament texts. There was no difference in their view between the truth and figures of the truth derived from a divine source; each makes his selection from that source and molds it according to his own bent.

The literary relations of the Gospels to the Old Testament are as close and intimate as any that one can imagine between two texts. In establishing this intimacy the evangelists not only authenticated their story but discovered its materials. In constructing a realistic, historylike narrative in such an unusual way they created a distinctive genre; and in terms of that genre they produced unique works of art.

THE ACTS OF THE APOSTLES, though it is Luke's second volume and a sequel to his Gospel, does not belong to that genre. That it is separated from the Gospel of Luke by the Fourth Gospel is significant; the four belonged together, and had to be kept together, even at the cost of splitting Luke's work in two. There is a sense in which the Gospels could be described as propaganda, but Acts is much more obviously propagandistic. In describing the action of the Holy Spirit through Paul and Peter as it was expressed in the early missionary activities of the Church, it continually deals with urgent matters of contemporary Church politics, such as the relations of Jew and Gentile. Moreover its Hellenistic connections are stronger than those of the Gospels, and it calls for the sort of literary treatment here given it in James Robinson's essay on Acts and in Helen Elsom's essay on the Greek influences.

Acts is the last of the wholly narrative books of the New Testament; obviously it was written later than Luke, and in all probability after all four of the Gospels. Perhaps a word on the dates of all these books is here in order. Mark is conventionally dated about 70 C.E., Matthew and Luke somewhat later, if Marcan priority is accepted; John is, conventionally, later still. All this is simply conjecture and depends to a large extent on internal evidence. The consensus was called into question by J. A. T. Robinson's *Redating the New Testament*, which argues for much earlier dates—45–60 for Mark, 40–60 for Matthew, 57–60 for Luke, 40–65 for John, 57–62 for Acts.[10] The arguments are very complex and need not here concern us except perhaps insofar as they suggest a much shorter temporal gap between the oral and written traditions than is usually taken for granted.

Again, conventionally, it is usually assumed that the earliest written parts of the New Testament were the Epistles: 1 and 2 Thessalonians, Galatians, 1 and 2 Corinthians, Philippians, Philemon, Romans, Colossians, Ephesians, with Hebrews coming later, and 1–3 John, 1 and 2 Peter, James, Jude, and the Pastoral Epistles (1 and 2 Timothy and Titus) later still. Robinson challenges these dates also and places James in 47–48, making it the earliest of all the writings, and as much as a century earlier than some suppose. It is certainly interesting to reflect that Mark and Matthew may, in some form, have been as early as the first Epistles of Paul; but the matter is not very important in the context of this volume.

Twenty-one of the twenty-seven books of the New Testament are letters. They are by no means always spontaneous communications, though most do have an occasional quality; however elaborate their construction and however weighty their doctrine, they belong to the genre of the letter and simulate the formal gestures and the stylistic informality of ordinary letters. It has been suggested that we should reserve the term *epistle* for literary documents in the form of letters, and the term *letters* for works that were not the product of such literary elaboration, in short for genuinely spontaneous writings; but the division proves too hard to maintain.[11]

The letters of Paul are all upon urgent occasions. They address a variety of situations and local problems and formulate a variety of doctrines, the implications of which have occupied his successors ever since. He might be thought not to have concerned himself very deeply with matters of style; though he rose on occasion to great eloquence and poetic force, he was not an artist in the sense in which that term might reasonably be used of the evangelists. Of course he was not writing history or narrative, or at least that was not his primary concern. He uses as a liturgical formula words that refer to a central event in the life of Christ—for instance, the institution of the eucharist, in 1 Corinthians 11:23–26. Or he sometimes speaks of his own life. Or he refers to Old Testament episodes, such as the veil of Moses at Sinai already mentioned or, in the complex allegorical arguments of Romans 9, the relations of Abraham's grandchildren. Telling the story of Abraham's sons by Sarah and Hagar, he explains why he is doing so: "which things are an allegory" (Gal. 4:22–31). With Paul narratives beget not more narratives but theology. It has often been remarked that he shows little interest in the life and works of the living Jesus. His authority, and that "glory" he so often deprecates, derive from a single historical moment, his personal encounter with his master on the road to Damascus.

This is not to say that he could ignore the past. His interest in the Torah is of course profound, his view of the Law a very complicated matter; but it has not the narrative aspect of the evangelists' reading. They were interested in a vast and complex plot, a narrative development culminating in a great scene of recognition, a recognition that depended on the working out of what had gone before. But Paul does not care to "build upon another man's foundation" (Rom. 15:20) or to speak of things not wrought by himself (Rom. 15:18). Indeed, as Karl Barth observed in his famous commentary on Romans, "Paul's thought is altogether unhistorical . . . surely no one would wish to contradict this by appealing to his use of the Old Testament!"[12]—or indeed to the traditions concerning the life of Jesus.

This being so, the relation of the Pauline Epistles to the rest of the Bible is quite different from that of the Gospels. It differs also from that of Hebrews (though this was once attributed to Paul), the typologies of which are more elaborate and more structural; it really is a transformation of Old Testament material. Yet Hebrews has not the narrative qualities of the Gospels; it does not operate with the figures of truth discovered by historylike narrative, though it has its figures of truth, more abstract, more of the intellect. And indeed it is true (and obvious) that from a purely literary point of view the rest of the Epistles have at best a secondary interest (as, for instance, the relation between 1 John and the Fourth Gospel). Of course there are other points of view; we are not, in speaking thus, judging their value.

Revelation presents a different set of problems. For a long time it was regarded with deep suspicion; early commentators had serious doubts about it, and so had Luther and Calvin. But it was sealed into the canon, and it seems an appropriate ending to the New Testament, indeed to the whole Bible: as distinctly an end as Genesis is a beginning.

The genre of apocalypse was already well established when Revelation was written, and it has an Old Testament representative in the Book of Daniel. It is very unlikely that Revelation was written by the evangelist John, but it was customary to attribute apocalypses to some great man in the past, Daniel for instance. There is always reference to some state of affairs contemporary with the author, but the material is presented as belonging to a remoter time. It is represented as occurring in a dream or vision, and the figures of the dream are very artificial and obscure, somewhat in the manner of medieval dream poetry. Readers are always of necessity interpreters; the text is deliberately vague or sometimes bewilderingly precise, and what one gets out of it depends to a large extent on what one puts in, which is why the Beast can be thought to represent not only Nero but also Napoleon or Hitler or a wicked pope. The mysterious numbers allow one to select the date on which the obscure events prophesied will take place, so the work is never out of date; it can be mapped on to almost any set of circumstances, which is why it has had so profound an effect not only on lunatic schismatics but also on serious political thinkers through the centuries. Apocalypse is always a literature of crisis; the known past is coming to a catastrophic end, the unknown future is upon us; we are placed, as no one ever was before, at precisely the moment in time when the past may be seen as a pattern and the future, amply predicted in the numerals and images of the text, begins to take exact shapes. It is hard to see how one can study this book without studying the interpretations it has attracted; it is incomplete without them, a strange collection of interpretanda and, because literally inspired, offering always not only mystery but also the possibility of finally making sense.

Revelation is not the only part of the New Testament that deals with the last things. There are the Synoptic "little apocalypses" (Mark 13, Matt. 24, Luke 21) and the famous eschatological passage in 1 Thessalonians 4:16–17 (the so-called rapture beloved of modern fundamentalists). And there is a sense in which the entire New Testament exhibits the eschatological attitudes that are an important element in apocalypses. It was mostly the work of men upon whom the ends of the world had come, and stemmed from the teaching of a master who may have believed that the end was inaugurated by his ministry, with its message of the kingdom of God at hand. The interval between his departure and the *parousia* grew longer, but in the first century at least Christians must have conceived themselves as at the crisis between one age and another. Their works show that they understood the past and the fullness of its relation to the present; that they understood, in short, the fullness of time (Gal. 4:4). Indeed the idea of fullness, *plērōma*, is essential to the New Testament. From the point of view of its writers, of generations of interpreters, and, in their own way, of modern literary critics, it is the part of the book in which the plot laid down earlier comes to fulfillment. The endings of all stories are in a certain fashion images of the general end; here is an ending which consciously transforms all that went to the making of it, so that it is rightly bound in one volume with the Old Testament, with its divinely controlled narrative, its clues, types, and promises. Literary critics are as apt as theologians to see this, for they too must be, according to their kind, eschatologists, students of endings.

NOTES

1. W. G. Kümmel, *Introduction to the New Testament*, 17th rev. ed., trans. Howard Clark Kee (London, 1975).

2. For an account of various theories, see Charles H. Talbert, *What Is a Gospel? The Genre of the Canonical Gospels* (London, 1977).

3. See Richard Longenecker, *Biblical Exegesis in the Apostolic Period* (New York, 1975); and Geza Vermes, *Jesus and the World of Judaism* (London, 1983), *Jesus the Jew* (London, 1973), and "Bible and Midrash," in *The Cambridge History of the Bible*, vol. I, ed. P. R. Ackroyd and C. F. Evans (Cambridge, 1970), pp. 199–231.

4. Stephen Neill, *The Interpretation of the New Testament 1861–1961* (Oxford, 1964), p. 107.

5. See Colin H. Roberts, *Manuscript, Society and Belief in Early Christian Egypt* (Oxford, 1979).

6. See Frank Kermode, *The Genesis of Secrecy* (Cambridge, Mass., 1979), chap. 6.

7. Michael Goulder, *Midrash and Lection in Matthew* (London, 1974), p. 326.

8. Werner H. Kelber, *The Oral and the Written Gospel* (Philadelphia, 1983).

9. Howard C. Kee, "The Function of Scriptural Quotations and Allusions in Mark 11–16," in E. Earle Ellis and Erich Grässer, eds., *Jesus und Paulus: Festschrift für Werner Georg Kümmel zum 70. Geburtstag* (Göttingen, 1975), pp. 165–168; cited in Kelber, *The Oral and the Written Gospel*, pp. 196–197.

10. John A. T. Robinson, *Redating the New Testament* (London, 1976).

11. Willi Marxsen, *Introduction to the New Testament*, 3d ed., trans. G. Buswell (Oxford, 1968), p. 24.

12. Karl Barth, *The Epistle to the Romans*, 6th ed., trans. Edwyn C. Hoskyns (1933; reprint, Oxford, 1968), p. 533.

Matthew

Frank Kermode

THE opening of Mark announces a gospel, suggesting an entity that already existed, the substance of his book rather than the book itself. And ancient custom designated the Gospels as versions of that original gospel, for each of them was described as "the Gospel according to . . ." But although they all have the same basic subject and are in various other ways related to one another, they differ to a remarkable extent. The differences no doubt arise in part from variations in the traditional material available and in the needs of the communities for which each of the evangelists was writing. But it is equally certain that each of them saw the basic material differently, worked it differently, and impressed upon it a distinctive literary method and talent.

Matthew's Gospel is much longer than Mark's and adds to the record a great deal concerning the teaching of Jesus, as well as providing a Nativity story totally absent from Mark and significantly different from Luke. All the evangelists had to deal with one problem in particular: they seem to have had highly developed and consecutive accounts of the last phase of the life of Jesus, but the material on his earlier years was more anecdotal, assembled on principles that were largely nonnarrative, and so more difficult to organize into a coherent and continuous story. Miracles, accounts of controversies with opponents, sayings of Jesus perhaps collected by topic or key word rather than given historical contexts—all these had somehow to be disposed in a new order and accommodated to narrative; for there is little doubt that each saw the telling of the *story* as his most important and influential task. Each writer meets the ensuing difficulties differently, and it could be said that none quite overcomes them, not even Luke, a self-consciously resourceful narrative historian, or John, whose narrative is probably the subtlest, despite the interruptions by long nonnarrative discourses.

It seems that we can internalize the rules of the gospel genre, so that the mixture of exhortation, isolated bits of narrative, and more continuous narrative exhibiting great depth and connexity simply strikes us as characteristic of a kind of writing we value and find no odder than, say, the presence of long catalogues in classical epic or lists of the names of dwarfs in Icelandic poetry. And we have before us, as these writers had, the example of the Jewish Bible, with its mixture of narrative, law, and poetry. So it is as unnecessary as it is useless to seek in Matthew's Gospel some principle of structural organization that would explain convincingly the relationship between its parts by reference to some external model. There is a theory that its structure is modeled on the Pentateuch, but few can bring themselves to endorse it, and it may be a nuisance if it tempts us to look awry at the whole book. Certainly the Old Testament is a very powerful shaping influence; certainly there are large allusions, as when Jesus is treated as a second Israel, and local allusions of very great importance, as in the narrative use of Old Testament testimonies, but we should not look for the large-scale literary dependence exemplified, for instance, by the relation of Joyce's *Ulysses* to the *Odyssey*.

It remains true, nevertheless, that the all-pervading allusiveness of Joyce's book and Matthew's dependence on the Jewish Bible have something in common. And from this dependence we may learn something about the right way to read Matthew, something about what might be called the logic of his imagination. His relation to Old Testament material is nearly always of the same kind. He grants the old text its sanctity and its perpetual force, but he always assumes that in an important sense it is not complete in itself. The event or saying foreshadowed in the old text is fulfilled in the new, and the new is therefore validated by it; but it also contains and transcends it. The relation of the new to the old is a typological relation; though the old was complete and invited no addition it must nevertheless be completed. It is as if history and story acquired a new and unexpected dimension.

Although typology is sometimes said to be a Christian invention, it is clearly derived from Jewish habits of thought and reflects Jewish rhetorical modes, some of great antiquity. It has been argued, for example, that the habitual parallelism of Hebrew verse is not so much a way of enforcing a point by means of repetition as of saying "A, and, what's more, B"; the second colon or verset provides something in excess of the first. And this formula could describe not only the general structure of Matthew's thought ("Israel A, and, what's more, Israel B") but also the texture of his prose. Indeed it is this quality above all others that provides us with a sense of the unity of this Gospel. The "what's more" of his texture reflects the "what's more" of his argument. The excess of B over A is what transforms A and fulfills it.

Fulfillment requires transformation, and transformation entails a certain excess. We can observe the operation of these three in Matthew's dealings with the Jewish Law. The nature of these dealings has been and remains the subject of minute and intense scholarly debate, caused in part by apparent contradictions in Matthew's treatment of the theme. But there is nothing equivocal about the famous pronouncement in 5:17–18: "Think not that I am come to destroy the law, or the prophets: I am not come to destroy, but to fulfil. For verily I say unto you, Till heaven and earth pass, one jot or one tittle shall in no wise pass from the law, till all be fulfilled." Here the "jot" (*iōta*) and the "tittle" (*keraia*) refer to the Torah, a writing so sacred that not even the smallest letter or the least important extratextual indication can be dispensed with. They are themselves sacred. The letter of the Law is complete in the minutest detail; one must believe that, exactly as a devout Jew believes it, yet still believe that the Law must be transformed, that it must unexpectedly bear the weight of Jesus' gnomic excess, must though already full be fulfilled. In Romans 10:4 Paul had described Christ as the *telos* of the Law, meaning its end (in every sense, both termination and perfection). Paul had to contend with the problem of libertine antinomianism in some of his congregations—they rejoiced in the thought that the Law was superseded, that they had unbounded ethical freedom. Matthew, however, is concerned not with supersession but with fulfillment, the fulfillment of a law that must remain intact, its prohibitions still in place; indeed it is to be more strictly observed than even the most observant Jews suppose.

Mark (7:2) says the Pharisees found fault with the disciples because they ate their bread "with defiled, that is to say, with unwashen, hands" and adds by way of explanation that the Pharisees follow "the tradition of the elders" and frequently wash not only their hands but also their utensils. Jesus in reply calls them hypocrites who "reject the commandment of God, that ye may keep your own tradition" (7:3–9). Matthew, reporting the same occasion, omits the explanation and proceeds at once to the countercharge, that the Pharisees neglect central parts of the Law. Then (15:20) he goes on to correct false pharisaic notions of defilement, and of the Law itself, which is by no means the same thing as their "tradition." There is a sharp contrast between what "ye say" and "the commandment of God" (15:5–6). And if Mark really commented a little later in his version that Jesus "declared all meats clean" (7:19; but the translation is very doubtful), he was, like Peter in Acts 11, proclaiming the abrogation of an important part of the Law, as Matthew certainly does not; probably he regarded the dietary rules as much more important than a jot or tittle.

One or two further instances will show that Matthew meant it when he said the Law was not to be destroyed. Luke has Jesus say: "The law and the prophets were until John [the Baptist]: since that time the kingdom of God is preached, and every man presseth into it" (16:16). He means that since John announced the coming of the kingdom, men seek that kingdom rather than the Law. But Matthew (11:12) gives the same traditional saying a quite different sense: "from the days of John the Baptist until now the kingdom of heaven suffereth violence, and the violent take it by force." The verb translated by "presseth" and "take . . . by force" is the same in each case (and it certainly connotes violence). But Luke's notion of a liberated urgency animating all men is quite absent from Matthew, for whom the Law and the prophets survived the coming of John; for him the suggestion of a migration from Law to kingdom is more threat than promise. When Matthew writes in the next verse that "all the prophets and the law prophesied until John" he is only preparing for the assertion (11:13) that John was the returned Elijah; that is, John is continuing the prophecies, not replacing them. Luke in 16:17 reaffirms the permanence of the Law, giving his version of Matthew 5:17–18, but the verse is so oddly placed in its context that it has been thought to be ironical, or perhaps an afterthought, a caveat against antinomianism. At best it is vague, as, in regard to the Law, Luke often is by comparison with Matthew. One more instance of Matthew's punctiliousness: Mark, describing the terrors of the Last Days, prays that they will not arrive in winter (13:18). Matthew adds the hope that they will not arrive on the sabbath either, when presumably the injunction to flee could not be obeyed (24:20).

Although Matthew arranges the ethical teachings of Jesus in consolidated nonnarrative sections, he is as determined as the other evangelists to give narrative force to his Gospel whenever he can. The controversy about the Law is therefore concretized in the incident of apparent sabbath-breaking by the disciples. The sabbath is a suitable focus for discussion of transgression and transformation; and Jesus first defends the disciples by citing the precedent of David eating the shewbread, and by observing that the Law exempted the priests in the Temple from rigid observance. The defense elicited by this anecdote is not only that the transgression was less apparent than real. "But I say unto you, That in this place is one greater than the temple" (12:6); the Greek means *something* greater, not only Jesus as lord of the sabbath but also the Second Temple, in which mercy is preferred to sacrifice. The Temple is transcended, though not reduced by a jot or a tittle; it is the Temple plus the excessive sense it must now bear.

So in the teaching about divorce (5:31–32) Jesus may seem to be overruling Deuteronomy by allowing divorce only in the case of adultery. His answer to the Pharisees on this subject (19:1–12) is again a counsel of excess. The authority for his stricter doctrine is Genesis 1:27, so that the Mosaic regulation turns out to be a concession to weakness: "from the beginning it was not so." The appeal is to a fuller law, now becoming evident but implicit in the original creation; it will now be restored in the excess of a new order of creation (19:28). The Law is transformed (as Passover will be transformed) with many consequences of paradox and excess. When seen in its fullness it holds one guilty of murder or adultery if one simply hates or lusts, even without acting out the emotions (5:28). No wonder the disciples fear that this transformed Law is excessive, beyond human capacity (19:25). Men are simply being asked to be perfect (5:48).

Ethical injunctions similar to these may be found in the rabbinic schools, as Geza Vermes points out;[1] but it is the concentration of similar formulas in Matthew that gives a distinctive literary effect. His habitual rhetoric is a rhetoric of excess. "If ye salute your brethren only, what do ye more *than others?*" (5:47) is only an approximate translation, as the italics of the King James Version indicate. Literally the Greek words mean "what excess do ye?" Excess is constantly demanded. Whereas Mark says, "But many that are first shall be last; and the last first" (10:31), and Luke says, "there are last that shall be first" (13:30), Matthew, having followed Mark when first using the expression, tells the parable of the Laborers in the Vineyard and, fortified by this narrative example, strengthens the saying: "So the last shall be first, and the first last" (20:16).

In the Sermon on the Mount the Beatitudes are nearly all paradoxes: blessed are the poor, mourners, the meek, the persecuted, the reviled. The righteousness of those who would enter the kingdom must exceed that of the Pharisees. Again and again righteousness must be produced to excess. The formula "You have heard . . . But I say" is sounded repeatedly (5:21–22, 27–28, 31–32, 33–34, 38–39, 43–44). Everything must be in excess: to love your neighbor is not enough; you must love your enemies too. When you give alms you must do it secretly, thus exceeding the excess of the more ostentatious giver. "Let not thy left hand know what thy right hand doeth" (6:3) would make the deed secret even from yourself. Also you must pray in secret, thus achieving more than the public display of the hypocrite achieves. And pray in plain language, a sort of paradoxical rhetorical excess, since plainness requires the skillful suppression of all florid persuasion (6:7–13).

A more explicit demand for excess is the formula "How much more . . . ?" "Behold the fowls of the air . . . Are ye not much better than they? . . . Consider the lilies . . . shall he not much more clothe you?" (6:26, 28–30). "How much then is a man better than a sheep?" (12:12). And akin to these rhetorical questions are the familiar "oriental" exaggerations: the beam in the eye (7:4), the camel and the needle's eye (19:24), questions such as "what man . . . if his son ask for bread, will . . . give him a stone? Or if he ask a fish, will . . . give him a serpent?" (7:9–10). The formula "how much more . . . ?" is a rhetorical device used by the rabbis as well as by the Greeks, and the absurd questions and the questions demanding the answer "no" are also familiar stratagems in the discourse of place and period. But cumulatively they have, in the Sermon on the Mount and elsewhere in Matthew, a quite unusual intensity. Sometimes it is the righteous who must defy common sense—leave their dead unburied, turn the other cheek; sometimes it is the others who are shown to be fools, building their houses on sand, choosing the wide gate that leads to destruction, refusing to be as little children. We may recall that the word "silly" once meant "holy," and that the foolishness of the holy is a quite different matter from the folly of the knowing. Matthew in his own way makes as much of this distinction as Paul.

Excess is a matter not only of word but also of deed. When excessive deeds or mighty works are in question we are confronted with the problem of *authority*. What is the nature of the authority of the teacher whose extraordinary feats support his announcement of a new dispensation? The Greek word *exousia* is translated sometimes as "authority" and sometimes as "power." The power displayed in miracles proceeds from the same authority as the power displayed in the language of Jesus; "he taught them as one having authority [*exousian*] and not as the[ir] scribes" (7:29). The nature of the power and authority of Jesus is demonstrated by the story of the centurion's servant (8:5–13). Jesus offers to go to the centurion's house and heal the servant; but the centurion understands that the journey is strictly unnecessary, that Jesus need only "speak the word." For he is himself "a man under authority, having soldiers under me"; he understands that authority comes from above, and that he can exert it on those under him merely by issuing commands. Authority gives him that power. And as he in his sphere can count on disciplined compliance, so he understands that Jesus in his sphere can do the same. This understanding arises from confidence in the authority of Jesus, which is faith: "and as thou hast believed, so be it done unto thee." The healing of the leper in the immediately preceding pericope has demonstrated that such uses of authority are compatible with the Law; the story of the centurion explains that authority is nevertheless relevant to Gentile as well as to Jew, indeed that the Roman's understanding of it is in excess of any shown by the Jews, so that this excess may bring the Gentiles to sit down with Abraham, Isaac, and Jacob, while "the children of the kingdom," the Jews themselves, will be cast into outer darkness. So important is it to recognize *exousia*. The power exercised in the healing of the paralytic (9:2–8) is *exousia*; "the Son of man hath power [*exousian*] on earth to forgive sins . . . they marveled and glorified God, which had given such power [*exousian*] unto men."

Obviously Matthew needed to explain this *exousia* as a manifestation of something new which was yet an extension of, or excess over, something old, namely the Law, the ancient and unchangeable source of authority; and he uses his account of the ministry to enforce this apparent paradox. Thus the Pharisees challenge Jesus on his sitting at the table with sinners (9:10–13). His reply is the sharp saying "They that be whole need not a physician, but they that are sick." This piece of common sense depends of course on the assumption that the speaker has authority as a healer, and probably reflects Hosea 6:1–2: "he hath smitten, and he will bind us up. After two days will he revive us: in the third day he will raise us up." Hosea speaks not only of healing but also of the last victory over death. In justifying the authority of Jesus in this particular case, Matthew extends that authority silently until it rules over death—a defilement greater than any the Pharisees fear from contact with publicans and sinners. They think the power of Jesus to be not of heavenly but of demonic origin, and they say so when he cures the dumb man (9:32–34). But this cure refers to Isaiah 35:5–6; it heralds a new order as the prophet described it, a transformation that will be brought about by an authority quite unlike that of the *goēs* or magician they take him to be. And this the crowd, though not the Pharisees, seems to perceive, thus preparing for the Triumphal Entry, when Jesus will be recognized as the lowly Messiah. Those who continue to deny his authority will become its instruments, and ensure that ultimate sacrificial excess which will be its sign and seal.

The character of this new and transcendent authority is adumbrated in various episodes. Jesus says there is a need for more laborers at the harvest (a stock figure for the Last Days) and so delegates authority to the disciples, giving them "power [*exousia*] against unclean spirits, to cast them out, and to heal all manner of sickness and all manner of disease" (10:1). He sends assurances to John the Baptist that he, Jesus, is truly "he that should come" (that is, the Messiah) (11:3), but the exercise of messianic authority will produce a situation very different from any that might have been expected of the Messiah, for there will be a conflict between those who accept this new authority and those who mistakenly adhere to the old idea of it. Sons and fathers, mothers and daughters, will be divided, and the sheep sent against the wolves. This new world is to be a world of paradox. Jesus' followers are of more value than sparrows, yet God, who is with the sparrows when they fall (10:30), will nevertheless not prevent men from falling; for, according to the most bleakly majestic paradox of all, "He that findeth his life shall lose it: and he that loseth his life for my sake shall find it" (10:39). Under this new authority the world is turned upside down; it becomes unacceptable to "the wise and prudent" and acceptable only to the simple or silly, to "babes" (11:25). Indeed, to accept it requires ignorance of all that the new authority does not vouchsafe (11:27); yet by another disorienting paradox this apparently impossible charge becomes an easy yoke and a light burden (11:28–30). The Torah was called a yoke, and not an easy one; yet these more absolute demands made by the transformed Torah have mysteriously become easy.

On this matter of accepting the easy yoke (which is nevertheless more demanding) there are some significant differences between Matthew and Mark. Mark represents the disciples as not very good at it. Usually they understand nothing. When Jesus walks on the water Mark's disciples are bewildered and their hearts are hardened (6:51); but Matthew's cry out that Jesus is "of a truth . . . the Son of God" (14:33). They understand that authority can be bewildering. When Jesus makes his uncompromising demand of the rich young man, Matthew's report again differs significantly from Mark's. From Mark we learn that when the man addresses

Jesus as "Good Master," Jesus replies, "Why callest thou me good? there is none good but one, that is, God" (10:17–18). Matthew changes the question: "What good thing must I do?" and also the answer: "Why question me about what is good? There is one who is good" (19:16–17). Mark's reply presumably had implications unacceptable to Matthew, who presses the idea of *exousia* much further. We might also ask why Matthew ignores Mark's observation that Jesus, looking upon the man, loved him (10:21).

MATTHEW ENFORCES upon us in various ways the themes of excess, transformation, and the authority by which excess is demanded and transformation achieved. He must also show that all this is done for the sake of fulfillment; at the end of time what must be seen to have been fulfilled is the Law. Consequently the demonstration of fulfillment must bind Matthew's book very closely to the Law and the Prophets, that is, to what we call the Old Testament, which of course was to Matthew the whole Bible. This necessity was obvious to all the evangelists, though each went about meeting it in his own way. Matthew wanted to show that Jesus was the new Israel, his words and deeds echoing the story of the old. His history must have details assigning it to its own moment of time; but it would lack significance if it did not appear also to be a transformation of an earlier history known by divine warrant, as explicated by the sedulous commentary of the learned, to be full of promises, oracles to be explained only later by correspondent divine events. There would be no sense in a narrative that lacked these validating correspondences, testimonies to the divine control of history. Narrative must, given the extraordinary novelty of the life and ministry, be new and astonishing; but it must also comply with *données* to be sought in the Old Testament. Indeed this compliance is the deepest source of its astonishing novelty.

It therefore seems likely that the best way to discuss Matthew's narrative treatment of the theme of fulfillment is to look at certain phases of his story: the Nativity, the Temptation, the Transfiguration, the Triumphal Entry, and the Cleansing of the Temple. (The parables are discussed in the essay on Luke, and the Passion narrative in the essay on John.) Matthew and Luke offer different versions of the Nativity story; Mark, Matthew, and Luke, of the Temptation; and all four evangelists, of the Entry and the Cleansing.

The popular imagination has blended the Nativity narratives of Matthew and Luke, but they are really independent attempts to establish that the birth of Jesus was of a nature appropriate to a divine child. They are best thought of as free narrative compositions based on selected Old Testament *données*. The method has something in common with the Hebrew *midrash aggadah*, in which new narrative embellishments could be provided to update or augment the original story; here, however, the purpose is to show that the true implications of the old story are only now brought out, fulfilled, in the new dispensation. Matthew has the episode of the Magi, Luke that of the shepherds. They agree that the birth took place in Bethlehem, the city of David, that the prophecy of Micah (5:2) might be fulfilled; but Luke alone offers an explanation as to why the Galilean family should happen to have been in that city, supplying the detail of the Roman census. It is to him that we owe the story of strangers in a town which could offer them no room at the inn. The details of the manger and the swaddling clothes come from Isaiah 1:3 and Ezekiel 16:4. Luke is always interested in fluent story, and it is he who doubles the nativities of Jesus and John the Baptist, describes the meeting between Elizabeth and Mary—the virgin and the old woman, each in her own way incapable of natural conception. Luke also writes Mary's hymn, the Magnificat, modeled closely on Hannah's hymn (1 Sam. 2:1–10), and bases the Benedictus of Zacharias (1:68–79) and the Nunc dimittis of Simeon (2:29–32) on Old Testament texts and themes. Following different Old Testament types, Matthew tells of the Annunciation made to Joseph; Luke's is made to Mary.

Perhaps the stories of the Annunciation can best illuminate the narrative methods used. Matthew's Joseph, like his namesake in Genesis, is a dreamer. What the angel says to him comes from the story of Abraham and Isaac ("Sarah thy wife shall bear thee a son indeed, and thou shalt call his name Isaac"; Gen. 17:19). Paul had treated the birth of Isaac from Sarah's barren womb as a type of the Resurrection, and Matthew takes it with at least equal plausibility as a type of the birth of Jesus. And, in the rabbinic manner, he recalls a similarity of phraseology in a remote passage of Isaiah (7:14): "Behold, a virgin shall conceive, and bear a son, and shall call his name Immanuel." In the Greek version the Hebrew *almah*, "young woman," is rendered *parthenos*, "virgin." If Mary was a virgin, some explanation was required of the nature of her marriage to Joseph; and this was provided in much the same spirit as Luke's story of the census and the journey to Bethlehem. A similar invention is Matthew's Slaughter of the Innocents, which recalls Pharaoh's murderous plot against the Hebrew boys (Exod. 1:22) and Moses' flight from Egypt (Exod. 2:15) and subsequent return to his people (Exod. 4:20). The infant Jesus escapes Herod's plot by fleeing to Egypt, but likewise returns to his people Israel, so fulfilling Hosea 11:1: "When Israel was a child, then I loved him, and called my son out of Egypt."

Luke, following the more usual Old Testament type, has the Annunciation made to Mary, and, not content with a fulfillment citation of Isaiah, he writes a dialogue between the angel and Mary: "How shall this be, seeing I know not a man?" (1:34). Both evangelists intend to establish Jesus as a son of David and the Son of God, but each takes his own way; Luke is the more discursive and goes on to describe the circumcision and presentation in the Temple; he has no flight into Egypt, but instead the annual visit of Jesus and his parents to Jerusalem at Passover, with the young boy arguing in the Temple.

Although both writers construct their narratives on biblical testimonies, Luke is the more inventive and Matthew the more insistent in his citation of the texts here fulfilled. "That it might be fulfilled . . . ," "Then was fulfilled . . ."; five times this formula occurs in the Nativity narrative, including 2:23, where the text cited is uncertain: "And he came and dwelt in a city called Nazareth: that it might be fulfilled which was spoken by the prophets, He shall be called a Nazarene [*Nazaraios*]." This last word may be related to the Hebrew word for "branch" (of the house of David) or to *Nazir*, a holy one, separate to God, like Samson (Judges 16:17), or to both. And by no means every element of the narrative deriving in this way from the Old Testament is fully signaled by the evangelist. He is constructing figures of the truth, and doing it by methods presupposing a full, intimate relationship between these founding texts and the events of Jesus' life, which fulfills them by transforming them.

IMMEDIATELY AFTER the Baptism Jesus is forty days in the wilderness and tempted there. Mark disposes of this episode in two verses (1:12–13): "And immediately the spirit driveth him into the wilderness. And he was there in the wilderness forty days, tempted of Satan; and was with the wild beasts: and the angels ministered unto him." Mark then proceeds with his narrative: the imprisonment of John and the beginning of Jesus' ministry. Matthew and Luke are much more extensive, though it is more usual for Matthew to reduce the detail of Mark than to expand it. From Matthew we learn that the temptation was triple: to turn stones into bread, to throw himself off the pinnacle of the Temple, to receive the kingdoms of the world in all their glory. Jesus rejects all three, each time with an apt quotation from Deuteronomy. Luke spreads the temptations over the forty days, whereas Matthew puts them all at the end. Luke reverses the order of the second and third. He omits the ministrations of the angels, common to Matthew and Mark, saying instead that Satan, defeated on this occasion, left Jesus "for a season" (4:13) or "until the proper time," meaning the Passion.

Mark is, as so often, enigmatic; presumably he is suggesting some sort of trial or initiation experience. Matthew augments this bare statement with material based on Old Testament texts. That the time in the wilderness was forty days must already have been traditional, and the number echoes that of the years spent in the wilderness by Israel, whose original temptation occurred at a place known as Temptation or Testing. Here are types and antitypes, fulfillments; the angelic ministrations recall the manna of the original, and the rejection of the temptations echoes the *shema*, prescribed in Deuteronomy, and ever since prayed daily: its triple commandment is to love God with heart, soul, and might. We see Jesus, like the centurion later, under authority, tested by authority before he begins to assert authority.

Luke is less interested in making explicit the biblical references, and he wants a more flowing narrative. He changes the order of the temptations to get the most violent at the end. He powerfully links the Temptation with the climax of the whole story, the Crucifixion, so decisively that in later times the first was called Christ's victory over sin, and the second his victory over death. (Satan reappears in Luke 22:3 to renew his assault.) Moreover he affirms the *totality* of the temptations, and later commentators were to point out that "all the temptation" (4:13), or "every temptation," meant that all possible temptations were included under the head of these three. Jesus' resistance thus becomes exemplary, as Hebrews 2:18 says it is ("For in that he himself hath suffered being tempted, he is able to succour them that are tempted"), and James 1:12 confirms it by saying that he who endures temptation will receive the crown of life. It is hardly to be wondered at that Milton, in *Paradise Regained*, based his own interpretative narrative mainly on Luke's. But here the point is that the tradition could be interpreted and developed according to the desires and needs of the writer. Others, the Gnostics for instance, understood the Temptation quite differently, as an allegory of demonic assaults upon the newly baptized. Luke concerns himself with shapeliness of narrative, with the relation of this part to the design of his whole book, and with the exemplary quality of the episode. Matthew, as always, favors fulfillment, to be demonstrated by the establishment of occult connections between his narrative and the master narrative it must somehow echo and transcend.

SOME MEASURE of this interpretative freedom is also observable in the accounts of the Transfiguration, in Mark, Matthew, and Luke. Moses and Elijah, who appear with the transfigured Christ, represent the Law and the prophets; so this moment is truly climactic, an emblem of the homogeneity of our whole Bible and of the fruition or perfection of its earliest parts in its end. Yet Mark's account has little of the majesty we might expect of such a moment: "he was transfigured [metamorphosed] before them. And his raiment became shining, exceeding white as snow; so as no fuller on earth can white them" (9:2–3). And Peter, confronted by Elijah and Moses and the radiant Jesus, babbles: "Master, it is good for us to be here: and let us make three tabernacles; one for thee, and one for Moses, and one for Elias. For he wist not what to say; for they [Peter, James, and John] were sore afraid" (9:5–6). Matthew and Luke speak of the dazzling clothes, but Mark's fuller seems too humble a tradesman to be mentioned in this sublime context; Matthew mentions the offer of the booths without comment, and Luke adds "not knowing what he said"

(Matt. 17:4, Luke 9:33). Mark and Matthew both include the command to silence "till the Son of man were risen from the dead," but only Mark adds that the disciples questioned "one with another what the rising from the dead should mean" (Mark 9:9–10, Matt. 17:9). It is an important theme of Mark's that the disciples throughout have very little understanding; Matthew's line is different, so he emphasizes the awe of the three disciples rather than their bewilderment; and when they are afraid Jesus, instead of leaving them baffled, comforts them (17:6–7). Luke alone reports the conversation of Moses and Elijah: they "spake of his decease [*exodos*] which he should accomplish at Jerusalem" (9:31).

Luke is again interested in narrative structure; his opening address to Theophilus promises that he will "write . . . in order" (1:3), and his deliberate linking of the detachable Transfiguration narrative to the Passion and Crucifixion is made in the interest of that resolution. Matthew is not concerned with such devices—he has as little time for them as for Mark's obsession with mysteriousness, silence, and incomprehension. He has his own different interests. The visit of Elijah, herald of the Messiah, calls for some remark connecting him with John the Baptist, so Matthew includes an explicit allusion to this link (17:13), which the disciples understand. In Mark the connection is much more enigmatic (9:12–13) and there is certainly nothing to indicate that the disciples saw the point. To Matthew the coming of John was a fulfillment of Malachi 3:1: "Behold, I will send my messenger, and he shall prepare the way before me," and he wanted his Elijah firmly related to this promise. For the rest, Matthew is content with the cloud, a recurrent apocalyptic property, with the voice repeating the divine statement at the Baptism, and with some additional Old Testament references absent from the other evangelists. The disciples fall on their faces like Daniel in his vision (Dan. 10:9); and like Daniel they are given comfort and told not to fear (Dan. 10:11–12). Moses coming down from Sinai with the two tablets had this radiant face, so that Aaron and all Israel were afraid (Exod. 34:29–30). As Luke strengthens the narrative structure, so Matthew strengthens possible links with the Jewish Bible. His Transfiguration is a figure for what becomes of the Law under the new, transforming authority. Here, as everywhere, the very existence of Matthew's book and its power to make sense depend on the prior existence of another book, which always tells the sacred truth yet always, despite its apparent completeness, needs completion.

LATER CHRISTIAN ASSUMPTIONS concerning Holy Week, the period between Palm Sunday and Easter, derive chiefly from John, though memory mixes elements from all four Gospels. The Triumphal Entry is a moment of the utmost importance to all of them, for it is a declaration of messiahship, though of a paradoxical sort. Jesus has his royal entry into Jerusalem but at the same moment asserts his humility; he is a lowly Messiah, not

a Davidic liberator, though properly hailed as the son of David. He is a
king, recognized as such by the people yet bound, within a few days, to
suffer a criminal's death. From this point forward the Gospels have a
powerful narrative impetus, and the story is full of paradox and irony.
Yet it remains, for all its urgent realism, a fulfillment of other stories and
prophecies.

All the accounts look back to, or fulfill, the prophecy of Zechariah:
"Rejoice greatly, O daughter of Zion; shout, O daughter of Jerusalem:
behold, thy King cometh unto thee: he is just, and having salvation; lowly,
and riding upon an ass, and upon a colt the foal of an ass" (9:9). Zechariah's
book—or books, since there seem to be at least three of them—is, or are,
extremely obscure, yet the importance of some of their visionary and
parabolic pronouncements in the formation of the last sections of the
Gospels is very great, and comparable with that of the Suffering Servant
passages in Isaiah. Matthew, as usual, seeks to intensify the fulfillment
relation already present in the tradition and, unlike Mark, is anxious that
the correspondences should be noted. Unlike both Mark and Luke he
quotes a version of Zechariah 9:9 (Matt. 21:5). And he follows the citation
so closely that his Jesus sends not only for the ass but also for the colt;
thus a characteristic Hebrew parallelism is given a plausible narrative
existence in two animals. Matthew does not want the "realistic" dialogue
between the disciples sent for the ass and the bystanders who ask why
they are untying it, though Mark and Luke report it. It is the messianic
detail he attends to. His crowd alone cries "Hosanna to the Son of David"
(21:9), a cry repeated by the children in the Temple (v. 15). By itself
"Hosanna" was not messianic and might be a tribute to a great teacher;
the addition of "Son of David" makes it so, this being, like "he that
cometh" (in the same verse), a messianic title.

John's account of the Entry is briefer, though still related to the
prophecy of Zechariah, which he loosely cites; but he gives a narrative
reason for the coming out of the crowd, namely that they had heard of
the raising of Lazarus (12:18); that story is unknown to the Synoptics, but
even if it had not been so, its telling represents an interweaving of narrative
motifs of a kind that hardly interested Matthew. Yet Matthew tells us that
"all the city was moved" (21:10) and that the chief priest and scribes "were
sore displeased" (v. 15)—and he does so not merely to accommodate an
apt quotation from Psalms 8:2 but out of narrative necessity. The enemies
of Jesus are for a moment restrained from acting against him for fear of a
tumult (21:46). But the story must move on and this tension be resolved,
as it is by the Cleansing of the Temple, which in the Synoptics is the act
immediately succeeding the Entry. "Crowd" in Matthew is a different
word from that used to mean "people," and, like a Shakespearean mob,
his crowd may be easily swayed. Here it must change from a mood in
which it acclaims Jesus to another, in which it demands his execution.

The Cleansing of the Temple is the main instrument of this change. After it, Matthew arranges several confrontations between Jesus and his enemies, and as late as two days before Passover (26:5)—and indeed because the Passover approaches and Jerusalem is full of crowds—they are talking of biding their time; it is the intimate relation of Passover, Last Supper, and Crucifixion that makes it necessary, from the point of view of narrative, to introduce another plot function to complete what the Cleansing began, and the choice is of Betrayal; hence the Judas story, developed from more verses in Zechariah.

John places the Cleansing at the beginning of the ministry, right after the messianic miracle at Cana, and his narrative explanations are therefore different, but their purpose is much the same. Each evangelist has his own needs, and their satisfaction produces wide deviations. John has his discourses, Matthew his parables and fulfillments. But they must converge at certain climactic moments; and it is at those moments that we may often perceive, by the less obvious differences between them, the idiosyncrasies of each: as Matthew's Passion narrative includes the dream of Pilate's wife, Mark's the naked boy who fled, Luke's the repentant thief on the Cross, and John's the piercing of Jesus' side. The first and last of these are manifestly "christological"; it is Matthew's imagination that allows a Roman lady to refer inadvertently to Jesus by an ancient messianic title ("that just man [or 'that righteous One']," 27:19) thus emphasizing the guilt and blindness of the Jews; and John (19:31–37) writes a narrative based on texts in Psalms (3:20), Zechariah (12:10), and Exodus (12:10). Mark's fleeing boy may be all his own work, another instance of his penchant for the unexplained mystery. Luke writes a characteristic embellishment, adding interest to the episode. All these bits of narrative are firmly embedded in our general harmonized notion of the Passion story; when we look at them in the context of each Gospel we can see that they illustrate different literary approaches, and begin perhaps to see each as characteristic of a peculiar style of composition. (The various versions of the Passion narrative are more fully considered in the essay on John.)

ALTHOUGH MUCH of the information in this essay derives from the tradition of biblical exegesis, it is being used for the purposes of secular literary criticism. Matthew has served for two millennia as a manual of devotion, a source of liturgical readings, and a historical record, and of course a literary approach need not impinge upon those uses. The concern here is with the manner, not with the message as interpreted by the faithful; the Gospels are writings first of all, whatever use is subsequently made of them.

Like the other Gospels, Matthew presents some special difficulties to the purely literary reader. It belongs to a genre with a very limited membership and, like its fellows, contains several different sorts of writing;

only the last quarter of it has the structural and dynamic qualities we associate with historical, quasi-historical, or functional narrative. The want of these qualities is responsible for the common observation that the Gospels are Passion narratives with nonnarrative prologues. And yet the peculiarities of the genre are so familiar that they cease to seem peculiar. Several varieties of discourse—parable, sermon, controversy, miracle story, to name only some—are brought together in a fashion that long acquaintance has robbed of its arbitrariness, and we are able to think about the constituent forms of discourse as contributing to a whole. We stand in a long tradition of interpretation, a tradition to which the writers themselves belong; Matthew is certainly under one aspect an interpretation of the Jewish Bible, which is itself, as we have it, an interpretation of precedent traditions. And later every generation could read him differently, without ever doubting his coherence, though without ever supposing that any one could search out all the implications of what he was doing.

NOTE

1. Geza Vermes, *Jesus and the World of Judaism* (London, 1983), pp. 45–48.

SUGGESTED FURTHER READINGS

Robert Banks, *Jesus and the Law in the Synoptic Tradition* (Cambridge, 1975).
Günther Bornkamm, Gerhard Barth, and H. J. Held, *Tradition and Interpretation in Matthew*, trans. Percy Scott (London, 1963).
J. C. Fenton, *The Gospel of St. Matthew* (Harmondsworth, 1963).
Michael Goulder, *Midrash and Lection in Matthew* (London, 1974).

King's College, University of Cambridge,
and Columbia University

Mark

John Drury

WHAT sort of literature is the Gospel according to Mark? It is sacred Scripture: a categorization long since and officially given to it by its inclusion in the Christian biblical canon. This venerable presupposition for reading it is certainly apt to a book which instructs its readers in the structure of the world's spiritual reality. It is about the holy. All the times, places, and people in it, together with their connecting movements, are concerned with the sacred as a way of life. It has the practicality and the mystery of religious writing.

But religious writing is an enormous category and in the Bible alone spans a wide spectrum of different forms: laws, letters, lyrics, proverbs, oracles, and various kinds of narrative. Every important literary or oral category had a religious use for the writers of the library of books which became the Bible. No book was under any obligation to keep to one category. In Mark Jesus legislates, speaks oracularly and proverbially, appeals to myth and compassionate common sense. But everything is carried and given significance by the story it is in. Mark is obviously and emphatically a narrative.

The narrative classification narrows the field slightly but not enough. Biblical narratives include court histories of kings, priests' myths about the origins and ends of things, and legends of heroes such as Jacob or Elisha, which had a more popular appeal. Mark best fits this last class. His tale is folktale. Before its official canonization as holy Scripture, it first lived among unofficial people and delighted them by having virtually nothing good to say about officialdom—high priest, procurator, or even apostle.

According to Walter Benjamin, folktale is the ordinary person's way of shaking off the nightmare which myth puts on his chest.[1] Mark's Jesus is typically a folktale hero, a wanderer going through ordeals which commandeer, disrupt, and reorder the established myths. He is unaccommodated and unofficial. He performs the miracles beloved of popular piety because they change lonely misery to social happiness at a touch; and of course these miracles are suspect to philosophy precisely because of their instant wish fulfillment. In teaching he uses the parables which rabbinism classed as *aggadah,* in distinction from *halakah,* the instruction of the elite. *Aggadah* was the junk jewelry of the pedlar, fine of its kind but not the same as the gems of leisured scholarship. He poses the riddles which delight children and the illiterate: tough, polemical little utterances which subvert the mind's accustomed order. He challenges the authorities and suffers from their malevolence and disregard, as the children and wayfarers of folktale suffer from wicked step-parents or witches and are put to the test by kings. And like them, he emerges from the ordeal triumphant. The official histories and the myths have their say. Jesus is no king, but he is David's son and lord. He is not God, but he is his son. Such powerful touches from other kinds of story have to be played out, however, within the folktale which they momentarily enhance. In view of Mark's apocalyptically dualistic frame of mind and his attachment to such apocalyptic myths as Doomsday and resurrection, it is particularly striking that myth does not get more of a showing than it does. Even in chapter 13, where it is a powerful force, it is firmly tied into the human incidents of the narrative. Mark's loyalty to popular narrative and the common human scene is all the more impressive in a writer so positive about the supernatural and the secret. His angels and devils do not interact in their own sphere. They serve people or batten on them. Women, children, fishermen, lepers, publicans, sinners, the sick, the unclean, and the mad: these matter to Mark as much as the powers that be—secular, religious, or (Jesus and God excepted) supernatural. His Jesus is a fitting hero for Christianity in its first and unofficial phase, housebased and taken by wayfaring missionaries to those whom the established faiths and cults did not satisfy; those who were glad to hear of the subversion and transgression of a religion which had never appealed to them.

From the reader's point of view, what matters most about folktale is the close attention it demands. A few of the Grimms' folktales would give good practice for reading Mark's. There is no unnecessary digression in such stories. They are lean, close and complex in articulation, with a precision which we tend to associate with science rather than with art. They are almost formulaic. Everything in them matters and has functional relationship to every other thing. So every, even momentary, negligence in reading them is disabling. They should be read no faster than the pace of speech, and not once only. For they belong to the people clustered round the storyteller who brings out of his narrative treasure things new and old, rather than to the rapid browser in the armchair.

The Text

Mark's is generally believed to be the first written gospel. Granted the truth of that belief, something momentous happened when Mark wrote his first word: *archē,* "beginning." A welter of oral and fluid tradition about Jesus got fixed into text. Stories which had been the property of

Christian preachers, teachers, and prophets were appropriated by a Christian writer. This written gospel is next-door neighbor to thirty or forty years of oral gospeling.

But in literature as in life, old habits die hard and new beginnings are not entirely new. Major features of oral gospeling impinge on Mark's text. It was meant to be read aloud to a circle of listeners: an external setting which matches the frequent scenes in the book, where Jesus questions and instructs his followers by word of mouth. This is a written text about a man who, according to its credible testimony, wrote nothing but spoke with an authority unofficial but divine: "They were astonished at his doctrine: for he taught them as one that had authority, and not as the scribes" (1:22).

Mark's book occupies a threshold between the evanescent spoken word and the more permanent and fixed written word. Yet very soon after Mark had written, two other Christian writers, Matthew and Luke, broke up the fixity of his text—amplified it and reduced it—with the same magisterial freedom with which Mark himself had treated his oral sources, in order to incorporate more material from oral or written sources.

Yet again text may not be utterly fixed, particularly in a culture used to oral narrative or in as creatively unstable an environment as primitive Christianity; but it is more stable than speech, a more solid referent for meditation than the liquidity of hearsay. Matthew's and Luke's Gospels were made possible by Mark's. They could operate with his document. Mark himself seems to have been conscious of the advantages of literary over oral gospeling; for why else did he go to the trouble of writing at all? We may even detect in his writing a certain animus against the very people who had fostered the preceding oral tradition about Jesus: his family and his disciples. According to him, they understood little or nothing of what Jesus told them or of what his actions implied. Indeed, he presents them as so obtuse and wrongheaded that it is extremely difficult, within Mark's own terms, to account for his having any coherent or dependable tradition to use at all. Certainly in this matter his successors, Matthew and Luke, seem to have noticed a difficulty amounting to inconsistency. They modified Mark's blockheads into more historically probable transmitters of tradition. In Matthew they have "little faith" but do *understand* Jesus. Luke is always conscious that he is dealing with the future leaders of the Church, men who may have erred but who always got things right in the end.

The stupidity of Mark's disciples seemed as historically questionable to Matthew and Luke as it does to us. But within his book it has its highly effective uses. It is both flattering and instructive to his readers. We understand Jesus better than the people in the text usually do. Their incomprehension assists our comprehension. It signals the dead-end paths—namely, any routes other than the road to the Cross, which the

disciples, naturally, do not want to know about (for example, Peter at
8:31–33). For Mark is after an extraordinary kind of comprehension. He
locates it at death, the world's edge, so that the centurion at the Cross is
given the correct insight: "Truly this man was the Son of God" (15:39).
In the course of the narrative Jesus is rightly identified by demons and
enemies, momentarily by Peter—who immediately errs by trying to
swerve Jesus from the way to the Cross. Genuine understanding, Mark
is telling us, is supernatural. So within the continuities of this world, and
within the continuities of a narrative set in this world, it is discontinuous
and sudden. People listen to Jesus' teaching and see his actions—and fail
to get it. Yet the truth about Jesus is peremptorily barked out by an
unclean spirit (1:24), suspected by a hostile high priest at the end of his
tether (14:61), and definitively pronounced by the centurion at the Cross,
who endorses what God has said at the outset (1:11): this is the holy one,
the Christ, God's Son. Identifications of Jesus within the narrative are
incidental (in a strong sense) and unmotivated. They simply occur. Their
source or ground, and therefore any continuity they could have, is elsewhere. Some sense of it is given by Jesus' being designated Son of God
by God at the very beginning of the book and by the centurion at its very
end: that is, at the thresholds of narrative entry and exit. There is ground
at the start and finish. Jesus is called "Son of God" in its first verse, the
caption which labels the entire book and gives us the identifying key.
Having put it so firmly in our hand at the outset, having virtually made
us into Christian initiates there and then and given us the ground of
understanding, Mark can safely and properly make his story as perplexed
and jerky as narrative can stand. So long as we hold on to what we were
told in the first verse, the story holds—and all the more dramatically for
its discontinuities and obscurities. Similarly, the lurid symbols of Rim-
baud's provocatively titled *Illuminations* are an intelligible sequence to the
writer/reader, who boasts "I alone have the key of this wild parade!"
Between the secure understanding given us in its first verse and the radical
insecurity and incomprehension of the subsequent tale, Mark's book gets
its energy.

Mark 1:1 gives divine knowledge to his readers. It is all-important.
Mark lived among people who believed the timetable of another world
to be pressing upon mundane time. Each touch of its pressure was a
promise of its eventual triumph over ordinary time and the defeat of
death, mundane time's most dreadful marker, by resurrection. God was
the master storyteller, the ultimate referent of every moment, the significance of which could be got from taking bearings back upon the sacred
past recorded in the Old Testament Scriptures, and forward upon Doomsday and God's kingdom to come. This cluster of beliefs—history articulated into divinely ordained epochs which were discernible by scriptural
exegesis and drove toward the divine ending—belonged to the apocalyptic

Judaism exemplified by the Book of Daniel. It is a major part of the matrix of Christianity. Paul's thought is drenched in it, and its influence on Mark is strong and sustained.

The importance of such a clear and rigid picture of the reality which shapes history is all the more urgent if we consider the physical appearance of Mark's text. It did not look the same as it does in a modern printed Bible. We do not possess Mark's autograph, but we can rightly suppose that he used the conventions of his time which survive in papyri. He wrote without punctuation, without paragraphing, even without spaces between words. His text consisted simply of letters, usually the same number to every line. It lacked the nonverbal aids to narrative structure which give us nowadays so much help in understanding the shape and rhythm of what is before us. So the only indication to his contemporary readers of the shape of what they were reading was in the words themselves. If somebody spoke, Mark had to write "And Jesus said unto them . . . ," because he had no quotation marks at his disposal. The word "and" served him as a colon or stop. Topographical movement such as going into a house or over water, leaving a place or arriving at one, divides his narrative text much as paragraphing divides ours. This is a reason for the austerely conventional character of Mark's scenery, for which Duccio would be a more apt equivalent in Christian painting than Holman Hunt. When Mark says "house" we do better to imagine a simple perspectiveless box around the characters concerned than a realistic dwelling. When he says "sea," heraldic wavy lines are more appropriate than Monet or travel posters. But the conventional is not at all the same as the perfunctory or the negligent. It bears structure and meaning simultaneously. A text without our repertoire of punctuation had to be all the more firmly and cleverly shaped by the words alone. The subtle divisions and connections made by our typographic conventions—divisions and connections without which there could be no narrative and which the speaker could make by pause or gesture—these had to be accomplished by Mark with words. In a nutshell, they had to be internalized within the flow of words, from which alone signals of the flow's articulation could be beamed to the reader.

Mark used narrative techniques common to all practitioners of the craft, but the layout of his text and the strength of his apocalyptic beliefs combine to make his use of them unusually (to us) diagrammatic. And his iconic austerity can sustain rich complexity of reference. The seeds of the end of a tale are planted in its beginning, the seeds of intervening events shed by other intervening events. For example, the healing miracles in the book are a cumulative series. By the end they have included men, women, and children; diseases of hands, feet, ears, eyes, and mouths (cardinal parts of the body in Jewish tradition; see Ps. 115:6–7); even death. Mark sets up a tale, then teasingly interrupts it with another tale before resuming it. Some examples of this are the death of John the Baptist, between the going and returning of the twelve apostles (chap. 6); the healing of the bleeding woman, between Jesus' setting out to heal a girl and his doing it (chap. 5)—an interruption which tightens the tale it is in because the girl dies in the meanwhile and has to be resurrected; the overthrow of the Temple traders, between the cursing of a fig tree and the finding it dead (chap. 11); and Peter's denial, between the two trials of Jesus (chaps. 14 and 15). This is a fundamental and indispensable narrative ploy, a way of engaging the reader and knotting the story into multiple strength, without which the tale might revert to mere chronicle. It is not usually as often or as boldly used as here.

Sometimes Mark's devices are more technically sophisticated. His account of the death of John hints at the death of Jesus. It is also narrated with almost Proustian temporal complexity. The train of events must have been: reason for John's arrest, John imprisoned, John killed, John possibly resurrected. But Mark goes backward. He starts with Herod guessing that Jesus is John resurrected from the dead at 6:14, mentions John's death at 6:16, his imprisonment at 6:17, and the reason for it at 6:18: the order of recall is the reverse of the historical order. Only at 6:21 do actual time and narrated time move forward together. But when they eventually synchronize they do so with all the more energy for having been sprung by this coiled beginning. The resulting complex and horribly fascinating little tale appealed to Flaubert, Wilde, and Richard Strauss for further development. Beginning by dragging backward: this powerful opening gambit is obvious here. It is concealed, at least to modern readers, in the Gospel's prologue, which, as a key to the whole subsequent story, is worth close attention.

Structures and Codes

The first fifteen verses of the book have unity. Jesus' gospel is announced in 1:1 just before the story begins, and in 1:14–15 Jesus comes into Galilee preaching it. Between those two pointed occurrences of the word "gospel" lie the events which form the starting motor of the whole gospel narrative. In other metaphors, Mark 1:1–15 is the overture which keys our mind into an atmosphere, the tabulation of the codes and ciphers used in the rest of the book. How does it move?

Verse 1 belongs in the present of Mark's Christian readers. "The gospel of Jesus Christ, the Son of God," is their book about their master. From that near present they are suddenly taken far back in time. Verses 2 and 3, quoting Exodus, Isaiah, and Malachi, fasten Jesus' story to the sacred past as strongly as verse 1 has fastened it to the sacred present. These three verses mark out a temporal span much greater than the narrated life of Jesus. Much of the energy in the telling of Jesus' life and death derives from that longer story on either side of it—and much of the significance, too. The Jesus announced as Son of God by the voice of Christian evangelism in verse 1 appears in verse 9 and is designated "beloved Son" by the divine voice quoting ancient Scripture in verse 11. The messenger announced by ancient Scriptures in verses 2 and 3 as a "voice . . . crying in the wilderness" to herald the Lord gets embodied in verse 4 as John preaching repentance and proto-Christian baptism in the wilderness. The pattern is a chiasm. The first to be announced, Jesus the Son of God, is the last to arrive. The second announced, John the herald, appears penultimately; the structure is *ABBA*. Its subliminal effect is to rouse us to the possibility that something momentous is happening in 1:1–15—something to do with John that brings Jesus into the lead. What happens is threefold: baptism of all Jewry, Jesus' baptism, Jesus' temptation. The central event, Jesus' baptism, is likely to be central in more than a formal way. And its powerful significance will become clear from the events on either side of it.

Before Jesus was baptized, everybody was baptized: "all the land of Judaea, and they of Jerusalem" were baptized in the Jordan (1:5). City and land stood empty, the Jordan thronged. It is a startling picture, and all the more so if, like Mark and his first readers, we know the old story behind it. There, after the Exodus from Egypt, the nation entered the Land by crossing the threshold of Jordan. After many years, David took Jerusalem and made it the capital. Here in Mark, the movement is reversed, the film rolled backward, and the nation is back at its beginning again, at its baptismal birthplace. It confronts a man whose appearance and diet signify the wild world before culture, an animal-like man. So rapid and momentous a backtracking could be taken as a climax, but it is immediately marked as a buildup by John's prophesying a greater man and a higher baptism.

No sooner said than done, as ever in the serendipity of legend. Jesus came from the edge of Judea, Galilee, and was baptized in the Jordan. So far this river has been the threshold of new beginnings, the thin line between contrasting states. But there is a thinner, the mathematical line, without thickness, where water touches land. As Jesus comes "up" over that, the spirit comes down ("descending") on him through the sky, the ceiling which separates divine and human worlds, splitting it in the process. The divine voice is heard below, authenticating Jesus. Mark uses his "coming up" and "descending" deliberately. Strong vertical movements strike through the horizontal narrative and open it to its meaning, its ground or height. The national baptism has been capped. Yet neither is this more powerful scene the end. The story is only beginning!

Its next phase is driven (Mark's own word in 1:12) by the greatest known force, the spirit which impels Jesus into the wilderness. In the old story which codes Mark's, the nation was forty years in the Wilderness, tested by God and testing him, before coming to the Jordan. It seems as though Jesus steps up out of the river onto that wild far side, and so is taken further back into the original story than everyone else in Mark's story, who comes only as far as the river. This is confirmed by Mark's mention of temptation and forty days. Jesus is tested in the wilderness beyond Jordan like old Israel, tested by Satan like Job, tested among wild beasts and ministering angels like Daniel.

From this ordeal of the primitive, Jesus emerges with his gospel, Mark having cleared the way for him by a proleptic note about John's imprisonment (1:14). The prologue ends with the actual announcement of the "gospel" of the first verse, and the story is set on its way (which, interestingly, runs first along the sea's edge; 1:16).

This prologue introduces us to, among other things, the rapidity and condensation of Mark's style, and to his hectoring narrative intensity, which is unrelieved except by the emphatic downbeat and the flagging of Jesus' power at 6:5, after the resurrection of the little girl and his return to his own country. "Straightway" is Mark's favorite adverb; "run," "arise," "shout," and "amaze" are among his favorite verbs. His shuttle moves fast through present moments, back and forth between precedents and effects. Events follow upon one another apparently helter-skelter. But they are linked by deliberately concealed significances.

We have already cracked one of these, the Exodus-in-reverse in the prologue, entailing the religious shift from the old religion to the new. Another in the same passage is the synchrony of Jesus' story beginning at the same point with the Christian reader's story *qua* Christian: with baptism for both. So how did Mark and his first readers understand baptism? The answer will make legible more of the book by uncovering a code which they knew. It is fundamental and simple. Baptism was a ritual of dying to live anew. Paul, writing before Mark, appeals to this as common knowledge in Romans 6:3: "Know ye not, that so many of us as were baptized into Jesus Christ were baptized into his death?" Mark shows that he shares that knowledge when, at 10:38, baptism is paired with the cup of death which Jesus will accept in Gethsemane (14:36). The baptism at the beginning of the verse and the cup at the end (which is also the eucharistic cup of 14:23) are linked. So baptism at the outset of Jesus' story is a secret and symbolic guarantee of how it will end. This matters because the Gospel is more about that end than about anything else. The prologue holds the book's genetic programme, a pattern of ordeal and crossing-over, of power unleashed after withdrawal and eclipse. Its climax and fulfillment are death and resurrection. On the same theme, many commentators have recognized a midstory seclusion in the events of 8:27–9:13, where, in the remote settings of the way to Caesarea Philippi and a "high mountain" (9:2), Jesus' secret identity is displayed and bound into his coming sufferings.

At both the beginning and the end of the book, days are marked out, together with times of day, with a precision lacking elsewhere. And in both the familiar pattern is discernible. The early passage 1:21–38 covers some twenty-four hours from morning to morning. On the sabbath morning Jesus cures a man in a synagogue and a woman in a house. "At even, when the sun did set," he heals "all that were diseased" among the crowd at the door (1:32). "And in the morning, rising up a great while before day" (1:35), he withdraws to the wilderness to pray, where Simon finds him and returns him to public life. It is, very precisely, a full day. Action is followed by withdrawal leading to further action. Jesus departs from the world and returns to it via its margin: the wilderness as a place of prayer, of contact with God. For the Christian, Easter is the classic example of this pattern. And it is in Mark's mind. Jesus "rising up a great while before day" (1:35) on this first day prophesies (more precisely in Greek than in the KJV) his early-morning resurrection at the end. The last chapters cover a series of days and of times within them, beginning at 14:1. There is unprecedented precision about the time of Jesus' death. He is crucified at the third hour, dies at the sixth, and is buried at evening. There follows a sabbath when nothing happens at all before the tomb is found empty in the early morning of the first day of the week. In the tomb a young man points to reunion in Galilee, where Jesus began.

The great hinge of the Easter week-end and week-beginning imposes its pattern on more than the first day of Jesus' work. The Resurrection occurs "after three days" (8:31). At 8:2 Jesus notices that the Gentile crowd which he is about to feed has been with him for three days. The number of days gives a resurrection gleam to the meal. A double measure of the same significance is given to the Transfiguration at 9:2 by its occurrence "after six days." The fig tree at 11:13 dies overnight in prophetic contrast to Jesus' overnight revival: the end of the old religion synchronized with the beginning of the new.

For Mark, as for Paul, Jesus' death and resurrection was the decisive point at which divine meaning had invaded human history and turned its course. But for neither of them was it the end. The new (Christian) course of history drove toward the coming of the divine kingdom which Jesus had inaugurated. The end of Mark's story is outside his text; hence one of its most extraordinary features, the abruptness of the ending, which is neither happy nor resolved. Women flee from the tomb shaking with terror; "neither said they any thing to any man; for they were afraid" (16:8). Such endings are very rare in ancient literature. However, Mark has already done something of this sort. Jesus' apocalyptic sermon in chapter 13, his longest continuous speech, ends as suddenly: "and what I say unto you I say unto all, Watch." These incomplete endings,[2] impressively fortissimo, are poised toward an ending—*the* ending—which is beyond the text. Chapter 13 prophesies the stages leading to it. In the first phase, the sufferings Jesus is about to face are promised to his disciples in their turn: betrayal, arrest, trial, torture, and death (13:9–13). The second phase is the horror of the war of 66–70 C.E.: desolation of the Temple, refugees, false messianic pretenders. In the third phase the cosmos collapses and the Son of Man comes to gather the elect. Mark wrote in the second phase, with the Roman conquest of Judea confirming his Christian apocalyptic convictions or prejudices: the destruction of the old is part of the validation of the new.

People

After all that, we may as well go back to the prologue again to open another topic, Mark's understanding of human nature. He believed the boundaries of individuality to be highly permeable. Baptism joined Christ and disciples in a single destiny. For Paul baptism was "into Christ" (Gal. 3:27), as Israel before had been "baptized unto Moses in the cloud and in the sea" (1 Cor. 10:2). So real was this communion that Christians in Corinth were accustomed to getting themselves baptized on behalf of their dead (1 Cor. 15:29—a precedent for today's Mormons); and on the threshold of his death Jesus gave his body and blood to be consumed by his disciples. Participatory sacraments, baptism and eucharist, frame the story. Compared with such vivid interpersonal communion, the Pharisaic baptism of pots and pans (7:4) was trivial and dead.

With Mark, it is never entirely certain who people are. In the prologue he presents John the Baptist, Jesus, and Satan as named characters. But John the Baptist is also Elijah, wearing his costume and leather belt (2 Kings 1:8). This identification is repeated as a common view at 6:15, immediately after Herod's opinion that Jesus is John resurrected—another doubling of roles. Elijah, having ascended to heaven and not died, was believed to be still in the wings of history. He might come to take Jesus down from the Cross (15:36). So Elijah, John, and Jesus merge into one another, and the grand riddle of Jesus' identity is soluble by way of a correct understanding of John's (11:28–33), to which the key is Elijah. Satan is a particularly interesting instance of the same fluidity. He is also called "Beelzebub," and according to the Jerusalem scribes, Jesus "hath Beelzebub, and by the prince of the devils casteth he out devils" (3:22). However unforgivable, even this identification is feasible. At 8:33 Jesus uses it on Peter when Peter has remonstrated with him: "Get thee behind me, Satan." Jesus might be Satan. Peter is, at least for a moment. People are lived by others, most spectacularly the demoniac of 5:1–20 who calls himself "Legion: for we are many" (v. 9).

Mark often signals personal changes by changes of clothes, which were conductors of the power in a person ("If I may but touch his clothes, I shall be whole"; 5:28). At the Transfiguration Jesus' garments radiate heavenly light. After his condemnation the soldiers mockingly clothe him in imperial purple, then strip him of it and put him back in his own clothes. The young man who fled naked from the garden at 14:51, leaving his garment (Greek *sindon*) behind, could be the young man at the end in the tomb wearing a white garment (Greek *stolē*). A *sindon* (the young man's?) has been used in the meanwhile to wrap Jesus' corpse (15:46). There is an echo here of the former demoniac sitting, as does the young man in the tomb, clothed and in his right mind after his exorcism and the drowning in water of his infesting demons (5:15). There is still a clearer echo of the theology of baptism, which turned upon Jesus' death and resurrection. There was a *sindon* which the young man left behind in the garden. A *sindon* was the clothing of the dead Christ. The *stolē* which the young man wears in the tomb after Christ's resurrection is the hieratic garment worn by redeemed believers in Revelation 6:11 and 7:9, 13. Christians moved from one to another, from being clothed in death to being clothed in redemption, through the baptismal rite. They had the code of this part of Mark's story.

Mark's people can surprise in other ways. We expect the disciples to be, if not heroic, at least fairly exemplary. They obey Jesus' brisk commands and follow him everywhere. Yet, as we have seen, they show little understanding of the events they are dragged through. They even exemplify the hardness of heart which characterized outsiders to the Gospel and against which Jesus hurls his words (see the volley of six angry questions at 8:17–18) and actions. Their obduracy is a frustration which heightens tension in the narrative like a repeated discord in music. They all abandon him at the end. James and John betray an obsession with status which is clean contrary to the Gospel. Peter is worse. Jesus' "friends" try to stop him, believing him mad (3:21). He disowns his mother and family. Yet his mother is there at his end, though "looking on afar off" (15:40), and at his empty tomb. The chief priests are wicked, the Pharisees and scribes hostile and wrong, the Sadducees just wrong. Yet at 12:28–34, after a denunciation of traditionalists, Jesus congratulates a scribe on being "not far from the kingdom of God." The crowd which follows Jesus about is seen in various moods: pressing on him so violently as to threaten to crush him (3:9), arousing his compassion (6:34), acclaiming him as he enters Jerusalem (11:9), then preferring Barabbas and howling for his death (15:11). Jesus seems most at home with outcasts: publicans, sinners, and lepers. Transgression of the boundaries of the taboo, like the crossings of the boundaries of personality, gives the story much of its force.

Transgression

A world is ordered and structured by its boundaries. It is changed when those boundaries are crossed. They are social fictions, myths which await their demythologizers. A narrative can draw even tidier boundaries than exist in the world, but only to violate them the more dramatically. The Christians were heirs of the magisterial transgressions of their founder, the outcast Messiah. From the standpoint of traditional Judaism these were blasphemies. Blasphemy, the crime for which Jesus is condemned (14:64), is an eruption of religious energy from the depths below orthodox structure, which it threatens by its primal force. It was for the Christians to show that what was, from the traditionalist point of view, a destructive evil, was truly a divinely authenticated salvation of the lost. Mark's story begins and ends with the sort of major transgressions which were needed to justify Christianity: that is, transgressions approved or done by God. The sky was split at Jesus' baptism, the Temple veil at his death. With the tearing of that veil, which marked off the Temple's inner sanctum and which only the high priest penetrated once a year with sacrificial blood, a huge profanation occurred. Simultaneously (15:36–39) a new holiness appeared with the Gentile centurion speaking Jesus' divine identity, previously spoken by the divine voice. The Temple and Golgotha were far apart. Only text makes these things simultaneous—to the mind's eye. The greatest shock of violation comes at the end. It is the empty tomb, a gaping hole in the supremely important boundary between dead and living. Through it divine power, of a most suspect and untoward sort, is loosed into the world. Hence the terrified flight of the mourners.

Fear, astonishment, and amazement are frequent reactions to Jesus' words and deeds throughout Mark's restless narrative. They surround his first miracle, the exorcism of a demoniac in the synagogue at Capernaum at 1:21–27. The excitement comes from forces breaking bounds. Jesus' teaching in the synagogue is authoritative and unofficial—and therefore astonishing. No sooner is that said than we are presented with an alarming breach of religious propriety as a *fait accompli*: "And there was in their synagogue a man with [Mark says 'in'] an unclean spirit" (v. 23). In the clean building there is an unclean presence, and out of it bursts, in utter contradiction of expectations, the sacred truth: "I know thee who thou art, the Holy One of God" (v. 24). This double shattering of conventional order is followed by a climactic tearing as the unclean spirit tears the man and bursts out of him, screaming. The rapid series of burstings has the effect of one of Dostoyevsky's "skandal" scenes: embarrassment pitched up to terror.

And so it goes on. At 2:1–12 a roof is "broken up" to get a paralytic into Jesus' presence. Jesus forgives the sufferer, and the scribes are scandalized by the blasphemy of his doing what only God should do. But the man is healed and goes out, and again the bystanders are "all amazed." At 2:15–17 there is further scandal at Jesus' eating with "many publicans and sinners." At 2:18–22 Jesus gives a parabolic justification of tearing and bursting: new cloth tears old cloth, new wine bursts old leather bottles, and the norms of everyday existence are overwhelmed by the carnival of the wedding day. Jesus goes on to disregard the sabbath regulations so integral to traditional order. He does not care that his disciples fall foul of them, for "the sabbath was made for man, and not man for the sabbath," and he, the "Son of man," is "Lord also of the sabbath" (2:27–28). He heals a man with a withered hand in a synagogue (adding to the scandal) on the sabbath, and the Pharisees decide to revenge his destruction of their orthodoxy by destroying him (3:6). The great breakings which are at the climax of Mark's Gospel are in sight: Jesus' death and his resurrection from death. In the intervening narrative the holy moves decisively from its accustomed places to new ones, from synagogue to house and, above all, from tradition to Jesus.

The Riddle of Bread

No guide to Mark's Gospel should take leave of his readers without some attempt to help them with one of its most baffling passages, 8:14–21. It is very difficult, but in a way entirely characteristic of this book of secrets, codes, and revelations. There is no mistaking the urgency with which Mark forces it on the reader. And the light of its meaning reflects far into the surrounding narrative. It reads:

> Now the disciples had forgotten to take bread, neither had they in the ship with them but [AT] one loaf. And he charged them, saying, Take heed, beware of the leaven of the Pharisees, and of the leaven of Herod. And they reasoned among themselves, saying, It is because we have no bread. And when Jesus knew it, he saith unto them, Why reason ye, because ye have no bread? perceive ye not yet, neither understand? have ye your heart yet hardened? Having eyes, see ye not? and having ears, hear ye not? and do ye not remember? When I brake the five loaves among five thousand, how many baskets full of fragments took ye up? They say unto him, Twelve. And when the seven among four thousand, how many baskets full of fragments took ye up? And they said, Seven. And he said unto them, How is it that ye do not understand?

The scene is simple but symbolic: Jesus and his (presumably twelve) disciples in a ship at sea with one loaf of bread. It is a classic little icon of the primitive Christian Church. In Jesus' weird harangue which follows, he emphasizes numbers in the course of recalling two incidents already narrated, the miraculous feeding of crowds (6:35–44, 8:1–10).

6:35–44   5 loaves among 5,000 left 12 baskets of bits.
8:1–10   7 loaves among 4,000 left 7 baskets of bits.

To understand the significance of these numbers we must take a series of steps backward.

The first step is to the sabbath-day controversy about Jesus' disciples plucking ears of grain—the material from which bread will be made. Jesus defends their action by asking: "Have ye never read what David did, when he had need, and was an hungred, he, and they that were with him? How he went into the house of God in the days of Abiathar the high priest, and did eat the shewbread, which is not lawful to eat but for the priests, and gave also to those that were with him?" (2:25-26). This David story has, for Mark, a double appeal. First, it is a legitimate transgression of cultic taboo; second, it is about David, and Jesus is both David's son and David's lord (12:35-37).

The regulations for the shewbread are set out in Leviticus 24. It is to consist of twelve loaves. The David story to which Jesus refers is at 1 Samuel 21. It says that David took five of these loaves. Seven would have been left. So these steps backward yield three of the numbers which occur in Mark's enigmatic text: five, twelve, and seven. Adding this Davidic material to the earlier list yields:

1 Samuel 21	12 loaves;	5 taken;	7 were left.
Mark 6:35-44	5 loaves among 5,000 left	12 baskets of bits.	
Mark 8:1-10	7 loaves among 4,000 left	7 baskets of bits.	

Now we can see that the first of Mark's miraculous meals takes two numbers from the story of David and the shewbread (which Mark has made part of his own story). They are twelve and five. There were twelve shewbread loaves and David took five. But with Jesus the numbers go another, and more wonderful, way. He too takes five loaves: he is David's son. Like father, like son. But he leaves—and this can only be supernatural miracle—twelve baskets of fragments. He is not only, even not really, David's son. He is the Christ who is David's lord (12:35-37). So what Jesus does numerically resembles what David did, but also numerically transcends it. This is polemical arithmetic in a story about the relation of the new Kingdom of Christ to the old Kingdom of David, the continuity and the discontinuity between them. It fits the topographical setting, which is a desert somewhere in Jesus' own and Jewish country.

The second miraculous meal, at 8:1-10, is set abroad and is part of an excursion into Gentile territory. In the region of Tyre and Sidon Jesus heals the daughter of a Greek woman (7:24-30). He is reluctant to do this at first and parries, with imagery directly related to our problem here: "It is not meet to take the children's [the Jews'] bread, and to cast it unto the dogs" (v. 27). But she takes up the figure wittily and rejoins: "Yes, Lord: yet the dogs under the table eat of the children's crumbs" (v. 28). This looks very much like a story which we ought to take into account. Between it and the second miraculous meal, Jesus opens the ears and looses the tongue of a deaf and dumb man. The channels of understanding are cleared and liberated. Now to the meal itself.

In the previous Jewish meal the number seven from the Davidic story was not used. David left seven of the twelve shewbread loaves and they were, as it were, left sitting there. But now they are used: seven loaves which leave seven baskets of fragments. This is a little less miraculous than with the Jewish meal, but only quantitatively. Qualitatively the symmetry of seven and seven, the sacred number of fulfillment, is more resolved. The David story was somewhat fulfilled in the Jewish meal; it is more completely fulfilled in this. (This notion of the somewhat-complete or somewhat-fulfilled is logically faulty but indispensable to story-telling.) The miraculous feeding of Gentiles is a consummation even greater than the miraculous feeding of Jews. This crescendo is in line with the Gentile centurion at the Cross (15:39) who transcends and resolves all previous human attempts to identify Jesus. And it reflects the great question which faced the Church after Jesus, of whether or not to admit Gentiles to its sacred meals, and the positive answer to it.[3] This, however, is a resolution not yet achieved, and Mark knows it, for all the influence it exerts on his mind. So five thousand Jews are fed, in contrast to four thousand Gentiles. The Gentiles are less in the kingdom *until* Christ's death has opened it to them. This is a theology Mark has learned from Paul, and his shortfall of a thousand in this story which comes before Christ's death reflects it. There is, after all, one loaf still to be given, and it will matter more than any of the others. At his last meal of all Jesus will take the loaf and say: "Take, eat: this is my body" (14:22). All the other loaves lead to that. The "one loaf" in the ship at 8:14, apparently uneaten, prefigures it.

With the miraculous meals so replete with major significance, the controlled fury of Jesus' interrogation of his disciples in the ship is understandable and apt: "How is it that ye do not understand?" (8:21). He is desperate. They have missed so much. The argument in the cornfield and the Davidic precedent, the lively exchange with the Greek woman and the miraculous meals before and after it—all have been lost on them. More than that, they have lost track of the holy and divine, which, in this long train of coded events associated with bread, has shifted from its accustomed setting into a new place: from old tradition into Christ's life and body and the new community which will be nourished by it.

This solution to the riddle of bread is not exhaustive or exclusively correct. The riddle is too deeply tangled into the fabric of the book for that to be likely. But at least this attempt to unravel it has been done within the book and by means of the hints and symbols it provides, not least those mind-bending numbers. It has shown that to understand a little bit of Mark we need to have attended very carefully to the incidents before it and to be sensitive to what is to come. It is a book which demands no knowledge except of the Bible, but makes very strict and precise demands on our attention. Then it can surprise us by its austere art and the radical force of its message. The darkest secrets of divinity and humanity lurk in its complex and taut story, waiting for agile and dedicated readers to glimpse them as they follow its way along the edges of the world.

NOTES

1. Walter Benjamin, "The Storyteller," in Hannah Arendt, ed., *Illuminations* (London, 1973), p. 102.

2. The last of them, 16:8, is the more incomplete in the Greek, where Mark writes "for" (Greek *gar*) after "they were afraid." So "for" is the last word Mark writes, leaving his whole text trailing, incomplete, into whatever is to come.

3. The most authentic trace of this crisis is at Gal. 2:11–21. Acts 10 gives a deceptively smooth and glamorized version.

SUGGESTED FURTHER READINGS

W. H. Kelber, *The Oral and the Written Gospel* (Philadelphia, 1983).
Frank Kermode, *The Genesis of Secrecy* (Cambridge, Mass., 1979).
R. H. Lightfoot, *The Gospel Message of St. Mark* (Oxford, 1950).
D. E. Nineham, *The Gospel of St. Mark* (Harmondsworth, 1963).

King's College, University of Cambridge

Luke

John Drury

THERE are space, light, and long perspective in Luke's Gospel. Like the painter Claude Lorrain, he is a master of the long view. This is noticeable straightaway, in the leisurely sentence which makes up the preface of his first four verses. Between the moment of his beginning the work and the events he is on the point of telling, "those things which are most surely believed [Greek, 'fulfilled'] among us," a lot has happened and he knows it. There have been "many" previous narrators. Before them there were "eyewitnesses, and ministers of the word." And there has been time for him to mature the "perfect understanding" of this large Christian inheritance which he advertises with some complacency. Now he is going to provide "the certainty of those things," the complete and definitive version. Neither Mark nor Matthew, the previous narrators whose work he builds into his own, enjoyed such calm literary self-confidence and self-consciousness. It is something new.

Time

Lucid articulation of historical process is Luke's skill. In the preface he moves from the "things" themselves (v. 1), through the intermediate period of tradition (v. 2), to his own writing (v. 3). His grand strategy is equally clear, sequential, and expansive. He is aware that history does not begin and end with his Gospel. It flows out of the Old Testament's Jewish past and into the Christian future of the Acts of the Apostles.

Luke's narrative begins further back in time than his predecessors'—not with Jesus as an adult man (as in Mark), nor even with Jesus' birth (as in Matthew), but with the still-childless parents of Jesus' herald, John the Baptist. Only at verse 13 is John's birth promised by the angel. (By the time Mark had written twelve verses he had got Jesus baptized and divinely authenticated.) It takes Luke another forty-four verses for John to be born. Within this clearly marked space between the prophecy of John's birth and its fulfillment, Luke does two things: he starts another story, and he connects it to the one which is already running. Jesus' birth is promised to Mary by the same angel that promised John's to Zacharias, and the two miraculously pregnant mothers meet. The narrative pauses

418

at 1:56 with three uneventful months, of which we are told only that Mary and Elizabeth were together. Then John is born, circumcised, and named, and his father prophesies his destiny. After this come Jesus' birth, more wonderful and more circumstantially described, his circumcision, and his naming. The prophecy of Jesus' destiny is made to outshine John's by being given both a prophet and a scene of its own: old Simeon is "waiting for the consolation of Israel" in the Temple (2:25, 27), where the whole story began—two suggestions of things coming, momentarily, back to base. But it is a point of repose from which Simeon sees far into the future. In the last episode of this two-chapter prologue, the Temple is the setting yet a third time: the twelve-year-old, *bar mitzvah* Jesus sits "in the midst of the doctors, both hearing them, and asking them questions" (2:46). It is an evocative scene—youth among the aged, religious tradition heeded and interrogated—again full of promise for the greater narrative which is about to unroll.

The magisterial shaping and pacing of the prologue vindicate Luke's claim at 1:3 to be a storyteller perfectly in charge of his matter. There is still more in the prologue to admire. When Luke writes at 1:1 of "the things *fulfilled* among us," he reveals the historical presupposition that runs through and energizes his whole work: that time's structure consists of prophecies made and fulfilled. The warnings and promises of prophets were the nexus of divine will and narrative time. This basic grammar dominates Luke. Every episode in his prologue is planted with the seeds of episodes to come and rings with the poetry of prophets and psalms. Are we reading a new Christian text or an old Jewish one? If we wonder, then Luke has succeeded. His prologue is a revival of the antique as deliberate as any neoclassical or neogothic building of the nineteenth century, and as motivated by the desire to demonstrate the august antiquity of the new. It contrasts with the shock of the new in Mark, already somewhat softened by Matthew with his genealogy and frequent recourse to fulfilled prophecy.

It is not just pattern and pace in the prologue that derive from the ancient Scriptures. So do the language, characters, and actual events. The language imitates the Septuagint and is full of its stock phrases: "the house of," "before the face of," "and behold," "and it came to pass," "in the days of." All the speeches are in the form of Jewish poetry and are stuffed with quotations from it. The deliberate datings follow old precedent. The characters are revivals of old Jewish types. Elizabeth and Zacharias are "righteous before God" like Noah, childless like Abraham and Sarah. Mary greets Elizabeth with an "occasional poem" very closely modeled on Hannah's (1:46–55; cf. 1 Sam. 2:1–11). The angel Gabriel, the most important personage in chapter 1, last appeared to Daniel (Dan. 9:21). Simeon and Anna are paragons of traditional piety. Abraham, Moses, and Elijah are invoked. More than all this, what happens to the characters revives events of the sacred past: miraculous births, angelic visitations, pilgrimages to the Temple, ceremonies in the Temple and at home in obedience to the Law. It is, incidentally, a sign of Luke's subtlety that the child Jesus and the events immediately surrounding him are a little less determined by the ancient than those associated with the child John. He grows further out of it and into the new. But the major point remains. Luke's way of establishing the historical "certainty" of the Christian Gospel is to appropriate sacred history lock, stock, and barrel. He both refers to it as past and makes it recur. This is far from the sort of certainty sought in modern historical criticism, but that Luke believed it to be utterly valid is as evident in his last chapter as in his first two. On the road to Emmaus, "beginning at Moses and all the prophets [which includes the histories] he expounded unto them in all the scriptures the things concerning himself" (24:27). "All the scriptures": Luke's literary confidence is imperial.

The thorough scriptural neoclassicism of the prologue is not maintained throughout the rest of this Gospel. Luke can change styles as time and place demand. In Acts, for example, he manages the official letter, the sermon, and the adventure story. The aptness of the particular character of the prologue to its place in his scheme of history is obvious. It establishes a link between the yesterday of Jesus' life and the day-before-yesterday of the Scriptures which "concern" him. Luke's long historical view is far from monotonous or monochrome. It is a flow through different but connected phases. So history before Christ, while coloring and shaping the prologue altogether, also provides shapes and tones at important points in what follows. The beginning of Jesus' public life is a tableau very different from the sudden irruption of Mark 1:15. The scene is synagogue, to match the Temple in the prologue. The subject is Scripture, with Jesus as both exegete and fulfillment of its prediction and precedents (4:16–30). Jesus' momentous departure to his doom at Jerusalem at 9:51–52 draws on the Exodus (the very word which is translated as "departure" at 9:51) and Ezekiel (Ezek. 21:2: "Son of man, set thy face toward Jerusalem, and drop thy word toward the holy places, and prophesy against the land of Israel"; compare "he stedfastly set his face to go to Jerusalem" at Luke 9:51 again). His last prophecy on the way to execution recalls Hosea and Ezekiel (23:30–31; cf. Hosea 10:8 and Ezek. 20:47). Stephen's apologia in Acts 7 is a résumé of ancient history. Among these fulfillments of past prophecy in the narrative present there are also prophecies made in the narrative present to await future fulfillment. So in the synagogue scene in 4:16–30, with its past-to-present references, there is also present-to-future prophecy of mission to the Gentiles. This will be fulfilled nowhere in the Gospel but only in Acts. With yet another traverse of the shuttle this prophecy of Gentile Christianity draws on the precedents of Elijah and Elisha. The miraculous apostolic fishing at 5:1–11[1] and Jesus' discourse at the Last Supper (22:24–36) also recall the past and look to the

Christian future. So past, present, and future, our usual divisions of time, are connected by prophecies made and fulfilled.

In view of all this we may regard it as a personalized focusing of complex temporal references that in Luke Jesus is himself a prophet. This interpretation of the central figure may surprise Christian readers, who are accustomed to other and later designations of him, but it should not surprise Jewish or Islamic ones. For Luke, Jesus is a prophet, not incidentally but first and foremost: "a prophet mighty in deed and word before God and all the people," as the two on the road to Emmaus call him (24:19). Their description is justified by Jesus' having raised a widow's son from death (7:11–17), as Elijah had done (1 Kings 17:17–24), with the witnesses acclaiming: "a great prophet is risen up among us" (7:16). Like Elijah, Jesus leaves the world by heavenly ascension, and, also like him, his return at the end of time is expected. Perhaps Jesus is nowhere more substantially a prophet and Elijah's antitype than in his expense of time and energy in attempting to bring the nation at large to repent and change its ways before it is too late.[2] The call to repentance occupies the greater part of Jesus' teaching on the way to Jerusalem in chapters 10–16—a large proportion of the book. He curses unrepentant Jewish towns (10:13–15); he compares this unrepentant generation unfavorably with Jonah's Ninevites (11:29–32); he recalls ominously the murder of prophets (11:47–52); he holds up local disasters as warnings of worse to come if repentance fails (13:1–5); and a series of parables of repentance, beginning with the fig tree at 13:6–9, has its climax with the great parables in chapters 15 and 16, which are not aimed only or chiefly at private persons. The Jewish revolt and its cruel suppression by the Romans is always in prophetic view. Jesus refers to it overtly at 21:20.

Prophets are inspired from above. But the energy derived from that vertical source is deployed horizontally. Prophetic thinking and utterance move back and forth along the stream of time. Luke's Jesus is the fulfilling last of the ancient prophetic line, foretelling its end and the beginning of a new dispensation in history. He is a historical axis or watershed, time's midpoint.[3] Luke is as horizontally minded about things concerning Jesus as about Jesus himself. Gabriel in chapter 1 does not speak of such stock angelic topics as heavenly mysteries or the end of time but of imminent historical events. That was his message in Daniel too, but here he proclaims, not the vast Danielic eras of world history, but the two births. Luke loves the domestic. He shows the angel, sent from God above, crossing the floor of a room in courteous greeting with his news. This telling of tidings is a major theme which also betrays Luke's interest in horizontal movement. It moves his pastoral birth story at 2:8–19. Here again, though the source is the "above" whence the angel comes upon the shepherds, we are shown movement on the earth's surface. The shepherds go to Bethlehem, see the child, make "known abroad the saying which was told them concerning this child" (v. 17), and return to their work. The Acts of the Apostles will be occupied with just this: greater journeys out and back with the news of Christ. It is symptomatic that Zacharias' punishment for his incredulity in chapter 1 is dumbness, inability to tell people what he has been told. For Luke that, along with impenitence, is a grave incapacity causing an eddy in the flow of his tale.

A comparison with John's Gospel will clinch all that has been said so far. John and Luke share tradition not found elsewhere (such as the fishing miracle and Lazarus), and both occupy the phase of gospel writing after Mark and Matthew. But they differ radically about history. John starts with myth where Luke starts with circumstantial tale. John has a word-incarnate christology of which there is no trace in Luke, who is occupied with his more down-to-earth prophet christology. John is more preoc-cupied with vertical movement and Luke with horizontal movement. It is as if John had seen the theological danger in Luke's historicism: Jesus held in a past which got remoter every day. Certainly his strategy is appropriate to his having a sense of the problem. He takes the long line of history and bends it into a curve around his vertically understood Jesus. That done, every point in history is equidistant from its center: whether the Creation, or Abraham, or the apostle Thomas, or readers like our-selves, or Doomsday. In these Johannine terms Luke's note that Jesus "increased in wisdom and stature, and in favour with God and man" (2:52), that he developed, would be quite unthinkable.

Beginning and Ending

John and Luke agree on one incontrovertible thing: there is more in the world than there is in any book. John even muses on this state of affairs in his last verse: "And there are also many other things which Jesus did, the which, if they should be written every one, I suppose that even the world itself could not contain the books that should be written. Amen." The glimpse of the world collapsing under an overwhelming weight of literature is memorably ridiculous—a librarian's nightmare, perhaps. It is apt that it should come at a book's ending, because it is when books begin and end that their relation to the world is most problematic. In mid-reading we are in the book's world, but starting and finishing we are in transition between world and book. At these exits and entrances the artificiality of texts is troublesome. They have to be modified so as to connect the text with what is not in it. John does it by myth and philos-ophy. He is writing about whatever was, is, or will be outside his book. Luke does it by his kind of history. Events outside his text on either side connect to it by prophecy and fulfillment. We have seen him doing it in his first two chapters. Now we will look at his last.

It is carefully structured to hold a tension between ignorance and recognition, confusion and clarity, in which uncertain identity and skepticism about news and evidence provide much of the drama. The first eleven verses of chapter 24 show the women at Jesus' empty tomb. The story is borrowed from Mark, but Luke makes telling amendments. Instead of meeting one man, as in Mark, the women meet two. I have suggested an identity for Mark's mysterious one man in my essay on Mark (see the section "People"). What can be suggested, since definition stronger than suggestion would be inappropriate to the tale, about Luke's two "in shining garments"? The shining garments are a clue. At his transfiguration Jesus' "raiment was white and glistering" (9:29). Luke uses words more closely akin to one another than glistering is to shining: *exastraptōn* and *astraptousē* are held together by assonance. Jesus himself is, crucially, not there in the tomb. The shining garments borrowed from the Transfiguration clothe the two men. But there were two men at the Transfiguration too. Then Jesus "talked with two men, who were Moses and Elias: Who appeared in glory, and spake of his decease [Greek *exodos*] which he should accomplish at Jerusalem" (9:30–31). Now we are at Jerusalem and that exodus is in train. The suggestion has to be that the two men may be Moses and Elijah, present at the event which they discussed before. It is at least clear that Luke refers backward in pointing up the significance of this scene. Where Mark has his man say "he goeth before you into Galilee" (Mark 16:7) and looks *forward* beyond the end of his text, Luke edits this into "remember how he spake unto you when he was yet in Galilee, Saying, The Son of man must be delivered . . ." (24:6–7) and looks *back* into his text. Recalling Moses and Elijah would be within the same reverting movement. The case for this interpretation is not weakened by the testimony of those other two men, the ones on the way to Emmaus at 24:23, that what the women had seen at the tomb was "a vision of angels" (not men, an indefinite number, and a curious agreement with Matthew, who had an angel at the tomb), for the apostles, who started this version of "a vision of angels," did not take the women's evidence seriously and "their words seemed to them as idle tales" (24:11). Their witness is secondhand and careless. Also the two on the way to Emmaus who retail the mistaken apostolic version are themselves mistaken and muddled. Misapprehension is of the dramatic essence of this chapter, and the "vision of angels" is, ironically, an "idle tale" of the very apostles who mistakenly considered the true report of the women to be just that.

The threads with which Luke ties story to story in 24:1–11 have already taken us into the Emmaus tale. It forms a bridge between the empty tomb (disbelieved by the apostles) and the revelation of Jesus himself to the apostles (before they have time to exercise on these male witnesses the glum skepticism which they have visited on the women). Set between the unbelieved empty tomb and the incontrovertible revelation of Jesus himself "flesh and bones," the Emmaus story juggles skepticism and positive recognition.

It begins with two men on "that same [empty tomb] day" traveling from Jerusalem to Emmaus. They are moving away from the locality where the decisive events are happening toward a place of no significance. They are on a dispirited narrative detour which, quite unexpectedly, will be revelatory. It is typical of Luke that Emmaus, as a place which is nowhere in particular, should be lit up with marvelous significance: Nazareth was like that too. On their way the two men talk "of all these things which had happened" (v. 14). Surreptitiously and incognito, Jesus joins them and asks them what they are talking about. The irony of this is very tense. He, and all that has happened to him, is the subject of their conversation, yet he appears as nobody in particular knowing nothing of any importance (that masterly "What things?" at v. 19). He gets, he of all people, the sort of rudeness which the depressed and preoccupied deal out to prying ignorance. It is a cue for further irony: they tell him what has happened to him! Perhaps, in their telling of it, they may happen on the truth of it. Luke believes much in the virtue of telling. But their account mixes falsehood ("vision of angels") with truth and ends with the inconclusive report that "certain of them which were with us" went to the tomb "but him they saw not." So their telling does not get them to the truth. Now it is the turn of the previously modest and reticent stranger to get rough: "O fools, and slow of heart to believe all that the prophets have spoken" (v. 25). They have been musing hopelessly because they have confined their attention to the recent past only. If, the stranger tells them, they would but take a longer, more Lukan, historical view, if they would but tell a longer tale, they would find in prophecies told long before the elucidation of the events which baffle them. He does what they have neglected to do, reaches into the dark backward of time and, in an enormous exegetical lesson of which the reader gets only the briefest note, expounds "in all the scriptures the things concerning himself" (v. 27). As at the beginning of his career (4:16–21), so, symmetrically, at its close comes Jesus' self-application of Scripture.

Hermeneutics take the two men to the edge of Emmaus and the threshold of certainty. But theirs is not the stranger's destination. "He would have gone further" (v. 28). There is symbolic as well as commonplace reference to the great exodus he is accomplishing. But he stays in biddable response to their constraining. Previously he has stopped them in their tracks with his ingenuous question (v. 17). Now they stop him in his tracks, and all three sit down to table. For the reader, who has heard so much of Jesus' teaching at table and his parables about sitting at table, who has so recently witnessed the "last" supper of which this one is reminiscent, it is a signal to arouse expectation. It is fulfilled: first by Jesus' eucharistically deliberate blessing and giving of the bread, second by the opening of the eyes of the two men (v. 31), answering to their "holden" eyes at verse 16. With climax mounting upon climax, Jesus vanishes at this moment. The two are left to tumble to the truth of everything and take the news to the apostles.

In the Emmaus story the happiness of the present moment of recognition floods back into the unhappy past by means of interpretation, changing it utterly. Good exegesis plucks from the mind a rooted sorrow and sets the heart aglow (v. 32). Present happiness carries into the next scene with Jesus himself among the apostles at last. He asks for food and eats before them. The meal at Emmaus, for all its wonder, was incomplete. He gave them bread but vanished before eating. Now he eats: fish, recalling the great catch at 5:1–11;[4] and honey, the food of the Promised Land toward which the original exodus traveled. All is complete. But in temporal process, to which Luke is as attentive as ever, it is never quite so. The most fulfilled present is not outside time or without reference to past and future. In the last ten verses of this last chapter both the remoter past of Moses, the prophets, and the psalms and the nearer past of Jesus' suffering and rising are once again recapitulated into fulfillment. And the future worldwide travels of Christian missionaries "in his name among all the nations, beginning from [not the KJV's 'at'] Jerusalem" are initiated.

So the end of the Gospel is also a beginning. As the first two chapters gravitated toward Jerusalem centripetally, so from now on the news will spread out from Jerusalem centrifugally. For a little while the apostles are to wait in Jerusalem, but only until the power to work comes upon them. Then their journeys away from it will be creative, not evasions of disaster as in the sad walk from Jerusalem to Emmaus. Given all this, the sketchy ascension in verse 51, even the satisfyingly symmetrical return of the apostles to the Temple, where the whole Gospel began, are expedients too temporary to amount to an ending. Perhaps for Luke, with his awareness of the long flow of time and his belief in Doomsday, an ending described in a historical book written by a man in history would not be appropriate anyway.

Crises

So much does the long historical perspective matter to Luke that beginnings and endings are shaped to find their places within it. They punctuate but never disrupt it. Mark was different. He rejoiced darkly in the disruptive power of the Christian gospel. He presented a Jesus energetically breaking bounds, transgressing rules and hopes. His work was framed by the vertical descent of power and authority at the outset, and by the twin disturbances of torn veil and empty tomb at its conclusion. "And suddenly" is as favorite a catchphrase of his as "And it came to pass" is of Luke's. Matthew did a good deal to calm Mark's detonations into a story of prophecy fulfilled and new energy emerging from old tradition. He began with a genealogy going back to Abraham, ended with the risen Jesus commissioning the apostles. That last Matthean scene is, for Luke, the germ of his Acts of the Apostles. He exploits further Matthew's extensions of Mark, and the resulting Gospel-with-Acts is a sequel and corollary to the epic sweep of Old Testament history.

In Luke the source of narrative movement is the pattern formed around a midterm crisis. In terms of the metaphor of flow, it is as if a stream encounters an obstacle. It swirls and eddies, momentarily going back on and in on itself, as it seeks a way round or through. Then it goes on, though in a different course from that which it might have taken otherwise.

The biography of Jesus which takes up the Gospel is, when seen within the context of Luke's whole scheme, one such extended crisis. Into it flow, as into a funnel, all the prophecy and precedent of the past, all the warnings and all the promises. Out from it on the other side fans the worldwide mission of the apostolic Church. In between the two is the narrative of resistance to Jesus from central or orthodox Judaism and acceptance of him by pariahs and heretics. This central narrative is what makes the difference. It is, in terms of Luke's central image of Jesus as prophet, a difference made by some people repenting and some not. The people of God before Jesus are not the same as the people of God after him. Nation has given place to universal Church.

A similar change affects the city of God, Jerusalem. Traditional enthusiasm for it glows in Luke's prologue. The Temple and its liturgy are as devoutly attended as any Deuteronomist could wish. Jesus' long journey toward Jerusalem (9:51) is decidedly ambiguous, however. Doom and hostility turn it into a strange pilgrimage. He dies there and rises. Around this great hinge between Gospel and the Acts of the Apostles there is much to-ing and fro-ing, starting with the Emmaus story, which eventually (very eventually) resolves itself in Acts through a series of missionary journeys from Jerusalem into the last and most adventurous journey of all, to Rome. Only at the end do we guess that Luke has had in mind a tale of two cities. Behind the gradual abandonment of Jerusalem which occupies the whole of Luke's *oeuvre* stands the catastrophe of 70 C.E., making urgent sense of this new religion's finding itself an urban center other than the rebellious and ruined capital of Judea which was, in happier days, its home.

The shape of Luke's historical macrocosm is also discernible in the microcosm of stories within it. His parables, for example, turn on the axis of a midterm crisis as decisively as Matthew's drive toward the ultimate crisis of Doomsday and stop there. We can see Luke making the necessary redistribution of incident when he adapts Matthew's Lost Sheep parable at 15:3–7. Matthew ended it with "and if so be that he find it, verily I say unto you, he rejoiceth over it" (Matt. 18:13). There is no conjectural "if so be that" in Luke. With his usual concreteness he substitutes "when he hath found it, he layeth it on his shoulders, rejoicing" (v. 5). Having made Matthew's rejoicing into fact instead of possibility, he extends it into a happy party of friends and neighbors in the shepherd's home. There was no such scene in Matthew. Luke's addition changes the parable radically. Retrieval is not an ultimate possibility but a current actuality with current consequence. This midterm finding of the lost sheep is paralleled in numerous other parables found only in Luke: the kind Samaritan breaking his journey (10:29–37); the tower builder and the king, who preempt disaster by prudence (14:28–33); the Prodigal Son coming to himself in the far country; the steward getting himself some support (16:1–18; Matthew would surely have brought down the curtain on the terrifying audit and consigned the man to hell).

As in parables, so in narrative incident, Luke's transforming crises take the place of Matthew's endings. The supper at Emmaus is an obvious instance (another broken journey). So is the resurrected widow's son at Nain, handed back to his mother and his future (7:11–17). Luke's treatment of Peter is particularly revealing. Mark was prepared to leave him in his abject failure (Mark 14:72) with only a hint of anything beyond it (Mark 16:7). In Luke that failure is taken in the narrative stride and a creative future for Peter is promised and (in Acts) enacted. At the Last Supper Jesus looks beyond Peter's denial to his episcopate: "I have prayed for thee, that thy faith fail not: and when thou art converted, strengthen thy brethren" (22:32). Peter is as important for the time just after Jesus as John the Baptist was for the time just before him. John was the last of the proclaimers of the Messiah to come; Peter is the first of the proclaimers of the Messiah who has come. That Luke, unlike either of his predecessors, should represent him as penitent and convertible shows that he regards the human heart and mind as axial in the movement of history. That is where the repentance, the change, can happen which surfaces in external history as new action beginning at the point where old energies ran out.

Parables

Luke's Good Samaritan and Prodigal Son parables show him to be as much a master of the short story as of the long. The full measure of his achievement becomes clearest from comparison of his parables with those of his predecessors, Mark and Matthew. Much of his achievement derives from them. An appreciation of his parabolic inheritance will allow us to gauge his innovative power.

Narrative engages its readers by feeding them a mixture of the hidden and the open. We are told enough to get us interested because we understand it. Enough is kept back from us to keep us interested by the presence of things which we do not understand, but hope to understand by reading on or reading again more carefully. It happens horizontally, along the story line: how will it end? Or, how does this bit which I am reading connect with what is before and after it? It also happens vertically: what is the deep and mysterious ground or source of these events which I am reading about? When parables occur in narratives they, as parts of the story, share these properties. As stories within the story they take stock of its movement along the line of time by reflecting, from the moment in between which they occupy, on the past, which has been told, and the future, which has yet to be told. They work vertically too. The space occupied by a parable is a temporary halt in the narration which is used to explore the depth and ground of what is past and impending. As we take time off from the obvious business of living to read stories which make some sense of it, so a story takes time off from *its* obvious business (saying what happens next) to tell another little story which makes some sense of the tale at large. Parables clarify—but without blowing the narrator's cover or exhausting the underlying mystery of his subject matter. According to Flaubert, a narrator should be submerged in his tale, but only up to the waist. He takes advantage of that position by looking about him and seeing much further than the submerged creatures in his story. He can look up and down into the sky and water which affect their little lives, around for anything that may be coming at them unawares.

Mark

As an author is to the whole story, so is anyone within it to the phase of it in which he tells a parable. By doing so he wraps himself for the occasion in the mantle of prophecy and stands aloof: like Ivan in *The Brothers Karamazov* when he tells his disturbing parable of the Grand Inquisitor to his believing brother Alyosha. It matters very much who tells a parable. By the very act of doing so he invests himself with some of the godlike percipience of the author himself—but usually with only so much as suits him as a character. It is his point of view that informs his parable, not the author's pure and simple, so the precious element of obscurity is preserved by the limits of speaking within character. But here we bump into what is distinctive and odd about the Gospels. All the parables in them, except for some little parabolic utterances by John the Baptist, are told by Jesus. And he is not a character like the rest of them. As the Son of God, he has the divine status of the one in the story who knows it all. Mark makes this status fiercely exclusive in his chapter 4, where nobody understands his parables, nor is meant to, though he explains them to his disciples in private. Whereas in *The Brothers Karamazov* the truth of human existence is pluralized and relativized by being portioned out among the four brothers, here it is concentrated on the single Son of God. This concentration holds the danger of overexplicitness, of blowing the narrative cover. It is counteracted by the extraordinary obtuseness of everybody else, hearing and hearing but not understanding. The easiest example is the parable of the vineyard at Mark 12:1–12. It is the easiest and the clearest, immediately understood by its hearers, because, unlike the previous seed parable in chapter 4, it occurs at a point in the narrative when the cards are down and the dénouement in sight. Yet everything in it refers to something else, in the manner of allegory, and does so in order to justify the transition from old religion to new which drives the whole book. It is clinched by the text from Psalms 118:22–23:

> The stone which the builders refused is become the head stone of the corner.
> This is the Lord's doing: it is marvellous in our eyes.

Old Testament imagery provides most of the code: Israel as vineyard, God as owner of it, the leaders as tenants, the prophets as emissaries of God. Christian imagery gives the rest: Jesus as the well-beloved son, his death and rejection as the climactic outrage which legitimates God's giving the vineyard to others (Gentiles).

The seed parable in Mark 4 is obscure because it is placed early in the story. The mystery is as deliberate as it is provocative. The reader knows who Jesus is because of what has happened before. He has heard the voice from heaven at 1:11: "Thou art my beloved Son, in whom I am well pleased," and the acclamations of demons at 1:24 and 3:11. There is no doubt about who Jesus is in the realm of the spirits to which the reader is privy. But men, apart from Jesus himself, are ignorant of it. So the demonic acclamations erupt into the story to be pushed back again by Jesus' commands to be silent, and only the reader is any the wiser. Likewise, the parables in Mark 4 are set in narrative consisting of repeated failures to recognize Jesus, of which the argument with scribes from Jerusalem about Beelzebub (3:21–30) is the sharpest. So Jesus tells parables which drive toward a harvest beyond failure—revelation beyond concealment, greatness beyond littleness—but do not get there. Even though Jesus explains them to the disciples privately, nothing is said about their understanding them, and the legend of the storm at sea which follows immediately (4:35–41) shows that they have not understood by having them ask: "What manner of man is this, that even the wind and the sea obey him?" The characters do not get the gospel secret of who Jesus is, not only because their hearts are hardened but also because the narrative in which they exist has not got there. Only in the events at the end, Jesus' death and resurrection, is his identity revealed, and Mark 4 is a long way from that. Precisely because of that distance it is necessary that the characters in the story cannot see the end—and that the reader *should* catch a parabolic glimpse of it.

Mark has Jesus say that he speaks in parables so that "seeing they may see, and not perceive; and hearing they may hear, and not understand; lest at any time they should be converted, and their sins should be forgiven them" (4:12). He puts Jesus at a decisive distance from the crowd to utter it: "he entered into a ship and sat in the sea; and the whole multitude was by the sea on the land" (4:1). It needs Jesus' interpretation, alone with the disciples, in order to be understood. That interpretation, together with the mystery and the pessimism about human nature, is well within Mark's apocalyptic world-picture. The seed parable in 2 Esdras 4, similar to and contemporary with Mark's, has the same features. The apocalyptic mind sees people frogmarched by fate and keeps its hold on history only by looking to the time when history's appalling contradictions of theology will themselves be contradicted by decisive divine action. The power and the glory—the meaning—will strike into the historical world from without. Meanwhile "we see through a glass, darkly" (1 Cor. 13:12), and the enigmatic parable is the aptest medium. Only divine beings, angels or Sons of God, know; and even they do not know everything (Mark 13:32). So Jesus interprets his parable. As he does so he locks it into the narrative text, in which the failures of which the parable speaks in advance will be actualized. These show Jesus' interpretation to be the indispensable carrier of the events in the parable into the events of the narrative proper.

At Mark 4:15 Jesus says: "these are they by the way side, where the word is sown; but when they have heard, Satan cometh immediately, and taketh away the word that was sown in their hearts." At 8:27–33, within the story's momentous midterm, Peter is on the way with Jesus and speaks the true word of Jesus' identity. But when Jesus tells him about his coming fate and Peter rebukes him, Jesus rebukes him in return with "Get thee behind me, Satan" (v. 33). Peter is Satan because he tries to take away that word.

At Mark 4:16–17 Jesus says: "And these are they likewise which are sown on stony ground; who, when they have heard the word, immediately receive it with gladness; And have no root in themselves, and so endure but for a time: afterward, when affliction or persecution ariseth for the word's sake, immediately they are offended." That "offended" is taken up later (14:27), when Jesus prophesies his imminent desertion by his disciples. They are not rooted in his gospel of death and resurrection: evidently, because in the Garden when those events were begun by the arrival of Judas and the posse "they all forsook him, and fled" (14:50).

Finally, at Mark 4:18–19 Jesus says: "And these are they which are sown among thorns; such as hear the word, And the cares of this world, and the deceitfulness of riches, and the lusts of other things entering in, choke the word, and it becometh unfruitful." At 10:17–22 a rich man, eager for eternal life, hears Jesus' word of fulfillment through renunciation and "went away grieved: for he had great possessions."

The only possible candidate for narrative actualization of the success-ful sowing is the centurion at the Cross, presented at 15:39 as the first of the crowd of Gentile Christians whom Mark preferred to any other human group. So it might be more accurate to say that that fulfillment lies beyond the text and in life.

Mark's parables are, then, controlled horizontally by being placed where they are on the temporal line, and vertically by his belief in two parallel levels of activity: the mundane and the supernatural or spiritual. The moment of the final coincidence of these two levels can be plotted precisely: at Mark 15:36–39 Jesus dies, the Temple veil which separates the mundane from the supernatural is split, and the centurion utters the truth ("Son of God") which none of the merely human characters has reached before, though the supernatural ones and the reader knew it all along.

Matthew

Matthew's Gospel is the earliest commentary on Mark and also, at least in the matter of parables, the best. In Matthew 13, which is his expanded version of Mark 4, we get a more explicit and rationalized explanation of the function of parables than Mark's. To the end of his version of Mark 4 Matthew adds his own reason for the parables: "that it might be fulfilled which was spoken by the prophet, saying, I will open my mouth in parables; I will utter things which have been kept secret from the foun-dation of the world" (13:35).

Matthew is never more in earnest than when he says that something fulfills prophecy. Jesus' birth and infancy are built of such fulfillments, and so here is his use of parables. To invoke prophecy and its coming to pass is to use a scheme of history. Matthew's is of a mythological sort common to many religions. Before the foundation of the world all was clear and simple. At the end of the world all will be simple again, as is shown in the parables which follow this assertion of fulfillment: the re-covery of the hidden treasure and pearl, the sorting into good and bad of plants and fish (13:44–50). But between the simplicities of Genesis 1:1 and Revelation 22:5, those twin parameters of the Bible where there is only God or "simplicity itself," stretches our ambiguous story. Here we are "under conditions that seem unpropitious"[5] and baffle clear explanation. They tease us by telling us a certain amount, but not enough for our satisfaction or repose. They arouse the weird intimation that "everything transitory is but a parable" (Goethe, *Faust* II). Goethe's word for the kind of utterance appropriate to the times is Matthew's too—parable. So Jesus, the Son of God, who alone knows about the start and finish of things, fulfills prophecy by opening his mouth in parables which speak what has been hidden from the beginning and what will be uncovered at the end

(Matt. 13:35). In that way he stands over and above the midtime narrative he is in. At the same time, and as a historical character within it, he can only be paradoxical and parabolical in his revelation.

It is appropriate to the historical myth of a transitory world of enigmatic ambiguity set between eternal simplicities, that the basic form of parable for both Matthew and Mark is historical allegory: historical because the parables are parts of the story, allegorical because they are not complete in themselves. Jesus alone tells them because he is the whole subject of the story, and because in him the two worlds meet. So things in the parables stand for things elsewhere. In the vineyard parable in Mark 12 the meaning of the allegorical figures is so well known from Old Testament Scripture and Mark's recent Church history that no explanation is needed. Matthew, still using historical allegory, more often makes the "elsewhere" to which they refer into the day of doom at the end of time. An example is the interpretation of the parable of wheat and tares at 13:37–43: Jesus has sown the good seed, the devil the bad seed, the angels are the reapers, and the fire is the Last Judgment. Another example is the set of parables about divine justice at the end of the world which Matthew adds to his version of Mark 13. They explain Jesus' final gnomic summons "Watch" (Mark 13:37) by parabolic examples of what sort of conduct it requires (Matt. 25). Watching becomes ethics, not haruspication.

So both Mark and Matthew have parables which are allegories of history. Mark, by concentrating more on the history within his tale which is history of the incognito Son of God, is necessarily the more obscure, enigmatic, and riddling (the parables at Mark 2:18–22 and 4:21 are riddles). Matthew, by adding parables about the Last Judgment, is necessarily the plainer.

Luke

Luke is plainer still. In his Gospel, and only there, occur those lucid and realistic tales which have such immediate appeal to moderns (who are generally much less fond of allegory than the ancients were) that they are often treated as normative. The Good Samaritan (10:30–35) and the Prodigal Son (15:11–32) are honored by historical critics as Jesus' own work, whereas the allegories of Mark and Matthew are often imputed to less enlightened early Christian teachers. Painters, writers, composers, and choreographers have taken up the Prodigal Son or the Good Samaritan as fit material for their arts. Luke's parables are, however, decidedly Lukan in their realism, humanism, and more optimistic view of history. These are features of Luke's whole outlook and show that the parables are very much part of his work. So is Luke very original? In gospel terms, yes. But in terms of the whole Bible, no. Mark and Matthew, with their often bizarre allegories of history, drew on the apocalyptic tradition of Ezekiel and Daniel, with its marked surrealism and allegory, which were appropriate to their gloomier view of human history. Luke draws on an older and Jewish tradition which was more cheerful about it. In the stories of Joseph and David we find a world confident in the justice of history, in its transparency to the divine. For the apocalyptists this confidence had broken down under catastrophic contradictions such as the sufferings of the righteous and the success of the wicked. Luke revives it. Indeed, the Good Samaritan draws copiously on 2 Chronicles 28, in which compassionate Samaritans tend the wounded and take them on their asses to Jericho. And the Prodigal Son has numerous echoes of the Joseph story: the journey to a far country where there are sexual temptation and famine, the reunion of father and son in which one runs to greet and kiss the other, the investiture with robe and ring, and the feasting. Luke learned his narrative craft, not from apocalyptic seers (though as a versatile stylist he could imitate them: see 10:18), but from the older realistic historians who rejoiced in the ambiguities of human nature, writ so large in David and Joseph, as the very material with which divine providence worked, rather than as something regrettable awaiting its Doomsday correction.

The best place to see Luke at work as a teller of parables is chapter 15. To the chagrin of Pharisees and scribes, Jesus is instructing publicans and sinners. He justifies his historical action by the parables which follow; reflection on history is still their function. The first is the Lost Sheep, which is adapted from Matthew 18:10–14. There it was applied to the Christian pastor among his flock. Here it is applied to Jesus in the more ordinary world at large. Thus Luke, the better historian, avoids Matthew's anachronism. He also increases the human and happy element by adding the celebration party given by the shepherd at his homecoming. At the same time, as we have seen above, this addition changes the structure from Matthew's twofold pattern (lost–found) to Luke's threefold pattern (lost–found–social consequence). This middle-of-time pattern carries into the subsequent parables in chapters 15 and 16, as well as being a reduced replica of the pattern inherent in the whole of Luke–Acts. After his adaptation of Matthew's Lost Sheep, Luke adds—it takes no great skill—the companion parable of the housewife and her lost coin. Luke makes more of women and of money than did Mark or Matthew. There is allegory in both these parables, most noticeably at the end of the second, where the joy in the household signifies the joy of the angels in heaven when a sinner repents. Luke can do allegory if he chooses. The trouble here is that it doesn't work. Matthew's Lost Sheep parable gives him trouble which his own, and derivative, Lost Coin parable makes worse. For his subject is the most urgent of all subjects to him—repentance. Sheep hardly repent. Coins certainly do not. Only that more complex entity, the human being, can repent. Jesus must tell a tale about a man who is bad but in the end good. The Prodigal Son fills the bill triumphantly and is followed by that masterpiece of moral ambiguity and blessed opportunism, the Unjust (better, Enterprising) Steward. As a result Luke's great parable section has a character quite different from the equivalents of his precursors. It is as full of domestic detail as a Dutch painting, draws its characters with a subtlety rivaled only by John, and presents the one thing needful as not endurance nor the penetration of supernatural secrets but the resilience to face up to and cope with the problem in front of one's nose. This is the wisdom of daylight, not nocturnal vision. On the way to it something has been achieved in the way of parables which may be ranged with what Mozart did for opera with *The Marriage of Figaro*: a grand and basically mythical genre has been transposed into the complexities of the commonplace. Luke does not reject the historical allegories of his predecessors. He includes many of them, usually with his own innovations—including improvements of the allegorical fit (compare his version of the Strong Man at 11:21–23 with Mark 3:27 and Matt. 12:29). And there are elements of allegory in the Prodigal Son itself: God as the father, the elder brother representing traditional Judaism and the younger representing Gentile Christianity. But the tale is quite intelligible to readers who miss these elements, and the Unjust Steward seems to have none at all. Luke's achievement is the naturalistic, unallegorical parable which breaks the mold. Perhaps it should not be called "parable" at all but rather "moral tale." Yet in one way he keeps faith with his tradition and, as a narrator, could scarcely do otherwise. His parables still refer to the greater story unfolding around them. The Prodigal Son and Unjust Steward are told *when* they are told because Jesus is on his way to Jerusalem, giving the nation its last call to repentance and a change of heart in the face of the disasters impending there: his own death and the defeat of 70 C.E. The turnabouts of the antiheroes of his tales are exemplary in a historically precise way because they refer to what the early Christians understood as the crux of history: the events between 30 and 70 C.E. which they saw (wrongly) as fatal to unbending Judaism and (rightly) as the origin of their adaptable religion. The Gospels, and the parables within them, are part of that vigorous Christian exercise in the interpretation of history.

Ethics

The function of parables in historical thinking, their status as stories to elucidate history, is not so obvious as their moral function. But the two are connected: parables usually elucidate history by moralizing it. Their moral aspect is more likely than the historical to engage the attention of an ordinary modern reader. What happened in the first century C.E. and what sense the Christians made of it is not nearly so urgent a concern for most of us as how we ought to behave. So parables lead us into morality and stay with us while we think about it. However, history in the sense of where we have just come from is always a very important factor in our understanding of where we are now, whether as readers or as social-political persons. As we leave thinking about history to concern ourselves with ethics we keep our historical or narrative frame of mind. And it is very apt to the Gospels that we should do so, because their moralizing is in the stream of narrative. Thus it is just as productive to address the issue of goodness by asking "When is it?" as by asking "Where is it?"

The question "Where is it?" refers to the stationary world-picture. For the evangelists this picture includes God, the human mind or heart, and manifest behavior in the world. Though they all use this structure their emphases differ—and emphasis is determinative in religion and literature. We have just seen, for example, Luke's interest in the human heart and mind. He even reports debates there in the form of soliloquies: the Unjust Steward's "what shall I do? I cannot dig; to beg I am ashamed. I am resolved what to do" (16:3–4); and the Prodigal Son's "how many hired servants of my father's have bread enough and to spare, and I perish with hunger? I will arise and go to my father" (15:17–18). Then each acts: the Steward settles leniently with his master's debtors, and the Prodigal Son goes home. Inward resolve carries into manifest behavior.

So Luke deals with two parts of the tripartite structure (God, human heart, behavior) in which goodness exists. If we suspect that he is light on the first of them, God, we are right. He is light on God, but not negative. God is over and above all. The best thing for human beings to do is not to speculate about divinity (that is more John's emphasis, which is heavily divine) but to cope with the crises which confront them; for such crises are the key points of the historical process, which for Luke *is* theology. Doing what is necessary in the face of historical necessity is obedience to God. The rich man in the parable at 12:16–21 is a fool because he fails to take account of the whirligig of time bringing its revenges. He thinks that his accumulation of goods is stable. For Luke this is tantamount to atheism: "so is he that layeth up treasure for himself and is not rich towards God" (12:21). He is using the commonplace of Old Testament wisdom, that practical atheism is the height of folly, within the traditional Old Testament belief that the phases of history and its crises are God's dealings with humanity and humanity's with God. Repentance is, for Luke, simultaneously adjustment to untoward circumstances and knowledge of God. It is, in his narrative mode, perhaps the *summum bonum,* certainly the first necessity for historical beings.

Luke's down-to-earth ethic has its literary manifestation in the three-fold narrative pattern so integral to him: life running into crisis, crisis, life on a new course. So the question "When is goodness?" is already answered for Luke. It is when a person copes realistically and resourcefully with what has come upon him. At such times it is a mistake to stick to stable norms and convention—indeed, a mistake to stick at all. Hence the congratulations of the Steward and his tricks. Another manifestation of the ethical importance to Luke of the mundane is the rich realism in which so many of the parables are presented. The Good Samaritan exemplifies the philanthropy to which Luke reduces Matthew's more diffuse Sermon on the Mount (compare Luke 6 with Matt. 5–7). His story is full of visual detail: stripped, wounded, half dead, oil, wine, beast, inn, two pence. The circumstances of the Prodigal Son, both in want and restored to comfort, are similarly vivid. As a result, of the four evangelists Luke has the largest number of words which appear only once in the Gospels. The other evangelists inhabit much less richly stocked worlds.

We can confirm what we have already noticed about the form of Luke's ethics, and gain some other insights, too, by comparing him with Matthew and Mark.

Matthew has a concern with human inwardness similar to Luke's. In each of the antitheses in the Sermon on the Mount—"Ye have heard that it was said by them of old time . . . but I say unto you" (Matt. 5:21–48)—the new ethic is an interior disposition: not being angry or lustful, not swearing or resenting, loving. There is some sense of narrative time: in the antinomy "it was said by them of old time . . . but I say unto you," and there is some suggestion of time just because things are happening—quarreling, going to the Temple, seeing a woman, having a cloak stolen. But the stark antinomy "old time . . . I" is not as developed as Luke's sense of historical change, the incidents are much sketchier and more general than Luke's rich examples. The persons involved lack Luke's particularity of character. Portrayal of character is highly indicative of ethical view. Matthew simply has good people and bad people. Sometimes the bad people disguise themselves as good people, "wolves in sheep's clothing"; but such efforts are useless, for the actions which spring from their inward dispositions (their moral "fruit") betray them (Matt. 7:15–20). Luke, though, has ambiguously good-cum-bad people whose actions are not so much moral achievements to be marked by the ultimate censor on Doomsday, as rescue operations which result in survival and vivacity in the present and some future after all. It is congruous with Matthew's less happily mundane and humanized ethic that his God is more intrusive: in the Sermon on the Mount he rewards, sees in secret, knows, forgives, provides food and clothes, sends down indiscriminate rain and sunshine. God is suddenly and decisively there at the end of Matthew's parables, after which no human action is possible.

The differences between Luke and Matthew are matters of nuance and development. Those between Luke and Mark are more extreme. Mark's determinism contrasts with the importance of human choice in Luke: not exactly free choice—Luke is too realistic to posit that—but the ability to change within the constraints of circumstances. In Mark divinity overrides and drives the action to its appointed end, and no one can do anything about it. Grim simplification results, as in the sower parable of Mark 4, in which people are reduced to types of terrain; and in Mark's somewhat strained convention of the invincible stupidity of the disciples. But there is also a paradoxical depth of tragic force at Mark 14:21:

> The son of man indeed goeth, as it is written of him:
> but woe to that man by whom the Son of man is betrayed!
> good were it for that man if he had never been born.

The colon in that verse divides the two opposing insights which together grip our minds in the face of tragedy: that fate is irresistible and that nevertheless we are culpable. And the last line, echoing Job, faces us with the morally destructive possibility of a life not worth living at all. Where is goodness in such a world? Even Jesus, addressed as "Good Master" and asked the great ethical question "What shall I do to inherit eternal life?" first parries the designation "good" with "Why callest thou me good? there is none good but one, that is, God" (Mark 10:17–22)—implying that goodness has no human or earthly resting place—and then indicates total self-impoverishment as the way to life. No wonder that both Matthew and Luke edit here! Mark's is the ethic of desperation, savage and austere in its expression, disruptive in effect.

Luke emerges as the most genial of the evangelical moralists, not least because his ethic is the most adapted to interesting narrative. Its particularity of characterization and richness of incident all turn on a crisis which, precisely because his characters are ambiguous and unstable, could go any way. Divine presence and plan are as lightly, subtly, and firmly kept in play without intrusion as in the Joseph story (to which as we have seen his Prodigal Son parable is much indebted). Tragedy is subsumed in comedy, which takes the worst in its stride as it moves on into a happier world. His confidence in the moral purpose and lucidity of history is remote to late twentieth-century minds. But for people enjoying fairly lucky lives of minor historical importance his lessons in adaptability and social responsibility are to the point. His admonitions to cope with necessity in all its forms (poverty, disappointment, interruption, mortality) are never unseasonable. And his greatest parables seem likely never to lose their moral appeal.

Goodness and evil in John's (which is usually held to be the last canonical) Gospel are understood within its cosmic vision: the light of divine being shines within the dark world of becoming. Goodness is coinherence within eternal life, participation in Jesus and the Father. Evil is the condition of being outside it or, still worse, leaving it for the outer darkness. "Abiding" is good. Apostasy is evil. When, in the trial and death of Jesus good and evil confront each other, Jesus is monumentally stable while his betrayer, accusers, judges, and even disciples swirl around him in restless agony.

All this Johannine stability contrasts strongly with Luke's positive theology of movement and time. For John, "Where is goodness?" is a much more appropriate question than "When is goodness?" The ethical implications can be seen in the long prelude in the Passion which begins with John 13, set at the Last Supper. Coinherence, being-together, is the reality subserved by the foot washing at the outset. When Peter protests this menial action by the Son of God, Jesus explains its sacramental value: "If I wash thee not, thou hast no part with me" (v. 8). As washing joins Jesus and believer, so it joins believer to believer and cements their community: "ye also ought to wash one another's feet" (v. 14). Communion in goodness having been established by washing, Judas's eating of the sop given him by Jesus is immediately followed by another coinherence: "Satan entered into him" (v. 27). This evil participation is not communion, not the stability of being maintained by mutual love and service. It is possession, a satanic drive from within, a parasitic force, which impels its host "immediately out: and it was night" (v. 30). Yet it seems that even here Jesus is sovereign: he has given Judas the sop and told him to go. Reality, God, is ultimately not dual but single.

There is enormous ethical strength in John's concentric diagram of the world, but its stability and inwardness bar any energetic exploration of ethical action. We hear of works to be done in Jesus' name, but they are not specified. Rather, they are subsumed under the rubric of love—"If ye love me, keep my commandments" (John 14:15)—and those commandments are compressed into the single one of love (John 15:12), which is itself circumscribed by the inner ring of divine belonging: "Greater love hath no man than this, that a man lay down his life for his friends" (John 15:13). Yet in Luke we see a still greater love than that, in a Jesus who loves his enemies (Luke 23:34). It is a measure of the limits of Johannine illumination. John's strength is centralized, presented in the parables of sheepfold (John 10:1–8) and vine (John 15:1–7), which hold goodness tightly within Christian community. The ordinary ethics of philanthropy get a poor showing. Between Jesus' giving Judas the sop at John 13:27 and Judas's departure into the night at verse 30 the author briefly and dismissively obtrudes: "some of them thought, because Judas had the bag, that Jesus had said unto him [that is, when Jesus said 'that thou doest, do quickly'], Buy those things that we have need of against the feast; or, that he should give something to the poor" (v. 29).

How banal to be thinking of religious or "charitable" provision when the fundamental issue of goodness and evil is at stake! Every evangelist pays the price of his achievement. John's metaphysic of eternal being, even the light of Johannine charity, leaves little room for Luke's Good Samaritan or almsgiving Zacchaeus. But the choices which constrain a writer's achievement are not always starkly exclusive. Whereas Luke has the most memorable stories about change of conduct (Zacchaeus, the

Prodigal Son, the Steward), John has psychologically penetrating narratives about change of understanding (the Samaritan woman, the man born blind, Thomas) to put beside Luke's Emmaus story on the same theme. John is concerned not so much with ethics as with the intellectual perception from which they come and, beneath that, with the being and belonging which are the ground of understanding.

NOTES

1. See Edmund Leach's essay, "Fishing for Men on the Edge of the Wilderness," in this volume.

2. By transferring the role of Elijah from John the Baptist, as in Mark and Matthew, to Jesus, Luke characteristically increases the temporal space at his disposal. Elijah was the prophet to come before Doomsday (Mal. 4:5). So if John is Elijah the end is closer and there is less history to run than if Jesus is Elijah.

3. Hans Conzelmann appropriately called the book in which he published this insight *Die Mitte der Zeit* [The middle of time] (Tübingen, 1954); Geoffrey Buswell's English translation (London, 1960) unfortunately changed this title to *The Theology of St. Luke*.

4. John (21:1–14) actually has the great catch after the Resurrection, with Jesus giving the apostles the fish cooked for breakfast. The two Lukan tales are run into one, with typical Johannine economy and compression.

5. T. S. Eliot, "East Coker," in *Collected Poems 1909–1962* (London, 1963), p. 203.

SUGGESTED FURTHER READINGS

H. J. Cadbury, *The Making of Luke–Acts* (London and New York, 1927).

Hans Conzelmann, *The Theology of St. Luke*, trans. Geoffrey Buswell (London, 1960).

J. M. Creed, *The Gospel According to St. Luke* (London, 1930).

John Drury, *The Parables in the Gospels* (London and New York, 1985).

———, *Tradition and Design in Luke's Gospel* (London, 1976).

King's College, University of Cambridge

John

Frank Kermode

SOME of the problems arising from the differences between the Fourth
Gospel and the three Synoptic Gospels were discussed in the Introduction to the New Testament. There are also, of course, problems arising
from its resemblance to those other Gospels. Indeed there is a long list of
questions calling for answers from historical critics, and it is fair to say
that the answers are always changing, and the list of questions always
lengthening. Earlier in the present century there were those who strongly
believed John to have been related to a particular form of Gnosticism, the
Mandean. This belief was abandoned after the discovery of the Dead Sea
Scrolls, which were the work of Jewish writers before the time of John,
and which anticipated some of his characteristic imagery and habits of
thought. John is now seen to derive from a tradition that is fundamentally
Jewish, however influenced by Hellenistic ideas. Such considerations and
others, such as the accuracy of his Palestinian topography, have induced
most scholars to reject the view that John's was a late theological reworking of the material, lacking direct contact with the original tradition. It is
now commonly thought that the Fourth Gospel has sources as old as,
though largely independent of, those available to the Synoptics.

Although in certain historical respects John clearly differs from the
other Gospels, and although one needs to take some account of this fact
when studying his practice as a writer, such considerations affect the
present essay only obliquely. Literary critics can reasonably avoid many
of the arguments which orthodox biblical criticism cannot. There is, for
example, a protracted discussion concerning which verses of the Prologue—a feature unique to John—are original, and which are interpolations. Literary critics may not feel disposed to substitute for the poem as
it now stands some hypothetical predecessor that fits better their views
on John's theology or his historical situation. They may attach much
importance to the long existence of the Gospel in its present form and
wish to see it in its immemorial contexts as a member of a set of gospels,
as part of a Testament, and as part of the Bible. They may suppose that
its career in these contexts has conferred upon it a certain cohesiveness
and integral force that are dispersed when the book is detached from its

neighbors, distributed among redactors, and purged of supposedly intrusive elements.

They are therefore likely to assume a real and intelligible relation between the Prologue and the narrative it introduces. They will not be troubled by fine theological differences between this poem and the Gospel as a whole, or postulate a different author for each, or maintain that the incorporation of the Prologue in the Gospel has been none too neatly achieved, or explain what the Prologue originally consisted of before the meddling began. For declining, whether from indifference or incapacity, to take part in such exercises they may be condemned as "precritical," that is, ignorant of the scientific advances made in biblical criticism over the past two hundred years. But there is a case for preferring the label "postcritical." In deciding not to be hindered by this immensely powerful tradition of largely disintegrative commentary, one hopes, without forgetting its importance, to regain some of the advantages of the precritical commentators who knew nothing about the Higher Criticism. For example, Chrysostom, sixteen centuries ago, remarked at the outset of his commentary on John that when we read this Gospel, we are not after all conversing with a particular person, so there is no point in asking where he lived or what sort of education he had.[1] Chrysostom gives his attention to other matters; not for him those arduous modern inquiries into sources Jewish and Greek and into the beliefs and needs of some hypothetical community. He is content to study what God says in the words that are there in front of him, as they strike him in his own life, in his own time. Augustine remarked, with much relevance, that we understand this difficult work only according to our restricted capacities[2]—restricted not only by what we are but also by when we are.

It would of course be foolish to deny what detailed study of the text has made obvious: some of it has gone awry. For example, 14:31 indicates a closure but the discourse continues; the pericope of the woman taken in adultery doesn't belong; some transitional verses are carelessly introduced; possibly some chapters are not in the original order. The last chapter is obviously not from the same hand as its predecessors. But it must also be said that long continuance has endowed the book as it stands with a certain unchallengeable integrity. It is substantially as it has been for many ages, and during most of its history people thought of it as inerrant, coherent, and urgently applicable to readers in their own situation and according to their powers of reading, which might include the skill of reading poetry— a skill calling for close attention to the words as they stand in the text rather than attention to their hypothetical antecedents. All the evangelists insist, by proceeding as they do, that we take an interest in stories, and we neglect that insistence when we take the stories apart with the purpose of deciding which of them is earliest, closest to actual historical events. There is a sense in which the critic who attends to the story rather than

to some lost narrative it perhaps replaced is attending to the first requirement of the Gospels. In much the same way biblical poems need to be
read as poems before they are disassembled or treated simply as clues to
a theology.

It may be helpful here to glance at Luther, an important though
"transitional" commentator, a herald of the critical though in many ways
still of the precritical world. Luther tells us, with suitable expressions of
contempt, that in popish times it had been the custom to write the words
"In the beginning was the Word" on a piece of paper, place the paper in
a quill or other container, and "hang it around one's neck or somewhere
else; or to read these words as a protective charm against thunder and
storms." What folly! If faith is wanting, there is no power in words. They
were not provided for magical purposes, and our business is merely to
believe them; we may then get our wish, not through incantations and
spells but "in and through faith."[3]

Luther, we see, is well aware that the words are mysterious; indeed
he says they are beyond the reach of human understanding without the
aid of faith. But their efficacy is not inherent in them; it lies in something
beyond, to which they merely point. Thus he wishes poetry away. Yet
his commentary cannot altogether dispense with it, as we see from the
curious figures he uses to express the relation between God and the Word.
God, he says, is as it were pregnant with the Word; and then, shifting the
figure, he adds, like a man's heart when it is filled with love or anger.
"There was in God a Speech or Word which occupies all of God," he says
more plainly.[4] But Luther's business is less with such musings than with
the correction of heretics, from Cerinthus (against whom he supposed the
Gospel to have been written) to the ruling pope. He is a theologian; he
will employ reason, aided by faith, to ask what beyond themselves is
signified by the words. That the Prologue should have the qualities of a
poem, *carmen* (itself related to charm and incantation), is a superstition or
accident to be discoursed away.

Calvin is yet more prosaic. Following Erasmus, he wishes to translate
logos not as *verbum* but as *sermo,* "speech": "In the beginning was the
Speech, and the Speech was with God, and the Speech was God." Phil-
ologically there is something to be said for this version, and Calvin likes
it because "as Speech is said to be among men the image of mind, so it is
not inappropriate to apply this to God, and to say that he reveals himself
to us by his *Speech.*"[5] *Sermo* is as far from *carmen* and incantation as
papistical magic from human rationality. It brings the Word out of dangerous poetry into rational discourse. Reason, dimmed though it was by
the Fall, had the task of establishing the coeternality of the Speech and
God because the doctrine of the Trinity depends on it, and that doctrine
must not be thought to have anything to do with charm or magic. So
Calvin is severe on Augustine, who on this text allowed himself to indulge

the Platonic fancy that God first created the forms. That was a philosoph-ical-poetic irrelevance with which Calvin would have nothing to do.

Calvin, incidentally, was a little troubled by the tense of the verb *to be* in the first verse. Does its *was* suggest that the state of affairs alluded to did not continue, that it was so only for a time? This is, in fact, an ancient problem. Chrysostom, as it happens, dealt firmly with it, and his precritical explanation has much appeal to readers of poetry. "It is not the expression *was* alone that denotes eternity," he says, "but that One was in the beginning." Used of men, he adds, the word *being* only distinguishes present time (as when we say "for the time being"), but when used of God it signifies eternity; just so, *was,* when used of our nature, signifies past time, indeed limited past time; it *was* but it stopped being; but when used in respect of God it signifies eternity.[6] What could be more apposite than this affirmation that *was* is here and throughout the Prologue a word specially and peculiarly illuminated, taken out of ordinary usage, by its immediate and mysterious context? And that context is extensive. God in the Old Testament and his Son in the New have special rights over the verb *to be*; for them to say "I am" is to assert divinity. And we may remind ourselves of the sentence with which Jesus ends the discussion concerning his stature in relation to that of Abraham: "Before Abraham was, I am" (8:58). In the Greek the words translated as "Before Abraham was" really mean "Before Abraham *became*" (came into being).

The words for "being" and "becoming" are, of course, as common in Greek as they are in English. When we think about their function in John's proem (and about their shaping influence on what follows) we must hold on to Chrysostom's insight: the initial context gives them a peculiar coded force. No doubt the implications of these special senses will in the end be theological; but the means are poetic.

The normal view of historical-critical exegetes is that in the first eighteen verses of John there are intrusions, premature splicings of sub-sequent narrative into a Prologue that probably existed before they did. The verses in question are 6–9 and 12–13; 6–9 are often said to be the original opening of the book before it was attached to the proem, displaced when the proem was, as it were, stuck on top. And for those who look at the matter in this way the next question is what sort of a document the original hymn was. From what "conceptual grid" does it come? It may have some resemblance to the *Hermetica:* should we therefore treat it as of Hellenistic origin? How does it relate to Philo, how to the Dead Sea Scrolls? Perhaps it is Jewish after all, but, as Kümmel supposes, the expression of a peculiarly Jewish form of *gnōsis,* related to the old Wisdom literature but opposed to the docetic element in other forms of Gnosti-cism?[7] These are real questions, but they are not of the kind I am com-petent, or wish, to ask. They are all concerned with origins, or with the relation between the text and a conjectural external order, the order of religious and intellectual history at large. The assumption is contrary to that of Chrysostom: if you discover what John *could* originally have intended you can reorganize his book to make it conform more closely to that possible intention. The notion that nobody ever thought anything that had not been thought before is curiously strong in biblical studies; it is an illegitimate inference from a much more defensible position, that there are linguistic and cultural constraints on what can be intended. These are controversial matters, but my claim here is merely that we may properly ask what the poem in its internal relations—in its language and also in its connection with the subsequent narrative—means to us, now, reading it as Augustine said we have to, in accordance with our restricted capacities. To do that we must treat verses 6–9 and 12–13 as part of the poem.

It will be helpful at this point to have the text on the page.

1. In the beginning was the Word, and the Word was with God, and the Word was God.
2. The same was in the beginning with God.
3. All things were made by him; and without him was not any thing made that was made.
4. In him was life; and the life was the light of men.
5. And the light shineth in darkness; and the darkness comprehended it not.
6. There was a man sent from God, whose name was John.
7. The same came for a witness, to bear witness of the Light, that all men through him might believe.
8. He was not that Light, but was sent to bear witness of that Light.
9. That was the true Light, which lighteth every man that cometh into the world.
10. He was in the world, and the world was made by him, and the world knew him not.
11. He came unto his own, and his own received him not.
12. But as many as received him, to them gave he power to become the sons of God, even to them that believe on his name:
13. Which were born, not of blood, nor of the will of the flesh, nor of the will of man, but of God.
14. And the Word was made flesh, and dwelt among us, (and we beheld his glory, the glory as of the only begotten of the Father,) full of grace and truth.
15. John bare witness of him, and cried, saying, This was he of whom I spake, He that cometh after me is preferred before me: for he was before me.
16. And of his fulness have we all received, and grace for grace.
17. For the law was given by Moses, but grace and truth came by Jesus Christ.
18. No man hath seen God at any time; the only begotten Son, which is in the bosom of the Father, he hath declared him.　(1:1–18)

Commentators ancient and modern would agree that the poem is what might be called a "threshold" poem. It is concerned with what *was* (in Chrysostom's sense, eternally) and how that which *was* crossed over into *becoming*. So the key words of the poem, its axis, are *was* and *became*, in Greek *ēn* and *egeneto*, common words used in an uncommon way. The first sentence of the book asks us to remember the opening words of the whole Bible, verse 1 of Genesis (known in Hebrew simply as "In the Beginning"); it tells how things became, at the behest, at the Word, of the God who is and was from the beginning. This beginning, the one that concerns John, is an older beginning than that of Genesis. *Was* is thrice repeated: the Word *was*, it *was* with God, it *was* God. It is traditional to explain that *was* is here used in three distinct grammatical senses: as denoting existence, relationship, and predication. This triplicity strongly reinforces the special sense of the word; its multidimensional quality, the variety of its aspects which are ignored in ordinary speech, is emphasized, and it is as it were abstracted from such speech. It draws attention to itself in the way of poetry. It stands for the condition of the eternal at the threshold of that which is not eternal but *becomes*—the eternal on the point of an unheard-of participation in that which cannot be eternal because it is created, because it has or will become. It is in contrast with this becoming on the other side of the threshold that the uniqueness of this *was* is affirmed.

The second verse is strongly placed on the *was* side of the threshold, strongly echoes the *was* of the first verse. But the third verse shows us the other side of the threshold: "All things were made by him, and without him was not anything made that was made." "Were made" translates *egeneto* ("became"); "was not" is also *egeneto* ("became not one thing"); and the final phrase, "that was made," is another form of the same verb ("not one thing that has become"). So we have three "becomings" to set against the triple *was* of eternity.

Some scholars argue that the last bit of verse 3 should really be the opening of verse 4, the change having been made for doctrinal reasons, perhaps to disarm Arian heretics. However—as sometimes happens in poetry—the phrase can equally well belong to either or both verses. If the words "that which has become" are taken with verse 4 we have, instead of "In him was life," the more complicated proposition, "that which has become was in him life," which brings together *become* and *was* in a vivid antithesis representing the created and the creator, itself a threshold. It was life in no other way save in him; that measured the extent of its being, its degree of freedom from becoming. The issue is philosophical but the method is the method of poetry.

"The life was the light of men": *was* now means both "was" and "is." Why is "life" identified with "light"? When the life-creating Word was spoken in Genesis, the first being created was light: "God said, Let there be light: and there was light." The light shines in the darkness as in Genesis the light *was* when ordered to be, when the earth was without form and only about to become. The darkness is still the darkness of that primitive chaos which, as later thinkers remarked, had only the potentiality of becoming. The pronouns of verses 3 and 4 do not let us know whether their antecedent is "God" or "the Word"; and that is poetry, for it is right that they should not at this point be separated by grammar. The Word and God, like light and life, are, at any rate in the poem, indivisible.

At this point we might almost suppose the poem to be over, for an apparently unconnected narrative begins: "There was a man sent from God, whose name was John." *Egeneto anthrōpos*: "there became, there came into existence, a man . . ." So the narrative actually begins—comes into being—with a verb that has already been given special weight by John, as it had in the Greek version of Genesis, which he is remembering. John the Baptist is at once firmly labeled as belonging to *becoming*. He was witness to the light (= the Word that *was*) but he *was not (ouk ēn)* that light now coming into the world. Verse 10 tells us that light *was* in the world; the positive form surely remembers the negative form applied in verse 8 to John.

It may well be that these verses were meant to limit the influence of John the Baptist or cut the ground from under the feet of some surviving Baptist sect. It remains true that the newly arrived John is here firmly associated with the *becoming* end of the axis; insofar as the form *was* can be used of him it must be used in the negative. Hence his introduction by means of *ouk ēn*; it is what he is *not* that links the narrative to the poem. And as the hymn continues it goes on distinguishing between the positivity of *was* and the negativity of the world upon whose threshold the Word stood. He, the Word, *was* in the world which *became* ("was made," *egeneto*, v. 10) through him but which failed to recognize him. That world was his own (v. 11)—his own property, of his own making—and his own (his own people) received him not. In other words, Being is treated as an alien by that which it caused to become. In these verses one may find something of that incantatory buildup of semantic pressure that Robert Alter distinguishes as a characteristic of some ancient Hebrew poetry.[8] For the general pathos of the first "verset," to use Alter's term—the creation denies its creator—grows more specific, and "his own" in the second part means "his own people," the neuter giving way to the masculine plural. And then in verse 12 exceptions are mentioned, those who did receive him and so earned the right to *become* sons of God and so to *be*. And this process is related semantically and in other ways to the paradigmatic moment of becoming, namely birth; but this is a different birth, a birth into being, a birth from above, of the spirit and not of the flesh.

It is now that we reach the most remarkable moment of the poem. We have met a paradoxical style of becoming (of birth) which is actually a form of being—one must be born not out of the stuff of becoming, but into being. In verse 14 the paradox is inverted, and we have the violent conceit of the incarnation, *being* surrendering to *becoming*: "The Word was made flesh." And here for the first time we find *egeneto* associated with the Word, for the Word which *was,* in that very special poetic sense, now *became*—became flesh. Such a union of being and becoming must be transient, which is why in the expression "dwelt among us" the Greek verb really means something like "pitched his tent," "camped," as Wisdom did in Ecclesiasticus 24:8. It may well strike the layman as strange that there is a good deal of argument as to whether this verse is really part of the poem.

Like Wisdom again, the Word is known by its glory—*doxa,* a word of many senses in John as elsewhere, though John uses it as a poet might, exploiting its ambiguity. The glory of the Word is distinguished from the world's glory; for example, in 5:41 Jesus says he receives not honor (*doxa*) from men, and in 5:44 that it is impossible for men to believe if they receive *doxa* from one another but do not seek the *doxa* that comes from God. There are other instances, as we shall see. The word *doxa* contains within itself antithetical senses, as antithetical as *ēn* and *egeneto,* the world of the dying generations. *Doxa* is related to the verb *dokeō,* which means "to seem" or "to appear"—it can be a glory by means of which being shines out amidst becoming, or it can be a mere semblance, an attempt on the part of becoming to simulate that true glory.

Here John cuts again to the Baptist, now bearing witness: "This [man] was he of whom I spake" ("was" when we expect "is," perhaps to remind us of the special status of *was* in the poem). The verse is generally regarded as intrusive, a renewed polemic against the followers of John who made excessive claims for him. But its language is the language of the hymn carried over into the incipient narrative: "the one coming after me has *become* before me, because he *was* before me," or rather "because before me he *was*" [AT]. In the order of becoming, and only there, does the Word made flesh *appear* to be the follower; by right of the eternal *was* he takes precedence over all that merely becomes. If this is an attack on false claims made for John it is still made in these high terms. It does not matter whether the voice speaking in verse 16 is that of the character John or of the hymn singer. Both know where the fullness of being resides, and that the grace received is superadded to such grace as was formerly available, for instance under Moses and the Law. The whole narrative, its past and its future, must fall under the rule of the great antithesis of being and becoming, be governed by the presence of the *was* in the *become,* the light in the darkness.

All will agree that the hymn ends and gives way to the narrative when, after a clean break, John is questioned about his status ("And this is the record of John, when the Jews sent priests and Levites from Jerusalem to ask him, Who art thou?" v. 19). His relationship to Jesus, first expressed in terms of the metaphysical plot of the hymn, is now given a narrative explanation. John repeatedly affirms his role as witness to the Word. He makes the first announcement of Jesus' paschal and eschatological role: "Behold the Lamb of God" (v. 29), and at once repeats the disclaimer of verse 15: he has become before me because he *was*.

The threshold quality, the liminality of the poem is now deepened into myth, and the myth is dressed in representations of actuality. Jordan is an archetypal threshold. Crossing over its water is baptism; the dove that descends is a figure not only of the spirit from above but also of that *pneuma* that brooded over the formless waste of waters in the beginning, at the great threshold between darkness and light. The ladder by which the angels will descend and reascend (as Jesus tells Nathaniel) is another bridge between chaos and spirit. Being can cross over or descend into becoming; it will participate in becoming until it reaches its end, a death which restores it to its former unencumbered state. Yeats remarked that Being was "a property of the dead, / A something incompatible with life"—the thought is similar, except that for John the "something" is the *true* life ("true" is another of his heavily loaded words), whereas the life with which Yeats says Being is incompatible is in fact a form of death. So the liminal antitheses of the poem extend themselves into the book as a whole.

THERE FOLLOW some instances of this process of extension. It is well known that John selected a relatively small number of miracles, or "signs" as he calls them; and that he seems to have gone to a good deal of trouble to relate them both to one another and to the discourses which he appends to them. For example, he is gently insistent on the connection between the first and second signs, the miracle at the Cana wedding where the water was turned into wine, and the healing of the nobleman's son, also at Cana. These miracles are explicitly described as the first and second signs (2:11, 4:54). Between the two comes John's version of the Cleansing of the Temple, the visit of Nicodemus to Jesus, and Jesus' interview with the woman of Samaria.

John has a few lucid allegorical parables—the True Vine, the Good Shepherd—but, as many have remarked, he uses the signs parabolically as well. His miracle stories yield different senses to "insiders" and "outsiders," and these early miracles have that characteristic in common. They also have a certain similarity of structure, one aspect of which has troubled the commentators. In the first miracle Jesus seems to speak rather sharply to his mother, refusing to do anything about the wine shortage because, he says, his hour is not yet come. In the second story he appears to rebuff the nobleman, who seeks a cure for his son (or servant). These moments of gruffness are not without parallels in the Synoptics, but it is odd that in both cases Jesus goes on to do as he was asked. This hesitation in the narrative may be related to the proper understanding of signs: people want to see conjuring tricks, thaumaturgy, demonstrations of power in the realm of becoming, wonders of a palpable sort. These miracles can be taken as magical displays, meant to impress the bystanders; yet it is clear that they are much more than that when interpreted by insiders (though sometimes insiders, like the disciples in Mark and on occasion in John also, show little understanding of any secret sense, any sense that has to do with being rather than with becoming).

The first Cana miracle, whatever else it may be, is a threshold; it corresponds to the Temptation story told in the Synoptics but not in John. At one moment the hero's hour is not yet come, as he tells his mother; then, abruptly, it *has* come. Many commentators on the Temptation have assumed that it was meant as a sort of rehearsal for the Passion, the victory over sin that preceded and was necessary to the victory over death. Milton was thinking of this pattern when in *Paradise Regained* he said that after the first victory in the Temptation Jesus could undertake the "great work before him set," or, as the angelic chorus expresses it at the end of the poem, he could on his "glorious work / Now enter, and begin to save mankind." In John's more abstract version the transformation of water into wine has the same force: it is the first act of the Word in the world, and a type of the greater transformation to come. Perhaps it is the grace beyond grace, the messianic wine of being that replaces the inferior wine of the Torah, which is appropriate only to becoming. Or perhaps it describes the metamorphosis of the merely created by the creator as he enters into its sphere. It foreshadows—is a type of—the final transformation of becoming into being, the last victory that restores the Word to God. The master of the feast tastes the miraculous wine (literally, he tastes "the water having become wine") and knows not whence it *is*—we might have expected *was*. The water, that is, *becomes* wine; the wine simply *is*. Thus the miracle exhibits the *doxa* of Christ; there is a direct quotation of 1:14. The parabolic narrative is telling us to remember the Prologue, as well as foreshadowing the end.

The setting is a wedding, perhaps because this provides a plausible occasion for the consumption of a very large quantity of wine, perhaps because weddings are obviously liminal ceremonies. (Jesus is more than once compared to a bridegroom.) A parabolic narrative must have this measure of contact with the ordinary world as well as larger and more obscure implications. Reports of events occurring in the public world—historical events—must of course be more unequivocally represented as having that contact with everyday reality, but they may also bear latent meanings. For example, John's treatment of the Cleansing of the Temple—

the first act of Jesus in a hostile Jerusalem—is such a factual report, much less parabolic in tone than the wedding at Cana, and he does not number it among the signs; but it has its penumbra of unobvious senses.

John's version of the Cleansing differs from those of the Synoptics in that it occurs at the outset rather than near the end of the ministry. It differs also in that John alone arms Jesus with a whip. The anthropologists tell us that temples are always liminal and that the cleansing represents a decisive moment of crossing, a confrontation with the other side. The incident fulfills a prophecy of Zechariah, that on the day of the Lord no merchant will be found in the Temple (Zech. 14:21). The day of the Lord will see a restored plenitude of being, an end of change. So the episode works rather like the wine miracle; an hour has come, a choice has been made, and the hour and the choice are themselves of decisive importance; but they also offer powerful premonitions of the end of the story. John does not call the Cleansing a sign, but "the Jews" think it is, and ask: "What sign shewest thou unto us?" (2:18). They are like Mark's crowd, which sees but cannot understand; to the Jews the answer of Jesus is dark, and they harden their hearts. He who wields the scourge will himself be scourged and the temple of his body destroyed; then, after a three-day pause, being will supervene on becoming. Such is the hidden sense of the signs, the sense conferred upon them by the plenitude of the end.

The failure of the crowd to understand such senses is, as R. E. Brown has remarked, an important aspect of John's narrative technique.[9] He uses it again in the episode of Nicodemus, an episode which also converts to narrative the language of the Prologue. The darkness under cover of which Nicodemus arrives to question the light (= life = the Word) is the uncomprehending darkness of 1:5 as well as the darkness of those who mistake the signs. Nicodemus, an educated but unenlightened Jew, has difficulty in understanding the parable of rebirth "from above," taking the expression to mean "born again"—literally to be reborn after the earthly manner of generation or becoming. He enters from the night, as later Judas will go out into it; and he is told that the knowledge which belongs to generation, genesis, flesh, becoming, is irrelevant to the being of eternal life. Having an economical sense of narrative, John will reintroduce Nicodemus at 7:50, where he is suspected of being a follower of Jesus, so that he can bring him in for the third and last time at the end of the story, when he brings myrrh and aloes to prepare Jesus' body for burial. This is another of John's matches between narrative sequence and abstract pattern, for the first appearance of Nicodemus is used to make a point about birth and the last to mark with appropriate ritual the threshold between life that is death and death that is life.

It is characteristic of John's method that two discourses intervene between the story of Nicodemus and the next narrative episode, the encounter with the woman of Samaria. This scene has been much admired for its dramatic elegance. It is based on certain Old Testament texts which have the character of "type-scenes," to use another expression of Robert Alter's. In Genesis and Exodus, meetings of men with women at wells on foreign soil are regularly followed by the marriage of the parties. And it has been conjectured that the woman has marital designs on Jesus; but this is probably a Nicodemean misunderstanding that misses an allegorical significance. Perhaps there is here a reprise of the wedding theme already sounded, not only at the Cana marriage but also in John the Baptist's allegorical description of himself as best man at the wedding of Jesus. The idea of some sort of intimate union is undoubtedly present. Luke chose the Samaritan as the least likely of good neighbors; and perhaps the hint of a union with Samaria—its perverse religious history represented by the woman's irregular sex life, and its denial that salvation is of the Jews— suggests another oblique reference to the day of the Messiah. The living water of Jesus surpasses that of Jacob, at whose well the meeting takes place, as being surpasses becoming and eternal life the life of generation. The woman is impressed by the easy miracle (Jesus knows all about her past) but his reply to her has deeper implications. She is chosen to receive the news that the hour cometh and now *is*; since the hour now is, she can recognize the Messiah and name him and have her recognition confirmed. As in the Cana miracle, we see enacted the coming of that hour. When the woman leaves her waterpot and goes off to fetch the chorus of Samaritans, Jesus fills the interval with talk of apocalypse already come, of the fields white to harvest. The Samaritans hail him as the Christ and savior of the world. For once there is no misunderstanding. The evangelist does not need to say of the Samaritans what he said of the Jews, that their response to the being of Jesus was unworthy of trust. It was his own who received him not, throughout the whole story and at its end. In considering these apparently serial elements in John's narrative we should be prepared to see each of them as relating not merely to a sequence of discrete events leading up to the Passion, but as self-contained symbolic moments which encapsulate the entire theme and story.

After the Samaritan episode there occurs a much debated link passage: "Now after two days he departed thence, and went into Galilee. For Jesus himself testified, that a prophet hath no honour in his own country. Then when he was come into Galilee, the Galileans received him" (4:43–45). The difficulty arises from the apparent irrelevance of the saying about the prophet in his own country. In the Synoptic parallels it is well motivated, but here Jesus is on his way from Jerusalem, where he has incurred enmity, to Galilee, where he is well received; and Galilee is his own country. The easy answer is that somebody has clumsily inserted the verse. Another explanation is that Judea, at a pinch, could be referred to as Jesus' home country. But the saying is surely an allusion to the great honor paid to Jesus by the discerning Samaritans, the strangers. If anything here is redundant it must be verse 43, "Now after two days . . . ," for we have already been told in verse 40 that he remained two days with the Samaritans. The contrast in verse 44 is between foreigners and Jews, and the clue is in the Prologue: "He came unto his own, and his own received him not" (1:11), now made more pointed by the consideration that Samaria was not his own country nor the Samaritans his own people, yet there and by them he was received.

Much the same point—others, but not his own, received him—is made in the story of the second Cana miracle. We are not told whether the nobleman or courtier was a Jew or a Gentile, though in the Synoptic parallels he is explicitly the latter. He does seem to be a marginal figure of some sort, certainly rich and possibly a sort of Galilean antithesis of Nicodemus. He accepts the rebuff of Jesus just as Mary did at the wedding; he understands that true belief is not in signs and portents but in the Word ("And the man believed the word [*logos*] that Jesus had spoken unto him," 4:50); his son lives. The Prologue told us that the Word was life.

This emphasis on the association between the Word and life is continued in the next chapter. The Word transcends the curative powers of the pool of Bethesda, just as the living water transcends the still water of Jacob's well, the wine of Messiah the inferior wine or water of the Law, the bread of life the manna of mere existence. Those who eat of the bread that is the Word will live forever, but those who fed on manna died. And here the being and becoming of the poem acquire a sacramental force. Bread stands for two things, one spiritual and the other mere substance. Later Jesus dips bread in wine and hands the sop to his betrayer (13:26) in a sinister parody of the Eucharist, which, with wine transformed as at Cana and bread from heaven, is the means to eternal life for those who receive the Word.

I have been trying to show how the Prologue and the narrative—or narratives, since the episodes are not only elements in a sequence but self-contained exempla—are related, how the *ēn/egeneto* axis of the Prologue is also the armature of the stories and of the larger story. Few would deny that John of all the evangelists has the strongest grasp on what he is doing. We sense this control even when the discourses threaten, as in chapters 14–17, to become too extensive, interrupting the narrative at a critical moment. But the discourses, in their own way, make the points made by the carefully ordered narrative, and in the end we feel them to be inseparable, a combination that complies with rules uniquely established for this subgenre—the Johannine type of Gospel—by its sole member. We can say that the discourses are fundamental to our sense of the distinctive qualities of John without implying that for him as for the others the story was the most important thing. And he writes narrative of remarkable variety, subtlety, and freedom.

John's storytelling has the virtues of economy, connexity, and depth.

He is bent upon making his narrative hang together, but in so doing he is always attending to his deepest purpose, which is the representation of the eternal in relation to the transient, of the manifestations of being in a world of becoming. To put this another way: although there is an exceptional amount of talk in John—his Jesus, in discourse and dialogue, is by far the most communicative of the four—he has still in greater degree than the others a concern for thematic organization of narrative, the creation of historylike detail, and what is sometimes called "the effect of the real." We see something of these distinctive characteristics in chapter 6, where he treats of two moments familiar to us from the versions provided by the Synoptics: the Feeding of the Multitude and the Walking on Water. John contents himself with a single Feeding, whereas Mark and Matthew have two. They had reasons for their choice, but John cared more than they for verisimilitude. And he makes different use of the Feeding. He associates it with Passover ("the feast of the Jews" he calls it, stressing as always a certain distance between the Jews and Jesus) and loses no opportunity to convert a celebration that belongs to the old time into one that is proper to the new, to a time in which being or eternity has penetrated history or becoming. The subsequent discourse distinguishes between manna and the bread of heaven. Between the Feeding and this related discourse he places the story of the Walking on Water. John has nothing to say about Peter's attempt to emulate the feat of Jesus, though he does say the disciples are afraid, which leads to Jesus' announcement, "It is I," the Johannine *egō eimi,* the divine self-proclamation characteristically veiled by ordinary language usage. John supplies a context different from that of the Synoptics; we hear nothing of Mark's hardened hearts and the failure of the disciples to solve the numerical riddle of the loaves. We have instead something that interests John more than such puzzles; a traditional episode is given his own kind of symbolism. The discourse on bread that complements the Feeding gives bread a special symbolic force, with those eucharistic overtones that will be more clearly sounded later. Again we have a half-hidden *egō eimi*: "I am the bread of life . . . I am the living bread which came down from heaven: if any man eat of this bread, he shall live for ever: and the bread that I will give is my flesh, which I will give for the life of the world" (6:35, 51). Like Luke, but in a manner entirely his own, John can make a narrative incident look back to the old world (manna) and forward to the altered future (Eucharist: the meeting point of the transient and the eternal). Plain as this may appear, the Jews do not understand it; "Jews" in this Gospel is a synonym for "those who cannot understand." They are given plenty of opportunities, and John even uses their own methods, goes about his business in familiar ways. The scholars tell us that 6:31–50 has the form of a synagogue sermon, with a text from the Pentateuch ("He gave them bread from heaven to eat," 6:31; see Exod. 16:4) followed by a new reading of it

(6:32) and then by a homily on the subject with supporting quotation from the Prophets (v. 45; see Isa. 54:13), with a conclusion that returns to the original text. Moreover it has been pointed out that the Torah readings prescribed for the time of Passover include the story of the manna, and there is a Passover *aggadah* which speaks of three breads: manna, the Passover bread, and the bread of the life to come. John builds his whole argument on this basis, using Jewish methods to explain the transcendental bread the Jews, he claims, cannot understand.

From all this we can see with what care John gave the episode of the Feeding his own shape and color, how he fit it into his own thematic patterns. The same moment of his Gospel may illustrate another of his qualities. It is John the novelist who chooses this moment to introduce, much earlier than the Synoptics, the theme of betrayal. One of the disciples will, like others who heard this discourse, "go away" (v. 67), but the charge of defection is in this case stepped up to one of betrayal (vv. 70–71). There is even a curious suggestion that Judas was chosen one of the Twelve in the full knowledge that he was a devil; indeed when you think about it there is no alternative to this view, since Jesus chose from a position of complete understanding and John writes from the position of omniscience. When Judas is directly accused, which happens only much later, the accusation is accomplished with a piece of bread—more evidence of the density of John's composition. We can guess, perhaps, how all these links were imagined in the first place: first the Psalms testimony (Ps. 41:9), as used in the Synoptics also; then the incorporation of that testimony into the narrative, but simply as a citation suitable to the occasion; then, in John, the memorable dramatizing of the citation, the handing of the sop; and finally the insertion of these pre-echoes in chapter 6. Synoptic allusions to Judas before the Last Supper are rather inert—he comes last in the lists of disciples and is tagged as the betrayer. But John, with his feeling for the possibilities of character in the development of story, puts Judas to work, just as he gets all that he can out of the bread or out of the simple expression "I am." The method by which he arranges those inconspicuous repetitions of word, idea, or incident—the literary devices which add up to what E. M. Forster called "rhythms"—may well owe something to Jewish liturgical practice. In the Passover readings the bread of the ceremony is said to replace the forbidden fruit of Genesis 2 and to foretell the manna which will again descend at the coming of Messiah. It has sometimes occurred to me that the subtleties of construction, the more or less occult relationship of parts, that we admire in favored novels owes a largely unconscious debt to ancient liturgical practice. This is part of one's justification for calling John a protonovelist. The other evangelists also know about this balancing of incident and theme and develop relationships within their books, or with the books of the Old Testament, that are not obvious on the surface but give structural strength to their work. Matthew's figure of the second Israel is an example, and so is Luke's technique of reticent backward and forward suggestion. But John's practice seems at once more delicate and more powerful.

With other instances I must deal more briefly, but in each case the method is much the same. John likes to associate chosen episodes with particular feasts, which is not surprising if I am right about the liturgical element in his architectonic habit. In this way he can release into his text many unspoken suggestions. In chapter 7 the feast is Succoth, or Tabernacles, and John alludes to the ancient texts concerning water which are associated with the feast. The extent of these allusions is indeterminate, the network of possibilities being so complex; but some idea of it can be got from the relevant pages of Raymond Brown's commentary.[10] Tabernacles was an important feast, associated with the Temple (figuratively a fountain of cleansing water) and, by way of harvest and fertility, with rain. There was also a tinge of messianism in both early Christian and Jewish attitudes to this feast. John's principal biblical reference is to Zechariah 14, but Isaiah 12:13 was chanted during the festal ceremonies at the fountain of Gihon, which fed the pool of Siloam. In John, Jesus is thinking of himself as the Temple from which the healing streams will flow as from the rock struck by Moses in the Wilderness. He is Isaiah's fountain of living waters (Isa. 55:2). By associating this part of the gospel story with Succoth, John is suggesting the presence in it of shadowy themes and images, never clearly expounded; the reader must make of them what he can. He must understand how much depends on the vast contextual resources of the Jewish Bible—that the harmonics of John's tones are inaudible except in relation to that background. According to an important rule of Jewish exegesis every mention in the Bible of any word—water, for example—is related to every other mention of it; and it is John's assumption that his allusions will join all these texts in a harmony that must defeat simple paraphrase. He uses the doubtful collocations, the difficult or ambiguous relations, as he does the multiple senses of single words.

One such word is "glory," *doxa,* which first occurs in the Prologue, where it represents the presence of Being, but there are distinctions that have to be made. Glory of the heavenly sort is light in darkness like the Word, but it can be confounded with an earthly *doxa.* In Plato *doxa* means error-prone opinion (perhaps represented in this story by the Jews). But when it refers to heavenly glory *doxa* is inseparable from *alētheia,* truth, another favorite theme of John's. (Plato has several celebrated discussions of the relation between *alētheia* and *doxa*; his conclusions are different, but it seems possible that John knew of them.) John associates true glory with the coming of the hour, another of his repeated "rhythms." Thus in 13:31–32, immediately after Judas goes out into the night, Jesus says: "Now is the Son of man glorified," presumably because the plot of betrayal, the instrument of the ultimate glorification, is now fully afoot. So in chapter 17 *doxa* is again associated with the hour that has come, with reciprocal glorification of Father and Son. Verse 5 is especially remarkable in this connection: "And now, O Father, glorify thou me with thine own self with the glory which I had with thee before the world was." There are differences of opinion about the exact sense of some of the prepositions, but the general sense is clear. And it may be noted that the expression "which I had with thee" might, on the evidence of some witnesses, be translated "the glory which was [*ēn*] with you" or "by which I was with you"; and that "before the world was," which is the King James Version's rendering of a Greek phrase meaning something like "before the being [*einai*] of the world," might well be replaced by "before the world became," since another attested reading is "before the becoming of the world." These alternatives stress, as the received versions cannot, the thematic opposition of being and becoming in relation to the word "glory."

The complexities of *doxa* are given narrative expression in the story of Lazarus. As in *King Lear* insistent references to eyes and to violence suffered by eyes suddenly irrupt into the action when Gloucester is blinded, so here the glory of which we have heard so much is represented in surprising, even shocking, action. The raising of Lazarus is not, like comparable incidents in the Synoptics, an isolated event. In John it is a great hinge of his plot. It makes his account of the causal sequence leading to the Passion very different from those of the other Gospels, in which of course there is no mention of Lazarus. We are told that the sickness of Lazarus is for the glory of God and the glorification of the Son (11:4). There is even a suggestion that Lazarus has been allowed to die for this very purpose. When at last, after unexplained delays, Jesus reaches the house Lazarus has been dead four days, and Martha comes close to reproving Jesus for his tardiness (11:20). It is her misunderstanding of Jesus' remark "Thy brother shall rise again" (v. 23) that provides the occasion for his proclamation (and here the *egō eimi* has unequivocally divine force) "I am the resurrection and the life." Jesus has still not reached the tomb, and when Mary comes out she utters the same reproach as Martha. This sounds rather like a folktale repetition; but there is a surprising twist. Jesus does not repeat his reply to Martha; he does not ask Mary if she believes, and he says nothing about resurrection. Instead he weeps. In the first encounter he is divine and says *egō eimi*; in the second he is a man grieving, a strange role for The Life, the victor over death, but it adds great force to the sequel. The victory, when it is enacted, is the painful emergence of the dead man from the tomb, a spiritual parody of fleshly birth; and its purpose is to demonstrate "the glory of God." The response of the chief priests and Pharisees is to demand that the giver of life be put to death. Jesus, calling forth Lazarus, "cried with a loud voice," *phōnē megalē* (v.

43), the very expression used of his dying cry in Matthew 27:46. In each case the cry paradoxically signals a new birth.

Time and again, as here, we find John giving his own emphasis to material from the common stock. For example, all the Gospels tell of the anointing of Jesus at Bethany. In Mark and Matthew the anointing is done at the house of Simon the leper by "a woman" (Mark 14:3, Matt. 26:7), and in their version she pours the ointment on his head. Some (Mark) or all (Matthew) of the disciples are indignant at the waste, but Jesus reproves them and explains that the woman has done a beautiful thing, and prepared his body for burial (Mark 14:3–9, Matt. 26:6–13). Luke, who places the event earlier in the ministry, says it happened in the house of a Pharisee called Simon and that the woman was a "sinner" (7:36–50). She washes his feet with her tears and then wipes them with her hair; then she anoints his head. The Pharisee says to himself that a genuine prophet would have known the woman was a sinner, and Jesus replies with a parablelike saying that the woman's love is greater than his and that her sins, though many, will be forgiven. This is an interesting variation—Luke is modifying the story to make a point about the forgiveness of sins and the mission of Jesus to sinners. His point would have been lost if he had followed Mark and Matthew and made Simon a leper, himself unclean, for the needed contrast is between the Pharisee and his comparatively loveless virtue and the sinning woman with her faith and devotion. John, in his economical way, identifies the woman with Mary the sister of Lazarus. She anoints his feet and wipes them with her hair, a much more extraordinary thing to do; and the protest against waste, omitted by Luke, is made not by some or all of the disciples, as in Mark and Matthew, but only by Judas, now characterized as a thief and ripe for an act even more criminal.

In the pre-Passion parts of the narrative John excels the others in his concern for connexity. Like them he is interested in the general implication of each anecdote considered alone, but far more than they he desires to hold the episodes together in a plot. The process of establishing economical relations between events and characters seems to be inherent in the interpretative tradition of Christianity. Later, postscriptural harmonizations make John's Mary a sinner also, and specifically Mary Magdalene; and the Roman Catholic liturgy celebrates the three women—the unnamed sinner, Mary of Bethany, and Mary Magdalene—in one feast. John appears to have known Luke's version of the story (anointing the feet is unusual, and loosening the hair could be taken as the act of a prostitute) but he converted it to quite a different purpose.

It would be wrong to exaggerate the differences between John's literary methods and those of the other evangelists. For example, he is, like them, very dependent on Old Testament sources. But he is more reticent in his use of them, and more suggestive. He is less insistent than Matthew on announcing fulfillments, though on occasion he does so. And he combines the record of fulfillment to a greater degree than the others with attention to narrative plausibility. In chapter 10, for instance, he speaks of Jesus preaching in Solomon's Porch in the Temple. It is the feast of Hanukkah, the winter solstice, and that sheltered place is therefore a plausible setting. And what Jesus says is closely related to the sabbath readings prescribed for that time. They make many references to sheep and shepherds. Most of these derive from Ezekiel 34, but John does not say so, preferring to work the allusions into a highly developed parable of the sort he favored, in which Jesus himself is (*egō eimi*) shepherd or sheep-door as appropriate. So also with the parable of the True Vine in chapter 15, which is adapted without acknowledgment from Psalm 80.

Even when John does acknowledge the text that is being fulfilled his method tends to be more complex than those of the Synoptics. For example, in 12:32 Jesus says "And I, if I be lifted up from the earth, will draw all men [or possibly 'all things'] unto me." The next verse explains that "lifted up" has a double sense; it can be used of the Ascension as well as of the Crucifixion, and there is a covert allusion to the Suffering Servant in Isaiah 52:13, where the Greek version uses the same verb and means that the Servant will be "lifted up and glorified exceedingly." The crowd fails to understand what is meant by this lifting up from the earth, pointing out that the Law asserts that "Christ abideth for ever." Their questioning is answered by another gnomic expression, "Yet a little while is the light with you," which reminds us again of the Prologue. Thereupon Jesus withdraws, as if miming that putting out of the light. And it is at this point that John writes in the text from Isaiah used by the Synoptics about the failure of the crowd to understand the parables. His verse 40 is parallel to Mark 4:12 and Matthew 13:13. But John adds (v. 41): "These things said Esaias, when he saw his glory, and spake of him." In fact Isaiah 6:1 says that the prophet saw the Lord, and then (6:3) that the seraphim said the earth was full of his glory. Combining the two, and making the glory belong to Jesus, John has converted the old text into another testimony to the misunderstood glory that was now on the point of achievement (see 12:2, 28) because the hour had come. All these subtleties are folded into the normal narrative—the political narrative, so to speak—when we are told (v. 42) that some of the chief rulers believed in Jesus but could not say so for fear of reprisals from the Pharisees; that is, they preferred the glory (*doxa*; KJV: "praise") of men to that of God (v. 43). In conclusion Jesus affirms his dependence on God and restates the commandment of everlasting life. It is a construction of much delicacy; the encounter is between *ēn* and *egeneto* and concerns the difficulty experienced by those who belong to the second realm in understanding the intrusion of the first. And the question as to what will be the situation of those left in the darkness of becoming when the light of the world departs from the world and resumes its former glorious being, is answered uniquely by John in the messages concerning the Paraclete, representative of the departed glory, its witness and advocate.

Most of the allusions to the Paraclete occur in chapters 15 and 16, after the point (14:31) where we have to think the Farewell Discourse originally ended and the Passion narrative resumed. One of the purposes of this lengthy insertion may have been to develop an answer to questions urgently raised but hitherto denied a sufficient reply, questions relating to the time between the present moment and the promised end—that is, between becoming and being. No doubt it could be argued that 15:1–17:26 is a damagingly lengthy interruption of the narrative as it nears its earthly climax, though in other respects the content of the passage will hardly be thought dispensable. It is, however, true that if chapter 17 in particular were absent it would not be possible to guess that it had ever been there. The end of chapter 16 would have made a good transition into the story resumed at 18:1.

The Passion Narratives

In their accounts of the Passion all four Gospels treat of what is basically the same series of events, but John is again distinctive; and each of the others has its idiosyncrasies. Scholars continue to debate the sources of the four versions: did Mark have two, did Luke have one entirely of his own, was John's independent of the others, and did he take something from Luke? These concerns reflect the slightly surprising fact that even where the four are closest there are many differences of detail and emphasis. Just as with the birth narratives of Matthew and Luke, we mix up all the versions in our heads and produce for ourselves a rough-and-ready harmony, so that our idea of the Passion story includes Matthew's earthquakes and resurrections, his thirty pieces of silver and his tale of Pilate's wife and her dream; Luke's scene at the court of Herod; and John's philosophical Pilate with his memorable sayings "What is truth?" and "Behold the man" and "What I have written I have written." In fact we have four versions of the same scenario, treated according to the skill and creative powers of the writers. For each of them this is the culmination of the narrative, an event of incomparable importance which must be made to seem real. But each has his own manner, his own sense of what the real looks and sounds like, his own style of narrative explanation. Each is saying as best he can that this was the way it was and also the way it had to be if the prophecies and testimonies were truly fulfilled, as they were.

Here are a few of the differences between John and the others. He omits the Agony in the Garden, the rending of the Temple veil, the enlistment of Simon of Cyrene to carry the Cross, and the cry of the centurion. Although all four mention the wounding of the slave's ear at the time of the arrest, and Luke says that Jesus healed it, only John tells us that the slave's name was Malchus and that it was Peter who wielded the sword. He remembers to identify the man with whom Peter conversed in the courtyard as a cousin of Malchus, liking, as many writers do, coincidences that suggest by their very triviality a high degree of plotting. He may have given the sword to Peter because he thought of him, here and elsewhere, as the most impetuous of the disciples. What the others tell us about the hearing before the Sanhedrin John disperses over earlier contests between Jesus and his enemies. Presumably his sense of drama led him to concentrate on one central trial scene, the interrogation by Pilate. Probably the most important of all the differences concerns the dating of the events described. John does not agree with the Synoptics that the Last Supper was a Passover meal. They use the occasion to show how Jesus transcends Jewish expectations that the Messiah will come at Passover, and intend to suggest that he transformed the Passover meal into the Eucharist. Indeed their words at this place are already strongly liturgical and parallel with 1 Corinthians 11:23–25. John's institution of the Eucharist comes much earlier (6:51–58). His reason for placing the Last Supper before Passover must have been that he wanted the Crucifixion to coincide with the killing of the paschal lambs before the feast. Whether or not this was so historically, as some argue, it will be conceded that to make the death of the Lamb of God occur at the same time as the killing of the Passover lambs is a brilliant narrative device.

The Synoptics do not wholly agree among themselves about what happened at the supper. Their accounts of the accusation of Judas vary, though each cites in some form the text from Psalms 41:9, "Yea, mine own familiar friend, in whom I trusted, which did eat of my bread, hath lifted up his heel against me." Matthew alone makes Judas ask "Is it I?" and provides the ambiguous reply, "Thou hast said." Luke intrudes a dispute among the disciples about precedence, with which Matthew and Mark dealt earlier. The prediction of Peter's denial is substantially the same in all three, though Mark muddles the tale by having the cock crow twice. Luke alone has the passage on the two swords and omits from the Gethsemane episode the request that the disciples watch with Jesus. All of them have Judas's kiss at the arrest, but Mark alone has at this point the enigmatic story of the fleeing boy. Only Luke has the trial before Herod, to which he shifts the mock coronation. That Herod and Pilate thereafter became friends is also Luke's idea alone. Only Matthew has Pilate's wife and her dream.

It is worth remarking that traditional Jewish narration, as Meir Sternberg has demonstrated, requires an omniscient narrator,[11] and Matthew is omniscient when he tells us about that dream and the conversation which followed it. The others, of course, have the same privilege, as when John is privy to Pilate's talk with Jesus and with the deputation that asks him to alter the wording of the legend on Jesus' cross, or when Luke knows what is going on inside the head of Simon the Pharisee. Writers in this tradition of storytelling are privy to the plot of God and to the thoughts of men and women. But omniscience, as Sternberg remarks, does not entail omnicommunication. One can be omniscient and reticent, as the Old Testament narrators are, and as Mark is; even John, as we have seen, does not tell all. It is a natural consequence of this traditional privilege that each teller may reveal and also withhold whatever he chooses so long as he is faithful to the fundamental story, which, in the case of the Passion, is a rigorous condition. But even here information may be reserved or inventively expanded. For example, Matthew tells us that Pilate publicly, and as it were ritually, washed his hands to demonstrate his guiltlessness concerning the fate of Jesus (27:24); this is a storyteller's device, giving more concrete form to Pilate's other protestations, making him *do* something as well as say it. It seems certain that Romans did not use this symbolic gesture.

A similar narrative refinement is discernible in the way Luke treats the two thieves (or bandits, or guerrilla fighters) crucified with Jesus. In Mark and Matthew they revile Jesus, but in Luke one of them is repentant and is promised a place in paradise (23:39–43). There is no doubt about which is the more memorable version. Luke achieves it by contrasting the behavior of the two thieves, writing some dialogue, and so introducing a little narrative melisma where none existed before. Narrative is a good mnemonic, and our recollection of the thieves is likely to be as Luke tells the story. In the same way our memory of Judas will depend most on Matthew's development, though doubtless with some touches of John. Conversely, an evangelist may omit what seems to him for some reason undesirable; so Luke leaves out the cry from the Cross, "Eli, eli," reported by both Mark and Matthew, perhaps because he did not like or was not interested in the pun (the hearers suppose Jesus to be calling on Elijah). He also does without the uplifted sponge, the centurion's observation that Jesus must be the Son of God (in Luke he merely calls him "innocent," 23:47). He does not name the women at the Crucifixion, and when later they come to the tomb they are still nameless. Matthew alone speaks of the Jewish scheme to cover up the news of the Resurrection, and he alone requires (another) earthquake to roll back the stone from the sepulcher. Inside the tomb Mark places a young man, Matthew an angel, and Luke two angels. Matthew's women, and Luke's more fully, give the disciples the message entrusted to them by the angel or angels; Mark's women, notoriously, do not, for being terrified they say nothing to anybody. In Matthew Peter is first to reach the tomb and first to meet the risen Jesus; Luke gives this honor to Mary Magdalene, while his Peter is still wondering what is happening. Luke alone has the Emmaus story and the Ascension.

A good deal more could be said about the variants in the Synoptic accounts, but this will be enough to show that each writer, within the constraints of the common scenario, made certain narrative choices and decisions, not only for theological reasons but because this is the way stories get told. Gaps are filled, points of potential interest developed, less suggestive points omitted.

A few final words on the innovations and omissions of John may help to make the point that these generalizations apply also to the most accomplished of the four authors. As we have seen, he preferred to deal with named persons and to distinguish one from another. The differences between the sisters Martha and Mary, implied in a few lines, have always been remembered. And perhaps by looking more closely at his handling of Judas we can get a workable notion of John's method. John describes his progress from petty theft to total evil, and when he accepts the sop we are expressly told that Satan possesses him. John has already cited the Psalms testimony he shares with the other evangelists (13:18) and he gives it dramatic form with the story of the sop. But he is reticent as well as omniscient, and his Judas says nothing. Peter's question about the name of the betrayer is relayed through the Beloved Disciple (closely associated with the narrator), and it is to this disciple that Jesus tells the facts. When Jesus says to Judas, "That thou doest, do quickly," everybody is puzzled and all the conjectures are wrong (13:29), so they throw into relief the knowledge of the narrator and his power to withhold that knowledge. There is, moreover, a mysterious causality in the sequence of these events, which the English translation obscures. In 13:27, where the King James Version has "Then said Jesus," the Greek really means "Jesus therefore said," which makes his gnomic remark a direct consequence of the dia-bolical possession of Judas. Still not replying, Judas immediately goes out: "and it was night." The Greek is as terse as possible; six words cover this exit. Judas leaves the light for the darkness. It is a key moment in the plot. Judas accepts his role; he is what ancient theorists of drama used to call the person designed to bring about the catastrophe. He was therefore necessary, in a sense a helper more than an enemy, for something or someone necessarily had to act in this way. Jesus at once celebrates this turn of events: "*Therefore,* when he was gone out, Jesus said, Now is the Son of man glorified" (v. 31). And this motif of betrayal, thus transmuted into a person acting, is at once associated with the motif of desertion in the prediction of Peter's denial which follows without interruption and which works in the same way.

We might even conjecture that this subtle writer excluded from this part of his narrative the institution of the Eucharist and placed it earlier, so that he could make a less overt but no less demonic allusion to it in the episode of the sop of bread and wine. There is an extraordinary finality about that moment. Judas, in this Gospel, never speaks again. He does not kiss Jesus at the moment of the arrest. Everything necessary has been said, and reticence prevails.

This reticence is, as I have suggested, as essential to the art of the Fourth Gospel as its chosen moments of expansiveness. There is in the whole tradition of writing about Jesus a tendency to adorn and elaborate the tale. Later authors, such as the writer of the apocryphal Acts of Pilate or Gospel of Nicodemus, report conversations between Pilate and Nicodemus and between Nicodemus and the Jews in the presence of many other scriptural characters—the man born blind, the woman with an issue of blood, and so on. Pilate washes his hands because the Jews have identified Jesus as the child Herod failed to kill. Some of these extensions of the story are very silly; though their authors could be said to be working in the same narrative tradition as the evangelist, they have a tendency to imitate the Greek romances. It is difficult to understand how anybody who knows these romance gospels could think the canonical Gospels had any real resemblance to the Greek novels or to Hellenistic tales of divine men. Obviously they could have been developed in that direction, but they were not so developed by their authors, among whom John in particular seems to have had the power of *not* speaking at strategic moments, of knowing where to leave gnomic gaps, and of qualifying omniscience by using multiple points of view. Even when he appears to have decided to tell all, as in the remarkable dialogue between Jesus and Pilate (18:33–38), he arranges for the participants to answer each other very obliquely; questions are answered with questions, and the central question, "Art thou a king?" is turned aside and depoliticized by the reply, "Thou sayest that I am a king." *Sy legeis,* "thou sayest," can also mean "yes," but that possible sense is smothered by the rest of the sentence, which switches the discussion from kingship to truth; and the dialogue ends with Pilate's question "What is truth?"—which Bacon seems to have thought intended for a joke, while others regard it as an expression of philosophical skepticism or of many other attitudes. John seems expansive here—the Synoptics give Jesus nothing to say except *sy legeis*—but he has not lost the capacity for gnomic reticence. Here we may mention two other instances of expansive dialogue: John's development of the theme of the superscription on the Cross, with Pilate's gnomic reply to the complaints of the chief priests (19:21–22); and the speech of the crucified Jesus to the Beloved Disciple concerning Jesus' mother (19:26–27). The power of the first lies in Pilate's tacit endorsement of the claim in the superscription, if that is what it is—it might be another joke, or an expression of his irritation with the chief priests. John knows when to leave something to his interpreters. The Beloved Disciple has certainly exercised them, and still does. He comes in at certain important moments—the Last Supper, Peter's denial, the Crucifixion—but we do not know him, or why Jesus' mother should be consigned to his care. He is in general a producer of enigmas;

he is also a movable narrative focus, lending credit to the detail of places, acts, or speeches provided by the narrator; at once the instrument of explanation and of reticence.

John's control of detail is often remarked, as when he says the Jews could not enter the Praetorium because of the approach of Passover—a detail not available, of course, to the Synoptics. He provides circumstantial detail about Pilate's judgment seat and the Pavement, all of which enhances the sense that these events are happening in a real, specifiable place (archaeologists, incidentally, have fairly recently shown that these details are correct). That John possessed such topographical information is certainly interesting, but from the literary point of view it is equally interesting that he knew so well how to use it.

His use of the testimony material is also discrete. His Jesus, unlike the Synoptics', carries his own cross—John is explicit about that. Of course he may not have known about Simon of Cyrene; or it may be that he wanted Jesus to go to his death the master of his own destiny, as R. E. Brown suggests;[12] or perhaps he feared that Simon could be enlisted in support of Gnostic explanations of the Resurrection. But possibly he was remembering that Isaac was said to have carried the wood that was to be used in his own sacrifice (Gen. 22)—this last is the conjecture of Chrysostom. It has always been understood that John's crucifixion scene was strongly influenced by Old Testament texts. It was he who gave Jesus the seamless garment proper to a high priest; and he combines this theme with the theme of the casting of the lots (Ps. 22:18). He alone includes the spear thrust and the decision not to break Jesus' legs, remembering the prohibition against breaking the legs of the paschal lamb (for example, Exod. 12:46) and Zechariah 12:10: "they shall look upon me whom they have pierced." There is a notable reconciliation here of testimony and probability, for it was customary to break the legs of the crucified in order to hasten their deaths, but here it was found to be unnecessary since Jesus was already dead; and so the testimony was plausibly fulfilled.

In John no centurion proclaims Roman acceptance of Jesus as Son of God, or as innocent; Pilate has seen to that business. He describes no agony in the Garden, and no death throes. There is no loud cry (as there was at the tomb of Lazarus), only the announcement "It is finished"—*tetelestai,* it is fulfilled, at the hour when becoming reaches its end in being. It is sometimes said that for John the Passion is a triumph; but he does not say so, and such a view is an interpretation of the sort his method imposes upon his readers. Wherever he thinks it necessary he helps by the tried method of embodying abstractions, as he does in the scene of the accusation of Judas and the prediction of Peter's denial, and as he does again when we must be told that after the Crucifixion the disciples experienced doubt. Would we have so sharp a picture of their state if John had not made Thomas the doubter and written that brilliantly economical scene?

And now, once again, talk of economy raises the matter of the very expansive and sometimes repetitive discourses. I will only add that in the Jewish Bible, without which the New Testament is inconceivable, narrative and poetry are continually interspersed with law, prophecy, and preaching. And that Bible also makes the powerful assumption that the language of narrative, like that of poetry, can hide sense as well as reveal it. John not only knew that Bible, but made the same assumption.

Appendix: The Epistles of John

This may be an appropriate place to mention the three Epistles attributed to John. Of the second and third nothing much need be said. Expert opinion varies as to their authorship, and their entry into the canon was very uncertain, but it may be that they are from the same hand as the first Epistle, which was quite probably the hand that wrote the Fourth Gospel. The first Epistle is by far the most imposing. It has no particular addressee, and it lacks most of the normal characteristics of letters at the time. It warns against false preachers, antichrists (a term used here but not in Revelation) whose current numbers and activities suggested the imminence of the *parousia*. The Epistle calls for the maintenance of pure doctrine and good conduct and issues special warnings against Gnostic deviations. The language and imagery of these exhortations are often reminiscent of the Fourth Gospel, but the literary interest of the Epistle is manifestly not of the same order.

NOTES

1. *Patrologiae Graecae Cursus Completus*, ed. J.-P. Migne, LIX (Paris, 1862), 29.

2. *Patrologiae Latinae Cursus Completus*, ed. J.-P. Migne, XXXV (Paris, 1841), 1569.

3. Luther, *Works*, ed. Jaroslav Pelikan, XXII (New York, 1957), 3.

4. Ibid., p. 10.

5. *Commentaires de Jean Calvin sur le Nouveau Testament*, ed. M. Reveillard, II (Geneva, 1968), 12.

6. Chrysostom, *Patrologiae Graecae*, LIX, 40.

7. W. G. Kümmel, *Introduction to the New Testament*, 17th rev. ed. (1973), trans. Howard Clark Kee (London, 1975), p. 228.

8. Robert Alter, *The Art of Biblical Poetry* (New York, 1985), and his essay "The Characteristics of Ancient Hebrew Poetry" in this volume.

9. R. E. Brown, *The Gospel according to John*, 2 vols., Anchor Bible, XXIX, XXIXa (Garden City, N.Y., 1966, 1970), cxxxv–cxxxvi, etc. I owe a large debt to this commentary.

10. Ibid., pp. 320–329.

11. Meir Sternberg, *The Poetics of Biblical Narrative: Ideological Literature and the Drama of Reading* (Bloomington and Indianapolis, 1985), pp. 99 ff.

12. Brown, *John,* 917.

SUGGESTED FURTHER READINGS

R. E. Brown, *The Gospel according to John,* 2 vols., Anchor Bible, XXIX, XXIXa (Garden City, N.Y., 1966, 1970).

C. H. Dodd, *Historical Tradition in the Fourth Gospel* (Cambridge, 1963).

——, *The Interpretation of the Fourth Gospel* (Cambridge, 1953).

John Marsh, *The Gospel of St. John* (Harmondsworth, 1968).

King's College, University of Cambridge,
and Columbia University

Acts

James M. Robinson

FOUCAULT has drawn attention to the political dimensions of literature to an extent unprecedented in previous literary criticism; yet critical biblical scholarship has given the Acts of the Apostles a political interpretation for at least a century and a half.

According to the Hegelian interpretation of the New Testament, the so-called Tübingen hypothesis, the appropriate critical way to study the New Testament was to determine the tendency of each text in terms of thesis, antithesis, and synthesis. Acts was taken to be a prime example of the synthesis stage of this process; that is, it was concerned with presenting a harmonious view of the antithetic poles represented by Paul and his Judaizing opponents. For Acts represented the synthesis prevalent in Luke's own day, which Luke's presentation then cast back upon the beginnings of Christianity.

Although the Hegelian schematism has long since been discarded, biblical scholars have continued to build upon its basic insights. Whereas Paul's authentic letters reveal the tension characteristic of the first generation of Christians, Acts presents Paul as much more moderate in outlook (as are Peter and James). This basically political interpretation of Acts is evident in the 1950 article by Philipp Vielhauer, "On the 'Paulinism' of Acts."[1]

At the end of the last century Franz Overbeck reacted against the uncritical historical assumptions of his contemporaries by arguing that primitive Christianity was in its self-understanding unhistorical, more an anticipation of monasticism than a real precursor of the Church of Christendom. The first Christians would not have been able to grasp the concept of Church history. Overbeck first introduced into New Testament scholarship the insight that the literary form of a work is more revelatory of its ultimate intent than is many a statement of theological content. He presented the Gospels as generally unliterary, uninterested in the literary style of their day, which he took to be a basic indication of the otherworldliness of primitive Christianity. The Gospel of Luke is the first to exhibit literary pretension. It is therefore no coincidence that it is Luke who perpetrates what Overbeck considered a "tactlessness of world-historical dimensions" in following up his Gospel with a history of the Church.[2]

This insight introduced another political dimension to the study of Acts. Not only did Luke have his ax to grind in the internal Church politics of his own day; he was also actively involved in the political claims of early Christianity on contemporary Greco-Roman society. He is therefore credited with the somewhat dubious distinction of being the first Christian apologist, eager to present the Jews as the cause of the Church's troubles and the Roman authorities as basically recognizing the legitimacy of Christianity. Luke is saying, in fact, that Christianity is of world-historical importance. Its founding did not just happen "in a corner" (Acts 26:26). Quite consciously he dates the beginning of Jesus' ministry (Luke 1:5, 2:1, 3:1–2) to the Augustan age.

Between the two world wars it was primarily Martin Dibelius who advanced the understanding of Acts, by applying to the book the form-critical method that had proved so successful with regard to the Gospels. This approach showed how little, compared with the Gospels, Acts was shaped by the oral transmission of materials in the nascent Church, and hence how much of it is to be ascribed to Luke himself. An outstanding instance has to do with the various places in the second half of Acts where the narration in the third person suddenly shifts in and out of the first-person plural. Earlier scholars had taken the so-called "we sections" as strong evidence that the author of Acts was an eyewitness of at least the Pauline part of the narrative, which of course fitted well with the Luke whom Colossians (then ascribed to Paul, but today regarded as deutero-Pauline) identified as Paul's travel companion. Dibelius made it clear that the "we sections" were at best limited to an itinerary of ports of call and lacked relevant historical narration. Subsequent research has shown that such eyewitness accounts were a literary convention of antiquity.

Just after the Second World War Dibelius published a final and definitive essay on the speeches in Acts, which make up a surprisingly high percentage of the book.[3] He argued successfully that they do not reflect primitive Christian preaching, as the preceding historicizing generation (represented belatedly by C. H. Dodd) had assumed, but rather present what Luke thought the significance of the occasion to be. Dibelius found that Luke shared this trait with historians of antiquity; it was clear that Acts was not to be seen as history in a modern sense. Rather it was Luke's way of presenting what Christianity is and has to say. He was more interested in influencing history in his own day than in giving a faithful account of past history. That is to say, he had political motives and would seek the most appropriate literary means to realize them.

Between the two world wars Henry J. Cadbury carried on equally important and somewhat parallel studies in Acts, analyzing the way in which Luke proceeded as an author of a literary work.[4] For example, at the turn of the century scholars had interpreted places where the same incident was reported more than once as seams revealing the use of sources that did not fully agree with each other or with Luke. Cadbury made it clear that Luke diversified the narration both to achieve variety, itself a trait of good style, and to score different points at different places in the story. From this perspective Luke the creative author or storyteller tended to replace Luke the historian, whereas earlier critics had assumed that Luke collected and carefully transmitted written sources prepared in the various centers of primitive Christianity such as Jerusalem and Antioch. Cadbury showed that the verisimilitude of such narrations as Paul's trip by sea to Rome, far from demonstrating that the author was an eyewitness, merely revealed him to have been familiar with popular sea adventures in Hellenistic novels and the maritime life of his day.

After the Second World War the study of Acts was indirectly but decisively influenced by Hans Conzelmann's *The Theology of St. Luke.*[5] Conzelmann made it clear that Luke was less interested in history in the modern sense than in a theology of history, divided doctrinally into three parts: the Law and the Prophets, recorded in the Old Testament; the middle of time, represented by Jesus and recorded in the Gospel of Luke; and the time of the Church, recorded in Acts. That is, Luke's theology was the formative principle in his literary composition.

Ernst Haenchen's commentary in 1956, echoed by Conzelmann's in 1963, provided close readings showing that in Acts Luke was a literary craftsman rather than a historian.[6] Haenchen's work made the literary rather than the historical approach the consensus of critical scholarship.

This critical consensus has not gone unchallenged, especially in Britain. The major English commentary of this century, by F. F. Bruce, ignores this perspective altogether.[7] C. K. Barrett's survey *Luke the Historian in Recent Study* (1961) is less decidedly conservative but, as the title suggests, also regards Acts as a historiography rather than as a piece of Hellenistic literature.

Some of the literary conventions of Acts serve to illustrate this approach. Both the Gospel and Acts are dedicated to Theophilus (Luke 1:1, Acts 1:1). Such dedications were a Hellenistic literary convention that elevated the literary work to the cultural level of the patron. The resemblance between the prologue to the Gospel (1:1–4), the flashback in Acts 1:1–2, and prefaces to Hellenistic histories has been much discussed. Luke uses all the phrases currently popular in the genre of contemporary historiography. He also employs correct letter form. James 1:1 and Acts 15:23 and 23:26 are the three instances in the New Testament of strict conformity with the Hellenistic convention of epistolary salutation; the letters of the Pauline corpus and those of Revelation have been characteristically modified in a Christianizing way. Luke presents himself as a well-informed, cultured person, aware of Queen Candace of Ethiopia (8:27) and familiar with the well-known curiosity of the Athenians (17:21). The speeches in Acts say no more than what Luke thinks his readers need to learn at each juncture. Other Hellenistic conventions in presenting speeches are employed, such as reporting that a speaker said much more than is recorded (2:40), letting a speaker be interrupted at the appropriate moment (2:37, 4:1, 22:22), and inserting historical examples into speeches (5:36–37).

Just as the classicism of the day could imitate an earlier literary style to accredit a Hellenistic text as belonging to the grand tradition, so Luke can shift from the Hellenistic Greek he normally writes into the ghetto Greek of the Septuagint translation of the Old Testament, to give a scriptural flavor—and authority—to his presentation. And he does this not indiscriminately, but where it counts: the elegant Hellenistic historian's preface to the Gospel is followed, in sharply contrasting language and style, by the biblical world of the infancy narrative (Luke 1–2), where there can be no mistaking, at the level of feeling, that the Jewish Scriptures are here being continued. And in the early chapters of Acts, the sermons are more biblical in tone than the surrounding narration. This scriptural tone results not only from the citation of biblical proof-texts, though they are of course in evidence, but also from the use of an archaic language to convey mood. Luke knew that one system prevails in one epoch, another in another, and could express this periodization of history not only in doctrine (for example, the christology of the early chapters of Acts is more primitive than the later treatment of the Gentile mission) and in Church practice (the "communism" of the early chapters of Acts does not characterize the later parts of Church history in which Paul—and Luke— functioned), but also in the atmosphere created by the language used. Luke was very aware of what language does and made good use of rhetoric to achieve his goals. He knew he could gain consent subtly by the way he expressed himself, as well as (or at times better than) by the content of what was said. This is a sophistication that critics do not usually ascribe to the New Testament but that is fully characteristic of Acts.

Luke did not present his views abstractly; he preferred to narrate. But his interest was not just to record the past; his primary purpose was to give a convincing account of the opinions he thought important. Oral tradition offered no sequential narration, only isolated episodes that the first evangelists arranged for their own purposes. By his own time Luke could draw for his Gospel on two sources, Mark and a now-lost collection of sayings (also used by Matthew) and usually called Q. But the tradition of Church history available to him when he was writing Acts was not in the form of connected written sources; it resembled more the discrete anecdotes that were available to Mark, for example, in writing his Gospel. For here, too, individual episodes do not normally have an interlocking cause-effect relationship; each stands on its own. Acts does contain some programmatic episodes to which later appeal is made, such as the conversion of the pagan Cornelius as a precedent of relevance to the Jerusalem Council (15:7–11, 14) and the conversion of Paul as relevant to his later autobiographical speeches. But such interlocking of stories is the exception rather than the rule. Usually Luke is not concerned to see how one episode leads to the next; that is, he is not in a modern sense trying to arrive at the historical nexus that elevates anecdotes to history. Luke's treatment of episodes becomes intelligible when we recognize that he convinces not by argumentation, but by the interspersing of vignettes among events. Eckhard Plümacher has recently shown that this style is dependent upon a form of Hellenistic-Roman historiography that had a purpose somewhat like that of Greek tragedy—to portray in dramatic narrative the points to be made, so as to arouse the desired feeling in the audience or reader.[8] This style Luke adapted to his own purposes.

Luke was in the somewhat awkward situation of having as his narrative material a tradition which began the story with the Roman execution of Jesus and went on to include the Roman execution of Paul, in the broader context of Nero's persecution. Jesus' death could not be ignored, only presented in as palatable a way as possible; but more recent Roman violence is simply bypassed. In the stories that he included, Luke repeatedly made the point that the persecutors were not the Roman authorities; rather it was the Jews who were responsible (Acts 13:50; 17:5–7, 13; 21:27). When they plot persecution (23:12–15, 25:3), it is the Roman authorities who maintain law and order. When the Jews turn the Christians in to the Roman authorities (18:12–13, 24:1, 25:5), the state comes to the Christians' defense. Justice is on the Christian side: Gallio makes it clear that he will punish injustice or crime but will not intervene in internal Jewish squabbles concerning doctrine, persons, or Torah (18:14–15). Festus makes the same distinction in explaining the situation of Paul to Agrippa (25:18–19), thereby acquitting Paul of any capital crime (25:25).

Luke is concerned to argue, as a kind of first advocate of the separation of Church and state, that the state has no jurisdiction over religious preferences. But he does not present this as an abstract theory, as did second-century apologists; his anticipation of their theory is expressed in story form. To be sure, the Roman officials more or less state for the Christians the principle of noninterference in purely religious matters (18:15; 25:20, 26–27). But this principle is then carried through in lively narrative scenes that stick in the memory, such as the Jews' attempts to evade this apologetic argument of the Christians by falsely accusing them of state crimes for which they could be prosecuted (17:6–7, 24:5).

Paul's appeal to Caesar is based on his unbounded trust in the system (25:11). When Paul is mistreated by the authorities in Philippi, he appeals to his Roman citizenship to demand not only that the mistreatment end, but also that his release be accompanied by a formal apology (16:37).

When Paul tells another Roman official he is a Roman, the official is terrified that he may not have treated Paul correctly, especially when Paul points out that he is a Roman by birth, whereas the official is only a naturalized citizen (22:25–29). With right on its side, the Church cannot fail. Paul was taken seriously by important people, such as Asiarchs in Ephesus (19:31), Epicurean and Stoic philosophers and the Areopagite in Athens (17:18, 34), proconsuls in Cyprus and Palestine (13:12, 24:24), even King Agrippa and his sister (25:22–23, 26:27–28). These are the kind of people who think well of Christians, who are even inclined to join the Church! One can only be amazed at the boldness of such a posture, at a time when persecutions were not uncommon. For the reality of Christian experience must have been a far cry from this utopian ideal, though it was made to sound all the more convincing by being presented as the real, what typically happens, rather than as a gratifying fantasy.

Acts does not confine this dramatized theology to the politics of Church and state, but applies it, though in less secular language, to internal Church politics itself. The outline of Acts is not in the preface, where we might expect it, but in the scene that connects directly to the preface, the Ascension, where Jesus himself presents the outline: in Jerusalem, in all Judea and Samaria, and to the end of the earth (1:8). This development from a Jewish sect into a world religion is a theme to which Luke repeatedly returns, not in the abstract, but in scenes in which the divine authorization (in the case of the Ascension, by the resurrected Jesus) is made clear through the action itself. The Ethiopian eunuch is converted by Philip, sent for this purpose by "the angel of the Lord" (8:26–40). In addition to the tradition of Paul's conversion, Luke narrates a subsequent audition, in which the Lord commissioned him to go to the Gentiles (22:17–21). Thus the doctrine of a legitimate Gentile Church is argued in narrative form at a series of decisive turning points.

The conversion of the centurion Cornelius in chapter 10 is the *locus classicus* for this main theme of Lukan political theology. Perhaps the best way to grasp this point is to consider this part of the text in reverse order, beginning with the political applications in chapters 11–15, which make clear the tendency at work in the way the historical narrative of chapter 10 itself was cast. For the whole Cornelius story is designed to function as Exhibit A at the Jerusalem Council. James brings the council to its conclusion with a speech that begins with the conversion of Cornelius, though generalized as a basic principle: "Simeon hath declared how God at the first did visit the Gentiles, to take out of them a people for his name" (15:14); he then buttresses this doctrine with proof from Scripture (vv. 15–18). James's conclusion is based on Peter's presentation to the council, which begins: "Men and brethren, ye know how that a good while ago God made choice among us, that the Gentiles by my mouth should hear the word of the gospel, and believe. And God, which knoweth the hearts, bare them witness, giving them the Holy Ghost, even as he did unto us; And put no difference between us and them, purifying their hearts by faith" (vv. 7–9). Here again the allusion to the Cornelius story is evident, not as a single isolated occurrence, but as a generalized principle of basic importance.

What is here alluded to decisively at the Jerusalem Council is anticipated in chapter 11 in more narrative form, but for much the same reason, to prepare for the description of the Antiochene mission that in turn led into the Jerusalem Council in Luke's presentation. In chapter 11 the debate is between Peter and the circumcision party. The narration of Cornelius' conversion is now briefer than the immediately preceding story, when it was presented as actually "happening," and the language that is retained focuses on the story's normative role: Peter was praying; he fell into a trance; he saw a vision from heaven; he heard a voice from heaven; he addressed the heavenly voice as Lord (compare Paul's dialogue on the Damascus Road); it is God who has cleansed; the vision recurs three times; the Spirit commands him to go to Joppa and not discriminate; an angel tells Cornelius how to be saved; the Holy Spirit descends as Paul speaks. The saying of Jesus concerning the spirit baptism to which John's water baptism only pointed is recalled to identify what occurred to Cornelius with the legitimation of the original disciples, so that any potential opposition (to Gentile baptism) is branded as opposing God (11:5–17). This pointed summary of the Cornelius story did in fact silence the circumcision party, which could only glorify God and state the Lukan principle: "Then hath God also to the Gentiles granted repentance unto life" (11:18).

In the account of the conversion of Cornelius itself in chapter 10, the narrative's repetitiousness and its focus on just this legitimizing language show that Luke has slanted it to his own purpose. The whole section, chapters 10–15, is a carefully composed unit, devised to present in extensive detail a story that can be immediately validated in miniature in the brief exchange between Peter and the circumcision party. Thereupon the Antiochene Gentile mission can be narrated and its practice welcomed not only by Phoenician and Samaritan Christians visited on the way to Jerusalem (15:3), but also in a formal sense by the Jerusalem authorities as the outcome of the Jerusalem Council in chapter 15.

The Jerusalem Council, in its definitive legitimation of the Gentile mission, is thus the basic turning point for Luke's conception. But more is involved than such an abstract principle. Ernst Haenchen has noted that the Jerusalem Council served to begin the shift away from the original organizational structure led by Peter and the apostles to the subsequent structure directed by James and the elders. As early as 12:17 the expression "James and the brethren" is used (by Peter) for the Jerusalem authorities. At the council itself, Peter represents only the missionaries who have come in from the field, whereas James presides. The scene provides a harmonious transition from one system of government to the other, in that both agree on the outcome. Thus the Jerusalem Council legitimizes the shift in the form of government, not just the theological point on which they agree. Transition language occurs when the elders are introduced in 11:30 as the recipients of the collection brought by Barnabas and Saul, and when the leadership of the Jerusalem Council is expressed in the recurrent phrase "the apostles and the elders" (15:2, 4, 6, 22, 23). The apostles are mentioned for the last time at 16:4; thus the Jerusalem Council is their swan song. By 21:18 the Jerusalem Church is led only by James and the elders.

Even this shift in the form of Church government is not merely Lukan theology about past changes. For the future belongs to the new form of government, presumably including also Luke's future. On the return trip from the so-called first missionary journey, Barnabas and Paul install elders in each church they have founded (14:23). On his final return to Jerusalem, Paul convenes at Miletus the elders of the Ephesus church (20:17). Thus it is apparent that Luke conceives of this form of Church government as standard practice for the Gentile Christianity of which he is a part.

Acts uses narrative to present even more abstract doctrine than the Gentile mission and Church government: Christian truth is revealed truth not always readily intelligible even to Christians. For example, the vision of unclean food that Peter should eat, according to an angel's command (10:14, 17), is so new that he at first refuses. Thus the reader is led through the shock of having admitted Gentiles into the Church. They come to accept the new revelation by accompanying Peter through the story.

Christian truth as divine revelation is even more inaccessible, indeed unintelligible, to the worldly mind; thus the inability of the Roman authorities to understand that Christianity is not a detraction or a weakening of the Christian apologetic's obvious appeal to sensible people, but indirectly a confirmation of Christianity's status as a revealed religion. Festus hears Paul's gospel and can only shake his head and say that Paul is out of his mind (26:24). Festus' own secular version of Paul's gospel could hardly have failed to amuse the Christian reader by its factual accuracy but complete lack of understanding; he reports that the issue between the Jews and Paul had to do with religion and some dead person named Jesus whom Paul claimed was (still) alive, which Festus conceded he could not understand at all (25:19–20). This inability of the carnal mind to understand the things of God does not prevent Luke from claiming, in the same context though quite inconsistently, that such truth is of course well known to worldly authority figures such as Agrippa (26:26–28). Luke is determined to maintain both apologetic values: Christianity is revealed truth, but Christianity appeals to important people, important in purely worldly terms. Such inconsistent claims would be less convincing in a more theoretical form of presentation, but when merely implicit in narrative contexts the inconsistency is blunted. Readers who sense the problem can resolve it, for example, by assuming that Festus missed the point and Agrippa saw the point. But the average reader is not so critical.

Another variant of this dialectic is the description of Paul playing the role of a Pharisee. Whereas the historical Paul roundly repudiated his pharisaic past (Phil. 3:6), Luke has Paul present himself before a hostile Jewish audience including Pharisees as himself still a Pharisee being persecuted by the opposing Jewish party, the Sadducees (Acts 23:6). The Pharisees fall for the ploy and rise to Paul's defense, suggesting that his views may well come from a spirit or angel (23:8–9). But this is the beginning of the series of stories in which the Jews with one mind seek to do away with Paul, as if the sympathy of the Pharisees did not exist— not they, but only the Romans will rescue him! Even if by Luke's time Pauline theology was so fully forgotten that his readers no longer appreciated the theological impossibility of this scene of Paul's rescue by the Pharisees, only a reader with very little critical acumen could take it at face value. Such a story shows how little Luke was concerned to present history in such a way that its factuality would be beyond question. Rather he was thinking in terms of presenting Christianity as the enlightened position that intelligent persons would obviously support, in the teeth of the evidence that Christians were not supported in such a way at all.

Several instances demonstrate Luke's lack of concern for normal historical treatment and thereby emphasize the primacy of his literary concern.

First, Paul reveals his identity as a Greek-speaking Jew with citizenship in Cilicia in order to avoid confusion with an Egyptian troublemaker, thereby also associating himself with the Roman official—he reverts to Aramaic only to address the "natives" (21:37–40). But he omits reference to his Roman citizenship until he is on the brink of receiving the third degree (22:25–28). Why did he not mention this right away? The answer is purely literary: the tension and excitement of the story would have been lost, for the threat of torture could not have arisen (23:34).

Second, the Roman authority is terrified to learn he has bound a Roman citizen (22:29), but he releases him only the next day (22:30). This delay is not to be explained in terms of different kinds of binding or imprisonment, or in terms of Roman procedure, but simply by the fact that one story was oriented to the revelation of Paul's Roman citizenship, and the other to bringing him before the Sanhedrin the next day, in which context Paul is released to go to the meeting. Did the Romans have the authority to convene the Sanhedrin? Could a Gentile attend it? Could the Roman authorities not have clarified the cause of the tension by interviewing Paul without illegal torture? The Sanhedrin is introduced to provide an instance of official Judaism's being put on trial for its illegitimate practices toward Christians, for the uproar has not taken place in the presence of the Sanhedrin, but in the Temple. When the high priest has Paul struck on the face, Luke the historian may be excused for not knowing that Paul, when reviled, blesses (1 Cor. 4:12), but hardly for presenting him as not recognizing the high priest when the latter places a curse on him (Acts 22:3–5). Either Luke really lacks literary skill, in producing so many dangling questions, or his interest lies elsewhere than in such historicizing questions.

Luke is much more interested in the situation of Christians between Jews and Romans in his own day than at any time in the past. The Temple was no longer standing; hence the original charge that Paul was desecrating the Temple was no longer relevant. But at his arrest, the Jews from Asia brand him first as one who speaks against the Jewish people and the Torah, both live issues in Luke's time, and only then as one who opposes the Temple (21:28). It is the issue of the Gentile mission, still acute in Luke's time, that causes the crowd, calm up to that point, to interrupt Paul in rage (22:22). It is as a leader of the sect of the Nazarenes (24:5) that Paul is to be defended, for in reality it is Lukan Christianity that is being defended.

Like the Gospels, in which the evangelists rarely speak directly of their own times, though the texts are slanted to address their times, Acts comes to a conclusion a generation or two before the time of its writing. But just as the apocalypse in Mark 13 and its adaptation in Luke 21:20–24 foretold the destruction of Jerusalem with remarkable clarity, so Acts presents a prediction by Paul, before his passion narrative begins, that reports on Luke's own time. When returning to Palestine for his arrest and execution (the latter not narrated in Acts) Paul convenes the elders of the church of Ephesus to meet his boat at Miletus, there to receive his last will and testament (Acts 20: 17–38). He says he knows that after his death wolves will come and not spare them, and that even some of their own number will lead their followers astray (20:29–30). This is apparently the clearest statement by Luke of what transpired between Paul's death and the writing of Acts. Since the focus is on Ephesus, we may assume that Luke had some knowledge of things there. Indeed, these imprecise suggestions of emergent heresy are not hard to place among the scattered documentation about Ephesus during this period, from Colossians, Ephesians, Revelation, and Ignatius. By the slanting of historical material Luke indirectly reports on what they more directly report.

Acts has succeeded to a remarkable degree in making history, which we have seen was more central in Luke's intention than the recording of history. The version of primitive Christian history presented in the book has been taken at face value down through the centuries, so that today we hardly realize how many of the seemingly unchallenged facts are Lukanisms, facts perhaps more literary than historical. Jesus ascended forty days after the Passion, and his appearances later, to Paul and to the John of Revelation, quite apart from appearances to Gnostics, somehow fail to conform to the scheme of resurrection appearances set up by the canonical Gospels. Luke forestalled the consequences of this dangerous challenge to the authority of the tradition regarding resurrection appearances by invalidating appearances after the first forty days, and the Church (with the exception of such heretical movements as the Gnostics) has simply taken him at his word.

The expectation of the imminent end of the world that gave primitive Christianity its apocalyptic focus was already blunted in the Gospel of Luke by sometimes rather drastic editorial operations. This blunting is continued in the opening Ascension story of Acts, where two speakers (presumably from heaven) stress that one should not look longingly up to the heaven into which Jesus has disappeared, but follow the course of the Book of Acts, with the assurance that in due time he will return. Thus the delay of the imminently expected kingdom of God is canceled as a problem for Luke's generation and replaced by an engrossment with the history of the Church.

Luke was in a sense the first Christian politician, in that he seems to have been the first consciously to think through the fact that the world is here to stay; Christianity must make its way in the world and do so on the world's terms. Thus to a degree he anticipated, indeed paved the way for, the conversion of the Roman Empire under Constantine more than two centuries later. He also anticipated two literary genres: that of (apocryphal) Acts and that of Church history as written by Eusebius, who was inspired by the real success of Christianity under Constantine.

Realizing that Christianity must change with the changing times, Luke introduced into his presentation a periodizing that anticipated the philosophy of history. He thus achieved the flexibility that a more theoretical presentation would probably have excluded. The theology of Paul hardly survived Paul's death, and by Luke's time it seems to have been forgotten. But Luke stands on our side of the cleft separating all subsequent Christianity from its beginnings.

Luke's political achievement is thus not merely that he produced the archetypes of Christianity, the superseded quasi-idyllic time of the Jerusalem Church and the more contemporary time of the Gentile mission of Paul. He undertook a much more subtle, more pervasive politicizing: he changed Christianity from a religion appropriate to a world existing in the last remnant of time to one which took it as it was, and tried to make it conform to his Christian vision of reality. Paul, confronting specific problems of practice and thought in Asia Minor and Greece, or Jesus, appealing to the Palestinian Jews to reshape their life and thought in accordance with his vision of the kingdom of God, were intelligible as holding operations, fifth-column tactics in an otherwise meaningless or hostile context. Luke, in contrast, did not argue that his *politeuma*, his citizenship, was of heaven rather than of this world (Phil. 3:20), but, anticipating Augustine, concerned himself with transforming society into the *civitas Dei.*

NOTES

1. Philipp Vielhauer, "Zum 'Paulinismus' der Apostelgeschichte," *Evangelische Theologie*, 10 (1950–51), 1–15; English translation by William C. Robinson, Jr., and Victor P. Furnish, "On the 'Paulinism' of Acts," *Perkins School of Theology Journal*, 17 (1963), reprinted in Leander E. Keck and J. Louis Martyn, eds., *Studies in Luke–Acts: Studies Presented in Honor of Paul Schubert* (Nashville and New York, 1966), pp. 33–50.

2. Franz Overbeck, *Christentum und Kultur* (1919; reprint, Darmstadt, 1963), p. 78. His formulation was introduced into the modern discussion by Karl Ludwig Schmidt, "Die Stellung der Evangelien in der allgemeinen Literaturgeschichte," *Eucharisterion*, II (Göttingen, 1923), 132.

3. Martin Dibelius, "The Speeches in Acts and Ancient Historiography," in Heinrich Greeven, ed., *Studies in the Acts of the Apostles*, trans. Mary Ling (London and New York, 1956), pp. 138–191.

4. Henry J. Cadbury, *The Style and Literary Method of Luke*, vol. I, *The Diction of Luke and Acts* (Cambridge, Mass., 1920), and *The Making of Luke–Acts* (London and New York, 1927).

5. Hans Conzelmann, *The Theology of St. Luke*, trans. Geoffrey Buswell (New York, 1960).

6. Ernst Haenchen, *The Acts of the Apostles: A Commentary*, rev. trans. R. McL. Wilson (Oxford and Philadelphia, 1971); Hans Conzelmann, *Die Apostelgeschichte* (Tübingen, 1963).

7. Frederick Fyvie Bruce, *The Acts of the Apostles* (London, 1951).

8. Eckhard Plümacher, *Lukas als hellenistischer Schriftsteller* (Göttingen, 1972).

SUGGESTED FURTHER READINGS

Henry J. Cadbury, *The Style and Literary Method of Luke* (Cambridge, Mass., 1920).

Martin Dibelius, *Studies in the Acts of the Apostles*, ed. Heinrich Greeven, trans. Mary Ling (London and New York, 1956).

Ernst Haenchen, *The Acts of the Apostles: A Commentary*, rev. trans. R. McL. Wilson (Philadelphia, 1971).

Leander G. Keck and J. Louis Martyn, eds., *Studies in Luke–Acts: Studies Presented in Honor of Paul Schubert* (Nashville and New York, 1966).

Charles H. Talbert, *Literary Patterns, Theological Themes, and the Genre of Luke–Acts* (Missoula, Mont. 1974).

Charles H. Talbert, ed., *Luke–Acts: New Perspectives from the Society of Biblical Literature Seminar* (New York, 1984).

Claremont Graduate School

The Pauline Epistles

Michael Goulder

O F the fourteen letters in the King James Version claiming Pauline authorship, seven are widely agreed to be authentic and four pseudonymous; the remaining three are disputed. Authentic are 1 Thessalonians, 1 Corinthians, Galatians, 2 Corinthians, Romans, Philemon, and Philippians, probably in that order. Pseudonymous (at least in their present form) are 1 and 2 Timothy, Titus, and Hebrews; 2 Thessalonians, Colossians, and Ephesians are disputed, Ephesians heavily so. However, because literary considerations may make it more likely that Paul wrote the last three letters, I have included some discussion of them. If Paul wrote them, Colossians and Ephesians belong with Philemon, and Ephesians was written to Laodicea.[1]

Community letters were a familiar feature of Jewish life. It was necessary for the national leaders to keep the Diaspora communities informed about the calendar each year, and innovations and ad hoc decisions would require such communication. Luke believed that Paul himself carried such letters to Damascus (Acts 9:2). We have two examples in 2 Maccabees 1:1–9 and 1:10–2:18, in which the Jerusalem authorities urge the Egyptian Jews to adopt the new feast of Dedication. These letters are prefaces to an account of the Maccabean War, after which the new festival was instituted. They give us an idea of the six-part model from which Paul could have developed his own epistolary style:

1. Salutation: "The brethren, the Jews that are in Jerusalem . . . send greetings to the Jews throughout Egypt, good peace" (2 Macc. 1:1; cf. v. 10)

2. Thanksgiving: "Blessed be our God in all things" (1:11–17)

3. Prayer for the recipients' well-being (with covert sermonizing): "May God do good to you" (1:2–6)

4. Account of the situation (1:7–8, 11–16 with the thanksgiving)

5. Encouragement/command to follow the senders' wishes: "and now see that ye keep the days of the feast . . . of the month of Kislev" (1:9, 1:18–2:16)

6. Pious conclusion: "Now God . . ." (2:17–18)

479

In Acts 15:23–29 Luke represents the apostolic council as sending out an encyclical letter consisting of features 1, 4, and 5.

First Thessalonians conforms to such a model: (1) "Paul and Silvanus, and Timotheus, unto the church of the Thessalonians . . . Grace be unto you, and peace" (1:1). There follow (2–3) thanksgiving with prayer (1:2–10) for their conversion and perseverance, extended in 2:1–16; (4) an account of the situation—Paul's waiting, anxiety, and joy at the news of their steadfastness (2:17–3:13); (5) some instruction on Christian sanctity (4:1–5:22); and (6) a pious conclusion: "And the very God of peace . . ." (5:23–28). The whole letter shines with Paul's warmhearted concern for them, his affectionate anxiety for their perfection, and his triumphant joy at their faithfulness. It lacks any artifice or rhetorical structuring: the thought flows naturally. He has had two major anxieties concerning them. The first is the fear that under persecution they would give up the faith. To counter this peril he speaks of his own sufferings at Philippi, his hard life while preaching to them, their joyful acceptance of the gospel and sufferings, the sufferings of other churches at the hands of the Jews, his frustrated wish to visit them, his sending of Timothy, and his warning that persecutions were inevitable (2:1–3:5). Now that Timothy has returned with the happy news of their faithfulness and love, he is exultant. He is comforted for all his present pains and pressures by their faithfulness: "now we live if ye stand fast in the Lord" (3:8). Night and day he prays for them; all he wants is to visit them (3:6–13). He has been really worried, and he is triumphantly happy that they have stood the test.

But the good pastor knows no peace: there is the second anxiety still—are they walking blameless in holiness (3:13)? There are the standard temptations to which Gentiles are liable (4:5), sex and sharp practice in business. Then there is the special Christian duty of providing for each other's needs, and of quietly earning a living to this end (4:1–12). In particular there is the Christian virtue of hope: there is no place for grief when our friends die, since they will rise to meet Christ when he comes to gather us all. We must ever be ready for that coming (4:13–5:11) and respect Paul's church officers, see that order is kept in church, pray, and honor those who prophesy in the Spirit (5:12–22). "And the very God of peace sanctify you wholly . . ."

First Thessalonians is so perspicuous a letter that the centuries drop away: we are looking over the shoulder of a good and genuine man who has staked all he has on his religious experience and been rewarded with a few hours of intense happiness. The community he has founded has not succumbed to hostile pressure: his work is not in vain. The clarity of this brief writing enables us to see its literary structure without difficulty; and we may notice a second feature now: Paul's anxieties show themselves in advance, like the preview of a film. Even in the thanksgiving he mentions first their work of *faithfulness* and *patience* of hope (1:3): "ye became followers of us, and of the Lord, having received the word in much affliction, with joy of the Holy Ghost" (1:6). The ethical nervousness is still more pervasive: "That ye would walk worthy of God, who hath called you" (2:12), "To the end he may stablish your hearts unblameable in holiness before God" (3:13). The particular point over Jesus' coming is similarly previewed in the thanksgiving: "And to wait for his Son from heaven . . . Jesus, which delivered us from the wrath to come" (1:10). It comes up again at 2:19: "For what is our hope . . . ? Are not even ye in the presence of our Lord Jesus Christ at his coming?" There is more than one reference to faith and love (3:6, 5:8), with hope as a different matter.

The discrimination of even these few literary features must affect our judgment on the authenticity of other letters. Paul begins 1 Thessalonians with a thanksgiving (*eucharistein*), and the same feature is found in Romans, 1 Corinthians, Philippians, and Philemon—and also in 2 Thessalonians and Colossians. Second Corinthians has a thanksgiving too, introduced by "Blessed be God" (1:3), as does Ephesians. Only Galatians has no thanksgiving: Paul is too angry and begins with a sardonic "I marvel that ye are so soon removed" (1:6). None of the eleven non-Pauline letters in the New Testament has a thanksgiving with *eucharistein*. Only 1 Peter has the formula "Blessed be the God" (*eulogētos*), and 2 Timothy has "I am grateful" ([AT] *charin echō*). The structure in 2 Thessalonians is not unlike that of 1 Thessalonians. The thanksgiving fills chapter 1, after an almost identical salutation; then comes the earnest discussion of the latest situation in the church—not so happy this time, as "deceivers" have been at work, and the teaching of the coming of the Lord has to be amplified (chap. 2); and chapter 3 discusses practical living. The thanksgiving is primarily for their faithfulness, as in 1 Thessalonians, but there is an extensive preview of the revelation of the Lord Jesus Christ from heaven to punish their persecutors (1:6–10, with a view to chap. 2), and another in prayer that "our God would count you worthy of this calling, and fulfill . . . the work of faith with power" (1:11, with a view to chap. 3). There is the same zeal for the practical working out of faith at 2:17: "and stablish you in every good word and work." The work in this case is an extension of 1 Thessalonians 4:11, earning one's living and not expecting the church to keep one. Phrases like "Now we beseech you, brethren," "pray for us," "Now the God/Lord of peace himself . . . ," which occur in both Epistles, are easily imitated (though they are not imitated in the pseudo-Pauline Pastorals): but the more subtle elements, the structure and previews, are important indications that 2 Thessalonians (as well as Ephesians and Colossians) is by Paul himself.[2]

The same essential structure—salutation, thanksgiving, discussion of the church's situation, practical holiness, pious conclusion—is developed in 1 Corinthians. The thanksgiving, as before, gives glimpses of what is to come. "That in every thing ye are enriched by him, in all utterance, and in all knowledge" (1:5) strikes the reader as unintentionally ironic; for at 4:8 Paul will wax sarcastic about those who think they have become rich, and they will be told at 8:1 that "Knowledge puffeth up, but charity edifieth." But the apostle is without guile. In chapter 1 he intends to be friendly, but his feelings get the better of him later, and very properly too. "So that ye come behind in no gift; waiting for the coming of our Lord Jesus Christ" (1:7) foreshadows the discussion of the gifts of the Spirit in chapters 12–14—and also, more subtly, the idea that has got around at Corinth that the kingdom has already begun (4:8 again: "ye have reigned as kings without us"). And of course there is the ethical anxiety, expressed in the hope that the Lord Jesus Christ will "confirm you unto the end, that ye may be blameless" (1:8). Blame can arise only from misbehavior; and thereupon Paul launches into the unhappy reports he has received of factions in the church and does his best to straighten matters out in 1:10–4:21. With chapter 5 he turns to ethical questions, and, as in 1 Thessalonians, the first one concerns sex. He shames the church with the particularly scandalous cases of a man living with his (dead?) father's wife, and of Christians who have been whoring on the basis that "All things are lawful" (6:12) (now that the kingdom has begun). But there are more serious sexual questions from an extraordinarily devout group (chap. 7): should married couples abstain from sex, or the engaged from marriage? These questions and others have been posed to Paul in a letter from Corinth, and he carries on answering them till chapter 15. Can a Christian eat of food which has or may have been offered to an idol? (chaps. 8–10). How is the church's worship to be conducted in face of competing spiritual gifts (chaps. 12–14, with an introduction in 11)? Is there really to be a resurrection of the dead (chap. 15)? Paul closes the letter in a welter of affectionate messages: his collection for Jerusalem, which they are to prepare for; his plans to visit; Timothy's coming; "Watch ye" (16:13); the commendation of Stephanas; greetings, especially from Aquila and Priscilla; and a personally written postscript. For all its problems, the same loving, fatherly care pervades 1 Corinthians as 1 Thessalonians, and the detail shows us the life of the Church in 50–60 C.E. more clearly than any other New Testament document.

Paul's pastoral tone is attractive. He uses personal, affectionate metaphors. "We were gentle among you, even as a nurse cherisheth her children" (1 Thess. 2:7); "we . . . charged every one of you, as a father doth his children" (1 Thess. 2:11); "being bereaved of you" (1 Thess. 2:17 [AT], *aporphanisthentes*); "And I, brethren, could not speak unto you as unto spiritual, but as unto carnal, even as unto babes in Christ. I have fed you with milk, and not with meat" (1 Cor. 3:1–2); "as my beloved sons I warn you. For though ye have ten thousand instructors in Christ, yet have ye not many fathers: for in Christ Jesus I have begotten you through the gospel" (1 Cor. 4:14–15); "shall I come unto you with a rod?" (1 Cor.

4:21). The same parental images recur later: "I beseech thee for my son Onesimus, whom I have begotten in my bonds" (Philem. 10); "My little children, of whom I travail in birth again until Christ be formed in you" (Gal. 4:19); and in every other Epistle.

In pastoral mood Paul tries to be tactful, but he finds this a strain. "We beseech you . . . that as ye have received of us how ye ought to walk and to please God, so ye would abound more and more" (1 Thess. 4:1)—the tactful pastor says not "so ye would walk," but "so ye would abound": but he then proceeds to an exhortation to abstain from fornication! The news that there are Cephasites and Apollosites at Corinth draws from him the tactful "was Paul crucified for you? or were ye baptized in the name of Paul?" (1 Cor. 1:13). Later in the same letter he says: "I hear that there be divisions among you; and I partly believe it" (11:18); the "partly" is masterly. "I write not these things to shame you," he says of their pretensions at 4:14, but that is in fact his precise intention; and he says so—"I speak to your shame"—about a lesser matter at 6:5. The opening of Romans is especially transparent in this way: "For I long to see you, that I may impart unto you some spiritual gift, to the end ye may be established; That is, that I may be comforted together with you by the mutual faith both of you and me" (1:11–12)—he remembers their contribution just in time.

Leadership is a tricky business, and it is too easy to accuse Paul of manipulation;[3] but he can still teach modern managers a thing or two. The Corinthian church is riven with disputes, and these are handled on the highest level for fifteen chapters. Only at 16:15–16 does he say: "I beseech you, brethren, (ye know the house of Stephanas, that it is the firstfruits of Achaia, and that they have addicted themselves to the ministry of the saints,) That ye submit yourselves unto such." We just happen to know from 1:16 that Stephanas and his household were the only people in the church baptized by Paul, and thus are probably his loyal supporters (compare 16:17). There is some extremely adroit handling of the issue of spiritual gifts. As chapter 14 reveals, the real question is whether the time of worship should be given to ecstatic and incomprehensible "tongues" or to edifying and excitable "prophesying." Paul favors the second but wisely evades any confrontation. First he muddies the issue by multiplying the gifts in chapter 12: apostleship (which only he has), teaching, healing, miracles (the same?), washing up ("helps") (vv. 8–10; cf. v. 28). Next he applies the parallel of the parts of the body with exhaustively repetitive sweet-reasonableness (vv. 11–27). Then he lists the gifts, with apostleship first (of course), prophecy second, and tongues eighth and last (v. 28). Then he fires off at a tangent with marvelous eloquence on charity (chap. 13). He has won the battle before ever he comes to fight it at 14:1. We probably have a second instance of the same brilliant tactic in chapters 1–4. From 1:12 it would be natural to infer that different groups followed

Paul and Apollos, but in 4:6 it appears likely that they are the same: "And these things, brethren, I have in a figure transferred to myself and to Apollos for your sakes; that ye might learn in us . . . that no one of you be puffed up for the one against the other" ([AR] *tou henos kata tou heterou*). The bogus multiplication saves confrontation; it muddies the issue and helps to bring peace to the church (and victory to Paul).

Another characteristic of Paul's pastoral style is the taking up of catchphrases. "Grace and peace" in the greetings is an instance of this, a Christianized version of the standard Greek (*chaire*) and Hebrew (*shalom*) salutations. "All things are lawful unto/for me" was a slogan of Paul's opponents (1 Cor. 6:12, 10:23), which he caps both times with "but all things are not expedient." "Meats for the belly and the belly for meats," they said (1 Cor. 6:13)—eat as you please, whether or not the meat has been offered to an idol: "but God shall destroy both it and them," he replies. We have this technique more subtly with their claims to wisdom (1:19–2:16). At first Paul is dismissive: "the foolishness of God is wiser than men" (1:25). But then his quick mind turns to exploit the claim in just the opposite sense: "Howbeit we speak wisdom among them that are perfect: yet not the wisdom of this world . . . But we speak the wisdom of God in a mystery" (2:6–7). Paul has wisdom too, but it is *divine* wisdom. We find the same double move, first dismissal and then appropriation on a higher level, in 2 Corinthians with commendatory letters and other matters. Claims to knowledge he upstages similarly: "And if any man think that he knoweth any thing, he knoweth nothing yet as he ought to know. But if any man love God, the same is known of him" (1 Cor. 8:2–3). It is not our knowledge of God that matters, but his knowing us. So again at 13:12: "then shall I know even as also I am known."

A strategy similar to these is an artificial evenhandedness which could be helpful to many a modern chairman, especially when taking the less controversial point first. Should couples live together without sex? Paul can see where that will lead: "Let the husband render unto the wife her due: and likewise the wife unto the husband" (1 Cor. 7:4 [AR]). But it is not actually the wife's sexual demands which would normally put the first strain on such relations, but the husband's. Paul studiously gives the wife parity throughout chapter 7, as he is far from doing in chapters 11 and 14; and he puts the lady first in the discussion too. In this way the reader gains the bogus impression of fair-mindedness, which continues as long as the alignment is not relevant to real life. The same tactic is used doubly in discussing circumcision. Paul is not frightened that a few ascetics will expel sex with a fork (and he would be delighted if they could, 7.7); he is frightened that the Jerusalem leaders will force the circumcision issue. How wise, then, to take the two points together, and to solve them with the bracketing conclusion, "Brethren, let every man, wherein he is called, therein abide with God" (7:24). He covers the sexual point first, because he has been asked about it, and includes the circumcision issue with studied casualness at 7:17–20. Furthermore, when he comes to the latter, he uses again the same device of taking the unreal option first, as if the two were on a par: "Is any man called being circumcised? let him not become uncircumcised. Is any called in uncircumcision? let him not be circumcised" (v. 18). How many people might there be wanting to get their circumcision reversed? But ostentatious evenhandedness, and slipping the controversial in as an afterthought, are spells which will charm the most powerful genie back into the bottle—for a season.

Our ability to isolate one or two of the apostle's rather transparent (and effective) techniques should not mislead us into thinking that we have the measure of him. He has a great mind, and it is a constant wonder to see how the most everyday problems draw from him profound theological arguments, often from the primary biblical chapters in the beginning of Genesis, or from the great fact of Christ. Should women be free to pray with their hair loose? "I would have you know that the head of every man is Christ; and the head of the woman is the man; and the head of Christ is God" (1 Cor. 11:3). Should a Christian settle a point with a fellow churchman in the secular courts? "Know ye not that we shall judge angels?" (6:3). Is there any harm in a man who has been baptized and who takes the true sacrament, eating meat which has been offered to gods who do not exist? "Brethren, I would not that ye should be ignorant, how that all our fathers were . . . baptised unto Moses in the cloud and in the sea; And did all eat the same spiritual meat . . . But . . . they were overthrown in the wilderness" (10:1–5). Perhaps the Corinthians have been ignorant until now, and perhaps Paul is making up his theology as he goes along; but it is not less genuine for that. From later Epistles we have splendid examples of everyday needs evoking theological profundity, such as the great Philippian "hymn" (discussed below). When he fears his dear Corinthians may have been seduced, he writes: "I am jealous over you with a godly jealousy: for I have espoused you to one husband, that I may present you as a chaste virgin to Christ" (2 Cor. 11:2). He encourages a generous contribution to his Jerusalem collection by saying: "ye know the grace of our Lord Jesus Christ, that, though he was rich, yet for your sakes he became poor, that ye through his poverty might be rich" (8:9). Paul is not afraid to appeal to sayings of Jesus when they are needed, concerning such matters as divorce (1 Cor. 7:10) or the payment of apostles (9:14); but he could think of a better way to raise money than Luke's "remember the words of the Lord Jesus, how he said, It is more blessed to give than to receive" (Acts 20:35).

Paul's metaphors and images are sometimes biblical, just as in these appeals. Sex offenders must be excommunicated: "Purge out therefore the old leaven, that ye may be a new lump, as ye are unleavened. For even Christ our Passover is sacrificed for us: Therefore let us keep the feast

. . ." (1 Cor. 5:7–8). The standard equivalence corruption/leaven suggests the paschal image, which is then developed. Similarly an apostle's rights are argued from the priest's right in Scripture to share in the sin offering (9:13) and the ox's right to share the corn he treads (9:9; Deut. 25:4), as well as from the secular examples of soldier, plowman, farmer, shepherd, and the like (9:7–13). The relation between Christ's resurrection and ours is fixed by the biblical relation of the firstfruits offering to the full harvest (15:20–23). But the distinction—and opposition—we draw between the sacred and the secular would be strange to Paul. He solves the problem "with what body do the dead come?" first with the secular analogy of the grain seed, which he understood as first "dying" and then being "quickened" with its own new body; and then with an analogy from the stars (15:35–42). The images of sowing and harvest recur often. The Corinthian church has been planted by Paul and watered by Apollos, who are fellow laborers on God's farm (3:6–9). "If we have sown unto you spiritual things, is it a great thing if we reap your carnal things?" (9:11). "He which soweth sparingly shall reap also sparingly" (2 Cor. 9:6; cf. Gal. 6:7–9). "The fruit of the spirit is love, joy, peace" (Gal. 5:22): the Spirit here has been sown in the Christian's heart, and the fruit is the harvest (cf. Phil. 1:11, 4:17). Paul is famous for taking his agricultural imagery too far with the grafting of wild onto cultivated olives in chapter 11 of Romans.

Planting and building are an Old Testament pair, and in 1 Corinthians 3:9–17 Paul elaborates the building image: "ye are God's building . . . as a wise masterbuilder, I have laid the foundation, and another [man] buildeth thereon." Paul's foundation stone is Jesus Christ, and the full building is the Church, God's temple, indwelt by his Spirit. He exploits the image to good edifying effect. Solomon's temple had been built of precious stones (actually ashlars) with gold and silver. Paul draws on this to warn his successors at Corinth to build similar materials on his foundation (v. 12), not wood, hay, and straw, which will be burnt to nothing in the fire of Judgment Day; they will be punished for their poor job, and (only a half-serious threat) they will be destroyed if they destroy his structure. Building (= edifying) is a favorite metaphor: "edify one another" (1 Thess. 5:11); "knowledge puffeth up, but charity edifieth" (1 Cor. 8:1); "all things edify not" (10:23).

It is important to notice how supple Paul's mind is: he can turn an image this way or that as occasion may demand. In 1 Corinthians 3 the *Church* ("ye") is the temple of God, and the Spirit dwells in it, because the threat is that false teachers will mar its holiness. At 6:19 ("What? know ye not that your body is the temple of the Holy Ghost which is in you . . . ?") the temple is the *individual Christian's* body—the threat is that a personal sin, fornication, will mar its holiness. Paul does the same with the harvest, which is sometimes money, sometimes righteousness, and sometimes the resurrection of the dead. Or the firstfruits is Christ in 1

Corinthians 15, the Holy Spirit at Romans 8:23, and the Jewish Church at Romans 11:16 (and I list more examples below). So we would be mistaken to take a different exploitation of an image in the doubtful Epistles as evidence against Pauline authorship. The opposite is true. It would be entirely in character for Paul to develop the Temple image in Ephesians for new needs. The Gentile issue became acute as the fifties wore on, so Ephesians 2:14 speaks of Christ as breaking down "the middle wall of partition between us," the barrier between the Court of the Gentiles and the central Temple area at Jerusalem. As other missionaries circulated with variant doctrines (2 Cor. 10–12), Paul's apostleship became more important. Ephesians 2:20–21 speaks of the Church "built upon the foundation of the apostles and prophets, Jesus Christ himself being the copingstone [AR]; In whom all the building fitly framed together groweth unto an holy temple in the Lord." Jesus Christ is the foundation in 1 Corinthians 3, because Paul would not have other teachers preach another gospel, and he can make a sermon out of their building materials. In Ephesians the problem has grown more acute; so the author keeps appealing to the (holy) apostles and prophets, and Jesus Christ takes the alternative vital position in the building, the copingstone. The Christians are then sermonized as fitting together smoothly and growing up to the keystone which will unite them. On literary grounds this looks just like Paul.

A similarly invalid argument is adduced from the image of the body of Christ. In 1 Corinthians 12 and Romans 12:5 the Church is the body, the idea being suggested no doubt by the presence therein of the Spirit; each "member" is then a Christian, including the head (1 Cor. 12:21b). Paul uses the metaphor to stress the interdependence of Christians, the value of all the gifts the Spirit gives. In Colossians Christ is "the head of the body, the church" (1:18), and the other missionaries do not hold "the Head, from which all the body by joints and bands supported [AR], and knit together, increaseth" (2:19). But then Colossians was written to oppose the doctrine that Christ was one of a number of heavenly powers (1:15–20), and the author, whether Paul or no, wants to stress that he is the beginning and the head in every sense. So the Christians are now all the other parts except the head, and there may be some muddle over the increase stemming from the head. But it is no argument against Pauline authorship that the body metaphor is now developed for a different purpose, with the identity of the head changed (nor that there is a muddle!).

Other images range widely. In 1 Corinthians 9:24 there is reference to the (Isthmian?) Games: "Know ye not that they which run in a race run all, but one receiveth the prize? So run, that ye may obtain"—and so to the need for training, to the imperishability of the Christian's crown, to the purposefulness of his running ("not as uncertainly," 9:26), to the pain of his boxing (9:26), and the fear of disqualification (9:27). He often thinks of the Christian life like this: "Ye did run well," he tells the Galatians (5:7), or he wonders whether he "should run, or had run, in vain" (2:2). The image becomes insistent in his last letter, Philippians (discussed below). Sometimes he appeals to the colorful military world: "Who goeth a warfare any time at his own charges?" (1 Cor. 9:7); "if the trumpet give an uncertain sound, who shall prepare himself to the battle" (14:8); and breastplates of light and helmets of salvation are put on at 1 Thessalonians 5:8. Paul varies the "putting on" image too: the Romans are to "put on the armour of light" (13:12; also 1 Thess. 5:8; Eph. 6:11, 14) and to "put . . . on the Lord Jesus Christ" (13:14; see also Gal. 3:27, Eph. 4:24); and we shall "be clothed upon with our house which is from heaven" hereafter (2 Cor. 5:2). The trumpet which shall sound and raise the dead is not drawn directly from battle, but is the angelic *shofar* to be blown in the eternal New Year, and is taken from the Jewish festal liturgy. In 1 Corinthians 14 Paul makes use of several musical images, pipes and harps as well as trumpets.

The Thessalonian letter(s) and 1 Corinthians belong to the springtime of Paul's mission. He has founded thriving churches and is happy, confident, and paternal; there are problems, but he knows himself to be loved and respected, and he is in no real doubt that all will be well. But during the second half of his long stay at Ephesus (three years, according to Acts 20:31), three long shadows fell across his path. A visit to Corinth was a disaster: a church member "wronged" Paul (2 Cor. 7:12)—perhaps hit him—and the church did not support him (2 Cor. 2:5–11, 7:8–12). News came from the Galatian churches in central Turkey, probably those whose foundation is described in Acts 13–14, that Jewish-Christian missionaries had come, insisting on circumcision and the full Mosaic law. Finally, it seems that people of the same kind, already in evidence when 1 Corinthians was written (15:56, 16:9), took over the Ephesian church, the Pauline citadel: Luke carefully excludes Ephesus from Paul's itinerary down the Asian coast in Acts 20, and the tradition soon after was that "all they which are in Asia be turned away from me" (2 Tim. 1:15). Paul left Ephesus with a broken heart and nearly died (2 Cor. 1).

The result of these three reverses, all stemming from the Jewish-Christian countermission, was the composition of the three letters of Paul's middle period, Galatians, 2 Corinthians, and Romans. All three respond to the challenge, albeit in different modes, and all three betray a shaken confidence and a tendency to anger and despair, which alternate with the fatherly tone which is Paul's natural self. Galatians begins without a thanksgiving: it is haughty ("I marvel that ye are so soon removed," 1:6), aggressive ("let him be accursed," 1:8–9), defensive ("before God I lie not," 1:20), abusive ("false brethren unawares brought in," 2:4), sarcastic ("these who seemed to be somewhat," 2:6; cf. v. 9), and self-justifying. Only at 3:1 does the real Paul reassert himself with the more winsome

"O foolish Galatians, who hath bewitched you?" (cf. 4:19). Second Corinthians was written after Paul had left Ephesus, and it marks the nadir of his life. The labors of two decades are nearly in ruins following "our trouble which came to us in Asia" (1:8), and "we had the sentence of death in ourselves" (1:9). The apostle is indomitable in defeat, and his charity to the man who humiliated him earlier (2:1–11) commands our admiration; but his spirit is not far from exhaustion, and his mood swings wildly, from a fevered joy that the Corinthians are supporting him, to an intemperate abuse of his opponents ("dishonestly . . . deceitfully . . . blinded . . . false apostles, ministers of Satan"). Romans was written a few months after this low point. Paul has traveled from Macedonia to Corinth to consolidate his support, and to pick up the money which he is taking to Jerusalem so as to sweeten the Jewish Christians (2 Cor. 8–9), and in Romans he is about to set off with it (15:25–32); Luke allows three months for the visit to Greece (Acts 20:3). It is astonishing how quickly Paul has regained his confidence, and he approaches the unknown Christians of the capital with dignity and apparent serenity: it is only in passages like the grossly unfair diatribe in chapter 2 that we can still descry the strain.

Galatians may not have time for giving thanks, but the opening foreshadows the themes of the letter no less than elsewhere. "Paul, an apostle, (not of men, neither by man, but by Jesus Christ . . .)" (1:1) is the opening broadside of a battle running from 1:11 to 2:14. Paul is a divinely commissioned apostle, unlike the countermissionaries (1:7) and their leader (5:10), commissioned by Jerusalem; and the "pillars" there accepted Paul's apostleship to the Gentiles at the council meeting (2:6–10). "Jesus Christ, who gave himself for our sins" (1:3–4), looks forward to the long debate on the basis of salvation in 2:15–5:12. Dependence on circumcision and the Law is a total error: we are saved by Christ, who bore our curse on the tree, and by faith we are crucified with him, and live.

The argument of Galatians is a sequence of preposterous sophistries. The countermission has the Bible, the Church, and reason entirely on its side. Genesis plainly provided that the people of God were the descendants of Abraham, and whether or not that descent was by blood, it must be sealed by circumcision. The way in which God willed his people to live was clearly set out in the Torah, stated in Scripture, and expounded in tradition. Paul himself concedes the Church's acceptance of these truisms: when the issue was forced, at Antioch, the Pauline Christians totaled one (Paul), the Jewish Christians the rest—Barnabas also was carried away with their dissimulation (2:13). Paul won the fight against all the odds by a dazzling display of intellectual pyrotechnics, reinforced by his own saintliness and force of character and his converts' loyalty and distaste for the knife.

Four times Paul appeals to Scripture to confuse his opponents' clear picture. Genesis 15:6, Abraham "believed in the Lord, and he counted it to him for righteousness," means in its context that God approved Abraham's acceptance of the prophesied birth of his son. Paul elevates it to imply that faith alone is the basis for God's righteous-ing[4] man, Gentiles included. Habakkuk 2:4 in the Greek version, "The righteous shall live by faith(fulness) to me," is allowed to override Greek Leviticus 18:5, "he who does [the commandments] shall live by them"; Paul makes faith, not law, the basis of life, an opposition not required or implied by the text. In Genesis 17:8 the promises are made to Abraham "and to thy seed"; Paul insists on the force of the singular, as meaning the one man, Christ. Genesis 21 speaks of the conflict between Hagar the slave-girl and her son, and the free wife Sarah and her son Isaac. Paul says that the Jews are the descendants of Ishmael, born after the flesh, while "we, brethren, as Isaac was, are the children of promise" (4:28). We may be grateful to him for this outrageous logic and for so enabling Christianity to become a world religion; but we should concede that theology deserves a bad name if an acceptable universalism has to be bought at such a price.

The fight over the validity of the Law leads Paul into a new field of metaphor, the law court, which plays a negligible part in the earlier letters but exercises a primary influence in Galatians and Romans, and on through Luther into Christian history. "Man is not justified [= acquitted] by the works of the law, but by faith in [AR] Jesus Christ" (2:16); "Christ is become of no effect unto you, whosoever of you are justified by the law" (5:4). In discussing salvation here Paul uses the analogy of a Roman court of law: the countermissionaries taught that if you kept God's Law you would be held innocent ("justified") before his judgment seat, and Paul is disputing this. At its fullest exposition, in Romans 8:31–38, God is the judge, Christ is our counsel "who also maketh intercession for us," the angelic powers ("neither death nor life nor angels") are our accusers and also agents provocateurs to separate us from Christ by tribulation, persecution, and so on. God acquits us, not on the basis of keeping the Law at all, but through Christ's death. At other times we stand before the judgment seat of Christ (2 Cor. 5:10) rather than of God, a further testimony to Paul's flexibility of mind. The status of the Law is a constant problem to Paul, and he never reaches a satisfactory solution. In Galatians he tends to be dismissive: the Law is merely a set of police regulations "ordained by angels" (3:19). These (hostile) angels, sometimes spoken of as "the elements of the world" (4:3, 9; perhaps the stars, or perhaps the cosmic alphabet), have had us in bondage (4:1–9). Paul repeatedly appeals to the imagery of slavery both here and in Romans. We have been "shut up" (Gal. 3:23), slaves (4:1, 7), enslaved (4:3), doing slave service (4:8); Judaism is the offspring of a slave-woman, we of the free; we are redeemed (4:5) and should "stand fast in the liberty wherewith Christ hath made us free," not becoming entangled again with the yoke of slavery (5:1). So too 2 Corinthians 6:14: "Be not unequally yoked with the faithless" [AR]. An alternative image is the minor, who "differeth nothing from a servant, though he be lord of all" (4:1). Before faith came we were guarded under the Law, which was attendant and tutor to us "until the time appointed of the father" (3:23–4:2). We are *sons* of God, adopted heirs, with the Spirit of God's Son crying in ecstasy through us, Abba, Father (4:6). Ancient educators, both the attendant (*paidagogos*) and the tutor (*epitropos*), included the birch among their sanctions and might be oppressive: the day of majority would in any case be a cause of rejoicing comparable to the day of manumission. Whatever the limits of Paul's scriptural arguments, his instinct that Christ's death had brought freedom found expression in the most moving of symbols, slavery and sonship. We have indeed been "bought with a price" (1 Cor. 6:20), but such new service is perfect freedom.

Second Corinthians presents many problems and is often believed to be a compound of several letters rather than a unity. However, the difficulties of this interpretation seem to exceed those of the unitary view, and the parentheses, disjunctures, and violent swings of mood can be seen as effects of the disaster Paul has sustained. As usual, there is an opening thanksgiving (1:3–7), this time for God's comfort in sufferings; and Paul's sufferings are the leitmotif of the letter, together with the comfort he has received from the Corinthians' support. But as soon as he begins to tell them his situation, his strong feelings drive him to interrupt himself. He breaks in on his "trouble in Asia" and his recovery (1:8–11) with a passionate defense of his motives in not coming to Corinth (1:12–2:11). He resumes with his situation at Troy (2:12–16), only to launch into an attack on those who "water down [AR] the word of God" (2:17), "handling the word of God deceitfully" (4:2). A soaring piece of scriptural allegorizing in chapter 3 makes it clear that these demons are Jewish Christians, and that their handling of God's word is what we should call common sense. Paul is as unfair as he was in Galatians, in saying that Moses put a veil on his face lest the sons of Israel gaze on the end of what was passing away (3:13): Exodus 34:35 suggests only that God's reflected glory was too bright to be seen. In 4:7–6:10 he has recovered his poise and rises to heights of pastoral eloquence on the hope of resurrection and the ministry of reconciliation. But in 6:11–7:16, where he returns for the third time to the concrete situation, the poise is in peril once more: the lovely, affectionate, fatherly tone of the whole is interrupted by the requirement that the Corinthians "separate themselves" (6:17 [AR]) from—that is, excommunicate—the immoral, the faithless (*apistoi,* not "unbelievers") and lawless, to be compared with darkness, Belial, and idols (6:14–16). It is best to attribute these alternations of mood to the fightings without and fears within to which he testifies in 7:5. In 8–9 he gives himself to the raising of a worthy collection for the Jerusalem saints, a signal that the end of the letter is not far off (cf. 1 Cor. 16:1–4, Rom. 15:25–33).

There remain, however, four more chapters, 10–13, mostly given to even more violent and sarcastic altercation. They begin, "Now I Paul myself beseech you," and this address echoes a Pauline habit of finishing a letter with a peremptory summing up. Examples include Galatians 6:11–18: "Ye see how large a letter I have written unto you with mine own hand. As many as desire to make a fair shew in the flesh, they constrain you to be circumcised . . ."; and 2 Thessalonians 3:14: "And if any man obey not our word by this epistle, note that man, and have no company with him." This time the peremptory summing up has taken the author over, and the hurt feelings of years spill the miserable facts over the page. It is the same fear of the Jewish-Christian countermission ("Are they Hebrews? So am I," 11:22) evidenced in 1:12–2:11 and 2:17–4:6, only the optimism of chapters 2 and 7 has evaporated in the harsh light of experience: the bitter charge of walking after the flesh still rankles and gets its answer.

Passionate feelings sometimes stir the apostle to disputatiousness, but sometimes also to sublimity, and 2 Corinthians perhaps contains more that is sublime than any other letter. His tenseness expresses itself in frequent rhetorical repetition: "what carefulness [the letter] wrought in you, yea, what clearing of yourselves, yea, what indignation, yea, what fear, yea, what vehement desire, yea, what zeal, yea, what revenge!" (7:11). This is not the vacuous rhetoric of the politician seeking time to find the next cliché: every noun means something, and there is movement from the first self-justification to the final punishment of the offender, each *alla* ("but" = "yea") spurring the reader to mark a stage in the movement, from the more self-regarding indignation and fear to the more outgoing desire and zeal, and the final action. The challenge to live without offense in 6:1–10 is an example of Paul's nobility:

> But in all things approving ourselves as the ministers of God, in much patience, in afflictions, in necessities, in distresses, In stripes, in imprisonments, in tumults, in labours, in watchings, in fastings; By pureness, by knowledge, by longsuffering, by kindness, by the Holy Ghost, by love unfeigned, By the word of truth, by the power of God, by the armour of righteousness on the right hand and on the left, By honour and dishonour, by evil report and good report: as deceivers, and yet true; As unknown, and yet well known; as dying, and, behold, we live; as chastened, and not killed; As sorrowful, yet alway rejoicing; as poor, yet making many rich; as having nothing, and yet possessing all things. (6:4–10)

The simultaneous piling up and variation of prepositional phrases reflect the genuinely manifold trials, graces, and paradoxes of the Christian vocation; and the sense that the writer has experienced all these things himself drives the reader irresistibly to recognize that this is authentic religion.

The Greek has in fact nineteen *en* phrases (= both "in" and "by") in succession, but none of them is synonymous. "In all things" and "in much patience" are specified in the following nine: the afflictions include being flogged, being imprisoned, and being lynched; the necessities and distresses include working till one drops and doing without sleep and food. The last six, from pureness to the power of God, mark the Christian's response—it is not in loose (12:20–21) or arrogant (11:18–20) living that such trials are to be met. The master varies his art, first by four two-word phrases, from "by the Holy Ghost" to "by the power of God," and then with three *dia* (= "through") phrases; and moves to his climax with seven paradoxes of the form "as A and yet non-A." Variation again plays its part, as in "as dying, and, behold, we live," or in the number of phrases, whose change emphasizes the writer's freedom. But the eloquence derives primarily from the multiple spiritual reality to which the climactic chains of particles point. A true Christian will have to accept all these tribulations and respond to them with all these graces, and the effect will be this series of amazing riches which stand earthly values on their head.

A similar succession of changing repetitions gives movement to Paul's celebrated chapter on charity in 1 Corinthians 13. There are three clauses to open, of the form "Though I *x* (and though I *y*), and have not charity, I am (nothing)"; then follow four clauses beginning "Charity . . . ," the first with two positive verbs, the second with a negative, the third with seven negatives and a converse, followed by four positives with the object "all things." The final "Charity never faileth" is contrasted with the weakness of prophecies, tongues, and knowledge, each with a different verb; the contrast then moves to the partial against the perfect, using oppositions of child/man and of darkly/face-to-face (from Moses in Num. 12:8); and finally the three abiding graces, and the greatest charity. We moderns want to use the passage as a lesson for a wedding, or something equally foreign to the apostle's intention, and should be quite happy to stop with "Charity never faileth." But Paul did not lose his touch halfway through. First Corinthians is a pitched battle against the enthusiasts with their "tongues" and their "knowledge" (*gnōsis*), and his climax is a real climax in which the secondary gifts of the Spirit are reduced to their partial status, while charity is shown to be a more excellent way than even the primary gift, prophecy (12:31). The effect of the multiple "though" clauses in verses 1–3 is to display the weakness of all the gifts, and verses 8b–12 reinforce this message. The sequence of sixteen verbs after the noun "Charity" convinces the reader of the overwhelmingly sane, all-embracing, and magnetic quality of the grace and leads on naturally to his climax at verse 13. Paul reaches sublimity because his cataract of Charity-verb sentences conveys the richness and attractiveness and down-to-earth quality of the Christian life, and because they take their place between earlier and later rapids of the river of his eloquence.

A final example of the same technique may be seen in the autobiographical passage in 2 Corinthians 11:23–32:

> Are they ministers of Christ? (I speak as a fool) I am more: in labours more abundant, in stripes above measure, in prisons more frequent, in deaths oft. Of the Jews five times received I forty stripes save one. Thrice was I beaten with rods, once was I stoned, thrice I suffered shipwreck, a night and a day have I been in the deep; In journeyings often, in perils of waters, in perils of robbers, in perils by mine own countrymen, in perils by the heathen, in perils in the city, in perils in the wilderness, in perils in the sea, in perils among false brethren; In weariness and painfulness, in watchings often, in hunger and thirst, in fastings often, in cold and nakedness. Besides those things that are without, that which cometh upon me daily, the care of all the churches.

There is no artifice here, for the confessor's heart is pouring over; but there is art, the greater for its naturalness. We note the climaxes in the opening: labors, stripes, prisons, deaths; more, more abundant (= above measure), more frequent, oft; the limited synagogue thrashing, the merciless Roman caning, the stoning, the shipwrecks, the twenty-four hours overboard—all of them "deaths" which the victim does not know if he will survive. Then comes the move from the dire to the everyday, the frequency being urged in part by the eight "in perils" and the four *en* phrases, and in part by the masterly controlled use of "often." Even here we are not without climaxes. The most shocking of the perils is that arising from false Christians; the most continuous of the stresses is the daily care of all the churches. Who could resist such an appeal?

Several more examples of the suppleness of Paul's mind, which is able to turn his opponents' claims to his advantage by taking a higher spiritual ground, are to be found in 2 Corinthians. The first of these is "Ye are our epistle" (3:2). How much better than the letters of commendation which his opponents brought from Jerusalem! Paul warms to his theme, not without some crossing of wires:

> Ye are our epistle written in our hearts, known and read of all men: Forasmuch as ye are manifestly declared to be the epistle of Christ ministered by us, written not with ink, but with the Spirit of the living God; not in tables of stone, but in fleshy tables of the heart. (3:2–3)

If the Corinthian church ("ye") is the epistle known and read by the world, then the epistle has not been written in Paul's heart; rather, Paul has "ministered" the letter which the Spirit has written in their hearts. But the heart leads on to a reflection on Ezekiel's prophecy, "I will give them one heart, and I will put a new spirit within you; and I will take the stony heart out of their flesh, and will give them a heart of flesh" (Ezek. 11:19; cf. 36:26). "Stony heart" recalls the tables of stone on which the Law was cut (Exod. 31:18), and so opens the way to an onslaught on the hard hearts of Jews and Jewish Christians, which will fill the rest of the chapter.

Two other examples come in chapter 10. Paul's opponents have accused him of being courageous (*tharrō*) when he is far away and meek when on the spot (10:1). The implication of cowardice is galling, and he takes up the military metaphor:

> For though we walk in the flesh, we do not war after the flesh: (For the weapons of our warfare are not carnal, but mighty through God to the pulling down of strong holds;) Casting down imaginations, and every high thing that exalteth itself against the knowledge of God, and bringing into captivity every thought to the obedience of Christ; And having in a readiness to revenge all disobedience, when your obedience is fulfilled. (vv. 3–6)

The web of association is drawn in effectively: courage, war, weapons, strongholds, captivity, and the punishment of rebellion once sovereignty has been reestablished. Particularly clever is the move from strongholds to "high things" (*hypsōma*), since a stronghold in the ancient world was commonly an acropolis or high place, and Isaiah 2 had made familiar the destruction which God had reserved for all high things exalted by man. I have noted Paul's use of war and trumpets in 1 Corinthians; and there are arms of righteousness and light in Romans 6:13 and 13:12 and at 2 Corinthians 6:7, a triumph at 2 Corinthians 2:14, and a breastplate and helmet at 1 Thessalonians 5:8. So it should be added that the magnificent passage in Ephesians 6:11–18, "Put on the whole armour of God . . . ," is in every way Pauline. It draws on his familiar images of arms, breastplate, and helmet; it develops the metaphor in a single-minded way, just like 2 Corinthians 10:3–6; and it attains sublimity. Such matters are not lightly to be ascribed to imitators, and are more dependable than counts of particles and loose clauses.

Further on, in verse 12, Paul is reproaching the countermissionaries with "measuring themselves by themselves," and the metaphor proves suggestive:

> But we will not boast of things without our measure, but according to the measure of the area [AR] which God hath distributed to us, a measure to reach even unto you. For we stretch not ourselves beyond our measure, as though we reached not unto you: for we are come as far as to you also in preaching the gospel of Christ: Not boasting of things without our measure . . . and not to boast in another man's area [AR]. (vv. 13–16)

Measuring makes Paul think of the section of the mission-field which God has allotted to him. The word which I have rendered "area" is "rule" in the King James Version (Greek *kanōn*); so he is able to appeal both to their gratitude, in that he brought the gospel as far as Corinth, and to their sense of impropriety that other men have invaded his preserve.

Second Corinthians includes a wealth of other images, developed or not. Noteworthy among these are the *business* images: "Who hath also sealed us, and given the earnest of the Spirit in our hearts" (1:22; "earnest" was a down payment, and the contract for it would be sealed with a signet); "we are not as many, which water down [AR, *kapeleuousin*] the word of God" (2:17); Paul is partner with the Corinthians (1:24, 6:1), as Titus is to him (8:23); "though he [Christ] was rich, yet for your sakes he became a beggar" (8:9 [AR], *eptōcheuen*). The "earnest" recurs at 5:5 and Ephesians 1:14; the seal at 1 Corinthians 9:2 ("you are the seal of my apostleship") and at Romans 4:11 (circumcision "the seal of righteousness") and 15:28 ("When . . . I have sealed to them this fruit," that is, the collection). So there are four different uses of the seal metaphor; the seal of the Spirit recurs in Ephesians 1:13 and 4:30. He similarly varies the Adam-and-Eve image. At 11:2–3, "I have espoused you to one husband, that I may present you as a chaste virgin to Christ. But I fear, lest by any means, as the serpent beguiled Eve through his subtilty, so your minds should be corrupted . . ." At Romans 7:9–11, "when the commandment came, sin came to life [AR, *anezēsen*], and I died . . . For sin, taking occasion by the commandment, deceived me, and by it slew me"; here "I" stands for mankind, sin should be Sin, that is, Satan, "deceived" is the same word as "beguiled" in the first text and at Genesis 3:13. In Ephesians 5:25–32 the Church-Christ idea of 2 Corinthians 11 is expanded as a homily for married couples.

The fact that Romans was written so soon after 2 Corinthians, and probably within two years of 1 Corinthians and Galatians, is a key to its interpretation. The basic structure of the letter follows that of 1 Corinthians:

Rom.		*1 Cor.*
1:16–32	"Greek" claims to wisdom are folly	1–2
	and lead to materialism and depravity	5–6
2–3	Jews also refuse the Cross	1:18–2:9
	and do not boast in Christ their righteousness	1:30–31
5–6	All men died in Adam; there is life for all in the death and resurrection of the new Adam	15:20–55
7	Sin, law, and death belong together since Eden	15:56–57
12	We are one body in Christ, members of each other	12
13	Love is the central commandment	13
14	Therefore, when eating meat, act in love of weak brothers	8, 10
15:22–16:24	Collection, commendation, greetings, grace	16

First Corinthians is an occasional letter, and Paul takes up the topics as he comes to them. Romans is his attempt to set out his gospel systematically to an important church he has never visited, and is written in the vain hope of staving off the same troubles he has been facing in Asia and Greece. So he begins with the same centerpiece, the Cross, and its offense to Greek and Jew. The wisdom-enthusiasts of 1 Corinthians 1 "knew" that "all things are lawful" (6:12), and such attitudes lead to prostitutes and lawsuits (5:1–6:20); so the moral quagmire of 1 Corinthians 5–6 is now made a feature of Romans 1 and is viewed as a "Greek" (non-Jewish) peril. Indeed in 1 Corinthians 1:22 Paul said, "the Greeks seek after wisdom," and the pagan idolaters of Romans 1 are described as "professing themselves to be wise" (v. 22). Jewish rejection of the Cross has not yet become an important issue in 1 Corinthians (1:22), but it does later, and receives the full treatment in Romans 2–3. Paul's only statement of his fundamental theology in 1 Corinthians was in chapter 15, where the Cross and Resurrection (vv. 3–4) are "the gospel which I preached to you" (v. 1), and this gospel is summed up in verse 22: "For as in Adam all die, even so in Christ shall all be made alive." The exposition of this concept is made the central doctrine of Romans: the Adam/Christ antithesis is set forth rather lengthily in chapter 5, the sacramental transfer at baptism from being "in" the one "into" the other in chapter 6, and the law/sin/death complex (from 1 Corinthians 15:56: "the sting of death is sin; and the strength of sin is the law") in chapter 7. The remainder of 1 Corinthians 12–16 forms the basis for Romans 12–16 but is set out there more logically. We are one body in Christ, *so* we should love one another, *and in particular* we must love the weaker brethren in questions of diet and calendar; and so to the collection, to personal messages, and to the grace.

But much has happened since 1 Corinthians, and warnings are needed against Jewish Christians as much as against the "wise"; so Paul uses the arguments of Galatians to amplify 1 Corinthians as the basis for his structure of Romans:

Rom.		Gal.
3:9–23	All are under sin, the promise is to faith	3:22
4:1–17	Abraham, faith, and righteousness	3:6–18
7:14–8:17	Flesh and spirit, bondage and freedom	5:16–18
	Sonship, crying Abba	4:5–7
9:7–9	Isaac the child of promise, not flesh	4:21–31
13:9	Law summarized in love of neighbor	5:14

Many other passages in Romans demonstrate its dependence on Galatians. Both use the same Old Testament texts, especially Genesis 15:6 ("Abraham believed God . . ."), Habakkuk 2:4 ("The just shall live by faith"), Genesis 21 on Isaac and Ishmael, and Leviticus 19:18. These are reproduced with extended and less bellicose commentary and fill the major gaps in the 1 Corinthians framework. But the extensions, especially in chapters 9–11, show how inadequate Paul now feels Galatians to have been. He wants many more texts to show that God always meant salvation to include the Gentiles and that Jewish rejection of Christ was part of the divine plan, indeed its masterstroke; and Romans 9–11 and 15:7–13 supply these. He probably has to reckon with a difference of proportion too: we have the impression that there were very few Jews in the Galatian churches, but they may have been a majority at Rome.

A further problem is the Cross. Paul was taught that "Christ died for our sins according to the scriptures" (1 Cor. 15:3), and he thought the Cross was central; but in 1 Corinthians 1–2 he does no more than revel in the paradox. Galatians 3 makes a first weak attempt to offer a theology: God had set a curse on anyone who did not keep the Law (Deut. 27:26), and Christ redeemed us from this curse by becoming a curse for us on the "tree" (Deut. 21:23). Second Corinthians 5 offers an improvement on this idea: God was in Christ reconciling the world to himself—him who knew no sin he made sin for us, that we might become the righteousness of God in him. Now almost the entire 2 Corinthians 5 passage is restated in Romans 5–8: reconciliation by Christ's death, living to him who died for us, no condemnation/a new creation if anyone is in Christ. But the mysterious abstracts, "becoming a curse," "made sin," are now interpreted by sacrificial imagery: God sent his own Son as a sin offering (8:3), God set Christ forth as an expiation (3:25). Even so, Paul feels ill at ease with the whole line of argument and never uses these terms again, just as he uses the Passover sacrifice image only once (1 Cor. 5:7) and the term "blood" rarely; the burnt offering is implied at Ephesians 5:2, and the peace offering at Ephesians 2:14. Nor is he much happier with the notion of the Cross as a victory over the powers: God "condemned Sin in the flesh" (Rom. 8:3), but this idea is not amplified until Colossians 2:15: "having spoiled principalities and powers, he made a shew of them openly, triumphing over them in it [the Cross]." The real thrust of the appeal to the Cross in Romans is that it "righteouses" us; that is, primarily, it wins our acquittal in the Last Judgment (and secondarily makes us good people); and it does this because God listens to the advocacy of his suffering Son— what Paul can do for Onesimus before Philemon, pleading his love given in a life of apostolic tribulation, Christ has done for mankind before God (Rom. 8:31–39). The sacrificial imagery comes more easily to Paul of his own life: "God . . . maketh manifest the savour of his knowledge by us in every place. For we are unto God a sweet savour of Christ" (2 Cor. 2:14–15); "that my service which I have for Jerusalem may be accepted of the saints" (Rom. 15:31); "that ye present your bodies a living sacrifice, holy, acceptable unto God, which is your reasonable service" (Rom. 12:1); "Yea, and if I be poured forth [AR] upon the sacrifice and service of your faith, I joy" (Phil. 2:17). In the last case his life is a wine offering poured over his converts' sacrificial lives.

As a literary achievement, Romans is a mixed success. Writing to strangers is not easy, and Paul takes several chapters to settle down. His opening is perilously close to being unctuous, and the unhappy (and unnatural) influence of the philosophical diatribe is marked, with its apostrophes ("And thinkest thou this, O man . . . ?" 2:3) and its assonances (*phthonou/phonou, asynetous/asynthetous*). He soon suffers the nemesis of rhetoric, as the flood of language takes over from the meaning: anyone critical of homosexual practice does the same himself (2:1), and all pious Jews commit adultery and rob temples (2:17–22)! Worse still, there are good Gentiles who on Judgment Day will be found to have kept the Law (2:13–16); so it is hard to see how *all* have sinned (3:23). Nevertheless, Paul is the final master of his words, and he is able to produce that sequence of lapidary antitheses which has persuaded Lutherans, and other Christians too, that Romans is the closest we have to the voice of God: "For as many as have sinned without law shall also perish without law: and as many as have sinned in the law shall be judged by the law" (2:12); "For the good that I would I do not: but the evil which I would not, that I do" (7:19); "Christ being raised from the dead dieth no more; death hath no more dominion over him. For in that he died, he died unto sin once: but in that he liveth, he liveth unto God" (6:9–10). By the eighth chapter he holds us wondering:

> For whom he did foreknow, he also did predestinate to be conformed to the image of his Son, that he might be the firstborn among many brethren. Moreover whom he did predestinate, them he also called: and whom he called, them he also justified: and whom he justified, them he also glorified. What then shall we say to these things? If God be for us who can be against us? He that spared not his own Son, but delivered him up for us all, how shall he not with him also freely give us all things? Who shall lay any thing to the charge of God's elect? It is God that justifieth. Who is he that condemneth? It is Christ that died, yea rather, that is risen again, who is even at the right hand of God, who also maketh intercession for us. Who shall separate us from the love of Christ? shall tribulation, or distress, or persecution, or famine, or nakedness, or peril, or sword? As it is written, For thy sake we are killed all the day long; we are accounted as sheep for the slaughter. Nay, in all these things we are more than conquerors through him that loved us. (8:28–37)

It is the same pattern we have seen repeatedly in Corinthians, the ascent from climax to climax with unrivaled variety—first the catena of clauses with "foreknow," "predestinate," "call," "justify," "glorify"; then the sequence of seven rhetorical questions, with occasional staccato replies; then the accumulated trials with the climax at death; a Scripture to prove it all; and, finally, the apostle's cry of defiant triumph. What Christian would not go with him to his martyrdom on such a note?

For it is to martyrdom that the road from Corinth was to take him.

Philemon was written by "Paul a prisoner of Jesus Christ" (v. 1) wearing "the bonds of the gospel" (v. 13). (The author to the Ephesians speaks of himself similarly at 6:20 as "an ambassador in bonds.") Paul writes to ask him to take back his runaway slave Onesimus, now a Christian; and few more delicate appeals have been penned. "Though I might be much bold in Christ to enjoin that which is convenient, Yet for love's sake I rather beseech thee" (vv. 8–9); "Whom I would have retained with me, that in thy stead he might have ministered unto me in the bonds of the gospel: But without thy mind would I do nothing" (vv. 13–14); "perhaps he therefore departed for a season, that thou shouldest receive him for ever; Not now as a slave [AR], but above a slave [AR], a brother beloved" (vv. 15–16). The preservation of the letter and its inclusion in the Bible are our reassurance that Paul's plea was accepted.

It is the same serenity which characterizes Philippians. The old man in chains (1:7) writes to thank his most faithful church for a further gift of money—they have done the same for him from the beginning (4:15–16). He knows he is a step from death, but he is "in a strait betwixt two [death and life], having a desire to depart, and to be with Christ; which is far better: Nevertheless to abide in the flesh is more needful for you" (1:23–24). What worries him is the same double anxiety he has known so long: that they should be of one mind, one spirit; not submitting to Jewish-Christian claims on the one side (1:15–16, 3:2–16), nor lapsing into greed and sex on the other (3:17–19). Even so, the old fire flashes as he thinks of the interfering countermissionaries; dogs, evil workers, knife-men, as he calls them (3:2). The indignant tone is like that of 2 Corinthians 10–11. He has been drawing the letter to a close, with friendly personal messages (2:19–30) and a concluding "Finally, my brethren, rejoice in the Lord" (3:1; cf. 1 Thess. 5:16, 2 Cor. 13:11). But then he thinks it "safe" to underline a point or two, and for a few lines there are abuse, "confidence in the flesh," and a list of his achievements. However, by 3:7 the anger has burned itself out, and all that matters is Christ, and pressing on together. Even the immoral group "of whom I have told you often, and now tell you even weeping, that they are the enemies of the cross of Christ" (3:18), stirs him to no more than sadness. The dominant note of the letter is joy (1:4, 18; 2:17–18, 28; 3:1; 4:4, 10): "Rejoice in the Lord alway: and again I say, Rejoice." Heroes deserve to die happy.

The approach of death carries Paul back to the athletic imagery of 1 Corinthians 9; "striving together" (synathlountes, 1:27, 4:3), "having the same conflict" (1:30), "I have not run in vain" (2:16); "Not as though I had already attained . . . but I follow after, if that I may apprehend . . . I count not myself to have apprehended: but this one thing I do . . . reaching forth unto those things which are before. I press toward the mark for the prize" (3:12–14); "my brethren dearly beloved and longed for, my joy and crown" (4:1). We might add his colleague Epaphroditus' "having wagered his life" (2:30 [AR]). Life's end also brings the thought of profit and loss, and true riches. "For to me to live is Christ, and to die is gain" (1:21); "But what things were gain to me, those I counted loss for Christ. Yea doubtless, and I count all things but loss for the excellency of the knowledge of Christ Jesus my Lord: for whom I have suffered the loss of all things, and do count them but dung, that I may gain [AR] Christ" (3:7–8). I have already mentioned the libation image of 2:17, another foreshadowing of death. New images are: community life (*politeuesthe*, 1:27; *politeuma*, 3:20; "our commonwealth [AR] is in heaven"), "lights in the world" (2:16), initiation (4:2). To the idea of fellow worker, he adds that of "fellowsoldier" (2:25) and "yokefellow" (4:3).

It is once again the simple ethical demand which sends the apostle's imagination to the theological heights. Just as the raising of the collection drives him in 2 Corinthians 8:9 to think of Christ's being rich and making himself poor in the Incarnation, so here the need for humility takes him to the thought of Christ's humility in the Incarnation. It is a shame that the quest for pre-Pauline hymns has so often led to the denial that Paul wrote 2:6–11.[5] Not only is the manner of development from an ethical requirement in line with the Pauline doctrine of the imitation of Christ, but the language is his own idiom—"being" (*hyparchōn*), "in the likeness of [men]" (Rom. 8:3), death and obedience (Rom. 5), "highly" (*hyper*–), "confess that Jesus Christ is Lord" (Rom. 10:9). There is a quotation from Isaiah 45:23, "Every knee shall bow and every tongue confess," which comes again in Romans 14:11. Some of the language recurs later in the letter without reference to 2:6–11, for example at 3:21: "Who shall change the fashion of our body of humiliation to the form of his glorious body" [AT]. Much of the doctrine is Paul's own—the cost of incarnation, obedience to the Cross, the entitlement at the Resurrection (Rom. 1:4), the subjection of the powers to Christ and, ultimately, to God (1 Cor. 15:24–28)—and what is not found elsewhere is not appreciably dissimilar. We ought to see in 2:6–11 the apostle's own farewell masterpiece, his eloquence stirred for the last time. The noble theme leads him to lapse into the poetic cadences of Hebrew parallelism, applied so effectively in Romans. The cosmic grandeur of the theology has the same power of movement as in 2 Corinthians—eternity, incarnation, crucifixion, resurrection, exaltation. There is the same piling up, first of participles, then of genitives, the same appeal to Scripture, and the same climax as in Romans 8:

> Let this mind be in you, which is [AR] in Christ Jesus: Who, being in the form of God, thought it not a prize [AR] to be equal with God: But emptied himself [AR], taking [AR] the form of a servant, becoming [AR] in the likeness of men: And being found in fashion as a man, he humbled himself, becoming [AR] obedient unto death, even the death of the cross. Wherefore God also hath highly exalted him, and given him the [AR] name which is above every name: That at the name of Jesus every knee should bow, of things in heaven,

and things in earth, and things under the earth; And that every tongue should confess that Jesus Christ is Lord, to the glory of God the Father.   (2:5–11)

NOTES

1. "In Ephesus" is missing from the text of some of the oldest manuscripts, and our earliest witness, the heretic Marcion, lists the letter "to the Laodiceans." The author writes as a stranger to the recipients; Paul lived for years at Ephesus. For a critical discussion of the Epistles see W. G. Kümmel, *Introduction to the New Testament,* trans. A. J. Mattill, 14th ed. (London, 1966).

2. On Col. see T. Y. Mullins, "The Thanksgivings of Philemon and Colossians," *New Testament Studies,* 30 (1984), 288–293.

3. See Graham Shaw, *The Cost of Authority* (London, 1983).

4. The Greek verb *dikaioun* can be translated as both "count righteous" (i.e., acquit) and "make righteous." To avoid the use of two translations it has become customary to use the artificial verb "to righteous"; see E. P. Sanders, *Paul, the Law, and the Jewish People* (Philadelphia 1983), pp. 13–14, n.18.

5. The theory that Phil. 2:6–11 is an independent pre-Pauline hymn goes back to Ernst Lohmeyer, *Kyrios Jesus* (Heidelberg, 1928).

SUGGESTED FURTHER READINGS

H.-D. Betz, *Galatians: A Commentary on Paul's Letter to the Churches in Galatia* (Philadelphia, 1979).

W. G. Doty, *Letters in Primitive Christianity* (Philadelphia, 1973).

A. T. Hanson, *Studies in Paul's Technique and Theology* (London, 1974).

University of Birmingham

The Epistle to the Hebrews
and the Catholic Epistles

Gabriel Josipovici

One of the things I tried to bring out more fully, as I went along, was the pure narrative interest of the thing as a story. It's Aeneas's story, some of which he tells himself, and most of which he doesn't. The narrative, if it's properly rendered, is extremely interesting and exciting. What happened to Virgil (partly because of the curse of his being a text in the fourth year of secondary school, and also because of his having supplied so many tags for speakers in the House of Lords) is that the poem has been fragmented. The arc, the really quite magnificent arc of the original narrative, has been rather lost to view. Nobody ever reads the entire *Aeneid*. They read in school, if they read anything, Books Two, Four, Six, *maybe*, if they're lucky. Nobody ever reads the last six books. Yet in the last six books the whole thing happens, really. That's the man at war. That's the *arma* and the *virum*. I would love to think that the whole story will be restored to view. People can read it, and will read it, because it turns out to be readable.[1]

THUS Robert Fitzgerald, in an interview given shortly before his death, on his translation of the *Aeneid*. It is not difficult to substitute the Bible for the *Aeneid* throughout, since everything he says applies to that much bigger and more complex book. For secondary schools and the House of Lords one could substitute Scripture classes and sermons; for books two, four, and six, the Gospels and possibly Genesis. Of course with the Bible the problems are more complex, partly because it is made up of so many different elements and nearly all of them are anonymous, and partly because it is the sacred book of the West. As such it has been bedeviled by unique problems of reading and interpretation, since lurking at the back of every interpreter's mind is the awful problem of the truth or otherwise of what he or she is reading. This problem has had the perhaps surprising effect of reinforcing the drive toward fragmentation, since the book has been seen as either obviously and literally all true, so that it doesn't matter where the phrase or episode one picks on comes from; or, once people became aware of the fact that it contains a number of distinct documents which are themselves probably made up of other documents, of rendering irresistible the desire to distinguish and account for all the strands.

Yet the "pure narrative interest of the thing as a story," stretching from Genesis to Revelation, is quite as strong in the Bible as it is in the *Aeneid*. Stronger, I want to argue, because, as in certain modern works such as Proust's *A la recherche du temps perdu* and Beckett's *Trilogy,* the problem of the nature of the narrative shape itself becomes the central theme. As a result the questions usually posed by biblical scholars—"Why is this section as it is, and for whom is it written?"—deny one of the fundamental facts about the Bible, that it asks us to understand the relation of what has gone before to what comes after.

A good place to test this argument is in the Epistle to the Hebrews and the Catholic Epistles. For the biblical scholar the key questions have been: "What are their points, and to whom are they addressed?" Biblical scholarship, in its optimistic heyday, imagined that the second question could, with enough work, be answered, and that once we knew the answer, once we understood what community or group was being addressed by the authors, we would have the answer to the first question. However, as so often in biblical scholarship, the optimism proved ill founded. Scholars still cannot agree as to whether the Epistle to the Hebrews is addressed to a tight community of recently converted Jews, a whole synagogue perhaps; or to a much looser group, or even to separate individuals; to recently converted Christians disillusioned by the failure of Jesus to reappear; or to any group of Judaic Christians. They cannot even decide whether it predates or postdates the destruction of the Temple in 70 C.E. It turns out in practice that what scholars think the letter means is what governs their choice of setting and date, which are then used as evidence establishing what the letter means—a circular argument common in biblical scholarship, which is so frequently at once meticulous and fantastical.

On the other hand, the question which the simple reader of the Bible will want to ask, the question about the place of the Epistles in the larger book, yields much greater dividends, for the simple reason that it is the very theme of the Bible at this point. For the Epistle to the Hebrews is the most profound and sustained exploration in the Bible of the relation of Jesus to the Old Testament, and of "now" to "then." As Graham Hughes, one of the most astute recent students of the Epistle, has observed: "the writer of Hebrews is the theologian who, more diligently and successfully than any other of the New Testament writers, has worked at what we now describe as hermeneutics. The question which has preoccupied him more deeply than any other . . . has been that of saying how we may conceive of the Word of God . . . as being subject to historical processes, and yet remaining, recognisably, God's word."[2]

I wholly endorse this general description of the Epistle, but its theme, as Hughes describes it, is one that cries out for understanding in literary, not historical, terms. In the following discussion, therefore, I concentrate on the Epistle to the Hebrews and refer to the other Catholic Epistles only when the argument requires.

To understand the context of this theme it is necessary to go back a little—to chapter 24 of Luke's Gospel, to be precise.

And, behold, two of them went that same day to a village called Emmaus, which was from Jerusalem about threescore furlongs. And they talked together of all these things which had happened. And it came to pass, that, while they communed together and reasoned, Jesus himself drew near, and went with them. But their eyes were holden that they should not know him. And he said unto them, What manner of communications are these that ye have one to another, as ye walk, and are sad? And one of them, whose name was Cleopas, answering said unto him, Art thou only a stranger in Jerusalem, and hast not known the things which are come to pass in these days? And he said unto them, What things? And they said unto him, Concerning Jesus of Nazareth, which was a prophet mighty in deed and word before God and all the people: And how the chief priests and our rulers delivered him to be condemned to death, and have crucified him. But we trusted that it had been he which should have redeemed Israel: and beside all this, to day is the third day since these things were done. Yea, and certain women also of our company made us astonished, which were early at the sepulchre; And when they found not his body, they came, saying, that they had also seen a vision of angels, which said that he was alive. And certain of them which were with us went to the sepulchre, and found it even so as the women had said: but him they saw not. Then he said unto them, O fools, and slow of heart to believe all that the prophets have spoken: Ought not Christ to have suffered these things, and to enter into his glory? And beginning at Moses and all the prophets, he expounded unto them in all the scriptures the things concerning himself. And they drew nigh unto the village, whither they went: and he made as though he would have gone further. But they constrained him, saying, Abide with us: for it is toward evening, and the day is far spent. And he went in to tarry with them. And it came to pass, as he sat at meat with them, he took bread, and blessed it, and brake, and gave to them. And their eyes were opened, and they knew him; and he vanished out of their sight. And they said one to another, Did not our heart burn within us, while he talked with us by the way, and while he opened to us the scriptures? And they rose up the same hour, and returned to Jerusalem, and found the eleven gathered together, and them that were with them, Saying, The Lord is risen indeed, and hath appeared to Simon. And they told what things were done in the way, and how he was known of them in breaking of bread. (24:13–35)

This could be a parable about the reading of books. The two men walk toward Emmaus, deeply troubled by the events of the past few days. They are so concerned with trying to understand what *has happened* that they pay no attention to what *is happening*: the risen Jesus walks beside them, but "their eyes were holden" (*hoi de ophthalmoi autōn ekratounto*). We learn then how they see the events which have just come to pass: Jesus, a mighty prophet, has been put to death by the authorities. And yet "we trusted that it had been he which should have redeemed Israel." (The Jerusalem Bible translates *ēlpizomen* by "our hope had been" and *lutrousthai* by "set free," rather than by the KJV's more loaded "trusted" and "redeemed.") We are left to infer the effect of the events on their expectations, for the narrative, typically, does not elaborate. The men simply go on to say that the tomb has been found empty and that though the women who first went there had a vision of angels who told them that Jesus was alive, the men who followed merely "saw him not." At this point the stranger addresses them, calling them fools and "slow of heart" to believe what has long since been written. To back this claim he reminds them of what Scripture has said about the coming of Christ and what would happen to him.

The narrative does not tell us either how the men reacted to this, not because it is elliptical but because the men *themselves do not know*. Like all men everywhere their reactions were probably so mixed that they could not sort them out and felt no need to. Moreover, they did not have much time, they were walking, they were presumably getting tired, and they had a lot on their minds—they were, in fact, in precisely the sort of situation in which information comes to us in life unless we happen to be acquiring it from a book or a lecture. When they arrive at the village the stranger wants to press on, but they persuade him, because it is late, to enter with them. At table he blesses the bread, breaks it, and gives it to them. At this point their eyes are opened and they suddenly grasp the identity of their companion, whereupon he vanishes. However, they can now understand in retrospect what they experienced on the way: "Did not our heart burn within us, while he talked with us by the way, and while he opened [*dienoigen*; Jerusalem Bible: 'explained'] to us the scriptures?" Something which they would have forgotten because it fitted into no pattern of meaning is given meaning by another, apparently unrelated event, the blessing and breaking of the bread. And once the flash of illumination has occurred, all locks together and every element reinforces every other: the crucifixion, the empty tomb, the words of the angels to the women, the words of Scripture, the stranger at their table, the blessing and breaking of the bread. And so they rise and return at once, late though it is, to Jerusalem, to report what they have learned to the other disciples. And, with wonderful honesty, they relate what happened on the way and how it was only subsequently that they recognized Jesus. Then, in immediate confirmation of the truth of what they say, and which we knew all along, since the narrative told us from the start who the stranger was, Jesus stands in their midst, shows his wounds, eats a piece of fish they offer him, and explains that "all things must be fulfilled, which were written in the law of Moses, and in the prophets, and in the psalms, concerning me." So "opened he their understanding, that they might understand the scriptures," saying to them: "Thus it is written, and thus it behoved Christ to suffer, and to rise from the dead the third day" (vv. 36–47).

We thus have four stages: the confused events leading to Jesus' death; the disappearance of the body; the giving of information which is clear but not understood, though the two disciples are presumably familiar with Scripture; and final illumination through a specific action by someone present to them, which casts a retrospective light over all that has gone before. None of the pieces by itself would make sense, yet if one takes away any single element—the death, the empty tomb, the Scriptures, the living presence—the whole collapses. Taken together they have the incontrovertible ring of absolute truth: the events give meaning to Scripture, and Scripture in turn confers meaning upon the events.

The remaining portions of the New Testament only develop and repeat this climactic scene of the Gospel. Different aspects of it form the focus of John's Gospel, the Acts of the Apostles, the Epistles, and Revelation. The Epistle to the Hebrews focuses mainly on the third stage, the way Scripture confirms the events of Jesus' life and those events give meaning to Scripture. Its argument could be summarized thus: God, in times past, spoke to us in shadows and enigmas, but the sacrifice of Jesus, his Son, has now made his meaning plain. The men of the Old Covenant were, like us, pilgrims, moving toward their goal and final resting-place, but never quite reaching it. We, on the other hand, now know our goal and are in a position to reach it. That is why a letter like this is needed, to comfort and encourage those who might, through fear or laziness or both, be falling back, losing faith, refusing to see the obvious truth. Like the disciples on the road to Emmaus, the people addressed in the letter have all the evidence before them and have even at moments understood, yet their eyes still tend to be "holden."

How, then, to open those eyes once and for all? Partly by explanation and partly by exhortation: "Look!" "Be!" "Do!" But is that not always the way with arguments? The speaker wants the listener to see things his way, and for this to happen it is necessary both for him to lay out the facts and for the listener to make the imaginative effort to understand what is being shown. How persuasive, then, is the argument? We, like the men on the road to Emmaus, know the Scriptures. And we know of the life and death of Jesus. Can we be persuaded to see these things in the way the author of Hebrews wishes us to see them?

The author of Hebrews begins by drawing a contrast between Jesus and the angels. Through scriptural proof drawn from Psalms, Samuel, and Deuteronomy he demonstrates Jesus' superiority: he is the Son, the inheritor of everything and the one through whom God made everything; he is the radiant light of God's glory and the perfect copy of nature, and now that he has destroyed sin he has gone to take his place at God's right hand in heaven: "Being made so much better than the angels, as he hath by inheritance obtained a more excellent name than they" (1:4). Pay careful attention, he exhorts, lest you drift away. Jesus was a son, like us, and his death redeems us: "Forasmuch then as the children are partakers of flesh and blood . . . For verily he took not on him the nature of angels; but he took on him the seed of Abraham," thus becoming "a merciful and faithful high priest in things pertaining to God" (2:14–17).

Scholars have argued that the author was concerned to combat a current Judaic belief in the power of angels and the danger of confusing Jesus with the angels. But we should also, in the light of the letter's inclusiveness, see this as part of the author's strategy of systematically going through the Scriptures and setting Jesus against them. Just as the first few chapters of Genesis tell of the Creation and then of the sons of God mingling with the daughters of men and the production of the race of giants, before we move on to Abraham and the generations of the Hebrew people, so here the author will start with the angels before he moves on to Abraham and then Moses. At the same time the author introduces what will in effect be one of the central themes of the letter: the relation of Jesus to the high priests of the Temple.

Having adumbrated the central tenet of the incarnation by stressing that the Son "took not on him the nature of angels; but he took on him the seed of Abraham" (2:16), the author now develops a contrast between Jesus and Moses. Moses was a faithful servant to God, but Jesus is faithful not as a servant but as the son and master of the house of the faithful; "whose house are we," he reminds his listeners, "if we hold fast the confidence and the rejoicing of the hope firm unto the end" (3:6). The argument here is not factual, as it was with the angels, but metaphorical and imaginative, the contrast between servant and son in a household merely allowing the author to lead his listeners to an understanding of the special nature of Jesus' role and of our own link to him. But the mention of Moses leads naturally to thoughts of the Promised Land and to the fact that Moses and his generation failed to enter it because they lacked faith: "For unto us was the gospel preached, as well as unto them: but the word preached did not profit them, not being mixed with faith in them that heard it" (4:2). Under Joshua the Hebrews did reach their goal, but in a deeper sense they did not. Playing on the fact that Jesus and Joshua are one and the same name, he goes on: "For if Jesus [Jerusalem Bible: 'Joshua'] had given them rest, then would he not afterward have spoken of another day. There remaineth therefore a rest to the people of God. For he that is entered into his rest, he also hath ceased from his own works, as God did from his. Let us labour therefore to enter into that rest, lest any man fall after the same example of unbelief" (4:8–11). Yet there is no reason why we should, "Seeing then that we have a great high priest, that is passed into the heavens, Jesus the Son of God" (4:14).

With the reiteration of the high-priest theme the author moves into his next set of comparisons and contrasts. Every high priest, he points out, is taken from among men and appointed to act as mediator, making sin offerings for himself as well as for the people. Yet the high priest is chosen by God, as Aaron was. Christ, however, is more than Aaron. You recall, he goes on, how Melchisedek came out to meet Abraham, and Abraham gave him tithes. This king of righteousness (*melek zedek*), this king of peace (*salem/shalom*), was no ordinary mortal. He was, we are told, "for ever," and the fact that he is given no ancestors or descendants confirms his immortality. Jesus is a high priest "after the order of Melchisedek" (6:20). He is of a different order from the high priests of the Temple, for they succeed each other, but Jesus is forever; they offer sacrifices repeatedly, but he sacrificed himself once and for all; they offer animals, but he offers himself (7:1–8:5).

Now he can develop his argument: "if that first covenant had been faultless, then should no place have been sought for the second" (8:7). This is driven home by a quotation from Jeremiah:

> Behold, the days come, saith the Lord, when I will make a new covenant with the house of Israel and with the house of Judah: Not according to the covenant that I made with their fathers in the day when I took them by the hand to lead them out of the land of Egypt; because they continued not in my covenant . . . I will put my laws into their mind, and write them in their hearts: and I will be to them a God, and they shall be to me a people.   (Heb. 8:8–10 = Jer. 31:31–33)

This in turn leads to an elaboration of the contrast between Old and New Covenants, the Old Law and the New, and to the reassertion that whereas the high priests sacrificed continually, Jesus sacrificed himself once and for all. In a dazzling passage he plays with these ideas:

> Having therefore, brethren, boldness to enter into the holiest by the blood of Jesus, By a new and living way, which he hath consecrated for us, through the veil, that is to say, his flesh; And having an high priest over the house of God; Let us draw near with a true heart in full assurance of faith, having our hearts sprinkled from an evil conscience, and our bodies washed with pure water. Let us hold fast the profession of our faith without wavering; (for he is faithful that promised;)   (10:19–23)

The reiteration of the word "faith" opens the way to the climactic chapter of the book: "Now faith is the substance of things hoped for, the evidence of things not seen" (11:1) it begins, and then develops into a mighty roll call of the Old Testament champions of the faith: Abel, Enoch, Abraham, Sarah: "These all died in faith, not having received the promises, but having seen them afar off, and were persuaded of them, and embraced them, and confessed that they were strangers and pilgrims on the earth" (v. 13). The list continues: Abraham again, Isaac, Jacob, Moses, Rahab,

Gideon, Barak, Samson, Jephtha, David, the prophets. Hardly a single major Old Testament figure is omitted, and to these are joined all the recent martyrs who died for their faith in Christ. "Wherefore," concludes the author, "seeing we also are compassed about with so great a cloud of witnesses, let us lay aside every weight, and the sin which doth so easily beset us, and let us run with patience the race that is set before us, Looking unto Jesus the author and finisher of our faith" (12:1–2).

The Epistle is drawing to its end. There is a final reminder to the members of the audience not to be like Esau, who sold his birthright for a mess of potage and, when he later wanted to obtain the blessing, was rejected though he begged with tears that his father change his mind; and a final comparison of the revelation to Moses on Mount Sinai with the revelation from the new Sion, the "city of the living God, the heavenly Jerusalem," into which the audience has arrived (12:18–22). "See," he warns them, "that ye refuse not him that speaketh" (v. 25). With that reiteration of the central theme of a God who speaks and must be listened to, the Epistle moves into its final exhortation and prayers.

As we have got to know more about the background to the New Testament we have learned what fierce intellectual struggles were taking place among the different Jewish sects to gain control of the interpretation of Scripture. Pharisees, Sadducees, Essenes, and Christians were all firmly convinced and bent on convincing others of the rightness of their views. After all, on the interpretation of Scripture depended not just happiness in this life, but the possibility of eternal joy or torment. We can see this clearly in the closing lines of the Second Epistle of Peter:

> But the day of the Lord will come as a thief in the night; in the which the heavens shall pass away with a great noise, and the elements shall melt with fervent heat, the earth also and the works that are therein shall be burned up. Seeing then that all these things shall be dissolved, what manner of persons ought ye to be in all holy conversation and godliness? . . . Wherefore, beloved, . . . account that the longsuffering of our Lord is salvation; even as our beloved brother Paul also according to the wisdom given unto him hath written unto you; As also in all his epistles, speaking in them of these things; in which are some things hard to be understood, which they that are unlearned and unstable wrest, as they do also the other scriptures, unto their own destruction. (3:10–17)

It is in Hebrews, however, that we find the most powerful and inclusive attempts to read the Hebrew Scriptures from a particular point of view. No one, reading it, is ever likely to be able to read what comes before it in the Bible in quite the same way again. Not only does it mirror many present-day scholarly and theological concerns, as theologians such as Moule and Hughes have argued;[3] it also mirrors for us what is involved in the reading and interpretations of any text. And for the simple reader of the Bible, as opposed to the first-century Christian or the twentieth-century theologian, it raises problems which neither its author nor his apologists seem to recognize.

Hughes argues persuasively that Hebrews is profoundly Christian in its desire to see the coming of Christ in the context of salvation history and in its effort to justify its arguments by an appeal to truth "out there." "The greatest part of [the author's] exegetical work is built around the eminently sound principle of hearing what the scriptures have to say about themselves."[4] It is not a Gnostic or a Neoplatonic document, he says, because it is concerned with real events in real history. If someone were to prove one day, for example, that Jesus was descended not from Judah but from Levi, then we would have to face the fact that one whole strand of the author's argument had been destroyed, for he asserts that Jesus is different *in kind* from the Levitical priesthood, since, like Melchisedek, he does not belong to any Priestly tribe. "Though history does not 'prove' faith's claims, it nevertheless both provides the opportunity for faith and, certainly, informs the content of faith. That is why this particular fact is seized upon so triumphantly by the writer."[5] Similarly, the Epistle's whole argument would be affected if its view of Jesus' inner sufferings were ever proved factually wrong; "That," says Hughes, "is what it means, in part, to have a theology of incarnation."[6] In discussing the use of biblical quotations he dismisses the strictures of scholars on the Christianizing of nonmessianic texts, pointing out, for example, that though neither Genesis 22 nor Psalm 8 has ever been claimed to be directly messianic, the Epistle's use of them in 6:14 and 2:6–8 shows that "the object of the author's concern is the possibility of despair . . . ; he counters the possibility by directing his readers' attention to the accomplished eschatology of Jesus's exaltation." In other words, "this prophetic word of God (1:1) is now allowed to function in a new way in the light of the more recent event of God's address through his exaltation of Jesus . . . It is no more the concern of the writer to force an identification of Jesus with the 'son of man' than it was to identify the content of the Christians' promise with that given to Abraham."[7] The necessary first element is the Old Testament passage, with its crucial phrases "a little lower than the angels," "thou . . . hast crowned him with glory and honour," and "thou hast put all things under his feet" (Ps. 8:5–6); but "these are to become vehicles for the new logos, and without them it would not have come into existence."[8]

This seeing the New Testament in the Old should not be too difficult for the student of literature to grasp. After Eliot and Borges we are perhaps more aware than nineteenth-century scholars were that what comes after has the power of altering our apprehension of what came before; that knowing Kafka's work, for example, we do not simply read Kafka into older authors but actually *uncover* him there. Before, we had eyes but could not see; now our eyes have been opened. So we do not need to be believing Christians today to understand that the sacrifice of Isaac or Virgil's Fourth Eclogue can carry a Christian message, as the Middle Ages believed, though positivistically minded scholars naturally dismissed this as the result of credulity and Christian propaganda.[9]

And yet both Hughes's persuasive arguments and those of the Epistle itself leave one uneasy. The travelers on the road to Emmaus listened to what the stranger had to say and, later, when they recognized Jesus in their midst, understood why they had burned as they listened, though had Jesus not made himself known to them they would probably have forgotten the entire incident. The reader of the Bible who has not broken bread with Christ must, I think, remain unpersuaded by all these scholarly arguments.

This is a difficult and delicate area. I phrased the remarks above with deliberate ambiguity, for I am not sure if what I mean is "the reader who has not had the privilege of dining with Jesus at Emmaus" or "the reader who is not a Christian." The best way to probe the problem is to look in some detail at how the author of Hebrews deploys his quotation from Jeremiah and his references to Abraham and Melchizedek, on which much of his argument turns. Once we understand their implications we can see if indeed, as Hughes says, the work is built "around the eminently sound principle of hearing what the scriptures have to say about themselves."[10]

Jeremiah 31:31–33, quoted earlier, seems to say unequivocally that the Lord will in days to come make a new covenant with Israel, an internal one this time, engraved on the hearts of his people, and not merely an external one. The author of Hebrews uses this passage to develop his theme that those days have now come and that the new covenant has been sealed by Jesus' sacrifice rather than by the blood of slaughtered animals. But is this indeed the point of the passage? The context is the promised restoration of Israel after the carnage which accompanied its overthrow. "Again I will build thee, and thou shalt be built, O virgin of Israel," says the prophet (Jer. 31:4), and then describes in detail how the vines will once more flourish and the young will come forth to sing and dance: "Behold, I will bring them from the north country, and gather them from the uttermost coasts of the earth, and with them the blind and the lame, the woman with child and her that travaileth with child together: a great company shall return hither" (31:7). He digresses to criticize Israel for backsliding, but quickly returns to his promise:

> As yet they shall use this speech in the land of Judah and in the cities thereof, when I shall return their captivity . . . Behold, the days come, saith the Lord, that I will sow the house of Israel and the house of Judah with the seed of man, and with the seed of beast. And it shall come to pass, that like as I have watched over them, to pluck up and to break down, and to throw down, and to destroy, and to afflict; so will I watch over them, to build, and to plant, saith the Lord. (Jer. 31:23–28)

Then comes the passage quoted in Hebrews about making a new covenant with the house of Israel and Judah. This is followed by another hymn of praise. The chapter ends thus:

> Behold, the days come, saith the Lord, that the city shall be built to the Lord from the tower of Hananeel unto the gate of the corner . . . And the whole valley of the dead bodies, and of the ashes, and all the fields unto the brook of Kidron, unto the corner of the horse gate toward the east, shall be holy unto the Lord; it shall not be plucked up, nor thrown down any more for ever. (31:39–40)

With a psalm or a self-contained narrative such as Genesis 22 it is possible to extend the meaning because meaning is not circumscribed in the first place; with prophecy it is a little different. Jeremiah's words apply specifically to the restoration of Israel after devastation. Restoration here is no abstract or purely internal notion; it involves vineyards, animals, towers, and gates. The law may be inscribed in the hearts of men, but here a real Jerusalem and real fields and farms are being referred to. To apply the prophecy to the newly arrived kingdom of God requires metaphor, and the fact remains that when we know the context of the Jeremiah prophecy we can only feel that the author of Hebrews has given it a meaning which the original did not have, and *in the process obscured the meaning it did have*. The concreteness of God's dealings with Israel, his concern not with an abstract entity but with such details as animals and trees and buildings, has completely vanished from Hebrews. It is not so much that an old meaning has been subsumed into a new one as that a new meaning has blotted out the old.

A rather different kind of scriptural passage is the episode recounted in Genesis 14:17–20 and touched on in Psalms 110:4, the meeting between Abram (he is not yet Abraham) and Melchizedek. In Genesis this meeting occurs at the end of Abram's rather surprising involvement in the military and political events of the Middle East. Abram joins an alliance against another grouping of chiefs, and when he returns triumphant from the wars he is met first by the king of Sodom and his confederates. Then "Melchizedek king of Salem brought forth bread and wine: and he was the priest of the most high God. And he blessed him, and said, Blessed be Abram of the most high God, possessor of heaven and earth: And blessed be the most high God, which hath delivered thine enemies into thy hand. And he gave him tithes of all" (Gen. 14:18–20). In chapter 7 of Hebrews the author, having in his usual manner slipped the name of Melchizedek into the argument a little earlier and returned to it at the end of the previous chapter, proceeds thus:

> For this Melchisedec, king of Salem, priest of the most high God, who met Abraham returning from the slaughter of the kings, and blessed him; To whom also Abraham gave a tenth part of all; first being by interpretation

King of righteousness, and after that also King of Salem, which is, King of peace; Without father, without mother, without descent, having neither beginning of days, nor end of life; but made like unto the Son of God; abideth a priest continually.   (vv. 1–3)

Consider, he goes on, how great such a man was, "unto whom even the patriarch Abraham gave a tenth of the spoils" (v. 4). The priests of the tribe of Levi, who take tithes from the people, are descended from Abraham, but "he whose descent is not counted from them received tithes of Abraham, and blessed him that had the promises. And without all contradiction the less is blessed of the better" (vv. 6–7). Here, he goes on, it is mortal men who receive tithes, but there the receiver was immortal; and Levi, who was, so to speak, already there in Abraham's loins, paid tithes at that moment to the immortal high priest of Salem. Thus we can see that the priests of Levi are by no means perfect; but Jesus, who sprang from the tribe of Judah, is perfect and immortal, like Melchizedek, "for that after the similitude of Melchisedec there ariseth another priest, Who is made, not after the law of a carnal commandment, but after the power of endless life. For he testifieth, Thou art a priest for ever after the order of Melchisedec" (vv. 15–17). So the chapter rises to its climax: "For the law maketh men high priests which have infirmity; but the word of the oath, which was since the law, maketh the Son, who is consecrated for evermore" (v. 28).

This key passage has been the subject of much scholarly debate.[11] It does not, however, seem to matter very much whether the author of Hebrews was using Genesis 14 or Psalm 110 or both. Nor does it seem to affect our reading of Hebrews to know that the rabbis had developed a mode of arguing "from absence," which would lead to the belief that since nothing is said here of Melchizedek's birth or death he must be immortal and must have always existed. We might indeed ask why, if Levi is already there in Abraham's loins, Judah is not there as well; but that, after all, is an extra little twist, not perhaps central to the author's argument. However, there are other aspects of the passage and its interpretation which might worry the attentive reader of Genesis. At 14:20 the King James Version has: "And he gave him tithes of all." This is a precise translation of the Hebrew: *wayiten-lo ma'aser mikol.* The Jerusalem Bible tries to sort out the pronouns: "And Abram gave him a tithe of everything." This is clearly how the author of Hebrews reads the passage, since he too says "to whom also Abraham gave . . ." Indeed, the Jerusalem Bible no doubt clarifies the ambiguity of the pronouns in this way precisely because of the passage in Hebrews. The Septuagint faithfully retains the ambiguity: *kai edōken autōi dekatēn apo pantōn.* But to the reader of Genesis the sense is surely quite different. Melchizedek brings out food and drink for the exhausted but triumphant Abram, blesses him and his god, and gives him one tenth of all he has. The context requires this; any other reading would contradict common sense.

It is not enough to say that already in Hebrew midrash Melchizedek is linked to David and set over against the line of Aaronite priesthood, that Rashi too read "he" as Abraham. Two errors do not make a correct reading. Moreover, for the author of Hebrews a great deal depends on our reading the episode his way and not the natural way. But we can do this only as a kind of metaphysical conceit. The author, however, is no Donne or Marvell; he is in deadly earnest. Unfortunately, the more earnest he is, the more foolproof his argument should be. That, as Hughes so rightly says, is what it means to have a theology of incarnation.

Even so, all this might not be too serious. We might feel that these are small blemishes, the product of an overzealous attempt to persuade or simply of the fact that no man can rise above the modes of interpretation current at the time he is writing. But it is, I think, part of a deeper problem, a problem perhaps more visible to the reader of the Bible as a whole than to the scholar or theologian. The best way to approach the issue is by way of chapter 11, the great and justly famous roll call of the Old Testament heroes of the faith:

> Now faith is the substance of things hoped for, the evidence of things not seen . . . By faith Abel offered unto God a more excellent sacrifice than Cain, by which he obtained witness that he was righteous . . . By faith Enoch was translated that he should not see death . . . By faith Noah, being warned of God of things not seen as yet, moved with fear, prepared an ark to the saving of his house . . . By faith Abraham, when he was called to go out into a place which he should after receive for an inheritance, obeyed; and he went out, not knowing whither he went . . . Through faith also Sara herself received strength to conceive seed, and was delivered of a child when she was past age, because she judged him faithful who had promised . . . By faith Abraham, when he was tried, offered up Isaac . . . accounting that God was able to raise him up, even from the dead . . . By faith Isaac . . . By faith Jacob . . . By faith Joseph . . . By faith Moses . . . refused to be called the son of Pharaoh's daughter; Choosing rather to suffer affliction with the people of God, than to enjoy the pleasures of sin for a season; Esteeming the reproach of Christ greater riches than the treasures in Egypt . . . By faith the walls of Jericho . . . By faith the harlot Rahab . . . And what more shall I say? for the time would fail me to tell of Gedeon, and of Barak, and of Samson, and of Jephthae; of David also, and Samuel, and of the prophets; Who through faith subdued kingdoms, wrought rightousness . . . turned to flight the armies of the aliens. Women received their dead raised to life again: and others were tortured, not accepting deliverance; that they might obtain a better resurrection . . . And these all, having obtained a good report through faith, received not the promise: God having provided some better thing for us, that they without us should not be made perfect. (11:1–40)

This is a powerful and rousing call, but it must leave readers of the Old Testament a little uneasy. Reading this chapter, we inevitably ask ourselves whether it corresponds to our own memory of the text. Is this all there is to say about these people? We remember Sarah laughing when God tells Abraham in her hearing that she will bear a son, a scene important enough to be commemorated in the very name of the child, Yitzhak; we remember the early life of Moses; we remember the enormously complex and ambiguous relations of David to his God—and we wonder: can it all be subsumed under the rubric of faith? And it is not enough to answer that faith was the most important element in their lives and that the author of Hebrews was clearly not going to recount the entire Old Testament. It is not enough, because the effect of Sarah's laugh, of David's passion for Bathsheba, is precisely to deny us the possibility of summing up their lives or their relations to God in terms of any single concept. These Old Testament stories seem almost designed to leave us with a baffling but fruitful ambiguity: they are clearly meaningful, not mere random chronicles; and yet meaning, in a strange way, inheres in them inextricably. Jacob is not necessarily better than Esau, Judah is hardly above reproach, David sins as much as or more than Saul. Yet they and not the others are the chosen ones. How can that be? we ask, and that seems to be the question the Old Testament again and again wants us to ask. Hebrews 11, by providing an interpretation, removes the question. And it is a fact of interpretation that once something is presented to us in one way it becomes very difficult to see it in any other way. Gombrich has demonstrated this often enough in relation to vision, but Wallace Stevens perhaps provides a more helpful example here. For when he placed his jar in Tennessee

> It made the slovenly wilderness
> Surround that hill.
>
> The wilderness rose up to it,
> And sprawled around, no longer wild.[12]

And just as the jar "takes dominion everywhere," so does the notion of faith in this passage. Yet, for readers of the Bible who have lived through the agony of Abraham on his way to Moriah or of David pleading with God to spare his son, such an interpretation can seem only a travesty. It turns these episodes into clear black and white, like those of Christian martyrdom with which the catalogue so movingly ends. And it finally confirms us in our feeling that if the author does indeed see Jesus in terms of the Old Testament past, his notion of that past is remarkably *thin*.

I take the term *thin* from Mary Douglas, whose *Natural Symbols*, though actually a critique of Protestant internalizations of ritual and of its anthropological significance, is directly relevant to this discussion. "We arise from the purging of old rituals," she says, "simpler and poorer, as was intended, ritually beggared, but with other losses. There is a loss of articulation in the depth of past time. The new sect goes back as far as the primitive church, as far as the first Pentecost, or as far as the Flood, but the historical continuity is traced by a thin line. Only a narrow range of historical experience is recognised as antecedent to the present state."[13] Christian theologians have always insisted that what distinguishes Judaism and Christianity from other religions is their stress on story and on history. It has become almost a ritual for those writing on the New Testament to pay homage to this fact. But too often the theory is taken for a fact. Even so sensitive a reader as Amos Wilder can write, "Those expressions of Christian hope are most vital which relate themselves most fully to the biblical past," but then support this claim only by asserting that Paul appeals to David, Moses, Abraham, and Adam.[14] Similarly Graham Hughes, at the end of his book, asks what the differences are between the Old Testament and the New, and replies that the Old Testament writings "manifest, and address themselves to, a situation which is predominantly one of expectation."[15] This assertion hardly fits Genesis or Judges or Samuel. In fact he is clearly thinking only of the prophets (and it is hardly true even of most of them). In both cases we feel that the authors' sense of the Old Testament is, in Mary Douglas's word, thin. And it is a thinness which is particularly striking because what is most characteristic of the Old Testament is precisely its density.

Of course this is not simply a criticism that should be leveled only at Paul or the author of Hebrews or even modern Christian scholars. We find it in rabbinic interpretations of the Old Testament, with their almost manic need to explain everything. We find it in portions of the Old Testament itself. First Chronicles, for example, is, like Hebrews, a retelling of stories we already know from other parts of the Bible. Like Hebrews it cuts a swathe through these stories in the interests of a single argument. And, as with Hebrews, such a strategy is likely to backfire with any readers already familiar with the material. For example, when we read in the opening chapter "Adam, Seth, Enosh, Kenan, Mahalaleel, Jered, Henoch, Methuselah, Lamech, Noah, Shem, Ham, and Japheth," we can see what the author is up to: he wants to give us a clear sense of the line from Adam to Abraham down to Solomon without any distractions. But the effect is to make us ask at once: What of Cain and Abel? What of the Flood? Omission brings the omitted material back even more vividly because it suddenly grows precious when we realize how easily it might never have come down to us. And the same is true of Hebrews.

There is, however, a difference. The argument of Hebrews is part of the continuing argument of the New Testament, whereas in the Hebrew Scriptures different and even contradictory material lies side by side. We are not asked to choose, to resolve contradictions. Individual books of the Old Testament form single strands of a very thick rope.

As in the cases analyzed by Mary Douglas, the thinness of the line of history in Hebrews (and in the other Catholic Epistles) reflects a persistent contrast between inner and outer, New Covenant and Old. We have already seen the author using selective quotation from Jeremiah to establish the contrast between the Old Covenant, with its merely external rituals and the New, graven on the heart of each man. In the two following chapters he develops this theme in a way which shows his familiarity with Hebrew Temple ritual, or at least his concern with it: "The first covenant had also ordinances of divine service, and a worldly sanctuary. For there was a tabernacle made; the first, wherein was the candlestick, and the table, and the shewbread; which is called the sanctuary. And after the second veil, the tabernacle which is called the Holiest of all" (9:1–3). The priests went into the first sanctuary but into the second only the high priest ever entered, and only once each year:

> But Christ being come an high priest of good things to come, by a greater and more perfect tabernacle, not made with hands, that is to say, not of this building; Neither by the blood of goats and calves, but by his own blood he entered in once into the holy place, having obtained eternal redemption for us. For if the blood of bulls and of goats, and the ashes of an heifer sprinkling the unclean, sanctifieth to the purifying of the flesh: How much more shall the blood of Christ, who through the eternal Spirit offered himself without spot to God, purge your conscience from dead works to serve the living God? (vv. 11–14)

This dismissal of the old priestly ritual is of course part of something larger, of a view of the Old Testament as having to do with mere externals and revealing confusion and imperfection, while Christ reveals to us the inner man and brings clarity and perfection, an end to doubt and the fulfillment of what had been promised:

> For the law having a shadow of good things to come, and not the very image of the things, can never with those sacrifices which they offered year by year continually make the comers thereunto perfect . . . For it is not possible that the blood of bulls and of goats should take away sins . . . But this man, after he had offered one sacrifice for sins for ever, sat down on the right hand of God . . . For by one offering he hath perfected for ever them that are sanctified. (10:1–14)

The conclusion is clear:

> Having therefore, brethren, boldness to enter into the holiest by the blood of Jesus, By a new and living way, which he hath consecrated for us, through the veil, that is to say, his flesh; And having an high priest over the house of God; Let us draw near with a true heart in full assurance of faith, having our hearts sprinkled from an evil conscience, and our bodies washed with pure water. (10:19–22)

This contrast between the old Jewish ritual and the new Christian one, between the sacrifice of animals, the complex topography of the Temple, the high priest and the rest, and the mystic sacrifice in Christ causes modern commentators no difficulty. In fact it seems like common sense. Thus Moule remarks that "Jesus was satisfied with nothing but the absolute sincerity and spirituality of which the Temple was meant, but too often failed, to be the medium."[16] And Hughes comments: "[The author of Hebrews] has actually replaced the sacrificial ritual with the infinitely more profound concept of the sacrifice of the will."[17] But was the Temple really meant primarily to be the medium of "absolute sincerity and spirituality"? And why is the concept of the sacrifice of the will "infinitely more profound"? Much of the work of anthropologists in the past half-century, as well as that of historians of the medieval Church such as Peter Brown and Richard Southern, has been directed toward making us see that such distinctions hold good only for those who already accept nineteenth-century liberal and Protestant assumptions.[18] Moule and Hughes, so sophisticated elsewhere, are, in their view of ritual, still subscribing to the long-discredited views of the positivist anthropologists of the nineteenth century.

There is no better discussion of the assumptions that lie behind those attitudes and the distortions they impose, than the opening chapters of Mary Douglas's *Natural Symbols*. "Ritual is become a bad word signifying empty conformity," she points out. Ritual, "defined as a routinized act diverted from its normal function, subtly becomes a despised form of communication . . . The ritualist becomes one who performs external gestures which imply commitment to a particular set of values, but he is inwardly withdrawn, dried out and uncommitted. This is a distractingly partisan use of the term. For it derives from the assumptions of the anti-ritualists in the long history of religious revivalism."[19] It is distracting because "to use the word ritual to mean empty symbols of conformity, leaving us with no word to stand for symbols of genuine conformity, is seriously disabling to the sociology of religion"[20]—and, she might have added, to the study of ancient literature, of which the Bible is a prime example.

What is fascinating about *this* ancient book, though, is that it contains both old and alien ways of thought *and* hints of precisely those attitudes of mind we associate with Protestantism and nineteenth-century liberal positivism. Of course the mystic ritual alluded to in Hebrews 10 cannot be simplified, as Moule and Hughes do, into a simple contrast between inner and outer, the spiritual and the fleshly. The author's vision is much richer than that. Yet it is not as rich as, say, Ephesians, and within Paul as well as the Catholic Epistles it is possible to see the emergence of a tone and even a vocabulary which makes the kind of reading I have criticized above seem eminently plausible. Even the Gospels, which retain so much of the quality of the Old Testament narratives, mark, by their insistence on the fact that the kingdom of Heaven is not of this world, a fundamental shift in the way we are to conceive of human culture. Christianity, after all, was from the start a religion not of a nation but of individuals. It was natural, therefore, that despite its attempt to retain much of the vocabulary of the Hebrew culture from which it sprang, it would be forced to drain that vocabulary of its original meaning.

Those who have read the Bible through from Genesis to the Catholic Epistles will have no difficulty in seeing this transformation at work. They will note that the Law invoked by Paul and the author of Hebrews seems to resemble Roman law much more than that Law or Torah in which so many Old Testament figures are said to have walked and which was an entire way of life rather than an externally imposed code of restrictions. Readers who have any Hebrew will note that a word like *berit* simply means "treaty" and is so used for treaties between kings as well as between man and God, so that to use the word "covenant" for the latter is already to separate the two domains, is already, that is, a small and unobtrusive but decisive step on the road to the splitting of inner and outer which culminates in Descartes. The Old Testament figures invoked in Hebrews and the Catholic Epistles have been transformed from historical characters living out their often confused and contradictory lives into moral exemplars. Be patient, James exhorts his readers; remember the patience of Job. Obey your husbands, Peter counsels the women in his congregation, "even as Sara obeyed Abraham, calling him lord" (1 Peter 3:6). Love one another, says John; don't be like Cain. "Even as Sodom and Gomorrha, and the cities about them in like manner," says Jude, "giving themselves over to fornication, and going after strange flesh, are set forth for an example, suffering the vengeance of eternal fire" (Jude 7).

Many of the themes and arguments of the New Testament are found in Jewish apocalyptic. Nevertheless, coming where it does in the large book we call the Bible, the New Testament has a peculiar potency. For a struggle is taking place within this book, a struggle over meaning. Once you claim, as Jesus does at the end of Luke's Gospel, for example, that in one person (himself) all that was written is fulfilled, you perform a major act of colonization. Those elements which do not fit disappear into the darkness, and only those which do appear to fit remain. It is like one of Gombrich's diagrams: one cannot see both pictures at once, however fast one's eyes move between them. What is confusing is that for the Old Testament as well as for the New history is meaningful. The difference is that the New Testament claims to know what that meaning is, whereas for the most part the Old Testament merely claims that there *is* meaning. Its insistent message is: remember—remember how the Lord delivered you from Egypt, remember how the Lord made a treaty with Abraham and how an angel wrestled with Jacob. By contrast the insistent message of the New Testament is: see, know, understand, for "the darkness is past, and the true light now shineth" (1 John 2:8). The very variety of the Old Testament texts, their frequent contradictoriness, keeps them in a kind of fruitful dialogue: Lamentations with the Song of Songs, Job with Genesis, Chronicles with Joshua–Kings. The New Testament, on the other hand, is single-minded: everything makes sense, and those who refuse to see that sense must be accused of willful blindness.

We gain a strong sense of this from all the Catholic Epistles, as from the other New Testament writings. But it is in Hebrews that we really see the power of such notions as perfection and fulfillment as hermeneutical tools. Once we ask of an Old Testament event, What does it mean? once we say, This is the fulfillment of that, it is very difficult to retain our sense of the plenitude and even contradictoriness of what went before. But, as Nietzsche tried to show in relation to Homer and Plato, and as later classical scholars such as Eric Havelock have made clear, the will to truth and clarity is itself in need of justification.[21] By the same token it is necessary to find ways of letting the *Iliad* or Genesis speak in the face of the interpretative tyranny of a Plato, a Jesus, a Paul, or a document such as the Epistle to the Hebrews. It is not enough to point out that *figura* operates in the Bible; we have to assess the gains and losses involved in reading the Old Testament figuratively. It is not enough to say that because the Bible is full of patterns we must read it ahistorically, as a set of such patterns. It is not enough, because what is at issue in much of the Bible is precisely the nature of patterning, of God's *design* for the world.

The Epistle to the Hebrews is fascinating just because it forces us to ask such questions as: Is clarity better than unclarity? fulfillment than nonfulfillment? What does "better" mean in this case? By giving such a convincing and powerful reading of the Old Testament, Hebrews forces readers who have responded to the earlier stories and events to ask themselves: Is *this* what they were about? What they were *really* about? And what does "really" mean here?

Perhaps we do not need to choose. But we should at least recognize the price of Truth.

NOTES

1. Robert Fitzgerald, "The Art of Translation," *The Paris Review,* 94 (1984), 58.

2. Graham Hughes, *Hebrews and Hermeneutics* (Cambridge, 1979), p. 3.

3. Hughes, *Hebrews*; C. F. D. Moule, *The Birth of the New Testament* (London, 1962).

4. Hughes, *Hebrews,* p. 56.

5. Ibid., p. 93.

6. Ibid., p. 95.

7. Ibid., p. 58.

8. Ibid., p. 59.

9. See Jorge Luis Borges, "Kafka and His Precursors," trans. J. E. Irby in *Labyrinths and Other Writings,* ed. Donald Yates and James Irby (New York, 1964), pp. 199–201; T. S. Eliot, "Tradition and the Individual Talent," in *Selected Essays* (London, 1951), pp. 13–22; and Stephen Medcalf, "Virgil's Aeneid," in David Daiches and A. K. Thorlby, eds., *The Classical World* (London, 1972).

10. Hughes, *Hebrews,* p. 56.

11. See F. L. Horton, Jr., *The Melchizedek Tradition* (Cambridge, 1976).

12. E. H. Gombrich, *Art and Illusion* (London, 1968); Wallace Stevens, "Anecdote of the Jar," in *Collected Poems* (London, 1955), p. 76.

13. Mary Douglas, *Natural Symbols* (Harmondsworth, 1973), p. 41.

14. Amos Wilder, *Jesus' Parables and the War of Myths,* ed. James Breech (London, 1982), p. 151.

15. Hughes, *Hebrews,* p. 133.

16. Moule, *Birth,* p. 17.

17. Ibid., p. 89.

18. See especially Peter Brown, *The Cult of the Saints* (London, 1981) and *Society and the Holy* (London, 1982); and R. W. Southern, *The Pelican History of the Church: Western Society and the Church in the Middle Ages* (Harmondsworth, 1970).

19. Douglas, *Natural Symbols,* pp. 19–20.

20. Ibid., p. 21.

21. Eric Havelock, *Preface to Plato* (Oxford, 1963). John Jones, *On Aristotle and Greek Tragedy* (London, 1962), has some relevant remarks on our misreading of Aeschylus when, for example, we take Agamemnon's carpet as an image of or metaphor for hubris rather than literally as the concrete manifestation of the wealth of the *oikos* or household, the trampling on which *is* a blow to the *oikos*. Jones's central argument, that we misread the Greeks when we do not recognize how different they are from us, applies to my discussion of the Old Testament in this essay.

SUGGESTED FURTHER READINGS

Peter Brown, *The Cult of the Saints* (London, 1981).

————, *Society and the Holy* (London, 1982).

Mary Douglas, *Natural Symbols* (Harmondsworth, 1973).

Eric Havelock, *Preface to Plato* (Oxford, 1963).

Graham Hughes, *Hebrews and Hermeneutics* (Cambridge, 1979).

John Jones, *On Aristotle and Greek Tragedy* (London, 1962).

C. F. D. Moule, *The Birth of the New Testament* (London, 1962).

Jacob Neusner, *Judaism and the Beginning of Christianity* (London, 1984).

Friedrich Nietzsche, *Twilight of the Idols,* trans. R. J. Hollingdale (Harmondsworth, 1968).

Geza Vermes, *Jesus and the World of Judaism* (London, 1983).

University of Sussex

Revelation

Bernard McGinn

READING the Book of Revelation has tended to be more of an obsession than a pastime. Those readers who could dismiss it, either with a quip like George Bernard Shaw ("a curious record of the visions of a drug addict") or with studied indifference like John Calvin, have been few. Many who have hated the book have been unable to escape it. D. H. Lawrence, for instance, felt compelled to write his own form of commentary to try to exorcise it from his mind. Suspect in its origins, controversial throughout its history, even today Revelation raises the question of how it is to be read in a more dramatic way than perhaps any other book of the New Testament. The insistence of many commentators, both early and late, that they alone have found the real key to this unveiling of the mysteries of the end has served only to compound the enigma as history has demonstrated the errors or insufficiencies of various readings. St. Jerome showed more wisdom than most, not only in merely revising someone else's commentary rather than writing his own, but also in remarking that "Revelation has as many mysteries as it does words."[1]

The variety of modern readings testifies that the obsession persists and that there is still no commonly agreed upon approach. Millions of Christian fundamentalists read Revelation in a highly literal way as a blueprint for coming crisis, while liberation theologians and others look to it for a political if less literally prophetic message. Biblical scholars advance interpretations based upon the historical-critical method, theologians and literary critics experiment with more existential or immanent readings dependent upon diverse hermeneutical theories, while artists and poets are content to mine the book for its rich symbolism. Ends are as necessary to all literary works as beginnings, and the absolute end of that library of books we call the Bible has provoked as much controversy as the Bible's account of the absolute beginning in Genesis. It sometimes appears that Revelation is a book whose literary interest has been transferred from the text to the readers. In itself arcane and full of secret allegories at whose original reference we can only guess, it has offered all the more opportunity to researchers who can with impunity discover in its pages the message they themselves put there out of a sense that so menacing a document, full of hitherto misunderstood detail, can have application only to the unprecedented world-historical crisis of their own moment in time. Consequently the meaning of the book is, almost uniquely, identical with its various applications. We learn most about it from later interpretations which may be manifestly unacceptable to us.

Yet at first glance Revelation seems a less difficult book than its history has proved. Both its author and its purpose are clearly proclaimed at the outset. Most Christians have believed that the John of Patmos who announces himself as the author (1:1, 4, and 9; 22:8) was none other than John the beloved disciple. Though the identification had been doubted in antiquity, not until the end of the eighteenth century was it challenged by critical scholarship. Debate continues about the social setting and ecclesial identity of John of Patmos, but most current scholarship views him as an itinerant Christian prophet of Asia Minor who wrote in the last decade of the first century.

All classic interpreters conceived of Revelation as a literary unity, the work of a single author. The same wave of historical-critical scholarship, largely German in inspiration, that questioned traditional views of authorship also attacked the book's unity, claiming that it was either composed of a variety of sources (frequently seen as Jewish rather than Christian in origin) or was a mélange of different redactions. Though the denial of literary unity won the day among critics at the end of the nineteenth century, it has recently come under increasing fire to the point where most biblical scholars would hold that Revelation is indeed the work of one author, whatever fragments of earlier traditions and materials he might have incorporated. Thus both scholars and those critics who believe that the passage of time as well as authorial intention affects the meaning of a work now admit the literary integrity of the text.

Revelation was traditionally conceived of as a prophetic book in accordance with its opening words: "The Revelation of Jesus Christ, which God gave unto him, to shew unto his servants things which must shortly come to pass" (1:1). Its author identifies himself as a prophet and speaks of his book as "words of prophecy" (1:2; 22:18, 19). Many interpreters, taking this claim at face value, tended to read Revelation in accordance with a simplistic understanding of prophecy; they held that just as the Old Testament prophets foretold things to come, Revelation prophesies the coming events of the end of time. On the basis of this understanding, John's book offers many difficulties in relating history and prophecy. Granted that Revelation discloses the final events, does it also reveal the course of history leading up to the end? If the message revealed embraces the whole of history, as many have thought, the complex structure of Revelation makes it exceedingly difficult to correlate its profuse symbolism with historical events in any simple way. It is not so much that the commentators have to match individual symbols with particular historical events, but that sequences of images need to be correlated with sequences of events.[2] Both ancient and modern readers have been perplexed by the relation between the book's structure and its message. How does Revelation say what it is trying to say?

Interpretations of the structure of Revelation are almost as many as its readers, but three general tendencies are discernible. One view, found among many classic Christian exegetes and modern fundamentalists, insists that the structure and message of the book is basically linear and prophetic, that is, that the images reveal the course of history, or at least the events imminent to the end of time. A second and rarer approach (represented today by the theologian Jacques Ellul) sees Revelation as a carefully crafted theological treatise containing a complex moral message and theology of history. Most modern scholars, however, view John's Revelation as a cyclical presentation of visions repeating, or recapitulating, the same basic message of present persecution, imminent destruction of the wicked and reward of the just.

The basic element in this recapitulative structure is the pattern of seven, a sacred number indicating fullness and completion. Sequences of sevens determine the course of the book: the seven letters (2:1–3:22), the seven seals (6:1–8:1), the seven trumpets (8:2–11:19), seven unnumbered visions (12:1–15:4), the seven vials (15:1–16:21), and a final seven unnumbered visions (19:11–21:8). These sequences are made more complex by such literary devices as inclusion, whereby a sequence can be seen as part of the final act of its predecessor (for example, the relation of the seven trumpets to the seventh seal in 8:1–2), and the method of "intercalation" in which two episodes that belong together are interrupted by another incident (for example, 8:2–6, in which the angels with the trumpets are introduced, but a heavenly liturgy intervenes before they begin to blow).[3] Nor is it always clear how these series of sevens relate to the general structural principles of the work, such as that discerned in the two great books: the "closed book" with the seven seals (5:1), which can be taken as containing what is revealed in chapters 6–11; and the "open book" that the "mighty angel" gives John to eat in chapter 10, which can be seen as the message of the second half.

The difficulties in relating the sequences of Revelation to the external text of history largely explain why many early interpreters eventually abandoned historico-prophetic readings of the text to concentrate either on internal or on purely future ones. In modern times this tendency has been encouraged by the discovery of the differences between Old Testament prophecy and intertestamental apocalyptic literature. In order to grasp the divergence between most older Christian interpretations of Revelation and contemporary historical-critical understandings it is necessary to take a look at both apocalyptic eschatology and the genre of apocalypse, the most potent but also most problematic literary contribution of intertestamental Judaism to Christianity.[4]

Since the late eighteenth century, scholars have recognized the importance of the new form of eschatology, with its deliberately opaque imagery, that arose among the Jews in the centuries immediately before Christ. This form of belief about the end centered on a divine revelation concerning God's coming intervention to do justice upon the wicked and to reward the good in a new aeon. The backdrop to this conviction, implicitly or explicitly expressed (sometimes through a sketch of the ages of the world), was a deterministic view of universal history seen as culminating in the triple drama of crisis-judgment-vindication. The vindication was conceived of in many ways, though it usually involved some kind of personal immortality, at times even the hope of resurrection from the dead (Dan. 12:2), a concept that apocalyptic eschatology introduced into Judaism. One of the frequent features of this new view of history was a sense that contemporary events, if correctly understood, could be seen as "signs of the times" that would reveal the imminence of the appointed end.

Though the identification of the groups and situations in which apocalyptic eschatology arose has proved difficult to ascertain in particular cases, there is general agreement that this view of history and the end was produced for purposes of consolation and theodicy among a subject people frequently laboring under a strong sense of persecution. This sense of opposition helps explain the dualistic elements found in the apocalyptic view of the world. Its colors, as can be seen in the Book of Revelation, are generally strong ones—blacks and whites, rather than muted tones.

General agreement about the meaning of apocalyptic eschatology has masked significant confusion about apocalypse considered as a literary genre. In recent years it has become increasingly evident that the Jewish and Christian apocalypses were part of a range of revelatory and oracular texts that proliferated in the Hellenistic world, and that the contents of the texts that can be called apocalypses included a wealth of heavenly mysteries broader and more diverse than just historical and eschatological secrets. One current view would define an apocalypse as a revelation mediated by a heavenly messenger and presented in written form (and in Jewish examples always pseudonymously ascribed to an ancient seer) containing both a horizontal, or historical, dimension and a vertical one concerning the relation of the terrestrial and celestial realms.[5] It is also becoming evident, as more work is done on early apocalypses and their later influence, that this genre not only introduced a new conception of history into Western religions but also was central in the development of the visionary tradition in Western literature and mysticism.

Apocalypses, by their very nature, were designed both to reveal (to believers) and to conceal (from the unworthy). The pseudonymity that characterizes all Jewish apocalypses, though not John's Revelation, was designed to heighten this sense of concealing and revealing. Secrets hidden long ago by the sages now were seen to uncover the course of history and what was to come. Perhaps the ancient apocalypses concealed much even from their original readers. Some scholars seem to assume that the first readers of the apocalypses had a magic key that unlocked the full meaning of the text in some exemplary fashion, but the nature of the genre itself and the evidence of the apocalyptic tradition, which from the start showed a concern for revising, interpreting, and adding to what had been revealed, points in the other direction. John's Revelation was probably at least partly mysterious even to its early audience.

No small part of the difficulty of interpreting apocalypses such as Revelation has to do with the way in which they make use of mythological symbolism. The apocalyptic authors used the ancient Near Eastern combat myth, which saw the formation of the world as the result of the victory of the divine warrior over the monsters of the watery chaos, to give meaning to present and future events. Thus in the apocalypses myth and history became inextricably intertwined as the "old story" of the myth and the "new story" of recent history enriched and transformed each other like two voices in a line of polyphony.[6] (An example in Revelation is the way the career of the persecutor Nero and expectations of his return have colored the picture of the seven-headed eschatological monster in 13:1–3 and 17:8–13). Of course, there is a sense in which even the most realistic narrative blends myth and the representation of contemporary fact; but the relation is special in the apocalypses because the writers' purpose is not to submerge the old in the new, but to give a higher meaning to history by relating it to transcendental mythic patterns. Along with the basic cosmogonic symbolism came a host of other symbols, spatial and temporal, human and animal. All too often these symbols have been read as ciphers for some one hidden message, but such reductive interpretations are usually too simple. By tapping into the deep mine of myth in order to give meaning to history, apocalyptic literature introduced ambiguity and polyvalence that increase fascination while compounding obscurity and that help explain why modern theorists of symbolism, both psychological and literary, have been so interested in the Book of Revelation.

Apocalypses belong to a literary form that absolutely requires to be read as containing more than apparent senses. But because of the difficulties just described, opinions about the character of these concealed senses vary greatly; and, in view of the association of the apocalyptic genre with theories of world history, it is not surprising that much interpretation has taken the form of historical prophecy.

Given this situation, the history of the ways in which Revelation has been read can provide a useful starting place for contemporary readers who wish to approach the book from a perspective that is both informed and modest. Such a history of interpretations may seem a distinctly secondary enterprise both to scholars who believe that the historical-critical method has canceled out all other readings, or to those critics who insist that to decipher a text correctly one need take no notice of either its original historical situation or its subsequent use. I side with those who argue that the history of the interpretation of a text is an integral part of its meaning, especially in the case of works that have been as influential and as controversial as Revelation. History constitutes the beginning of a fruitful reading, if not its end.

The inherent difficulty that all eras have found in reading Revelation is evident in the writings of some of its most noted interpreters.

In the *City of God* St. Augustine admits that he had once held to a futurist millenarian reading of 20:1–6, but that after seeing the error of literal or "carnal" interpretations of the millennium he came to identify the thousand-year reign of Christ and the saints on earth with the history of the Church.[7] The difficulty he had in dealing with Revelation, he tells us, was not only that the book, like all prophecy, mingles literal and figurative expressions, but also that it has few plain passages to help illuminate the obscure ones and that it frequently repeats the same things in different forms.[8] Augustine's solution was to adopt a spiritual interpretation based on that of the Donatist exegete Tyconius, which reduced the prophetic part of Revelation to the minimum and read the symbols as messages about moral conflict within each person and in the Church in general. The shift from ends conceived of as mythically imminent to those seen as fictionally immanent, which Frank Kermode has suggested is central to the influence of apocalyptic eschatology on Western literature, had an analogue in early Christianity in the writings of Augustine and the other spiritual interpreters.[9]

Joachim of Fiore, a Calabrian abbot of the twelfth century, studied Revelation with unmatched passion, but he too found the book difficult and at first intractable. In his massive *Exposition on Revelation* he reports that as early as the tenth verse of the first chapter he was stymied by the mysteries of the text. Then, early on Easter morning in 1183 or 1184, he was granted a divine revelation: "About the middle of the night's silence, as I think, the hour when it is thought that our Lion of the tribe of Judah rose from the dead, while I was meditating I suddenly perceived in my mind's eye something of the fullness [*plenitudo*] of this book and of the entire harmony [*concordia*] of the Old and New Testaments."[10]

Joachim may have been the first (though he was certainly not the last) exegete to claim that the meaning of Revelation had been divinely revealed to him. He described this divine gift not as the charism of prophecy itself, but as a "gift of understanding" (*donum intellectus*), the ability to see what the text really meant to say. The abbot's discovery of a new interpretation that remained influential for centuries might have made him the patron saint of critics had he been canonized rather than condemned.

Martin Luther was a third influential reader who confessed his initial difficulties with Revelation. In his 1522 Preface he almost excluded it from the New Testament canon as "neither apostolic nor prophetic," because "Christ is not taught or known in it." But eight years later, chastened by Rome's obduracy and Münzer's radicalism and with a greater grasp of Church history, the Reformer performed a *volte-face* in a new Preface to the German Bible.[11] Here Luther offered a brief sketch of the meaning of Revelation that proved central for Protestant interpreters for centuries, both because it identified the papacy with the Antichrist and because this identification was made within the context of a historically progressive reading of the text. Earlier interpreters, such as Joachim (but not Augustine), had also claimed to find a consonance between Revelation's prophecies and the events of Church history, but they had begun with Scripture and used it as the key to unlock history. Paradoxically, Luther, the great champion of the biblical word, claimed that history enabled him to make sense of Revelation:

> Since it is meant as a revelation of what is to come, and especially of coming tribulations and disasters for the Church, we can consider that the first and surest step toward finding its interpretation is to take from history the events and disasters that have happened to the Church before now and to hold them up alongside these pictures and so compare them with the words. If, then, the two fit and agree with each other, we can build on that as a sure, or at least an unobjectionable, interpretation.[12]

For Luther, even though it is the text of history that illuminates Revelation's obscure pictures, the message that is revealed is fundamentally an evangelical one, the trials and tribulations of the "one holy, Christian Church."

The difficulties that Augustine, Joachim, and Luther experienced in dealing with Revelation go back to the origins of Christianity. The earliest debate over Revelation, one that almost prevented its inclusion in the canon, concerned a central feature of its message about the future, the prediction of the thousand-year (that is, chiliastic) reign of Christ and the saints on earth in 20:1–6. This prophecy developed elements found in Jewish apocalyptic eschatology and was echoed in a famous saying, attributed in a number of early Christian sources to Jesus, about the physical abundance of the coming kingdom. Major Christian writers of the second century, such as Justin and Irenaeus, read Revelation historically and interpreted literally its images of things to come, especially the reign of Christ and the saints; but a reaction against literal readings of the coming rewards, particularly when pictured as a millennium of banqueting and the propagation of children, is evident from the end of the second century. The delay of the expected return of Christ made historical interpretations and calculations based on Revelation more difficult, and the book's strident anti-imperial stance was increasingly uncongenial to Christians seeking accommodation with Rome. Furthermore, the expectation of some Christians that the coming kingdom would be in a restored earthly Jerusalem seemed dangerously close to the political aspirations of Jewish messianism. All these factors contributed to the first great debate over how to read Revelation.

Although Greek writers were the first to begin working out principles for a spiritual, or immanent, interpretation of Revelation, it was more fully achieved in Latin Christianity, and the book long remained marginal in the East. The early third-century commentary of Hippolytus, surviving today only in fragments, rejected attacks on Revelation on the basis of a synoptic understanding of eschatological texts from both the Old and the New Testaments. Origen used Revelation freely, giving it the same highly spiritual reading he gave to all Scripture; but the fact that he did not live to write the commentary he promised was a sore blow. The greatest of the Greek exegetes decisively rejected Christian chiliastic hopes for an earthly kingdom in a restored Jerusalem as delusions of those who "understand the divine scriptures in a Judaistic sense."[13]

Methodius of Olympus, like Origen, provided spiritual interpretations for key passages. His *Symposium* outlined a spiritual reading of one of the most powerful but challenging passages in Revelation, the account in chapter 12 of the battle between the woman in heaven and the great red dragon with the seven crowned heads and ten horns. The woman is identified with the Church bringing forth "those who are washed in baptism," while the dragon is the devil, whose heads and horns are given an allegorical interpretation as vices. Significantly, the 1,260 days of the woman's sojourn in the wilderness (v. 6) are taken not as a real historical period, but as a symbol of the Church's perfect knowledge of the Trinity.[14]

The earliest surviving complete commentary is the work of a Greek martyr bishop writing in Latin about 300 C.E. Victorinus of Pettau has received less attention than he deserves. His commentary may be inelegant in style and pedestrian in particulars, but it tries to give a coherent reading of the whole book and uncovers one of the fundamental principles still used for dealing with its structure, the notion of recapitulation. "Do not regard the order of what is said," he writes, "because the sevenfold Holy Spirit, when he has run though matters down to the last moment of time and the end, returns again to the same times and completes what he has left unsaid."[15] The idea that the structure of Revelation is recapitulative rather than linear or progressive has remained a major option for readers ever since. Since its revival half a century ago, it has been increasingly influential in historical-critical studies.

Victorinus does not deny a historical aspect to Revelation, but he stresses moral and theological applications. In chapter 12, for example, he agrees with Methodius, and indeed the whole tradition of the Fathers, in seeing the woman as the Church and the dragon as the devil; but he identifies the dragon's seven heads with six persecuting Roman emperors and the coming Antichrist, and he views the 1,260 days of verse 6 as a real three and a half years of the preaching of Elijah. Victorinus' highly literal interpretation of the coming kingdom described in 20:1–6 was also increasingly suspect at the time.

It was left to the late fourth-century Donatist exegete Tyconius to cap the spiritualizing reading of Revelation by providing a fully comprehensive interpretation based upon coherent exegetical principles (including recapitulation) that excluded any hope for a coming earthly kingdom. Many aspects of Tyconius' approach can be recaptured in his *Book of Rules* for interpreting Scripture and in the surviving fragments of his *Commentary*. He is concerned exclusively with the struggle between good and evil throughout the history of the Church, which he conceives of as the "twofold body of the Lord." Current events such as the persecution of the Donatists are a part of the revealed story, but in only a general way, that is, as exemplifications of something that has and always will be the case. Tyconius does not historicize the text by showing how it correlates with the Church's history; rather, he synchronizes images and symbols to show how they have meaning for each moment in the Church's life. (For example, the 1,260 days of the woman's flight into the desert signify the entire age of the Church's existence in the world of the wicked.) Although he does not deny a final personal Antichrist, he is much more interested in Antichrist conceived of as the increasing body of evildoers within the Church. From his perspective, even the mildest forms of chiliastic expectations are gross misreadings—the thousand years of 20:1–6 are nothing else but the Church's rule in living and dead down to the coming of Doomsday. Though Augustine and Jerome were largely responsible for spreading this ahistorical, moral, ecclesiological, and antimillennial interpretation to later commentators, it originated with Tyconius.[16]

The Tyconian-Augustinian tradition dominated Latin readings of Revelation for seven hundred years. Although it did not deny all prophetic dimension to the book, it tended to eschew attempts to read current events as signs of the end in accord with the Lord's command, "It is not for you to know the times or the seasons, which the Father hath put in his own power" (Acts 1:7). Those who followed the tradition did not engage in historical readings of Revelation, but in finding moral messages to encourage the struggle against vice and error. Though the centuries from 400 to 1100 saw many events that heightened people's sense that the approach of the end was imminent, and though the same period produced considerable apocalyptic literature in both the East and the West, the Tyconian-Augustinian tradition did little to encourage these ideas. There were, to be sure, innovation and variety within the tradition, especially after the eighth century, when Bede introduced an analysis based upon seven recapitulative visions rather than the line-by-line readings preferred by former exegetes.[17] At the end of the same century, the Spanish monk Beatus of Liébana penned an extensive if unoriginal commentary that soon came to be richly illustrated with a series of vibrantly colored illuminations. The surviving Beatus manuscripts of the tenth through twelfth centuries are priceless examples of medieval art.

The Tyconian-Augustinian reading of Revelation began to be questioned about 1100. Rupert of Deutz, a reforming German monk, saw the conflict between the woman and the dragon in chapter 12 as a prophecy, or at least a type, of the struggle between Gregory VII and Henry IV; his massive commentary made unprecedented use of parallels between historical events and the symbols in Revelation. Exegetes in the rapidly expanding new schools of the twelfth century addressed the problem of Revelation within the context of their desire to systematize Bible reading and study, though apparently with only fairly traditional results. The great innovator was Joachim of Fiore, the Calabrian abbot who owed his new reading to divine inspiration.

Joachim's interpretation, most fully set forth in his *Exposition on Revelation* but present in almost all his works, is among the most complex ever attempted. Without giving up the ecclesiological and moral dimensions of the Tyconian-Augustinian line, and while fully agreeing that recapitulation was an essential feature of the text, the Calabrian produced the first fully developed historical reading of Revelation, one which showed in detail not only how the symbols of the book correlated with the major events of Church history, but also how they enabled the reader to see, at least in broad lines, what was to come. Although Joachim sees the Bible as a whole as revealing the trinitarian structure of the world-historical process, its last and most important book is the culminating disclosure of the "fullness of history" (*plenitudo historiae*). It is "the key of things past, the knowledge of things to come; the opening of what is sealed, the uncovering of what is hidden."[18]

For Joachim the meaning of history is tied to the growth of the spiritual understanding (*intellectus spiritualis*) of the Old and the New Testaments. This spiritual understanding was first revealed at the Resurrection (hence the abbot's Easter revelation). Its painful progress through centuries of conflict with carnal understanding is to reach a culmination in the dawning third *status,* or age of history, when, after the Antichrist's defeat, the Holy Spirit will reveal the fullness of Scripture and thus the ultimate meaning of history in the reformed and purified monastic Church. In this conception of the third *status* Joachim broke with Augustine and his followers and reintroduced millenarianism into Christianity, claiming that although the bishop was right to attack a literal reading of the thousand years, belief in a coming more perfect age of uncertain duration was no error but "a perfectly evident interpretation" (*serenissimus intellectus*). Joachim's millenarianism presupposed a detailed historicizing of the entire symbolism of Revelation; thus, for example, he analyzed the seven heads of the dragon of chapter 12 as seven persecutors culminating in the imminent Antichrist of the second *status*.

The Calabrian abbot's powerful and original exegesis not only introduced a new understanding of history into the West but also influenced and challenged interpreters of Revelation for centuries to come. During the thirteenth century, the debate between the two great protagonists, Augustine and Joachim, grew and intensified among their followers.

Joachim's followers took over the novel exegetical techniques and startling views of the abbot and extended them in ways that he might well have rejected, especially in their virulent criticism of the papacy and in their willingness to see a particular form of current religious life (usually Franciscan) as identical with the form to be realized in the imminent millennial age of the Church. The best example of this approach is the Franciscan Peter Olivi's *Postil on Revelation,* finished shortly before his death in 1298 and still unedited. The work was considered dangerous enough to merit papal condemnation in 1326.

Building on hints in Joachim's own writings, the radical Joachites emphasized a dialectical view of the papacy's role in the coming crisis that would mark the transition to the better state of the Church. On the one hand, the see of Peter was central to the destiny of Christianity and would therefore have an important part to play in both the crisis and the age to come; on the other hand, given the prediction that the Antichrist would be a false teacher enthroned in the Temple (2 Thess. 2:3–4), it was possible to regard unspiritual popes, especially those who attacked the evangelical Franciscan way of life, as predecessors or embodiments of the Antichrist. The eschatological conflict between good and bad popes (the *pastor angelicus* and *antichristus mysticus*) was among the major innovations of late medieval commentary on Revelation. Unlike the Reformation commentators and their Hussite predecessors, however, the Joachite exegetes never lost faith in the essential importance and eschatological role of what they conceived of as the highest office in Christendom.

Alongside the Joachite commentaries on Revelation, increasingly bold in their historicizing use of the symbols of the book, there was a broad middle range of exegesis that used both the Tyconian-Augustinian tradition and more recent methods of interpretation. These commentaries, though rarely exciting, were widely used by those afraid of the excesses of the Joachites and also influenced the profuse use of Revelation in late medieval art.

Finally, Joachim's complex reintroduction of a historical dimension opened the way to less complicated views of the relation between history and prophecy in Revelation. In the fourteenth century the most famous of late medieval exegetes, the Franciscan Nicholas of Lyra, popularized a new form of linear prophetic reading of Revelation in his *Postil on All Scripture*. According to Nicholas, "In the Spirit through images he [John] saw the Church's course from the time of the apostles down to the end of the world."[19] In his precise correlations between symbols and past events, the Franciscan appears even more arbitrary and bizarre than Joachim, as when he says that the book John is commanded to eat in 10:9 is Justinian's *Digest,* or when he interprets chapter 12 as prophesying the Emperor Heraclius' defense of the Church against the Persian persecutor Chosroes symbolized by the dragon. Nevertheless, Nicholas wisely forbears from attempting to find any correspondence between current events and Revelation and also avoids any hint of millenarianism. Concerning chapters 17 through 20 he drily remarks: "Because 'I am not a prophet, or the son of a prophet' (Amos 7:14), I will not say anything about the future, except what can be taken from Scripture or the words of the saints and the established teachers. Therefore, I leave the interpretation of this to the wise. If the Lord were to grant me its understanding, I would be glad to share it with others."[20]

Although late medieval sectarians, especially the Hussites in Bohemia and the Lollards in England, abandoned the Joachite dialectical view of the apocalyptic role of the papacy and identified it only with the evil symbolic figures found in Revelation, they did not create any new principles for interpreting the relation between history and prophecy in the mysterious last book of the Bible. On the eve of the Reformation there were, then, three broad ways to interpret the book: the Tyconian-Augustinian model (recapitulative, moral, and ecclesiological, but resolutely ahistorical and antimillenarian); the Joachite (also recapitulative, moral, and ecclesiological, but progressively historical and millenarian); and that disseminated by Nicholas of Lyra and his followers (linear-historical, ecclesiological, and antimillenarian). All three models would influence sixteenth- and seventeenth-century readers, though they were radically transformed by the energies and passions unleashed by the split within Western Christendom.

Although Luther's reading of Revelation was linear-historical (and thus not unlike Lyra's), his insistence that history enabled him to make sense of Revelation introduced a tension into Reformation commentary that is evident in the following centuries. Joachim, Nicholas of Lyra, and other medieval authors had searched for correlations between historical events and the symbols of Revelation, but history took on a new and more important role in classic Reformation commentary. The Protestants' need to demonstrate the evangelical claim that the papacy itself (along with the dread Turk) constituted the institutional embodiment of the Antichrist was at the heart of this new historicization. It has been suggested that the fulfillment of apocalyptic prophecies in the rise of the Reformed churches against Rome served the Protestant cause as a rebuttal to a Roman Catholic apologetic based on miracles.[21]

This is not to say that Protestant interpretations were uniform, especially on such questions as the meaning of the millennial kingdom. Luther's own reading was historical and evangelical in its stress on the preaching of God's word in history. The three "woes" announced by the eagle in 8:13 were central to his understanding of the progress of history revealed in the book. The first woe (9:1–12) was the heretic Arius, the second (9:13–21) the Muhammadan attack on the Church, the third the papal empire announced in 11:14 and described in chapter 13. Thus Luther gave the woman who bears the man-child in chapter 12 a more spiritual interpretation; she signified that "some pious teachers and Christians will continue under the first two woes and under the third which is still to come."[22] Luther was resolutely antimillenarian. His experience with the radicals had convinced him that the thousand years of chapter 20 had begun at the time when the prophecy was written. Not all of his contemporaries or successors were so sure.

The emphasis on history that Luther made central to Reformation reading of Revelation was variously appreciated by his followers and by the other Reformers. Heinrich Bullinger, in his influential *Hundred Sermons on Revelation* (1557), was less interested in drawing correlations with historical events than in creating an evangelical version of the old moralizing Tyconian interpretation; but others were more historical in orientation. Lutherans soon began to find a place for Luther himself in the scheme of history, identifying him with the angel bearing the Eternal Gospel in 14:6–7. Joachite exegesis, with its historicizing tendencies and reformist stance, influenced many Reformation commentators. But binding all the classic Reformation commentaries together was their anti-Romanism—Revelation, correctly understood, showed how the papacy through history had functioned as the persecuting Antichrist.

Nowhere was Revelation more avidly studied and more vociferously debated than in Reformation England. The reasons for this are complex, but part of the explanation lies in the close linkage established between the English national identity and the cause of the Reformation, and the growth of the radical Puritan strain that eventually led to a revival of millenarianism. The Anglican mainstream, like the Continental Reformers, justified their break with the pope by equating Rome and Babylon; but those groups that came to question the Elizabethan settlement turned the tables on the moderates by viewing the established episcopal Church as Laodicea the lukewarm (3:16) or even as Babylon on native shores.

John Bale originated the mainstream English interpretation with *The Image of Both Churches* (1548), a rather disorganized work in three parts which showed how Revelation disclosed the struggle between the true evangelical Church and the false Babylonish Church down through seven ages of history. In his first part Bale asserted that the binding of the dragon (20:2) began with the Reformation, but under the influence of the Continental commentators he later abandoned this view with its millenarian implications, giving an allegorical reading of chapters 20–22. Like Luther, Bale was concerned with relating historical events and the prophecies found in Revelation. His reading of the seven heads of the dragon was an original historicizing one, viewing them both as seven figures of deceit spanning all of world history and as seven periods of attack on the Church since the coming of Christ. Unlike Luther, Bale insisted that "the text [is] a light to the chronicles, and not the chronicles to the text."[23]

Bale's interest in martyrdom as a sign of the true Church was developed by John Foxe in his famous ecclesiastical history *Actes and Monuments* (1563). Foxe had a powerful influence on Edmund Spenser and on the development of an English variant of the imperial apocalyptic myth in the Elizabethan period. At his death Foxe left an unfinished commentary on Revelation called the *Eicasmi,* which was more mathematically precise and historicizing in its attempts to correlate history and prophecy than Bale had been. This concern for chronological accuracy was even more marked in the case of the noted Scottish mathematician John Napier, who wrote *A Pleine Discovery of the Whole Revelation of St. John* in the wake of that singular historical "proof" of the Protestant view of history, the defeat of the Armada in 1588. Napier demonstrated how precise a timetable could be uncovered in Revelation, even down to the determination that the seventh and last age of history had begun in 1541 and would last until 1786. Although Napier saw this age as concluding with a harvest period of peace from 1688 on, he rejected a millenarian reading of chapter 20, placing the thousand-year binding of Satan in the past, as the classic Reformed tradition always had.

The revival of truly millenarian readings of Revelation, which often included a sense of England as an apocalyptically elect nation, did not become popular until the seventeenth century. In the 1640s and 1650s hundreds of sermons and pamphlets, frequently based on texts from Revelation, fueled the fires of social and political unrest.

The academic commentators of the previous generation initiated this new millenarianism. The chief figures were Thomas Brightman, a Bedfordshire parson, whose *Revelation of the Revelation* was published posthumously in Latin in 1609; and Joseph Mede, a Cambridge don and teacher of Milton, whose *Key of Revelation* first appeared in 1627, also in Latin. Brightman's work, written partly in response to Jesuit attacks on Protestant exegesis, differed little from its predecessors in method but introduced some important new ideas. The parson not only emphasized the role of England as a chosen nation but also reintroduced hopes for a millenarian era, to be fully realized after the defeat of Rome and the dragon (in 1650 and 1695, respectively). Brightman did this by distinguishing between two millennial ages, one (prophesied in 20:2) lasting from 300 to 1300, and the other (found in 20:4–5) beginning in 1300. He was convinced that the patristic chiliasts "did not wander much from the truth."[24]

Mede's method of interpretation was more original and his millenarianism, though guarded in expression, no less real than Brightman's. Mede adopted an internal, philological method which gave the various symbols of Revelation consistent historical and political meanings (for example, "winds" always means "wars"), so that the repetition of an image indicated a return to the same topic. On this basis Mede worked out a scheme of temporal repetitions, or "synchronizations," that were really nothing more than ancient recapitulations with a new twist.[25] In Mede's scheme the third woe, seventh seal, seventh trumpet, and seventh vial all corresponded to the coming millennium, when Christ would return to earth, bind Satan, and reign with the saints, an event which Mede predicted would occur between 1625 and 1716.

The great age of English commentary on Revelation did not end with the Restoration, but there was little innovative thought. Henry More, the Cambridge Platonist, defended Mede's views against the rising tide of more critical scholarship, and Isaac Newton perfected the mathematical approach to prophetic calculations of world history with a monotony that led Voltaire to remark that "Sir Isaac Newton wrote his comment upon the Revelation to console mankind for the great superiority he had over them in other respects."[26] One change of note did occur in the eighteenth century, when interpreters such as Daniel Whitby turned away from Mede's premillennial position (that Christ's second coming would inaugurate the reign of the saints) in favor of a postmillennial view that saw Christ's return as following a new and better age soon to dawn for mankind. This position influenced the first great American commentator, Jonathan Edwards, who wrote extensively on Revelation in the first half of the eighteenth century.

In the nineteenth century the American and British heirs of the millenarian tradition of interpreting Revelation, reacting to such dramatic events as the American and French Revolutions and the careers of Napoleon I and III, continued to produce apocalyptic treatises and commentaries. Among the most influential figures on both sides of the Atlantic was John Nelson Darby, the founder of the Plymouth Brethren and in many ways the originator of present-day fundamentalism.

While Protestants, both on the Continent and in England, were developing their distinctive readings of Revelation, Jesuit exegetes were also busy. From 1581 to 1593 Cardinal Bellarmine published his three-volume *Controversies* attacking Protestant theology and exegesis. Several generations of Jesuits furthered this theological counterattack, not least by showing that the Protestant readings of Revelation based on a historical interpretation of the text and the identification of the papacy with the Antichrist were erroneous. The Jesuit commentators of the late sixteenth and seventeenth centuries were hampered by a hankering after Joachite exegesis that helped them to provide their own order with a unique historical status; but the best of the group—notably Franciscus Ribeira, who published his commentary in 1591, and Ludovicus ab Alcasar, whose work came out in 1614—are regarded as the ancestors of the historical-critical interpretation of Revelation. Not only did they bring vast erudition to bear in showing that there was no evidence for identifying the papacy with the Antichrist, but they also denied the basic premise of exegetes since Joachim and Nicholas of Lyra that Revelation foretold the course of history. For them the book was to be understood in the light of what we could know about the original early Christian context in which it was written. The fulfillment of whatever prophecies it contained still lay in the future.

This new literary and critical reading of Revelation soon influenced Protestant scholars, first Hugo Grotius in his *Notations to the New Testament* (1644), and then Henry Hammond in England in 1653. During the eighteenth century, despite commentaries such as Johann Albrecht Bengel's, which combined philological erudition with exact chronological predictions and fervent millenarianism, the strengthening current of Enlightenment criticism further eroded the foundations of traditional historical readings of Revelation. By the century's end, when Johann Salomo Semler and others denied the Johannine authorship of the book and emphasized the Jewish background of its apocalyptic imagery, the era of modern critical study of Revelation had begun.

In the great proliferation of commentaries on and readings of Revelation since 1800, almost all of the traditional interpretations have continued to exert an influence. Today, however, the primary question confronting readers of Revelation seems to have shifted from the relation between history and prophecy to that between prophecy and science. Is it possible to give a reading of the book that is both prophetic and also in some sense scientific?

The term *scientific,* of course, can be understood in various ways. The desire for greater mathematical accuracy among commentators such as Napier and Newton could be said to be a scientific claim, just as the philological approach of Brightman, Mede, and Bengel made an appeal to scientific learning. But the historical erudition and use of literary criticism introduced by the Jesuits, developed by Grotius and others, and eventually pushed beyond the theological boundaries which held that Revelation must always be seen as a book in some way prophetic, won the day. By the nineteenth century historical science had overcome prophecy in interpretations of Revelation, at least in the scholarly world. The victory, of course, has been at least in part a pyrrhic one. The academic triumph of the historical-critical method has not produced any one generally agreed-upon explanation of the structure of the book and the meaning of the mysterious sequences of symbols of which it is composed, even among scholars, and outside the academy many continue to read and to use Revelation in very different ways.

Two kinds of reaction to the dominance of scientific approaches to Revelation have been evident in the past two centuries. First, the book, having long exerted so strong an influence on art and literature, might itself be viewed primarily as an imaginative creation, as a work of literature rather than as a repository of truths about the course of history and the events of the end. Johann Gottfried von Herder, the Romantic philosopher, pioneered this approach in his effusive commentary on Revelation, *Maranatha* (1779). The nineteenth and especially the twentieth centuries have seen numerous examples of this tendency, as well as an abundance of studies of the influence of Revelation and the apocalyptic mentality upon Western literature. In recent years most historical-critical interpreters of the book have discovered the importance of literary criticism, and many commentaries and studies now employ at least some elements of contemporary literary theories.

The other reaction to the victory of the historical-critical method was the rise of the fundamentalist interpretation in the nineteenth century, a kind of inverted scientific approach in its adherence to a crudely literalistic reading as providing the only true "objectivity."[27] Modern critical readers of Revelation tend to forget that most of those who ponder the book today see it through the eyes of the Hal Lindseys and the Billy Grahams as the divinely given plan for the coming Armageddon. The conflict of interpretations between academic readings carried on in schools of divinity and religion and in departments of English on the one hand and the mass of general readers on the other is probably greater now than ever before.

This cleavage of viewpoints may give some scholars cause for despair, but it also can be taken as a message of hope: at least it indicates that Revelation is still widely read and greatly treasured. When the book ceases to be controversial, it is likely to be forgotten. Those who value Revelation, though they will doubtless continue to quarrel about the meaning of its bold and provoking symbols and its intricate recapitulative structure, can agree with the words of the American divine Cotton Mather: "I confess *Apocalyptic Studies* are fittest for those Raised Souls, whose *Heart Strings* are made of a Little *Nicer* Clay than other mens."[28] Perhaps the last word can be left to Herder, who for all the disorder of his own reading was among the first to recognize that although Revelation may be many things, we cannot afford to forget that it is a great symbolic work of literature, more of a poem than a philosophical or historical treatise: "Where a book, through thousands of years, stirs up the heart and awakens the soul, and leaves neither friend nor foe indifferent, and scarcely has a lukewarm friend or enemy, in such a book there must be something substantial, whatever anyone may say."[29]

NOTES

1. Jerome, *Letter* 53.8.

2. As pointed out by Michael Murrin, "Revelation and Two Seventeenth Century Commentators," in C. A. Patrides and Joseph Wittreich, eds., *The Apocalypse in English Renaissance Thought and Literature* (Manchester, 1984), p. 126.

3. On the importance of intercalation see Elisabeth Schüssler Fiorenza, *The Book of Revelation: Justice and Judgment* (Philadelphia, 1985), pp. 172–174.

4. An important recent study on the genre is John J. Collins, ed., *Apocalypse: The Morphology of a Genre, Semeia* 14 (Missoula, Mont., 1979). More recent debate on definitional questions can be found in David Hellholm, ed., *Apocalypticism in the Mediterranean World and the Near East* (Tübingen, 1983).

5. See Collins, *Apocalypse,* p. 9.

6. These terms are taken from Adela Yarbro Collins, *The Apocalypse* (Wilmington, 1979), p. xi.

7. Augustine, *City of God* 20.7 and 9.

8. Ibid., 20.21 and 17.

9. Frank Kermode, *The Sense of an Ending: Studies in the Theory of Fiction* (New York, 1967).

10. Joachim of Fiore, *Exposition on Revelation* (Venice, 1527), fol. 39v.

11. Luther's 1522 Preface is found in *Luthers Werke,* vol. VII, *Die Deutsche Bibel* (Weimar, 1931), p. 404. For the 1530 Preface see ibid., pp. 407–421. Luther's views on Revelation have recently been treated by Hans-Ulrich Hofmann, *Luther und die Johannes-Apokalypse* (Tübingen, 1982).

12. Luther, 1530 Preface, *Deutsche Bibel,* p. 408.

13. Origen, *On First Principles* 2.11.2.

14. Methodius, *Symposium* 8.4–13. On the history of the interpretation of chapter 12, see Pierre Prigent, *Apocalypse 12. Histoire de l'exégèse* (Tübingen, 1959).

15. Victorinus, *Commentary on Revelation* 8.2–3.

16. On the Tyconian-Augustinian tradition see Wilhelm Kamlah, *Apokalypse und Geschichtstheologie* (Berlin, 1935); and Bernard McGinn, *The Calabrian Abbot: Joachim of Fiore in the History of Western Thought* (New York, 1985), chap. 2.

17. On these two types see Robert E. Lerner, "Joachim of Fiore's Breakthrough to Chiliasm," *Cristianesimo nella Storia,* 6 (1985), 500–501.

18. Joachim, *Exposition,* fol. 3r. On Joachim's exegesis see McGinn, *Calabrian Abbot,* chaps. 4 and 5.

19. Nicholas of Lyra, *Postil on All Scripture,* 6 vols. (Basel, 1506–08), VI, fol. 246v.

20. Ibid., fol. 270v.

21. Katharine R. Firth, *The Apocalyptic Tradition in Reformation Britain 1530–1645* (Oxford, 1979), p. 178.

22. Luther, 1530 Preface, *Deutsche Bibel,* p. 412.

23. John Bale, *The Image of Both Churches,* in *Select Works of John Bale, D.D.,* I (Cambridge, 1849), 253.

24. Thomas Brightman, *The Workes* (London, 1644), p. 825.

25. On Mede's method, see Murrin, "Revelation and Commentators."

26. Newton's *Observations upon the Prophecies of Daniel and the Apocalypse of St. John* appeared posthumously in 1733. Voltaire's remark was quoted in Bishop Thomas Newton's *Dissertations on the Prophecies,* III (London, 1759–60), 4.

27. See Ernest R. Sandeen, *The Roots of Fundamentalism: British and American Millenarianism 1800–1930* (Chicago, 1970), especially pp. 110–112.

28. Quoted by Stephen J. Stein, "Transatlantic Extensions: Apocalyptic in Early New England," in Patrides and Wittreich, *Apocalypse in English Renaissance Thought and Literature,* p. 277.

29. Quoted in Moses Stuart, *Commentary on the Apocalypse,* II (Andover, 1845), 501.

SUGGESTED FURTHER READINGS

Wilhelm Bousset, *Die Offenbarung Johannis* (Göttingen, 1906; reprint, 1966).

Adela Yarbro Collins, *Crisis and Catharsis: The Power of the Apocalypse* (Philadelphia, 1984).

John J. Collins, *The Apocalyptic Imagination: An Introduction to the Jewish Matrix of Christianity* (New York, 1984).

Austin Farrer, *A Rebirth of Images: The Making of St. John's Apocalypse* (Gloucester, Mass., 1970).

Elisabeth Schüssler Fiorenza, *The Book of Revelation: Justice and Judgment* (Philadelphia, 1985).

Katharine R. Firth, *The Apocalyptic Tradition in Reformation Britain 1530–1645* (Oxford, 1979).

Frank Kermode, *The Sense of an Ending: Studies in the Theory of Fiction* (New York, 1967).

D. H. Lawrence, *Apocalypse* (New York, 1960).

Bernard McGinn, *The Calabrian Abbot: Joachim of Fiore in the History of Western Thought* (New York, 1985).

C. A. Patrides and Joseph Wittreich, eds., *The Apocalypse in English Renaissance Thought and Literature* (Manchester, 1984).

University of Chicago

GENERAL ESSAYS

The Hebrew Bible and
Canaanite Literature

Jonas C. Greenfield

THE biblical writers drew in various ways and to varying degrees on the literary traditions of the surrounding Near Eastern world, Mesopotamian, Egyptian, Hittite, and Canaanite. The most immediate contact, however, was with Canaanite culture: hence a consideration of what the Hebrew writers adopted from their Canaanite predecessors provides an illuminating instance of their relation to contiguous and antecedent literatures.

Little was known about Canaanite culture before the discovery of the texts from Ugarit. Biblical references were sparse and on the whole negative, and the later Greek and Roman writers usually concentrated on limited aspects of Phoenician civilization, painting a picture of luxury and decadence. The corpus of Phoenician inscriptions was, and remains, small. A major source of information was the excerpts, in the works of later writers, of the *Phoenician History* of Philo of Byblos, who lived in the late first century–early second century C.E.

In 1929 Ras Shamra, a site in northern Syria not far from the port of Latakia, was accidentally discovered and then excavated by the French until 1939. This site proved to be Ugarit, a locality known from ancient texts; it was an important international trading center, significantly involved in the cultural and political life of second-millennium Syria. The 1930s saw the discovery of many texts written on clay tablets in a cuneiform alphabet of thirty letters. The language, called Ugaritic by scholars, proved to be a Canaanite dialect older than Hebrew, Phoenician, and the other known Canaanite dialects but sharing with them many common traits of morphology, vocabulary, and syntax. The tablets contained myths and epics, tales, legal and commercial documents, omen-texts, ritual and administrative texts, and correspondence. Some years after the Second World War, when excavations were resumed at Ras Shamra and expanded to nearby sites, new documents—including many in Akkadian and some in Hurrian and Hittite—were discovered. There has not been another major find of literary texts in Ugaritic.

Most of the literary texts in Ugaritic include the Ba'al epic, dealing with the leading figures in Canaanite mythology. There are also the tales of Aqhat and Keret and a series of minor stories. Although ritual texts have been found, no real liturgical text is known. The major literary texts were written down, as dated colophons inform us, during the reign of King Niqmaddu, around 1375. Many scholars assume that they were composed orally earlier and written down when, at about that time, the Ugaritic alphabet was devised. Although Ugarit was geographically not part of Canaan, it was a northern outpost of Canaanite culture. The tablets uncovered there provide us with a view of the pantheon, religious practices, mythology, and literature of the Canaanites. There were surely local variations and differences of emphasis; the Canaanites of Ugarit, Tyre, Ashkelon, Shechem, and Jerusalem surely had their own versions of various myths and rituals; but as the following pages will show, the version available in Canaan proper could not have differed much from that known in Ugarit. Contact with Canaanite culture continued long after the Canaanites had effectively disappeared from Judah and Israel. It remained the culture of the neighboring countries and formed the basis for popular beliefs and practices. But although Canaanite influence was strong and constant, considerable portions of the biblical corpus are free of it.

Varied use has been made of the Ugaritic texts in the study of the Hebrew Bible. Some discussions focus exclusively on the influence of these texts; others merely allude to their importance as reflections of Canaanite culture and literature; and still others neglect the texts entirely. Most studies of the texts from Ugarit concentrate on the following categories: the divine world of the Canaanites, the mythology of the Canaanites, the literary means available to the Canaanites, and the daily life of the Canaanites.

The Hebrew Bible refers in passing to a variety of Canaanite gods. These allusions are often lost on modern readers even if they know Hebrew, for the gods and their deeds (mythology) have been defunctionalized and are hard to recognize. In the Canaanite world of the second millennium, the formative period for Israel's development, the pantheon of Canaanite gods was still vital; their deeds were told in tales, hailed in epics, and praised in hymns. This tradition continued in the first millennium B.C.E. among the neighbors of Israel, primarily among the Phoenicians but also among the Aramaeans and the other inhabitants of the bordering lands. We cannot be sure how long these native traditions endured in Judah and Israel; some of them surely became part of the folk religion and survived into much later periods.

Before the discovery and publication of the Ugaritic corpus we were dependent upon disparate sources for information about Canaanite religion. The discovery of the Ugaritic texts has enhanced the usefulness of the scanty Phoenician corpus and of Eusebius' excursus on Phoenician religion in *Preparatio evangelica,* excerpted from the *Phoenician History* of

Philo of Byblos; but this material must still be treated with caution. Despite its pretensions to stem from ancient sources, it often reflects the Hellenistic tendencies of the author rather than reporting accurately the contemporary state of Phoenician or Canaanite religion. Philo reconstructs the genealogy of the gods as Elioun (= Elyon, the Most High), Ouranos (Heaven), Kronos (El), Zeus (Ba'al). The first two deities do not have a place as such in known Canaanite texts. However, in the witness list of the Aramaic Sfire treaty the gods El and Elyan (Elyon) are mentioned as a unit. We may assume that the scheme presented by Philo of Byblos was a later construct based on the need to match the divine genealogies known from the Hellenic and Hellenistic world, and that Elyon was an epithet of El. Thus in the oath taken by Melchizedek in Genesis 14:18–19, "Abram is blessed to El Elyon, creator of heaven and earth."[1] Melchizedek is called a "priest of El Elyon." In Phoenician, the epithet of El is *qoneh 'arets*, which may be translated "creator (or possessor) of the earth." This epithet may stand behind the enigmatic term *Elkunirsha* known from a Hittite text containing a Canaanite story and is found in both Punic and Palmyrene texts, as well as on an ostracon excavated in Jerusalem.

In the second millennium, to judge by the Ugaritic texts, the god El was the high god, but he had become otiose, transferred as it were to a sort of Olympus where he ruled over an assembly of the gods. Three younger gods were in dispute over the succession. Contrary to what some scholars have maintained, there was no conflict between El and his successors. It would seem that on one side there was Yam, the prime candidate, called Prince Sea and "friend of El"; and after him Mot, Death. On the other there was Ba'al, the storm god, a valiant hero and warrior who brings fertility to the land. Eventually Ba'al emerges ascendant. El is described as goodhearted and kindly, and at this stage weak, bullied by both his wife, Athirat, and his "daughter," Anat (although "daughter" may be used loosely); even so, one Ugaritic text credits him with a sexual escapade. The Ugaritic texts record no creation or flood story, although fragments from Akkadian texts excavated at Ugarit deal with elements of these stories. Some scholars have assumed that such stories were told at Ugarit, since El had the epithets "creator of creations" and "father of man." The first of these is indeed ambiguous, and the best that can be said is that El shares many traits with the Mesopotamian Enki/Ea, who according to the Atrahasis epic helped in man's creation. In the second epithet the word for "man" is the equivalent of Hebrew Adam, both a common noun and the name of the first man, but it would be foolhardy to build too much on that. El is responsible for health and well-being. It is to El that one turns when one is childless, as in the Aqhat tale; and in the Keret tale El blesses the newlywed Keret with fertility and later creates a goddess who removes Keret's serious illness. El is portrayed with very human attributes: his passions aroused, he may be cajoled to grant wishes;

he mourns the death of Ba'al; and he rejoices when Ba'al's resurrection is heralded in a dream.

The assembly of the gods is a well-known institution in ancient Near Eastern religion. It is in the assembly of the gods that the decision is taken to punish tumultuous mankind by means of the flood, and in the Babylonian creation epic it is the assembly that commissions Marduk to defeat Tiamat the sea goddess and her chaotic henchmen; Marduk is elevated to head of the assembly, a sort of *primus inter pares,* after accomplishing this feat. El is described as presiding over the assembly, with Ba'al waiting upon him. The assembly takes place in El's holy mountain, which is not to be confused with Ba'al's Mount Sapunu or Mons Casius; it was called *m'd,* Hebrew *mo'ed,* "assembly." Even after Ba'al becomes head of the gods, the assembly remains the domain of El. The assembly is mirrored in various forms in the biblical corpus, the most obvious reference being Psalms 82:1, where the gods are described as assembled in the congregation of El. The mountain of the assembly (*har mo'ed*) is also mentioned in Isaiah 14:13, with further reminiscences in Psalms 89:5–8 and 29:1–2, 1 Kings 22:19, and Isaiah 6:1–8. It is before the assembly of the gods that the dramatic scene of Daniel 7:9–14 takes place. The "tent of the assembly," *'ohel mo'ed,* originally partook of this meaning, since this was the place where God was to meet with the children of Israel.

Although Ba'al's mountain, Sapunu, is easily locatable at Jebel el-aqra', to the north of Ugarit, the location of El's remains a matter of speculation. The texts indicate that it must be approached by water, "toward El at the source[s] of the rivers / in the midst of the headwaters of the two deeps." Perhaps it is the Amanus, which ranges along the southern shores of present-day Turkey, between Iskenderun and Antakya, and is now called Nur. These mountains literally descend into the sea.

Ba'al is a more aggressive god than El; he is a warrior, as his epithets reveal, and in the Ugaritic tales he eventually defeats both Yam and Mot (Death). With the aid of Anat he also defeats Yam's henchman. During these travails Mot for some time has power over Ba'al, who is "swallowed up" by Mot's open mouth. Ba'al goes down to the netherworld to return only after seven years, years in which the earth suffers drought. Ba'al lives on Mount Sapunu (biblical Zaphon), and part of the Ba'al epic deals with the fact that he does not have a proper dwelling place there. With the intervention of Athirat (the Ugaritic form of Ashera) El grants him the right to a palace built by the master craftsman god Kothar-and-Hasis. In the course of Ba'al's exploits he also commits bestiality. The cause of Ba'al's death is not clearly stated; his corpse is found and buried by Anat with the help of the goddess Shapash.

Athirat/Ashera is El's consort, her numerous offspring are called children of El, but she lives apart and looks to her own affairs, seeking to make one of her children ruler after Ba'al has vanished. The first candidate is too weak to take Ba'al's place, and the second, though described as a hero, cannot sit on Ba'al's oversized throne. Ashera has essentially two epithets: *qaniyatu ilim,* "creatress of the gods," descriptive of her function as the leading goddess; and *rabbatu 'athiratu yammi,* which has not been convincingly interpreted. We may translate it simply as "Lady Athirat of the sea." The god Yam (Sea) would in all likelihood have been El's choice for a successor. Indeed when Yam's emissaries demand Ba'al's surrender, El and the council of the gods succumb without resistance; Ba'al, however, battles Yam and defeats him. Mot's role is different; late in the epic Mot challenges Ba'al and it is clear that Ba'al fears him; there is almost a degree of inevitability in this relationship. At one point Ba'al even offers to become Mot's eternal servant in order to save his own life. Mot is described as having a very wide mouth, which swallows up those who go down into it, and his habitation is described as miry. Although Ba'al's corpse is found and buried, it is as if he has been swallowed by Mot. After Ba'al's resurrection he has a dire struggle with Mot and emerges victorious. This sequence perhaps indicates that the struggle between life and death is to be viewed as a continuous battle.

Ba'al's consort in the Ugaritic texts is the goddess Anat, who has been called, following the model of the Mesopotamian Inanna/Ishtar, a "goddess of love and war." Most scholars assume that Ba'al was her lover, although there is no explicit reference in the texts to such a relationship; she is called his "sister/daughter of his father," but this would not have constituted a taboo (cf. Abraham and Sarah, Gen. 20:12). Anat aids Ba'al in his battle with Yam, mourns and buries Ba'al after Mot vanquishes him, and in turn harrows and destroys Mot. In the texts she is characterized by both ferocity and tenderness and her chief epithet is "virgin," indicating that she does not bear children. Except for the name of the town Anatot and the enigmatic Shamgar ben Anath (Judges 3:31, 5:6) she is not mentioned in the Hebrew Bible, in contrast to Ashtart (Ashtoret), who plays only a slight role in the extant Ugaritic texts but is the leading Canaanite goddess in the first millennium B.C.E.

Of the host of minor gods in the Ugaritic texts, three deserve mention: Shaḥru (Hebrew Shaḥar), Shalmu (Hebrew Shalem), and Rashpu (Hebrew Reshef). Shaḥar is known to stand behind the second component in the name Helel ben Shaḥar in Isaiah 14:12, but the mythological referent remains unclear. Shalem is a component of the name Jerusalem (Gen. 14:18, Ps. 76:2). Rashpu is the god of pestilence and equated with the Akkadian Nergal. In the Hebrew Bible the word *reshef* is used for a demon (Deut. 32:24, Hab. 3:5), disease (Ps. 78:48), and sparks and fiery arrows (Ps. 76:3, Job 5:7, Song of Songs 8:6).

One of the most fruitful areas of research regarding the influence of Canaanite literature on biblical literature has concerned poetic technique. What poetic and rhetorical devices did the Hebrew poets inherit from their Canaanite predecessors? Or, if we do not want to speak in terms of influence or even of a heritage, the question becomes, What did the Hebrew writer share with the Canaanite writer?

On the simplest level are the numerous word pairs known from Ugaritic that are found later in Hebrew and, to a more limited degree, because of our lack of sources, in Phoenician. At least fifty such word pairs are known to us, and some scholars would claim more than twice that number. Sometimes the pairs are used simply in parallel—"house/court," "house/palace," "orphan/widow," "father/lord," "gold/silver," "chair/throne," "hand/right hand," "smite/strike," "smite/destroy," "smite/hack," "build/raise," "eat/consume," and so on; sometimes three verbs are used, forming a triad instead of a pair. Ugaritic poetry combines some of these pairs in a construct relationship (two words that are connected morphologically in Hebrew to form a phrase or concept) such as "land of his inheritance" (as in Isa. 49:8; Jer. 2:7, 16:18) or in chiasms. All these devices are found in the biblical corpus. Indeed, most Ugaritic word pairs are also known from the biblical corpus. The biblical writers rang their changes on the inherited material and, on the whole, used it with great subtlety.

A good example is the word pair 'oz/zimrah, "strength/might," whose Ugaritic counterpart occurs in a text published some years ago. In that text is also found the Ugaritic equivalent of sir/zammer, "to sing/sing hymns" (literally, "to tell the mighty deeds of"). The first pair is known from Exodus 15:2, "the Lord is my strength and my might" (see also Isa. 12:2, Ps. 118:14), and the second pair is frequent in Psalms. In Psalms 59:17 the first word pair is transformed, "O my strength [uzzi], to you I sing hymns [azammera]." Psalms 18:37–40 (= 2 Sam. 22:38–41) provides an example of the use of an extended word pair; that is, two related pairs are used together and blend into each other. The pairs are "smite/destroy" (mhs/klh) and "smite/strike down" (mhs/smt): "I pursued my enemies and overtook them, and did not turn back till I destroyed them [kallotam]. I smote them ['emhasem], and they could rise no more; they lie fallen at my feet. You have girded me with strength for battle, brought my adversaries [qamay] low before me; made my enemies ['oyebay] turn tail before me; I struck down my foes [mesann'ay wa'asmitem]" [AT]. In these lines there are two other shared and blended word pairs, "adversary/enemy" and "enemy/foe," as well as the phrase "fall at the feet of," known from Ugaritic. The use of the word pair mhs/smt also has an internal chiastic effect on this unit.

In addition to the use of word pairs, a variety of other rhetorical means were shared, such as the use of the same verb in parallelism in the perfect and imperfect tenses, or of the same root in the active and passive voices. Knowledge of this device has served as a corrective to the tendency, easily observed in the notes to the various editions of the Biblica Hebraica, to equalize the tenses and the verbal voice. Thus when the Hebrew says "he has acted/he will act" or "he will build/let it be built," there is no need to put both parts of the parallelism into the same tense or the same voice. Another important feature of both traditions was the posing of rhetorical questions. The double rhetorical question in Ugaritic would be "Is it kingship like the Bull, his father, he desires, or authority like the Father of Man?" In Ugaritic, where there is no interrogative *he,* the first part begins with a zero element (with voice intonations), and the second is introduced by *hm,* "if, or"; while a good Hebrew example would be "Will you really reign over us, or indeed rule over us?" (Gen. 37:8), with the first part introduced by the interrogative *he* and the second by *'im.* The two traditions also use the triple rhetorical question, achieved by the addition of "why" (*ik* in Ugaritic, *maddu'a/lama* in Hebrew). The Hebrew poets greatly expanded the possibilities of this device.

Word pairs are found throughout the Hebrew Bible, in the Aramaic Book of Daniel, and in later literature too. Thus "laughter/joy" and "reach/come," found in the Ba'al epic, also occur in Ecclesiastes 2:2 and Daniel 7:13, respectively. Other word pairs in the Hebrew Bible are not known from Ugaritic, but since word pairs are also known from Akkadian and Arabic, it is clear that this is a constitutive element of Semitic poetry.

Another feature of Hebrew poetry that has been noted in recent years is the break-up of stereotyped phrases. This device, as far as we know, is rarely used in Ugaritic, but it sometimes occurs in a phrase inherited from Canaanite poetry. An example is *srrt spn,* "the fastness of Sapunu," referring to the remote parts of the mountain on which Ba'al made his home. The two elements of the phrase are found in Hosea 13:12: "Ephraim's guilt is bound up [*sarur*], his sin stored away [*sefuna*]"; another example occurs in Job 26:7–8.

The use of word pairs depends naturally upon parallelism. Parallelism has long been recognized as a feature of biblical poetry, but it was Bishop Lowth (1710–1787) who gave it its deserved prominence. In recent years some scholars have disputed its importance, and others have made of this relatively straightforward feature a complex and quasi-mathematical process. Ugaritic poetry shows a developed use of parallelism with sufficient examples of the major types familiar to us from the analysis of Hebrew poetry: synonymous, antithetical, synthetic, semantic, and climactic parallelism. The parallel units may consist of two or three versets, the latter often consisting of the "expanded colons" that have been much discussed in recent studies of Hebrew and Ugaritic poetry. As with the other rhetorical techniques discussed above, the biblical writers displayed more virtuosity than the Ugaritic writers in the use of parallelism.

The issue of meter in Hebrew and Ugaritic poetry also deserves mention. Although the presence of meter in Ugaritic poetry would not necessarily imply its existence in Hebrew poetry, it would make it more

probable. The recent fashion of syllable counting is at best a dubious
exercise, for we have no means of determining the correct vocalization of
the Ugaritic text or of pre-Masoretic Hebrew, not to speak of the actual
vowel quantities, so vital in such an attempt. There is no way to assign a
purely quantitative (that is, metric) system to Ugaritic poetry; there is no
fixed meter. Probably there was a basic stress system which could tolerate
many variations, a sort of free rhythm equally suited for singing or
recitation and allowed for great flexibility in length of line. There were
undoubtedly basic rules by which the poet worked, but these were determined by parallelism and word pairs and by syntactic and phonetic needs.
The same is true both of biblical passages that clearly show a Canaanite
background and of those that seem free of such influence.

Discussions of parallelism and word pairs often quote the following
passage from the Ba'al epic:

> Now, your enemy O Ba'al
>   now, you smite your enemy
>   you strike your adversary;
>   you will take your eternal kingdom
>   your everlasting dominion.

The first group of three versets is a good example of triadic parallelism.
These five lines contain four word pairs: "enemy/adversary," "smite/
strike," "eternal/everlasting," "dominion/kingdom." The first three pairs
also occur in biblical Hebrew; in the last pair Hebrew substitutes *memshala*
for Ugaritic *drkt*. The triad has long since been compared with Psalms
92:9: "Surely, Your enemies, O Lord, / surely, Your enemies perish; / all
evildoers are scattered." It is clear that from the purely formal point of
view the two verses resemble each other only in the invocation, in the
use of the pair "enemy/adversary," and in rhythm. Yet closer analysis of
Psalms 92:8 and 93:4 reveals still stronger resemblances. Psalms 92:8 reads:
"but You are exalted [*marom*] O Lord for all time." In Psalms 93:4 *marom*
recurs, translated "on high." *Mrym*, the Ugaritic cognate of *marom*, describes the highest point of Ba'al's holy mountain, Sapunu. In Hebrew
marom, besides meaning simply a height, is also the height of Zion (*merom
Siyyon*, Jer. 31:12); the "heights" are the heavens in which God dwells (2
Sam. 22:17 = Ps. 18:16; Isa. 33:5, 57:15; Jer. 25:30; Ps. 102:19, 144:7).
Therefore, the use of *marom* to designate God along with the adverb
le'olam, "for all times," connects Psalms 92:9 to the idea expressed in the
dyad of the Ugaritic text quoted above. Indeed, if we consider Psalm 93
as a sequel to Psalm 92, following liturgical usage, "your throne stands
from of old: from eternity You have existed [that is, reigned]" (93:2)
echoes clearly the sentiment of the Ugaritic text.

Psalm 92 constitutes what I have come to call a cluster: the psalmist
consciously or unconsciously reuses and reshapes phrases from Canaanite

literature. Psalms 21:2–4 provides another example. In verse 3 of this royal psalm, the rare word 'areshet, "desire, request," occurs with natatta, "you gave." Both echo the Ugaritic tale in which Anat, trying to get Aqhat's bow (a possible sexual reference), first says to him: "Ask for silver and I'll give it to you / for gold, and I'll bestow it on you." After Aqhat rejects her first offer, she raises the stakes: "Ask ['rsh] for life, O Aqhat the youth / ask for life [ḥym] and I will give it to you [atnk] / for deathlessness, and I'll bestow it on you." Psalms 21:2–4 says of the king:

> "You have given him [natatta] the desire of his heart
> You have not denied the request ['areshet] of his lips . . .
> You have set upon his head a crown of fine gold.
> He asked for life [ḥym]; You granted it;
> a long life, everlasting.

Three of the vocables used in the Ugaritic text are found here: 'areshet, "request"; ḥayyim, "life"; and ntn, "to give, grant." The psalmist, knowing that deathlessness is not attainable, has substituted "long life," strengthened by the modifier "everlasting." "Gold" is adduced in the form of the royal crown. In verse 13 nashira wanezammera, "we will sing hymns," is also known from Ugaritic.

Two of the themes in Psalm 24 are God's supremacy and the need for purity in order to go up to the mountain of the Lord: "Who may ascend to the mountain of the Lord? / Who may stand in his holy place?" (v. 3). Both "mountain" and "holy place" are epithets of Mount Sapunu. The psalmist's command "O gates lift up your heads" (v. 9) was noted in the early days of Ugaritic studies as echoing Ba'al's encouragement to the gods when they cowered before Yam's emissaries: "Lift up, O gods, your heads from your knees." In verse 2 God has "founded the world on the seas / and established it on the rivers"—that is, after the defeat of Yam; and in verses 7–8 God enters the gates and is hailed as a hero, mighty and valiant.

Psalm 27 contains many disparate elements and themes, but there is a cluster of Canaanite terms. Verse 2 uses the word pair "foes/enemies." Verse 4 contains an inverted reminiscence of the phrase from Aqhat quoted above: the psalmist asks not for life as such, but "to sit in the house of the Lord all the days of my life." In the next phrase he expresses his desire "to gaze upon the beauty of the Lord, to frequent His temple." No'am, translated "beauty" here, is used in Ugaritic as an epithet for the sanctuary (qdsh) of Ba'al: "in the midst of my mount, godly Sapunu / in the sanctuary (qdsh) mount of my possession, / in the pleasance [n'm], the hill I possess." Therefore, no'am YHWH should be translated "YHWH's pleasant place" and is a parallel to "temple" (hekal). The cluster continues into verse 5, which begins with yispeneni, "he will shelter me" and finishes with besur yeromemeni, "he will raise me high upon a rock." For the ear tuned to

Canaanite the first word in the verse echoes Sapunu, Ba'al's mountain; the last word echoes *mrym* in *mrym spn*, "the height of Sapunu," mentioned above, and is thus another example of the break-up of a stereotyped phrase; and in *sur* there is an echo of the Ugaritic/Canaanite word for mountain, also known in Hebrew. All told, Psalm 27, which unlike Psalm 29 does not have an explicit Canaanite background and does not directly use any of the usual mythological themes, nevertheless exhibits a cluster of words and phrases that relate it to the Canaanite tradition.

Deuteronomy 32:6–7 closes one unit (vv. 5–6) and opens another (vv. 7–9): "Do you thus requite the Lord, O dull and witless people? Is not he the father [*'abika*] who created you [*qaneka*], who formed you and made you endure [*wayekoneneka*]? Remember the days of old. Consider the years of ages past; ask your father, he will inform you; your elders, they will tell you." The language comes, on the whole, from the description of El. The people are called "witless," *lo' hakam*, that is, lacking the basic characteristic of El. The first and third verbs—*qny*, "create," and *knn*, "establish"—are used of El; "eternity ['*lm*]/ages past [*dr dr*]" is a well-known word pair, but both words are also epithets of El. Verse 8, which mentions "the most High" (Elyon) and "the sons of Adam [man]," presents on the one hand another epithet of El and on the other reminds us that El was called "father of man" (*ab adm*). The author of Deuteronomy 32 has skillfully woven into his covenant poem these and other elements of antecedent literary tradition.

One final good example of a cluster occurs in Ezekiel 28:2–6, the last of three poems dealing with Tyre. It derisively accuses the king of Tyre of likening himself to El, and just as El's dwelling was in the midst of the sea, so is the dwelling of the king of Tyre (an allusion to Tyre's location on an island). The prophet then upbraids the king for considering himself wise, indeed wiser than Daniel/Danel, who is praised for his piety and his role as a judge in the Ugaritic tale of Aqhat and is also known from Ezekiel 14:14 and later material. Judgment, as the story of Solomon shows, is one of the clearest signs of wisdom (1 Kings 3:16–28). The prophet tells the king of Tyre that he is proved to be a man and not a god by the hands of those who will kill him (v. 9). The contrast between the king of Tyre and El goes back to the role of El as father of man, but himself deathless. The prophet uses against the king of Tyre his sharpest rebuke, invoking language from Canaanite epic tales that were surely familiar to Tyrians. The "Lament on the king of Tyre" in 28:12–19 must also be based on Canaanite material as yet unknown to us; one reference, verse 14b, must go back to a reference to El's holy mountain, the place of the divine assembly, known to us from Ugarit.

The similes used by Ugaritic poets are often the same as those encountered in biblical poetry. For example, four lines of a recently published Ugaritic text from Ras Ibn Hani, a site near Ugarit, call on the evildoers to leave "like smoke from a lattice / like a snake on a pillar / like a mountain goat/ibex to its rock / like a lion to its lair." All of these except the second image have biblical parallels. Although the word for smoke is different, Hosea 13:3 provides a good typological parallel:

> Therefore they will be like a morning cloud
> and like early-morning dew that disappears,
> like chaff driven from the threshing floor
> and like smoke from the lattice.

The ibex and its mountain haunts are mentioned in 1 Samuel 24:3 (with the same word for rock as in the Ugaritic text) and Psalms 104:18. The last Ugaritic simile, "like a lion to its lair," raises interesting questions of interpretation. The Ugaritic word for lair or thicket is *sk*. Its Hebrew equivalent, *sok*, occurs in Jeremiah 25:38, where it is said of God: "like a lion He has gone forth from His lair," and also in Psalms 10:9 and Job 38:39–40. On the basis of Jeremiah 4:7, "The lion has come forth from this thicket [*subko*]," various scholars have proposed emending *sukko*, "his lair," to *subko* in the verses referred to above. The Ugaritic text demonstrates that the word for "lair" is indeed *sk* rather than *sbk* (*sobek*), and indeed it may be Jeremiah 4:7 that needs emendation. Psalms 27:5 may also require additional study, for *sukkoh* is usually translated "his pavilion" because of its parallelism with *'ohalo*, "his tent," in "grant me the protection of his tent." But in light of the pairing of "rock" with "lair" in the Ugaritic text, may there not be a trace of intended ambiguity here with *sukkoh* standing parallel with both *'ohalo*, "his tent," and *sur*, "rock," in the last verset? Clearly, we cannot appreciate the actual complexity of a seemingly simple text without knowledge of the Ugaritic material.

Among the epithets of El reflected in biblical texts is *abu shanima*, "father of years." This image of El recurs vividly in Daniel's vision (7:9), where God is called in Aramaic "the Ancient of days," his garment is "white as snow, and the hair of his head like pure wool." In Psalms 102:24–28, where the poet asks that his days not be shortened, he addresses God as *'eli*, which may be translated "my God," but it is clear that the choice of divine name was deliberate. He continues: "do not take me away in the middle of my *life*, You whose *years* endure generations on end." He goes on to say that even heaven and earth—usually considered eternal—will pass away, "but You are He whose *years* are without end." This theme is also found in Job 36:26: "See, God [El] is greater than we can know / the number of his years cannot be counted." El has both great age and wisdom. In an interesting passage, after he has approved of building a palace for Ba'al he is told by Ba'al: "You are aged, O El, and indeed wise; / your hoary age has instructed you." Are we to hear in Psalms 105:22b ("to . . . teach his elders wisdom") an ironic reflection of this phrase? And is the sentiment echoed and challenged in these verses from

Job: "Is wisdom in the aged, and understanding in the long-lived?" (12:12) and "I thought, 'Let age speak, let advanced years declare wise things' . . . It is not the aged who are wise: the elders who understand how to judge" (32:7, 9)?

Elsewhere in Job, an understanding of the text depends on recognition of its ancient source, El's connection with wisdom. In chapter 27 Job begins a long peroration with a declaration of God's (El's) injustice toward him and then describes how God treats the wicked. Chapter 28 describes mankind's uncovering of the earth's mineral wealth. In verse 11 Job says: "He dams up the source of the streams," thus echoing the description of El's dwelling place, quoted above. In verse 12, as if the scene has been set by the reference of El's dwelling place, Job asks: "But where can wisdom be found: where is the source of understanding?" Two answers are given: the deep/the sea (Yam) says: "I do not have it, it is not with me" (v. 14); and perdition/death (Mot) says: "We have only a report of it" (v. 22). Yam and Mot have a special relationship with El, according to the Ugaritic texts: both are "beloved of Yam." Philo of Byblos tells us that since they were the children of El, it was therefore only natural that they would be asked about the whereabouts of Wisdom. The answer given in Job 28:23 is that only God understands.

In the Ugaritic texts, Ba'al begins as a sort of underdog, with Yam courting success as the favorite; but, if the interpretation which seems most plausible is correct, Ba'al emerges as the hero who batters Yam, dries him up, and makes an end to him. The triumphant cry was "Yam is truly dead, Ba'al will reign!" Elsewhere the Ba'al epic tells of the smiting and destruction of Ba'al's henchman, who is called either Lotan (a conventional reading of *LTN*, long recognized as the equivalent of biblical Leviathan) or *tunnanu*, "dragon" (= Hebrew *tannin*). One of Lotan's epithets is "the elusive serpent"; the text also informs us that Lotan had seven heads. This mythological figure has become the source of a powerful series of images in the biblical corpus. The most straightforward parallel is Isaiah 27:1: "On that day the Lord will punish with his great, cruel and mighty sword Leviathan the elusive serpent, Leviathan the twisting serpent, and will slay the dragon of the sea."

The biblical texts take up this topos in a variety of ways. The monster becomes a metaphor for the personification of chaos or, as in Isaiah 27:1, for the forces of evil. In Psalms 74:13–14:

> It was You who drove back the sea with Your might,
>> who smashed the heads of the monsters in the waters;
> it was You who crushed the heads of Leviathan,
>> who left him as food for the denizens of the desert.

Mentioning the heads of Leviathan makes the referent clear, but there is a serious distinction between the two traditions, for in the biblical account

Yam is not destroyed. He is rebuked, restrained, dried up (for example, Isa. 17:13, 50:2, Nahum 1:4; Jer. 5:22; Hab. 3:8; Ps. 89:10; Job 7:12, 26:12–13). In the biblical writers' realistic sense of things it was impossible to describe the sea as dead. The distinction is drawn between Yam's henchman, who is destroyed, and Yam himself; thus in Isaiah 51:9–10: "it was You who hacked Rahab in pieces, that pierced the Dragon;/it was You who divided up the waters of the great deep."

In the Ugaritic tale Ba'al must defeat Yam in order to achieve rule, but there is nothing more than that in the text, notwithstanding scholars' efforts to interpret those texts as indicating that Ba'al imposed order on a chaotic world, and the battle with Yam as thus taking on cosmogonic significance. There are two reasons for this line of thought, the first being that in the Hebrew Bible the theme of the defeat of the sea is connected with creation, as in Psalms 74:16–17:

> The day is Yours, the night also;
>   it was You who set in place the orb of the sun;
> You fixed all the boundaries of the earth;
>   summer and winter You made them.

Defeat of the monster symbolizing chaos, followed by creation and the ordering of the universe, is known also from the Babylonian creation epic, a work which may have come under western Semitic influence before it was written down, which happened after the composition of the Ugaritic texts. Be that as it may, this creation theme is lacking in the Ugaritic texts that have reached us.

This theme is also used by prophet and psalmist for historical and eschatological purposes. The "splitting of the sea" ceased to be a literal bashing of Yam, but the passing of the Israelites through the Reed Sea in the Exodus was viewed as a reenactment of that event; so Isaiah 51:10b reads: "that made the abyss of the sea a road that the redeemed might walk." The theme then becomes part of an eschatological promise to bring the exiled back to the Promised Land. A high point in the development of the theme is Exodus 15, the "Song of the Sea," in which the battle with the sea is transferred to one between Pharaoh and his forces at the sea. The sea is metamorphosed into a weapon with which to overwhelm and destroy the Egyptians. In this "song" the might of the Lord is praised and he is called a "man of war." Exodus 15:2–3 contains many items that can now be associated with the Canaanite poetic tradition through a known Ugaritic equivalent; thus *'ozi wezimrat Yah*, "the Lord is my might and strength"; and verse 17 presents a cluster of phrases from the Canaanite repertoire: "the mountain of your inheritance," "the place of your abode," and "the sanctuary which your hands established."

Some scholars have compared the "Song of the Sea" and the Ugaritic Ba'al epic in great detail, seeking a "deep structural" connection. But these efforts seem exaggerated. The receding of the Reed Sea, the "turning back" of the river Jordan (as in Psalm 114), and the various references to the drying of the sea/river are later reflexes of the myth historicized and used as part of either the prophetical repertoire or the liturgy.

The elements in the description of the construction and destruction of the Golden Calf can also be traced back to the Ugaritic corpus. The biblical accounts are contradictory. In Exodus 32:4 a mold or a bag seems to have been used to hold the gold rings when they were thrown into the fire, from which the molten calf emerged; but in 32:24 Aaron simply states that he took the gold, threw it into the fire, and the calf emerged. The latter version has been compared with the formation of Ba'al's palace, which emerged fully built from a conflagration of choicest cedars in which gold, silver, and precious stones were burned for seven days. The destruction of the calf as described in 32:20—"he took the calf that they had made and burnt it; he ground it to powder and strewed it upon the water and made the Israelites drink it"—has been compared typologically with the treatment of Mot at the hands of vengeful Anat, after Mot has swallowed up Ba'al: "she seized divine Mot, she hacked him with a sword, she winnowed him with a sieve, she burnt him with fire, she ground him with millstones, she scattered him in the field, his flesh was eaten by the birds, his pieces by the fowl." In this case nothing in the content connects the two elements, but the typology of the action taken in disposing of the Golden Calf is clarified. Some have also pointed to the image in Ezekiel 5:12—"a third will die in the plague . . . a third will fall by the sword, and a third I will disperse" (see also Ezek. 12, 14–15; 30:26)—as echoing the motif known from the same Ugaritic text about Mot. It would be at best a faint echo, but an interesting one, for the Hebrew counterpart of the Ugaritic word for "flesh," *she'er*, can be mistaken for the phonetically similar Hebrew word for "remainder," (*she'ar*) found in some of these texts.

An image that has its origin in Canaanite mythology is that of the mouth of death (Mot). After Ba'al defeats Yam and receives permission to build a palace, the threat of Mot remains. The gods are here portrayed in very human likeness. Mot is described as having "a lip to the earth, a lip to heaven." At death, then, one is swallowed by Mot and thus descends into the netherworld. In Numbers 16:30 Moses says of Korah and his band that "if the Lord act, and the earth open wide its mouth and swallow them and all that belongs to them, and they go down alive into Sheol" it will be understood that they have provoked the Lord; and in verses 32–33 "the earth opened its mouth and swallowed them . . . and they went down alive into Sheol." As many commentators have noted, the word *'erets* means both "earth" and "underworld."

This image of engulfment is found in a variety of texts. Examples include: "Who has made his maw as wide as Sheol, who is insatiable as death" (Hab. 2:5); "Sheol has opened wide its gullet and parted its jaws in a measureless gape" (Isa. 5:14). "Going down to the pit" is one of the usual terms for death (Ezek. 32:29; Ps. 28:1, 88:5–6; Prov. 1:12). When death is defeated the image is reversed: "He will surely destroy [literally, 'swallow'] death forever, and the Lord God will wipe the tears away from all faces" (Isa. 25:8).

The Ugaritic texts allow us to trace the background of some modes of action recorded in the Hebrew Bible. They often assume narrative significance even for readers who are unaware that the action recorded is traditional. Thus in the story of the divine messengers' visitation to Abraham in Genesis 18:1–8, Sarah is assigned the task of preparing loaves of bread for them, and Abraham goes out to get a calf for the dinner and prepares other food. This sequence has often been taken as a sign of Abraham's hospitality; however, the same action is known from the Aqhat story, in which Danel sends his wife to get a calf to feed the craftsman god Kothar-and-Hasis. The Ugaritic story has the double narrative often adopted by the biblical writers, in which a person is told what to do, and the action is then recounted.

The Ugaritic texts provide us with descriptions of what was normative under certain circumstances. A good example is the detailed account of the mourning scene after El is told that Ba'al is dead (repeated verbatim in the description of Anat's reaction to the news). El descends from his throne and sits first on his footstool, then on the ground; he puts on a loincloth, pours dust on his head, cuts his body and face, harrows his chest and back, and cries: "Ba'al is dead . . . after Ba'al I will descend into the netherworld." Biblical descriptions of mourning are found in 2 Kings 18:28; Jeremiah 16:6; and Job 1:20; 2:8, 12. Ezekiel in his lamentation over Tyre makes excellent use of the mourning *topos*. In 26:16 he describes how the naval magnates will sit on the ground with their finery removed, and in 27:29–31 he carries the image further by having the sailors leave their ships to pour earth on their heads, dress in sackcloth, tear their hair, and lament (see also 7:18). El's lament, "after Ba'al I will go down into the netherworld," has been compared with Jacob's. After he is shown the bloody cloak and concludes that Joseph is dead, Jacob tears his garments, dresses himself in sackcloth, and declares: "I will go down to the netherworld in mourning for my son" (Gen. 37:35). In the Aqhat tale, after the death of Aqhat is established and his remains buried, female mourners, called "wailers and mourners," enter Danel's home accompanied by men who slash their skin. The female mourners are known from biblical (Jer. 16–17) and later tradition. Gashing the skin and cutting the flesh in mourning are mentioned in Jeremiah 16:6, 1 Kings 18:28, and elsewhere and are forbidden by biblical legislation (Deut. 14:1). Of numerous other instances of the continuity of customs, mores, and beliefs, two others are worth noting here: the *marzeah*, a sort of association or club known from Amos

(6:7) and Jeremiah (16:5), is mentioned in both Ugaritic and Akkadian texts found at Ras Shamra and in Phoenician and Aramaic texts as late as the third century c.e.; and the *rephaim*, "shades," who dwell in the underworld (for example, Isa. 14:9, 26:14; Ps. 88:11; Job 26:5) play a role in Ugaritic texts and are mentioned in a late text from Carthage.

Many of the features discussed above can also be found in the available Phoenician inscriptions, as well as in early Aramaic texts. The Hebrew writers have been called "good students" of their Canaanite predecessors, but it is more accurate to designate them as active participants in a broader literary culture: they were participants and also innovators.

NOTE

1. All translations of the Bible are based on the New Jewish Publication Society's *Tanakh: A New Translation of the Holy Scriptures according to the Traditional Hebrew Text* (Philadelphia, 1985).

SUGGESTED FURTHER READINGS

J. C. L. Gibson, *Canaanite Myths and Legends* (Edinburgh, 1978).

H. L. Ginsberg, "Ugaritic Myths, Epics and Legends," in J. B. Pritchard, ed., *Ancient Near Eastern Texts Relating to the Old Testament* (Princeton, 1969), pp. 129–155.

My indebtedness to W. F. Albright, André Caquot, M. D. Cassuto, F. M. Cross, T. H. Gaster, H. L. Ginsberg, C. H. Gordon, Moshe Held, Agnes Herder, Arvid Kapelrud, B. A. Levine, S. E. Loewenstamm, J. C. de Moor, D. G. Pardee, M. H. Pope, Stanislau Segert, Maurice Sznycer, and others will be apparent to those familiar with the literature.

Hebrew University of Jerusalem

The New Testament and Greco-Roman Writing

Helen Elsom

THE New Testament is written in Greek and is addressed—explicitly in Luke's dedications and the Epistles—to an audience which lives in the world of the Greek-speaking eastern Roman Empire. The expectations of its intended readers, which we should understand when we read the text, are influenced by this fact. The Greek language, with its literary and philosophical traditions, was part of the "official" culture of the empire, in that administrators were expected to have at least a smattering of Greek language and literature. Moreover, although the New Testament is a rewriting of Jewish Scripture, the actual text to which it alludes is the Septuagint version, which had already begun the process of rewriting the Scriptures for the Hellenistic world. The later history of Christianity suggests that it was helped on its way to becoming the dominant religion by the fact that its sacred texts were written in Greek and in literary forms which, if not Greek themselves, could be understood in Greek terms, popular as well as learned.

Although the substance of the Jewish scriptural background was also important, the special nature of Greek literary writing in the Greco-Roman period made it possible for non-Greek texts to be assimilated to the Greek classics and used as models in the same way. By the Roman period, Greek prose had—superficially at least—become highly derivative and was produced almost mechanically by variation on and combination of set themes, often taken from classical Greek history, drama, or philosophy. But this writing often reflected interests very different from those of the classical period. During the Hellenistic and Roman periods, for instance, interest in the individual arose and increased, perhaps as a result of the significance for the history of their times of the personalities of Hellenistic monarchs and Roman emperors. Three new genres—biography, prose fiction, and biographical romance—provided a means of exploring the character of a historical figure or the experiences of an individual. But these works were written in classical Attic Greek and took their subjects and themes as well as their language from the classical past.

The New Testament also reorganized traditional material, reworking

561

Jewish texts and ideas in forms accessible to Greco-Roman readers. The narratives of the Gospels all use texts from Scripture which concern the Messiah, but the events which "enact" these texts (that is, "fulfill the prophets") are organized as a narrative of the active life of an individual, in the same way that the synthetic Hellenistic biographies of classical figures focus on the significant actions of their adult lives. Similarly, Paul employs letters, a literary medium used by Greek philosophers and Roman rulers as well as by the Jewish religious authorities, to convey his teaching about the life and significance of Jesus. His rhetorical technique and philosophical themes recall those of Greco-Roman philosophical rhetoric. In fact the New Testament represents the transformation of the world in history by means of the transformation of the Messiah of Scripture into a Greco-Roman culture hero.

Of the works in the New Testament, the Synoptic Gospels, Acts, and Paul's Epistles to the churches can be most easily analyzed in Greco-Roman terms, since they contain formal elements which suggest that they should be read in these terms. The remaining works are excluded from the discussion for very different reasons. The Pastoral Epistles can be seen to fit into the broad pattern of Greco-Roman letters, but they are too brief to require a complex reading. The Apocalypse and the Gospel of John both represent special cases: both have Hellenistic Jewish antecedents, but each represents a completely different concept of history and theological outlook.

The Gospels and Acts: Narrative Genres

Biblical scholars are still discussing the question of the "genre" of the Gospels, of the composite Luke–Acts, and of the Apocalypse in relation to both scriptural and Greek genres. Often they attempt to show that the Gospels are like other specific Greek texts, and therefore of the same "kind." For instance, similarity to Plato's Socratic dialogues and Xenophon's *Memorabilia* is used to justify a label such as "memoirs of a great teacher."[1] But if the Gospels are read with this model alone in mind, much of the text will appear irrelevant, including the narrative of Jesus' passion, death, and resurrection, which has nothing to do with his teaching.

The Gospels obviously do not have a simple meaning of the kind that "memoirs" or a similar one-word description would imply; nor is it essential for readers to have knowledge of any particular classical Greek works in order to understand them. So labels and comparisons of this type do not, without some further analysis of the nature of the texts involved, afford much help to the reader of the Gospels, although this is what scholars often require from such descriptions. On the other hand, the literary background which is explicitly available to readers of the Gospels—the Jewish Scripture—does not provide models for their narrative form but rather a key to the interpretation of the events within it. To some extent the texts of the Gospels direct their own reading: Jesus prophesies his own death (Mark 8:31, Matt. 16:21–28, Luke 9:22–23) and confirms hints from the start of the narrative of his ministry that his teaching will get him into trouble; and the "mystery" of his identity is problematized and finally resolved in a way which requires attention and a knowledge of Scripture on the part of the reader; but it is not necessary to know about pagan philosophical martyrdoms or the recognitions of romance.

Nevertheless, such conventions were part of the literature in Greek which was likely to be familiar to the urban citizens of the Roman Empire who read the Gospels. This fact suggests strongly that where the latter works have similar characteristics to the pagan texts, they also have a similar function and require a similar reading. The function and significance of the works which most resemble the Gospels are far from uncontroversial in themselves, however. Romance and biography are both problematic genres which can have a strange and possibly parodic religious quality; and uncertainty about their literary merit has tended to impede an assessment of their social function. Thus the following discussion is of necessity speculative and partial. Nevertheless, an analysis of the Gospels and Acts in terms of Greco-Roman biography, which is the narrative of the significant life of an important individual, and in terms of romance, which could be described as a narrative of the self-discovery of typical individuals, casts useful light on the ideal reading of these New Testament texts.

Hellenistic and Greco-Roman Biography

Each of the Gospels provides an account of the significant actions of Jesus' life in terms of his identity as the Messiah. The identification of an individual in this way is typical of Greek biography. There have been various attempts to describe the relationship between the Gospels and three general "kinds" of Greek biography: the "memoirs of a great teacher by a student," on the model of Xenophon's *Memorabilia*; a more general divine-man biography, on the model of various lives of philosophers, especially the *Life of Apollonius of Tyana* by Philostratus, and the traditions concerning Plato; and "aretalogy," or a collection of the miracles of a divine figure.[2] These three categories are neither well defined nor necessarily mutually exclusive. The first two depend upon a very limited number of examples, and the third is purely hypothetical, extrapolated from the Gospels and later works. The problem with this approach is that the history of Greek biographical writing is not the history of the independent development of different kinds of biography with well-defined functions. It consists rather in the transformation of individual major texts which may also spawn derivative imitations. An account of the major works and developments in biography is therefore the appropriate background to this aspect of the Gospels.

Greek and Greco-Roman biography formed part of a tradition in which the interests of historiography were combined with those of systematic ethics. The subject of a biography is important in the history of his times, but biography looks at the experiences and motives which make up the individual and form the backgound to his life's actions. The biographer, of course, uses a set of ethical assumptions which are not necessarily those of the subject to describe the latter's life. For example, in Xenophon's and Plato's contrasting accounts of the life of Socrates, both aim to record what Socrates was like, and in particular to show that he was a good man, but the two writers have such diverse concepts of what it is to be a good man that, beyond a desire to live virtuously, their respective depictions of Socrates share only external qualities. Xenophon's work consists of short dialogues in which Socrates is shown clearly to endorse the same conservative values as Xenophon himself. His execution is thus blamed on the degenerate nature of the democracy.

Plato's approach is both more dramatic and more systematic. In the *Apology,* Socrates is on trial for his life. He does not present the kind of argument which will get him acquitted, but reasserts his conviction that he would be doing wrong not to live as he does, to give up his investigation of the nature of virtue and his criticism of the received moral values of Athens. In the *Crito,* Socrates is offered the chance to escape to Thebes or Crete and avoid execution, but he argues dialectically that he must obey the laws of Athens and stay and die. In the *Phaedo,* Socrates on the day of his death tries to persuade his friends by arguments that death is not to be feared. He recapitulates his intellectual career, describing how he progressed from natural science to dialectic in the quest for truth which has brought him here to prison and execution. He refutes several theories of the soul which deny its immortality and then presents his own argument. Phaedo concludes his narrative with the words "thus died the best and wisest of men then living." Socrates' choice of death proves that he is a model for emulation: he values the truth which he is seeking so much that he would rather die than give up his quest.

Both works, then, show that Socrates was "good" by representing him as enacting the ideals of a particular ethical system. Socrates is analyzed as an individual acting within history, and the virtue of his action depends on the importance that he places on doing what is right. His place as the founder of a philosophical tradition is earned by his choice of death, which proves his goodness. This context for the representation of a person, which could be described as the characteristic crisis of an individual, was used by many subsequent writers. The first seems to have been Isocrates in the

Antidosis. The forensic speech is an obvious format for such an account.

Aristotle's systematization of ethics provided a more formal basis for the analysis and description of "a life" in terms of dispositions and choices of action, and such an analysis lies behind the "classical" form of systematic biography. This is foreshadowed by Theophrastus' *Characters,* a collection of descriptions of ethical types based partly on Aristotle's ethical doctrines and partly on New Comedy. The later Peripatetics seem to have been obsessed with the collection of information as well as with its systematization, and with them biography became a collection of historical facts organized to show the subject's place in an overall chronology, in his family, or in the philosophical succession of his school. None of this biography survives in its original form, but it is reflected and often presumably cannibalized in the *Lives* of Suetonius, Plutarch, and, later, Diogenes Laertius.[3]

Alongside this encyclopedic kind of biography, however, the figure of Socrates continued to serve as the model of a philosopher in various kinds of literary work. By the Roman period, it was possible to portray a philosopher who criticized the Roman Empire as a latter-day Socrates, especially if he was executed, or for an exiled philosopher so to portray himself.[4] His suffering "guaranteed" his virtue and ensured his lasting good name.

This pattern recurs in another class of pagan biographies from the first and second centuries C.E. (almost all of which postdate the Gospels). Their subjects are actual or would-be culture heroes or holy men, some of whom perform miracles of healing or are persecuted, or both. For instance, Lucian's *Life of Demonax* (written sometime in the mid-second century) claims to present "one of the great men of modern times." The account of Demonax's family and his devotion to philosophy from an early age resembles in a more succinct form the childhood of Jesus in Luke. The bulk of the *Life* consists of short anecdotes about his encounters both with the establishment and with more extreme and ostentatious Cynics, which again recall similar episodes in the Gospels. His death is described briefly with a few words of eulogy. Lucian's *Death of Peregrinus* provides a more extended death scene, though its hero is a negative example, a fraudulent Cynic sage.

It has occasionally been suggested that these works, and others like them, especially Philostratus' *Life of Apollonius,* are in fact pagan responses to the popularity of the Gospels, since in some cases the resemblances are striking. As well as a miraculous birth and childhood and scenes of teaching and healing, the *Life of Apollonius* also includes a confrontation with the emperor Domitian (*Life of Apollonius* 7.31–34) which recalls Jesus before Pilate and Herod in Luke, and a miraculous death with post-mortem appearances (8.30–31). But these works clearly have antecedents in Hellenistic collections of sayings and of biographical anecdotes and in imitations of the death of Socrates.

Although all the Gospels use recognizably Greek components in their accounts of the life of Jesus, Luke is a special case in that it uses explicit Greco-Roman generic markers to confront the Greek concept of history and to show that Jesus has in fact altered the ethical nature of human life. Luke begins with a characteristically Greek dedicatory paragraph:

> Since many before have tried to set in order an account of the fulfillment of prophecy that has been handed down to us by those that were eyewitnesses and the servants of the word, I have decided after careful observation to write down all in detail from the beginning.   (1:1–3 [AT])

Similar language can be found, for example, in the opening of Josephus' *Jewish Wars*:

> Since many of those who have written about the war waged by the Jews against the Romans—a major historical event—were not there but write speculative, inconsistent, and meretricious accounts from hearsay, while others were there but give a false account, either because they are toadying to the Romans or because they hate the Jews, and their versions contain rhetorical praise and blame but not a trace of historical accuracy, I have decided to translate my history into Greek for the subjects of the Roman empire, since I myself fought against the Romans.

Both refer to previous versions, both claim accuracy, and both define their relationship to their sources. Luke's aim is to establish not merely truth but certainty. He writes, he tells Theophilus, "So that you may know the truth for certain of the account that you have already heard" (1:4 [AT]). Luke is using historical method in order to "make certain" what was hearsay before. He makes it clear, however, that his account concerns the fulfillment of prophecy. In other words, he promises an account of the Jewish Messiah in a Greek historical work.

The birth stories of Jesus and of John again integrate the methods of history and biography. The narratives of the two births are interconnected so that on one level the effect is that of mimetic chronological accuracy: events are related in order, month by month, from Zacharias' vision onward. This creates a set of paired accounts. Zacharias' vision of Gabriel is followed by Mary's, and his skepticism is contrasted with her positive acceptance. Gabriel's appearance to Zacharias recalls God's words to Abraham (Gen. 15:1–5) and establishes John the Baptist's credentials as the last of the Old Testament prophets. Jesus' conception, by contrast, is like that of a Greek sage. Plato, Alexander the Great, and Apollonius of Tyana are all credited with having been fathered by a god, and in each case a dream vision announces the fact.

Luke, however, treats the birth of Jesus not simply as the birth of a holy man, but as a major historical event. The (apparently fictitious) census which takes Mary and Joseph to Bethlehem is dated with bureaucratic precision and also serves to place Jesus in the Roman world from the start. So the prophecy of Scripture, replicated by Gabriel within the Gospel narrative, is fulfilled in Greco-Roman history.

The birth stories thus require two parallel readings. Jesus is the savior of the world both as the Messiah of Scripture and as a Greco-Roman culture hero. His life is a turning point in history; hence the chronological and historical framework. Two "bridge" passages reinforce this point. Jesus is found "teaching" in the Temple at the age of twelve. This foreshadows his future activity and conforms to a Greek biographical topos which requires that a great man should have a prodigious childhood. John the Baptist's teaching in the following passage, by contrast, is historical and is given a detailed chronology in Roman terms, which carries the Old Testament prophecy into historical temporality. So when John baptizes Jesus, since he has been established as a historical figure, he introduces him not only to adult life, but also to history.

In the remainder of Luke's Gospel Jesus' career is divided into two parts, the first extending from his time in the wilderness to his transfiguration and confirmation of the apostles (9:50) and the second consisting of his journey to Jerusalem. It is clear that Luke's account is organized around the historical fulfillment of prophecy, a principle alien to Greek biography, but that within this organization it uses many of the same elements, notably teaching and miracle cures. Both involve conflict with established authority figures—scribes, Pharisees, and lawyers—and provide a motive within the narrative for Jesus' execution.

It is also significant that Luke preserves a historical sense of temporality throughout the narrative. Jesus' and John's public careers are dated from the rules of Herod and Pilate, and these two figures, who will recur in the narrative of Jesus' trial, are mentioned at intervals in the Gospels. Herod's connection with John is mentioned in passing, but his fear that Jesus is John risen from the dead (9:7–9) occurs at a crucial point: Jesus has sent out the twelve as his ministers, and Herod's fear confirms the authority of the apostolic succession, as well as reminding us that Jesus fulfills John's prophecy and hence those of the ancient prophets. Pilate, likewise, is mentioned as the murderer of the Galileans (13:1–5).

As well as serving as historical reference points, the figures of Pilate and Herod are representatives of the two temporal authorities. Jesus' confrontation with them after his arrest recalls a common element in the biographies of philosophers. Socrates, of course, was tried before the Athenian people; later philosophers occasionally oppose "tyrants" (including Roman emperors) face to face, though the best example of this (Apollonius of Tyana confronting Domitian) is post-Gospel.[5] Jesus' opposition to temporal authority, however, is of a different kind. Like the narratives of his death and resurrection, it is to be explained in theological terms. Although the narrative character of the Gospels is formally analogous to that of Greco-Roman biography, its significance is completely different. But the Greco-Roman elements have helped to make an important theological point—that the fulfillment of the prophecies happened inside history.

Romance

The fact that the Gospels can be read as "quests" for individual identity suggests that, like the *Life of Apollonius of Tyana,* they can also be read in the light of the fictional narratives that were apparently very popular during the first four centuries of the common era. These works, namely the Greek romances and the Latin novel *The Golden Ass,* share with the Gospels the quest for identity which Aristotle refers to in the account of recognition in the *Poetics.*[6] In Mark's Gospel, for instance, we are confronted with the problem of Jesus' identity in a narrative which creates the "messianic secret" before resolving it. In the action this finally takes place when Jesus identifies himself before the council (Mark 14:62) and is confirmed when the centurion acknowledges his identity (15:39).

Except possibly for *The Golden Ass,* the romances are all said to share a popular origin. Like the Gospels, however, they include a great deal of inventive rewriting of classical texts, and there is no question that they are literary and literate by any modern criterion. They were written for the entertainment of private readers, and their ordinary language and comparative psychological realism allow their readers to relate the contents more immediately to universal human experience.

There are opposing views about these works. It has been asserted that they are disguised versions of cult myths of Isis. Their appeal lies in the fact that if you have been initiated into the cult, you will recognize the things which were revealed to you in the process of initiation, disguised in the narrative, and the status which your initiation gave you will be confirmed. If this is the case then these works are genuine sacred texts, in the way that the Gospels are, though it is worth noting that the romances are directed at individual readers rather than at performance within the community. But it has also been claimed that the romances use religious myths and ideas in a trivial way to justify their existence, to add a veneer of intellectual respectability to a work of gratuitous sex and melodrama.[7] In either case, however, it is clear that their popular appeal was based on the dramatization of the crises of every life and of everyday experience, which acquire a kind of mythical status through their appearance in the novel. It is possible that the process of reading these texts provided a vicarious introduction to such experiences and helped to condition readers' reactions to them.[8]

The nature of the plots of the romances further suggests that this is the case. Although the texts which survive may not be strictly a representative sample, it is striking that all five which are written in Greek concern a heterosexual couple who end up happily married after various adventures and dangers. These episodes are fantastic and melodramatic, and both they and the happy endings are engineered by the intervention of appropriate deities such as Isis and Artemis. But the problems of marriage, of transition from childhood to sexual maturity, and of the "discovery" of one's adult identity, are universal. Even more tellingly, perhaps, *The Golden Ass,* a novel in Latin, presents a first-person account of a young man's transition from adolescent worldliness to adult respectability. The process by which this happens is fantastic: he dabbles in magic and is turned into a donkey by mistake; finally he is rescued by the goddess Isis. But, as in the Greek romances, he undergoes a particular change of status which is common to most people, certainly to most upper-class men, that of becoming a responsible adult. Although the final status of Lucius, the narrator, is not entirely free of problems, his narrative offers the likely readers of the novel a reminder or a preview of the process of growing into a respectable citizen with a religious consciousness. Readers would either be reassured of their adult status or experience (vicariously) what it is like to grow up.

The narrative of the Gospels is concerned with the identification of Jesus as the Messiah. Although the content of Jesus' life is organized around a different set of texts, the experience of reading the Gospels is similar to that of reading a romance: each individual reader follows the identification of a suffering hero. Although Jesus is the sacrificed deity of myth, his human form and place in contemporary history allow us to identify with him to some extent, and to react emotionally to his sacrifice. The "full" reading of the text will lead to a conviction that the world has been changed by these events; that is, readers will identify themselves as Christians. In the Gospels, however, there is no distinction between recognition of Jesus' personal identity (as foundlings are recognized by tokens in drama) and recognition of his status: the formal "tokens" of Jesus' identity are his fulfillment of the prophecies—he explicitly rejects identification as his parents' son—and he cannot be identified in any way except as the Messiah.

The obvious resemblance of Acts to romance suggests that the Gospels were indeed read like romances. Acts involves travel in the same geographic area as the setting of the romances, and some of the incidents, notably the shipwrecks and formal trials, which afflict the apostles in their quest to found the Church recall the adventures of the heroes of romance. (Many critics have commented on the similarity between the speeches in

Acts and those in Greek historiography. The romances also make use of classical Greek historiography, and it is likely that both they and Acts are drawing on a common stock of elements for narrative prose.) Acts, however, is comparatively succinct for a romance, and the succession of heroes is not typical. Three apostles fulfill their lives in different ways: Stephen's martyrdom is most like the death of Jesus and is marked as such; but after his death Peter and Paul continue the mission, suggesting survival or even resurrection of a single hero. Paul's travels, in particular, cover the geographic and sometimes ethical ground of those of the heroes of romance. The narrative of Acts is a quest to found the Church. The narrative is resolved not by the recognition of the identity of an individual, although the heroes could be said to identify themselves by their martyrdom, but by the reader's recognition that the Church will become a historical force because Paul reaches Rome and is therefore in a position to consolidate his previous work of preaching and of establishing churches, from the center of temporal power. All these resemblances suggest strongly that the authors of the Gospels and Acts are using Greek forms in order to give Christianity a place in the Greco-Roman order.

The Epistles

With Paul's Epistles we move to a different mimetic mode, but once again the aim of the texts is to place the revealed truth within the Greco-Roman order through the use of Greco-Roman forms. The letter was one of the most common kinds of writing in the Roman period. It was the means by which monarchs and emperors administered their domains, and by which the Jewish authorities in Jerusalem held together the cult and the community of the Jewish people until the destruction of the Temple. It also provided a useful literary frame for philosophical teaching, since the fiction of the letter suggests that the absent teacher is speaking to every reader individually and so providing concerned personal guidance about the way to live. Because it could "create" the personal presence of the real or presumed writer, the letter also provided a useful vehicle for biography and autobiography in antiquity. People could create any personality they chose for themselves by writing and selecting for publication letters which seemed to allow readers to spy on their actions unobserved. And friends and enemies could do the same for anyone important.

These various aspects of the letter are not mutually exclusive: Cicero, for example, writes business letters with a glance at posterity but mainly to do business; the Younger Pliny writes business letters to famous people mainly to show the world that he is the sort of person who does business with famous people, although it is possible that he also sent the letters he chose to publish; and Seneca's correspondence with Lucilius is a philosophical drama in letter form which is made to resemble Cicero's correspondence with Atticus by the addition of some circumstantial details. Yet all three sets of letters represent their writers and correspondents in a similar way, and each could be said to reveal the chosen persona of its writer and a valid account of his views. It therefore seems artificial to draw a distinction between "letters," that is, documentary letters, and "epistles," or literary letters.

In antiquity, as today, the conventions of the letter were conservative but not always observed. The handbooks from later antiquity offer form letters with blank spaces for the appropriate details to be inserted for a variety of purposes. These range from a simple friendly letter, which is all greeting and no message, to letters of criticism and of recommendation, whose purpose is to establish or confirm a specific kind of relationship.[9] But these treatments are very schematic; ancient letters in fact say anything that their writers want to say, and the conventions are adapted accordingly. For example, letters almost always begin with an address, "A to B, greetings," to establish a relationship between writer and addressee. But when the emperor sends a letter to a city in his official capacity, the address includes all his titles to show his authority, for example, to legislate for the city or to grant benefits. Similarly, Paul glosses his own name in order to authorize the teaching in his letters. The pro forma wishes for health and the acknowledgment of a previous letter, which often follow the initial greeting, can likewise be adapted. In his letters on moral philosophy, Seneca makes his hope for the health and philosophical well-being of Lucilius a substantial part of each letter, and by commenting on Lucilius' reports of his progress "documents" the effect of his own teaching.

Paul's letters are roughly contemporary with those of Seneca and in many respects belong in the same world. (An early tradition of correspondence between the two sages exists.) His general method of self-representation is also similar: he dramatizes the effect of his teaching on his addressees and adopts the familiar persona of a Greco-Roman authority figure. In an important respect, however, he is like Pliny: his letters place him within the full sweep of history and in the broader geographic context of the Roman Empire. The authoritative nature of the letter places Paul's personal voice firmly in the Greco-Roman world alongside the voices of emperors and philosophers. The communities to which he writes are both disciples of a philosopher and cities of the kingdom of God, administered by means of Paul's letters. He thus depicts a realistic relationship with his addressees which implies a historical situation on which the reader is in a sense spying. The world in which Paul depicts himself writing includes the social and literary institutions of the Roman Empire along with its physical realities. Paul's implied audience consists of religious groups in the major cities of the Roman Empire, people who are aware of their position in Roman and Jewish history. Paul places himself in the historical context of the Roman Empire, on its roads and in its prisons. His letters are delivered by people traveling about the empire, taking advantage of the mobility permitted by Roman rule. But their purpose is to describe and encourage the historical process by which Paul's addressees are to come to live in a new world, differentiated from that of the past and from the Greco-Roman order. Admittedly, this new phase of history is brought about partly by a synthesis of Greek and Jewish systems of thought; but a new dynamic is introduced into history. Paul's letters are both the causes and the documents of historical change.

Let us now examine in more detail the ways in which Paul uses the conventions of Greco-Roman letters to transform pagan philosophical wisdom and the Roman and Jewish laws into a single religious doctrine.

Scholars have discussed in detail the formal elements of Paul's letters.[10] Paul often has liturgical rather than epistolary forms in mind, so that the letter is also a religious service and homily performed at a distance, but the flexibility inherent in the letter form often allows the same element to have several functions. The opening of Paul's letters is fairly consistent, however, and similar to the conventions found in other letters. He uses the basic formula "N to the assembly of the P" but adds attributes both to his own name and to his addressees. For instance, Galatians begins with the following salutation:

1. Paul, apostle, not by human gift
            or through human agency,
            but through Jesus Christ
            and God the Father, who raised him from the dead,
    and all the brothers here with me,

2. to the community of the Galatians,

3. grace to you and peace, from God the Father and the Lord Jesus Christ,
    who gave himself for our sins . . .   (Gal. 1:1–4 [AT])

The salutation continues into a liturgical blessing which recapitulates the redemption of the world. It thus helps to define both the sender and (particularly) the addressees in terms of their membership in a group to whom the redemption of the world has been revealed. To establish his authority to speak in this context, Paul describes himself as an apostle, authorized by the same act of redemption. In this he differs from the emperor, whose titles are constitutional, and from philosophers, whose authority depends on their knowledge of the doctrines of a particular school. Paul's authority derives directly from the way things are.

The same pattern occurs in a more complex salutation in Romans, but with greater stress on the act of communication itself:

1. Paul, the slave of Christ,
       called as an apostle
       set apart for the gospel of God,
       which he declared in advance through his prophets in holy Scripture
    concerning his son, born from the line of David in the flesh
    the son of God set apart in the power of the spirit of holiness,
       from the resurrection of the dead, . . .
    from whom we receive grace and our apostolic mission,
       for the obedience in faith among all the nations
       for the sake of his name
    among which nations you, too, are called
       as belonging to Jesus Christ,

2. to all the beloved of God in Rome,
       called as saints,

3. grace and peace . . .   (Rom. 1:1–7 [AT])

The repetition of "called," *klētos,* which suggests both naming and summoning; the use of *aphorismenos* and *horisthentos,* both from the verb *horizō,* from the Greek root signifying definition or setting apart; and the repetition of "obedience," *hypakoē,* with the dual implications in its Greek etymology of "listen and obey," stresses again that Paul is in a sense the word which is sent out by God and heard by men. Both his travels and the journeys of his letters convey the word of God and so are part of the historical process.

Romans, like many surviving Greek letters, consists of an essay in an epistolary frame. Paul's salutation introduces the major themes of an essay on Jesus Christ, but he does not begin it immediately. Instead, he next introduces another element familiar from private Greek letters, a thanksgiving, which fulfills a function similar to the wish for health often found at this point. In Romans, as in several other of Paul's letters, this clearly also has a function similar to the acknowledgment of a previous communication: "First I thank my God . . . that your faith is proclaimed throughout the whole world. God is my witness that I make unceasing mention of you in my prayers . . ." (1:8–9 [AR]). The commonplaces of acknowledgment and hopes for good health are integrated with the theological content of the letter, the mediation and intercession of Jesus Christ between God and man. Paul's wish to visit Rome to help break down the distinctions between Greeks and barbarians, wise and foolish (Rom. 1:14), which characterized the historical world before Christ and the Church as it was developing in the world, reinforces this point: his act in writing is also a symbol of Jesus' redemption of the world, but Paul is still a human being, and he must work on the particular problems of the world as he comes to them. Neither he nor any other individual can bring about a change in the whole nature of the world of the kind that Jesus in the Gospels brought about, but he can perform actions within history which are symbolic of Jesus' redemption of the world, and which are part of the new course of history because they help communicate this redemption to others in the world.

The complex organization of the body of Paul's letters is largely beyond the scope of this essay. But it is worth commenting briefly on one aspect of them which is often discussed: the features his "sermons" share with popular moral philosophy, both in content and in form.[11] Paul makes considerable use of the Platonic "two worlds" system based on the dichotomy between the flesh and the spirit; and the form of the essays may be related to the kinds of dramatic public lecture or epideictic speech which are often a medium for popular ethical teaching.

Scholars since the nineteenth century have tried to define the characteristics of a genre in which this kind of teaching appears; and Paul's letters, especially Romans 1–11, have been analyzed in terms of their "diatribal" qualities. In Greek the label "diatribe," derived from *diatribein,* "to pass time," was used to refer to philosophical discussion, often between a teacher and pupils, in a leisurely setting—or at least not in one of political activity—but on moral issues of some importance. Its use in Greco-Roman texts seems to have followed from depictions of Socrates' philosophical activity, and many of the texts retailing popular morality have something of the Socratic manner. More generally, they share a number of characteristics which suggest an urgent moral purpose. They are aggressive in manner, and the speaker often dramatizes a conflict between himself and a hypothetical opponent or else denounces an abstract vice. Scholars have identified the address to a hypothetical opponent and devices such as the rhetorical question as typical of the diatribe, but in fact these features characterize a broad range of writing, including verse satire and some speeches in comedy and tragedy. It seems more reasonable to assume that there was an accepted way of conveying "practical" teaching on moral and religious topics in literary works than to try to define precisely which works qualify as diatribes. This way of teaching involves the use of dramatic elements which draw the audience in. Sometimes (for example, in some of Dio's less polished dialogues) a neutral interlocutor is included in the performance in order to suggest the appropriate reaction; but most often the speaker or writer directs the audience's reaction himself, as, for instance, Seneca directs the reader's reaction to his teaching by his depiction of Lucilius' reaction. Note, too, that he uses the same devices in works which are explicitly letters rather than lectures.

Other examples of this kind of work are numerous. Many of Dio of Prusa's so-called orations are in fact lectures of this type: he uses Diogenes the Cynic and Socrates (in his apologetic speech *On Exile*) as his mouthpieces as well as speaking *in propria persona* when he denounces the pursuit of wealth in preference to virtue, and other vices of the age. The discourses of Maximus of Tyre are more perfunctory examples of the same genre; and a number of other works which include rhetorical denunciations of the evils of the age could also be compared with Paul's telegraphic sermons.

A particularly instructive example of this type of writing is Apuleius' *On the God of Socrates*. In this flamboyant lecture Apuleius outlines Plato's cosmology, with special attention to the place of the gods and intermediary powers which appear in Greek and Latin literature. One of these is the personal deity of Socrates—his "divine sign"—which Apuleius brings into the presence of his audience by impersonating it himself. The sign, using Apuleius as a mouthpiece, launches into a dramatic tirade against greed and worldliness. The content of Paul's teaching is not as easily articulated, and he does not insulate himself from responsibility for his attack on his audience, as Apuleius does; nevertheless, there is a strong resemblance here in the way in which he constructs himself as a speaker, and also in the sustained imagery—often based on the difference between appearance and reality—which he uses to reinforce his teaching.

Indeed Paul's rhetorical use of imagery, especially of self-referential imagery, is typical of Greek didactic discourse. The Platonic tradition has, of course, a well-established repertoire of images which derives for the most part from the text of Plato. Socrates uses a number of famous images and examples, both in argument and as myths. For instance, he often uses the doctor as an example of someone who knows what is good for someone's health, in contrast to a pastrycook, who will simply please the belly; and the image which he uses in book 1 of *The Republic,* of the mind as the helmsman steering through a sea of misfortunes, was particularly popular as a political and ethical image later. In general, such images are concrete and commonplace, although the tenor can be more exotic or can be extended into an allegory. For example, Dio describes in unpleasant detail a Libyan monster which he then allegorizes as a figure for tyranny; but the description is also an exuberant piece of horror fiction for its own sake. Orators and philosophers also tried to adapt classical commonplaces to refer to the contemporary world. For instance, the many images which describe the tyrant's condition reappeared with special significance for the autocratic Roman emperor.

Paul's aim is to transform imperial legislative writing, and so he often uses the imagery of imperial rule explicitly. This practice, too, has analogues in Greek texts. For example, the Hellenistic Pseudo-Aristotle and Apuleius (who translates him into Latin) compare the place of God in the universe to that of the Great King in his palace-city of Ecbatana: both are invisible at the center and control the visible world by means of intermediaries, messengers, and ambassadors.[12]

The most prominent image in Paul's teaching is the image of the legal document in all its forms, including the legislative letter itself. The discussion of the Law and "sonship" in Galatians 3:1–4:7 is a good example. In this extended metaphor, the law, that is, Jewish and Roman (human) law, both represents divine law and is an antecedent state that must pass away before the divine law can be enacted. Jesus as a scapegoat has ransomed us from the "curse of the Law"—the penalty of criminality prescribed by the Law—by becoming cursed himself, although he is innocent and therefore not subject to the Law. But the image which Paul uses to help try to explain this paradox comes from the civil law: a will is not challenged until it is enacted, that is, until the principal is dead and the heirs are in a position to inherit. Another legal image follows immediately (3:15–18): the law is a contract made by an intermediary; in the world after Christ, God acts directly without need of agents or guarantors. Paul's preoccupation with the status of the Law is due largely, of course, to the fact that he is addressing audiences who are preoccupied with the Jewish Law, and who may well be having institutional difficulties with the status of the Jewish religion. But the status of the law was also seen as a problem in the Roman Empire. For instance, Plutarch discusses the issue in his *Life of Solon,* a work which seems to reflect Greco-Roman philosophical interests rather than those of the sixth century B.C.E.

Paul's letters conclude as they begin, with conventional elements which help to anchor the writer to the historical world whose transformation they depict. The famous ethical imperatives in 1 Corinthians 7:1–11:38 are appended to the main letter as responses to subsidiary questions. In this case the questions—concerning the attitude of members of the community to the categories of the outside world—are so closely related to the content of the body of the letter that their treatment becomes an extension of it, but they also serve as a link between Paul's abstract teaching and his historical self-representation. The promise of a visit which occurs in most of the letters likewise serves as a pivot between Paul's voice as a mediator when he is teaching and his historical persona: the letter signifies that he is present only as the persona created by the text but by wishing to be present he points to the possibility of his real presence. The letters often end, like private letters, with simple imperatives: "Watch ye, stand fast in the faith, quit you like men, be strong. Let all your things be done with charity" (1 Cor. 16:13–14); and with greetings for and from other members of the community. Some have a final greeting in Paul's own hand, as in the "big letters" in Galatians 6:11, which recalls the imperial manner: emperors often appended a brief greeting to official letters produced by their secretaries.

Paul, then, transforms the conventions of the Greco-Roman letter so that they are, as it were, written in the spirit: he administers the law of the kingdom of heaven by transforming the law of the Roman Empire, and replaces rationalist popular moral philosophy with revealed truth. As with any other mystery cult, the revelation cannot be expressed in writing, but unlike other cults, Paul's justifies itself by its effect within the world, which he documents in his letters. The content of the revealed truth is the same as that of the Gospels, but the Epistles show the act of redemption of the Gospels replicated within the subsequent history of the Greco-Roman world, not narrated by a quasi-historian's voice, but documented by texts which are part of the action of redemption.

NOTES

1. V. K. Robbins, "Mark 1:14–20: An Interpretation at the Intersection of Jewish and Greco-Roman Traditions," *New Testament Studies,* 28 (1982), pp. 220–231, uses this label for the Greco-Roman tradition represented in Mark.

2. See Patricia Cox, *Biography in Late Antiquity: The Quest for the Holy Man* (Berkeley, 1984), who includes a survey of the discussion. In general, I follow Cox on the nature of Greco-Roman biography, although her study is concerned with texts of a later date.

3. For a more detailed account see Arnaldo Momigliano, *The Development of Greek Biography* (Cambridge, Mass., and London, 1971).

4. Tacitus depicts Seneca's enforced suicide in a parody of the death of Socrates (*Annals* 15:62–63); Dio of Prusa bends the story of his exile to make himself like Socrates (*Oration* 13).

5. Philostratus, *Life of Apollonius* 8.32–34.

6. *Poetics* 1452a22–b13, 1454b1–1455a20.

7. The definitive statement of the view that the romances are disguised cult narratives is Reinhold Merkelbach, *Roman und Mysterium in der Antike* (Munich, 1962). It has been influentially opposed by B. E. Perry, *The Ancient Romances* (Berkeley, 1967).

8. This position is well outlined in J. T. Trembley, "The Beloved Self" (Ph.D. diss., Princeton University, 1981).

9. These texts are collected at the beginning of Rudolph Hercher, *Epistolographae Graeci* (1873; reprint, Amsterdam, 1965). For a convenient collection of private letters with translation, see A. S. Hunt and C. C. Edgar, *Select Papyri,* I (London and Cambridge, Mass., 1932), nos. 88–169.

10. See J. L. White, *New Testament Epistolary Literature in the Framework of Ancient Epistolography, Aufstieg und Niedergang der Römischen Welt* II 25.2 (Berlin, 1984), pp. 1730–56, especially 1733–51.

11. For a recent survey of this topic see S. K. Stowers, *The Diatribe and Paul's Letter to the Romans* (Missoula, Mont., 1981).

12. The description of the city originates in Herodotus (1.98). See Pseudo-Aristotle, *De mundo* 398a11–b10; Apuleius translates the *De mundo* in such a way as to make it reflect the mystification of imperial bureaucracy.

SUGGESTED FURTHER READINGS

H. H. O. Chalk, "Eros and the Lesbian Pastorals of Longus," *Journal of Hellenic Studies,* 80 (1960), 32–51.

Patricia Cox, *Biography in Late Antiquity: The Quest for the Holy Man* (Berkeley, 1984).

Frank Kermode, *The Genesis of Secrecy* (Cambridge, Mass., and London, 1979).

Arnoldo Momigliano, *The Development of Greek Biography* (Cambridge, Mass., and London, 1971).

B. E. Perry, *The Ancient Romances* (Berkeley, 1967).

J. L. White, *New Testament Epistolary Literature in the Framework of Ancient Epistolography*, Aufstieg und Niedergang der Römischen Welt II 25.2 (Berlin, 1984), pp. 1730–56.

J. J. Winkler, *Auctor et Actor: A Narratological Reading of Apuleius' Golden Ass* (Berkeley, 1985).

Clare College, University of Cambridge

Fishing for Men on the Edge
of the Wilderness

Edmund Leach

M Y purpose is to offer a demonstration of a personal style of biblical
exegesis which derives from my experience as an anthropologist.[1]
The method owes a great deal to the structuralist technique which Claude
Lévi-Strauss has applied to the analysis of the oral mythology of preliterate
peoples, but, as far as the Bible is concerned, it is closely related to the
typological style of argument employed by the majority of early Christian
writers. I should emphasize that I lack most of the qualifications of an
ordinary biblical scholar. In particular I do not read Hebrew.

I start with a picture (see the drawing).[2] The original is brightly
colored, and, in context, the colors have symbolic significance, but the
drawing alone will make my point. Even if it had carried no title, almost
all readers of this book would have immediately recognized that the
principal theme is the baptism of Jesus by John the Baptist which is
reported in all four Gospels. The event is specified as taking place in the
river Jordan in the Wilderness. In Mark it is the first incident of Jesus' life
history (Mark 1:9–11).

But what else does the picture represent? The answers that might be
given to that question will depend upon the individual reader's personal
background. Different readers will, quite legitimately, interpret the picture
in different ways. For example, some will notice that John is anointing
Jesus and will recall that the words *Messiah* in Hebrew and *Christos* in
Greek both mean "the anointed." This and other details may suggest that
Jesus is being initiated as both a king and a prophet. And then there are
the fish. They are there, of course, to show that Jesus is immersed in the
waters of the Jordan. But do they signify anything else? Well, perhaps,
perhaps not. This optional and multilayered character of symbolic associations is one of my principal themes.

But how about my title? The problem may seem deceptively simple.
Why does the author of Mark tell us that the apostles Simon-Peter, Andrew, James, and John are two pairs of brothers and all fishermen? The
obvious answer is that it was so. The first four Christians really were
fishermen who plied their trade on the Sea of Galilee. Why not? It is

perfectly possible. But Mark 1:17 makes this detail into a trope: "And Jesus said unto them, Come ye after me, and I will make you to become fishers of men." So we still have a problem. Why should Mark have attributed this remark to Jesus at this particular point in his ministry?

First let me summarize my theoretical assumptions. I regard biblical texts as strictly on a par with the sacred texts of other major religions such as Islam and Buddhism. The common feature of such texts is that they presuppose that the discourse concerns two levels of experience, the physical and the metaphysical. Religious texts are concerned with the relationship between the physical world of here and now and the metaphysical, dreamlike, experience of the Other, and they must necessarily incorporate literary devices whereby the two may be distinguished. The Bible is not a history book even though many devout believers, both Jewish and Christian, treat it as such. It is a corpus of mythology which provides a justification for the religious performances of believers.

Drawing after "The Baptism," in the twelfth-century St. Albans Psalter, St. Godard's Cathedral, Hildesheim. Courtesy of Bellerophon Books.

The individual stories in the Bible have a manifest straightforward meaning, and, taken one by one, there is nothing very special about them. Some are plainly fabulous and have close parallels in the folklore of other societies worldwide. Others appear to contain elements of authentic history, though it usually requires a great deal of special pleading to make them dovetail with the findings of archaeology. But such discrepancies do not really matter. The religious truth that they are supposed to contain relates to the Bible as a whole, *considered as a unitary work of art*. So it is the stories as a collectivity that invite interpretation.

As with pictorial compositions, mythological texts have many levels of meaning. The reader/listener/observer makes his or her personal contribution to what such meanings are. It is never the case that any one interpretation is uniquely true or transparently false.

In saying that the Bible is not a history book but a mythology, I am not arguing that the events it records could not possibly have happened in real time. It is simply that spatial and chronological relations within biblical texts always have symbolic significance whether or not they happen to correspond to reality as ordinarily understood. The patterning is determined by literary-aesthetic considerations rather than by historical or geographic facts.

This literary-aesthetic structure of biblical texts has important implications. The readers of a novel or the audience of a play are always expected to apprehend the text as a whole, not just chapter by chapter or scene by scene. It is a mark of high aesthetic quality that nothing in the text is there by accident; everything has relevance for everything else. The task of the literary critic is to show where such relevances lie. This applies to the Bible also.

So my concern is with the biblical texts that we have rather than in the reconstruction of texts that we do not have. This perspective runs counter to almost all the major strands of biblical criticism that have been developed since early in the nineteenth century.

It is quite obvious that the texts we have are a surviving remnant from a much larger and more diverse body of earlier texts. During the past 160 years enormous erudition has been devoted to the reconstruction of these earlier texts, with the underlying assumption that, in some unspecified sense, the early texts were more "authentic" than the edited versions which survive.

My own position is just the opposite. I take it for granted that all surviving biblical texts have in the past been heavily edited and revised many times over. While editorial amendments may have come about in many different ways, the main purpose of the nameless editors was to achieve coherence; they were seeking to establish a mythological canon, a justification for the faith and for the performance of rituals as practiced in their own times.

It is possible, indeed very likely, that some of the texts existed in the form of oral legends before they were written down, but the documents which we now have are literary texts composed by authors who almost certainly lived in cities. When they wrote about nomads in the Wilderness or about fishermen sailing on the Sea of Galilee, they were exercising their literary imagination; they were not describing scenes of which they had direct experience.

Admittedly, the first sixteen books of the Old Testament are arranged as if they formed a more or less continuous history from the beginning of time until the building of the Second Temple in Jerusalem, but the historical framework is a literary device designed to exhibit the unfolding of the plot. At every stage, events are presented as a fulfillment of what has come before and as a foreshadowing of what will come after. This is what happens in a Shakespearean tragedy or in a novel by Tolstoy, but it is not the manner of a serious history book.

The faithful maintain that the whole of the Bible is true; for this to be possible, the truth has to be aesthetic rather than literal. This gives us the fundamental principle that underlies my style of interpretation. I assume that there is a symbolic congruence between any one part of the Bible and any other. The reader or auditor of any biblical text is expected to be familiar with all other biblical texts. Resonances from these other texts continuously influence whatever is heard or understood.

Moreover, the Bible is not a closed system of texts, complete in itself. We bring to our reading and listening echoes from all other parts of our individual cultural background. In particular, the resonances in the Old Testament that affect Jewish readers, whose memories are saturated with talmudic glosses, are likely to be very different from those of Christians who cannot read Hebrew. For Christian readers, on the other hand, the resonances of New Testament texts will vary according to the extent of their familiarity with Old Testament texts. That is why my picture of the baptism of Jesus does not have just one meaning but many different meanings, depending upon who looks at it.

There is nothing novel about such an argument. The interdependence of the Old Testament and the New has always been acknowledged and explicit. Every scholarly commentary on the books of the New Testament includes lists of the direct quotations or close paraphrases from Old Testament sources along with lists of cases in which passages from the Old Testament are used as "allegories" to justify passages in the New. Indeed, in all forms of biblical commentary it is standard practice to draw attention to cross-references in other parts of the biblical corpus. So why fuss about coherence?

It is partly a matter of degree. For example, all the more usual forms of biblical commentary take it for granted that the geographic environment presupposed in biblical texts is the geographic environment displayed in modern maps of the Near East. This is partly true, but features of this real geography are *regularly* put to symbolic use in a way that is not commonly understood.

The very diverse documents which make up the Bible were worked into their present canonical form over a period of some five centuries from about 250 B.C.E. onward. Throughout this period, the dominant external political milieu was that of the Greco-Roman-Alexandrine world. This political context is relevant because it may help us understand the mental attitudes of the canonical editors. But there is a negative aspect of such contextualization. We should not attribute to scholars of antiquity details of knowledge which they cannot possibly have possessed.

Modern maps are based on accurate cadastral surveys, and we possess a great deal of fully verified information about the historical chronology of major political events in the ancient world. But the geographic and chronological knowledge of biblical editors was much less precise. Roman itineraries arranged place-names in sequence and sometimes recorded distances, but they mostly ignored orientation. The names and reign dates of local monarchs were based wholly on tradition. There was no cross-checking of the kind that can now be provided by the archaeologists. We should accept such limitations.

For example, there is a massive body of modern scholarship, both Jewish and Christian, which assumes that the Exodus from Egypt under Moses was a historical event and that in the light of what is known from other sources it ought to be possible to give a precise date to this event, to plot on modern maps the exact details of the wanderings of the Israelites in the Wilderness, and even to give a historical identity to the daughter of Pharaoh who rescued Moses from the bulrushes.[3]

My own view is that the historical status of the Exodus is about on a par with the historical status of the Trojan War: it might have happened, but, almost certainly, it didn't. But that is not the issue.

Before the beginning of the nineteenth century very few theologians saw any conflict between their belief that the Bible is a record of historical events and their belief that this history conveys divine messages of a symbolic kind. It was almost universally believed, by Jews and Christians alike, that God had arranged matters so that history *should* provide just such a divine revelation.

In our present supposedly enlightened age such an attitude is hardly possible. Rational empiricism requires that we make a choice: *either* the Bible is a record of history *or* it embodies a symbolic message. The two views have come to seem mutually contradictory.

But if faced with such a choice, we must opt for a symbolic rather than a historical interpretation. The authors and editors of the Book of Exodus certainly believed that the stories which they were committing to writing were a record of history; if we are honest we must say that they had no good grounds for this belief. But this doesn't matter. The editors of the biblical canon were not fussy about the details of the real world. They were primarily interested in the divine message which they believed to be embedded in sacred history, and they arranged their stories accordingly. This is true of the New Testament as well as of the Old.

A New Testament example of such arrangement occurs in the first twenty verses of Mark's Gospel. On first reading, the text seems quite straightforward: Jesus is baptized in the river Jordan by John the Baptist; he is tempted by Satan in the Wilderness; he returns to Galilee and summons his first four disciples. The story is presented as a record of historical fact, yet every sentence looks either backward to Old Testament predictions about the coming of the Messiah in the last days or forward to Christian predictions concerning the second coming of Christ and the Day of Judgment.

This text in Mark is concerned with initiation: the initiation of Jesus himself by John and of the four senior apostles by Jesus. Water is involved in both cases; the river Jordan in the first, the Sea of Galilee in the second. In the case of Jesus, the Wilderness comes into it as well. These are the two major symbols discussed in this essay, but first I must make a theoretical digression.

Religious texts (and ritual sequences) must necessarily incorporate some device whereby the metaphysical Other can be distinguished from the physical here and now. Anthropologists have learned from experience that van Gennep's thesis about the three-phase structure of initiations ("rites of passage") serves just this purpose in a very wide range of applications.[4] Highly condensed, the argument runs like this:

The ordinary time and ordinary space of everyday experience are continuous; social time and social space are discontinuous. At an initiation the initiate moves from one position in social space/time to another by a discontinuous jump. This move occurs in three phases:

1. The initiate is separated from his or her original status in real world society (rite of separation).
2. The initiate is isolated from society in a state of limbo associated with taboos of various kinds (marginal state).
3. The initiate is brought back into real world society in his or her new (initiated) status (rite of aggregation).

The major social discontinuity is between the status of the initiate at phase 1 and the status of the initiate at phase 3. During phase 2 the initiate is in a "sacred" condition, not only outside society but also outside secular time.

Certain forms of symbolic expression appear very frequently but not invariably. Differences of social status, which are of crucial significance in the conduct of secular life, tend to be ignored; an egalitarian state of *communitas* prevails. Symbolism of death and rebirth is frequently worked into the ritual sequence. Death and rebirth also feature in the associated mythology. The disjunctures between the ritual phases are frequently marked by sacrifice in ritual or killings in myth.

When initiations are represented in story form, the timelessness of the marginal phase 2 becomes part of the plot. We can recognize its character when we note that everything that happens in phase 2 is abnormal when compared with the normal, real time, world of phase 1 and phase 3.

In the story of Moses, as recorded in Exodus, we encounter a series of these van Gennep sequences. Here are two examples.

First sequence:

1a. Moses is born as a Hebrew Levite of lowly status (Exod. 2:1).
  b. During a massacre of male Israelite children Moses is placed in an ark of bulrushes (sacrifice and rite of separation involving symbolic death [pictures of Moses' ark often show a kind of coffin]).
2. The ark floats in the river (marginal state).
3. Moses is discovered and lifted from the water by an Egyptian princess (symbolic rebirth). He becomes an Egyptian prince living in a palace (rite of aggregation).

Second sequence:

1a. Moses is now an Egyptian prince.
  b. He kills an Egyptian and flees from Pharaoh (Exod. 2:15) (sacrifice and rite of separation).
2. Moses takes refuge in the Wilderness (marginal state).
3. Moses returns to Egypt with the standing of a mighty prophet with magical powers (Exod. 4:29) (rite of aggregation).

In these examples Egypt stands for the here and now while the ark in the river and the Wilderness both represent the Other.

In this summary the reductionism is extreme but let us look at some of the component elements in greater detail.

The Wilderness

The Wilderness of the English-language Old Testament corresponds to several different Hebrew terms but is consistently called *eremos* in the Greek of the Septuagint. This term is translated into the English of the New Testament as both "wilderness" and "desert." It signified "wild" territory, untamed by man but not necessarily uninhabitable. *Midbar,* the usual Hebrew equivalent, included dry pasture land where sparse grazing was available for sheep; indeed, this was its principal meaning.

The prototype Wilderness is provided by the geographic environment of the wanderings in the Book of Exodus. If you are in Egypt, the Wilderness is where you get to if you cross the Red Sea; if you are in the land of Israel, the Wilderness is where you get to if you cross the Jordan. The Wilderness is the Other World. Entering or leaving the Wilderness symbolizes a metaphysical movement from the here and now to the timelessness of the Other or vice versa.

Any reader of John Bunyan's *Pilgrim's Progress* surely takes it for granted that both the topography and the chronology of the story have this sort of religious significance. Why should the Bible be any different?

How does this affect the details of the Exodus story? In chapter 2, Moses, a prince of Egypt by adoption, takes flight from Pharaoh. He marries the daughter of Jethro, a man of the Wilderness, and begets a son, Gershom. In chapter 3, Moses arrives at Horeb, the mountain of God, and becomes the chosen vehicle of God's word. In chapter 4, Gershom is circumcised. The rite is here presented as providing Moses rather than Gershom with a magical protection against mystical threat, though if we jump forward to Exodus 12:12–13 we may infer that Gershom is protected against the threatened destruction of "all the firstborn in the land of Egypt." In any case, as presented in Exodus 13:15, the rite of circumcision is a substitution for sacrifice. At the end of chapter 4, Aaron is likewise sent by God to the mountain of God in the Wilderness before he and Moses together return to Egypt to carry out their mission.

Chapters 12 and 13 provide the charter myth for the festival of the Passover, itself the story of a grand-scale rite of separation. At Exodus 13:17–18, the text makes the explicit point that the journey into the Wilderness (a marginal state) seems to be an irrational diversion, though it also shows that the authors/editors of Exodus were confused about the real geographic relationship of the land of Egypt and the land of the Philistines.

Then at chapter 14 the Israelites, who have been promised at Exodus 3:8 and again at Exodus 13:5 that they will be journeying to "a land flowing with milk and honey," move from Egypt, a land of suffering but of plenty, into the Wilderness, a land of potential starvation and death, by crossing water on dry land.

This is possible because of divine intervention. By further divine intervention Pharaoh and the Egyptian army are destroyed. Then in chapters 16 and 17 the Israelites are miraculously provided with food (manna) and water.

Extrabiblical sources attached special value to this water. According to legend, the rock of Horeb traveled with the Israelites on their wanderings. It was the water of life. It teemed with fish.[5]

In this Other World everything happens in reverse. The heavenly bread falls from the sky like rain; the heavenly water does not fall like rain but emerges from a rock. Perhaps you think this polarity is a structuralist fantasy? On the contrary, the point is noted in the Talmud.[6]

The end of the forty-year period of wandering in the Wilderness presents exactly the same set of motifs but in a different order: in Joshua 3–4 the Israelites cross the Jordan on dry land; in Joshua 5:2–9 there is a renewal of the rite of circumcision, which had been omitted during the wanderings in the Wilderness; at verse 10 the Israelites celebrate the Passover; at verse 12 the daily supply of manna ceases; in Joshua 6 the enemy (in this case the people of Jericho) are destroyed by divine intervention.

This symmetry cannot be accidental. The Wilderness is marked off as altogether Other. It is a world in which ordinary food is not available but in which God's chosen people are sustained with divine bread and divine water. It is a world in which the chosen prophets Moses and Joshua, and to a lesser extent Aaron and Miriam, converse directly with God. It is a world in which the rite of circumcision is *not* required (apart from the enigmatic exception of Gershom). It is a world with sharply defined water boundaries: the Red Sea on one side, the river Jordan on the other. In order to enter this sacred other world, ordinary people (other than chosen prophets such as Moses and Aaron) need divine intervention by which the water boundaries are made passable. It is a world which includes the mountain of God, Mount Sinai (Horeb), which is itself bounded, a world apart within a world apart (Exod. 19:12, 23–24).

Thus specified, the Wilderness, the Other World of things sacred, is in every respect the exact converse of the profane world that is familiar to ordinary people conducting their ordinary secular affairs.

It is not the case that whenever the term *wilderness* appears in the English text this invariably implies an abnormal/mythical/sacred situation as opposed to a normal/real world/profane situation, but the pattern recurs very frequently.

Another example in which the Wilderness provides the "marginal state" in a van Gennep sequence starts at 1 Kings 17:1, when Elijah suddenly appears at the court of Ahab in Samaria as a herald of God's vengeance. He comes from Gilead the country to the east of the Jordan. Gilead was not in the desert but it rates as Wilderness in terms of my definition. From Samaria God first sends Elijah eastward back across the Jordan into the Wilderness. There, at the brook Kerith (near Jericho), he is fed by the ravens. Thus sanctified and endowed with magical powers he withdraws to foreign territory in the far west at Sidon and is magically sustained by the inexhaustible flour and oil of his impoverished hostess, whose son he later restores to life. Later still, when Elijah has carried out his role as miraculous rainmaker and slaughtered the prophets of Baal, he again takes flight into the trans-Jordan Wilderness (1 Kings 19:3).

Again he is magically provided with food, and travels for forty days and forty nights to the mountain of God (Horeb/Sinai). God orders him to return to Damascus by way of the Wilderness to complete his prophetic role by anointing Jehu as king of Israel and Elisha as his own successor.

These incidents are all transformations of stories from the Books of Exodus and Joshua which refer to Moses and Joshua and the Israelites wandering in the Wilderness. In the Elijah versions the Wilderness is consistently presented as a reservoir of divine power to which the prophet withdraws when in need of spiritual sustenance.

The final episode in the Elijah story makes it clear that the structural similarity has been carefully worked out.

Elijah and Elisha start from Gilgal (2 Kings 2), a place-name which echoes that in Joshua 4:19, where the Israelites first camped after magically crossing the Jordan, before the magical destruction of Jericho. This earlier Gilgal was thus on the frontier of the secular world. Gilgal is now said to be close to Bethel on the frontier of Samaria. From Gilgal Elijah and Elisha go to Jericho. Both at Bethel and at Jericho the "sons of the prophets" warn Elisha that Elijah is about to be removed (vv. 3, 5). From Jericho they go to the Jordan. Elijah strikes the waters with his cloak, and the waters divide so that Elijah and Elisha walk over on dry land. Once they are in the Wilderness on the other side of the Jordan, Elijah and Elisha are separated from each other by "a chariot of fire and horses of fire." Elijah is swept up into heaven by a whirlwind. Elisha destroys his own mantle and takes over that of the departed Elijah. He then returns across the Jordan by the same supernatural means as before. Elisha forthwith proceeds to perform a miracle. He purifies a polluted well at Jericho, the paradigm of a polluted place (Joshua 6:17, 26) (compare Moses drawing pure water from the rock at Horeb, the paradigm of a sacred place, in Exod. 17:6).

As can be seen, the initiation in the Elisha sequence conforms perfectly to the classic van Gennep pattern already described. The new prophet (Elisha) is initiated into his new role by first discarding his earlier status in a rite of separation (passing dryshod across the Jordan), then temporarily moving into a state of limbo (marginal state) in the Wilderness, and then assuming his new role in a rite of aggregation in which he takes over the robe of office of his predecessor but which is otherwise the exact reverse of the initial rite of separation. Meanwhile the old prophet, who is replaced, disappears. But the supernatural crossing of Jordan echoes Joshua 4:22–24.

The Unfordable Stretch of Water

In these examples the boundary between the secular and the sacred is a stretch of water. It is represented as an obstacle which is negotiable but only with divine aid. But there are other biblical stories in which the water barrier itself is the focus of attention.

The first of these is the story of the Flood (Gen. 6:14–8:14). In Christian medieval typology Noah's ark was the Church, which provides a sanctuary for those who have been redeemed by the rite of baptism (the Flood), which washes away the sins of mankind. The implication of the original Old Testament story (and indeed of primeval flood stories in general) is the other way about. The survivors of the Flood, Noah and his family, are the first true men, the first inhabitants of the world as we know it; the giants and patriarchs of the pre-Flood era were people of another time, another world. But in either case the barrier which separates this world from the other is represented as impassable water.

Another water barrier appears in Ezekiel 47, in his account of his vision of the Last Days, when the theocratic rule of the Messiah in the rebuilt City of David will be restored. The imagery derives from transformations of passages in the Pentateuch and from the description of Solomon's Temple.

An unfordable river runs from the New Jerusalem to the Dead Sea. The waters of this river are so pure and copious that the waters of the Dead Sea itself become fresh and the vegetation luxuriant. The river and the revived lake teem with fish. All the varieties of fish in the world are to be found there. On the shore of the lake fishermen spread their nets.

This river, which "issued out from under the threshold of the house [temple] eastward" (Ezek. 47:1), recalls the river which "went out of Eden to water the garden" (Gen. 2:10). It is implied that, in the Last Days, a luxuriant Eden will reappear in the vicinity of Jerusalem.

This story is the converse of that in Isaiah 19:5–9, where it is predicted that, as we approach the end of time and the final triumph of Israel, the Nile will drain away and there will be no fish. The reversal is not inconsistent; the last days will bring damnation to the wicked as well as salvation to the elect.

Fish

So what about the fish? This is a very large topic and I shall have to be selective.[7]

At first sight the trope of the fish is quite simple:

fish:no fish::plenty:famine::blessings:damnation.

But Ezekiel 29:1–12 gives it a different twist. Here the prophet is predicting the total destruction of Egypt at the hands of Nebuchadrezzar, king of Babylon. Pharaoh is described as a great monster lurking in the streams of the Nile.

I will put hooks in thy jaws, and I will cause the fish of thy rivers to stick unto thy scales, and I will bring thee up out of the midst of thy rivers, and all the fish of thy rivers shall stick unto thy scales. And I will leave thee thrown into the wilderness, thee and all the fish of thy rivers: thou shalt fall upon the open fields; thou shalt not be brought together, nor gathered: I have given thee for meat to the beasts of the field and to the fowls of the heaven.　(vv. 4–5)

Two slightly different images are involved: (1) fish = men; (2) taking the fish from the water = men meeting their death. This links up with several other prophecies concerning the punishment of the wicked in the Last Days, such as Amos 4:2, Habakkuk 1:14–17, and Jeremiah 16:16. In Jeremiah, the gathering together of the sinners is described thus: "Behold, I will send for many fishers, saith the Lord, and they shall fish them; and after will I send for many hunters, and they shall hunt them from every mountain, and from every hill, and out of the holes of the rocks."

Most of these same metaphoric themes reappear in the New Testament.

New Testament Typologies

For the early Christians God's message to the New Israel as embedded in the Gospels was a fulfillment, and therefore a transformation, of God's message to the Old Israel as encoded in the Old Testament. This belief is repeatedly emphasized in the Gospel texts themselves and went almost unchallenged until the early years of the nineteenth century. My own assumptions are very similar; they include the following:

1. The religious meaning of the New Testament derives from the canon as a whole and not from the separate meanings of the twenty-seven different documents.
2. Mark is the earliest of our four Gospels. The other three evangelists borrowed extensively from Mark or from a text very similar to Mark.
3. All four Gospels are post 70 C.E.
4. John is probably, but not certainly, the latest to be written.
5. The geography of Gospel Palestine, like the geography of Old Testament Palestine, is symbolic rather than actual. It is not clear whether any of the evangelists had ever been there.
6. The Greek texts which we now have are original texts and not translations from Aramaic.

Certain inferences can be made from these assumptions—for example, that Luke was a well-educated Greek, though he might have been of slave status, and he might have been of Jewish origin; that Matthew was a Hellenized Jew of considerable education; and that even Mark, who was less educated than the others, was very far from being a peasant or a fisherman. All four evangelists were well versed in Jewish Scripture, which they knew in the Greek Septuagint form.

So what about Mark 1:1–20? The first sentence announces the "gospel [good news] of Jesus Christ." What is this good news? Surely not just a history of past events? Rather, the promise of things to come: the second coming of Christ, the end of time, the heavenly kingdom of the elect. The story of Christ's ministry, crucifixion, and resurrection is there only as a justification for the final promise of Mark 16:16: "He that believeth and is baptized shall be saved; but he that believeth not shall be damned."

The account of Jesus' ministry starts off with a classical rite of passage of exactly the same type as that which marks the initiation of Elisha. Jesus is baptized by John by immersion in the Jordan (rite of separation), he is in the Wilderness for forty days (marginal state), he returns to Galilee to commence his preaching (rite of aggregation in his new status as a prophet). Before he returns, John the Baptist, like Elijah, has been removed from the scene.

Then at verses 16–18 we get the following very significant piece of text: "Now as he walked by the sea of Galilee, he saw Simon and Andrew his brother casting a net into the sea: for they were fishers. And Jesus said unto them, Come ye after me, and I will make you to become fishers of men. And straightway they forsook their nets, and followed him."

This is not a plausible piece of history, but if it is a contrivance of art, then we must ask: Why the Sea of Galilee? Why fishermen?

As we have seen, the trope of fishing for men to gather them together at the Day of Judgment comes from Jeremiah 16:16 and other Old Testament prophets. It is a powerful metaphor.

The author of Mark was likewise concerned to present a message about the Last Days, the coming of the heavenly kingdom that will be heralded by the second coming of Christ. The imagery of Jeremiah 16:16 fits this message. Having decided to use it, the author had to have fishermen, a place where they could fish, the apparatus of fishing, boats, nets, and so on. He was not prepared to follow Ezekiel in creating an imaginary world in which the Dead Sea was full of fish, so Galilee was the obvious place since, as Mark must have known, there was a real-life fishing industry in the Sea of Galilee.

Mark's imagery was copied by the other evangelists, so that the apostles Simon-Peter, Andrew, James, and John are always fishermen. But the metaphor is elaborated in various directions. In Luke 5:2 (and Matt. 13:2) Jesus preaches from a ship standing offshore, thus marking off a sacred precinct separate from the land of the commonalty (ship:land::sacred:profane), as in the medieval Christian interpretation of Noah's ark.

In Luke the preaching is followed by Simon-Peter's obtaining a miraculous "great multitude of fishes" (5:4–11), which echoes the fishermen and the fish in Ezekiel 47:9–10. The miracle causes alarm among the disciples but Jesus then repeats the injunction from Mark: "Fear not; from henceforth thou shalt catch men." In Luke 8:22–24 (also Matt. 8:23–27)

Jesus is on a ship in the middle of the lake. He falls asleep. But there is a storm and the disciples are afraid. Jesus shows his power by stilling the storm. Once again metaphysical events occur in the betwixt and between.

Stories of the miraculous feeding of the multitude with bread and fish recur throughout the Gospels: (i) Matthew 14:15–21; (ii) Matthew 15:32–38; (iii) Mark 6:30–44; (iv) Mark 8:1–9; (v) Luke 9:12–17; (vi) John 6:8–13. The feedings take place in a Wilderness environment on the shore of the Sea of Galilee. They echo the stories of the supernatural feeding of the Israelites during their Exodus wanderings. Because of the very explicit elaboration in John 6:26–58, these stories, along with the more intimate miraculous feeding of the disciples in (vii) John 21:9–13, have always been seen as providing a model for the Eucharist. They reflect the fact that in early Christianity the Eucharist food consisted of bread and fish rather than bread and wine.

Each of these seven feedings is linked with an epiphany in which Jesus reveals himself as a supernatural being: (i) Matthew 14:24–33; (ii) Matthew 17:1–9; (iii) Mark 6:49; (iv) Mark 9:2–13; (v) Luke 9:28–36; (vi) John 6:19; (vii) John 21:9–13. In (i), (iii), and (v) the epiphany takes the form of Jesus walking on the waters of the Sea of Galilee after he has first gone onto "the other side" and withdrawn "up into a mountain to pray." In (ii), (iv), and (vi) the epiphany is a transfiguration on a high mountain in the Wilderness. The cross-reference to Horeb/Sinai is made explicit by the inclusion of Moses and Elijah (Elias). The scene is witnessed by the apostolic fishermen Peter, James, and John. In (vii) Jesus, after his resurrection, appears to the same apostles (and others) on the shore of the Sea of Galilee. In (i) Peter seeks to imitate Jesus. He is immersed in the process and saved by Jesus: a baptism in water. Something very similar happens in (vii) at John 21:7 when Peter jumps into water naked on recognizing the risen Christ.

Here I must insert a structuralist comment. The usual van Gennep triad puts the sacred in the middle:

normal status A	marginal state	normal status B
profane world	sacred Other	profane world

But here the duplicated epiphanies in Matthew and in Mark serve to put the profane in the middle:

sacred	profane	sacred
below (Matt. 14:24–33)	normal	above (Matt. 17:1–9)
boat on the sea	land	mountain in the Wilderness
(Mark 6:49)		(Mark 9:2–13)

I shall not pursue this particular transformation any further except to point out that in both the Old Testament and the New it is regularly implied that sheep:wilderness::fish:water. For example, Ezekiel 34:11–16 makes essentially the same point with respect to sheep and shepherds that Jeremiah 16:16 makes with respect to fish and fishers, and when John 21:11, which reports the catching of fish, is unexpectedly followed at John 21:15–17 by the threefold injunction "Feed my lambs . . . Feed my sheep . . . Feed my sheep," the author is not changing the subject so much as changing the key.

In any case, it seems quite plain from the text that the reader of Mark is expected to find significance in the fact that the senior apostles are fishermen. The text of Mark is in Greek. The Old Testament texts which Mark claims to quote are also in Greek, a pastiche of several different passages from the Septuagint. If the "fishers" of Mark 1:16 is substituted for the "messenger" of Mark 1:2, we get back to the text from Jeremiah, "Behold, I will send for many fishers." Mark and his editors were structuralists too![8]

But let us return to the apostolic fishermen.

How about the historical geography? It is not impossible. The Sea of Galilee is a lake, thirteen miles long and eight miles wide at its maximum breadth. In recent times, before 1948, the boats that were to be found there were few and small; in Gospel times they were numerous but were probably of a similar type. A boat photographed around 1909 could plausibly have held the five individuals required by Mark 1:19–20. But Mark's details are unsatisfactory. According to recent ethnography, fishing is a nighttime occupation; netmending takes place by day. Nets are mended onshore, not in a boat.[9]

So, taken as a whole, Mark's scene is imaginary. That implies that each implausible detail must "mean" something. So why does Mark introduce Zebedee and his hired servants? They do not appear again, but James and John remain "the sons of Zebedee."

The two pairs of brothers who are summoned as disciples in Mark 1:16–20 remain leading apostles throughout the Gospel story except that Andrew (who is here paired with Simon-Peter) fades into oblivion. The evangelists juggle with these names in different ways, thereby introducing a kinship factor which may not have been intended. Thus one widely accepted reading of a combination of Mark 15:40, Matthew 27:56, and John 19:25 would make the mother of James and John, the sons of Zebedee, the sister of the Virgin Mary.

But this is a complicated matter and I will not discuss it in detail though it can be connected with the rest of my argument. I will stick to the fish and the fishermen.

The initial problem is why the fishermen apostles of Mark 1:16–20 should be treated as two pairs of brothers. The pairing persists. James and

John in particular are treated as inseparable as if they were twins. They are frequently referred to collectively as "the sons of Zebedee" and once by the title "Boanerges," which is interpreted in the text as meaning "the sons of thunder" (Mark 3:17). In other contexts in which these same four original apostles are mentioned the order is rearranged to Simon-Peter, James, John, Andrew (as in Acts 1:13) but the names James and John are always adjacent.

But why sons of thunder? Why Zebedee?

It has been suggested that Boanerges was a corruption of *Bene regesh* and that *regesh* might have been Aramaic for "thunder," but that doesn't help much. Zebedee (Greek, *Zebedaios*) is presumed to be the equivalent of Hebrew Zebedaiah. The name is not unlike that of several undistinguished Old Testament characters. In Hebrew the name might mean "Gift of God." An implausible Greek etymology might produce *za-ba-dios*, which could mean something like "the divine king."

But the reference need not be biblical at all. The fishing-for-men symbolism was not confined to Judaism; it had widespread ramifications in the pagan mystery cults that flourished in the first century C.E., and heavenly twins were everywhere.

The mythology of the heavenly twins of Greco-Roman myth (Dioscuri/Gemini) is complex and inconsistent. In the commonest surviving version, they were the sons of Leda by different fathers but born on the same day. Kastor (Castor) was the son of the human king Tyndareus and initially mortal; Polydeuces (Pollux) was the son of Zeus and initially immortal, but because Polydeuces refused to be separated from his dead brother, they were eventually both made immortal but spent their days alternately in heaven and in the underworld. They were thus worshiped as a single incarnate mediating deity and jointly titled *Dios Kuroi* (that is, "sons of God"). Since Zeus was prototypically the god of thunder, "sons of thunder" would be an appropriate alternative title for the Dioscuri. There is no literary evidence that they were ever so named, but there is not much literary evidence of any sort on this subject.

All these associations are very thin, yet it deserves note that Zeus visited Leda in the form of a swan (that is, as a deity who walked on the water as Jesus did in Matt. 14:25–26) and that the Dioscuri were, among other things, the patron saints of sailors in distress. They were specially invoked in times of storm, when they manifested themselves as white birds and stilled the storm. Storm-stilling is one of the powers which Jesus delegates to his fishermen disciples, and the standard symbol for the Holy Ghost is a white bird.

I am not suggesting that the reader/listener is *required* to interpret "sons of thunder" in this way, but many of Mark's original Greek-speaking audience would surely have made associations along these lines.

Modern Jews and Christians have been brought up to believe that the

deity of the Bible is an entity of an entirely different order from that of
the pagan gods and goddesses of the Greco-Roman world. It would not
have seemed like that in the first century C.E.

But Zebedee and Boanerges are not central to my analysis. The key
point is that, from a structuralist point of view, all the New Testament
fishermen stories can be treated as component elements in the same myth/
dream story, a single theme with variations and repetitions. What sort of
story?

In Mark 1:16 two fishermen throw their net into the sea; in Mark
1:19 two fishermen mend their net while sitting in a boat; in Mark 4:37–
41 Jesus stills the storm; in Matthew 13:47–51 Jesus preaches the parable
of the net; in Matthew 14:24–33 Jesus walks on the waters and is joined
by Peter, who is submerged and saved in the process (he is baptized); in
Luke 5:2–11 one fisherman (Peter), with the sons of Zebedee as his partners, has a miraculous "draught of fishes," but their net breaks; in John
21:1–14 one fisherman (Peter), with the same and other partners, has a
miraculous draught of fishes, but his net does not break. In the last
reference Peter jumps into the sea naked (he is again baptized) (John 21:7).

The parable of the net makes the significance of the fishing for men
trope quite explicit, at any rate as it was understood by the author/editors
of Matthew.

> Again, the kingdom of heaven is like unto a net, that was cast into the sea,
> and gathered of every kind: Which, when it was full, they drew to shore,
> and sat down, and gathered the good into vessels, but cast the bad away. So
> shall it be at the end of the world: the angels shall come forth, and sever the
> wicked from among the just, And shall cast them into the furnace of fire:
> there shall be wailing and gnashing of teeth.   (Matt. 13:47–50)

I cannot do better than that. The mytho-logic of the apostolic fishermen trope is that the fish in the lake are the souls of men crossing over
from this world to the Other as they approach death (or the Day of
Judgment—as in Jeremiah). Those who are caught in the net are the elect,
who are saved; those who are not caught are the damned. In Luke 5 the
net breaks, some of the souls are not saved. In John 21 the net does not
break. Salvation is for all. But the fish number 153.

Down the centuries, Christian numerologists (and there have been
many) have had great fun with this "153." The earliest theory was that of
St. Jerome, which fits well with my argument. He claimed that it was
known to the ancients that there were in the whole world 153 kinds of
fish. No such statement occurs in surviving classical texts but this explanation would make the miraculous draught of fishes in John 21 echo
Matthew 13:47 as well as the teeming fish in Ezekiel's vision of the life-
giving stream:

everything . . . which moveth, whithersoever the rivers shall come, shall live: and there shall be a very great multitude of fish, because these waters shall come thither: for they shall be healed; and everything shall live whither the river cometh. (Ezek. 47:9)

If we accept that, then the message of the 153 is the same as that of the unbroken net: "salvation is for all."

But why should it be Peter who catches the fish? *Petros* in Greek and *cephas* in Aramaic both mean "rock." He was already so named by Paul. According to John 1:42 he is given the name by Jesus, for no obvious reason. The story here seems to contradict that of Mark 1:16–17. In this case Simon-Peter and Andrew are not fishermen but followers of John the Baptist who are at "Bethabara beyond Jordan" (that is, in the Wilderness) (John 1:28, 40–41). If the cross-reference implied by the name Cephas was originally to the rock in the Wilderness from which flowed the water of life teeming with fish, things would hang together. This seems to me much more plausible than the explanation offered in Matthew 17:18, which must date from a period when the bishop of Rome was already acknowledged as head of the Church and successor to Peter.

But the metaphors relating to the apostolic fishermen are multivalent and closely packed.

Any standard reference book about symbolism in Christian art will include the information that the fish stands for Christ himself and that the association is based on a cryptogram. The initial letters of the formula IĒSOUS CHRISTOS THEOU YIOS SŌTĒR (Jesus Christ, Son of God, Savior) read I.CH.TH.Y.S., the Greek for "fish."

But this appears to be a rationalization of the fourth century C.E., when Christian symbols on mosaic floors were becoming commonplace. There are much earlier associations of gods and fish in the eastern Mediterranean, and when Tertullian, writing in Latin at the end of the second century, described Christ as "our Ichthys" and baptized Christians as little fishes, he was referring not to an acrostic but to a very widespread conception of deity.[10]

But that lead could take us far afield. In *The Golden Bough* Sir James Frazer wrote twelve volumes about dying gods and divine kings. If he had chosen to write about dying gods and phallic fish, his book would have been just as long. I will mention only one nonbiblical example and two Old Testament cross-references.

The prototype of all dying god stories is the Egyptian myth of the murder of Osiris by his brother Seth and his subsequent rebirth in the form of Horus from the body of his sister-wife-mother, Isis.

There are many versions of this story, but all agree that Seth tore up Osiris' body and scattered the pieces. Isis and her sister reassembled the scattered pieces, but the penis was missing. In Plutarch's account this was because it had been swallowed by a fish. Isis made herself pregnant by means of the phallus of the dead Osiris and gave birth to Horus, who was hidden in the reeds of the Nile after the manner of Moses in the bulrushes. This complex story of death and rebirth includes the equation fish = penis = God.[11]

The first biblical cross-reference is that the name Jesus is the same as that of the Old Testament Joshua, the replacement of Moses. Joshua is called "the son of Nun" (Joshua 1:1). But in Hebrew *nun* means "fish."[12]

The second is the story in which Jonah spends three days and three nights in the belly of the great fish (Jonah 1:17). This was a very early and very common Christian "type" for Christ's resurrection and for the promise of future resurrection for mankind. It was frequently used as a decoration for elaborate Roman Christian sarcophagi (see Matt. 12:40).

That is enough. According to the early Christian Fathers the New Testament lies concealed in the Old. We know that, so why say it again? I am not claiming any originality, but I am arguing that biblical coherence is much more radical than most contemporary scholars seem to realize.

But I am also making a complementary point. It is only the professional theologians who have an interest in dissecting the total text into self-sufficient fragments. The ordinary, nonacademic reader of the Bible takes it for granted that the story has an overall unity and that one should read it as literature, as a total work of art, much as one listens to choral singing echoing from the vaulted roof of a gothic cathedral.

The reader/listener does not have to be a sophisticated scholar to proceed in this way, but if we pay close attention to the detailed patterning of the echoes, we shall perceive much that might otherwise be missed.

NOTES

1. Preliminary versions of this essay took the form of seminar papers and lectures presented at King's College, Cambridge; the Hebrew University of Jerusalem; Willamette University, Oregon; the University of Montana; the University of Lethbridge; and the University of Calgary. I have made use of helpful comments offered by members of the audience in all these institutions.

2. The colored miniature which serves as the original for this drawing is described in detail by Otto Pächt in *The St. Albans Psalter (Albani Psalter)*, Studies of the Warburg Institute, XXV (London, 1960).

3. G. I. Davies, *The Way of the Wilderness* (Cambridge, 1979), provides a scholarly assessment of the evidence. U. W. Mauser, *Christ in the Wilderness*, Studies in Biblical Theology, XXXIX (London, 1963), is an example of a totally different, much less prosaic, approach to a similar problem.

4. Arnold van Gennep, *Les rites de passage* (Paris, 1909); English translation by M. B. Vizedom and G. L. Caffee, *The Rites of Passage* (London, 1960). Van Gennep's original argument has been considerably expanded by later authors; see in particular V. W. Turner, *The Ritual Process* (London, 1969).

5. E. R. Goodenough, *Jewish Symbols in the Greco-Roman Period*, 13 vols. (Princeton, 1953–68), VI, 186.

6. Ibid., p. 184.

7. Ibid., V, 31–61, discusses the extensive literature, with supplementary material at XII, 96–101.

8. Mark 1:2: *idou egō apostellō ton aggellon* ("Behold I send the messenger"). Mark 1:16: *ēsan gar halieis* ("for they were fishers"). Jer. 16:16: *idou egō apostellō tous halieis tous pollous* ("Behold I will send the many fishers").

9. E. W. G. Masterman, *Studies in Galilee* (Chicago, 1909), plate facing p. 3.

10. For extensive discussion see Goodenough, *Jewish Symbols*, V, 32–35. The drawing bears on this point. Two other pictures by the same twelfth-century artist emphasize the importance of fish as part of the food in the Eucharist. In the drawing itself the cloak of water enveloping the naked Jesus is fish shaped. However, Adolf Goldschmidt, *Der Albanipsalter in Hildesheim und seine Beziehung zur symbolischen Kirchensculptur der XII Jahrhunderts* (Berlin, 1895), saw this enveloping cloak of water as mountain shaped. Tertullian, who was responsible for the *Ichthys*–little fishes metaphor, also insisted that the liturgy of the baptismal rite should include anointing with oil. In the drawing the angel on the left appears to be holding a towel and the angel on the right a coat. Goldschmidt saw the picture in this way. The original, however, is more ambiguous. Pächt, *The St. Albans Psalter*, considers that the angel on the left is holding not a towel but part of its own costume. In the colored original there is a sharp contrast: the angel on the left holds a dark cloth, the one on the right a bright garment. If dark:bright::old:new, then we may have a cross-reference to Zech. 3:3–4. In the baptismal rite of the Greek Orthodox Church the infant initiate is anointed with oil as well as immersed naked in water. After this baptism the infant is dressed in new clothes (provided by the godmother) which replace those worn at the beginning of the rite.

11. See R. T. Rundle Clark, *Myth and Symbol in Ancient Egypt* (London, 1959), chaps. 3–5.

12. W. Robertson Smith, *Kinship and Marriage in Early Arabia*, 2d ed. (London, 1907), pp. 255–256, appears to argue that Joshua's patronymic is based on that of the Syrian god Dagon, who was likewise named Ichthys in Greek but whose name had an Aramaic version corresponding to "son of *nun*", which, more properly, should have been "son of *nuna*" because the divine parent fish in question was the goddess Atargatis, who was closely associated with Isis/Ishtar.

SUGGESTED FURTHER READINGS

Most of the substantial literature of biblical Structuralism is in French and is freighted with jargon and elaborate formalistic designs. Much of the English-language material in this field has been published in the periodical *Semeia* or as monographs in the *Semeia Supplements*. Polzin's book below provides a comprehensive bibliography.

Robert M. Polzin, *Biblical Structuralism: Method and Subjectivity in the Study of Ancient Texts*, Semeia Supplements, no. 4 (Philadelphia and Missoula, Mont., 1979).

Edmund Leach, *Genesis as Myth and Other Essays* (London, 1969).
Edmund Leach and D. Alan Aycock, *Structuralist Interpretations of Biblical Myth* (Cambridge, 1983).

King's College, University of Cambridge

The Canon

Frank Kermode

THIS chapter offers some explanation of the processes by which the Bible came to include the books it does—insofar as that can be done in reasonable space, or indeed at all—and to venture some remarks on the consequences of their transmission to us as a single book. But it is necessary to begin by saying why we have chosen this particular version of the Bible; for there are many differently constituted Bibles, each with its own version of the canon, and it might be thought that our choice is quite arbitrary. Most obviously, the Jewish Bible lacks the twenty-seven books of the New Testament. The Jewish Bible in Greek—a collection of great antiquity and authority—differs as to contents, and frequently as to text, from the Hebrew Bible. The Latin Bible of the Roman Catholic tradition contains in its Old Testament books dismissed by the Bibles of the Reformed churches as apocryphal. Those churches include as their Old Testament the books of the Hebrew Bible and the twenty-seven New Testament books. This is the "Bible" treated in the present book; it is what most people think of when they think of the Bible; it is the collection to which modern literatures mostly refer; and the fact that all Bibles have them, no matter what else they include, gives them an importance greater than that of the disputed elements. This does not imply a literary judgment on the works excluded, nor does it reflect a belief that all the canonical books are of superior merit. We do not understand all the criteria of canonicity, but we know enough to be sure that modern criteria of literary quality have no relevance to them.

Even the most learned explanations of how the constituent books found themselves together in a canon are highly speculative and have to deal with an intractable mixture of myth and history. Once a sacred book is fully formed, deemed to be unalterable and wholly inspired, it acquires a prehistory suitable to its status and related only very loosely to historical fact or probability. The real history involves all manner of external influences: for example, the closing of the Jewish canon must be in some sense consequent upon the waning of Hebrew as a spoken language, and upon the destruction of the Temple in 70 C.E., when the book rather than the Temple cult became central to religion. Already there were more Jews in the Diaspora than in Palestine, so the time for such a change was ripe, and the Bible, already holy, acquired an extra cultic sanctity. In the case of the New Testament it seems possible that the lack of an appropriate technology prevented its achieving definitive shape until the fourth century. The Christians preferred the codex or leaf-book to the scroll, and during the earlier period these newfangled codices could not contain texts of any great extent; only in the fourth century did it become possible to produce a codex that would hold all the accepted Christian Scriptures. Thus canon formation is affected by what seem on the face of it to be political, economic, and technological forces without immediate religious or literary relevance.

The legendary account of the growth of the Bible tells of the destruction of the sacred books during the Babylonian Captivity and their reconstruction by the divinely inspired memory of Ezra. By his time (fifth century B.C.E.) the canon was virtually complete, though Daniel, traditionally ascribed to the sixth century, was added in the second. At the end of the first century C.E. a final list was established at the Council of Jamnia. A more scholarly account would say that the importance of the Law after the return from Babylon speeded the process by which all the disparate material in the Pentateuch acquired final form and authority; the other two sections, the Prophets and the Writings, developed at a different pace, and in some instances, notably that of the Song of Songs, there was dispute about a book's status well into the second century C.E.; tradition has it that the Song of Songs was saved by the advocacy of Aquiba, as a religious allegory. Although the proceedings at Jamnia are not nowadays thought to have been concerned with the canon, the learned still appear to accept the date, ca. 100 C.E., as about right for the closure of the canon. It was of course necessary to leave things out as well as let things in, and a distinction was drawn between books which "defiled the hands" because of their sacred quality, and "outside" books which presumably failed this test, though they might still be granted a certain extracanonical utility. Such was the practice as early as Ezra, who, according to legend, set aside for the use of the wise seventy books apart from the Scriptures proper. Books thus set aside or hidden away would be apocrypha in the original sense; the word later acquired dyslogistic overtones, and the apocryphal came to mean the false or inauthentic.

It would be wrong to suppose that all the constituent books were submitted to the same impartial examination. The Five Books of Moses were naturally of unassailable authority, as were the Psalms and the Prophets. The invocation of Old Testament texts in the Gospels is evidence, if such were needed, of the reverence accorded the Scriptures in a time before the canon was finally established. One might say that there was a canonical habit of mind before there was finally a canon, and that it was in evidence during the long centuries that separate Ezra from 100 C.E. There is some question whether it is proper to speak of a Jewish canon at all, and insofar as it has to be accepted as corresponding to real historical developments it may be thought of as a fictional construct concealing the historical truth. Thus the large redactive enterprises carried out on the Torah are concealed by its canonical form, and scholarship has to break it down again into its original components. It is true that revisions of the Old Testament books were carried out in response to external pressures— for example, the political needs of post-Exilic Israel, and, in the first century C.E., the centrifugal force of heresy and schism. But the fact that Judaism reacted to these forces by affirming the cohesion of the Scriptures and, ultimately, by effectively closing the canon is sufficient evidence not only of the significance of the individual books, but of the belief that their power was enhanced by membership in a whole greater than the sum of its parts.

The evolution of the New Testament is another story, though hardly less complicated and conjectural. The first Christians already had a Bible— the Jewish Bible in various forms, Hebrew and Greek and Aramaic—and saw no need of another. What was central to their beliefs was transmitted by oral tradition; indeed the authority of that tradition survived into the second century, although most of what was to become the New Testament already existed. The power of the oral tradition did not reduce the Christian commitment to the Jewish Scriptures; the faithful lived in the end time, history was coming to a close, and events would all occur "according to the scriptures," as they had in the life of Jesus. In a sense the oral tradition took its place beside the Scriptures, just as the Jewish tradition of oral interpretation filled out the implications of the written Torah. In the end both were written down, but the Christian writings came earlier, partly because Paul wrote letters which acquired general authority, and partly because as the years passed it must have seemed important to perpetuate the increasingly fragile oral testimony of the works and sayings of Jesus. One consequence of the growth of Christian Scripture was the transformation of the Old Testament into quite a different book, a sort of unintended prologue to the New Testament. Whether it should be retained at all became a serious question; and the reasons for keeping it were of a kind that had nothing to do with Judaism.

The gradual replacement of the oral tradition by writing was the necessary prelude to the establishment of a canon, with all the consequences of that development. Oral tradition is quite different from written; it is variable, subject to human memory (however aided by mnemonics), discontinuous, selective, and affected by feedback from audiences. It would encourage its transmitters to invent and to add interpretations. It has been suggested that Mark's Gospel—which we take to be the first of the canonical four—resulted from a conscious rejection of the oral tradition, which it represents as virtually extinct (the women at the tomb fail to transmit an oral message to the disciples) or as corrupted by the false preachers and prophets Mark assails in chapter 13.

Neither Paul nor the evangelists wrote with the object of adding to the existing Bible; indeed the only book of the New Testament that claims such inspired status is Revelation, with its threat of damnation to anybody presuming to add to it. Paul's earliest letters belong to about 50 C.E.; the Gospels are of uncertain date, the consensus being that they belong to some time between 60 and 90 C.E., though earlier dates have been proposed. It seems likely that the contents of the New Testament were written over a span of something close to a century, and none of them by writers who supposed they were candidates for entry into a fixed corpus of Scripture.

It is easier to understand why gospels got written (though less easy to see why they took the form they have) than to guess why four, no more and no less, were finally accepted. There must have been many more, and it appears that in the second century there were three versions of Mark available, one public, one reserved for the few, and another used by a Gnostic sect and condemned by the orthodox. Only the public version survives. John was also attractive to Gnostics, and there was accordingly stiff opposition to his inclusion in the canon. Here again we need to remember that "gospel" originally meant not a piece of writing but the good news proclaimed by Jesus; the evangelists wrote down their versions of this news, which were labeled "the Gospel according to X," and eventually the term came to mean also this new genre. The relation of these new documents to the existing Scriptures was a matter for dispute; the heretic Marcion wanted to do away with the Jewish Scriptures altogether, and to recognize as authoritative only a version of Luke and of some Pauline letters. It was conceivably in response to such ideas that orthodoxy felt it must decide what had authority and what didn't, settling on four Gospels as part of the New Covenant or Testament. The concept of a new covenant and of its fulfilling or even replacing an older one is immediately indebted to the Eucharist, for Jesus spoke of the cup as the new covenant (*hē kainē diathēkē*) (1 Cor. 11:25, Luke 22:20), and ultimately to the covenantal element in Jewish theology. When Paul (2 Cor. 3:14) talks about the Jewish dispensation as the old written covenant now replaced by that of Christ—the letter replaced by the Spirit—he is still thinking of the new testament (this is the Latin translation of *diathēkē*) as unwritten. Indeed the expressions *diathēkē* and *testamentum* (sometimes *instrumentum*) were not applied to the new writings until late in the second century, by which time the idea of a body of authoritative Christian writings, including the letters of Paul and the four Gospels, was well established. In the intervening period it is probable that the originals were altered or augmented for the sake of doctrine or inclusiveness; they were not thought of as inspired. Reasons for holding them to be so were provided later. Only when their inspiration became an issue did the discrepancies among the four seem to call for attention. Around 170 C.E. Tatian produced his Diatessaron ("Through the Four"), the first of many attempts to harmonize the Gospels. The idea of producing synopses to expose rather than eliminate the differences and facilitate research into relations and priorities arose many centuries later in modern biblical criticism.

Fanciful explanations were available for there being four Gospels, no more and no less: the compass has four points, the cherubim four faces; there are four covenants, associated with Adam, Noah, Moses, and Christ. The discrepancies among them could be explained as a test of faith. Perhaps the commonsense answer is that of Harry Y. Gamble, that the fourfold Gospels represent "a precarious balance between unmanageable multiplicity on the one hand and a single self-consistent gospel on the other."[1] At any rate the four came to be canonical.

Other books were scrutinized according to criteria on the nature of which there is still much dispute, though it is interesting to note that the tests applied were in part philological. It was noticed, for instance, that the Greek of Revelation is not that of the evangelist John, to whom it was attributed; and that the Greek of Hebrews is of a quality sufficient to prove that it was not written by Paul—perhaps, it was proposed, Luke wrote it up from notes. Doubts were entertained concerning 2 Peter and 2–3 John. These issues never quite died away and were important at the time of the Reformation, since *sola scriptura* requires one to be sure what *scriptura* really is. Luther at first rejected Revelation and had grave doubts about James. But all these works have survived in the canon.

As time passed Christianity also became to a great extent dependent on a book, and although the authority of the oral tradition survived—and continues to survive in the magisterium of the Roman Church—the written word acquired the greater power. There remained the need to close the canon, and the date given for this is 367 C.E., when Athanasius listed the twenty-seven books as the only canonical ones. He actually used the word, and also gave a list of rejected books, which he called apocrypha. Doubts persisted, and there may be argument as to whether the canon can really be said to be closed; but it has not been added to as yet, nor has anything been taken away from it; and it is hard to see how the Gospel of Thomas, discovered in this century, if added to the canon, could partake of the authority acquired by the others over the years.

Kanōn, a Greek word originally meaning "rod," came to signify many other things, including an ethical norm or a rule or criterion. It could also mean a list of books, sometimes—and this is the beginning of the biblical sense—a list of recommended books. By 400 C.E. it meant, for Christians, only those books held to be holy and of authority. The Jewish canon, even though it was not so called, had similar qualities. It is characteristic of the Jewish tradition that great care was taken over the transmission by copying of the sacred text, which was held to be unalterable and without corruption, though, as bibliographers know well, this is humanly impossible. The books contained within the canon or canons are held to be inspired and to be interrelated like the parts of a single book. Their relations with "outside" books are of a quite different order. It is important to understand the extraordinary privilege of these inside books. Religious and political history would have been unimaginably different if the apocalyptic prophecies of Daniel had been excluded from the Old Testament, or those of Revelation from the New. John Barton has some interesting observations on the overwhelming importance of inclusion in the canon: suppose Ecclesiastes had been turned down, lost, and rediscovered recently among the documents at Qumran—would it not be virtually a different book from the one we have?[2] Canonization can thus, as it were, alter the meanings of books.

The doctrine that the Bible is its own interpreter was held in different circumstances by both the rabbis and Luther, and the belief that one can best interpret a text by associating it with another text of similar authority clearly presupposes a canon; the idea of explorable correspondences between every part would be absurd if one had no certainty about the extent of the whole. If the entire text is inspired—a belief deeply held by the Jews, with their scrupulousness about every jot and tittle, and given formal expression for the Christian canon at the Council of Trent in the sixteenth century—then the most fleeting echo, perhaps only of a single word, is significant. And given that everything is inspired, all possible relations among parts of the text are also inspired. The poet George Herbert had these relations in mind when he wrote, in "The Holy Scriptures, II":

> Oh, that I knew how all thy lights combine,
>   And the configurations of their glorie!
>   Seeing not onely how each verse doth shine,
>   But all the constellations of the storie.
> This verse marks that, and both do make a motion
>   Unto a third, that ten leaves off doth lie:
>   Then as dispersed herbs do watch a potion,
>   These three make up some Christians destinie.

We can now specify certain characteristics of the mythical or magical view of the canon. Regardless of innumerable historical vicissitudes, redactions, interpolations, and corruptions, the canonical text is held to be eternally fixed, unalterable, and of such immeasurable interpretative potential that it remains, despite its unaltered state, sufficient for all future times. This perpetual applicability is established by a continuing tradition of interpretation, as the relevance of old texts to new times always is. Interpretation is controlled by changing rules but is remarkably free, for the canonical book, itself fixed in time and probably in a dead language, has to be made relevant to an unforeseen future. It must prefigure history: hence we have typological interpretations. The book becomes a mythical model of the world: the Torah is said to be identical with the Creation, the Christian Bible becomes the twin of the Book of Nature. And the exploration of these world-books requires interpreters who can study the subtle hidden structures just as physicists and chemists (or their ancestors, the alchemists and astrologers and magicians) studied the created world.

It is hardly surprising that the assumptions underlying these views collapsed with the onset of modern scientific philology. From the beginning the canon was seen as a late and arbitrary imposition on the books it contained. Those books should be studied like any other ancient texts, understood in their original senses, and valued for what they told us about the past, so that the work of the interpreter becomes primarily archaeological. It is not the book's membership in a canon that gives it authority, but its report of or allusion to various historical events and persons. And of course the true as opposed to the legendary history of the formation of the canons supports this commonsense view of the matter, for there is little reason to believe that such a series of accidents, unexplained judgments, decisions taken under who knows what political or ecclesiastical duress, should result in a divinely privileged, exclusively sacred, compilation. For the factitious context of the canon the scholars substituted the larger contexts of history. They knew by what methods the sacred texts had been made closely applicable to modern situations; if the New Testament had not already taught them that lesson, the Dead Sea Scrolls, which applied ancient Scriptures exclusively to the concerns of a particular sect at a moment presumed to be just before the End, must have made it plain. And thus the canon, despite its importance in the formation and continuance of the religious institutions which endorsed it, seemed to crumble away. It was no longer a separate cognitive zone, merely a rather randomly assembled batch of historical texts; really, one may say, no longer a Bible so much as a collection of *biblia*.

Such attitudes are as old as "scientific" biblical criticism, from the beginnings of which in the late eighteenth century it was assumed, by Michaelis among others, that the canon was not uniformly inspired, and that by historical analysis one could even assist religion by finding out which books were inspired and which were not. Later the question of inspiration was dropped, or the word acquired a new sense. It might be difficult for some investigators to devote themselves to pure historical truth when it involved the dissolution of the New Testament into a scatter of fortuitously assembled occasional writings; for in most cases these scholars were Christians, and the New Testament is after all the foundation document of their religion. But there were ways out of that dilemma which did not involve their subscribing to obsolete and false ideas about the canon.

In recent years the historical-critical tradition, now well over two centuries old, has been under challenge. That tradition also made hermeneutical assumptions of which its practitioners were not fully aware. For example, they were ready to believe that older views on the canon and the status of the separate books could be dismissed as peculiar to their time and as founded on assumptions now evidently false; but they took it for granted that they themselves were exempt from historical "situatedness," that they could, without interference from their own prejudices (of which they were unaware), transport themselves across history in a pure and disinterested way. As Hans-Georg Gadamer has put it, the historical critic is always seeking in the text something that is not the text, something the text of itself, is not seeking to provide; "he will always go back behind [the texts] and the meaning they express [which he will decline to regard as their true meaning] to enquire into the reality of which they are the involuntary expression."[3] But it is possible to take an interest in the text and its own meaning; that is literary criticism proper, and Gadamer believes that it has for too long (in these circles) been regarded as "an ancillary discipline to history."

The opposition that has lately developed to "scientific" disintegration of the canon is based on the idea that the Bible still ought to be treated as a "collection with parameters."[4] Brevard Childs, who uses these words, has studied both Testaments from the point of view of a revived but still moderate belief in canonicity. Childs wants to eliminate the tensions between historical criticism and an understanding of the Bible as canonical Scripture; he wants, not a return to precritical notions of the canon, but attention to its historical integrity; for he thinks it important that the canon was the product of historical interactions between the developing corpus and the changing community, not of some belated and extrinsic act of validation. And when fully formed the canon is not just an opaque wrapping that must be removed so that one can get at the contents and see them as they really were. Of course the constituents have their own histories, and it is good to know about them. But their preservation and their authority are owing not primarily to their usefulness as testimony to historical events. It is their capacity to be *applied*, their applicability to historical circumstances other than those of their origin, that has saved them alive.

Whatever one's view of the controversy now in progress between defenders of the tradition of historical criticism and practitioners of what is now called "canonical criticism," it is clear that the latter is not a primitivistic revival of precritical notions of plenary and exclusive inspiration. Since we are still living in an epoch in which the historical or "scientific" approach is normal, and therefore seems commonsensical or natural, we may tend to dismiss the opposition as merely eccentric. Yet its presuppositions are at least as defensible as those of the "normal" practitioners; both sides make large assumptions, the one believing that events and persons can be made available, as if by magic, to the reader, and the other that historical application can form a body of discrete writings into a whole—as if by magic.

This, of course, is a different kind of magic from the old one; yet the old one still exerts its attractions. It remains quite difficult to think of the wholeness of a canon without associating the idea with the wholeness of an organism or the wholeness of a world. We observe in the realm of secular literary criticism the powerful effect of canon formation on the kinds of attention paid to the books included, even though it is impossible to think of secular canons as closed with the same definitiveness as ecclesiastical canons. And it is undeniably attractive to be able to think of the canon as forming an intertextual system of great complexity, to be studied, by a weaker magic than was available in the past though it is still a kind of magic, as a fascinating array of occult relations, a world of words.

Goethe, commending *Hamlet*, said it was like a tree, each part of it there for, and by means of, all the others. Five hundred years earlier a Kabbalist said this of the Torah: "Just as a tree consists of branches and leaves, bark, sap and roots, each one of which components can be termed tree, there being no substantial difference between them, you will also find that the Torah contains many things, and all form a single Torah and a tree, without difference between them . . . It is necessary to know that the whole is one unity."[5] Moses de Leon and Goethe appear to have had the same thought, though we could make the two statements sound very different by examining their contexts: one of them belongs to what we think of as Romantic organicism, the other to Kabbalistic mysticism and a Jewish tradition that has always accommodated change and variety of interpretation but has always thought of the Torah as an entity, coextensive with the created world.

A flatter, more rational version of the holisms of Goethe and Moses de Leon might be thought to suit us better in our own time. It is true that both historically and actually we grant a different form of attention to canonical books, and that secular criticism has seriously entertained notions of the literary canon that might well be thought to give it a kind of wholeness and a high degree of intertextual relations. Examples include the canonical element in the criticism of T. S. Eliot and the stronger holistic claims of Wilson Knight. It is not surprising, therefore, that the professional biblical critics should feel a renewed obligation to save their canon. Schleiermacher, usually thought to be the founder of modern hermeneutics, was also a major New Testament scholar; he believed that the study of the constituents of the canon must be carried on by exactly the same methods and with the same object as the investigation of secular texts, but he also remarked that "a continuing preoccupation with the New Testament canon which was not motivated by one's own interest in Christianity could only be directed against the canon."[6] It was out of such a conflict of interest that new ways of thinking about the interpretation of ancient texts developed, and new ways of thinking about history in general. Whether the canon in question is Christian or Jewish or secular, we can no longer suppose that there is a simple choice between the historical and the canonical approach, since the two are now inextricably intertwined. It is an empirical fact that each book has its own history; it is also true that the association of many books in a canon was the result of a long historical process and owed much to chance and much to the needs and the thinking of people we know little or nothing about. But it is also a fact that works transmitted inside a canon are understood differently from those without, so that, if only in that sense, the canon, however assembled, forms an integral whole, the internal and external relations of which are both proper subjects of disinterested inquiry. Nor need we suppose that we have altogether eliminated from our study of canonical works every scrap of the old organicist assumptions, every concession to a magical view of these worlds and their profound, obscure correspondences. When we have achieved *that* degree of disinterest we shall have little use for the canon or for its constituents, and we shall have little use either for poetry.

NOTES

1. Harry Y. Gamble, *The New Testament Canon* (Philadelphia, 1985), p. 35.

2. John Barton, *Reading the Old Testament* (London, 1984), p. 102.

3. Hans-Georg Gadamer, *Truth and Method*, ed. Garrett Barden and John Cumming (New York, 1975), pp. 301–302.

4. Brevard S. Childs, *Introduction to the Old Testament as Scripture* (London and Philadelphia, 1979), p. 83.

5. Gershom G. Scholem, *On the Kabbalah and Its Symbolism*, trans. Ralph Manheim (London, 1965), p. 46.

6. Quoted in W. G. Kümmel, *The New Testament: The History of the Investigation of Its Problems*, trans. S. McLean Gilmour and Howard C. Kee (London, 1973), p. 425.

SUGGESTED FURTHER READINGS

James Barr, *Holy Scripture: Canon, Authority, Criticism* (Oxford and Philadelphia, 1983).

John Barton, *Reading the Old Testament* (London, 1984).

Gerald L. Bruns, "Canon and Power in the Hebrew Scriptures," in Robert von Hallberg, ed., *Canons* (Chicago, 1984).

Brevard S. Childs, *Introduction to the Old Testament as Scripture* (London and Philadelphia, 1979).

———, *The New Testament as Canon* (London, 1984).

Otto Eissfeldt, *The Old Testament: An Introduction* (Oxford and New York, 1965).

Hans-Georg Gadamer, *Truth and Method*, ed. Garrett Barden and John Cumming (New York, 1975).

Harry Y. Gamble, *The New Testament Canon* (Philadelphia, 1985).

R. M. Grant, "Literary Criticism and the New Testament Canon," *Journal for the Study of the New Testament*, 16 (1982), 24–44.

E. Hennecke, *New Testament Apocrypha*, I (London, 1963).

Werner H. Kelber, *The Oral and the Written Gospel* (Philadelphia, 1983).

W. G. Kümmel, *Introduction to the New Testament* (London, 1975), pp. 475–510.

Morton Smith, *Clement of Alexandria and a Secret Gospel* (Cambridge, Mass., 1973).

King's College, University of Cambridge

The Characteristics
of Ancient Hebrew Poetry

Robert Alter

EXACTLY what is the poetry of the Bible, and what role does it play in giving form to the biblical religious vision? The second of these two questions obviously involves all sorts of imponderables. One would think that, by contrast, the first question should have a straightforward answer; but in fact there has been considerable confusion through the ages about where there is poetry in the Bible and about the principles on which that poetry works.

To begin with, biblical poetry occurs almost exclusively in the Hebrew Bible. There are, of course, grandly poetic passages in the New Testament—perhaps most impressively in the Apocalypse—but only the Magnificat of Luke 1 is fashioned as formal verse. Readers of the Old Testament often cannot easily see where the poetry is supposed to be because in the King James Version, which has been the text used by most English-speaking people, nothing is laid out as lines of verse. This confusing typographic procedure is in turn faithful to the Hebrew manuscript tradition, which runs everything together in dense, unpunctuated columns. (There are just a few exceptions where there is a spacing out roughly corresponding to lines of verse, as in the Song of the Sea, Exod. 15; Moses' valedictory song, Deut. 32; and an occasional manuscript of Psalms.)

What has accompanied this graphic leveling of poetry with prose in the text is a kind of cultural amnesia about biblical poetics. Over the centuries, Psalms was most clearly perceived as poetry, probably because of the actual musical indications in the texts and the obvious liturgical function of many of the poems. The status as poetry of the Song of Songs and Job was, because of the lyric beauty of the one and the grandeur of the other, also generally kept in sight, however farfetched the notions about the formal character of the verse in these books. Proverbs was somewhat more intermittently seen as poetry, and it was often not understood that the Prophets cast the larger part of their message in verse. Finally, it is only in our century that scholars have begun to realize to what extent the prose narratives of the Bible are studded with brief verse

611

insets, usually introduced at dramatically justified or otherwise significant junctures in the stories.

Over the last two millennia—and, for many, down to the present—being a reader of biblical poetry has been like being a reader of Dryden and Pope who comes from a culture with no concept of rhyme: you would loosely grasp that the language was intricately organized as verse, but with the uneasy feeling that you were somehow missing something essential you couldn't quite define. The central informing convention of biblical verse was rediscovered in the mid-eighteenth century by a scholarly Anglican bishop, Robert Lowth. He proposed that lines of biblical verse comprised two or three "members" (which I shall call "versets") parallel to each other in meaning.

Like many a good discovery, Bishop Lowth's perception has not fared as well as it might. The realization soon dawned that some of what he called parallelism was not semantically parallel at all. This recognition led to a sometimes confusing proliferation of subcategories of parallelism and, in our own time, to various baby-with-bathwater operations in which syllable count, units of syntax, or some other formal feature was proposed as the basis for biblical poetry, parallelism being relegated to a secondary or incidental position. In another direction, at least one scholar, despairing of a coherent account of biblical verse, has contended that there was no distinct concept of formal versification in ancient Israel but merely a "continuum" of parallelistic rhetoric from prose to what we misleadingly call poetry.[1] Some of these confusions can be sorted out, and as a result we may be able to see more clearly the distinctive strength and beauty of the biblical poems, for an understanding of the poetic system is always a precondition to reading the poem well.

Semantic parallelism, though by no means invariably present, is a prevalent feature of biblical verse. That is, if the poet says "hearken" in the first verset, he is likely to say something like "listen" or "heed" in the second verset. This parallelism of meaning, which is often joined with a balancing of the number of rhythmic stresses between the versets and sometimes by parallel syntactic patterns as well,[2] seems to have played a role roughly analogous to that of iambic pentameter in Shakespeare's dramatic verse: it is an underlying formal model which the poet feels free to modify or occasionally to abandon altogether. In longer biblical poems, a departure from parallelism is sometimes used to mark the end of a distinct segment; elsewhere parallelism is occasionally set aside in favor of a small-scale narrative sequence within the line; and a few poets appear simply to have been less fond than others of the symmetries of parallelism.

Before attempting to sharpen this rather general concept of poetic parallelism, let me offer some brief examples of its basic patterns of development. David's victory psalm (2 Sam. 22) presents a nice variety of possibilities because it is relatively long for a biblical poem and it includes quasi-narrative elements and discrete segments with formally marked transitions. In the fifty-three lines of verse that constitute the poem, few approach a perfect coordinated parallelism not only of meaning but also of syntax and rhythmic stresses. Thus: "For with you I charge a barrier, / with my God I vault a wall" (v. 30).[3] Here each semantically parallel term in the two versets is in the same syntactic position: with you/with my God, I charge / I vault, a barrier/a wall. Though our knowledge of the phonetics of biblical Hebrew involves a certain margin of conjecture, the line with its system of stresses, as vocalized in the Masoretic Hebrew text, would sound something like this: *ki bekhá 'arúts gedúd / be' lohái adáleg-shúr*, yielding a 3 + 3 parallelism of stressed syllables, which in fact is the most common pattern in biblical verse. (The rule is that there are never less than two stresses in a verset and never more than four, and no two stresses follow each other without an intervening unstressed syllable; and there are often asymmetrical combinations of 4 + 3 or 3 + 2.)

It is hardly surprising that biblical poets should very often seek to avoid such regularity as we have just seen, through different kinds of elegant—and sometimes significant—variation. Often, syntactically disparate clauses are used to convey a parallelism of meaning, as in verse 29: "For you are my lamp, O Lord, / the Lord lights up my darkness," where the second-person predicative assertion that the Lord is a lamp is transformed into a third-person narrative statement in which the Lord now governs a verb of illumination. Even when the syntax of the two versets is much closer than this, variations may be introduced, as in two lines from the beginning of the poem (vv. 5–6) that describe the speaker having been on the brink of death. I will reproduce the precise word order of the Hebrew, though at a cost of awkwardness, for biblical Hebrew usage is much more flexible than modern English as to subject-predicate order.

> For there encompassed me the breakers of death,
> the rivers of destruction terrified me.
> The cords of Sheol surrounded me,
> there greeted me the snares of death.

The syntactic shape of these two lines, which preserve a regular semantic parallelism through all four versets as well as a 3-3 stress in both lines, is a double chiasm: (1) encompassed-breakers-rivers-terrified; (2) cords-surrounded-greeted-snares. In the first line the verbs of surrounding are the outside terms, the entrapping agencies of death, the inside terms of the chiasm (*abba*); and in the second line this order is reversed (*baab*). This maneuver, which, like the interlinear parallelism, is quite common in biblical verse, may be nothing more than elegant variation to avoid mechanical repetitiousness, though one suspects here that the chiastic boxing in and reversal of terms help reinforce the feeling of entrapment that is being expressed: as the two lines unfold, the reader can scarcely choose between a sense of being multifariously surrounded and a sense of the multiplicity of the instruments of death.

Another frequent pattern for bracketing the two versets together involves an elliptical syntactic parallelism, usually through the introduction of a verb at the beginning of the first verset which does double duty for the second verset as well, as in verse 15: "He sent forth bolts and scattered them, / lightning, and overwhelmed them." The ellipsis of "he-sent-forth" (one word and one accented syllable in the Hebrew) produces a 3-2 stress pattern, which also involves a counterposing of three Hebrew words to two. (It should be said that biblical Hebrew is much more compact than any translation can suggest, with subject, object, possessive pronoun, preposition, and so forth indicated by suffix or prefix; and most words have only one accent.) This rhythmic truncation of the second verset conveys a certain abruptness which the poet may have felt intuitively was appropriate for the violent action depicted. Elsewhere in biblical poetry, when ellipsis through a double-duty verb occurs while the parallelism of stresses between versets is maintained, the extra rhythmic unit in the second verset is used to develop semantic material introduced in the first verset. Here is a characteristic instance from Moses' valedictory song (Deut. 32:13): "He suckled him with honey from a rock, / and oil from a flinty stone." That is, since the verb "he-suckled-him-with" (again a single word in the Hebrew) does double duty for the second verset, rhythmic space is freed in the second half of the line in which the poet can elaborate the simple general term "rock" into the complex term "flinty stone," which is a particular instance of the general category, and one that brings out the quality of hardness. (The development of meaning within semantic parallelism is discussed in detail later.)

It is beyond my purposes here to classify all the subcategories of parallelism that present themselves in David's victory psalm, but two additional cases are worth looking at to round out our provisional sense of the spectrum of possibilities. Verse 9, like the one that precedes it in 2 Samuel 22, is triadic: "Smoke came out of his nostrils, / fire from his mouth consumed, / coals glowed round him." First, let me comment briefly on the role of triadic lines in the biblical poetic system. Dyadic lines, as in all our previous examples, definitely predominate, but the poets have free recourse to triadic lines with none of the uneasy conscience manifested, say, by English Augustan poets when they introduce triplets into a poem composed in heroic couplets. In longer poems such as this, triadic lines can be used to mark the beginning or the end of a segment, as here the triadic verses 8–9 initiate the awesome seismic description of the Lord descending from on high to do battle with his foes. Elsewhere, triadic lines are simply interspersed with dyadic ones, and in some poems they are cultivated when the poet wants to express a sense of tension or instability, using the third verset to contrast or even reverse the first two parallel versets. Now, the smoke-fire-coals series quoted above involves approximately parallel concepts and actions, but the terms are also *sequenced*, temporally and logically, moving from smoke to its source to an incandescence so intense that everything around it is ignited. This progression, too, reflects a more general feature of poetic parallelism in the Bible to which we shall return.

Finally, biblical poetry abounds in lines like the one immediately following the line just quoted: "He tilted the heavens, came down, / deep mist beneath his feet" (v. 10). Here the only "parallelism" between the second verset and the first is one of rhythmic stresses (again 3-3). Otherwise, the second verset differs from the first in both syntax and meaning. The fairly frequent occurrence of such lines is no reason either to contort our definition of parallelism or to throw out the concept as a governing principle of Hebrew verse. The system, as I proposed before, is rather one in which semantic parallelism predominates without being regarded as an absolute necessity for every line. In this instance the poet seems to be pursuing a visual realization of the narrative momentum of the line (and, indeed, the momentum carries down through a whole sequence of lines); first he presents the Lord tilting the heavens and descending, and then, as the eye of the beholder plunges, a picture in the locative second clause of the deep mist beneath God's feet as he descends. This yields a more striking effect than would a regular parallelism such as "He tilted the heavens, came down, / he plummeted to the earth," and is a small but characteristic indication of the suppleness with which the general convention of parallelism is put to use by biblical poets.

Now, the greatest stumbling block in approaching biblical poetry has been the misconception that parallelism implies synonymity, saying the same thing twice in different words. I would argue that good poetry at all times is an intellectually robust activity to which such laziness is alien, that poets understand more subtly than linguists that there are no true synonyms, and that the ancient Hebrew poets are constantly advancing their meanings where the casual ear catches mere repetition. Not surprisingly, some lines of biblical poetry approach a condition of equivalent statement between the versets more than others. Thus: "He preserves the paths of justice, / and the way of his faithful ones he guards" (Prov. 2:8). By my count, however, such instances of nearly synonymous restatement occur in less than a quarter of the lines of verse in the biblical corpus. The dominant pattern is a focusing, heightening, or specification of ideas, images, actions, themes from one verset to the next. If something is broken in the first verset, it is smashed or shattered in the second verset; if a city is destroyed in the first verset, it is turned into a heap of rubble in the second. A general term in the first half of the line is typically followed by a specific instance of the general category in the second half; or, again, a literal statement in the first verset becomes a metaphor or hyperbole in the second. The notion that repetition in a text is very rarely simple restatement has long been understood by rhetoricians and literary theorists. Thus the Elizabethan rhetorician Hoskins—might the King James translators have read him?—acutely observes that "in speech there is no repetition without importance."[4] What this means to us as readers of biblical poetry is that instead of listening to an imagined drumbeat of repetitions, we need constantly to look for something new happening from one part of the line to the next.

The case of numbers in parallelism is especially instructive. If the underlying principle were really synonymity, we would expect to find, say, "forty" in one verset and "two score" in the other. In fact the almost invariable rule is an ascent on the numerical scale from first to second verset, either by one, or by a decimal multiple, or by a decimal multiple of the first number added to itself. And as with numbers, so with images and ideas; there is a steady amplification or intensification of the original terms. Here is a paradigmatic numerical instance: "How could one pursue a thousand, / and two put ten thousand to flight?" (Deut. 32:30). An amusing illustration of scholarly misconception about what is involved poetically in such cases is a common contemporary view of the triumphal song chanted by the Israelite women: "Saul has smitten his thousands, / David, his tens of thousands" (1 Sam. 18:7). It has been suggested that Saul's anger over these words reflects his paranoia, for he should have realized that in poetry it is a formulaic necessity to move from a thousand to ten thousand, and so the women really intended no slight to him.[5] Such a suggestion assumes that somehow poetry conjures with formulaic devices indifferent to meaning. Saul may indeed have been paranoid, but he knew perfectly well how the Hebrew poetry of his era worked and understood that meanings were quite pointedly developed from one half of the line to the other. In fact the prose narrative in 1 Samuel 18 strongly confirms the rightness of Saul's "reading," for the people are clearly said to be extravagantly enamored of David as they are not of Saul.

Let me propose a few examples of this dynamic movement within the line, and then try to suggest something about the compelling religious and visionary ends that are served by this distinctive poetics. (For the sake of convenience, I have chosen almost all my examples from Psalms.) In the first group, the italics in the second versets indicate the point at which seeming repetition becomes a focusing, a heightening, a concretization of the original material: "Let me hear joy and gladness, / let *the bones you have crushed exult*" (Ps. 51:10); "How long, O Lord, will you be perpetually incensed, / *like a flame* your wrath *will burn* (Ps. 79:5); "He counts the number of the stars, / each one he *calls by name*" (Ps. 147:4). These three lines illustrate a small spectrum of possibilities of semantic focusing between the two versets. In the first example, the general joy and gladness of the first verset become sharper through the contrastive introduction of the crushed bones in the second verset, and bones exulting is, of course, a more vividly metaphorical restatement of the idea of rejoicing. In the second example, the possible hint of the notion of heat in the term for "incensed" (*te'enaf*, which might derive etymologically from the hot breath from the nostrils) becomes in the second verset a full-fledged metaphor of wrath burning like a flame. In the third example, there is no recourse to metaphor, but there is an obvious focusing in the "parallel" verbs of the two versets: calling something by name, which in the biblical world implies intimate relation, knowledge of the essence of the thing, is a good deal more than mere counting. The logical structure of this line, which is quite typical of biblical poetics, would be something like this: not only can God count the innumerable stars (first verset) but he even knows the name of (or gives a name to) each single star.

Since the three examples we have just considered move from incipiently metaphorical to explicitly metaphorical to literal, a few brief observations may be in order about the role of figurative language in biblical poetics. Striking imagery does not seem to have been especially valued for itself, as it would come to be in many varieties of European post-Romantic poetry. Some poets favor nonfigurative language, and very often, as we have seen, figures are introduced in the second verset as a convenient means among several possible ones for heightening some notion that appears in the first verset. In any case, the biblical poets on the whole were inclined to draw on a body of more or less familiar images without consciously striving for originality of invention in their imagery. Wrath kindles, burns, consumes; protection is a canopy, a sheltering wing, shade in blistering heat; solace or renewal is dew, rain, streams of fresh water; and so forth. The effectiveness of the image derives in part from its very familiarity, perhaps its archetypal character, in part from the way it is placed in context and, quite often, extended and intensified by elaboration through several lines or by reinforcement with related images. However, there is no overarching symbolic pattern, as some have claimed, in the images used by biblical poets, and there is no conventional limitation set on the semantic fields from which the images are drawn. Though biblical poetry abounds in pastoral, agricultural, topographical, and meteorological images, the manufacturing processes of ancient Near Eastern urban culture are also frequently enlisted by the poets: the crafts of the weaver, the dyer, the launderer, the potter, the builder, the smith, and so forth. This freedom to draw images from all areas of experience, even in a poetic corpus largely committed to conventional figures, allows for some striking individual images. The Job poet in particular excels in such invention, likening the swiftness of human existence to the movement of the shuttle on a loom, the fashioning of the child in the womb to the curdling of cheese, the mists over the waters of creation to swaddling cloths, and in general making his imagery a strong correlative of his extraordinary sense both of man's creaturely contingency and of God's overwhelming power.

As for the operation of poetic parallelism within the line, the possibilities of complication of meaning are too various to be discussed comprehensively here, but an important second category of development between versets deserves mention. In the following pair of lines, the parallelism within the line is of a rather special kind, involving something other than intensification:

> The teaching of his God is in his heart,
>   his footsteps will not stumble.
> The wicked spies out the just,
>   and seeks to kill him.   (Ps. 37:31–32)

In the first of these lines, the statements of the two versets do correspond to each other, but the essential nature of the correspondence is *causal*: if you keep the Lord's teaching, you can count on avoiding calamity. In the next line, causation is allied with temporal sequence. That is, to try to kill someone is a more extreme act of malice than to lie in wait for him and hence an "intensification," but the two are different points in a miniature narrative continuum: first the lying in wait, then the attempt to kill. We see the same pattern in the following image of destruction, where the first verset presents the breaking down of fortress walls, the second verset the destruction of the fortress itself: "You burst through all his barriers, / you turned his strongholds to rubble" (Ps. 89:41).

It is sometimes asked what happened to narrative verse in ancient Israel, for whereas the principal narratives of most other ancient cultures are in poetry, narrative proper in the Hebrew Bible is almost exclusively reserved for prose. One partial answer would be that the narrative impulse, which for a variety of reasons is withdrawn from the larger structure of the poem, often reappears on a more microscopic level, within the line, or in a brief sequence of lines, in the articulation of the poem's imagery, as in the examples just cited. In quite a few instances this narrativity within the line is perfectly congruent with what I have described as the parallelism of intensification. Both elements are beautifully transparent in these two versets from Isaiah: "Like a pregnant woman whose time draws near, / she trembles, she screams in her birth pangs" (Isa. 26:17). The second verset, of course, not only is more concretely focused than the first but also represents a later moment in the same process—from very late pregnancy to the midst of labor.

This impulse of compact narrativity within the line is so common that it is often detectable even in the one-line poems that are introduced as dramatic heightening in the prose narratives. Thus, when Jacob sees Joseph's bloodied tunic and concludes that his son has been killed, he follows the words of pained recognition, "It's my son's tunic" with a line of verse that is a kind of miniature elegy: "An evil beast has devoured him, / torn, oh torn, is Joseph" (Gen. 37:33). The second verset is at once a focusing of the act of devouring and an incipiently narrative transition from the act to its awful consequence: a ravening beast has devoured him, and as the concrete result his body has been torn to shreds. We see another variation of the underlying pattern in the line of quasi-prophetic (and quite mistaken) rebuke that the priest Eli pronounces to the distraught Hannah, whose lips have been moving in silent prayer: "How long will you be drunk? / Put away your wine!" (1 Sam. 1:14). Some analysts might be tempted to claim that both versets here, despite their semantic and syntactic dissimilarity, have the same "deep structure" because they both express outrage at Hannah's supposed state of drunkenness, but I think we are in fact meant to read the line by noting differentiation. The first verset suggests that to continue in a state of inebriation in the sanctuary is intolerable; the second verset projects that attitude forward on a temporal axis (narrativity in the imperative mode) by drawing the consequence that the woman addressed must sober up at once.

Beyond the scale of the one-line poem, this element of narrativity between versets plays an important role in the development of meaning because so many biblical poems, even if they are not explicitly narrative, are concerned in one way or another with process. Psalm 102 is an instructive case in point. The poem is a collective supplication on behalf of Israel in captivity. (Since it begins and ends in the first-person singular, it is conceivable that it is a reworking of an older individual supplication.) A good many lines exhibit the movement of intensification or focusing we observed earlier. Verse 3 is a good example: "For my days have gone up in smoke, / my bones are charred like a hearth." Other lines reflect complementarity, such as verse 6: "I resembled the great owl of the desert, / I became like an owl among ruins." But because the speaker of the poem is, after all, trying to project a possibility of change out of the wasteland of exile in which he finds himself, a number of lines show a narrative progression from the first verset to the second because *something is happening,* and it is not just a static condition that is being reported. Narrativity is felt particularly as God moves into action in history: "For the Lord has built up Zion, / he appears in his glory" (v. 16). That is, as a consequence of his momentous act of rebuilding the ruins of Zion (first verset), the glory of the Lord again becomes globally visible (second verset). Then the Lord looks down from heaven "to listen to the groans of the captive, / to free those condemned to death" (v. 20)—first the listening, then the act of liberation. God's praise thus emanates from the rebuilt Jerusalem to which the exiles return "when nations gather together, / and kingdoms, to serve the Lord" (v. 22). Elsewhere in Psalms, the gathering together of nations and kingdoms may suggest a mustering of armies for attack on Israel, but the last phrase of the line, "to serve [or worship] the Lord," functions as a climactic narrative revelation: this assembly of nations is to worship God in his mountain sanctuary, now splendidly reestablished. In sum, the narrative momentum of these individual lines picks up a sense of historical process and helps align the collective supplication with the prophecies of return to Zion in Deutero-Isaiah, with which this poem is probably contemporaneous.

This last point may begin to suggest to the ordinary reader, who with good reason thinks of the Bible primarily as a corpus of religious writings, what all these considerations of formal poetics have to do with the urgent spiritual concerns of the ancient Hebrew poets. I don't think there is ever a one-to-one correspondence between poetic systems and views of reality, but I would propose that a particular poetics may encourage or reinforce a particular orientation toward reality. For all the untold reams of commentary on the Bible, this remains a sadly neglected question. One symptomatic case in point: a standard work on the basic forms of prophetic discourse by the German scholar Claus Westermann never once mentions the poetic vehicle used by the Prophets and makes no formal distinction between, say, a short prophetic statement in prose by Elijah and a complex poem by Isaiah.[6] Any intrinsic connection between the kind of poetry the Prophets spoke and the nature of their message is simply never contemplated.

Biblical poetry, as I have tried to show, is characterized by an intensifying or narrative development within the line; and quite often this "horizontal" movement is then projected downward in a "vertical" focusing movement through a sequence of lines or even through a whole poem. What this means is that the poetry of the Bible is concerned above all with dynamic process moving toward some culmination. The two most common structures, then, of biblical poetry are a movement of intensification of images, concepts, themes through a sequence of lines, and a narrative movement—which most often pertains to the development of metaphorical acts but can also refer to literal events, as in much prophetic poetry. The account of the Creation in the first chapter of Genesis might serve as a model for the conception of reality that underlies most of this body of poetry: from day to day new elements are added in a continuous process that culminates in the seventh day, the primordial sabbath. It would require a close reading of whole poems to see fully how this model is variously manifested in the different genres of biblical poetry, but I can at least sketch out the ways in which the model is perceptible in verse addressed to personal, philosophical, and historical issues.

The poetry of Psalms has evinced an extraordinary power to speak to the lives of countless individual readers and has echoed through the work of writers as different as Augustine, George Herbert, Paul Claudel, and Dylan Thomas. Some of the power of the psalms may be attributed to their being such effective "devotions upon emergent occasions," as John

Donne, another poet strongly moved by these biblical poems, called a collection of his meditations. The sense of emergency virtually defines the numerically predominant subgenre of psalm, the supplication. The typical—though of course not invariable—movement of the supplication is a rising line of intensity toward a climax of terror or desperation. The paradigmatic supplication would sound something like this: You have forgotten me, O Lord; you have hidden your face from me; you have thrown me to the mercies of my enemies; I totter on the brink of death, plunge into the darkness of the Pit. At this intolerable point of culmination, when there is nothing left for the speaker but the terrible contemplation of his own imminent extinction, a sharp reversal takes place. The speaker either prays to God to draw him out of the abyss or, in some poems, confidently asserts that God is in fact already working this wondrous rescue. It is clear why these poems have reverberated so strongly in the moments of crisis, spiritual or physical, of so many readers, and I would suggest that the distinctive capacity of biblical poetics to advance along a steeply inclined plane of mounting intensities does much to help the poets imaginatively realize both the experience of crisis and the dramatic reversal at the end.

Certainly there are other, less dynamic varieties of poetic structure represented in the biblical corpus, including the Book of Psalms. The general fondness of ancient Hebrew writers in all genres for so-called envelope structures (in which the conclusion somehow echoes terms or whole phrases from the beginning) leads in some poems to balanced, symmetrically enclosed forms, occasionally even to a division into parallel strophes, as in the Song of the Sea (Exod. 15). The neatest paradigm for such symmetrical structures is Psalm 8, which, articulating a firm belief in the beautiful hierarchical perfection of creation, opens and closes with the refrain "Lord, our master, / how majestic is your name in all the earth!" Symmetrical structures, because they tend to imply a confident sense of the possibility of encapsulating perception, are favored in particular by poets in the main line of Hebrew Wisdom literature—but not by the Job poet, who works in what has been described as the "radical wing" of biblical Wisdom writing. Thus the separate poems that constitute chapters 5 and 7 of Proverbs, though the former uses narrative elements and the latter is a freestanding narrative, equally employ neat envelope structures as frames to emphasize their didactic points. The Hymn to Wisdom in Job 28, which most scholars consider to be an interpolation, stands out from the surrounding poetry not only in its assured tone but also in its structure, being neatly divided into three symmetrical strophes marked by a refrain. Such instances, however, are no more than exceptions that prove the rule, for the structure that predominates in all genres of biblical poetry is one in which a kind of semantic pressure is built from verset to verset and line to line, finally reaching a climax or a climax and reversal.

This momentum of intensification is felt somewhat differently in the text that is in many respects the most astonishing poetic achievement in the biblical corpus, the Book of Job. Whereas the psalm-poets provided voices for the anguish and exultation of real people, Job is a fictional character, as the folktale stylization of the introductory prose narrative means to intimate. In the rounds of debate with the three Friends, poetry spoken by fictional figures is used to ponder the enigma of arbitrary suffering that seems a constant element of the human condition. One of the ways in which we are invited to gauge the difference between the Friends and Job is through the different kinds of poetry they utter—the Friends stringing together beautifully polished clichés (sometimes virtually a parody of the poetry of Proverbs and Psalms), Job making constant disruptive departures in the images he uses, in the extraordinary muscularity of his language line after line. The poetry Job speaks is an instrument forged to sound the uttermost depths of suffering, and so he adopts movements of intensification to focus in and in on his anguish. The intolerable point of culmination is not followed, as in Psalms, by a confident prayer for salvation, but by a death wish, whose only imagined relief is the extinction of life and mind, or by a kind of desperate shriek of outrage to the Lord.

When God finally answers Job out of the whirlwind, he responds with an order of poetry formally allied to Job's own remarkable poetry, but larger in scope and greater in power (from the compositional viewpoint, it is the sort of risk only a writer of genius could take and get away with). That is, God picks up many of Job's key images, especially from the death-wish poem with which Job began (chap. 3), and his discourse is shaped by a powerful movement of intensification, coupled with an implicitly narrative sweep from the Creation to the play of natural forces to the teeming world of animal life. But whereas Job's intensities are centripetal and necessarily egocentric, God's intensities carry us back and forth through the pulsating vital movements of the whole created world. The culmination of the poem God speaks is not a cry of self or a dream of self snuffed out but the terrible beauty of the Leviathan, on the uncanny borderline between zoology and mythology, where what is fierce and strange, beyond the ken and conquest of man, is the climactic manifestation of a splendidly providential creation which merely anthropomorphic notions cannot grasp.

Finally, this general predisposition to a poetic apprehension of urgent climactic process leads in the Prophets to what amounts to a radically new view of history. Without implying that we should reduce all thinking to principles of poetics, I would nevertheless suggest that there is a particular momentum in ancient Hebrew poetry that helps impel the poets toward rather special construals of their historical circumstances. If a Prophet wants to make vivid in verse a process of impending disaster, even, let us

say, with the limited conscious aim of bringing his complacent and wayward audience to its senses, the intensifying logic of his medium may lead
him to statements of an ultimate and cosmic character. Thus Jeremiah,
imagining the havoc an invading Babylonian army will wreak:

> I see the earth, and, look, chaos and void,
>   the heavens—their light is gone.
> I see the mountains, and, look, they quake,
>   and all the hills shudder   (Jer. 4:23–24)

He goes on in the same vein, continuing to draw on the language of
Genesis to evoke a dismaying world where creation itself has been reversed.

A similar process is at work in the various prophecies of consolation
of Amos, Jeremiah, Ezekiel, Isaiah: national restoration, in the development from literal to hyperbolic, from fact to fantastic elaboration, that is
intrinsic to biblical poetry, is not just a return from exile or the reestab-
lishment of political autonomy but a blossoming of the desert, a straight-
ening out of all that is crooked, a wonderful fusion of seed-time and
reaping, a perfect peace in which calf and lion dwell together and a little
child leads them. Perhaps the Prophets might have begun to move in
approximately this direction even if they had worked out their message
in prose, but I think it is analytically demonstrable that the impetus of
their poetic medium reinforced and in some ways directed the scope and
extremity of their vision. The matrix, then, of both the apocalyptic imagination and the messianic vision of redemption may well be the distinctive
structure of ancient Hebrew verse. This would be the most historically
fateful illustration of a fundamental rule bearing on form and meaning in
the Bible. We need to read this poetry well because it is not merely a
means of heightening or dramatizing the religious perceptions of the
biblical writers—it is the dynamic shaping instrument through which those
perceptions discovered their immanent truth.

NOTES

1. James L. Kugel, *The Idea of Biblical Poetry* (New Haven and London,
1981).

2. On the interplay of different elements of parallelism—semantic, rhythmic,
and syntactic—see the incisive remarks by Benjamin Hrushovski in "Prosody,
Hebrew," in *Encyclopedia Judaica,* VII (New York, 1971), 1200–02.

3. All translations in this essay are my own [AT]. I follow the original rather
literally in order to make certain aspects of the underlying poetics more perceptible
in English.

4. Quoted in L. A. Sonnino, *A Handbook to Sixteenth-Century Rhetoric* (London, 1968), p.157.

5. See, for example, Stanley Gevirtz, *Patterns in the Early Poetry of Israel* (Chicago, 1963), pp. 15–24.

6. Claus Westermann, *Basic Forms of Prophetic Speech,* trans. H. C. White (London, 1967).

SUGGESTED FURTHER READINGS

Robert Alter, *The Art of Biblical Poetry* (New York, 1985).

John Bright, *Jeremiah*, Anchor Bible, XXI (Garden City, N.Y., 1965), pp. cxxvii–cxxv.

Benjamin Hrushovski, "Prosody, Hebrew," in *Encyclopedia Judaica,* XIII (New York, 1971), 1200–01.

University of California, Berkeley

Midrash and Allegory: The Beginnings of Scriptural Interpretation

Gerald L. Bruns

THE basic historical task of biblical hermeneutics is not simply to describe the techniques of exegesis that have been applied to the Scriptures but also to elucidate the conditions in which the understanding of these texts has occurred. For example, how were the Scriptures understood in the beginning, during the long transition from preliteracy to the rich Hellenistic culture in which the biblical texts received something like their present form? This is a very difficult question, because we know very little about the Scriptures during this period. One could perhaps mark the boundaries of this period (roughly) as follows. On the one side there is the story of the discovery of the Temple Scroll during the reign of Josiah (2 Kings 22:1–23:3). This is the period of the Deuteronomic scribes (late seventh century B.C.E.), and the text in question would have been an early version of the Deuteronomic Code. The story of its discovery represents the institution of the Torah as a sacred and binding text— a recovery of the Sinai Covenant in which the Covenant is now concretized, not just in the Decalogue, but in a complex collection of laws, regulations, and instructions governing the whole range of human life. On the other side there are the formation of the New Testament texts and the production of the Masoretic texts of the Hebrew Bible, that is, a period of textual standardization and formal ecclesiastical closure within divergent traditions. This is the beginning of the patristic period in Christianity and of rabbinic Judaism, which produced the Mishnah, the Talmuds, and the great midrashic collections that continued well into the tenth century.

However, between these two rough boundaries the Scriptures were in a state of great fluidity. We can speak only vaguely of the Deuteronomic scribes who produced the first Torah.[1] We do know, however, that when the exiles returned to Palestine in the late sixth and early fifth centuries, they brought with them a considerable library that already represented a long scribal tradition of inscription, borrowing, revision, compilation, glossing, amplification, and scholarly redaction. To this period belongs the production of the Pentateuch.

The crucial figure in the post-Exilic period is Ezra, priest and scribe, who is said to have supervised the writing of a second Torah after the original had been destroyed in a fire (2 Esdras 14:20–48). It is Ezra who gives the public reading of the Scriptures in the impressive canonization story of Nehemiah 8:1–8, in which the people bind themselves to YHWH in the Pentateuch. And it is Ezra who presides over the formal interpretation of the Scriptures when his priests and scribes and the Levites circulate among the people and instruct them in the Torah: "So they read in the book of the law [Torah] of God distinctly, and gave the sense, and caused them [the people] to understand the reading" (Neh. 8:8). Ezra, in other words, is essentially a hermeneutical character, a *sofer* or scholar of the sort portrayed vividly in the Wisdom of Sirach:

> He searches out the wisdom of all the ancients,
> And busies himself with prophecies;
> He observes the discourse of famous men,
> And penetrates the intricacies of the figures.
> He searches out the hidden meaning of proverbs . . .   (39:1–7)

The main point about Ezra, however, is that he produced the *texts* of the sacred Scriptures and not just the interpretation of them. Ezra is called "the second Moses." He is authoritative for what is in the texts without being authorial in the manner of (the first) Moses or the prophets. We can take him to signify that in the post-Exilic period the Scriptures were already so extensively revised and edited that a distinction between original authorship and secondary hermeneutics can no longer be made.

This means that the beginnings of scriptural interpretation are to be looked for within the Scriptures themselves. Scholars now recognize that the making of the Scriptures was already a hermeneutical process in which earlier biblical materials were rewritten in order to make them intelligible and applicable to later situations.[2] We know, for example, that Jeremiah's sermons were rewritten in the light of the catastrophes of the destruction of the Temple and the Exile in Babylon. In the soferic period this process of revision and amplification of received texts is exemplified by 1 and 2 Chronicles, which are essentially glosses on parts of Genesis, Samuel, and Kings—glosses, however, that take the form of an amplified rewriting. Thus in Greek the Chronicles are known as *ta paralipomena,* "the things omitted"—a sort of writing between the lines to fill in the gaps of what had previously been written. Perhaps one can see the same compositional principle in the production of the Gospel texts, which give us four versions instead of a single, homogeneous account.

This helps to explain an ancient hermeneutical insight. As the rabbis, Augustine, and Luther knew, the Bible, despite its textual heterogeneity, can be read as a self-glossing book. One learns to study it by following the ways in which one portion of the text illumines another. The generations of scribes who shaped and reshaped the Scriptures appear to have designed them to be studied in just this way. Thus Brevard Childs speaks of the "interpretive structure which the biblical text has received from those who formed and used it as sacred scripture."[3] This does not mean that redaction produced a unified text (or what we would think of as unified: a holistic text, free of self-contradiction, a systematic or organic whole; the Bible is everything *but* that); rather, it means that the parts are made to relate to one another reflexively, with later texts, for example, throwing light on the earlier, even as they themselves always stand in the light of what precedes and follows them. Thus a midrash on the Song of Songs preserved in the *Midrash Rabbah* characterizes Solomon explicitly in terms of his hermeneutical wisdom: "He pondered the words of the Torah and investigated [the meaning of] the words of the Torah. He made handles to the Torah"—where "handles" mean parables and sayings or proverbs. "So till Solomon arose," the midrashist says, "no one was able to understand properly the words of the Torah, but as soon as Solomon arose all began to comprehend the Torah."[4] Elsewhere in this same midrashic text the task of exegesis is characterized as "linking up the words of the Pentateuch with those of the prophets and the prophets with the Writings."[5] The following is worth quoting in full:

> Once as Ben 'Azzai sat and expounded, the fire played round him. They went and told R. Akiba, saying, "Sir, as Ben 'Azzai sits and expounds, the fire is flashing round him." He [R. Akiba] went to him and said to him: "I hear that as you were expounding the fire flashed round you . . . Were you perhaps treating of the secrets of the Chariot?" "No," he replied. "I was only linking up the words of the Torah with one another and then with the words of the prophets, and the prophets with the Writings, and the words rejoiced as when they were delivered from Sinai, and they were sweet as at their original utterance."[6]

However, the structure of the Bible as a redacted, self-interpreting text has this important exegetical consequence: the Bible effectively blocks any attempt to understand it by reconstruction of its textual history and a working back to an original, uninterpreted intention. This self-interpreting text is also self-effacing with respect to its origins. The whole orientation of Scripture is toward its future, not toward its past. The Bible is prophetic rather than expressive in its structure. This is perhaps why the Bible has proved such a stumbling block to historical criticism and the doctrine of romantic hermeneutics which says that understanding a text means understanding it as well as and even better than its author did. For what is at issue with respect to the Scriptures is not what lies behind the text in the form of an original meaning but what lies in front of it where the interpreter stands. The Bible always addresses itself to the time of interpretation; one cannot understand it except by appropriating it anew. Revelation is never something over and done with or gone for good or in danger of slipping away into the past; it is ongoing, and its medium is midrash, which makes the words of Torah rejoice "as when they were delivered from Sinai" and as "sweet as at their original utterance" (I.10.2).

The term *midrash* derives from *darash,* meaning "to study," "to search," "to investigate," "to inquire": it means "to go in pursuit of." More generally, it can be taken to mean "account," that is, giving an account of what is written, where the task of the account is to address whatever question or topic that arises whenever the Torah is recited or studied or applicable to the situation at hand. *Midrash* is the word for whatever occurs in a situation in which the understanding of the Torah is called for. The point, however, is that there is never a situation in human life in which the understanding of the Torah is *not* called for. This is the upshot already of those famous Deuteronomic texts such as the one that enjoins the king, as soon as "he sitteth upon the throne of his kingdom, [to] write him a copy of this law in a book . . . And it shall be with him, and he shall read therein all the days of his life: that he may learn to fear the Lord his God, to keep all the words of this law and these statutes, to do them" (Deut. 17:18–19). Meditation and application are the watchwords of midrash. "This book of the law shall not depart out of thy mouth; but thou shalt meditate therein day and night, that thou mayest observe to do according to all that is written therein" (Joshua 1:8).

Think of midrash not simply as a method of exegesis but also as a form of life; its concern is not just with meaning but also with action in the world. Talmudic tradition distinguishes between *midrash halakhah* and *midrash aggadah,* that is, between giving an account of what is at issue or at stake in a legal text and giving an account of a narrative (or, more accurately, any nonlegal text: not so much a narrative as a verse, a word, parts of a word, letters and textual embellishments like the *tagin* and *te'amim* that adorn letters and words). However, it is not always clear how the distinction between two kinds of midrash looks in practice, because the Torah is altogether a *binding* text, even though it is made up of heterogeneous materials and not just of legal texts, and even though "Law" is not an entirely adequate translation of "Torah." We must take this character of binding as crucial. Midrash is concerned everywhere with the *force* of the text as well as with its form and meaning. The sense of the Torah is always the sense in which it is binding upon life, that is, the way it bears upon human action and the quality of conduct in the everyday world. As Joseph Heinemann says, "while the rabbinic creators of the Aggadah looked back into Scripture to uncover the full latent meaning of the Bible and its wording, at the same time they looked forward into the present and the future. They sought to give direction to their own generation, to resolve their religious problems, to answer their theological questions, and to guide them out of their spiritual perplexities . . . The aggadists do not mean so much to clarify difficult passages in the biblical texts as to take a stand on the burning questions of the day, to guide the people and to strengthen their faith."[7]

This is a vital point for the understanding of the nature of midrash. In our modern tradition we tend to think of texts as documents or as formal or aesthetic objects—writings that we try to analyze or to operate on at a distance. But such distance is just what midrash seeks to overcome. Midrash illustrates a basic hermeneutical principle, which is that the understanding of a text can never remain simply a state of intellectual agreement with what is said; it is never simply a mental state or the conceptual grasp of the mental state of another. Understanding shows itself only in action in the world. Taking the scriptural texts as historical documents or as aesthetic objects (studying them, for example, as "literature") tends to repress this midrashic side of understanding. We will have missed the whole point about midrash if we divorce interpretation from action. Thus it would be a mistake to distinguish, as some scholars do, between "pure" and "applied" midrash, because in midrash interpretation is never purely analytical or philological but always entails application to the situation in which the interpretation occurs.[8] Midrash is not only responsive to the Scriptures as a way of coping with the text's wide-ranging formal problems; it is also responsive to the situations in which the Scriptures exert their claim upon human life. Think of midrash as the medium in which this scriptural claim exerts itself.

The hermeneutical task of mediating between text and situation helps to explain the excessiveness—the legendary extravagance—of midrashic interpretation. For midrash always seems to be going beyond the text in the manner of transgression—going too far, saying not only what the text does not say but also what the text, taken by itself, does not appear to warrant. But in midrash the text is never to be taken all by itself as a purely analytical object; the text is always *situated*. Thus the task of midrash is never merely reproductive; it is always productive of new understanding. It is a way of keeping the Bible open to the histories of those who answer its claims.

Astonishing examples of midrashic extravagance are to be found everywhere in the collections of rabbinical commentaries that extend from the fourth and fifth centuries C.E. Indeed, it is because of this extravagance that many scholars construe midrash as a literary rather than as a hermeneutical phenomenon: for them it is a genre of rabbinical literature. Midrash means the parables, sayings, puns, stories, and flights of eisegesis created by the rabbis, almost always at the expense of the biblical text. This is the aesthetic view of midrash. It argues that, since midrash cannot be taken seriously as interpretation, it can be appreciated only as literature or art; it is creativity rather than commentary.[9] Midrash in this respect is subjected to the same bracketing as the Scriptures themselves: since the Bible cannot be taken seriously as a sacred text, it can be of value only aesthetically; it is (like midrash) the uncritical product of wild or primitive imagination.

The rabbis themselves, however, were never embarrassed by hermeneutics: "the rabbis said: Solomon had three thousand parables to illustrate each and every verse [of Scripture]; and a thousand and five interpretations for each and every parable"[10]—which computes to a total of three million fifteen thousand interpretations for every scriptural verse. From a modern standpoint, which pictures a solitary reader isolated with the scriptural text and trying to divine an intention (or his or her own private understanding), this interpretive extravagance is outrageous; but the rabbis are not to be pictured this way. Their relationship to the text was always social and dialogical, and even when confined to the house of study (*beit midrash*) it was never merely formalist or analytical. They saw themselves in dialogue with each other and with generations of wise men extending both backward to Koheleth and Solomon (and beyond to Moses and to God himself, who is frequently pictured as studying his own texts) and forward to the endless openings of the Scriptures upon new questions that are put to them.

Thus the midrashic collections that have come down to us are structured as conversations rather than as systematic expositions. This makes a midrashic text often difficult to read (and unwieldy to describe), but not more so perhaps than any other text that tries to preserve the heteroglossia of living speech. For example, *Pesikta Rabbati* contains a long midrash on a text from the Book of Numbers. To make a point about this text a rabbi named Tanḥuma bar Abba applies to it a text from Ecclesiastes (a favorite verse of the midrashists): "The words of the wise are as goads, and as nails fastened [driven? planted?] by the masters of assemblies, which are given from one shepherd" (12:11). This quotation generates a long midrashic dialogue on the text from Ecclesiastes. This is not a digression, as it would be in a systematic discourse, which would presumably return to the text from Numbers, but a turn in the hermeneutical conversation— a new direction whose endpoint, however, cannot be foreseen (perhaps cannot ever be determined). Here is an extended part of this conversation:

> With regard to the effect of Jacob's decree, R. Tanḥuma bar Abba began his discourse as follows: *The words of the wise are goads* (Eccles. 12:11). Why *as goads*? Because as a goad directs the heifer to plow in the furrow it is meant to plow, so the words of the wise direct a man in the ways of the Holy One, blessed be He. How beautifully, then, did Solomon put it when he said, *The words of the wise are as goads!*
>
> As for the word *goad*, the Mishnah calls a goad *marde'a*, while the Bible calls it either *darban* or *malmad*, as is written *With an ox-goad* [*malmad*] (Judg. 3:31); and *To set the goads* [*darban*] (1 Sam. 13:21). Why, R. Nathan asked, is

the goad called *marde'a*? Because it imparts sense [*moreh de'ah*] to the heifer. And why is a goad called *darban*? Because it lodges understanding [*madir binah*] in the heifer. *Malmad*? Because it trains [*melammed*] the heifer to plow in the furrow it is supposed to plow. Even so the words of the wise lodge understanding in men, impart sense to them, and teach them the ways of the Holy One, blessed be He. So you see, *The words of the wise are as goads.*

Another interpretation: Why are the words of the wise described as *darbanot*? R. Berechiah answered: Like a shuttlecock flying back and forth [*dur banot*], or like a ball that children play catch with—one tosses it here and another tosses it there—so words fly back and forth when the wise come into a house of study and discuss Torah, one stating his view, and another stating his view, still another stating another view, and another stating a different view. Yet the words of these and of the other Sages, all of them, were given by Moses the shepherd from what he received from the Unique One of the universe. *They are given from one shepherd* (Eccles. 12:11). Now since one states one view, and one states another view, do their words merely fly about aimlessly in the air? Indeed not! Scripture goes on to describe the words of the wise *As nails planted by the masters of assemblies* (ibid.). Note that the text does not say "as nails set," but planted. Why? In describing the words of the wise as nails, Scripture is pointing up the fact that since a nail has a head it is easy to pull out. Hence the phrase *as nails planted* implies the following: The roots of a tree deep-planted are hard to pull out, yet they do not have strength like the strength of iron; a nail of iron, on the other hand, though it has strength, (can easily be pulled out). Therefore both the strength of iron and the tenacity of a tree's deep-planted roots are given to the words of Torah.

Another comment: As the roots of a tree spread in all directions, so words of Torah enter and spread through the whole body of a man.

As nails planted by masters of assemblies. Just when are words of Torah said to be planted like nails in men? When? When a master of Torah enters a house of study where men are assembled to hear him.

Another comment: Since a goad may be taken up and set aside at will, one might think that the same can be done with words of Torah; therefore the verse goes on to say *as nails planted*(—immovable).[11]

This text is instructive in several ways. It shows what the practice of commentary as the "linking up the words of Torah with one another" looks like. It means, of course, elucidating one text by means of another (basic philological practice), but it also means wordplay, in which the rabbis pick up on the ways in which the words of the Scriptures echo one another. The text just quoted gives an excellent illustration of rabbinical punning, where what the interpreter says is not so much a reading into the text as a way of opening it up by discovering in its language—in the interplay of its words—new sources of understanding.

More important, however, this text is a midrash on the nature and authority of midrash. The pun which turns a goad into a shuttlecock opens the way to the characterization of midrash as dialogical interpretation. Midrash is multiple, heterogeneous, and conflicting—"so words fly back and forth when the wise come into a house of study and discuss Torah, one stating his view, and another stating his"—but Rabbi Berechiah makes the crucial point that there is no conflict of authority in this conflict of interpretations, because it is *the whole dialogue* which is authoritative, not just the isolated interpretations that emerge from it. Midrashic interpretation is multiform and extravagant but also holistic as a social practice; no one interpretation stands by itself, because no one rabbi speaks as a solitary reader—no one rabbi speaks purely and simply in his own name and on his own private authority. The whole dialogue goes on in the name of God and the name of Moses: "the words of these and of the other Sages, all of them, were given by Moses the shepherd from what he received from the Unique One of the universe. *They are given from one shepherd.*" This means that there is neither occasion nor cause to determine the authority or correctness of this or that isolated interpretation. Interpretations are not logical propositions concerning which we have to decide for and against, true or false. They are modes of participation in the dialogue with Torah, such that the words of the wise as they engage the Torah cannot be isolated from the words of Torah itself. Hence the rabbinic tradition—which perhaps extends all the way back to the Pharisees and beyond them to the priestly Ezra—concerning the unity of the written and oral Torah. The meaning and authority of the word *Torah* extends itself to include not only the original Pentateuch, followed by the Prophets and Writings, but also the Mishnah, the talmudic commentaries on the Mishnah, and the whole tradition of midrash. Hence the claim that midrash makes for itself: "Matters that had not been disclosed to Moses were disclosed to R. Akiba and his colleagues."[12]

Again, we must think of midrash as a form of life—life with a text that makes claims upon a whole community (indeed, a whole nation)—and not just as a technique of exegesis that anyone might pick up or put down at any time. Midrashic interpretation is not a species of technical knowledge; it is not a methodological approach to texts that might be compared with other approaches ancient and modern. Thus it would make no sense to wonder whether one could "apply" midrashic techniques as a method of literary criticism, say, by interpreting wildly, saying whatever one pleases: saying whatever one pleases is *not* midrash. On the contrary, it would be more true to say that midrash gives us an insight into what interpretation always is (whatever the method) when interpretation *matters* to human life. In hermeneutical terms, midrash shows the historicality of understanding.

For example, the long midrashic text quoted above emphasizes that rabbinical conversation concerning Torah is not just talk. "Now since one states one view, and one states another view, do their words merely fly about aimlessly in the air? Indeed not!" The rich punning on "goad" and the complicated unpacking of a strangely mixed metaphor—"Note that the text does not say 'as nails set,' but planted. Why?"—concerns the *force* of midrash, that is, the hermeneutical function of the application of Torah as a *binding* text. The words of midrash not only illuminate the understanding of those who hear them; they also take hold so that they become even part of the flesh of those who understand: "so words of Torah enter and spread through the whole body of a man." Here is a superb metaphor of appropriation. The insight is that understanding is something more than a mental state. The words of the wise "impart sense" not by filling the mind with concepts (true doctrines, divine ideas, Revelation as a spiritual package), but by directing the one who understands along a certain path. Understanding here means following a way of life, walking in "the ways of the Holy One." Midrash in this sense is not *technē* but *phronēsis,* wisdom rather than knowhow. Ultimately midrash would thus concern itself with the question of what it is to be a Jew (a question, it turns out, in which Christianity is profoundly implicated).

Accordingly, in order to grasp the nature of midrashic understanding, we ought not to think of the Scriptures and their interpretation in terms of an original meaning that gets preserved twice over, latently in a text and explicitly in tradition. Indeed, from a hermeneutical standpoint it is not clear what sense it makes to distinguish between text and tradition; and this, in fact, is the whole argument of Pharisaic-rabbinic Judaism, which makes this distinction only in order to efface it, that is, to obscure the boundaries between composition and interpretation. The word *Torah* encompasses both the sacred text and how it is taken by those who answer to it. In the same way a legal text cannot be isolated from its interpretive tradition, where how a text is understood means how we act upon it. Thus although the text was composed in a situation very different from our own, it must be taken in relation to *our* situation if it is to have any force. Taking a text this way is what appropriation means, which is the source of so-called excessiveness (as opposed to literalness) of interpretation. If the text does not apply to us, then it is an empty text, even though we can read it well enough to say how its words work; but we cannot say that we understand it—understand it, that is, midrashically. Midrashic understanding is reflexive and reciprocal: we take the text in relation to ourselves, understanding ourselves in its light, even as our situation throws *its* light upon the text, allowing it to disclose itself differently, perhaps in unheard-of ways. "Matters that had not been disclosed to Moses were disclosed to R. Akiba and his colleagues." What this claim means is that Revelation is not something that occurs once for all and is now over and done with; it is a claim about the historicality of Revelation, that is, its openness to the history of those who receive it.

The key to midrash lies in this reciprocity between text and history. Midrash is a dialogue between text and history in which the task of giving an account—giving a midrash—does not involve merely construing a meaning; it also involves showing how the text still bears upon us, still speaks to us and exerts its claim upon us even though our situation is different from anything that has gone before. The task of midrash is to keep open the mutual belonging of the text and those who hear it. There is a common accord between ourselves and what is written, and the task of midrash (indeed, the task of any biblical interpretation that is hermeneutically informed) is to bring this accord into the open.

This same point can be made with respect to another literary activity of rabbinic Judaism, the Targums, the various Aramaic translations of the Hebrew Scriptures that began to be made perhaps as early as the last two centuries B.C.E. These translations are sometimes fairly literal (as in the Targum Onkelos), but frequently they are periphrastic or appropriative in the sense that they amplify the original in order to say what has been left unsaid. The Targum Pseudo-Jonathan contains vivid examples of "midrashic" translation, particularly with respect to biblical tales which are laconic in the original but rich and detailed in the Aramaic. (What did Cain say to Abel, and how did Abel respond? The Targum Pseudo-Jonathan will tell you.) The point is not to see this embellishment simply as something added to a textual object that has been sealed off from time and history. "Midrashic" Targums must be understood in relation to the historical situation in which they work to mediate between the traditional text and those who, however differently situated, remain under the charge of what it says.[13]

Another related practice is pesher interpretation. It resembles midrash in one respect, in that it gives the text an intimate application to the historical situation of the interpreter.[14] It differs from midrash in that the relationship is exclusive; the text is related to one moment only, a moment thought of as occurring near the end of time. This is the way the Qumran sectaries read the Scriptures, as we know from the Dead Sea Scrolls, and it is also the basis of early Christian interpretation of the Hebrew Bible; the Scriptures were understood both as Torah and, eschatologically, as prophecy of the fullness of time. A striking example of pesher interpretation occurs in Luke 4:16–21, where Jesus reads the Scriptures in the synagogue at Nazareth:

> And he came to Nazareth, where he had been brought up: and, as his custom was, he went into the synagogue on the sabbath day, and stood up for to read. And there was delivered unto him the book of the prophet Esaias [Isaiah]. And when he had opened the book, he found the place where it was written, The Spirit of the Lord is upon me, because he hath anointed me to preach the gospel to the poor; he hath sent me to heal the brokenhearted, to preach deliverance to the captives, and recovering of sight to the blind, to set at liberty them that are bruised, To preach the acceptable year of the Lord. And he closed the book, and he gave it again to the minister,

and sat down. And the eyes of all them that were in the synagogue were fastened on him. And he began to say unto them, This day is this scripture fulfilled in your ears.

Similarly, in the episode on the road to Emmaus, Jesus begins elucidating the Scriptures to his companions, taking himself as the text's meaning: "And beginning at Moses and all the prophets, he expounded unto them in all the scriptures the things concerning himself" (Luke 24:27); and again, in John, Jesus says: "For had ye believed Moses, ye would have believed me: for he wrote of me" (5:46).

In pesher midrash the interpretation of the Scriptures becomes at the same time the medium of self-understanding and self-disclosure (not to say self-authorization). Historically, of course, the question here has to do with the way the community of Jewish Christians, faithful to Torah, made sense of Christ—or, indeed, how Christ made sense of himself to other people and indeed to himself as well. The answer is, not independently of history and tradition, as if by the invention of a new language, but within tradition and in the very language that the tradition makes available in its texts. The Gospel texts (but Luke especially) picture Christ as an observant Jew who enters into tradition, understands himself in it; in a certain way, he understands himself *in front of* the Scriptures, standing before them and answering to them and to a form of life that they project. For the basic hermeneutical principle of pesher interpretation is that Scripture makes sense, not by opening inwardly to an intention that lies behind the text, but by laying open (in front of itself or into its future) a possibility which the community takes it upon itself to actualize or fulfill in terms of action, that is, in its forms or way of life. Thus no Christian can read Isaiah 53 (to take the most obvious example of the figure of the suffering servant) without seeing how this text maps itself onto Christ's own history.

The patristic practice of typology, despite its frequently anti-Jewish point, is absolutely continuous with midrash and pesher; that is, it is rooted in the figure of Jesus as the sectarian midrashist who appropriates the sacred text, seeing its meaning in its application to himself. As Origen says, "Jesus reads the Law to us when he reveals to us the secrets of the Law. For we who are of the catholic Church, we do not spurn the law of Moses but accept it, so long as it is Jesus who reads it to us. Indeed, we can only possess a correct understanding of the Law when he reads it to us, and we are able to receive his sense and his understanding."[15] What Origen describes here is the hermeneutical circle of Christian understanding: the Old Testament is to be read as a midrash of the New, just as the New Testament is a midrash upon the Old. This midrashic circle gives the theological structure of promise and fulfillment. The two texts are in dialogue with and throw their light on each other—*and* on all those who come within their range. This last, of course, is the point that Luther and the tradition of reformist hermeneutics constantly stress, namely that to understand a scriptural text means to understand how it applies to oneself and one's own life. Understanding is always ultimately self-understanding. Hans-Georg Gadamer writes very much in the spirit of Luther when he says that "understanding always involves something like the application of the text to be understood to the present situation of the interpreter."[16] But now we see that this basic principle of philosophical hermeneutics is as old as midrash, that is, as old as interpretation itself. Indeed, as we have seen, the Scriptures themselves are structured precisely on this principle.

For the point is not that midrash is a special type of interpretation, a sort of primitive exegesis; rather it is exemplary of all interpretation that is open to the historicality of human life. Thus to read a text in the light of events that transpire long after the text was written is not a naive or uncritical way of reading—hence the shock of reading the Gospel according to John, with its strong anti-Jewish character, in the light of the Holocaust. This way of reading is the whole basis of legal understanding, where we always construe a text in terms of the situation in which we find ourselves and not just strictly in terms of the situation in which the law was originally handed down. The law is always being supplemented (not superseded or replaced) by the interpretation of it. In the law, as in midrash, we see a perfect illustration of the hermeneutical principle that we understand differently if we understand at all;[17] but this is just to say that the law is midrashic in its hermeneutical structure. It does not mean that we don't understand the law in its original context and first meaning; it is simply that this is not all that we understand, since, after all, we do not stand outside the law but in front of it, open to its questions, and always obliged to say how it is with us under such conditions. You cannot claim to have understood a legal text unless you see yourself in its light; but this self-understanding in turn sheds its light on the law, enlarges its intelligibility, and allows it to take into account what it had not foreseen. Interpretation always involves a dialectical movement of self-understanding and the understanding of the other, that is, of what comes down to us from the past. In this same way, the main point about midrash is not that it is free with the Scriptures but that it shows us how we are always within the embrace of what we seek to understand. Midrash means the interpretation of texts that are not kept like museum pieces under glass. The Scriptures, like the law, exist historically and are always entering into new situations in which the understanding of them requires that they be resituated in languages and forms of life different from the ones in which they were originally composed.

What is it to resituate a text in this way? The everyday example is obviously that of translation. Since languages are historical as well as grammatical, translation involves situating a text in a new conceptual framework—a new history—and not just transferring a meaning from one tongue to another. To be sure, translation implies synonymy, but we know that languages are not always cognate with one another, and in fact analytic philosophers of language have coined the phrase "radical translation" to characterize translation between languages with completely independent histories, or between which there has been no extended period of contact (for example, between ancient Hebrew and Greek rather than, say, between modern French and English).[18]

It is in the context of radical translation that the subject of allegorical interpretation needs to be examined. The translation of the Hebrew Bible into Greek in the third century B.C.E.—that is, the production of a version of the text that came to be called the Septuagint—is a good (if rough) example of radical translation, and allegory is a good example of what is called "radical interpretation," that is, not free interpretation, but the interpretation of a text or corpus that has been resituated within an alien conceptual framework.[19] Allegory presupposes a cultural situation in which the literal interpretation of a text would be as incomprehensible as a literal translation of it.

The best texts for the study of allegorical interpretation are found in the work of Philo, a Greek-speaking Jew and Hellenistic philosopher who lived in Alexandria, where the Septuagint had been produced in order to provide a text of the Scriptures for a large Jewish population that no longer used Hebrew. Philo flourished about the time of Christ, and his works include a number of elaborate commentaries on Genesis and a collection of questions and answers on puzzling words and expressions in Genesis and Exodus. This hermeneutical material is rooted in an ancient theory of signs which holds that such things as names and numbers have both a common usage and a usage which is proper to the schools, or to traditions of meditation, argument, and teaching. This theory was traditionally applied to the study of Homeric texts and, indeed, to any texts whose language was remote from familiar speech; but more generally it is related to a commonplace distinction between light and dark sayings, or between proverbs and enigmas, where the one is a truth which circulates widely and which everyone can recognize, whereas the other requires study, reflection, investigation, and the assistance of the sorts of special insight possessed by unique individuals such as Tiresias or even Oedipus: people who are required to cope (often as a matter of life or death) with riddles and prophecies. This notion is basic to Eastern antiquity, but we are perhaps most familiar with it in the sayings of Heraclitus ("*Physis* [Nature] loves to hide," fr. 123) and the Wisdom traditions of groups such as the Pythagoreans. This notion, moreover, antedates the development of rhetoric and grammar, and so ought not to be linked with the logical distinction between literal and figurative propositions with which we are most comfortable.

Indeed, even for someone as late as Philo the distinction between literal and figurative would be less applicable to the study of texts than would the more elementary distinction between the plain and the dark. Thus Philo's word for "figurative" derives from the Greek *trepein,* "to turn," which means not transformation (turning one thing into another) but conversion (turning something around): when confronted with a dark saying, you can make it plain by turning it toward you, because the light it sheds is on its nether side, shining away from you. Frequently, however, what requires turning is not the saying but the one who fails to understand it. If a saying shines its light away from you, you are not standing where you should be; you need to alter your place or condition in order to situate yourself in the light of what is said. This idea goes back at least to Plato's allegory of the cave, but an excellent example of what this entails can be found in Augustine's *Confessions.* Augustine's conversion placed him in a position to understand what had previously been incomprehensible to him. It is entirely appropriate, therefore, that the *Confessions* should conclude with two books of commentary on Genesis.

The interest of allegory, however, is rather more in names than in sayings (or stories or whole texts). For someone like Philo it would have been normal to assume that each name in Genesis, for example, belongs to two contexts. It names whatever it names in the biblical text ("Moses" just means Moses), but it also belongs to a second lexicon that derives from the language of moral philosophy that comes down from Plato's Academy. It is this language that defines the norms of rationality—or, more accurately, gives the theory of wisdom—for men of learning such as Philo. This philosophical language is also authoritative for the Christian tradition, not only for the early Fathers such as Clement of Alexandria and Origen, who were squarely within Philo's intellectual culture and recognized their kinship with him, but also for men of late antiquity such as Augustine, who had to contend with the strangeness of the biblical texts within the context of Ciceronian norms of literary and philosophical discourse.

Essentially, Philo's commentaries on the Scriptures try to explain how to translate biblical language into the language of moral philosophy (whence the Scriptures, strange as they are, can be counted as a book of Wisdom). In fact, manuals for converting the one into the other were widely circulating before Philo's time,[20] and they provided equivalencies such as: Adam = Natural Reason, Eve = The Senses, Egypt = The Body, Israel = The Soul, Moses = Divine Wisdom. A conversion manual of this sort (like a book of etymologies) would enable a Hebrew name to function like a Greek name such as Philo's, which is not only the name for Philo but also the name for love. The task of exegesis in this event would not be simply to know what Philo's name means but also to work out the sense (the conditions) in which it would be appropriate or, conceivably, inappropriate to call him by that name. Does he live up to his name? Exegesis would want to know what in his life would justify his name, just as, for example, it would want to know what in the life of Odysseus would justify both his name (*odyssasthai*, "to cause pain") and the various epithets that subsequently attach themselves to him (Sacker of Cities, Much-grieving Odysseus). Exegesis in this sense would extend beyond the name into the story or an account of action; it would move from *logos* to *praxis*, from words to deeds. The interpretation of names means understanding ways of life.

Philo's commentaries are not easy to read. For the Cain and Abel story, for example, Philo offers a verse-by-verse exegesis that expands without (apparently) systematic planning to four books. For Philo, however, exegesis is less a reading out than a crossing over or conversion in which he tries to justify as well as elucidate the biblical texts. His point of departure is always the perplexing word, name, or phrase, and his practice is to resolve this perplexity in two ways. For common names, his method is philological: he follows the standard procedures of Alexandrian textual criticism (which gives us both the Homeric texts and the Septuagint) by showing how a word is used in the various contexts in which it appears. For proper names, however, he has recourse to a manual of translation. Thus at the beginning of his book *On the Birth of Abel and the Sacrifices Offered by Him and by His Brother Cain,* Philo writes:

> In case these unfamiliar terms may cause perplexity to many, I will attempt to give as clear an account as I can of the underlying philosophical thought (*tēn emphainomenēn philosophian*). It is a fact that there are two opposite and contending views of life [*doxas*], one which ascribes all things to the mind as our master, whether we are using our reason or our senses, in motion or at rest, the other which follows God, whose handiwork it believes itself to be. The first of these views is figured (*ektypōsis*) by Cain who is called Possession, because he thinks he possesses all things, the other by Abel, whose name means "one who refers (all things) to God." Now both these views or conceptions lie in the womb of the single soul.[21]

Philo goes on to elucidate his point by correlating the Cain and Abel story with the story of Jacob and Esau and their conflict within Rebecca's womb (Rebecca = Patience). Later, in the book *That the Worse is Wont to Attack the Better,* he construes the Cain and Abel story as a story about the conflict between rhetoric and philosophy and also between true and false eloquence (Aaron versus Joseph). Abel in this context is the tongue-tied philosopher who is defenseless against Cain's sophistries, in contrast to Moses, who is true Wisdom: Moses remains silent, but he can depend upon his brother Aaron to give voice to the truth.

The Cain and Abel story can be turned this way and that, but throughout his commentaries or turnings Philo holds fast to his main theme of the opposition between self-love and love of God. This is the truth that the Cain and Abel story teaches: what happens to Abel is exactly what happens to the love of God when it is overcome by self-love. Hence the maxim embodied in the title, that "the worse is wont to attack the better": whenever you have two vital elements, one worse and one better, the one will attack the other: you can count on it.

It has become customary to call this sort of thing a "moralizing" of the Scriptures, but Philo did not think of himself as attaching a moral to a story. The technical term for "underlying philosophical thought" is *hyponoia,* literally, "a deeper or higher thought." *Hyponoia* is frequently translated as "allegory," but strictly speaking *allēgoria* is a rhetorical rather than a philosophical term and occurs only seldom in Philo by comparison with *hyponoia* and *symbolon.* Basically, *hyponoia* means that there is more for us to think about in a name or a story than simply what is said: *hyponoia* is what emerges upon reflection. It is a product of second thought as against first reading. Elsewhere I have made the point that in allegorical interpretation "the intelligibility of a text cannot be isolated from what occurs to the reader in the course of his meditations upon what is written." Allegory (so-called) is a function of spiritual life rather than a technique of reading: it is a type of contemplation that is practiced in front of or in the light of a traditional text. Our modern conception of exegesis as a type of objective analysis may incline us to dismiss allegory as pseudo-exegesis, but this view is simply unhistorical: it maps onto allegory the structure of romantic hermeneutics in which a subject deploys itself ana-lytically against an object. However, in allegory the text "cannot be figured as an objective entity that is subjected to some sort of mental operation. On the contrary, the concept of *hyponoia* seems to presuppose a Platonistic theory of knowledge as the recognition of what is already known to you. An allegorical reading of the Law is in this respect not the introduction of something alien or subjective into the Law but rather the recognition in it of what you know to be true. *Hyponoia* presupposes a memory-based epistemology, not an epistemology of subjects and objects and methods for certifying their correspondence."[22]

However, this does not mean that allegory was somehow prelogical or that it fell short of what we would count as norms of analytical reason. On the contrary, in antiquity allegory was preeminently a philosopher's way of reading: it was essentially a way of taking nonphilosophical texts philosophically, that is, in the spirit of a search for wisdom. And in keeping with its philosophical nature allegory exhibits a logic which, in fact, we resort to every day in the normal course of making sense of things.

The logic of allegory is the same as in metaphor as regards the truth of statements or propositions. When you encounter a proposition which, taken by itself or as it stands, is false, you try to find a way of reading it that will make it come out true. A metaphor does not exist by itself but only in the context of interpretation: it simply means that what you cannot take in one sense you must try to take in another.

To take something—to make sense of it—simply means to find a state of affairs in which it fits. What is a false statement in one context or situation will in another prove true. A sentence is true by virtue of the way it hangs together with other sentences held to be true. Truth is not just a question of logical form or empirical verification (or falsification). All this means, however, is that it is impossible to tell whether a sentence is true or not by considering that sentence in isolation. As W. V. O. Quine has said, the truth of a sentence is holistic: it presupposes a body or fabric of interwoven sentence within which it fits, or which it doesn't rend or tear. Quine calls such a fabric a "conceptual scheme."[23] It is a framework of interlocking true sentences, or sentences held to be true. Thus, for example, the statement "The law is an ass" is, taken by itself, false (or anyhow absurd), but we know it is not to be taken just in this way, because we also know of another sense (or context or set of conditions) in which it is true, namely the sense which Dickens gives it; that is, we know of circumstances under which it is true to say, "The law is an ass." Being literal-minded essentially means being ignorant of the manifold conditions in which our sentences, however figurative they sometimes are, are true (or anyhow not absurd).

Allegory operates on this metaphorical principle of saving propositions from the charge of falsehood or nonsense; the difference is that allegory is concerned with saving whole texts, or indeed whole fabrics of interlocking sentences. One might say that the task of allegory is the saving of whole systems of belief, like the Mosaic Law.

However, here is the point: basic to allegory is what logicians in Quine's tradition call "the principle of charity." Charity is required in all cases of radical translation (translation between two completely alien languages). How do you go about constructing a translation manual that will enable you to interpret sentences of a radically alien language? The principle of charity is your starting point. This principle is very ancient, but it was given its modern formulation by a logician named N. L. Wilson. The principle, according to Wilson, requires you, when confronting an alien text or corpus, to seek "that interpretation which, in light of what it knows of the facts, will maximize truth among the sentences of the corpus."[24]

Donald Davidson has put the principle this way: "Making sense of the utterances and behavior of others, even their most aberrant behavior, requires us to find a great deal of truth and reason in them."[25] The idea here is that for understanding to be possible, you have to assume that the alien is very much the same as you are, which simply means that the alien holds to be true what you hold to be true, even though you have obviously different systems of belief. Thus Davidson says that we must "assign truth conditions to alien sentences that make native speakers right when plausibly possible according, of course, to our own view of what is right."[26] Davidson calls this his theory of radical interpretation. The upshot of the theory is that "if we cannot find a way to interpret the utterances and behavior of a creature as revealing a set of beliefs largely consistent and true by our own standards, we have no reason to count that creature as rational, as having beliefs, or as saying anything at all."[27]

"Charity," Davidson says, "is forced on us; whether we like it or not, if we want to understand others, we must count them right in most matters."[28] It is easy to see that allegorical interpretation, as Philo practiced it, conforms pretty much to the basic structure of Davidson's theory. We must imagine Philo assigning truth conditions to the Mosaic text that will make that text right according to Philo's standards of what is right. (A truth condition is simply whatever has to be the case for a sentence to be counted as true. What *is* the case is essentially what conceptual schemes are about.) The modern complaint against allegorical interpretation is that it violates the basic principle of historical criticism, which is that you must situate a text in its own time and place before you begin to interpret it. But Davidson's theory would hold that you would not know how to do this unless you had already understood the text according to the logic of radical interpretation (that is, the logic of allegory), which requires you to have already found a great deal of truth and reason in the text that you seek to study historically. Allegory in this respect would be the precondition of historical criticism. There can be no understanding of the other except on the basis of an interpretation which maximizes or optimizes agreement between the other and yourself. And this in turn is consistent with the basic hermeneutical principle that you can understand only that with which you share a deep common accord, that is, a common ground, a mutual belonging. The task of hermeneutics would always be to work out this common ground where it isn't already in place. The ancient practice of allegory illustrates this principle. We must imagine Philo's allegorization of the Law not as a reading out or a reading in but as a laying open of a common ground between law and philosophy, or between Moses and Plato. Our task is to see that there is nothing strange in this, but that, on the contrary, it is what occurs in all understanding. Allegory is not a method of exegesis but a condition of understanding as such. For understanding is always historically situated; it always occurs within a horizon which is different from (but not closed off to) the horizon in which the text to be understood was originally composed.

Thus the logic of allegory stands behind the main principle of patristic exegesis, namely "the rule of faith," which holds that the Scriptures are always to be construed in a way that is consistent with apostolic teachings. This rule sounds imperious, and in Tertullian's *On Prescription against Heretics,* in which the rule is given a sharp, legal formulation, it *is* imperious, because Tertullian was concerned with the question of who has the right to quote from the Scriptures in support of a doctrinal position. For Tertullian, the primary question for the interpretation of the Scriptures is, Who owns them? This is a question of authority in interpretation: Who has the right to say what a text means? Yet the hermeneutical principle that this question implies is not imperious but commonsensical. In the idiom of analytic philosophy of language, the rule of faith simply assigns truth conditions to the Scriptures that will make the text right according to the apostolic (as against Jewish, Gnostic, or Platonic) view of what is right. Different traditions have different rules of faith, including the tradition of historical criticism. The question is, What counts as an interpretation that will stand as authoritative for Christian communities? In effect, the rule of faith defines the spirit—the presuppositions or conceptual framework or tradition: the fore-understanding—in which Christians read the Scriptures, including the Old Testament. As Irenaeus wrote,

> If anyone reads the Scriptures . . . with attention, he will find in them an account of Christ, and a foreshadowing of the new calling. For Christ is the treasure which was hid in the field, that is, in this world (for "the field is the world," Matt. 13:38); but the treasure hid in the Scriptures is Christ, since he was pointed out by means of types and parables. Hence his human nature could not be understood, prior to the consummation of those things which had been predicted, that is, the advent of Christ . . . For prophecy, before its fulfillment, is to men (full of) enigmas and ambiguities.[29]

Individual exegetes might disagree about which texts are to be taken as prophetic, but there could be no disagreement as to how the Old Testament is to be taken in principle. The alternative to typology is the Gnostic rejection of the Old Testament as just a profane text.

More generally, of course, the rule of faith means construing the Scriptures in light of Christian doctrine. This is how Augustine conceives it in his *On Christian Doctrine:*

> It is to be understood that the plenitude and the end of the Law and of all the sacred Scriptures is the love of a Being which is to be enjoyed and of a being that can share that enjoyment with us . . . Whoever, therefore, thinks that he understands the divine Scriptures or any part of them so that it does not build the double love of God and of our neighbor does not understand it at all. Whoever finds a lesson there useful to the building of charity, even though he has not said what the author may be shown to have intended in that place, has not been deceived.[30]

In practice, then, the rule of faith is a rule for determining whether a scriptural text is to be taken as it stands (or in its original sense) or whether it is to be tacitly rewritten as a figure of *caritas*: as Augustine says, "whatever appears in the divine Word that does not literally pertain to virtuous behavior or to the truth of faith you must take to be figurative."[31] And what this amounts to is a way of coping with the strangeness of the biblical text, that is, its cultural difference: "If Scripture commends something despised by the customs of the listeners, or condemns what those customs do not condemn, they take the Scriptural locution as figurative if they accept it as an authority. But Scripture teaches nothing but charity, nor condemns anything except cupidity, and in this way shapes the minds of men."[32] Here (as elsewhere) Augustine's eye is on the relationship between the text and the situation in which it is to be taken.

However, Augustine's is not therefore an unhistorical or uncritical view of the Scriptures, that is, one indifferent to the ways in which it is alien to the situation in which it continues to be authoritative for teaching. Indeed, Augustine is extremely sensitive to the tensions between the scriptural text as a historical document and its existence as a text for Christian teaching. The text for him was an intersection of multiple tensions because the text itself contains multiple inscriptions that show its Hebrew origins, its Christian history, and its Latin reception. Jerome gave him no end of trouble with his Vulgate, which was translated directly from the Hebrew text and so produced a Latin Bible sometimes dramatically different from the one with which Augustine's community was familiar. Throughout all this, however, Augustine's hermeneutical logic remained the logic of allegory: as Davidson says, "If we cannot find a way to interpret the utterances . . . of a creature as revealing a set of beliefs largely consistent and true by our own standards, we have no reason to count that creature as rational, as having beliefs, or as saying anything at all."

A historical view of the Scriptures, then, is not one that merely situates the text in the time, place, and circumstance of its composition. Such an approach is not so much historical as romantic; it assigns truth conditions that will make the text right according to nineteenth-century standards of what is right—namely, the idea that the understanding of a text means understanding it as well as or even better than its author. On the contrary, a historical view of the Scriptures is a view which sees their *historicality,* that is, their life in human time. Here the Bible is not an ancient artifact or museum piece but rather exists historically like a good law. There is always a dialogue of text and history, in which the one is adapted to new situations and the other (as Augustine says) is shaped by what the text has to say. The beginnings of scriptural interpretation illustrate this dialectical relationship between the text and those who stand (and understand themselves) in its light.

NOTES

1. Moshe Weinfeld, "The Scribes and the 'Book of the Torah,'" in *Deuteronomy and the Deuteronomic School* (Oxford, 1972), pp. 165–173.

2. P. R. Ackroyd, "The Old Testament in the Making," in *The Cambridge History of the Bible,* vol. I: *From the Beginnings to Jerome,* ed. P. R. Ackroyd and C. F. Evans (Cambridge, 1970), pp. 67–112.

3. Brevard S. Childs, *Introduction to the Old Testament as Scripture* (London and Philadelphia, 1979), p. 73.

4. *Midrash Rabbah,* trans. Harry Freedman and Maurice Simon (London, 1939). Quotation is from the midrash to the Song of Songs, I. 1. 8.

5. Ibid., I. 10. 2.

6. Ibid., I. 10. 2.

7. Joseph Heinemann, "The Nature of the Aggadah," trans. Marc Bregman, in Geoffrey Hartman and Sanford Budick, eds., *Midrash and Literature* (New Haven, 1986), pp. 48–49; originally published in Joseph Heinemann, *Aggadah and Its Development: Studies in the Continuity of a Tradition* [Hebrew] (Jerusalem, 1974).

8. See Geza Vermes, "Bible and Midrash: Early Old Testament Exegesis," in *The Cambridge History of the Bible,* I, 199–231.

9. A good example of this outlook is found in Jacob Neusner, *Midrash in Context: Exegesis in Formative Judaism* (Philadelphia, 1983), which is not about exegesis at all but about certain formal problems attaching to the compilation of midrashic texts in the fifth and sixth centuries. Neusner feels free to polemicize against midrash as an interpretive practice, which for him amounts simply to saying whatever one pleases about a text.

10. *Pesikta Rabbati: Discourses for Feasts, Fasts, and Special Sabbaths,* trans. William G. Braude, 2 vols. (New Haven, 1968). Quotation is from Piska 14.9.

11. Ibid., Piska 3.2. Cf. *Midrash Rabbah,* Numbers (Naso), XIV. 4, for a slightly different version of this conversation.

12. *Midrash Rabbah,* Numbers (Chukkath), XIX. 6.

13. John Bowker, *The Targums and Rabbinic Literature: An Introduction to Jewish Interpretations of Scripture* (London, 1969).

14. *The Midrash Pesher of Habakkuk,* trans. William H. Brownlee (Missoula, Mont., 1979).

15. *Selections from the Commentaries and Homilies of Origen,* trans. R. B. Tollinton (London, 1929), p. 54.

16. Hans-Georg Gadamer, *Truth and Method,* ed. Garrett Barden and John Cumming (New York, 1975), p. 274.

17. Ibid., p. 264.

18. See W. V. O. Quine, *Word and Object* (New York, 1960), pp. 26–30.

19. See Donald Davidson, *Inquiries into Truth and Interpretation* (Oxford, 1984), pp. 125–139.

20. See R. P. C. Hanson, "Interpretation of Hebrew Names in Origen," *Virgiliae Christianae,* 10 (July 1956), 103–123.

21. Philo, *On the Birth of Abel and the Sacrifices Offered by Him and by His Brother Cain,* in *Philo in Ten Volumes,* trans. F. H. Colson and G. H. Whitaker, II (Cambridge, Mass., and London, 1958), 95–97.

22. Gerald L. Bruns, "The Problem of Figuration in Antiquity," in Gary Shapiro and Alan Sica, eds., *Hermeneutics: Questions and Prospects* (Amherst, Mass., 1981), p. 151.

23. Quine, *Word and Object,* pp. 9–12.

24. Quoted by Ian Hacking, *Why Does Language Matter to Philosophy?* (Cambridge, 1975), p. 148.

25. Davidson, *Inquiries,* p. 153.

26. Ibid., p. 137.

27. Ibid.

28. Ibid., p. 197.

29. *The Writings of Irenaeus,* trans. Alexander Roberts and W. H. Rambaut (Edinburgh, 1883–84), p. 461.

30. *On Christian Doctrine,* trans. D. W. Robertson, Jr. (Indianapolis, 1958), p. 30.

31. Ibid., p. 88.

32. Ibid.

SUGGESTED FURTHER READINGS

Renée Bloch, "Midrash," trans. M. H. Callaway, in *Approaches to Ancient Judaism,* vol. I: *Theory and Practice,* ed. William Scott Green (Missoula, Mont., 1978), pp. 29–50.

Michael Fishbane, *Biblical Interpretation of Ancient Israel* (Oxford, 1985).

Joseph Heinemann and D. Noy, eds., *Studies in Aggadah and Folk Literature* (Jerusalem, 1978).

James L. Kugel, "Two Introductions to Midrash," in Geoffrey Hartman and Sanford Budick, eds., *Midrash and Literature* (New Haven, 1986), pp. 77–103; originally published in *Prooftexts,* 3 (1983), 131–155.

Wayne S. Towner, "Hermeneutical Systems of Hillel and the Tannaim: A Fresh Look," *Hebrew Union College Annual,* 53 (1982), 101–135.

Notre Dame University

English Translations of the Bible

Gerald Hammond

FOR one kind of reader the Authorized Version's "And God saw the light, that it was good" (Gen. 1:4), is a better translation than such modern equivalents as the New English Bible's "and God saw that the light was good" or the New American Bible's "God saw how good the light was," because it sounds better, more impressive in its slightly odd syntax. Another kind of reader prefers the modern versions because they are straightforward, and therefore probably more accurate. For this group the Authorized Version's oddness is an archaic obstacle to understanding. Also, the reader dedicated to the notion of narrative efficiency will find the modern renderings more attractive because they describe God's action neutrally, diluting *see* to the point where it means nothing more than "realize." The Authorized Version's rendering, in contrast, takes a definite view of what God actually does; its syntax gives "saw" its fullest sense, that of looking into the light. The difference is almost as great as the difference between saying "I saw the book he had written" and "I saw that he had written the book." The older version is the more anthropomorphic and, for that reason, is likely to be more attractive to many readers, but not to those who prefer an abstract God.

But do these aesthetic distinctions have any bearing upon the way we may judge the different versions' relative degrees of accuracy and fidelity to the original? The matter of anthropomorphism is one area to consider. In response to a traditionalist who asserts that the Authorized Version's rendering accords with a Bible whose representation of God is resolutely anthropomorphic, the modern theologian might counter with the view that it is so only because the Bible is written in languages which had no better way of expressing these things. Part of the essential accuracy of a translation should be to turn not only idioms but also ways of thought and casts of mind into their contemporary equivalents; since we are much less happy today than were the ancient Hebrews with a God who has eyes, it is better to weaken the sense of "saw" from "seeing with eyes" to "realizing." One reply to this, of course, is that there is no less anthropomorphism in the modern renderings, only that it is less noticeable.

Then there is the matter of accuracy at the actual level of words and phrases. The modern versions do not differ from the earlier ones here: all have "God," "light," "saw," and "good." This fact shows how most of the modern translations are constrained by a basic set of equivalents established by the Renaissance translators.[1] Thus they nearly all use "God," as the Authorized Version did, to translate *elohim* here, just as they use "Lord" to translate *YHWH*. Occasionally a translator tries to break with the tradition, but the rendering "And Elohim saw" is unlikely to succeed with the general readership of the Bible—a readership immeasurably greater than that of any other work of literature in the Western tradition, and one whose literary values, for narrative and poetry, are often conditioned by their early experience of it.

But what of the syntax which causes the difference in meaning between the Renaissance and modern renderings in this verse? As a rule, whenever we encounter a syntactic oddness or aberration in the Authorized Version—the kind of thing the word "archaic" is used unthinkingly to describe—we ought to assume that it reflects an attempt to reproduce the original's word or phrase order. William Tyndale, who originated the Renaissance English biblical tradition, said very little about the theory and practice of translation; but he did assert that in the matter of word order English was an excellent language to translate into from Old Testament Hebrew:

> They will say it cannot be translated into our tongue, it is so rude. It is not so rude as they are false liars. For the Greek tongue agreeth more with the English than with the Latin. And the properties of the Hebrew tongue agreeth a thousand times more with the English than with the Latin. The manner of speaking is both one, so that in a thousand places thou needest not but to translate it into the English word for word when thou must seek a compass in the Latin and yet shall have much work to translate it well-favouredly, so that it have the same grace and sweetness, sense and pure understanding with it in the Latin as it hath in the Hebrew. A thousand parts better may it be translated into English than into the Latin.[2]

Tyndale, like all other Reformation translators, worked hard to keep as close as possible to his original, for both the Renaissance cry *ad fontes* and the Protestant emphasis on the centrality of the text required Bible translation to be as transparent as possible. Thus the Authorized Version translators, who thought hard about every verse, kept Tyndale's "And God saw the light, that it was good," as the best possible rendering of the Hebrew. *Wayar elohim et-ha'or ki-tob* translates literally as "And-he-saw God the-light that-good." The Renaissance version keeps "the light" as the direct object of "saw" and makes "that it was good" a secondary element, entirely dependent upon that stark main clause.

But does "literal" here mean the same thing as "accurate" or "faithful"? It is arguable, for instance, that if this was not the only way to express in Hebrew that God saw the goodness of the light, it was at least a fairly common way. If we translate idiom for idiom rather than word for word, then it is more accurate to render this locution in a common English structure, and to use the odd "saw X that it was X" is misleading because it implies that the original construction is deviant. There are problems here, however. For one, it is not so easy to assert confidently that the Hebrew locution, as it occurs in Genesis, is common. So fundamental is this verse in the biblical tradition that later uses of the same construction, especially with the phrase *ki-tob* ("that-good"), may well be, if not in direct imitation, then at least strongly influenced by it. (This is particularly the case if we argue that all of our biblical texts are written in a literary language.) It would be more accurate, then, to render the English equivalent in a sufficiently unusual form to mark the primacy of the phrasing and to signal, by using it again, places where it is being imitated. And if we were to claim that there is no such noticeable deviation from the norm in the original, it is still arguable that idiom-for-idiom translation is as treacherous as translating word for word. Idioms are even more embedded in language and culture systems than single words are, so that what is offered is not translation, but only an equivalent.

Now the questions become more perplexing. How far was a Hebrew speaker of that period aware, when using the idiom "saw X that it was X," of any emphasis in the verb's meaning? This scarcely admits an answer, since it is not even easy for contemporary speakers to say how far they are aware of the act of seeing when they say "I saw that he had written it" instead of "I realized that he had written it." And if we could answer with confidence that they have no awareness of it, we would have to add to the equation the disturbing habit which poets and storytellers have, of giving life to dead metaphors and finding in our flattest phrases a cultural subconscious which they can bring to the surface. In the end, my preference for the Authorized Version's rendering to the modern ones comes from my sense that the opening chapters of Genesis are a carefully wrought narrative which uses language with unusual force and emphasis. "God saw the light, that it was good," is, after all, only a slight deviation from the English norm, but it is strong enough to reproduce this first great example of the sublime in literature.

TRANSLATION is one of the most influential forms of literary criticism, for it both interprets and recreates the text it addresses. Indeed, in its original uses in English the word *interpret* meant "translate." But most readers of the Bible who do not know Old Testament Hebrew or New Testament Greek—and that is all but an infinitesimal percentage—are unaware of the implications of this fact. Behind the joke "If the Authorized Version was good enough for St. Paul then it's good enough for me" lies the recognition of a real resistance to the idea that our Bible is a translation; betrayed too by the increasingly common slip which gives the Authorized

Version's alternative title as the St. James Bible. For many who rely upon the citation of word and verse to give literal support to dogma the fact of translation is an embarrassment, but it may also be perplexing to readers who approach the Bible as a literary achievement, for, without knowledge of the original languages, where can they find them best translated into English—"best" embracing both aesthetic appeal and accuracy? What, for example, are such readers to make of a volume like this, which uses the Authorized Version rather than any of the modern versions as its basic text?

Aesthetically there is no argument. Everyone concedes—the modern translators soonest of all—that the Authorized Version is itself a great work of art. It marked the culmination of nearly a hundred years of English Bible translation, beginning with Tyndale in the 1520s and 1530s, who translated all of the New Testament and large portions of the Old. He used Luther's German Bible as his main source but, astonishingly for an Englishman of that time, knew enough Greek and Hebrew to improve on Luther by bringing his English version closer to the original.[3] Major versions by Miles Coverdale—the Coverdale Bible in 1535 and the Great Bible in 1539—soon followed, and the rest of the century saw three more attempts to produce a definitive English version: the Geneva Bible in 1560, the Bishops' Bible in 1568, and the Catholic Reims-Douai Bible, begun in the 1580s.[4] But none of these, not even the Catholic one, marked a radical departure from what Tyndale had begun. And the Authorized Version, although it was instituted through Puritan demands for a new translation at the Hampton Court Conference, proudly proclaimed itself to be not a new translation, but simply an improvement of what already existed: "We never thought from the beginning that we should need to make a new translation, nor yet to make of a bad one a good one . . . but to make a good one better, or out of many good ones one principal good one."[5] The same spirit governed the Revised and Revised Standard Versions, and nothing could stand at a further extreme from the modern enterprises in biblical translation, each of which announces itself in its title or preface to be new. The newness of even the newest of these is, as we saw with "God" and "Lord," still likely to be a heavily circumscribed novelty, but it is stressed for two distinct reasons: to give readers what they popularly demand, a readable version; and to include the most recent findings of biblical scholarship.

Whether these are compatible desires is an open question. Those who try to play off the aesthetic qualities of the Authorized Version against its modern rivals usually favor the older translation, but lay it open to the charge that its very aesthetic superiority is a snare and a delusion. Not only does it repel a vast contemporary readership, who suspect any form of rhetoric as elitist, but, more seriously, it misrepresents in several ways the material which it professes to translate. For example, it elevates the prosaic to a poetic level, and its evenness of quality makes the large variety of biblical texts, written in many different periods, styles, and genres, all appear the same. The following pages explain some of the principles which seem to govern the Authorized Version's renderings and compare them in terms of accuracy and fidelity with the efforts of more recent translators.

MOST PEOPLE WILL probably fix their ideas of accuracy in translation on the text itself, and on the meanings of the individual words in it. In both cases it should be plain that any modern version is likely to be far more accurate than a Renaissance translation. Even though the Authorized Version translation panels were made up of scholars whose knowledge of Greek and Semitic languages was impressive, in the four hundred years of scholarship since we have learned far more about the semantics of biblical languages. In neither case, though, is the matter as simple as these assumptions indicate.

The earliest debates about English Bible translation centered on the meanings of words. Catholic polemicists throughout the second half of the sixteenth century accused Protestant translators of including deliberately heretical mistranslations in their versions. Even earlier, in the 1520s, Thomas More attacked Tyndale's New Testament for its mischievous renderings. Instead of "priest" he had used "senior"; instead of "church," "congregation." Tyndale's reply showed a delicious pragmatism: "Of a truth *senior* is no very good English, though *senior* and *junior* be used in the universities; but there came no better in my mind at that time. Howbeit, I spied my fault since, long ere Mr More told it me, and have mended it in all the works which I since made, and call it an *elder*."[6] This comment reveals how little concerned the Reformation translators were to defend their versions as inspired—but for our purposes the point is that semantic accuracy is largely an illusion. More's most famous charge was that Tyndale had translated *agape* in 1 Corinthians 13, not with the word "charity," as he should have done if he were paying proper respect to the Vulgate, but with the word "love." Such a word, having none of the traditional theological implications of "charity," and many undesirable ones, was too dangerous to be used in such a context. Tyndale replied by pointing out that no word is as immutable or uncontaminated as More pretended, and to restrict a translator in that way would lead to no translation at all. Ironically, "charity" did replace "love" later in the century, and in its use in the Authorized Version it became the definitive English rendering, only to give way to "love" again in most of the modern versions. But no reader who encountered "charity" in 1 Corinthians ever assumed that it had its normal English sense there—otherwise the idea that one could give away all one's goods and still not be the possessor of charity would be difficult to take—and whether a version uses "charity," "love," or some other word, such as "joy," makes little difference, for the context defines the word and gives it its specific meaning. This is an extreme example, but not a misleading one, for it is in the nature of a literary text that it constantly redefines and recontextualizes words. By ignoring this fact, translators frequently diminish the status of the text they translate; and usually their very desire to achieve semantic accuracy leads them to do so.

Here the demands of scholarship and translation are in competition. Consider another example from the early chapters of Genesis: how the Authorized Version renders the verb *yada*. Chapter 2 introduces us to the "tree of knowledge of good and evil," "knowledge" being a translation of the noun *da'at*, a cognate form of *yada*. This verb then rings through the narrative of the Fall. In 3:5 the serpent uses it twice: "For God doth know that in the day ye eat thereof, then your eyes shall be opened, and ye shall be as gods, knowing good and evil." The humans eat the fruit, and in verse 7 the narrator tells us: "And the eyes of them both were opened, and they knew that they were naked." In verse 22 God says that "the man is become as one of us, to know good and evil"; and then the narrator tells us, in 4:1: "And Adam knew Eve his wife; and she conceived." In each case the Authorized Version translates the verb with "know" or "knowing." A modern translator is unlikely to do the same, partly from a reluctance to reproduce the "archaism" of Adam knowing Eve, but also because of the scholarly instinct which perceives the word only as it appears in the lexicon.[7] Here *yada* is being used in three distinct meanings according to lexical definition: "to know," "to understand," and "to have carnal relations with." As a result modern versions, though they may keep the word *know* for the words of God and the serpent, will probably choose something more specific when they come to the narrator's words. Instead of "they knew that they were naked" they will use "discovered" or "realized," and instead of Adam knowing Eve, they tend to ring the changes through such euphemisms as "lay with," "had relations with," or "had intercourse with."[8]

For the doubtful gain in semantic precision, the literary loss is large. No readers of these modern versions can perceive, as they can easily in the Authorized Version, the narrative's economical linking, through this verb, of the fruit of the tree with shame, God's knowledge, and sexuality. It is at the least arguable that the Renaissance practice is more faithful to the original text, and the implications for the literary critic are large. Robert Alter, in showing how vital a part of biblical narrative technique is the repetition of key words, has warned that "most modern English translations go to the opposite extreme, constantly translating the same word with different English equivalents for the sake of fluency and supposed precision. Nevertheless, the repetition of key-words is so prominent in many biblical narratives that one can still follow it fairly well in translation, especially if one uses the King James Version."[9]

This is not to say that the translators of the Authorized Version were fanatically dedicated to the idea of a one-for-one equivalence. They probably had to resist strong pressures, from Puritan polemicists such as Hugh Broughton, to translate in this way, and their preface makes it clear that such a notion is an entirely unnecessary constraint:

> we have not tied ourselves to an uniformity of phrasing, or to an identity of words, as some peradventure would wish we had done, because they observe that some learned men somewhere have been as exact as they could that way . . . But, that we should express the same notion in the same particular word; as for example, if we translate the Hebrew or Greek word once by *purpose,* never to call it *intent*; if one where *journeying,* never *travelling*; if one where *think,* never *suppose*; if one where *pain,* never *ache*; if one where *joy,* never *gladness,* etc. Thus to mince the matter we thought to savour more of curiosity than wisdom, and that rather it would breed scorn in the atheist than bring profit to the godly reader. For is the kingdom of God become words or syllables?[10]

Nonetheless it is notable that in this respect the Authorized Version is the most conservative of the Renaissance translations. Tyndale and the Calvinist translators of the Geneva Bible took little care to maintain verbal equivalence. The Authorized Version, however, particularly in its use of the more common words—and these are the most likely to be "key words"—moved much closer to a formulaic principle of translation. Thus a relatively uncommon word such as *khiydah,* which occurs in about eight different contexts in the Old Testament, is rendered variously "riddle" (Ezek. 17:2, Judges 14:12–17), "dark saying" (Prov. 1:6; Ps. 49:5, 78:2), "taunting proverb" (Hab. 2:6), "dark sentence" (Dan. 8:23), and "hard question" (1 Kings 10:1). The context governs the small changes in sense. A slightly more common word, such as *la'ag,* is rendered more variously, ranging from "laugh to scorn" (as in 2 Kings 19:21) to "have in derision" (Ps. 2:4), although in all three of its occurrences in Proverbs it is translated as "mock": "I will mock when your fear cometh" (1:26); "Whoso mocketh the poor reproacheth his Maker" (17:5); "The eye that mocketh at his father" (30:17).[11] With common words there is great consistency of translation: *lekhem* is, more likely than not, rendered as "bread," *nefesh* as "soul," *leb* as "heart."

How we feel about this practice must partly be governed by our attitude toward canonicity. To a great extent translation encourages the idea that there is a canon, for to have both Old and New Testaments in the same language is only the most obvious example of the way it forces homogeneity upon books of very different kinds; thus the use of "heart" encourages the belief that similar assumptions and connotations lie behind both *leb* in Genesis and *kardia* in Corinthians. But there is little sign that twentieth-century translations have any other kind of aim, even if they are less likely to use "heart" in either place and despite their intent to reflect a decanonizing scholarship, aimed at pulling apart and fragmenting the original texts. Their repeated insistence upon a plain, readable style does as much to encourage the idea of a canon as might any formulaic translation of individual words. If the Bible is a collection of texts produced over a long period and widely diverse in genre and style, then to turn them all into "the language we use today" will inevitably mask such distinctions.

Within single books and parts of books, however, the specter of a delusory canonicity can be ignored, and it is here, perversely, that the modern translators' insistence upon a clear, readable style, while it disguises distinctions between books, now masks the techniques of repetition which are so basic to the literary effects of the Bible. As their use of "know" to translate *yada* shows, the Renaissance translators' practice worked better. They were, for a start, shrewdly perceptive of the need to reproduce very close repetition, as, for instance, within a single verse. Thus, where in Genesis 3:15 God describes the enduring enmity between Adam's and the serpent's offspring by using the same verb, *shup,* Tyndale takes care to convey the reciprocal process of revenge, even though it stretches the meaning of the English verb he uses far beyond its possible range of meanings: "and that seed shall tread thee on the head, and thou shalt tread it on the heel." This rendering is the more notable because neither of his principal sources had the stylistic sense to repeat the verb. The Vulgate has *conteret* and *insidiaberis,* Luther *zutretten* and *beissen.*

Because of the Renaissance translators' tendency toward formulaic renderings of common words, their versions are more likely than the modern ones to show up places where biblical writers had given new force to common phrases and idioms. Robert Alter discusses 2 Samuel 3 as an example of this sophisticated narrative technique, in which a pattern of repetition is suddenly subverted by an ominous variant of a familiar phrase. In verse 21 David sends Abner off, and the narrator tells us that he went in peace (*wayelekh bashalom*). In verse 22 the narrator uses the phrase again, also at the end of the verse: Abner was not with David, for he had sent him off and he went in peace. In verse 23 Joab is told what has happened, and the phrase is again used at the end. And then, in verse 24, Joab goes to the king, asks him why he has let Abner go, and finishes his remonstrance, not with the phrase which has ended the previous three verses, but with an intensification of the verb which they had used (*wayelekh halokh*). With such a formulaic narrative the Authorized Version translators are entirely happy, and the reader of their English rendering will, just like the reader of the Hebrew original, first become accustomed to the pattern and then find it suddenly subverted:

And Abner said unto David, I will arise and go, and will gather all Israel unto my lord the king, that they may make a league with thee, and that thou mayest reign over all that thine heart desireth. And David sent Abner away; *and he went in peace*. And, behold, the servants of David and Joab came from pursuing a troop, and brought in a great spoil with them: but Abner was not with David in Hebron; for he had sent him away, *and he was gone in peace*. When Joab and all the host that was with him were come, they told Joab, saying, Abner the son of Ner came to the king and he hath sent him away, *and he is gone in peace*. Then Joab came to the king, and said, What hast thou done? behold, Abner came unto thee; why is it that thou hast sent him away, *and he is quite gone*? (vv. 21–24)

In contrast, the reader of a modern version such as the New English Bible can find no such pattern, and so can register neither it nor its reversal. That version ends verse 21 with "granting him safe conduct" and verse 23 with "departed under safe conduct," and varies its translation with "after his dismissal" in verse 22. As a result the statement at the end of verse 24, "He has got clean away," bears no relation to what has gone before.[12]

The Renaissance translators' readiness to render the Bible in a formulaic way helps us recognize and respond to the individual style of the books. A simple, telling example is the constant use of the word *leb* in Ecclesiastes, in phrases and contexts which vary from the most idiomatic to the most heartfelt. So frequently is it used that the speaker's *leb* becomes a character, and the idiom takes on a new life. When he says, in the words of the Authorized Version, "I gave my heart to search and seek out" (1:13; see also v. 17), or "I said in mine heart" (2:1; 3:17, 18), or "I applied mine heart to know" (7:25), these virtual clichés lose their staleness because of the way *leb* is used in more imaginative contexts throughout the book: as in 2:10, "I withheld not my heart from any joy"; or 2:23, "yea, his heart taketh not rest in the night"; or 5:20, "because God answereth him in the joy of his heart"; or 7:3, "by the sadness of the countenance the heart is made better." Again, the modern versions do not allow their readers such an insight. Partly it is a matter of not wishing to sound archaic, partly a wish to avoid redundancies, so that in the New English Bible, for instance, only in the last two examples is "heart" used. Otherwise, all kinds of variations are used.[13]

Too often the contrast between old and new shows up not merely an imperviousness on the part of the modern versions toward the Bible's literary effects, but a real desire to suppress them. In 1 Samuel 15 we find what a modern literary critic will eagerly recognize as a narrative abrasion. The chapter closes with an account of Saul's reluctance to execute the king of the Amalekites, despite the divine command, by way of the prophet, to do so. The Hebrew presents us with a striking contradiction. In verse 11 God tells Samuel that he repents (*nikham*) having made Saul king. Then, in verse 29, the prophet tells Saul that God is not a man and therefore does not repent (*nikham*) his actions. Six verses later the narrative ends the chapter by stating that God repented (*nikham*) that he had made Saul king. No reader of the Authorized Version can miss the conflict between God's and the narrator's words on the one hand, and the prophet's on the other, for, as we would expect, it uses the same English word each time: "It repenteth me that I have set up Saul to be king . . . And also the Strength of Israel will not lie nor repent: for he is not a man, that he should repent . . . and the Lord repented that he had made Saul king over Israel." But in the twentieth-century versions the conflict is diluted by deliberate variations: the New International Version has "grieved . . . change his mind . . . grieved," the Jerusalem Bible "regret . . . go back on his word . . . regretted," the New English Bible "repent . . . change his mind . . . repented." In each case the prophet's words are made to seem distinct from God's and the narrator's, as if he had to be protected from the charge of some kind of duplicity in his statement to Saul. But of course it is this very duplicity which makes the narrative so powerful.

MORE IMPORTANT than the translation of words is the translation of syntax. Consider the way the Authorized Version and the New English Bible cope with Isaiah's spectacular list of wanton fripperies (3:18–23). The Authorized Version has:

> In that day the Lord will take away the bravery of their tinkling ornaments about their feet, and their cauls, and their round tires like the moon, The chains, and the bracelets, and the mufflers, The bonnets, and the ornaments of the legs, and the headbands, and the tablets, and the earrings, The rings, and nose jewels, The changeable suits of apparel, and the mantles, and the wimples, and the crisping pins, The glasses, and the fine linen, and the hoods, and the vails.

The New English Bible has:

> In that day the Lord will take away all finery: anklets, discs, crescents, pendants, bangles, coronets, head-bands, armlets, necklaces, lockets, charms, signets, nose-rings, fine dresses, mantles, cloaks, flounced skirts, scarves of gauze, kerchiefs of linen, turbans, and flowing veils.

Both translations have found English equivalents for the list of Hebrew clothes and ornaments, and we can be confident that here the New English Bible's scholarship will stand up to close scrutiny—in the details of the individual items its renderings are likely to be far more reliable than the Authorized Version's. But this is very nearly an irrelevance when we consider the different effects of the two translations. By suppressing the Hebrew syntax the New English Bible translators have made theirs virtually unreadable. It is nothing but a list, and its context, that of an articulated prophecy, is entirely lost. The Authorized Version translators have taken care to reproduce the syntactic details of the original. In this case it is not a matter of word and clause order and the disposition of clauses, but merely the recognition that in the Hebrew the list is punctuated by conjunctions—the ubiquitous Hebrew *waw*—and by definite articles. Every "the" in the Authorized Version's rendering is equivalent to the Hebrew definite article, every one of its fifteen "and"s in these verses reproduces the *waw,* and every time *and* is omitted, at the beginning of each verse, the Hebrew omits it too. Formulaic translation this may be—it is fascinating to note that the Geneva Bible, its chief predecessor in the Old Testament, had exactly the same syntactic structure except that it began verse 23 with "and," and the Authorized Version carefully took this away—but the consequence is an English rendering in which Isaiah's prophecy becomes a work of literature, a prophetic tirade with an evocative rhythmic patterning, and not a list to be hurried through as quickly as possible.[14]

It is not easy to overestimate the effect upon English prose, and through it upon English culture, of the Renaissance translators' close adherence to the word order of their original texts. T. S. Eliot's claim that a sophisticated prose style is the sign of an advanced culture is, principally, a syntactic observation. While English poetry was already developing a high degree of complexity, prose remained an unwieldy medium avoided by imaginative writers, who preferred verse for drama, and by scholars, who preferred Latin. The disposition of clauses in an English sentence of the first half of the sixteenth century is often a painful matter, the writer soon losing control over them, with the result that some sentences extend aimlessly over hundreds of words. Translating the Bible into English helped change this situation radically, largely because the early translators like Tyndale had the sense to follow closely the syntax of their originals. This is as much a cultural as a grammatical phenomenon, for the highly developed, sophisticated prose which comes naturally to any modern writer of English, and which bombards any modern reader, is based upon the syntactic patterns established by the writers of the sixteenth century. The temptation to regard biblical writings condescendingly, as coming from a more primitive culture, neglects to take into account how far our deepest structures of expression were formed by these more developed biblical texts. We can see the process at work in Tyndale's prose. In Genesis 24:14 he threads his way through a series of clauses, including both narrative and direct speech, and never loses control as contemporary prose writers were liable to do, because he follows his original, if not absolutely word for word, then certainly clause for clause: "Now the damsel to whom I say, stoop down thy pitcher and let me drink; if she say, drink, and I will give thy camels drink also, the same is she that thou hast ordained for thy servant Isaac: yea, and thereby shall I know that thou hast showed mercy on my master."

In his rendering of New Testament Greek, which has less in common with natural English word order than Old Testament Hebrew, Tyndale's success was largely the result of his having observed the original's ordering and disposition of clauses. Consider his translation—again very much the

basis of the Authorized Version—of the complicated syntax of Hebrews
1:1–4:

> God in time past diversely and many ways, spake unto the fathers by
> prophets: but in these last days he hath spoken unto us by his son, whom
> he hath made heir of all things, by whom also he made the world. Which
> son being the brightness of his glory, and very image of his substance,
> bearing up all things with the word of his power, hath in his own person
> purged our sins, and is sitten on the right hand of the majesty on high, and
> is more excellent than the angels, inasmuch as he hath by inheritance obtained
> an excellenter name than have they.

Now compare the New International Version's translation:

> In the past God spoke to our forefathers through the prophets at many times
> and in various ways, but in these last days he has spoken to us by his Son,
> whom he appointed heir of all things, and through whom he made the
> universe. The Son is the radiance of God's glory and the exact representation
> of his being, sustaining all things by his powerful word. After he had
> provided purification for sins, he sat down at the right hand of the Majesty
> in heaven. So he became as much superior to the angels as the name he has
> inherited is superior to theirs.

Essentially the difference is between a two-sentence and a four-sentence
rendering—and Tyndale's second sentence, beginning with "which son,"
is so intimately connected to the previous one that it would not be misleading to punctuate the whole thing as just one sentence. The Greek, as
we would expect, is a fairly exact model of the Renaissance rendering,
both of them threading their way through a series of clauses without
permitting the reader the kind of pause which the modern version's sentence division does. Of course the modern version is easier to follow—
this is its purpose, after all—but the implications for our canonical view
of the Bible are worth considering.

Because a writer's style is more intimately bound up with his syntax
than any other feature, modern versions, which maintain more syntactic
uniformity, make less of a stylistic distinction between books than do the
Renaissance versions, which allow their renderings to be molded by the
original syntax. Consider Matthew's account of the finding of the tethered
ass (21:1–3, 6–10), as given by the Authorized Version:

> And when they drew nigh unto Jerusalem, and were come to Bethphage,
> unto the mount of Olives, then sent Jesus two disciples, Saying unto them,
> Go into the village over against you, and straightway ye shall find an ass
> tied, and a colt with her: loose them, and bring them unto me. And if any
> man say ought unto you, ye shall say, The Lord hath need of them; and
> straightway he will send them . . . And the disciples went, and did as Jesus
> commanded them, And brought the ass, and the colt, and put on them their
> clothes, and they set him thereon. And a very great multitude spread their

garments in the way; others cut down branches from the trees, and strawed them in the way. And the multitudes that went before, and that followed, cried, saying, Hosanna to the Son of David: Blessed is he that cometh in the name of the Lord; Hosanna in the highest. And when he was come into Jerusalem, all the city was moved, saying, Who is this?

This is barely distinguishable from a piece of Old Testament narrative; most of its clauses are coordinate rather than subordinate. Now compare it with the Authorized Version's rendering of Luke's account (19:29–37):

And it came to pass, when he was come nigh to Bethphage and Bethany, at the mount called the mount of Olives, he sent two of his disciples, Saying, Go ye into the village over against you; in the which at your entering ye shall find a colt tied, whereon yet never man sat: loose him, and bring him hither. And if any man ask you, Why do ye loose him? thus shall ye say unto him, Because the Lord hath need of him. And they that were sent went their way, and found even as he had said unto them. And as they were loosing the colt, the owners thereof said unto them, Why loose ye the colt? And they said, The Lord hath need of him. And they brought him to Jesus: and they cast their garments upon the colt, and they set Jesus thereon. And as he went, they spread their clothes in the way. And when he was come nigh, even now at the descent of the mount of Olives, the whole multitude of the disciples began to rejoice and praise God with a loud voice for all the mighty works that they had seen.

This is still more paratactic than a piece of modern narrative prose would be, but not overwhelmingly so, and it is appreciably different from Matthew's account in its more frequent use of subordinate clauses. Both passages accurately reflect the Greek. Luke's syntax is the more sophisticated, Matthew's the more Hebraic; and, once more, this kind of distinction, important in any literary appreciation of the two narratives, is unlikely to be reproduced in a modern version.

Old Testament narrative is characterized by its almost exclusive use of the conjunction *waw* to link virtually every clause and sentence. Right from the beginnings English translators of the Bible were happy to render these links with "and," so that their narratives sometimes consist entirely of coordinate clauses. It is probable that this practice was something natural to early sixteenth-century writers of English prose, inheritors of a tradition going back to Anglo-Saxon's repeated use of *ond*. But this is distinctive to English, in contrast to the more sophisticated syntax of the Vulgate, and even of Luther's German. And that the English translators appreciated this harmony between Hebrew and English is borne out by the successive versions' increasing use of it through the century—despite the growing flexibility of English prose during this period, with its writers' increasing skill in the deployment of subordinate clauses and the construction of complex sentences. The Authorized Version's translators, rather than reducing the percentage of simple coordination, actually intensified it. For instance, in the developing narrative of Pharaoh's responses to the plagues visited upon his country, Tyndale renders the critical verse Exodus 9:7 like this:

> And Pharaoh sent to wit [that is, know]: but there was not one of the cattle of the Israelites dead. Notwithstanding, the heart of Pharaoh hardened, and he would not let the people go.

However, the Authorized Version has:

> And Pharaoh sent, and, behold, there was not one of the cattle of the Israelites dead. And the heart of Pharaoh was hardened, and he did not let the people go.

Syntactically Tyndale's is the more modern of the two. He renders the three conjunctive *waws* as "and," "but," and "notwithstanding," whereas the Authorized Version, written nearly a century later, uses "and" in all three places. The Jerusalem Bible translates the verse:

> Pharaoh had enquiries made, but it was true: none was dead of the livestock owned by the sons of Israel. But Pharaoh became adamant again and did not let the people go.

And the New International Version:

> Pharaoh sent men to investigate and found that not even one of the animals of the Israelites had died. Yet his heart was unyielding and he would not let the people go.

Here we can see the diminishments consequent upon tinkering with the original syntax. In its translation of the *waw* which introduces Pharaoh's obstinacy, only the Authorized Version conveys the strength of the narrative's portrayal. To have him hardening his heart in spite of the plague, which is the force of Tyndale's "notwithstanding" and the modern versions' "but" and "yet," is to miss the point of the narrative. He hardens his heart because of the plague. A character like Pharaoh responds to power with power, inevitably, and not, as the modern sophisticators of the syntax would have it, irrationally.

By heavy use of coordinating clauses the Authorized Version leaves its narrative structures open to the widest possible range of meanings, for such coordination imposes upon events only a relatively weak impression of sequentiality. More sophisticated syntactic structures, using all kinds of subordination, are more interpretative and insist upon such things as cause and effect, motive, and specific temporal relations between events. This is not to say that the Authorized Version attempts anything like a complete monotony of clause connection. It often uses "and when" or "but" rather than the simple "and," but its overall effect is still much more Hebraic than English. It begins Genesis in the way it intends to go on, merely placing one thing after another, and leaving us to interpret for ourselves the degree to which the things described are sequential or simultaneous, and whether, for example, the darkness was an intimate part of the formlessness (1:1–2):

> In the beginning God created the heaven and the earth. And the earth was without form, and void; and darkness was upon the face of the deep. And the Spirit of God moved upon the face of the waters.

In a more sophisticated rendering, such as the New English Bible's, the darkness is presented as a subsidiary part of the formlessness:

> In the beginning of Creation, when God made heaven and earth, the earth was without form and void, with darkness over the face of the abyss, and a mighty wind that swept over the surface of the waters.

And in the New International Version the hovering of God's spirit is not as ambiguous as in the Authorized Version, where it could be either simultaneous with the creation of the formless universe or consequent upon it. Here it all happens at the same time:

> In the beginning God created the heavens and the earth. Now the earth was formless and empty, darkness was over the surface of the deep, and the Spirit of God was hovering over the waters.

THIS OPENNESS to a range of meanings is one of the Authorized Version's great merits as a translation and extends far beyond the use of a heavily paratactic syntax. It seems to have been an important principle that its renderings be capable of embracing differing, even apparently incompatible, interpretations—partly, one assumes, because there were many Puritan and Catholic critics only too ready to accuse it of partiality. A translation which could admit ambiguity was nearly always to be preferred to a narrowly interpretative one—a practice completely opposed to the aims of most modern translators, and one which has significant literary consequences.

It has always been possible to get some idea of the way the Authorized Version translators worked simply by comparing their renderings with their predecessors'. This is a fascinating pursuit, because it repeatedly shows both how minute their changes often were, and also how these apparently trivial alterations could have unexpectedly large effects on both aesthetics—as in the well-known example of their changing "small still voice" to "still small voice"—and meaning. Recently, however, we have been able to add to our speculations about the reasons for these changes some hard evidence, thanks to the scholarship of Ward Allen, who unearthed and edited the notes of one of the members of a translation panel, John Bois.[15] Again and again these notes show how concerned the translators were to achieve as open a rendering as possible. Thus their translation of Romans 12:10 reads: "Be kindly affectioned one to another with brotherly love; in honour preferring one another." Earlier versions had rendered the verb in the last clause as "go before" or "preventing" (in Elizabethan English, *prevent* means "go before"), as in the Geneva Bible's "Be affectioned to love one another with brotherly love. In giving honour, go one before another." Bois's note shows that "prefer" was used in order to get two meanings into the verse: "Let each one of you strive to prevail in giving honour to another" and "in honour esteeming others before themselves."[16]

We have learned to prize ambiguity in poetry, and we see its roots in the English tradition largely in the work of John Donne and the Metaphysical poets who followed him. Bois's notes repeatedly remind us that the translators of the Authorized Version were Donne's contemporaries, men of a similar cast of mind. The Geneva Bible renders 2 Corinthians 10:16 thus:

> And to preach the gospel in those regions which are beyond you: not to rejoice in the measure, which is appointed to another man, that is, in them that are prepared already.

The Reims Bible has:

> yea unto those places that are beyond you, to evangelize, not in another man's rule, to glory in those things that are prepared before.

Bois's note shows that the translators tried to include another sense which they perceived in the Greek in the final clause: "This is said concerning those historians who through a certain laziness and weakness of mind, shirking the labour of seeking the truth of things, produced their own histories from others' writings."[17] Bois then turns to the word immediately preceding this clause, one we have encountered in another context earlier, *kanon*, which the earlier versions had rendered as "measure" and "rule." The note explains *kanon* as meaning "the space between the . . . place from which one jumps and the . . . pit" in a long-jumping contest. Several alternatives to "rule" are scouted, with "line" being the ultimate choice because it will convey both the athletic submetaphor and the sense that the final clause is concerned, among other things, with other men's writing.[18] Thus: "To preach the gospel in the regions beyond you, and not to boast in another man's line of things made ready to our hand." Translating the final Greek phrase as "things made ready to our hand" adds to the earlier versions' idea of other men's worldly authority the authority of earlier writers which historians had lazily acceded to—"line" being both imperial lineage and the lines of writing on a page. It is good to have the note, too, not only to show the verbal dexterity of these translators, but as a fresh view of the strenuous origins of canonicity.

One final example of the extraordinary economy of the translators' practice comes in 1 Corinthians 13:5, part of the continuing definition of charity: "Doth not behave itself unseemly, seeketh not her own, is not easily provoked, thinketh no evil." The earlier English versions had rendered the last clause as "thinketh not evil." Changing "not" to "no" undoubtedly promoted euphony—the two open vowels collide powerfully with each other—but Bois's note informs us that the translators had another purpose too. The note reads *non imputat malum* ("he does not impute evil");[19] in other words, "thinketh not evil" means that evil thoughts do not come into charity's mind. "Thinketh no evil" means the same but adds the second idea that charity never conceives of anyone else acting through evil motives; "no" has more to do with "evil" than with "think," whereas "not" attaches itself more closely to the verb.

All these examples can be seen to have doctrinal or theological implications, but they also have one distinct literary implication: that the Authorized Version's translators were artful and, in the best Renaissance sense, witty, contriving to make what they wrote have a variety of meanings. In their view the translator's task was not to assume that there is one clear meaning to which the text should be reduced, but instead to open out the text to include as much as possible.

Ambiguity is an inherently poetic ideal, and in this respect it is instructive to consider the Renaissance translators' response to the most poetic element of biblical writing, its imagery. The contrast between Renaissance and modern translators' treatment of *leb*, "heart," shows up how regularly the earlier translators reproduced the image whereas modern translators often feel constrained to suppress it. Many modern versions eschew anything which smacks of imagery or metaphor—based on the curious assumption, I guess, that modern English is an image-free language. When Christ, in the Sermon on the Mount, talks about those who *hunger* and *thirst* for righteousness, the Good News Bible drops the images of hungering and thirsting, and renders it "Happy are those whose greatest desire is to do what God requires." And where the Authorized Version has Christ warning that anyone who looks lustfully at a woman "hath committed adultery with her in his heart [*kardia*]," the New American Bible, disapproving of the idea that the heart should be conceived of as anything but a muscle, translates it as "he has already committed adultery with her in his thoughts"—quite a different idea. Again, it is unfair to imply that all the virtue is on one side. We will not find Job's splendid image of the "eyelids of the morning" (3:9) in the Authorized Version, which has "the dawning of the day," but in the New English Bible. But the general tendency is overwhelming, and as a result in the modern versions forms of expression of varying degrees of poeticality are reduced to the prosaic. The loss is measurable not only in terms of aesthetics but also in terms of meaning.

Particularly in the narrative sections of the Bible the Authorized Version emerges from comparison with twentieth-century versions as more attractive and more accurate. This success has much to do with the Renaissance translators' sense that they were translating works of literature, so that they brought to the task the same attitudes that they would have brought to constructing a sermon—one of the most impressive literary forms of the sixteenth and seventeenth century, delivered to larger audiences than the playhouses got. The Renaissance translators were still close to a Protestant Reformation which stressed the primacy of the Bible's literal sense, as opposed to the various allegorical readings which the Catholic Church had foisted upon it. Stressing the literal sense very often involves treating the story with as much care as any writer of narrative should do. And so the Authorized Version presents Christ on the hillside delivering his sermon and speaking like a popular preacher. Instead of saying aridly scholarly things like "How blest are those of a gentle spirit; they shall have the earth for a possession" (New English Bible) or "not the smallest letter, not the least stroke of a pen" (New International Version), he says "Blessed are the meek for they shall inherit the earth" and "one jot or tittle"; and instead of words which no mouth could ever utter, such as "And if one of the occupation troops forces you to carry his pack one kilometre, carry it two kilometres" (Good News Bible), he says the beautifully pithy "And whosoever shall compel thee to go a mile, go with him twain." And when Martha is ordered to open up Lazarus's tomb, she does not protest with the affected "by this time there is a bad odour" (New International Version) or "by now there will be a stench" (New English Bible), but registers frank revulsion: "by this time he stinketh" (John 11:39).

At its best, which means often, the Authorized Version has the kind of transparency which makes it possible for the reader to see the original clearly. It lacks the narrow interpretative bias of modern versions, and is the stronger for it. When the writer of Proverbs asserts that man is constantly aware of his own mortality and the mortality of those he loves, the Authorized Version translates a plain Hebrew sentence as plainly as possible: "Even in laughter the heart is sorrowful" (14:13). Versions which replace "is" with "may," as the New English Bible and New International Version do—"Even in laughter the heart may grieve" and "Even in laughter the heart may ache"—have already begun to interpret away the inconsolability of the original; just as replacing the Authorized Version's splendidly literal translation of the phrase which recurs in the historical books, "him that pisseth against the wall," with "every mother's son" (New English Bible) or "every last male" (New International Version) abandons any real attempt to reproduce its register and tone.

Through its transparency the reader of the Authorized Version not only sees the original but also learns how to read it. Patterns of repetition, the way one clause is linked to another, the effect of unexpected inversions of word order, the readiness of biblical writers to vary tone and register from the highly formal to the scatological, and the different kinds and uses of imagery are all, like so much else, open to any readers of the Renaissance versions, and best open to them in the Authorized Version.

NOTES

1. Although English translations are the topic here, it should be remembered that behind these lay earlier translators' efforts, in particular the Vulgate, whose "deus" and "dominus" match "God" and "Lord." There were earlier English versions than Tyndale's, notably the Wyclif Bible at the end of the fourteenth century, but these were not printed, and any influence upon the later tradition is not strong.

2. From Tyndale's preface to *The Obedience of a Christian Man* (1528).

3. See my argument for Tyndale's knowledge of Hebrew, "William Tyndale's Pentateuch: Its Relation to Luther's German Bible and the Hebrew Original," *Renaissance Quarterly*, 33 (1981), 351–385.

4. The best account of the relationship among the English Bibles is C. C. Butterworth, *The Literary Lineage of the English Bible* (Philadelphia, 1941). The most useful general history is still B. F. Westcott, *A General View of the History of the English Bible*, 5th ed. (London, 1905). For a more detailed study of the different versions' translation methods see Gerald Hammond, *The Making of the English Bible* (Manchester, 1982).

5. From the translators' preface. This and other basic documents relating to the Renaissance Bible are collected in A. W. Pollard, ed., *Records of the English Bible* (1911; reprint, Oxford, 1974).

6. William Tyndale, *Answer to Sir Thomas More* (1531; reprint, London, 1850), p. 16. Tyndale's use of "senior" instead of "priest" angered More by removing the biblical basis for the priesthood. Tyndale's second thoughts do the same thing, only better.

7. The *Oxford English Dictionary* describes *know* used in this sense as "chiefly an Hebraism" but points to parallels in other European languages.

8. The New English Bible, New American Bible, and Jerusalem Bible renderings, respectively.

9. Robert Alter, *The Art of Biblical Narrative* (London, 1981), p. 93.

10. In Pollard, *Records of the English Bible*, p. 374.

11. Modern versions vary. The Jerusalem Bible and the New English Bible have three different renderings: "jeer at," "mock," "look jeeringly"; and "deride," "sneers at," and "mocks," respectively. The New American Bible and New International Version have "mock" in all three places.

12. The Jerusalem Bible gets it wrong by rendering all four verses in the same way: "and he went unmolested" (v. 21), "and he had gone unmolested" (v. 22), "to go away unmolested" (v. 23), and "to go unmolested" (v. 24). The New American Bible is similarly obtuse, ending verses 21–23 with a variant of "go away in peace," and verse 24 with "go peacefully on his way." The New International Version is the best of the modern attempts: "and he went in peace" (v. 21), "and he had gone in peace" (v. 22), "he had gone in peace" (v. 23), and "Now he is gone!" (v. 24).

13. The New International Version renders five of these ten examples with "heart"; the Jerusalem Bible and the New American Bible, like the New English Bible, use "heart" only twice.

14. For a similar contrast in the New Testament between the Authorized Version's reproduction of the original's expressive syntax and the New English Bible's suppression of it, see their renderings of 2 Corinthians 6:4–10.

15. Ward Allen, ed. and trans., *Translating for King James: Notes Made by a Translator of King James's Bible* (Nashville, 1969). The notes seem to be those of one of the final revising committees.

16. Ibid., p. 43. The first quotation is Allen's translation of Bois's Latin, the second of his recasting of the Greek text.

17. Ibid., p. 53.

18. Ibid.

19. Ibid., p. 49. The note refers to Zechariah 7:10: "and let none of you imagine evil against his brother in your heart."

SUGGESTED FURTHER READINGS

Ward Allen, ed. and trans., *Translating for King James: Notes Made by a Translator of King James's Bible* (Nashville, 1969).

Walter Benjamin, "The Task of the Translator," in Hannah Arendt, ed., *Illuminations*, trans. Harry Zohn (London, 1973).

C. C. Butterworth, *The Literary Lineage of the English Bible* (Philadelphia, 1941).

Gerald Hammond, *The Making of the English Bible* (Manchester, 1982).

Werner Schwarz, *Principles and Problems of Biblical Translation* (Cambridge, 1955).

University of Manchester

GLOSSARY

INDEX

Glossary of Biblical and
Literary Terms

aggadah (Hebrew, "that which is told"). Anecdotal and legendary elements of rabbinic tradition, preserved both in the Talmud and very abundantly in the Midrash. Midrash that is sermonic and not primarily concerned with the interpretation of law is called *midrash aggadah*.

antinomian(ism) (Greek *anti* + *nomos*, "against law"). The doctrine among some Christians that the Mosaic Law had been totally superseded; revived in Europe, England, and America after the Reformation. A central discussion is Romans 3; see also 1 Cor. 9:21.

antitype. See *type*.

apocalyptic. Adjective: relating to apocalypse ("uncovering, revelation"). Noun: the study of apocalypse and apocalyptism (apocalypticism).

Apocrypha (Greek, "things hidden away"). Writings excluded from the canon(s). As a singular, the body of such writings. The books occurring in the Septuagint (q.v.) and Vulgate (q.v.) but not the Masoretic (q.v.) Bible; also a body of writings excluded from the New Testament. By extension, the spurious or inauthentic.

Catholic Epistles. James, 1 and 2 Peter, 3 John, and Jude—so called because they are addressed to the Church generally and not, like Corinthians and Ephesians, to individual congregations. 1 and 2 John do not fit the description exactly but are usually included, so that there are seven in all.

chiasm. A formal patterning of any literary or rhetorical unit that preserves symmetry while reversing the order of the terms, to produce the sequence ABBA.

Christology. The study of the person and nature(s) of Christ; by extension, the study of his supposed presence in the Old Testament and so related to *typology*.

Deuteronomic History (also Deuteronomistic History). According to scholarly consensus, the continuous history of Israel offered in Joshua, Judges, 1 and 2 Samuel, 1 and 2 Kings, if not composed, then edited by the writers or school responsible for Deuteronomy; perhaps completed in the Babylonian Exile; stresses importance of central cult, danger of exile as punishment; often uses hortatory style with certain characteristic formulas.

dyadic line. A line of Hebrew verse containing two parallel "members" or versets (q.v.); the most prevalent pattern in biblical poetry.

envelope structure. A formal organizing device frequently used by biblical writers in which the borders of a poetic or narrative unit are marked by repetition, at the end, of salient terms, phrases, or clauses that appear at the beginning.

eschatology. The study of the last things (Greek *eschatos*, last). Often used to describe the conviction of New Testament writers that the end of the world was approaching; but can be used of any theology of an end, even if not immediately expected. In later Christian theology the study of the four last things: Death, Judgment, Heaven, and Hell.

exegesis (from Greek, "to lead out, interpret"). The interpretation of passages in Scripture.

First Commonwealth. The first autonomous Israelite political presence in Palestine, beginning with the early phase of the conquest in the twelfth century B.C.E. and ending with the Babylonian destruction of the kingdom of Judah in 586 B.C.E.

form-criticism. In modern biblical scholarship, the analysis of the text into its stereotypical literary constituents, which variously correspond to what literary critics would describe as genre, subgenre, type-scene (q.v.), or topos (q.v.).

Former Prophets. In the traditional Hebrew division, the narrative books Joshua, Judges, 1 and 2 Samuel, 1 and 2 Kings.

halakhah (Hebrew, "going," "the way one should go"). Law as it is formulated by rabbinic tradition, the determinative stage running from the third to fifth century C.E. Midrash concerned primarily with legal interpretation of the Bible is called *midrash halakhah.*

hermeneutics. The general theory of interpretation governing exegesis and, by extension, all forms of literary, legal, and philosophical interpretation.

Hexateuch (Greek, "composed of six books"). The Five Books of Moses together with Joshua, considered by some scholars as a literary, or redactional, unit.

Higher Criticism. A nineteenth-century movement in bibical scholarship that raised questions about the origins, evolution, and fundamental character of the Bible; used in opposition to Lower Criticism, which deals with analysis of the text and philology.

hypotaxis. A kind of syntax—and hence literary style—that places related clauses in subordinating constructions and specifies the connections among them through subordinate conjunctions. The opposite of parataxis (q.v.).

key word. A common device in ancient Hebrew narrative and poetry in which a theme is advanced by repetition of a strongly marked term, often with a play on its different meanings or on words that resemble it.

Latter Prophets. Also known as the "literary" or "writing" prophets—Isaiah, Jeremiah, Ezekiel, and the Twelve Prophets.

logos (Greek). Word, speech, discourse; with a special sense in John 1, where it means the creative word of God.

messianic (Hebrew *mashiah*, "anointed"). Adjective referring to all forms of speculation and prophecy concerning a redeemer expected in the future. (The Greek Old Testament translates the Hebrew word *Messiah* as *Christos.*)

Masoretic (Hebrew *masoret*, "tradition"). The received version of the Hebrew text of the Old Testament as established by the grammarians of Tiberias, roughly sixth to tenth century C.E.; includes vocalization of the consonantal text and tropes for chanting.

midrash (Hebrew, "inquiry," "interpretation"). The activity of Jewish Bible interpretation, sometimes associated with actual sermons, that began in the third century C.E. or earlier; attained its earliest literary formulations at the end of the fourth century; and continued in various ways, in a mixture of Hebrew and Aramaic, until the twelfth century or later; characterized by imaginative interweaving of different biblical texts and by vivid parables and narrative materials.

Minor Prophets. Called minor not because of their stature but because of the brevity of their surviving work; in Hebrew they are simply called The Twelve—Hosea, Joel, Amos, Obadiah, Jonah, Micah, Nahum, Habakkuk, Zephaniah, Haggai, Zechariah, Malachi.

Northern Kingdom. The kingdom of Israel, formed through the secession of the ten northern tribes in 926 B.C.E. under the leadership of Jeroboam I; destroyed by the Assyrians in 721 B.C.E.

paronomasia. Punning used as a literary device.

parataxis. A kind of syntax—and hence literary style—that places related clauses in a series of parallel units without subordination, the links being indicated by "and" or by no term of conjunction. The opposite of hypotaxis (q.v.).

parousia (Greek, "presence" or "arrival"). The second coming of Christ, thought by early Christians to be imminent. Frequent in New Testament (e.g., Matt. 24:27, 37, 39, 43) (KJV: "coming").

Pastoral Epistles. 1 and 2 Timothy, Titus—so called because they instruct pastors in their ecclesiastical duties.

Pentateuch (Greek, "composed of five books"). The Five Books of Moses (Gen., Exod., Lev., Numb., Deut.), considered by Jewish tradition the core of all law. See *Torah*.

pericope (Greek, "section"). A self-contained section of Scripture.

pesher (Hebrew, "deciphering"). A form of interpretation that appears to have flourished in the intertestamental period, first clearly attested in the Dead Sea Scrolls, in which the meaning of a biblical text is construed to be revealed and fulfilled in imminent events of the interpreter's era.

Priestly (code, editors, etc.). Designates literary and editorial groups generally assumed to have played a crucial role in establishing the text and preliminary canon of the Hebrew Bible in the Second Commonwealth, especially fifth and fourth centuries B.C.E. One of the three major strands of the Pentateuch, P, has been identified as a product of Priestly circles, reflecting a distinctive style and distinctive theological and cultic concerns.

Primeval History. The biblical account of the origins of the world and of mankind until the advent of Abraham (Gen. 1–11).

prolepsis. An anticipation of events to be reported later in the narrative sequence; foreshadowing.

pseudepigrapha (Greek, "writings with false superscriptions"). A miscellaneous group of some sixty-five texts, not part of the Old Testament but often linked with it by ascription of authorship to an Old Testament figure; written by Jews or Christians in the last three centuries B.C.E. and the first two centuries C.E.

redactor. Any editor of a traditional text; for the Old Testament the redactors are generally thought to have belonged to Priestly circles (q.v.) and to have performed the work of selecting, stitching together, and revising older Hebrew texts during the Second Commonwealth.

resumptive repetition. A narrative or editorial device in which, after the interruption of a narrative line by digressive material, the return to the main line is formally marked by repetition of the last sentence or phrases used before the interruption.

Second Commonwealth. The revived national entity in Judah that began after the Persian emperor Cyrus permitted the return of Judean exiles in 538 B.C.E.; political autonomy was almost always limited by imperial powers, with the rebuilt Temple serving as chief national symbol; hence the definitive end of the Second Commonwealth is marked by the destruction of the Second Temple in 70 C.E.

Septuagint (Greek, "seventy"). The Greek translation of the Old Testament prepared for Ptolemy II of Egypt in the third century B.C.E.; so called because of ancient tradition that it was prepared in seventy days by seventy Jewish sages.

Southern Kingdom. The kingdom of Judah, with its capital in Jerusalem, after the secession of the ten northern tribes in 926 B.C.E.; destroyed by Babylonians in 586 B.C.E.

summary notation. A device that formally marks the conclusion of a textual unit by recapitulating its content through a series of catchphrases.

Synoptic Gospels (Synoptics) (Greek *synopsis*, "a general view"). Matthew, Mark, and Luke, so called because they give differing views of the same material and can be presented in parallel columns for a synoptic study. Each of the three Gospels may be called a Synoptic.

tagim (also *tagin*). The "crowns" or curlicues that adorn the Hebrew letters of Scripture in traditional calligraphy; mystic tradition considered them intrinsic to the meanings of the text.

targum (Hebrew, "translation"). Any of the Aramaic translations of the Old Testament done in the last centuries B.C.E. and early centuries C.E.; the targum style of translation often involves paraphrase and thus crosses over from translation to exegesis.

te'amim. The small markings above and below the Hebrew consonants in the Masoretic text (q.v.) that indicate tropes for cantillation in the synagogue and also provide some guidance to syntax and semantic relations among phrases.

testimony (Latin *testimonium*). A passage in the Old Testament thought to have a direct bearing on the life, death, and resurrection of Jesus; interpreted in the style of pesher; hence, applies also to parallel practice in the Qumran documents.

topos (Greek, "place," usage corresponding to English "commonplace"). In a system of rhetoric, a conventional subject, situation, strategy of persuasion, often entailing particular verbal formulas or set figures of speech.

Torah (Hebrew, "instruction"). In the Bible, teaching in general and Mosaic teaching in particular; from the latter usage, later often a designation for the Pentateuch.

triadic line. A line of Hebrew verse containing three parallel "members" or versets; used sparingly by most biblical poets.

type. An Old Testament passage or character whose hidden sense is made plain only when fulfilled by a New Testament antitype: e.g., the high priest Melchizedek is a type of Christ, the crossing of the Reed Sea a type of the Redemption. Interpretation through types is called *typology*. The typological habit spread far beyond the biblical texts.

type-scene. In biblical narrative, the marking of a crucial juncture in the life of the protagonist (birth, initiatory trial, betrothal, deathbed) by following a fixed sequence of familiar motifs.

United Kingdom. The short-lived monarchy, under David and Solomon (from about 1000 B.C.E. to 926 B.C.E.), that united all the Israelite tribes under a single government with its capital in Jerusalem.

verset. One of the two or three formal subunits or "members" that make up a line of Hebrew poetry; sometimes referred to in scholarly literature as bicolon or hemistych.

Vulgate. The Latin translation of the Bible (*editio vulgata*) made by St. Jerome and completed at the beginning of the fifth century C.E., first printed in 1456 (the Gutenberg Bible). It is still the basis of the Roman Catholic Bible.

Wilderness. The Sinai Wilderness or Desert in which, according to the traditional account, the Israelites wandered forty years after the liberation from Egypt until the entry into Canaan; Wilderness Tales are reported in Exodus, Leviticus, and Deuteronomy, but their main locus is Numbers.

Wisdom (Hebrew *ḥokhmah*). An international literary genre and intellectual activity in the ancient Near East that conceives wisdom pragmatically as a transmissible craft and is characteristically not nationalistic or cultic in its emphases; in the Bible, most clearly represented in Proverbs, Ecclesiastes, and Job.

Index